"Sicques, Tigers, or Thieves"

"SICQUES, TIGERS, OR THIEVES": EYEWITNESS ACCOUNTS OF THE SIKHS (1606–1809)

Edited by
Amandeep Singh Madra
and Parmjit Singh

"SICQUES, TIGERS, OR THIEVES"
© Amandeep Singh Madra and Parmjit Singh, 2004.

First published in 2004 by
PALGRAVE MACMILLAN™
175 Fifth Avenue, New York, N.Y. 10010 and
Houndmills, Basingstoke, Hampshire, England RG21 6XS
Companies and representatives throughout the world.

PALGRAVE MACMILLAN is the global academic imprint of the Palgrave Macmillan division of St. Martin's Press, LLC and of Palgrave Macmillan Ltd. Macmillan® is a registered trademark in the United States, United Kingdom and other countries. Palgrave is a registered trademark in the European Union and other countries.

ISBN 1–4039–6201–4 hardback
ISBN 1–4039–6202–2 paperback

Library of Congress Cataloging-in-Publication Data

"Sicques, tigers, or thieves": eyewitness accounts of the Sikhs (1606–1809) / edited by Amandeep Singh Madra and Parmjit Singh
    p. cm.
    Includes bibliographical references and index.
    ISBN 1–4039–6201–4—ISBN 1–4039–6202–2 (pbk.)
    1. Sikhs—History. I. Title: Eyewitness accounts of the Sikhs, 1606–1809. II. Madra, Amandeep Singh. III. Singh, Parmjit.

DS432.S5S42 2004
954.02'5'0882946—dc22   2003058037

A catalogue record for this book is available from the British Library.

Design by Newgen Imaging Systems (P) Ltd., Chennai, India.

First edition: November 2004

10 9 8 7 6 5 4 3 2 1

Printed in the United States of America.

CONTENTS

CHRONOLOGY OF ACCOUNTS

1606: A Jesuit Account of Gurū Arjan's Martyrdom. Father Jerome Xavier s.j. to Father Gasper Fernandes s.j., Lahore, September 25, 1606, *Relação Anual das Coisas que Fizeram os Padres da Compenhia de Jesus Nassuas Missõs*, ed. Father Fernão Guerreiro (Lisbon: 1609. Reprint, Coimbre Imprensa da Universidade: 1931), 4: 369–70.

1716: Execution of Bandā Singh Bahādur in Delhi. *Madras Diary and Consultation Book*, 1715–1719, 87 Range 239.

1757: Omīchand, the Plassey Protagonist. Robert Orme, *A History of the Military Transactions of the British Nation in Indostan, from the year MDCCXLV [1745]*, 2 vols. (London: Printed for John Nourse, 1780), 2: 50–1, 182–3.

1760: Of the Seikh's or Sikhan. Eur Mss OV173, part 10, 175–7, Orme Collection MSS, Oriental and Indian Office Collection, British Library, London.

1768: Wendel's History of the Jats, Pathāns, and Sikhs. Francis Xavier Wendel, *Memoires de l'origine et etablissement des Siks*, Eur Mss ORME OV8, part 14, 67–103, Orme Collection MSS, Oriental India Office Collection, British Library, London. Received by Robert Orme in 1772. Reprinted in the original French in François Xavier Wendel, *Les mémoires de Wendel sur les Jat, les Pathan, et les Sikh*, ed. Jean Deloche (Paris: École française d'Extrême-Orient, 1979), part III.

1770: Wendel's Letter Recounting a Battle between the Jats and the Sikhs. *The Doings of the Sikhs and the Jats*, Eur Mss ORME OV 147, part 11, pp. 51–4, Orme Collection MSS, Oriental India Office Collection, British Library, London.

1770: Ferishtāh's History of Hindūstān. Muhammad Kasim Ibn Hindu Shāh [Astarabadī Ferishtāh], *The History of Hindostan, from the Earliest Account of Time to the Death of Akbar; Translated from the Persian of Mahummud Casim Ferishtah . . . Together with a Dissertation Concerning the Religion and Philosophy of the Brahmins*, trans. Alexander Dow, 3 vols. (London: T. Becket and P.A. de Hondt, 1770–1772), 2: 81–3.

1776: "A Snake with Many Heads": Polier's Warning to the English. Antoine Louis Henri Polier, "Extract of a letter from Major Polier at Delhi to Colonel Ironside at Belgram, May 22, 1776," *Asiatic Annual Review for the year 1800* (London: 1801), pp. 32–5.

1776: Polier's Mughal Memoirs on the Sikh Incursions. Antoine Louis Henri Polier, *Shah Alam II and his Court: A Narrative of the Transactions at* *the Court of Delhy from the Year 1771 to the Present Time*, ed. Pratul C. Gupta (Calcutta: S.C. Sarkar and Sons, 1947), pp. 46–8; 56–60; 62–3.

1781: Visit to the Takht at Patnā. Charles Wilkins, "The Sicks and their College at Patna, dated Benares, 1 March 1781," *Transactions of the Asiatick Society.* (Calcutta: 1788), vol. 1, pp. 288–94.

1783: "Sicques, Tigers, or Thieves," George Forster. George Forster, *A Journey from Bengal to England, through the Northern Part of India, Kashmire, Afghanistan, and Persia; and into Russia, by the Caspian Sea*, 2 vols. (London: Printed for R. Faulder, 1798), vol. I: pp. 197–201; 215; 223–35; 248–50; 253–95.

1784: Warren Hastings's Memorandum on the Threat of the Sikhs. Forrest, *Selections*, III, 1123–5, National Archives of India, New Delhi, Secret Proceedings, December 14, 1784, pp. 537–44.

1784: Sikh Troop Movements in Patiālā. *The Morning Post and Daily Advertiser*, Tuesday, September 21, 1784 [p. 2, col. 2].

1786: Mahā Singh Sukkarchakīā. *The London Chronicle*, from Thursday, October 26 to Saturday, October 28, 1786 [p. 414, cols. 2–3].

1786: Memoirs of a Mughal Nobleman. Irādat Khān, *A Translation of the Memoirs of Eradut Khan, a Nobleman of Hindostan, Containing Interesting Anecdotes of the Emperor Aulumgeer Aurungzebe, and of his successors, Shaw Aulum and Jehaundar Shaw, in which are Displayed the Causes of the Very Precipitate Decline of the Mogul Empire in India*, trans. Jonathan Scott (London: for John Stockdale, 1786), pp. 58–64.

1787: A Treatise on the History, Religion, and Culture of the Sikhs. Antoine Louis Henri Polier, "The Siques," *History of the Seeks: A Paper Read before the Asiatic Society of Bengal December 20, 1787*, Orme Collection MSS, Oriental and India Office Collection, British Library, London, XIX, pp. 73–83.

1787: Sikhs Invade Delhi. *The London Chronicle*, from Thursday, July 31 to Saturday, August 2, 1787 [p. 109, col. 2].

1788: Du Perron's Indian Researches. M. Jean Bernoulli ed., *Description historique et géographique de l'Inde qui présente en trois volumes, enrichis de 64 cartes et autres planches 1. La géographie de l'Indoustan, écrite en Latin, dans le pays méme par Le Pere Joseph Tieffenthaler. 2. Des Recherches historiques et geographiques sur l'Inde & la Description du cours du Gange & du Gagra avec un très grande carte par M. Anquetil du Perron . . . 3. La carte générale de l'Inde, celles du Cours du Brahmapoutre & de la Navigation intérieure du Bengale, aves de mémoires relatifs a ces cartes publies en Anglais par M. Jacques Rennell . . . Le tout augmenté de rémarques et d'autres additions*, 3 vols. (London: 1788), 1: 109; 2: viii, 177, 192–205.

1788: Browne's Treatise on the Sikhs. Lt.-Col. James Browne, *India Tracts: Containing a Description of the Jungle Terry Districts, Their Revenues,*

Trade, and Government: With a Plan for the Improvement of Them. Also an History of the Origin and Progress of the Sicks (Logographic Press, Printing-House Square, Black-Friars, 1788), pp. 1–30.

1789: The Collapse of the Mughal Power in Lahore. *The Diary: or, Woodfall's Register*, Thursday, August 20, 1789 [p. 3, col. 2].

1789: A Muslim Account of Sikh History. Ghulām Hussain Khān, *A Translation of the Sëir Mutaqharin*, trans. M. Raymond [Hajee Mustapha, pseud.], 3 vols. (Calcutta: printed by James White, 1789), 1: 19–20, 22–3, 71–2, 87–97; 3: 137–9, 207–13, 319–27.

1790: Afghān Retreat Signals Sikh Prosperity. Quintin Craufurd, *Sketches Chiefly Relating to the History, Religion, Learning, and Manners, of the Hindoos: With a Concise Account of the Present State of the Native Powers of Hindostan* (London: Printed for T. Cadell, 1790), pp. 356–70.

1794: "Extraordinary Modern People": Dominions of the Sikhs. Mr Griffith to Mr Adamson, Bombay (dated Surat, February 17, 1794), *Containing Information Respecting the Characters of the Inhabitants on the Banks of the Indus* (Home Misc. Series 456b), Oriental and Indian Office Collection, British Library, London, pp. 625–99.

1794: Ferishtāh's History of the Deccan. Muhammad Kasim Ibn Hindu Shāh [Astarabadī Ferishtāh], *Ferishta's History of Dekkan from the First Mahummedan Conquests: With a continuation from Other Native Writers of the Events in that Part of India, to the Reduction of its Last Monarchs by the Emperor Aulumgeer Aurungzebe: Also, the Reigns of his Successors in the Empire of Hindoostan to the Present Day: and the History of Bengal, from the Accession of Aliverdee Khan to the Year 1780*, 2 vols., trans., Johnathan Scott (Shrewsbury: Printed for the Editor by J. and W. Eddowes, 1794), 2: 142–6; 236–7, 268–70.

1796: Massacre of Fakīrs, Hardwicke. Thomas Hardwicke, "Narrative of a Journey to Sirinagur," *Asiatick Researches*, vol. VI (London, 1799), pp. 309–19.

1796: An Artist's Impressions of the Sikhs, Balt Solvyns. Balthazar Solvyns, *A Collection of Two Hundred and Fifty Colored Etchings: Descriptive of the Manners, Customs, Character, Dress, and Religious Ceremonies of the Hindoos* (Calcutta: 1796, 1799), section I, number 9 "A Sic"; section VII number 8 "Naunuck Punthy"; and Balthazar Solvyns *Les Hindoûs* 4 vols. (Paris: Chez L'Auteur, 1808–12), vol. I, section 8, number 5 "Sics, A Hindoo Tribe"; vol. II, section 4, number 6 "Nanuck-punthy."

1798: Francklin's History of the Reign of Shāh Ālum. William Francklin, *The History of the Reign of Shah-Aulum, the Present Emperor of Hindostaun* (London: Printed for the author, by Cooper and Graham; and sold by R. Faulder, etc., 1798), pp. 71–8; 86–90.

1798: Zemān Shāh and the Sikhs. *The Times*, Monday, February 5, 1798 [p. 4, col. 1].

1799: Submission to Zemān Shāh. *The Times*, Friday, July 19, 1799 [p. 3, col. 3].

1800: Sikhs Gather to Oppose Afghān Rule. *The English Chronicle*, and *Universal Evening Post*, from Saturday, April 19 to Tuesday, April 22, 1800 [front page, col. 3].

1801: Attack on Fakīrs at Haridvār by Sikhs. *The Times*, Saturday, October 17, 1801 [p. 3, col. 3].

1802: A Character of the Sikhs. "A Character of the Sieks, from the observations of Colonel Polier and Mr Forster," *Annual Asiatic Review for the Year 1802* (London: 1803), pp. 9–12.

1802: An Account of George Thomas. *The Edinburgh Evening Courant*, Monday, October 11, 1802 [back page, col. 2].

1803: Ranjīt Singh's Correspondence with the British. The most noble and Marquis of Wellesley, *History of All the Events and Transactions which have Taken Place in India: Containing the Negotiations of the British Government, Relative to the glorious Success of the Late War* (London: J. Stockdale, 1805), pp. 133–4; 184–5.

1803: Memoirs of an Irish Mahārājā. William Francklin, *Military Memoirs of Mr. George Thomas; Who, by Extraordinary Talents and Enterprize, Rose from an Obscure Situation to the Rank of a General, in the Service of the Native Powers in the North-West of India, etc. Compiled and Arranged from Mr. Thomas's Original Documents* (Calcutta: 1803. Reprint, London: John Stockdale, 1805), pp. 100–14; 343–4; 352; 355; 369–70.

1803: A Modern History of Hindūstān. Thomas Maurice, *The Modern History of Hindostan: Comprehending that of the Greek Empire of Bactria, and Other Great Asiatic Kingdoms, Bordering on its Western Frontier: Commencing at the Period of the Death of Alexander, and Intended to be Brought Down to the Close of the Eighteenth Century* (London: Printed for the author, by W. Bulmer and Co., 1802–1803), pp. 508–12; 526; 617–20.

1806: Standoff in Ranjīt Singh's Punjab. William Thorn, *Memoir of the War in India Conducted by General Lord Lake and Sir Arthur Wellesley from its Commencement in 1803 to its Termination in 1806, on the Banks of the Hyphasis with Historical Sketches, Topographical Descriptions and Statistical Observations, Illustrated by maps and plans of operations* (London: 1818), pp. 478–503, 506–7.

1808: A Failed Spying Mission to Lahore. "Tour to Lahore. From the manuscript notes of an officer of the Bengal army, made from actual observation, during a late tour through the Punjab to Lahore; and affording, among much valuable matter, some illustrations of the character and manners of Sik'hs," *The Asiatic Annual Register*, vol. XI—for the Year 1809 (London: Printed for T. Cadell and W. Davies, etc., 1811), pp. 421–40.

1809: A Statesman's Note from the Afghān Frontier. Mountstuart Elphinstone, *An account of the Kingdom of Caubul and its Dependencies in Persia, Tartary and India* (London: 1815), pp. 75–6.

LIST OF ILLUSTRATIONS

PREFACE

It was with considerable relief that the statesman and traveler, George Forster, frantically scribbled in a letter of 1783 that "unhurt by the Sicques, tigers, or thieves, I am safely lodged in Nourpour." Forster was not comparing Sikhs to tigers or thieves but he was likening the comparable danger of these three very real threats during his travels. What Forster betrays is not just the perilous nature of his journey—he was after all a clandestine spy sent by Warren Hastings, the then governor-general of India, to procure information on the Sikhs of the Punjab—it also succinctly articulates the eighteenth-century worldview of the Sikhs. With these words amongst his long letters, Forster viewed the Sikhs with trepidation, occasionally fear, and often with a level of deference that had almost disappeared as evidenced by British writers a century later. Forster's Sikhs are rough-mannered rogues, living in the saddle, brusquely chasing interlopers from their territory. His frequent brushes with the Sikhs and the nervous relief with which he describes his escapes are testimony to the reputation of the Khālsā of the eighteenth century.

By contrast, in the mid- to late-nineteenth century, Sikhs were frequently described as "loyal stalwarts," "brave," and "steadfast," an illustration of their new position as citizens, albeit unequal, of a conquered Punjab within the British Empire. In the accounts presented in this book, the descriptors "formidable," "warlike," and "wild" are far more common adjectives. How that view of the Sikhs altered, and indeed, how they developed is the well-told story of the early- and mid-nineteenth century and is a product of the relative peace of princely Punjab, the gallantry of the Anglo-Sikh wars, and the loyalty of Sikhs during the Indian Mutiny of 1857.

The eighteenth century remains, to most writers of Sikh history, an enigma: a mysterious period between the sacred era of the Sikh Gurūs and the heady days of the Sikh courts. This is due largely to the dearth of historical material that supports this critical episode in the formation and development of the Sikh *panth*. Whilst the earlier periods have a wealth of religious liturgy that provides some view on early Sikh thought and the later periods aroused the curiosity of neighboring empire builders as well as court chroniclers, the eighteenth century occupies a dark phase in Sikh history. The need to improve our own understanding of the Sikhs who lived in this lawless century, and to take a closer look at traditions that are now almost foreign to the modern-day perception of the Sikh way of life, were our prime motivations for embarking on this work.

When Sir John Malcolm, military man and early empire-builder, first published his pioneering *Sketch of the Sikhs* in the *Asiatick Researches* in 1810 (published later as a book in 1812), he blew the cover on the Sikhs for the first time for most Europeans. Malcolm drew on primary accounts, local historians, and Muslim news writers and chroniclers to compile his treatise. The accuracy and breadth of his work sustain his writings as some of the most often quoted words on the Sikhs, even to this day. However, Malcolm was by no means the first writer to chart the progress, history, and fate of the Sikh people. For the previous two centuries, soldiers, travelers, administrators, scholars, missionaries, and empire-builders had borne witness to the development of the Sikh people. In letters, footnotes, and passing references, these men and women join to shed light on a little-understood period of Sikh history.

Whilst Malcolm's work certainly did not usher in a golden period in the study of Sikh history or religion, it does provide a convenient point at which to cease the collection of the accounts presented in this work.

The vast majority of the accounts presented within *Sicques, Tigers, or Thieves* are lodged firmly in the eighteenth century. However, the opening account dates to the early seventeenth century, which makes it not only the oldest in this collection but also the most intriguing. The letter, dated Lahore, September 25, 1606, from a Jesuit missionary to his monastery in Goa, recounts the ghastly martyrdom of the fifth Guru of the Sikhs, Guru Arjan, and provides the earliest surviving account of the Sikhs to the Western world, and the only European account—to our knowledge—from the seventeenth century. From this point, we have attempted to republish the extant canon of major pieces of surviving, written history that would have informed western consciousness of the Sikhs during the period 1606–1809, just prior to the debut of Malcolm's *Sketch*. However, there are a small number of accounts that were published after our cut-off point but they have been included by virtue of their having been penned prior to 1809. Accordingly, the chronological labels assigned to the accounts in chapter headings have been determined on the basis of either the date when the account was published for the first time or when the account was actually written, whichever is the earlier.

There are, of course, gaps in the history, some so tantalizing that the search for these significantly slowed the progress of publication. The Sikh historiographer, Dhian Singh, who otherwise rarely reverts to conjecture and hearsay, notes in *Daswen Pātshāh kā Antan Kautak* that the tenth Guru, Gobind Singh, was attended by a western physician in the Deccan in 1708. The man, supposedly called Call or Cole, treated the Guru at Nanded after the fatal knife wound sustained from a Pathān mercenary. Who was Cole? Did he actually exist? In whose employ was he? And most importantly, did he leave any writings or memoirs relating to one of the most critical points in Sikh history? Unfortunately, there appears to be no other reference to this man in existence and we can only conclude that either he did not exist or was so obscure a figure as to not leave a trace in the otherwise pedantic record-keeping of the English East India Company.

The accounts herein span some two centuries and only represent those written by European travelers to India. These early journeymen and women, formed the basis of the intelligence that the British establishment and interested general public would have received throughout the eighteenth century and well into the nineteenth. In some cases, the accounts are not first hand at all, but are translations of earlier works from Persian or local languages. These have been included where the translation was published prior to 1809, simply because they would have contributed to Western consciousness of the Sikhs. Later translations of earlier works were not included within the scope of this study.

Previous attempts at this type of study[1] have proven to be sources of inspiration for this work; however, where they have faltered in presenting either incomplete, judiciously edited, or simply missing accounts, we believe that we have tried to present as complete a picture as we possibly can of the earliest European accounts of the Sikhs.

Our attempt to try to collate every surviving written text on the Sikhs between 1606 and 1809, will inevitably reveal unpublished, undiscovered fragments and accounts that will further illuminate the early history of the Sikh people. For these gaps we apologize in advance, and hope to redress them someday in a further edition. There is a similar canon of texts that are drawn from Persian and the vernacular languages of Punjab, which form an incredibly important repository of information of the Sikh people viewed from Mughal eyes. Fortunately, many of these accounts have been critically examined and published in J.S. Grewal and Irfan Habib eds. and trans., *Sikh History from Persian Sources* (New Delhi: Tulika, 2001).

For the accounts reproduced here, we have prefaced each one with a short biography of the writer or translator, which is an important precursor to the text that follows. Often the authors have occupied a precarious position, finely balancing the weight of scholarship with the basic prudence and expediency of a politician. The background to the account, the authors' own vested interests and biases are vital pre-reading before their written work is entered into, and in each case within this text, these dimensions are articulated. Throughout the account, we have tried to clarify, illustrate, and cross-reference pertinent points that are being made. The resulting notes have been appended as endnotes to each chapter. These form the bulk of our work on this project and are by no means exclusive explicatory annotations on the subject. These references, together with the readers' own interpretation, form a useful link to further reading, research, or just food for thought.

There are a multitude of ways in which we could have arranged the accounts within this book. A simple chronology would have highlighted the development of the faith from the perspective of the European writers who encountered the Sikh people. However, grouping the accounts by the occupation of the writer is an altogether more powerful mechanism to observe this development as the writers generally share similar perspectives. Within each of the successive six parts, the individual accounts are placed in chronological order. Even in this arrangement, some compromises have had to be made. Few of the writers can be conveniently and simply typecast as either a missionary, Company man, traveler, military man, news writer, or orientalist.

However, we have had to make that judgment. The use of cross-references in the endnotes, we hope, will make the links between common observations and consonant themes easier to trace.

A bewildering list of characters emerge from these assorted accounts, ranging from long forgotten Sikh leaders and minor Mughal overlords, to Afghān invaders and a small army of English bureaucrats. In their day, they would have formed the caucus of the uneasy and precarious leadership that was a hallmark of pre-modern Punjab. Now they are long-forgotten characters, eclipsed in many ways by the courts of the Mahārājās that followed. The glossary of names that closes the book has been some attempt to contextualize the characters and their backgrounds.

A final note must be made of the accounts themselves. The initial charm of the original spellings, grammar, and typography quickly gave way to a huge headache while trying to manage the variant forms and spellings of words and the nature of the English that was employed. We have worked hard to ensure that we did not, in anyway, modify the primary material; the original texts retain their original spellings and the original footnotes (but with note cues converted to Roman numbering for ease of cross-referencing) are placed separately at the end of the original text rather than being incorporated with our endnotes. The spelling variants are manifold, with the word "Sikh" spelt in at least seventeen different ways,[2] and proper names having various interpretations when Latinized. Our glossary and index attempt to navigate the eager reader through this maze of spellings and adequately cross-reference the book. Within our own text, we have employed the common modern spellings and diacritical marks that are used for most vernacular terms; where disputes have arisen even with this policy, the excellent *Encyclopaedia of Sikhism* ed. Harbans Singh (Patiala: Punjabi University, 1992–1998) has adjudicated.

Running parallel with the objective of presenting early written works on the Sikhs, we also included some of the earliest examples of Sikhs in sketches and paintings. These images, many of them published here for the first time, reveal the diversity of late-eighteenth and early-nineteenth-century Sikhs: *Akālīs, Nānakpanthīs, Suthrāsāhīs, misl Sirdārs, Mahārājās*, and even a *Rānī*. Seeing these early visual representations contributed immensely to the research as many of them are mentioned in the accounts included herein.

"*Sicques, Tigers, or Thieves*" has been an immensely rewarding and exciting piece of work to be involved in. We hope that in presenting these long-forgotten accounts, we render some service to scholars, students, and general readers keen to better understand the early history of the Sikhs, and maybe inspire others to compile the next great challenge: that of the early Punjabi accounts of the Sikhs.

Amandeep Singh Madra
Parmjit Singh

NOTES

1. The most notable being Ganda Singh ed., *Early European Accounts of the Sikhs* (New Delhi: Today & Tomorrow's Printers & Publishers, 1974).
2. The seventeen variant spellings are: Sikh (common, Hastings, Du Perron); Scheick (Wellesley); Scheik (Wellesley); Seeck (Griffiths); Seek (Wilkins, Polier, Hardwicke); Seick (*The Times*); Seik (Dow, Craufurd, Maurice, Wendel, Polier, Francklin, Thorn); Seikh (Anon, Polier); Sic (Solvyns); Sick (Browne); Sicque (Forster); Siek (Polier); Sik (Wendel, Scott, Elphinstone); Sik'h (Matthews); Siques (Polier); Syc (Raymond); Syck (Raymond).

Acknowledgments

This book was the product of hundreds of hours of work, sifting through dozens of leads, thousands of pages of text, and millions of words. It was, of course, not a two-man task and it is a real pleasure to be able to acknowledge the contribution of those people who played a part in getting this book into print.

It is singularly appropriate to start by acknowledging the role of the Heritage Lottery Fund who sponsored a United Kingdom Punjab Heritage Association (UKPHA) project, which allowed us to copy and transcribe thousands of pages of text that form the core of the text in this work. Without the vision and support of this program, many of these important texts would have remained unavailable and inaccessible to most general readers.

A chance visit to New York and the offices of Palgrave Macmillan at St Martin's Press led us to meet with Gayatri Patnaik, who with great energy and commitment initially commissioned our work. We would also like to acknowledge the support, encouragement, and patience of Toby Wahl, Erin Ivy, and Heather VanDusen who guided the book to completion.

Our first foray into writing and eventual publication in 1999 was greatly encouraged by Susan Stronge at the V&A Museum. This second book was no exception and we are both extremely grateful for her continued support.

The massive library-based effort was made easier by a small team of volunteers who worked methodically through our lists of potential sources. Prime amongst these were Jagdeep Singh Bhambra and Davinder Singh Toor. This considerable task was assisted by the staff of the Oriental and India Office Collection at the British Library, British Library Newspaper Library in Collindale, and the Royal Asiatic Society Library. Dr Vidiya Nand Singh and his team at the Government Museum and Art Gallery in Chandigarh, Punjab, were a significant help in graciously allowing us to reproduce many early images of the Sikhs from their vast collection of paintings. We are grateful to Jean Frost for the transcription of most of the text, which was often latinized and frequently sent in a panic and Pali Madra for arranging the completion of the transcription effort in India.

The research for this book benefited from the assistance of the following, to whom we are indebted: Gurdit Singh, David Godrey, and Thomas Belz for providing valuable source materials; Sukhi Dosanjh, Nic Dent, and Hardeep Bath for their editorial advice; Neil Carleton was, as ever, the principal source of knowledge on Sikh guns; Rupe Dhindsa provided valuable insight into some of the early great gamers; Himadri Banerjee for his assistance on Omīchand; Prof. Robert L. Hardgrave, Jr. and Urmille De for detail on Solvyns; and Richard Cossow and Peter Bance for sharing their respective libraries of early Indian books with us.

A special mention must be made to Dr Jeevan Singh Deol for editorial support, translations, and overall guidance and input. Jeevan has come to be a good friend. Nidar Singh Nihang also deserves a special note of thanks for his insight into the Akālī Nihang oral traditions that form an important aspect of the commentary in this book. Francisco Jose Luis provided an expert translation of Father Xavier's letter that opens this book. With his insight and detailed notes, he has greatly deepened the understanding of this seminal text in the canon of early European writings on the Sikhs. The final editorial review was aided greatly by Kanwal Madra who also provided some incredibly helpful additional commentary. Lastly, the jacket artwork and website for the book (www.sicques.com) were wonderfully conceived and brilliantly executed by Suki Bains and Millan Handa respectively.

As ever, we would like to thank our families who have, once again, put up with our obsession and equally provided support, counsel, and encouragement. An enormous debt of gratitude goes to our respective parents, and our wives, Harpreet Madra and Dilgir Kaur. Lastly, Arjan Singh, Chetan Singh, Parambir Singh (Kharka), Nirlep Kaur, and Khem Singh were all unwitting sources of inspiration throughout the writing of this book, which tells the stories of their forefathers.

INTRODUCTION

The Indus valley, a panhandle of well-irrigated country draining its five eponymous rivers into the Arabian Sea, contends with the Nile Valley and the fertile crescent of the Euphrates for the tag "cradle of civilization." Here, from modern day Karachi to Ropar in East Punjab, the Harrāpan people created some of the world's first organized cities. Archeological remains point to a highly formalized and creative community that built remarkably ordered structures in primitive urban surroundings. Within walls thirteen feet thick and equally as high they perfected crafts and artistic traditions in addition to mastering the land. For centuries, these highly skilled and cultured people dominated the Indus Valley and its, then, seven rivers.

It was no accident, then, that the region of the Indus Valley that is now known as the Punjab[1] developed so rapidly during an age when man was mastering the land. With well-irrigated, fertile soil, a vast flat agricultural canvas in the plains, and a favorable climate, the scene was set for some of humanity's earliest and most successful social and agricultural experiments. A rich source of man's most basic commodities led to the rapid development of an agrarian community and eventually into a highly developed market economy. Coupled with the avaricious nature of human life, the Punjab inevitably developed into a source of conflict and conquest.

When Alexander the Great burst through the Himalayan ranges and into the Punjab in 326 B.C., he was an early proponent of what became an established tradition of conquerors and marauders—from the Ghaznāvīds and Ghurīds of Afghānistān in the eleventh century, through to the Mughals, and later still the Persians and Afghāns who entered from foreign lands in central Asia to variously plunder, conquer, ravage, and then leave. The continuity, viciousness, and inevitability of these incursions made a profound impression on the indigenous people of this unique area, informing virtually every aspect of life in the Punjab. The consequence is a land of continual conquest, migration, and settlement and a people congruent with these hard facts of life.

With its geographical position as one of the gateways into India, the Punjab also developed into a cultural melting pot; an environment within which the fertile and diverse traditions of different communities clashed and spawned a multitude of hybrids. Cultural fusions of musical traditions, religious expression, linguistic oddities, and even culinary styles inimitably identify the region. This milieu is the backdrop to the early history of the Sikhs.

The geopolitics of the Punjab since the fifteenth century arguably had a colossal impact on the resultant formation of the Sikh faith. The Punjab that

Gurū Nānak, the first of ten Sikh Gurūs, was born into was experiencing a rare period of stability between the devastating incursions of the Turkic Mongols and the invasions of Bābur, the first of the Great Mughals whose descendants so profoundly guided the subcontinent's fate for 300 years. Gurū Nānak's village, Talvandī Rāi Bhoe, was an insignificant village in the greater Punjab dominated by the rule of the Afghān Lodīs. The Lodīs had reigned supreme following the retreat of Tamerlane and, drunk on their own good fortune, toyed with their power forgetting that the roots of their authority lay, like so many before them, in the physical force that they could muster. As the soldier–poet, Bābur, turned his attentions from his beloved Samarkand to the potential riches of India and its capital Delhi, the Lodīs engaged in petty politics and allowed their armies to rot.

Bābur, a fifth-generation descendant of Timur the Lame,[2] and a leader of 12,000 battle-hardened and unscrupulous men, entered the Punjab at the behest of factious bodies of the Lodīs' own family in an exchange that can be best described as a standoff followed by a massacre. Distractions did not allow Bābur to mount a full invasion until two years later in 1525 when he led the invasion into the Punjab plains. In the lush greenery of the Punjab and with men paid only by the loot that they could carry, the country was laid to ruin wherever they went. The effect was devastating; temples were torn down, idols smashed, towns razed to the ground. The impact on the people was, as ever, far more destructive. Fuelled by the language of the Islamisists, the invasion took on the valedictory nature of a *jīhad*. The Mughals were expunging the east of infidels.

Eyewitness accounts of this invasion are few. However, Gurū Nānak's writings, preserved in the *Ādi Gurū Granth Sāhib*, make reference to the invasion in the celebrated *Bābar Vānī*. Later, Sikh tradition points to a meeting between the two men, some asserting that Bābur bowed at Gurū Nānak's feet. Like many traditions, this is likely to be apocryphal. What is certain is that the impact of the invasion on the Punjabi people gave Gurū Nānak the perfect illustration of just how low man can stoop in the name of religion. In four short hymns of immense clarity, Gurū Nānak denounces the duplicity of the claim of Bābur, adding what has been interpreted as a concluding prophetic note about the fate of the subcontinent in the coming years.

Gurū Nānak's message was a simple one of pure and honest living—the universality of man and God's message. The invasion of Bābur and his marauding hordes into Punjab drew a response that added a firm stand against social injustice and at the same time underlined the message of universality. In Gurū Nānak's hymns, all men are equal. At no time is this more poignant as when he referred to the plight of the people of the Punjab during the assault of Bābur.

The gateway had rapidly become a bloody corridor into the dominions of India and the capital Delhi. Over the next three decades, successive invaders marched into India. In each sweep into and out of the country, the Punjab was to bear the brunt of the invasions. In a land rich in history, confirmation of the incursions and the early bloody history of the Mughal interlopers is evidenced in the monuments, architecture, and even topography of the Punjab. The greatest mark, however, was on the people and the culture of the region itself. No strangers to invasion and constant change, the latest episode in their history certainly had one of the deepest impacts.

By the time of the later Sikh Gurūs, and the spiritual and cultural revolution that became Sikhism, the Punjab was ruled by the dynasty of the Great Mughals, whose influence dominated Northern India for over 300 years. They were not, however, a homogenous house with an array of leaders from despotic religious fanatics to introverted poet–kings. Continual Mughal intervention into the early history of the Sikhs informed the faith's very development like few other external influences could have done. Nowhere was this more apparent than in 1606, when Gurū Arjan Dev, fifth Gurū of the Sikhs and the most prolific poet among the Sikh Gurūs, was arrested and martyred in Lahore. His martyrdom sent shockwaves through the fledgling *panth* and eventually hastened a militarization that was formally and finally instituted into the Khālsā by Gurū Gobind Singh in 1699.

The chance observation by the Jesuit Jerome Xavier in 1606, gives historians the first extant European account of the Sikhs. From this seminal moment in Sikh history, soldiers, travelers, diplomats, administrators, scholars, missionaries, and empire builders bear witness to the Sikh people. In letters, footnotes, and passing references, these men and women join to shed light on a mysterious and little-understood period of Sikh history. Most of their accounts have only been published once, and some have never been published in their entirety. Together, these individual scraps of evidence help to generate a detailed understanding of the traditions and beliefs of eighteenth-century Sikhs—a period nestled between the sacred Gurū period and the heady days of the Sikh Empire under Mahārājā Ranjīt Singh.

However, each account is informed by the writers' own bias, political views, or position. Colonel Antoine Louis Henri Polier, one of the most prolific writers on the Sikhs, writes from the privileged point of view of a Mughal courtier and this clearly appraises his view of the itinerant Sikh bands that continually frustrated Mughal designs in the Punjab. Polier's Sikhs are opportunist, ill-mannered marauders whose hit-and-run tactics and surprise raids on the government trade caravans were nothing but the actions of thieves and highwaymen. Individually, the writers betray their own biases but together some union sense can be made of the accounts presented herein. Common threads naturally emerge: in most cases these are independent observations that corroborate each other to form a compelling picture of the idiosyncrasies of the eighteenth-century Sikhs.

Many of these remarks identify the Khālsā's common characteristics; the unshorn hair, the militarization, and the abhorrence of tobacco. However, within these varied accounts are also contained rather more contentious or unusual observations that demand notation in order to better understand the origins and impacts of these behaviors. Whilst these deviations from the accepted doctrines of the Khālsā may appear unorthodox or even sacrilegious, it should be noted that the commentators in virtually every case were not attempting to explore the Sikhs as a faith group but as a political force. This frequently led them to make judgments on the faith from the evidence of the Sikhs (and frequently non-Sikhs) whom they encountered rather than attempting, or wanting, to understand the doctrinal roots of the religion.

The most common observation is also one of the least contentious—that Sikhs are identifiable by the wearing of blue clothing. The reference to early Sikhs being clothed in blue is mentioned in eleven of the accounts. Sikh tradition holds that the army of the Sikh Gurūs dressed in blue—as the *Buddhā Dal* continues to this day. The source for this color is confirmed in some of the early liturgy of the Khālsā. Bhāī Gurdās II, writing about the creation of the Khālsā notes; "Thus came into being the *bhujangī* [youthful] Singhs dressed in blue."[3] Early visual heritage of the Sikhs in illustrated folios and wall paintings further supports the observation, showing Sikhs swathed in dark blue, even with blue *kachchh* or breeches—a phenomena that is now rarely seen.

There is only a minor variation with regards to color noted in these early accounts. In *A Translation of the Sëir Mutaqharin*, translated by M. Raymond under the pseudonym Hajee Mustapha (part VI, chapter 32), the French Creole translator writes in a footnote, "It is true that they wear only a short blue jacket, and blue longdraws: but they use likewise the yellow and the white in their turbans, as well as the blue, although by the by the latter is the general colour." Yellow, more likely a saffron colour, is an innovation borrowed from the Hindu pantheon as a symbol of sacrifice. In the martial liturgy of the Khālsā, saffron has a sacred place as it visually represents the giving of one's head for the Gurū and the Khālsā.

A short note in a diary of a lady traveler, in the first decade of the nineteenth century, gives some further dress detail on the more affluent Sikhs whom she witnessed at Haridvār. The party crossed the path of a Sikh group which included "Ranee Mutaab Kour [Mehtāb Kaur, d. 1808], wife of Rajah Rungeet Sing; Rajah Sahib Sing, of Patialah, and his wife; Rajahs Bodge Sing [probably Rājā Bhāg Singh of Jīnd (1760–1819)] and Burgwaan Sing." Her observations are no less interesting in understanding the clothing of Sikh nobles and courtiers. "The dresses of the Sieks we saw, were made of silk, wadded with cotton, reaching to their feet; the sleeves entirely obscuring the hands, and edged with a broad gold or silver lace all round the skirts. These dresses are made to fit the shape; the skirt to wrap across the front, and fasten by strings on one side; their throat being always exposed. Over this, they wear a long shawl, bound tight round the waist; a turban on their heads; and in cold weather, when they go out of doors, two square shawls, one plain, the other sprigged, envelope turban, face, and shoulders, leaving the smallest possible aperture, just that they may see their way: shawl socks, and shoes trimmed up at the points, either embroidered on scarlet or yellow cloth, or made of scarlet or yellow leather."[4]

This may well explain the origins of the tradition but does not fully explain the reason why the Sikhs would be disposed to wearing dark blue as part of their religious identity. One possible practical reason was its utility as camouflage, especially in the jungles and swamps used as hideouts by the

Sikhs. The Indian natural dyes of the period would have given their clothing an almost black appearance which would disappear into the shadows of a densely forested area. James Browne notes the dark color and the psychological effect that this had in his 1788 account: "their dress is dark blue, as ordered by Gooroo Gobind, and gives them, when collected in large bodies together, a very dismal appearance." The account of Ghulām Hussain Khān, *Seïr Mutaqharin*, puts an altogether different spin on the reasons for the uniform of the Khālsā. He points to the Sikhs imitating Afghāns in commemoration of the Afghān assistance to Gurū Gobind Singh. This he uses to establish the reasons for the Khālsā dress code. He writes: "For whenever any one put any question about this man which they payed so much respect to, they would answer, that he was a Pir-zada or Holy-man of their's, the Pir-zada of Ootch. Gooroo-govind having been so lucky as to extricate himself out of so great danger, conserved the Afghān garb in memory of that event; and he even made it henceforward the distinctive garb of his followers, no one of which could be admitted into it, unless his hair and beard proved of the proper length, and his garb of the proper pattern."

The peculiarities of the blue clothing associated with the Sikhs seems to be entirely attributable to the Khālsā, the martial, baptized fraternity constituted by Gurū Gobind Singh. The distinctiveness of the Khālsā uniform was matched by the peculiarity of the Khālsā mode of attack. This observation makes for a secondary common thread that is noted by many of the authors of these early accounts.

With small bands of men allied to a common goal but linked with their co-religionists in a loose set of fraternities, the pieces were in place for classic guerrilla warfare. The guerrilla warfare of the eighteenth-century Sikhs was dominated by the mounted soldier. Bands of Sikhs operating in small groups, living in the saddle would use the basic tactic of "hit the enemy hard enough to kill, run, turn back and hit him again; run again, hit and run till you exasperate the enemy, and then, melt away."[5] This tactic of fighting on the run is noted by a sizeable number of writers including Polier, Forster, Solvyns, Francklin, Thorn, and Dow. A letter from Colonel Polier (*Extract of a Letter from Major Polier at Delhi to Colonel Ironside at Belgram*, May 22, 1776—see part II, chapter 8) is also notable for its insight into the guerrilla strategies employed by the eighteenth-century Sikhs. As a vassal of Mughal rule, Polier writes with some frustration that they "satisfied themselves in making a kind of hussar [light cavalry] war of it, cutting off stragglers and intercepting provisions. In this they excel. To say the truth, they are indefatigable, mounted on the best horses that India can afford, each carries a matchlock of a large bore, which they handle dexterously enough, and with they annoy considerably, avoiding, at the same time, going in large bodies or approaching too near." This method of warfare developed by the Sikhs as horsemen was unique and referred to as *dhaī phat*, or two and a half strikes. Ratan Singh Bhangū, whose grandfather and father were involved in the Sikh struggle for survival in the eighteenth-century gives his definition of this term in his *Prachīn Panth Prakāsh*: "There are two and half strikes to battle.

The approach and escape from the enemy are one strike each. To fight and die fighting the enemy is only half a strike. Our Gurū [Gobind Singh] has told us to fight on the run. To fight on the run is a great stratagem. On the run did the true Gurū fight. To fight on the run is no sin."[6]

A common error by many writers of the time, and one that is repeated by Griffiths, Du Perron, Polier, Francklin, and Thomas is the confusion between Banda Bahādur and Gurū Gobind Singh. Many early chroniclers, when recounting the history of the Sikhs, attribute the audacious attack of Bandā Bahādur on Sirhind—a series of events that were reported and attributed widely by Persian news writers—to Gurū Gobind Singh. A possible explanation could be that the chroniclers of the Punjab would have noted the Gurū's departure from Punjab to the Deccan in 1708 as the head of a Sikh standing army that was mobilizing in order to support a campaign led by the then Emperor Bahādur Shāh. Unbeknownst to the chroniclers, the Gurū died in Nānded on October 7, 1708. When Bandā Bahādur returned again at the head of another armed militia of Sikhs, some may have mistakenly assumed that this was the return of Gurū Gobind Singh.

Another possible explanation is hinted at in Du Perron's account. He mentions a specific act under the very first example of Sikh rule, albeit short-lived, in 1710—when Bandā Bahādur (he confusingly refers to him as *gobindsingue*) captured Sirhind and immediately issued a silver rupee from his Mukhlisgarh fortress in the Śivālik foothills. His motivation for doing so was not entirely economic; the minting of coinage sent a revolutionary message to the Mughal overlords as well as announced his arrival as ruler of Sirhind. A Persian couplet on the coins reinforced the defiant message: *sikkā bar har do'ālam tegh-i-nānak wāhab ast fatah gobind singh shāh-i-shāhān fazal sachehā sāhib ast*[7] [the coin is struck in the two worlds (secular and spiritual), Nānak is the provider of the sword (power) by which Gobind Singh, the king of kings, is victorious]; the reverse: *zarb ba-amān ud-dahr musawarat shahr zīnat al takht mubārak bakht-2* (struck for the security and peace of the world and the walled town of the elegant throne and blessed fortune). In a final act of subversion, Bandā rejected both the Islamic and *Vikramī Samvat* dates and began a new calendar commencing from his victory at Sirhind, the numeral 2 pertains to this date. Bandā commenced a long tradition of Sikh rulers minting coins in the name of the Sikh Gurūs. With Bandā's rule being so close to Gurū Gobind Singh's presence in the Punjab, some would have been excused for interpreting the couplet as announcing the Gurū's rule as overlord of Sirhind.

The more problematic of the observations noted consistently by the early writers—in fact by Polier, Browne, Forster, Griffiths, George Thomas (Francklin), and Craufurd—was the observed practice amongst some Sikhs of using *bhang*, literally cannabis. The context in which it is mentioned is as a constituent part of a drink that is known as *sukkhā*, literally the bringer of comfort. The use of opiates and cannabis was seemingly prevalent amongst the guerrilla fighters of the eighteenth century. This observation is noted in connection with some of the cultural peculiarities of the Sikhs, in most cases these writers, who represent the most prolific and credible of the historic sources, mention the use of *bhang* while commenting on the Sikhs' abhorrence of tobacco or use of other intoxicants.

In modern Sikh doctrine, the use of cannabis is a strict taboo. However, in the Akālī Nihang pantheon, the consumption of *bhang* has always had a ritualistic role and retains an important place in their daily customs. *Sukkhā* is prepared as a *prasād* in the normal daily ceremonies and is used as a communal sacrament. The preparation involves grinding a dozen or more ingredients in a pestle while reciting morning prayers and selections of Akālī Nihang liturgy that remind the congregation of the hard days of battle which variously curse, hex, and abuse the enemies of the Khālsā. The ground concoction is tightly strained and the resultant liquid is shared in the same way that *karāh prasād* is shared in the traditional Sikh sense. Despite the offence that it engenders in mainstream Sikhs, it is vehemently defended by the Akālī Nihangs as an important tradition.

While they do reject the notion that *bhang* is an intoxicant, and therefore, it does not contravene the rules of the Khālsā, they do paradoxically acknowledge the analgesic properties of *bhang*. Tracing its origins to the early days of the Khālsā, the most likely explanations for its use are threefold; as a sustainer during the severe times of battle, as an anesthetic, and as a mechanism to aid respite between campaigns. In the harsh conditions of the battlefield, there was no set time for resting, sleeping, or eating; injuries from hand-to-hand, close quarter fighting were continuously sustained with little time to treat them properly in the thick of battle. In these conditions, there would only be enough time to simply bind the wound and stop the blood, maybe taking something to suppress the pain. All too easily, the heat, flies, and fine dust would lead to wounds festering and becoming infected, resulting in bouts of fever. The warrior would also have to deal with the emotional turmoil of living under the constant threat of death or injury, and seeing comrades fall in bloody battles. As a consequence, the Sikh warriors made use of what was, in effect, a natural pharmacy. Their motivation under these circumstances was certainly not one of recreational use, but in order to prevent being overwhelmed by the harsh realities that they were facing.

James Browne notes in his 1788 account that the Sikhs "smoke *Bang*." The smoking of cannabis (or tobacco) is viewed, even by Akālī Nihangs, as an anathema, and is one of the few strict taboos they adhere to.

Whist the consumption of *bhang* can be attributed to the somewhat archaic practices of the Sikh warriors, the Akālī Nihangs, the drinking of alcohol is generally regarded as taboo for all Sikhs. However, writers such as Polier, Browne, Matthews, and Thomas note the practice. Alcohol has never been endorsed by the Khālsā and remains that way. However, amongst Sikhs, it was not an uncommon practice, therefore these writers are noting their observation rather than the doctrinal view. It is still interesting to note that none of these writers, or indeed any of the early commentators on the Sikhs, specifically acknowledge that for the Khālsā, alcohol is a prohibited substance. However, this must be viewed as a result of the writers' focus

being on the practices and history of the Sikhs rather than the doctrinal pro-
hibitions of the Khālsā. Only a single reference in a piece of early Khālsā
liturgy, comments on alcohol as potentially permissible in extreme circumstances. The late-eighteenth-century Rahitnāmā, or code of conduct, by
Bhāī Desā Singh comments on the place of alcohol in daily life: "Another's
wife, gambling, falsehood, theft, and alcohol, know these to be the five vices
in the world. He who forsakes them, recognize him as a Singh." However,
in the very next line he goes on to specify the appropriate use of alcohol as
applied to the battle-hardened Singhs: "If going to battle, drink alcohol. Any
other day, do not even mention its name."[8]

Early writers were naturally preoccupied with drawing parallels and finding differences with other, better-known, faith groups in India. This obsession by early amateur anthropologists highlighted many of the doctrinal and
practical boundaries that existed between the faith groups who made up
northern India. One of the principal variances that many writers note
between the Sikhs and both Hindus and Muslims is in the dietary prohibi-
tions. The oft-repeated observation is that the Sikhs will consume meat, but
abstain from beef. This statement reflects the common practice amongst the
Sikhs in rural Punjab that continues to exist even today. This is not a doctrinal rejection of beef, but a reflection of the cultural norm in a predominately
Hindu society as well as a mark of respect to an important livestock animal
by a largely agrarian people. In the Hindu pantheon, the respect for the cow
is a well-recorded and understood practice. Regarding the sanctity of cows
amongst the Sikhs, an interesting story from the early eighteenth century has
been recorded by an Udāsī writer, Sevā Dās: "when the Guru adorned his
high seat, a man suddenly appeared and cried, 'O True Emperor, I have
become guilty of cow-slaughter.' The Guru instructed the attendant to conduct him nearer to him. On being asked the man repeated, 'O True
Emperor, I am guilty of the ultimate sin of cow-slaughter.' 'Don't be stupid.
You appear to be under influence of a *masand*. That is why you are upset and
are lamenting thus. So what if a cow has died. Go home and relax. It is the
Lord alone, and none else, who kills and revives,' said the Guru."[9]

Polier specifically mentions that the Sikhs eat pork, a comment that he
makes with some disdain. This is used by Polier to differentiate the Sikhs
from the Muslims and gives some evidence to his allegiances and personal
bias. Pork does not have any specific role in the Sikh diet, rather its
consumption stems from the hunting of wild boar.

Of more concern, and a practice that would now be abhorrent, is the
noted practice of forcing Muslim converts into the Sikh faith to take a form
of *amrit* which includes pig blood. Variants of this observation record that
Muslims are made to wear a boar's tusk as an amulet or to eat pork. This is
an extremely unorthodox practice that has not survived into modern times
and has no doctrinal roots. It is not known to have existed into the nineteenth century, which would imply that it was introduced in the mid- to late
eighteenth century as a practical measure for a particular set of circumstances, possibly to counter the threat to survival arising from the high risk

of infiltration by opposing forces. To detract any interlopers into the faith, especially those from the enemy camps who were predominately Muslim, the Sikhs may well have adopted a form of truth test by forcing the convert to defy the most basic practice of their former faith. Du Perron, while describing the ceremony of initiation, provides perhaps the most practical reason, centering on the necessary change of beliefs for the new initiate: "Then the senior Siks give them food to eat, and all that they eat is stirred with the tooth of a wild boar. This latter ceremony is especially done to a Musulman who becomes Sik in order that he no longer feel repugnance towards pork."

Emerging from this disparate band of writers, is a picture of the eighteenth-century Sikhs, both Khālsā and non-Khālsā. The writers represent the full gamut of Europeans who ventured east in the seventeenth and eighteenth centuries—soldiers, empire builders, missionaries, Company employees, bureaucrats, and academics—each one accompanied by their wits and by their own prejudices. The Sikhs whom they encountered were as various as the writers themselves—guerrillas, scholars, pious worshippers, warriors, artisans, and farmers. Each one left some impression on the world, a glimpse of the lives and the leanings of themselves as well as their community. A picture emerges of an upwardly mobile people, a faith group rooted in the modernity and liberation of the message of the Gurūs and hardened by their intransigence against Mughal rule and subsequent invasion. Chaotically governed by a succession of despots and interlopers, the eighteenth century sees the Sikhs standing on the precipice of power, a rudimentary political structure is in place, the origins of a government appear to be taking root, and the scene is set for, as Polier prophetically comments, "some ambitious chief, led on by his genius and success, [to absorb] the power of his associates, [to] display from the ruins of their commonwealth the standard of monarchy."

NOTES

1. Ancient accounts make reference to the original seven rivers of Punjab in the epithet *Sapt Sindhava* (the land of seven rivers). In early Sanskrit literature, only the five rivers are alluded to in the term *Panchanad*, and later Greeks accounts recounting Alexander the Great's travel through the country also define the region by its five rivers in the term *Penta Potamia*. Gurū Gobind Singh refers to Punjab fondly in the autobiographical work *Bachitar Nātak* using the ancient name *Madra Deś* as the Gurū recounts how he was brought from Patnā and lovingly cared for in the country of his forefathers.

2. Tamerlane (1336–1405), Turkic ruler and conqueror who accompanied the thirteenth-century conqueror Genghis Khān.

3. Bhāī Gurdās, *Vāran Bhāī Gurdās jī*, ed. Giānī Hazārā Singh (New Delhi: Bhāī Vīr Singh Sāhit Sadan, 1999), 667.

4. A. Deane, *A Tour Through Upper Provinces of Hindustan Comprising a Period Between the Years 1804 to 14, with Remarks and Authentic Anecdotes Annexed a Guide up the River Ganges with a Map* (London: 1823), 190.

5. Arjan Dass Malik, *An Indian Guerrilla War: The Sikh Peoples War 1699–1768* (New Delhi: Wiley Eastern Ltd, 1975), later published as Arjan Dass Malik,

The Sword of the Khalsa (New Delhi: Manohar Publishers and Distributors, 1999), 81.

6. Ratan Singh Bhangū, *Prachīn Panth Prakāsh* (Punjabī), ed. Bhai Vir Singh. (New Delhi: Bhai Vir Singh Marg, 1832), 310.

7. *The Encyclopaedia of Sikhism*, s.v. "Sikh Coins," "Divine coinage of the Sikhs," Jyoti Rai, Sikh Messenger, April 1999, 39–45.

8. Piara Singh Padam, *Rahitname* (Punjabī) (Patiala: Kalama Mandira, 1974), 49.

9. *Episodes from Lives of the Gurus: Parchian Sewadas*, trans. with commentary by Kharak Singh and Gurtej Singh (Chandigarh: Institute of Sikh Studies, 1995), 50–53.

PART I

MISSIONARIES

CHAPTER 1

A JESUIT ACCOUNT OF GURŪ ARJAN'S MARTYRDOM, 1606

Father Jerome Xavier s.j. to Father Gasper Fernandes s.j., Lahore, September 25, 1606, *Relação Anual das Coisas que Fizeram os Padres da Compenhia de Jesus Nassuas Missōs*, ed. Father Fernão Guerreiro (Lisbon: 1609. Reprint, Coimbre Imprensa da Universidade: 1931), 4: 369–70. Translated by Francisco Jose Luis.

A critical turning point in the early history of the Sikhs was arguably the martyrdom of Gurū Arjan, the fifth Sikh Gurū, at the hands of the then Mughal emperor, Jahāngīr. This marked the first of two Gurū-martyrs and remains an evocative symbol of martyrdom in the Sikh tradition. For Sikhs, this event marked the coming-of-age of the early *panth* when its own critical mass had sufficiently ruffled Imperial feathers and jolted their faith-based community to seriously consider the call to arms that was championed by the martyred Gurū's son, Hargobind. The origins of the primary self-image of the Sikh as a warrior have their genesis in this very act. However, from the point of view of the Imperial news writers, commentators, and diarists, the event was hardly worthy of mention.

Surprisingly, however, the martyrdom of Gurū Arjan is noted, albeit briefly, in a letter dated September 25, 1606 from a Jesuit, Father Jerome Xavier s.j. to the Provincial Superior of Goa, Father Gasper Fernandes s.j. Writing in Portuguese from Lahore, the letter was later rearranged and published by Father Fernão Guerreiro s.j. (d. 1617).[1]

These remarks form the earliest known European written account of the Sikhs although it is not clear that Xavier witnessed the events, and therefore the Gurū himself. Commenting on the letter, Dr Ganda Singh notes that "there is no indication that Father Xavier knew the Guru personally or that he was an eyewitness of what he has recorded."[2] The letter, which is a private correspondence rather than the official annual letter, covers a variety of topics commencing with notes on the pastoral activities of Jesuits working in Lahore and Agra. The contents then take a political turn as Xavier mentions the machinations at court, specifically Akbar's death and funeral, Xavier's relationship with the late emperor, and Jahāngīr's accession as the new emperor.[3]

Jahāngīr's reign is noted for its relative stability. However, a single event of rebellion by his son, Khusrau, marked his early years in power. This was not the first conflict that father and son had suffered, but now as emperor, there was a great deal more to lose and the errant son was placed under house arrest. Khusrau broke free from virtual confinement in court and on the pretext of visiting Akbar's burial place in Sikandrā near Agra, he commenced a tour north and west through Delhi to garner support and lay siege to Lahore. In his flight from Agra to Lahore it is said that Khusrau had met with Gurū Arjan, either at Goindvāl or Tarn Tāran.[4]

Jahāngīr's own recollections of the event shed light not only on what took place but also on the motives behind the subsequent arrest and martyrdom of the Gurū:

> In Goindwal, which is situated on the Bank of the river Biyah (Beas), there lived a Hindu, named Arjun in the garb of *Pīr* and *Shaikh*, so much so that having captivated many simple-hearted Hindus, nay even foolish and stupid Muslims, by his ways and manners, he had noised himself about as a religious and worldly leader. They called him *Guru*, and from all directions fools and fool-worshippers were attracted towards him and expressed full faith in him. For three or four generations they had kept this shop warm. For years the thought had been presenting itself to me that either I should put an end to this false traffic or he should be brought into the fold of Islam.
>
>   At last when Khusrau passed along this road, this insignificant fellow made up his mind to wait upon him. Khusrau happened to halt at the place where he was. He [Gurū Arjan] came and saw him, and conveyed some preconceived things to him and made on his forehead a finger-mark in saffron, which the Hindus in their terminology call *qashqā* (tīkā) and is considered propitious. When this came to the ears of our majesty, and I fully knew his heresies, I ordered that he should be brought into my presence, and having handed over his houses, dwelling places and children to Murtaza Khan, and having confiscated his property, I ordered that he should be put to death with tortures.[5]

Jahāngīr's own comments betray his long-standing desire to deal with Gurū Arjan, and the incident with his rebellious son provided a justification to do so.

The extract of Xavier's letter that makes mention of the Gurū commences by reasserting the Gurū's association with the rebel prince, Khusrau. A striking aspect of Xavier's letter is the inference that the Gurū was not tortured to death by the Mughals, as is stressed in Sikh tradition, but was murdered by a "gentile" who stood credit for the Gurū's fine of 100,000 *cruzados*. This is contradictory to Jahāngīr's own diary note that refers to a clear order to "be put to death by torture."[6] According to Xavier, this "gentile" murdered the Gurū after the surety could not be returned to him.

This startling explanation for the Gurū's martyrdom is in part corroborated by the only other contemporary account, namely, the *Dabistān-i-Mazāhib*, which quite clearly mentions the method of torture as being "inflicted by the collectors" and hastening the ultimate demise of the Gurū.

> When after the capture of [prince] Khusrau, His Majesty king Jannat Makānī Nūruddīn Muhammad Jahāngīr punished and mulcted *Gurū* Arjan Mal, on account of his having prayed for the welfare of Prince Khusrau, the son of His Majesty Jannat Makānī, who had rebelled against his father, and a large amount was demanded from him [Gurū Arjan], he found himself powerless to pay it. He was tied up and kept [in the open] in the desert around Lahore. He gave up his life there owing to the strong sun, summer heat and injuries inflicted by the collectors.[7]

Could it be that these "collectors" were associated with the "gentile"? Interestingly, this interpretation of the events of 1606 are supported to some extent by the *Udāsī*, Sevā Dās, who lays some of the blame on one Chandū Khatrī, a *dīwān* (revenue official) in the service of Jahāngīr, who was reeling from the rejection of the marriage of his daughter to the Gurū's son. Chandū is identified as feeding false reports against Gurū Arjan, thereby contributing to his arrest and torture.[8] Macauliffe also points to a Chandū Shāh as the main protagonist in the arrest and torture of the Gurū. Kesar Singh Chhibbar's earlier work of 1769 lays the blame at the feet of the Gurū's elder brother, Bābā Prithī Chand (1558–1618), who maintained a long-running claim for Gurūship. Hari Ram Gupta discusses the matter at great length[9] and counts the leader of the orthodox Islamic revivalists of the Naqshbandī order, Shaikh Ahmad Farūqī Sirhindī (1563–1625), as a key influencer of Jahāngīr and his courtiers against the Gurū. In a letter to Shaikh Farīd Bukhārī, Sirhindī says: "These days the accursed infidel of Goindwal was very fortunately killed. It is a cause of great defeat for the reprobate Hindus. With whatever intention and purpose they are killed, the humiliation of infidels is for the Muslims life itself."[10]

Xavier himself was no doubt under some pressure to retain cordial relations with the Mughal court to which he had been dispatched some years earlier and this may well have colored his opinions. Jerome Xavier followed in a long tradition of missionaries of the Jesuit order. The first Jesuit to land in India was Francis Xavier (coincidentally, Jerome Xavier's granduncle and later St Francis Xavier), who arrived in Goa in 1542. Francis Xavier was a zealous missionary on the move. In his ten years in India he established churches and congregations, and made some early links with the locals. Following his success in India, Jesuits were to be found in most Portuguese enclaves of the new trading country. They quickly impressed the Mughal emperor, Akbar, who invited them into the Mughal court. The Jesuit hope of converting him to Christianity failed miserably, but that first mission spawned further forays. The third mission was in May 1595. Here, Father Jerome Xavier accompanied by Father Manuel Pinheiro and Brother Bento de Goes, arrived in Lahore and into the court of the then aging Akbar.

Xavier spent twenty years in the Mughal court of Akbar and Jahāngīr, witnessing the ascendancy of Mughal splendor, dispensing spiritual leadership, and becoming a remarkable scholar in Persian. Having left the court, he spent his retirement as rector to the St Paul's College in Old Goa. He died in Goa on June 27, 1617 in a fire that engulfed his room and ignominiously suffocated him while sleeping.

The section reproduced below is a new translation into English.[11] In addition to the obvious historical importance of the account related to the martyrdom of Gurū Arjan, the account of Father Xavier's as a narrative reveals a great deal regarding how he perceived not only Sikhs but Indic religious traditions in general. The absence of the word "Hindu" when referring to non-Muslims is a striking feature of Xavier's text. The word used by Father Xavier and in other Portuguese and Catholic accounts about India is "gentile" (port. gentio). The concept of *gentile* included all religious practices that were neither Christian, Jewish, or Islamic. As such it is an all-inclusive term, heterogeneous in essence and devoid of any homogeneity. The concept of a homogeneous religious tradition called "Hinduism" appeared much later at the beginning of the nineteenth century when the Mughal concept of "Hindu" met Western Orientalist scholarship and the aspirations of the new emerging elites of the British Raj. Non-Muslim inhabitants of India were Shaivas, Vaishnavas, Shaktas, Smartas, or practiced non-denominational folk religions. Any sense of an underlying unity failed to exist amongst them but for the Christian or Muslim observer they were all "gentiles" or "Hindus." Sikhs were perceived as one group amongst the *gentiles* even though they perceived themselves, and were perceived by others, as clearly distinctive.

Father Xavier's observation that the Sikh Gurū was the equivalent of the Pope deserves special attention. The use of such a strong and unusual comparison from a Jesuit shows how important the influence of the Gurū was. Sikhism's influence was originally not just restricted to the Punjab but extended to all parts of Northern India. The many *Udāsī* and *Nirmalā* establishments throughout Northern India are clear proof of that influence. In fact, it seems that Sikhism had much more influence than most official historiographies, Indian or Western, would let one believe.

It seems that Father Xavier projects the difficult relationship between his order, the Pope, and the court of Portugal. The terms "coitado" and "pobre" clearly show sympathy toward the Gurū and his sufferings, so close to those of the martyrs of the Catholic tradition. This sympathy reinforces Father Xavier's statement about the importance of Sikhism at that period, far from being a marginal aspect of India's medieval history.

Father Xavier's account is, therefore, a most precious document regarding the way Sikhs were perceived during that period. It breaks preconceived perceptions of Sikh history and challenges the modern "Hindu" construct.

———————

When the Prince [Khusrau] came flying from Agra, he passed where a gentile called Gurū (Gorù), who amongst the gentiles is like the Pope amongst us. He was held as a saint and was as such venerated; because of this reputation of his and because of his high dignity the Prince went to see him, desiring, as it seems, some good prophecy. He gave him the good news of his new reign and gave him a tikka (otria) on his forehead; although this man (the Gurū) was a gentile and the Prince, a Moor; to the pontiff it seemed that it would be good to give this symbol peculiar to gentiles, as a sign of success in his undertaking; as the Prince was the son of a gentile woman and because of the prince's opinion of his saintliness.

The King [Jahāngīr] came to know of this and after having imprisoned the Prince he ordered for the said Gurū (Gorù) to be brought. Having him imprisoned, some gentiles interceded for their saint: finally they managed to get him sentenced to a hundred thousand cruzados, a petition of a rich gentile who remained his guarantor. This individual took care that either the King (El-Rei) annul this sentence or the saint have or at least negotiate that money; but in all he got frustrated; and he seized from his poor Pope everything he could find not sparing his clothes nor the clothes of his wife and sons; and seeing that all of this was not enough, as the gentiles don't have loyalty towards neither Pope or father regarding money, each and every day he gave new torments and gave new affronts to the poor saint. He ordered him to be beaten many times with shoes on his face and forbade him to eat, so that he (the Gurū) would give him more money, as he was not willing to believe that he did not have it, but he did not have it nor did he find anyone who would give it to him; and thus amongst many trials, pains and torments given by the very ones who adored him, the poor Gurū (Gorù) died. The guarantor tried to save himself, but he was imprisoned and killed after they had taken everything they could find.

NOTES

1. Annual Relation 1606–1607 (part IV, Book III, chapter V, fos 148–51r. Reprinted in Coimbra 1931 vol. II, 366–70). The original text of the letter is in the Marsden Manuscripts of the British Museum (BM Add MSS 9854, ff. 38–52r).
2. Singh, *Early European Accounts*, 181.
3. E.R. Hambye s.j., "A Contemporary Jesuit Document on Guru Arjun Dev's Martyrdom," in *Punjab Past and Present: Essays in Honour of Dr Ganda Singh*, ed. Harbans Singh and N. Gerald Barrier (Patiala: Punjabi University, 1976), 115.
4. Jahāngīr's own diary, *Tuzuk-i-Jehāngīrī*, notes that the Gurū was at Goindvāl when Khusrau passed through while Sarūp Dās Bhallā, *Mahimā Parkāś*, notes that the meeting took place in Tarn Tāran.

5. Singh, *Early European Accounts*, 182.
6. Ibid., 183.
7. Irfan Habib trans., "Sikhism and the Sikhs 1645–46: From 'Mobad,' *Dabistān-ī-Mazāhib*," in *Sikh History from Persian Sources*, ed. J.S. Grewal and I. Habib (New Delhi: Tulika, 2001), 67.
8. Singh, *Episodes from the Lives of the Gurus*, 87.
9. Hari Ram Gupta, *History of the Sikhs*, 5 vols (New Delhi: Munshiram Manoharlal, 1978–1991), 1: 144–54.
10. Shaikh Ahmad Farūqī Sirhindī, *Maktūbāt-i-Imām-i-Rabbānī* (Lucknow, 1889), letter 193, quoted in Yohanan Friedmann, *Shaykh Ahmad Sirhindī: An Outline of His Thought and a Study of His Image in the Eyes of Posterity* (Montreal: McGill-Queen's University Press, 1971), 74.
11. The Portuguese letter has been previously translated into English in John A. D'Silva, "The Rebellion of Prince Khusru According to Jesuit Sources," *Journal of Indian History*, vol. V (1927), 267–81 and also in Father Fernão Guerreiro, *Jahangir and the Jesuits* trans. C.H. Payne (London: George Routledge & Sons, Ltd., 1930), 11–12. A short paper with fresh translation in E.R. Hambye s.j., "A Contemporary Jesuit Document on Gurū Arjun Dev's Martyrdom," in *Punjab Past and Present: Essays in Honour of Dr Ganda Singh*, ed. Harbans Singh and N. Gerald Barrier (Patiala: Punjabi University, 1976), 113, sheds further new light on this account. Additional commentary on the portion relating to Gurū Arjan can be found in Dr Ganda Singh, *Early European Accounts of the Sikhs* (who reproduces John A. D'Silva's translation), Gopal Singh, *History of the Sikh People (1469–1978)* (New Delhi: World Book Centre, 1979. Revised and updated edition, New Delhi: World Book Centre, 1988), 194fn., and J.S. Grewal, and Irfan Habib, ed. and trans., *Sikh History from Persian Sources* (New Delhi: Tulika, 2001), 58.

CHAPTER 2

WENDEL'S HISTORY OF THE JATS, PATHĀNS, AND SIKHS, 1768

Francis Xavier Wendel, *Memoires de l'origine et etablissement des Siks*, Eur Mss ORME OV8, part 14, 67–103, Orme Collection MSS, Oriental India Office Collection, British Library, London. Received by Robert Orme in 1772. Reprinted in the original French in François Xavier Wendel, *Les mémoires de Wendel sur les Jat, les Pathan, et les Sikh*, ed. Jean Deloche (Paris: École française d'Extrême-Orient, 1979), part III.
Translated by Dr. Jeevan Singh Deol.

Father François Xavier Wendel was part of a much larger nexus of early European travelers to India who wrote about the Sikhs. He was intimately acquainted with Antoine Louis Henri Polier, Joseph Tieffenthaler, and Anquetil Du Perron (see part I, chapter 3). Wendel is a character of whom little is known. He came to India in 1751 with the Jesuit mission and was living in Lucknow in 1763. Like many of his Jesuit contemporaries, he served in one of the royal courts—in Wendel's case it was the Rājā Jawāhar Singh of Bhāratpur where, in March 1768, he was chosen to negotiate business with the English in Calcutta. Wendel is principally remembered for his role while in charge of the mission of Agra, where he negotiated several rights for the Jesuits of Mughal India. In his later life, he spent his time between Agra and Lucknow, where he died on March 20, 1803.

Throughout his life, Wendel was a prolific writer, commentator, and avid researcher. He certainly provided Polier with detailed information of a military nature but also sent scholarly papers to men such as Tieffenthaler. He mapped and sent geographical and topological data to the English geographer, James Rennell, who used them to prepare his map of India. His intimate knowledge of Persian allowed him to translate into French part of the memoirs of Jahāngīr.

Wendel's treatise on the Jats, Pathāns, and Sikhs remained an obscure, unpublished manuscript until relatively recently. It wasn't until 1979, some two centuries after it was first penned, that it was published in the original French with a short preface. The passages on the Sikhs have never before been translated into English and they go some way in explicating some interesting aspects of early European thinking on the Sikhs. Written in 1768, Wendel's notes were compiled while the Afghān King, Ahmad Shāh Durrānī, posed a real threat to the stability of the Punjab and the future of the Sikhs. The sections of Wendel's text that deal with the invading Shāh's impact on the Punjab and its people can be treated as the most precise while some of the earlier text is littered with mistakes. It is a great shame that these mistakes otherwise compromise an account that contains a great deal of fascinating points and intriguing details.

Primarily a religious figure and a spiritual leader, Padre Wendel recounts the history of the Sikhs from Gurū Nānak to Gurū Gobind Singh. He cannot reconcile Gurū Nānak's itinerant ministry with that of his own or that of the Catholic Church with its massive infrastructure and awesome power base. His history quickly disintegrates into a polemic on the Hindu yogi, but he resists further digressions to continue the story of the Sikhs. In his detail, Wendel, whose sources remain unclear from the introduction to his work, is remarkably consistent with Sikh tradition and later historians in his recounting of the execution of Gurū Tegh Bahādur at the hands of the then Mughal Emperor, Aurangzeb. In fact Wendel, who is not quick to praise non-Christians, remains sympathetic and respectful in his treatment of how the Gurū refused Islam in preference to execution. Whilst Wendel does not make any mention of the role that the Gurū played in defending the rights of the Kashmīrī *pandits*, he also does not support other contemporary writers (namely, Ferishtāh and Ghulām Hussain Khān in part VI, chapters 29 and 32 respectively) who regarded the Gurū as a renegade who was punished as a criminal rather than as a religious leader.

At this point, Wendel makes a most extraordinary statement and one that finds no other support or corroboration in other accounts. Wendel claims that the tenth Gurū, in return for the district of Sirhind, was prepared to accept conversion to Islam. However, according to Wendel, the emperor would not accept such terms and subsequently, the Gurū left the Punjab in some shame for the Deccan. Not only is this story uncorroborated by other writers but it is simply not supported by any other fact that we know either from the Mughal or Sikh perspective. Wendel allows his own prejudices to overshadow his short passage on the tenth Gurū. What is not apparent is the reason why Wendel, who otherwise is relatively complimentary about the Sikh faith, decides to regard Gurū Gobind Singh with such disdain although it is quite clear that Wendel is vociferous in his dislike for the Sikhs of his day who he considers "an assembly of wicked of all varieties and of every caste."

Wendel provides an interesting variant to the traditional narrative of the *Chandī* drama, which maintains that the Gurū invoked the benevolence of

Chandī with the aid of Brahmins in order to inspire the Sikhs to join his martial path in an uprising to overthrow the Mughal regime. Wendel implies that this was the precursor to the formal formation of the Khālsā in 1699.

It is another of Wendel's mistakes that actually provides fascinating early European reference to an aspect of the reign of Bandā Bahādur that is often quoted in traditional histories. Bandā Bahādur clearly riled the Mughal authorities with his peasant revolution but he also antagonized large numbers of the Khālsā. He was accused, in his own lifetime, of creating a schism within the united Khālsā by his innovations of the accepted doctrine. To some, this was too much and they vigorously fought against him. One of these innovations was the adoption of the war cry "Fateh Darshan." This literally translates as "bear witness to the victory," an enormously haughty statement especially given that Gurū Gobind Singh claimed "Vāhigurū jī kī Fateh" (lit. "Victory belongs to the creator"). Not unsurprisingly, this change caused great agitation amongst the Khālsā. Wendel in his writings incorrectly, but consistently, refers to Bandā Bahādur as Fateh Darshan or "Fate-dersan."

Despite the mistake of Bandā's name, Wendel provides a particularly accurate account of the capture and execution of Bandā Bahādur, and an especially chilling account of the execution of the Sikhs who accompanied him. Following the reference on Bandā Bahādur, Wendel's chronology moves to a contemporaneous account of the Sikhs who lived in the Punjab in the 1760s, the time of writing. Wendel, like many contemporaries, notes that the Sikhs were viciously divided and prophetically observes that should the Sikhs someday follow the Marāthās in uniting, they too could open "a road to their sovereign power."

Wendel provides the earliest known European account of the Sikh mode of mobile warfare which gives a valuable insight into the battle tactics used by Sikhs against the latter invasions of Ahmad Shāh Durrānī. He likens their hit-and-run tactics to those employed by the Parthians and notes their successes against the more formidable and sizeable armies of the Pathāns. Interestingly, he also contends that the Sikhs dread the use of firearms "in such a way as never to go near where there are cannonballs, bullets or sulphur." This contradicts many other eyewitness accounts which assert that the Sikhs were especially effective when armed with a matchlock.

Writing in 1768 Wendel remarks, like many other contemporaries, on the disunity of the Sikhs in the Punjab. As he put it "among 10,000 men there will be at least as many commanders and what is more, each is independent of the other." Remarkably, within the span of his own lifetime, the Sikhs would consolidate under the exceptional, but short lived, leadership of Ranjīt Singh.

Following Wendel's notes on the Sikhs, we reproduce one of the many letters written by Wendel that are preserved in the Orme collection of manuscripts at the British Library. This particular letter contains some of the more illuminating details on the Sikhs and their constant military engagements with their neighbors (in this case, the Jats), and is a good representative example of the information found within the body of Wendel's letters. This collection, a vast assemblage of information on the early European view of the Sikhs, demands a separate linguistic and historical study in order to gain a better comprehension of the Jesuit view of the Sikhs.

Whoever reads in the history of Indostan of our times the expeditions, construction and fortune that have been made so rapidly since the beginning of this century, after the Marathas, by the Jats and Rohélas during the general decadence of the Mogols will expect, I think, that this astonishing success must have made others desire to undertake to do the same. In effect, we know no more than that the most obscure people and men of the lowest condition have happily taken advantage, for their own gain, of the troubles of their neighbors or of those by whom their own country was troubled. Thus (without saying anything about events of this kind from a more remote age) the enterprise in Persia undertaken by the Afghans under Myr-Weis animated the famous Thamas-couli-kan or Nader-chah,[1] and this example gave occasion to the celebrated chah Thorrani[i] to invade and lay waste a number of times, under our own eyes, to Indostan. Such is mortal grandeur and fortune: to be born of nothing, to grow by violence and to consolidate oneself and subsist by the loss and ruin of others. The history of a troop of brigands, popularly called Siks, that today affects so strongly the centre of the empire of the Grand Mogol and menaces the vicinity, will serve as a new proof of this ancient truth.

Baba Nânec,[ii] a *kattri* by caste or extraction from the government of Panjab or Lahor, was in the sixteenth century the first originator or founder of this peculiar sect, called by him the *Nánek-band*. One must nevertheless beware of believing that the Siks of today and their way and manner of living are those that this venerable elder is reported to have kept up himself and left to the Siks or his disciples. This *kattri*,[iii] a wealthy man respected among those of his country and, we have grounds to notice

---

[i] *Sik* means in the language of the country the Persian *morid*, that is to say, devout person, disciple, sectator; thus *sikni*, a female devotee. In this discussion, *Siks* by antonomasia signifies or will signify the following: disciples or sectators of Bâba-Nânek. Today under this special name must be understood the new class of brigands who are the subject of this report.

[ii] *Bâba*: this is the name that is given in India to those old men or *faquirs*, withdrawn to some remote place, who have *tchélas*, *morids* and disciples of their sect. The meaning is nearly the same as in Europe, and everyone is sufficiently educated about it.

[iii] *Kattri*: the caste of *kattris* is that of the *divans*, *vaquils*, agents or public prosecutors and similar officers of the court, like that of the *kayts* is of the *mothatti*, or writers, inspectors, etc., although these two castes are indifferently employed for the same responsibilities. The *kattris* originate from Panjab, the *kayts* from Parrab or the country to the east, from Agra beyond the Gemna to the province (gouvernement) of Pattna. These two castes appear more skilful than any other at the offices mentioned above, either because they have carried out and occupied them for a long time or because their genius aided by the climate gives them something that makes them clever. The *kattris* are mostly well built, fair and easy to distinguish from the other inhabitants of Indostan. Both castes have the reputation of being shrewd, crafty and political. They eat meat and drink *arrac*, two things abominable to most of the other castes of the country. Their way of life in general has something that is indicative of the court. Ever since the Mogols have been established in Indostan, the Cachemirians, a flexible and duplicitous [?] people have been widely introduced in place of the *kattris*, at present they have once more begun to fall with the power that has been their support.

from his writings and doctrines, endowed with noble knowledge, weary of the world, removed himself to a remote place, in an area at the foot of the Gomaum, to the north-east of Lahor, where one can still see today a famous pond frequented annually by a number of his *morids* or devotees and other tokens of his residence hallowed since his death by the superstition of the inhabitants of the environs. The enthusiasm devoted to him at the end of his life, his precepts and instructions full of wisdom according to the ability of these people (who are mostly amazed by everything that has the appearance of the extraordinary), and the credibility of those who had visited or communicated with him acquired for him so high a reputation for wisdom, inspired from on high,[iv] for being holy and for being divine, since his words were the same as oracle for all Panjab and his renown also spread to neighboring countries: there are some compact volumes of his doctrine and they are still read today with devotion and admiration.[v] He was widely respected and, even though a gentile or hindu, had as many devotees among the mahométans. In order to make him more marvellous or to give greater credit to their belief in him, his devotees recount a good number of miracles from his life and after the death of this *pire*,[vi] in particular that there was a dispute about whether his corpse should be burnt or buried after his death, according to the different sentiments of his *morids*; before the decision about what should be done, the venerable deposit became invisible to the eyes of all and nothing was preserved of it, they say, but the memory.

Whoever has seen India must, I think, have seen a certain number of those solitary faquirs, a species, it seems, of those ancient solitary anchorites, or perhaps what is left of those famous and alleged wise men of whom histories of ancient times give us so favourable a report. And who knows whether the great and divine Bramah or Bermah, from whom some claim to derive the fundamental belief of the Indians, was not, in his time (perhaps not so remote), one of these *babas* that we see today.

[iv] To make this gourou their patriarch even more glorious, the Siks, disciples of Bâba-Nânec, claim that he had no education that could have helped him in the sublime doctrine that he taught afterward, but that he had been inspired and marvellous since his youth, or rather I have noticed of their belief in him that they clearly see him as God himself, transformed into this mortal being to teach to others things so elevated and above the understanding of men. And in general all these great *pires*, *gousayns* or *faquirs* of Indostan are seen as celestial spirits who live in the bodies of men so extraordinary. From that, without doubt, is the great and amazing veneration that the people everywhere have for them.

[v] I have seen several of these books written in verse, in Persian characters and in the Indian Panjâbi language, that is to say such as is spoken in the surroundings of Lahor. In them Bâba-Nânec expresses nobly enough and with an elevated spirit the essence of God and the divine attributes; the devotees were delighted by them. It would appear that he had knowledge of the doctrine of the ancient wise men or magi or those celebrated more modern *souphis* who are their remainder. His other works on moral doctrine are not less sensible. Many read them, few understand them without an interpreter, because of the way in which it is expressed as well as the language, being nothing but a very corrupt dialect of that of Indostan, which has moreover changed a great deal since the death of Nânec. Howerver it can be said about the doctrine of this *pire* or Indian wise man as about those of all similar phantoms of holiness that "*narraverunt mihi iniqui fabulationes, sed non ut lex tua.*"

[vi] *Gourou*, *pire*, are the same thing, that is to say, venerable, holy, master and interpreter of the law or divine preceptor. Mohammedans give to their *faquirs* or *pires* the surname of *chah* which is to say, great, *busurg*, or venerable, thus Chah-mathar, Chah-godbuddin, Chah-nezamuddin, etc, famous *faquirs* and holy Mohammedans in Indostan; from *pire* is *pirott* or *pirott-gi*, title of the household Brahmane of each family of distinction among the Gentiles of this country.

In effect, based on what we have learned of Baba-Nanec in recent times, he seems to be an author with whom we can agree, even though he conformed to the beliefs of Hindoustan. Whoever has seen this country, I believe, must know the respect and high veneration that Indians show to this sort of person in general and in particular to those who, for some time, have had the success of having some prestige in the vicinity and have grown old in their retreat. People come from afar to see and visit them; people revere and worship them; princes humble themselves before them, sit beside them with hands joined and with the utmost respect to hear them. I have been witness (and would one ever believe it in Europe?) that a great and powerful *raja* who marched at the head of an army of more than 240,000 men, descended from his elephant to give place to one of these semi-divine rurals, who, completely naked, hair dishevelled, with a long grey beard and his body smeared with ashes and cow dung, had the appearance of a completely wild Pan or Faunus. It is not unusual in India to send tambourines, troops, carriages, elephants—in a word the most magnificent train of the great—to call these divine men to their houses and, with this procession of the great at their disposition, one can easily judge what the veneration of the people for them must be. Also it would be a crime for a *raja*, not matter how great and illustrious he was, to not give up in his own hall of audience his *masnat* or carpet of honour, reserved only for him, to any one of these reputed *pires*, who was summoned or came of his own free will (which does not happen often) to do him the honour of his visit. We Europeans rebuke this condescension; they treat it with surprise and with blindness, I know. I do not want at all to defend it in all its extent. It should none the less teach these refined people of our hemisphere a little more with regard to those whom they see as the presidents, masters and directors of their religion, at the same time as we notice an indifference, coolness and open contempt that disheartens the last of the nations that it pleases us to treat as barbarians and savages. Egypte worshipped Joseph; Nebuchadnezzar, Daniel; Persia, the magi; Indostan the Brahmans; through all of antiquity, all peoples revered the wise men who were nothing but the masters of their beliefs; only Europe, to put it in this way, takes care not to do this and that is why we must believe that it has become wiser. And Nânec-gourou (because that is what he is normally called), although venerable during the space of about 150 years, from Baber-chah up to the reign of Aurangzeb, was not even so the type to make as much noise in Indostan as from the beginning of this century. When he passed away, his post and *pire's* chair remained with someone of his family who, by descent, delivered it in the end to one Deg-bahadr,[vii] under Aurangzeb, and once

---

[vii] As far as we can judge the establishments of these gourous until the time of Gourou-Govind, these *pires* were neither so poor or so lacking in things that make life convenient. It is said that Gourou-Govind had stables filled with horses and a large entourage [?] and fund to cover their expenses, which is neither new or rare in India, that is to say, to see these so-called *pires* kept like some great person of the country. I remember having seen in Gouzaratte one of these *tâcors*, as they are called, a type of patriarch among them who was marching with the following and accompaniments [?] of a prince and in the places where it pleased him to stop, usually outside cities, there was no one of any sex, age or condition who did not come to see him, make offerings to him and receive from his *dohas* (+) or benedictions and, during the time of his stay, a band of singers and musicians of the country (he sitting on a type of throne) gave audience to the crowd, which was fighting [?] to see him. During the time of raja Savaijessing, raja of Amber or Jépor, on the occasion of a feast he held in honour of a new incarnation (which, according to the day-dreams of the Bramanes, would manifest itself during his rule) among many others of all classes, there was one of these *gourous* or *pires* who had come there with 50 or 60,000 of his followers, most of them armed and capable of chasing out the raja if they wished.

more a number of devotees incorporated themselves into this sect and made so much of this gourou, at that time president, that this king, being besides a great enemy of things having a connection with gentilism, asked him to explain himself.

Having made Deg-bahadr come to his presence and, having questioned him a great deal on his conduct and way of living, this prince, it is said, asked of him a miracle in confirmation of the doctrine that he was claiming as divine, most of it in opposition to mahométisme [Mohammadanism]. Excusing himself due to inadequacy and because miracles are the work of the all powerful, Deg-bahadr had in the end to choose either to renounce the doctrine and become a musulman or confirm it by the death to which he had been condemned; he did not hesitate to refuse, graciously giving his head and arousing by his example his disciples to do as much at their turn, when the occasion would present itself, which they did not fail to do follow, as we shall soon see.

In the reign of Bahadr-chah,[2] Gourou-govind succeeded to the caliphate of the Sik sect and was the last of his race. He had neither the spirit nor all the self-control of his ancestors; having let himself be tempted by ambition (often the stumbling block or failure of the most firm resolutions and also of holiness, not only the false and apparent, as is that of most of these famous *pires* and *faquires* of Indostan), he was presented by the *amyr* Kan-kana, his friend, to Bahadr-chah: he was made to expect the government of Sirhind (in the vicinity of which he had his establishments) in exchange for accepting mahometanism, and he seemed well enough induced to this change. But this prince, by a sentiment more noble and contrary to that which had exercised his father, generously refused to make converts to Mohamed through such low designs and, as he thought, unworthy to the holy law of his prophet. Thus Govind, as well as the shame of losing his reputation among his own people, had the displeasure of being discouraged in his intentions at court where he nonetheless remained, supported by his friends, and in the company of this king left for the Deccan where, following the reports that we have of him, he was killed by a simple Pattan in a religious dispute in which he became involved.

For this ceremony, which succeeded in nothing but fattening up the Bramanes, I was assured that the raja, otherwise wise and philosophical enough, spent more than 50 lacs of his treasure, having had brought from all parts animals of every kind from humans to the least insect to sacrifice them, following the opinion of the Bramane director, to the divinity that was to be born. This same raja, having been told of the excesses that several of these *pires* committed with some of their devotees, in spite of the veneration that the raja himself had for these people, ordained that all should marry or leave his jurisdiction. Some submitted, several refused and instead left the establishment, among them the great *gourou* or *pire* of the *raja* himself, a man of great reputation throughout Indostan and leader of a large class of *gosayns*. (+) doah: the people of India are similarly persuaded that doahs or benedictions, vows or wishes of these *pires* cannot fail to be of advantage to them, just as they are stubborn in believing that their *bad-doah* or maledictions and imprecations will be followed by a certain misfortune, fast or slow in arriving. This belief is also founded on their books, valued as divine writings. In the Veidam, the adventures of Routren, famous for his amorous exploits (or rather debauches), like another Jupiter, at each step detail the regrettable sequels of imprecations or *bad-doah* that this god or *deüta* had to suffer from these *faquires* or solitary ones when he set himself to debauching with these women or concubines. It is without question in this persuasion that part of the great veneration that Indians have for their *faquirs* is founded; it is also from there that most of their indulgence for their impertinence comes and do not rebuff it except very rarely and with the greatest circumspection. The respect of Mohammedans for their *dorvechs*, not less than that of the gentiles, would also appear to bear relation to it, although at the same time we dare not deny that this sort of people is respectable in every time and every country.

It is because of this gourou that the Siks took courage and later made more noise. It is said that baba-Govind, before going to the court, had a meeting at his taquia, or dwelling place, with a famous Bramane come from the Decan (another impostor as regards sanctity); they made, in front of a numerous assembly of devotees, a type of sacrifice to Bâba-Nânec and after having thrown into a large fire a sabre and bow, which emerged from it without having been touched by the flames, with a marvellous brilliance, at the same time as an unknown voice was heard which said: fate gourou, fate gourou, that is to say: victory is Bâba-Nânec's; it belongs to our gourou and that the sabre and bow would henceforth be the arms that the *morids* of this gourou would have to use and, facing them, there would be no enemy who could resist. Gourou Govind himself remained dumbfounded for and outside of himself for some time, ordained some things like a man who had lost his mind—whether because the Braman sorcerer had actually made him mad or because he himself had resolved on this ruse to give greater credit to the farce that he had just played out—making him delighted and as if filled with a spirit from on high, which did not fail to have effect on his devotees, as he had intended. And admittedly having recovered so easily from this pretended madness and seeing the manoeuvres that he made soon afterward for possessing himself of greater power (perhaps again with other, vaster designs, had he been successful), these are very manifest signs of the delusion with which he had taken advantage of the credulity of the followers of his sect. He did more: having returned from his reveries, whether true or feigned, having showed his disciples the arms that Bâba-Nânec had presented them with, he himself limited their mode of dressing and colour that he said he had been inspired to make known to them, that is, to let their hair and beards grow, to dress in no colour but blue, made of indigo, and to have no regard to caste distinctions . . . that anyone could become Sik . . . and finally that all Siks were fit for anything . . . Hence this strange confusion and mixture of persons of all castes and extraction among the Siks of today, a thing so abominable and until then unknown to the gentilism of Indostan.

With Gourou Govind, the stock of Bâba-Nânec died out, but not, as we have said, the sect. In his absence or soon after his death, another calife or *pire* put himself in his place, although without right and without title. He was the leader of a troop of these *gousayns*, called *saniassi* (about whom we have spoken elsewhere), himself also a morid of Bâba-Nânec or feigning to be so to succeed him in authority and in rank among the Siks. Fate-dersan[3] (that was the name that he had taken), not content with introducing himself into the place and establishment of his predecessors, soon conceived the design of a broader domination. Having gathered a good number of these vagabonds of his extraction and others who joined themselves, he undertook in the name of the Siks and under the auspices of Nânec-gourou to make himself master of the lands in the vicinity of Tchaic[viii,4] and his bands started to make excursions there and to excite trouble within the country, in such a way that the governor of Lahore had need of all his vigilance, sustained by the forces of his government to stop or suppress their insolence and, since the entire army of Bahadr-chah also marched to this side after its return from the Decan, the governor did not have a difficult time destroying Fate-dersan and his troop. He was obliged to leave the plains and find a retreat in the mountains of Gomaum, where it was not so easy to pursue and capture him. There, he was confined and did not dare to appear so daringly at all, although

---

[viii] Tchaic or Tchaique: this is the place consecrated to the memory of Bâba-Nânec, 20 or 25 cosses to the east of Lahor where the Siks annually go to have their general assembly and make the sacrifice which is mentioned below.

he did not fail to consolidate himself there and make himself at the same time more numerous and stronger, while his bands took to the field in small numbers to extract from there their subsistence and spread terror. They continued to do this quite frequently, but not with as much success so as to appear so openly. The court being at Lahor and having so many troops under the princes, sons of the king, in the province, although it was nearly impossible for the Siks to leave their retreat without risking being pursued immediately, taken or powerfully chased, and they were also still too few and too new to the profession. It would take them some time to make themselves more skilful, and the troubles in the empire that would give them occasion to do more freely what they wished. With Bahadr-chah dead and Mozzodin, his successor, having left Panjab to take himself to the capital and take possession of the kingdom, Fate-dersan immediately took up his original intention. The indolence of Mozzodin and the troubles that arose shortly afterwards between him and Feroc-cher[5] gave enough leisure to the Siks to grow to the point where they openly attacked and became masters of several places, until Feroc-cher, having become the peacable possessor of the throne, sent a positive order to the governor of Lahor to join his forces and act in such a way as to seize the person of Fate-dersan in whatever way possible, break up his party and relieve the province at the soonest of a race so abominable and extravagant as was this new class of brigands under the name of Siks.

Abdoll-seman-kan,[6] at the time the governor of Punjab, partially stimulated by the damage that his government had suffered from them and partially to avenge himself on this sect that scorned so openly the law of Mohamed, and finally, to follow the orders of the court, took himself there quickly and pursued so closely the Siks and their leader that in the end he forced them to throw themselves into a mountainous place of difficult access called Loh-garr, which Fate-dersan had only recently made himself master of and had made into the centre of the exploits that he intended. He obstinately defended himself there, and the expedition cost Abdoll-seman-khan a great deal in difficulty and people to bring it to an end. He was however successful. Having been reduced to the utmost extremity in that place, Fate-dersan and the people who were left with him had no option but to surrender; he was taken with six or seven hundred of his followers and the governor, wanting to prevail at court because of his conquest, spared them all their lives; then, having locked Fate-dersan in a cage at Lahore, he sent him and the others, attached in pairs by fetters on their feet, on camels to be presented to the king at Dehly.

Some people worthy of trust who found themselves in Dehly on this occasion and everyone in general speak, with some exaggeration, of the gaity and contentment of these miserable ones when they entered in this condition, laden with chains, into the capital, which would yet become the scaffold of their torture. One cannot grow weary of praising the firmness and constancy with which they viewed and scorned the death that they would all suffer soon after, without exception. After having tried a great deal and needlessly to make them musulmans, promising them life and the emperor's mercy, a proposition which they did not want to listen to at all, the provost of the city ordered that they be beheaded, which would be carried out during the course of a week, and every day one hundred were taken from the place of torture to be executed, they became so joyous and pleased that they fought over turns and each wanted to be first. Just as their lives were being taken away, they were once more offered mercy on the condition mentioned above, but instead of accepting it, they pressed those who had to cut their throats to hurry and not postpone any longer the pleasure of finding themselves earlier with their Nânec, whose name they always had on their lips. Fate-dersan was the last who died; he was probably spared expressly to disturb him with the sight of so many of his followers who had been finished off before his eyes; but nothing was capable of affecting him, scorning with disdain every mercy and every offer that could be made to him, he protested that he would have been absolutely unworthy of commanding so many lives as had been sacrificed for his consideration, in front of and for him, if he did not have at least enough constancy to follow them in death. Thus died Fate-dersan with about seven hundred Siks, and one can say that this large number that had been wiped out instead of diminishing the sect actually served to augment it and make it more respectable and general.

It is not so easy to understand and explain how enthusiasm as regards a pure super-stition might be capable of making such an impression on the spirit of people, mostly unpolished, ignorant and not at all instructed in the mysteries of the sect for which they had died in throngs. Examples from every time and from every law true or crude have been well cited in this connection; other than the living faith, founded on a remunerative God, sustained in a law of mercy by the powerful and supernatural assis-tance of Jesus Christ, can it be sufficiently conceived, I ask, how people, lacking one and unsure of the other, scorn so constantly the appealing attractions of life and the horror of an ignominious death on no other principle than knowing of an uncertain hope of being afterwards happy in the society of a man perhaps deceptive, whom they did not know, in a state of felicity purely imaginary of which they have still less knowl-edge than of the author of the belief on which it is founded.[ix] One sees, it is true, in

---

[ix] A modern author (Z. Hollwell, *Interesting historical events*, part II) prides himself on having found the skeleton key of this enigma, of explaining with total ease this horrid sacrifice (or, as people like to call it, this act of national and pious principles) in the instruction of the *pirot* or domestic Bramane and in the persuasion of an imaginary bliss of their released spirit in the com-pany of their dead spouses, etc.; besides I will here point out in passing what this author has reported falsely about this custom, regarding the number, the precise time and other particulars on that subject 1. that the *pirot* or domestic Bramane is usually idiotic and ignorant, all his knowl-edge being limited to announcing the fasts and feasts of the family, to inform of the good and bad days and to undertake a journey or other affair of importance, to arrange and make marriages and other similar occupations of his profession. None or few instructions, above all for the sex, none of these persuasive predications that this author supposes; 2. there are not *pirots* or domes-tic Bramanes in every house and just in the houses of the rich and the very distinguished; 3. the interest of the domestic Bramane would instead be to encourage widows to survive their husband and, since women cannot remarry, perhaps the *pirot* could rather find his account with them alive rather than burnt; 4. it being completely against the customs of the gentiles to keep in their houses the corpse of a dead person from the house, how could the widow's decision wait twenty-four hours and afterwards burn herself with the body of the deceased? 5. the general belief of these *sattia* (+) or so-called martyrs to love and conjugal fidelity (which bind them to this terri-ble sacrifice) is that to transmigrate afterwards into the body of one of the *rânis* or princesses yet to be born, if she is a woman of low extraction, or into that of a person of higher rank, if she is the widow or concubine of a *raja*. They are little or not at all instructed about liberation and the state of purification of their migratory spirit and, since most of them know nothing about the superior and celestial type of felicity, it is futile to suppose them possible of being sensitive to it as far as we understand it [?]. Also, the most sensible people of Indostan ingenuously confessing that real *sattias* or strong and faithful women are those who after their husband dies keep them-selves in chastity, retirement and the exercise of other moral virtues suitable to their state, this famous sacrifice therefore being in ever sense an act of despair or at least of illusion rather than of piety and of a religion founded on reasonable and solid principles, but more can perhaps [be said] elsewhere on this topic. (+) *Satti*: steadfast, strong, faithful; sattia: believers; by antonomasy satti, a woman who burns herself alive with her deceased husband; the tokens that relations cus-tomarily erect on the place where this sacrifice takes place is also called satti: these are square stones, large or small, on which are ordinarily depicted pictures of those who burnt themselves there; each caste has their own particular ones.

Indostan examples of this sacred fury, so to speak, even more amazing, in the ghastly custom of wives' burning themselves alive with their deceased husband. In vain, I think, one calls to assistance the famed metempsychosis or transmigration of souls (in whatever fashion one dares to understand or explain it) to decipher this enigma, constantly obscure and, in my opinion, insoluble. The doubtful assurances of a Bramane, a thousand times found faulty, the precepts and promises or often reveries of an elder or *faquir*, often not better educated than the lowest of his *morids* (to whom his manner of living, a little extravagant and out of the ordinary for others, has given him all the credit of a wise man and the reputation of a holy man), are they enough to reject so stubbornly a good present, so natural, so flattering for the hope of a future happiness, doubtful and inconceivable? Yet one sees them nonetheless mistaking this grand, this unique good, life; one sees them sacrificing themselves to the cruellest and most repellent deaths. What is it that prompts them? What is it that encourages them, pushes them? We cannot presume that they were endowed with motives or powers from on high. It is necessary therefore to find others, and where can they be found except in the force of custom and example and in a living person, although erroneous conviction (actually given birth to by the ambition and honest love of having the reputation after death of being faithful, constant and holy in the eyes of those whom they make admirers of their false virtue and heroism rather than in the hope of a future greatness and felicity up there of which most are neither educated or certain). But let us return to our Siks and leave this matter for another occasion, although it too is worth of a very long argument.

Just as the constancy of so many people who had given their lives so generously affirmed the followers of Bâba-Nânec in their belief, so too did the harsh punishment and pursuit terrify the Siks to no longer dare to stir themselves for a long time. Nothing is heard of them until after the invasion of Nader-chah,[7] incident on so many revolutions that arose afterward, the one after the other, in this empire, that almost everyone knows. During almost the entire reign of Mohamed-chah, they remained quiet other than some troubles of little consequence that they incited concerning the son of Zacharia-kan,[8] governor of Lahor, who having fallen out with his father got himself involved with them; but it had no repercussions and the trouble was quickly quelled. There were no longer leaders of the sect, at least ones as famous as those about whom we have spoken, although at the same time it had already become more general and widespread through nearly the entire expanse of Panjab. Each of the *zamindares*[9] along the Gomau from the Zatalass[10] to the Jhelum, beyond Lahor, little by little made himself leader of a few hundred horsemen under his command, according to his power or his pretensions of standing up for himself or of extending his own boundaries and thus, in a short time, there was this number of brigands by whom Indostan is now spoiled. Abdina-beg-kan,[11] governor of Sarhind, spared neither haste nor expenditure to suffocate and extirpate this nascent pest, but he himself died in the end and, after this there was no one else who could oppose them. The sudden and repeated irruption of the Tourrani *chah* first of all obliged the *zamindares* to put themselves on their guard at the same time as it furnished them with frequent occasions to take to the field and ally themselves with one another for the common cause of defending themselves, falling in detached parties and in dangerous passages (which they knew perfectly) upon convoys, the front and rear-guard Tourranis, putting them in disorder and, before they could rush there, taking the booty by roads and tracks known only to them. The example of the Jats to the south of Dehly encouraged them and the success they had on different occasions magnified their audacity and their number. When they were pursued, the neighboring mountains and the forests by the side of the main road were their retreat; the chah, as powerful as he was, often did not know how to get away and deliver himself from them.

By the fiftieth year of this century it was known that the Grand-Mogul was no longer master nor able to bother himself with the provinces (*gouvernements*) around the Zatalass in the north of the empire. It was Ahmet-chah Tourrani or the Siks who had them at their disposal; it is true that they never dared to appear in front of the *chah* and attack him; nonetheless they chopped several of his detachments into pieces, destroyed some leaders and governors and more than one reduced him to having to turn back due to the shortage of food caused by the devastations made in the area where the army had to pass or halt. They also got all the way to the barrier fortress Attec on the Indus and, so as not to leave any strong places on the sides of the grand way of Indostan, there is almost no place that they had not lain waste to, broken down, plowed down and destroyed. After the celebrated defeat of the Marattes under Bhaou (1761), they profited greatly from the booty that the victorious Tourranis carried off from the expedition that they had just completed. At the end of the year 64, the *chah* having taken it into his head to return to Indostan, the Siks put into the field more than 80,000 men to prevent the Pattan army from pentrating to the heart of the country and effectively prevented them from going any further forward; Ahmet-chah was obliged to return home in spite of his efforts; the Siks followed him and harassed him up to the other side of the Indus. The next year, after they had forced the *chah* to withdraw, they had the audacity to have coins struck at Lahor, with this arrogant inscription whose sense can be rendered as:

> If there is a law in the world; if there were ever a master
> It was that of Nânec-gourou; only He is worthy of being it.[x]

In the way that all of Punjab and the country between the Gomaum and the rivers Zatalass and Indus already, despite the pretensions of the Tourrani chah, is nothing but the property of the Siks, subordinate to them and at their pleasure and arrangements.

In order to finish with this nasty race, at the end of the year 66 Ahmet-chah undertook a new expedition to Indostan with the intention of destroying them. Consequently they had not ever been attacked more sharply and pursued more closely than on this occasion. Leaving the great roads, the *chah* deliberately lead his army to the mountains on foot in order not to spare either any habitation or individual of the Siks. He effectively destroyed a great quantity of them and the Siks no longer had anywhere to hide except the places between the mountains where the Tourranis, who went everywhere to chase them, did not have the means to approach. Notwithstanding the number and the sharp force with which they had been pursued and pressed, a part of their cavalry, about 15 to 20,000, who were wandering in the field got ahead of the army, crossed the Zatalass and Jamna with a surprising rapidity and created terror up to the gates of Dehly. They threw all of the province beyond the Jamna to the northeast of Dehly into consternation and left it pillaged, laid waste to and set afire before a detachment of Tourranis, with the Rohélas of Nagib-kan[12] (who had joined the *chah* on the banks of the Zatalass) could pursue and chase them. Their outings had

---

[x] The Persian is: *Mazhab nanak kardim zahir vahm batinast*
    Badshahi dinu dunya ap hi sahib ast
that is to say in the meaning of the Siks: that the doctrine of Bâba-Nânec is so sublime and extensive that it includes things manifest and obscure, intelligible and incomprehensible, in a word, all that can be said and known: that this gourou is the real king of the world and lawmaker, that he is God himself.

become so frequent and so unexpected that the province of Delhy was taken by surprise and was already made half depopulated and deserted. It is they who turned the Rohelas into warriors, just as at the same time it is because of the Rohélas (although not much better than the Siks) and their wise and brave leader Nagib-kan that the rest of Indostan is up till now indebted for not having already been taken, like the Panjab, into misery and despair by these barbarians. Since Pannipatt, the towns of Sirhind, Lahor and some of the places subordinate to the *raja* of Jambou have nothing but the memory of their former splendour and grandeur. The great road blocked up, the convoys from Persia and Cachemire interrupted, the country-side depopulated and everywhere a dreadful appearance of devastation and desolation. It is moreover to be feared that this mass of marauders which will increase every year in power, by the booty that they have already amassed and the success that they have had, will quickly spread its rapine to very far off in the south of Indostan, since there is actually nothing but the fear of the Tourrani *chah* that can hold them back, or the forces of this side capable or united to resist them, all the more so in that they are called and even paid, for these agreeable expeditions in which they lay waste to everywhere they set foot.

It has been mentioned elsewhere (*vid. Mem. des Jats*) that the leader presently ruling the Jats (as good and as brave of the Siks) had called them twice to his aid for his mad expeditions and, after having been deceived and betrayed by them twice, the blind passion to avenge himself on his enemies has made him very recently engage to take them at great price, 25 or 30 thousand, after they themselves had spread out in his country, ravaged an entire province of revenue of more than 10 lacs per year, devastated and destroyed places in the surroundings which no enemy had touched up till now and of which the booty by a mediocre estimation could pass beyond 3 million, or 30 *lacs*. Having finally gone to the place where the combined armies of the Siks and the Jats were to meet in order to open the campaign and having had 11 lacs given to them in advance, they executed a complete turn around and commenced negotiations with the Rajpouts, the enemy that they had set out to attack, and declared themselves openly against the Jats who had called them, sought them and paid them. This entirely disconcerted the arrangement of the expedition that was forthcoming, but had by chance the desired long-desired effect that the Rajpouts and Jats reconciled themselves, something which until then had appeared very nearly impossible, so much that these two peoples, the one indebted to the other, had been embittered and stubbornly sought to destroy one another. It is surprising that all the great people of the middle of Indostan, in whose interest it was to have put in place a strong barrier against the influx of thieves, there is so little activity to prevent them or even to confront them and repel them. But that has been precisely the fate for so long of this large body of this empire: instead of supporting the other members on occasions when the consequences would be happy or disastrous for each one separately, they looked calmly upon the ravaging of a neighbour and a fire close by without being touched. They even thrilled in it and furnished it with material. Can we expect anything else of this except an impending and general revolution. The Marattes have already opened the road to their sovereign power in this way, and there is a great appearance that the Siks will follow them.

There is still a single thing that one can call capable of giving an obstacle to this power among the Siks, which is that up till now there are too many leaders or, to put it better, almost none at all among this vast multitude. It is only a vast but rough and shapeless body without a head; among 10,000 men there will be at least as many commanders and what is more, each is independent of the other and no more master of the troops of which he has command than the others are of him, each rules his party according to his whim; it is only when there was a journey to be undertaken that they are more or less united in standing by one another, in the case of being attacked or pursued. Their way of making war approaches that which is reported of the Parthians: to break through and flee in small groups, to show themselves in front and fall on the rear, to wander about, cut off and surprise convoys, this is the technique by which they have until today they have made their skill and bravery visible. They have no artillery and very often no other arms than the sabre, a bow and at most a lance. They have no luggage or vehicles, other than as many as they need to load and carry away the booty that they have taken. They commence an attack in the name of the Gourou, they come to life by it and become excited about the affair and, as soon as Gourou-Govind had the skill (as has been reported above) of imposing the pretended marvel of the sabre and the bow, they committed themselves very boldly in perilous circumstances even if they do not have the power to sustain it.

At first, they did not set themselves to anything but holding their own against pursuit by mahométans. It was a body of *gousayns* or *faquirs* on horseback, like there are so many others on foot, above all the *sanniassis* or *beraguis*, so numerous and so well known in all of India. They did not touch women or their clothes and jewels, they pillaged but did not kill at all and showed enmity only to mahomedanism. Today there are no infamies that they do not commit. To pillage, murder, lay waste to friends and enemies—all is equal to them. It is nothing more than an assembly of wicked of all varieties and of every caste who, under the name of Siks or disciples of Nânec-gourou, ordered under different leaders whom they obey as much as it pleases them, make a public profession of breaking down and destroying all that is still intact in this unfortunate country, exposed to their violences, and leaving everywhere marks of a brutal fury and inhumanity. Hindus and mohamedans, most of the lowest extraction and the most cursed in Indostan, are welcomed. There is no rank or definition among them. No more extravagant sect has been seen in India that one knows of. When they had had much success, they took it in their heads to change the name from *Siks* to that of *Sings*,[xi] the honorary appellation of Rajpouts and of the most noble castes, to give themselves some lustre after they had acquired some power. Hence the strange composition of the names of the chiefs with the greatest reputation, such as Tchersa-sing, Calâl-sing, Tocca-sing[xii,13] and others of this type. They do not preserve anything of gourou Nânec except the memory and the name, assembling generally every year at the end of the month of April near the famous Tchaic in the region of Lahor and make there a type of sacrifice[xiii] to this *pire* which consists of boiling in a vast cauldron which they call a *carrah*[14] some sugar, some flour, some butter and I do not know what other drugs and then eat it together and with ceremony, after having spread out on it a cloth under which they claim are invisibly imprinted the marks of a hand, a sign of benediction as also of consent from on

[xi] *Sing* or *Seng*: lion, appellation already general in Indostan, especially among the Rajpouts; thus Ajit-sing, Mahado-sing, etc., and of other castes who have takend it from them, like Badan-sing, Javaer-sing Jats, Man-sing, Saheb-sing, etc., *kattris* and *kayts*.

[xii] Tchersa-sing: *tchersa*, leather, animal skin; *calâl*, innkeeper; *tocca*, labourer who works with a hammer and by striking it, like a blacksmith, locksmith, carpenter, etc., all low castes in this country.

[xiii] A type of placenta of the ancients. This offering is used markedly among the Hindous and, on many occasions, the Mohammedans also use it in the name of their *pires* or alleged holy men and afterwards carry it to friends or members of their household as a sacred thing. It is perhaps this sacrifice that *Jerem*. C.VII v. 18 and others speak.

high; it is also on this occasion that they deliberate their public affairs and expeditions to undertake after the season of the rains.[15]

They and their horses are mainly of indifferent height, but robust, as is usual for people who live in the mountains or close to them. There is something fierce in their manner: a brown complexion, black beard and hair, often untidy and hanging on the shoulders, together with clothes all in indigo and often neglected, which gives them the overall appearance of barbarians and savages. Since they live from theft and plunder, they do not have either train or tent; they camp where they find plunder and always leave a solitude for 5 or 10 *cosses* around, as we have already noted. However they are no longer as light as before and they have slowly begun to live in a grander style, a natural effect of the power they have attained, perhaps the same prevents them from extending this power further, as one has seen happening to the Marattes, since they decided, contrary to their beginning, to come and take with them from the Decan this large train and din of artillery and baggage that in the end they left in the same country where they had just collected charges, to be maintained in the splendid manner to which it seems they were not suited. Do we also not know that Alexander the Great was the same, after his brave Macedonians had been loaded with the booty that Persia and India had furnished them. It is not beyond all plausibility that after they had collected so many *lacs* in so few years and had made themselves sought after and feared throughout Hindoustan, they could not decide to equip themselves with artillery and everything that is necessary for this great project to obtain sovereign domination over these countries, particularly priding themselves with a prophecy or oracle of their gourou, of which they are the heirs and in the end should become the possessors. The ambition has many attractions for following it, and it is a type of political hydropsy that increases by the amount that one gives it power and the means to satisfy it.

This is very nearly what one could wish to know or that I can say about this nasty race, better known for their plundering and similar infamies (which they have committed in the heart of this empire and which they will still commit nearby) than for their extraction or profession of the sect of which they carry the name. There are Siks in small or large number throughout all of Indostan, that is to say those who are *morids* or sectators of Bâba-Nânec, above all among those of the *kattri* caste in which this gourou takes his origin. Yet it is properly speaking Panjab, the country of the Siks by profession, that is still the meeting place and residence of these barbarians about whom we have been speaking. When the rainy season comes, they return to their homes and deal with the country over which each of the leaders had the skill or the strength to become master; when October is over, they set off again, and, if the fear of the Abdali *chah* does not hold them back, not having already dealt with the northern side that they have very nearly entirely subjugated and rendered tributary up to the final extremity of India this side of the Gomau for several years, they begin to expand in the southern territories, a country where there is more to take and where they do not yet find enough resistance to prevent them. It still must be said that, more or less strong with the sabre, they fear firearms in such a way as never to go near where there are cannonballs, bullets or sulphur. Since they have not yet had the occasion or the firmness to measure all their forces ranged in the field in battle, we cannot say much of their courage or military bravery, and it does not appear that they will ever do wonders there as long as they do not have a single leader capable of commanding them and whom they really wish to obey.

To say it all in a few words, the Siks of today are an assembly of brigands of every caste and of every condition, without laws and without faith, a new class of thieves, born of superstition and increased by disorder, in a word one of those monstrous powers who in recent years have elevated themselves on the debris of the power of the Great Mogol.

All things have their decline, and it appears that, more than others, domination and in particular that which has violence as its base, like the Mohammedan, as soon as it was founded. Asia is a country of revolution, and Indostan has for a long time been its theatre. As soon as Mohammedanism was introduced there, tyranny took over; attempts to topple the tyrannical regime necessarily followed and consequently, sooner or later, gave way to disorder and general confusion. Nothing remains of the Great Mogol except his name and the name would already have been extinguished if the prince who claims to bear it today had not found (as has already been said on other occasions) strangers to guarantee it. How long will the feeble shadow of his royalty last? It is a shame that this vast, rich and always fertile empire, in spite of suffering so many exhaustions, after so many devastations visited on it, should not have enough attractions for it to be conquered by those who have its key in their hands, the strength, the qualification and, might I say again, the right, while the Marattes, Jats, Abdalis, Rohélas, Siks and perhaps others after them grab hold of it, plunder it, lay waste to it and destroy it? Have they more right to do it? Do they have more strength for it? People everywhere desire a master: the great fear him and while there is not one there cannot be rest or tranquillity and (may I be forgiven for daring to add this at an inappropriate time) as long as there is no security at all for those who, being able to give it or be it, do not have enough audacity or enough courage, of union and of a wish to undertake it. We depopulate Europe to give inhabitants to savage lands. A peopled, polite, cultivated kingdom ready to receive a master—wanting one—has no beauties for a conquering nation to dominate it. Is there more justice in chasing the poor Americans out of their places of living, subjugating them and becoming master of their possessions than in destroying a perfidious, murderous, usurping, tyrannical race, avowed enemy of Christianity, under whom for more than 600 and more years have groaned, with many other nations, the supple, gentle, pacific peoples of Indostan? At the same time it would seem so easy to execute it by the means of those who live there; they will aid the enterprise, they will move it forward: it only needs to want and know how to involve them and govern them.

Wendel's Letter Recounting a Battle between the Jats and the Sikhs, 1770
The Doings of the Sikhs and the Jats, Eur Mss ORME OV 147, part 11, pp. 51–4, Orme Collection MSS, Oriental India Office Collection, British Library, London.

Padre Wendel
Agra the 3rd March 1770[16]
Sir

My little belov'd Justinus just now arrives; I am very glad to see him after the Tour I hazarded to make him make: My uneasiness on his behalf engag'd me to write you after on the same Subject, & I am hoping you will be pleas'd to behave [?] you accordingly. After my last you will have heard of a Reconnetre [?] arrived Saturday past 24 Febr[uar]y between the Jauts & Seiks, & of the success or victory obtain'd by the former: if you should have occasion to desire a further relation with some Circumstances & certainty, the fact is as follows. After about 14 days idle conferences for an amicable accomodement, those Barbarians suddenly returned to their former encampment near Hosel, about 40 Coss from Agra on the Royal Rout to Delhy. The Jauts followed them. Saturday in the morning an engagement soon arrived between the advanced Parties, almost without the Jauts advice & consentment. Two Chiefs of

the Jauts Army making the Avantgarde, Gopalroy the Mhorattah & the French Chief
Mr Maddock, with his Troop of light horse, 6 Companies of Sepoys, & 2 Pieces of
Cannon, 1 four Pounder & a 2 Pounder; took the resolution to make a decourát of
the Enemy's Parties, who robb'd almost in their sight. The Jauts Army being distant
about 4 Coss backwards, & their own remanent forces left in a notable distance; they
saw them suddenly surprized by about 20,000 Seiks on all sides: the Attack being
indispensable, & a retreat impossible, a fierce engagement soon ensued, which
brought upon this little Body the whole Seiks Army. After combating unanimously &
with surprizing entripidity as long as they had munition, & the Mharattah's Cavalry
being almost all wounded and kill'd. Gopaulroy himself by a Musket Shot render'd
inable for further Action, they were oblig'd to retreat & avail themselves of a little
Village behind them, where they retired. The Seiks attack'd them on all sides, but
with loss, & unsuccessfully. About 1000 Musketeers, & some Cavalry arriving at the
same time from the Army, they sustain'd, and repell'd all the Enemies endeavours 'till
about 3 O'Clock in the Afternoon the Engagement having commenced at 9 in the
Morning; yet their Loss had been very sensible: The French Chief's Party having
almost perish'd, all horses kill'd or catch'd by the Seiks; & so the Mharattah's Cavalry.
The Seiks gain'd a piece [of artillery]; who could not be brought back, the Animals
being kill'd or wounded: yet the same Piece was regained soon after: things being in
such a desperate situation on both sides, the Seiks seeing themselves unable to gain
the Village, as also the Defenders to sustain longer Efforts, the whole Jauts Army distant from the Field of Battle about 4 Coss, arrived, but too slow: & with some violence the Enemy begun to fly abruptly, the Jauts harass'd them about 5 Coss; having
to do no more than to catch some baggage Animals abandon'd by the Seiks on their
Deroute; & by this way a compleat Victory had been obtain'd by the Jauts, whose
greatest number had not ever seen the Enemy. Almost none of the both Chiefs men,
who engaged in the Attack, retired without Wounds, only excepted the French Chief,
with one or two of his Europeans; and of 6 Companies not 3 entire return'd: it must
be confess'd both Chiefs behaved them with extraordinary Courage, and having the
whole Seiks forces so long a time upon them they had the Fortune to make a Defence
almost thought impossible; being also much certain that they behaved too bold, &
inconsiderate to expose themselves to such unavoidable a danger to perish all without the least hopes of Recovery; they gain'd themselves great Reputation it is true, &
the Jauts seeing them now almost deliver'd of those plunderers, must attribute the
whole success to the personal bravery, & unparallell'd intrepidity of those Chiefs:
none of the others having contributed anything to the obtain'd advantage, which
nothwithstanding was a pure hazard.

Nowul Sing not being of resolution to attack the Seiks and had sent the same day
his Vakeel to those Robbers for accomodement, the morning the Battle commenced.
The Enemies loss must be great because they escaped in the utmost confusion &
rapidity from the Field of Battle; and retired in Full Course to upon 30 Coss from
thence, the following night & day. It is now reported that they lost 2 Principal Chiefs,
and their General Wounded, also 2 others, with a great part of their Detachments:
Yet their Kill'd & Found on the Field of Battle are not numerous: they sustain'd the
Attack more vigorously than could be expected from a Party of Robbers: party
jumped from their Horses combating with Fire Arms;[17] & making a good discharge
by Peletons,[18] reforcing & retiring, as they thought proper, having such prodigious
a number for their Supply. The whole loss of both Chiefs & Jauts perhaps amount to
4 or 500 kill'd and wounded: more than the double the Enemy left in the Field, and
afterwards perish'd in their precipitate flight. By this late Advice from Delhy, they

have now retired toward the Frontiers of the [?] Dominions, where they are ravaging the Country, as the Jauts made to show a motion for their pursuit as they should have done. This is almost the narration of the past success, of whom perhaps you may soon have heard from different Accounts.

With regard to the pretensions of the Grandee in our Neighbourhood: it appears that the Motion of your Forces had made strong effect against his designs: the Rajah of Ghohud observing with some Jealousy all its endeavours some Chiefs retired actually, and I am assured he pretends to retire himself to Gwaulear under the Mharattahs protection; perhaps it will cost him more than he seems to believe. At present no very great reason appears, to be anxious at all his endeavourings.

If you should think proper, & worth your leisure please to give a little Account of the Success to General Baske as perhaps he may be anxious to know some particulars, and more authentick accounts perhaps you will not be able to gain from other hands.

Permit me to be with truth.

Sir

Your etc etc etc

Pr. Wendel

NOTES

1. Nādir Shāh (q.v.).
2. Emperor Bahādur Shāh (q.v.).
3. Wendel has confused the name of Bandā Singh Bahādur with his salutation cum battle cry.
4. This is a reference to Chakk (also Chakk Gurū Rāmdās or just Chakk Gurū (q.v.)), the early name for Amritsar (q.v.).
5. Farrukh Sīyār (q.v.).
6. 'Abd us-Samad Khān (q.v.).
7. The first invasion was in 1738.
8. Zakariyā Khān (q.v.).
9. Land owners of the Jat caste.
10. The river Satluj.
11. Ādīnā Beg Khān (q.v.).
12. Najīb ud-Daulā (q.v.).
13. "Calâl-sing" is a reference to Jassā Singh Āhlūvālīā (q.v.) who was born into a family of *Kelāls* whose hereditary profession would have been distilling and dealing in spirits. "Tocca-sing" clearly points to Jassā Singh Rāmgharīā (q.v.) who came from a family of *Tharkhāns* or carpenters. The pejorative *Tokhā* is occasionally used for *Tharkhān*. It is not clear who "Tchersa-sing" refers to.
14. A *karāhī* or cooking pot.
15. Wendel gives us one of the earliest descriptions of the *Sarbat Khālsā* (q.v.).
16. Following the death, in 1769, of the Jat ruler of Bhāratpur, a succession struggle ensued between his brothers, Nawal Singh and Ranjīt Singh. The latter called upon the cis-Sutlej territory Sikhs and sought their assistance in the dispute. The Sikhs accepted and on their way to meet him, they plundered the lands around Delhi. Soon after, they entered the Doāb and encamped near Delhi. On January 26, Nawal Singh ordered a large body of the Jats to proceed toward Delhi to oppose the advance of the Sikhs. The Sikhs marched with such rapidity through the Jat country that consternation was produced among the populace, and the advancing Jat force retreated the following day

without even sighting the enemy. The Sikhs marched on to Chunar, south of Delhi. At this time, the deposed Nawāb of Bengal, was encamped near Gwalior trying to unite the Sikhs, Jats, and Marāthās under his banner to invade Bengal and fight against the British government. He sent agents to the Sikhs and Jats to bring about peace for his own ends. Nawal Singh also sent his agent to the Sikhs but after a fortnight's idle conference, the matter came to nothing. The Sikhs broke up their camp and returned to their former encampment near Ālīgarh. Father Wendel continues the story from this point.

17. This irregular cavalry maneuver, involving men dismounting from horses, was applied in an unorthodox way when Akālī Phūlā Singh and his men turned the tide of the Battle of Terī against the Afghāns in 1823: ". . . Phoola Sing ordered his men to dismount and let their horses go. This was done, and at the same instant the Akalees shouted their war-cry of *Wah Gooroojee!* which the Affghans as loudly answered with their *Allah! Allah!* The horses set at liberty, either from habit or alarmed by the tumult, rushed wildly forward and into the ranks of the enemy. This strange and unexpected attack caused some confusion in the Affghan host, observing which the Akalees, throwing down their matchlocks, rushed forward sword in hand with such impetuosity as to drive back the enemy, and to secure themselves a footing on the hill." Smyth, Major G.M. Carmichel, *History of the Reigning Family of Lahore* (Calcutta: Thaker and Co.-St. Andrew's Library, 1847. Reprint, Delhi: Parampara Publications, 1979), 189–90.

18. From the Hindi term *paltan*, a corruption of battalion. It is the usual Indian word for a regiment of native infantry. Henry Yule and A.C. Burnell, *Hobson-Jobson: A Glossary of Colloquial Anglo-Indian Words and Phrases, and of Kindred Terms, Etymological, Historical, Geographical and Discursive*, ed. William Crooke (London: Murray, 1903. Reprint, Sittingbourne: Linguasia, 1994), s.v. "Pultan."

CHAPTER 3

DU PERRON'S INDIAN
RESEARCHES, 1788

M. Jean Bernoulli ed., *Description historique et géographique de l'Inde qui présente en trois volumes, enrichis de 64 cartes et autres planches 1. La géographie de l'Indoustan, écrite en Latin, dans le pays méme par Le Pere Joseph Tieffenthaler. 2. Des Recherches historiques et geographiques sur l'Inde & la Description du cours du Gange & du Gagra avec un très grande carte par M. Anquetil du Perron . . . 3. La carte générale de l'Inde, celles du Cours du Brahmapoutre & de la Navigation intérieure du Bengale, aves de mémoires relatifs a ces cartes publies en Anglais par M. Jacques Rennell. . . Le tout augmenté de rémarques et d'autres additions,* 3 vols. (London: 1788), 1: 109; 2: viii, 177, 192–205.
Translated by Dr. Jeevan Singh Deol.

The work, *Description historique et géographique de l'Inde qui présente en trois volumes,* is the product of a complex series of relationships stretching over a number of years. The principal editor was the German, Jean Bernoulli, who consolidated and published a three-volume work consisting of single volume contributions from the Jesuit missionary and noted geographer Joseph Tieffenthaler, an oriental and linguistic scholar, Anquetil Du Perron, and cartographer Jacques Rennell. Of these three quite disparate characters, Father Tieffenthaler and Du Perron mention the Sikhs.

The first volume contains the manuscript of Father Joseph Tieffenthaler (1710–1785), a Jesuit missionary and scholar, who sailed to India in 1743 from Portugal and spent more than thirty years traveling, studying, and researching the geography, flora, and fauna of India. A prolific writer, the sheer volume of his literary output was not fully published until long after his death. His notes and sketch maps were sent in manuscript form to the celebrated French orientalist and geographer, Abraham Hyacinthe Anquetil Du Perron (1731–1805), whom he had met in Sūrat in 1759.[1] He published the Father's works in the *Journal des Scavans* and also in his own geographic work *Des Recherches historique sur l'Inde*. Du Perron also commenced his career in the priesthood but gave that up in order to pursue his deep interest in Eastern languages. His subsequent stay in India was short-lived due to the British conquest over the French in India. However, the eleven years that he did spend there were incredibly fruitful. He learnt Persian, Sanskrit, Zend, Avestan, and Pahlāvī, collected over 180 manuscripts that were later donated to the Royal Library, and translated various Zoroastrian and Hindu texts into European languages.

The three volumes appear to be three separate works, and are the result of a complex evolution of manuscripts and editing. Anquetil Du Perron used notes provided to him by the cartographer Colonel Jean-Baptiste-Joseph Gentil, agent for the French Government to the court of Shujā-ud-Daulā, and published in 1788. Bernoulli himself states that he received the manuscript on August 21, 1785, to which he later added Du Perron's own corrections.

The first extract, a brief note from Tieffenthaler's first volume, highlights the importance of Amritsar as the pre-eminent city amongst the Sikhs but is historically inaccurate.

The second and more detailed extract, taken from the second volume, is titled "On the Siks" and is from the notes section to the main work. Du Perron tells us that this extract along with two others "were sent to me by Mr. Gentil, Knight of the Order of St. Louis, Colonel of Infantry. I added to them the explanations that I thought appropriate for clarifying the subject matter. Everything that is in quotation marks is by Mr. Gentil, that which is not is mine." This curious mixture of Gentil's manuscript notes with a commentary by Du Perron is occasionally difficult to follow. However, it is similar to many other early contemporary accounts particularly because the information therein is useful but contains serious flaws of the Sikhs and their beliefs. The most obvious factual flaw is the confusion surrounding the nature of the reign of the ten Gurūs. He asserts that Gurū Nānak was the founder, and Gurū Gobind Singh the first chief. Presumably ignorant of the other eight Gurūs, and uncertain of the timeline between the first and tenth Gurū, he places Gurū Nānak in the reign of Aurangzeb. Most intriguingly, mention is made of a possible *Janamsākhī* manuscript "in Moorish" of the life of Gurū Nānak. Du Perron tells us that it "is one of the manuscripts with which M. Gentil enriched the Royal Library. When my affairs permit, I will publish a translation or at least an extract of it."

Gentil makes the common mistake, which Du Perron fails to correct, of confusing Bandā Singh Bahādur and Gurū Gobind Singh. A possible explanation for this phenomenon was the lack of widespread knowledge in the Punjab of the order to end the continuity of the human Sikh Gurūs. The last Gurū, Gobind Singh, had died on October 7, 1708 at Nānded following an earlier assassination attempt. Five days earlier, he had written to the Sikhs of Dhaul of his imminent return to the Punjab following a favorable meeting with the Emperor Bahādur Shāh: "We have met the emperor with all success, and received a robe of honor and a jeweled necklace worth Rs. 60,000 as a gift. We are returning shortly. Be at peace with one another. When we come to Kahlur let all the Khalsa come armed."[2] A further explanation could be due to the claim to Gurūship that Bandā is said to have made during his time as the head of the armed Sikhs that returned to the Punjab.[3]

Interestingly, Gentil refers to Sikhs in terms of the majority being Khālsā Sikhs and the rest as *Khulāsā* Sikhs. The latter term is now rarely used, but was a common term for *Sahajdhārī* Sikhs in the eighteenth and nineteenth centuries. Du Perron fails to translate the two terms satisfactorily. The word Khālsā is derived from the Perso-Arabic word *khalisah* (property under the direct management of a ruler)[4] and *Khulāsā* literally means "lesser."[5]

Gentil accurately records that the Sikhs "accept only one God, worthy of the adoration of all men" which Du Perron discusses in some detail, opening with the claim that "[t]he unity of God is not a new doctrine among the Indous," and elaborating on his point with several references to the *Vedas*. However, Gentil relies on Tiefentaller when he states that "coarse Sikhs see Nanek as a God" which is ample proof of the devotion and reverence reserved by Sikhs in the eighteenth century for Gurū Nanak, even though it contradicts the orthodox position today.

A figure who looms large in the historical part of this account is 'Abd us-Samad Khān (d. 1737) who was the governor of Lahore from 1713–1726. He had previously served in the court of the emperors Aurangzeb and Farrukh-Sīyār. Most notably, he was the governor of Lahore when he was charged to capture Bandā Bahādur, which he succeeded in doing as is mentioned in the text, although the author continues to refer to Bandā as *Gobinsingue*. Descended from a notable family of Samarkand, his son was Zakarīyā Khān (d. 1745) who was later to put a bounty on the head of all Sikhs, and order the execution of two prominent Sikhs in the early eighteenth century, Bhāī Tārū Singh and Bhāī Manī Singh.

In the closing part of the account, Du Perron acknowledges the inherent bias that exists in Muslims accounts on the history and nature of the political power of the Sikhs. He also shows much interest in the mission of Bandā, recounting his execution with obvious enthusiasm and admiration.

Volume 1, p. 119

Brief description of some places in the province of Lahor:

The headquarters of the Sikhs is Amarsar,[6] called Tschek[7] by others; the place is on the side of a pond. The town called Rámdáspour is 18 miles from Lahore. Rámtirat (another town of the Sikhs) is only 6 miles from there. The Sikh nation flocks to this place, which has a stone bank, every year and distributes many alms; that is because it is where Nanak, the founder of the Sikhs, led a solitary life.[8] A building has been constructed in his honour in the middle of the pond.

Volume 2, p. viii

Preface to section I "The state of India:

"I am not speaking either of the Siks,[c] neighbors of the Sind or Indus, nor of the Djats, settled around Agra; transient powers, if considered on their own, born out of the troubles of Indoustan and who, as Hindus, are included in those of the Marathas."

Volume 2, p. 177

Notes:

The following three extracts were sent to me by Mr. Gentil, Knight of the Order of St. Louis, Colonel of Infantry. I added to them the explanations that I thought appropriate for clarifying the subject matter. Everything that is in quotation marks is by Mr. Gentil, that which is not is mine.

Volume 2, pp. 192–205

[Note c] On the Siks:

"The Sikhs are idolaters[9] and of the Radjeput caste, and as a result always residents of India, in the province of Lahore, where they have been making themselves known with great reputation for nearly a century in the north-west of Delhi, 200 *kos* from that capital."

One understands that Radjepoute means "son of a Rajah" (rajah patré in Samskrétan) and that the four castes of the Indous are, Brahmes, priests; Settreas or Katteries, soldiers; Weinsjas, merchants; and Soudraes or Schoutres, labourers, workers, etc.

"The Radjepouts consider themselves descendants of the Katteries, according to Indians the second caste, from whom the sovereigns are also descended. They are the best well-known for bravery among the Indians. Ancient Indian legend or history says that in the time of the fourth incarnation of Ram, the half tiger and half man under the name of Narsing Outan, their ancestors were in twenty one battles, in which they were put to flight and almost destroyed by Ram. After many losses they withdrew to the province of Lahor. Subsequently the Patanes took possession of the country and subjugated them, and afterwards with the passing of time the Mogols did so."

Here the author confuses the manifestations of Vischnou in the form of the Boar and the Lion. In Samskretan, Nar means man and Simhouam, Sinhaha, Singham, lion. What he has written as Outan is Vara Schoutar, made of Vara, Boar and Schatrouhanta, victorious, in Samskrétam.

The manifestation of the god in the form of Narsingue was to punish a minor king who mistreated his son badly because he always had the name of the deity—Ram, Ram—on his lips.

The Patanes that are referred to here, are the Ghorides, masters of Lahore, etc toward the end of the twelfth century, and the Mogols are those of Tamerlan during the fourteenth century and subsequently.

"They (these Radjepouts) always follow the doctrine of the Brahmes [Brahmans], and the second Bed, give to the second caste, was their holy book."

The four Vedams or Beids (according to the pronunciation of the north of India) are the Rak Beid, the Djedjr Beid, the Sam Beid and the Athrban Beid. In Sanskrétam, Vedaha signifies "the law" or "the book of the law." According to the preface of the Oupnekhat, "the Rak Beid is a divine book in which the the measure of the letters of every four Messraas (each quatrain) is equal in number; the Djedjr Beid is the divine word, in which the letters of each four Messraas are not equal in number; the Sam Beid is the divine word which is read with consonance (rhyme); and the Athrban Beid is the fourth divine book.

The attribution of a certain Veda to a certain caste is arbitrary: each of these four books contains things that concern them all.

"At the end of the reign of Alamgir the first more than a century ago, since he began to reign in 1658, a monk named Nanek,[10] celebrated in the province of Lahor for his mildness, humane nature and selflessness brought a new doctrine to light, and little by little it gathered itself into a party of which Gobindsingue, his disciple, was the first chief. Nanek was called Goarou, Master, and his supporters Sinks or Siks, that is to say disciples."

There is in Moorish a life of this patriarch of the Sikhs. It is one of the manuscripts with which M. Gentil enriched the Royal Library. When my affairs permit, I will publish a translation or at least an extract of it.

Gourou signifies master in Sanskrétam, and Sevakaha, servant.

"They (the Sikhs) reject the eighteen Pourans or books of the Gentile [or 'of Gentooism'], viewing as fable everything that is said about Brahma, Bischen and Mahadeou, whose divinity they deny."

In Sanskrétam, Pouranam means knowledge, as Schastram does history, account in verse. The 18 Pouranams are the 18 books of the mythological history of the Indous, much later than the Vedes.

One understands that Brahma, creator; Bischen or Vischnou, preserver; and Routren, Isvaren or Mahadeo, destroyer, considered separately under each of their attributes, are the three primary agents of the second order in Indian theology.

"They accept only one God, worthy of the adoration of all men."

The unity of God is not a new doctrine among the Indous: but the Persian translation of the Oupnekhat was able to spread it further, Sanskrétan books being heard by very few people. This translation is from the year 1067 Hegira, 1656 of the Christian era, two years before the reign of Aurangzebe: as a result, it had long existed when Nanek appeared. We may recall that the second Beid, the Djedjer, is given as the divine book of the Ragepouts and the Siks.

Here are three passages taken from this Beid, from the third and the first, on the unity of the Primal Being that the reader will be very delighted to find here. I have reserved for the second part of this work, in the passage on Benarès, a long passage from the Oupnekhat that treats of the same subject.

"One should first observe," says the Italian author who furnished me with these three passages, "that among the Gentiles religion is free . . . Those who are opposed to the Brahmes, even though peasants, quote as maxims the following words from the Sam Beid and Giugiur Beid."

Apart from a single God, there is no other deity. There is no other sacrifice excepting the sacrifice of Param gioti (God of supreme light, but material), nor is there one due (*si conviene*) to any other. To sacrifice to Barmah or Mahadeo has no merit; on the contrary, it is a great sin; one should not even employ (*pigliare*) their name in any other manner. Among the human race there has never been a man more shameless (*disonesto*) than Mahadeo, nor a greater sinner than he; thus (in the words of the same Beids), we should see them all as a demon; and since it is a sin to make a sacrifice to a demon, it is also a sin to make a sacrifice to Mahadeo.

The same Sam Beid continues:

Barmah, Mahadeo and all the other gods are nothing but pure men (and, the master who instructs the disciple concludes): why then do you call them gods? Bischnou and Mahadeo were always sunk in (*involti*) sins. Do you not know that there is only one God, and that there can be no others? In what place did you find two gods? Other than a single God, you seek others in vain.

In the Giugiur Bed and the Rag Bed, the master says to the disciple:

O insane man, why do you sacrifice to the demon? This figure that you keep is no (*non è già*) god. And how could it have been God if there is no God other than Paramgioti?

In Samskrtam, param means "great" and Dyourta "flash." Hence the word Paramgiota, that is used for the Primal Being, the only God, refers in Indian theology the supreme light, material and immaterial, the universal light, source of all that exists.

The preceding passages, literally translated, are taken from a very curious Italian manuscript composed in 1770 by Father Marco Dalla Tomba, Capuchin missionary from Tibet, who passed more than 17 years in the country, was instructed by a Brahme from the University of Benarès and who had at his disposition the library of the King of Betia.

This work has as a title: *Osservationi sopra le Relationi chef a M Holwell Inglese de gl'Evenementi istorici ed interessanti toccanti le Provincie del Bengale e dell'Imperio del Grand Mogol del Indostano. Particolarmente sopra la 2ᵃ. Parte del suo Libro, in cui tratta della Mythologia, Feste & Digiuni de gli Indiani, che sieguono il libro, chegli chiama Shasta, tradotto in franchese e stampato in Amsterdam nel 1763.*

The author, in this passage that I received in Paris on 25 October 1784, does not discuss anything but the mythological portion of the work of Mr. Holwell. Mr. Etienne Borgia, Secretary of the Congregation of Propaganda, placed it in the library at Velitri on 12 February 1775. Guided by the enlightened love that he has for the arts, this learned prelate, judging the utility such a work could have for me in the course of my work, on his own and without my having asked, had the kindness to send it to me from Rome.[i]

This is the second literary service that I owe to the capital of the Christian world. The first is so important that I will not miss the opportunity to say a few words about it here. I will report the fact without adornment or remarks.

At the beginning of October 1783, I asked the Pope for a manuscript Indian dictionary, deposited in the Propaganda Library in 1704. This work had for a title *Thesaurus linguæ Indianæ* and is in four columns: Latin, Indoustan in Nagri characters, French and the characters of Indoustan. The author, Father François Marie de Tours, Capuchin missionary, composed it in Surate in 1703. I saw an abridgement of it in this city in 1758. Count de Vergennes, Minister and Secretary of State in the

---

[i] This worthy and learned prelate was honored with purple last year in 1785: fitting reward for his rare merit and useful works. Now prince of the Church, he is no longer Secretary of the Congregation of Propaganda; but he will not be any less inclined to follow his propensity to further on all occasions the progress of letters and the work of those who cultivate them. Having had, like Mr. Anquetil, the advantage of feeling the happy effects of it, I cannot stop myself from displaying my gratitude publicly. I even requested several enlightened travellers who visited Italy to run their attention to the museum of Cardinal de Borgia at Velletri, from where Mr. Anquetil received the manuscript in question. I know, partially from a letter from His Eminence, that it is still rich in Oriental curiosities, although the Congregation of Propaganda had already received many as gifts. One will find there, for example, some very rare paintings that represent the famous incarnations of the divinities of India: these paintings, made on the scene by artists of the country well versed in the mythology of Indoustan, are preferable to many of the engraved drawings of these incarnations. Two other very remarkable paintings from the Borgia Cabinet, which have already been engraved on two large leaves under the eyes of the illustrious possessor, are those which, as much I was able to judge without explanation, represent nearly the entire cosmogonic and mythological system of Tibet. One of them has the following Latin inscription: Cyclus transmigrationum ex Thologia Lhamarum, ex Linteo quod fixum est Velitris in Museo Borgiano Pictor Tibetanus Jon-de La-hu-ri ex Archetypa sacro in Lhapprauga Lasscusi asservato coloribus expressit. The other this: Figura mundi Tibetani ex linteo etc. ut sup. We see on the names of the 12 constellations and some other words in Tibetan characters. (Bernoulli)

Department of Foreign Affairs, was happy to send my letters and support them; that is to say that he himself made the request. Cardinal de Bernis took on the proposal and the negotiation at Rome; Cardinal Antonelli and Prelate Borgia seconded the request of the French Ambassador; and the Holy Father (Pius VI) ordered—until then an unprecedented favour—that the original itself should be sent out. All this was done without the courier losing a day. I received it by the post of 14 December in the same year 1783. It is a folio volume of 900 pages. If something had happened to it en route, the loss could never have been made good. I had it for four months. I copied it in its entirety, down to each comman, including also the Nagrie column; and I sent it back at the end of three months, on 12 March 1784. Enlightened religion will always be the support of literature: only fanaticism fears the progress of human knowledge.

I take up again the article on the Siks.

"Nevertheless coarse Sikhs see Nanek as a God, according to the Jesuit Father Tiefentaller. They do not accept images or sculptures. They wear a rosary of 109 beads around their necks. Poor or rich, they are always dressed in blue. The greater part of them let their beards grow and are called Colsa; the others shave and keep a moustache: these are called Colassa."[11]

We will see at the end of the second part of this work note B that Father Teiffentaler has written on the Indian religion. The word God is strong but is not surprising in speaking of the opinion that the coarse Sikhs might have about Nanek: everywhere those whom we properly call ordinary people are near enough idolaters and the people stretch themselves out in front of the crook and sceptre.

I did not find in Samskretam or in Indoustan the meaning of the words Colsa and Colassa; only that in Sanskretam Kalouchaha means dirt, filth. In Persian Koseh indicates a man with little or no beard; Kosch, Koschesch indicate moustache.

"They (the Sikhs) are good soldiers by reason of the constant wars that they have had to withstand, as much against Aabdali Ahmedchah[12] as against the Mogol governors. Their weapons are the lance, the sabre and the shield. They have a marked hatred toward Mahometans and have carried out many wars against them.

"After the death of Nanek Gourou, whom they see as their patriarch, Gobindsingue, his most famous disciple, seeing himself at the head of a large mob that used to gather every year around a great pond, which they saw as sacred, on a place made by Nanek their Master, attacked and pillaged Lahor, defeated the governor of Sarhind, Vasirkhan,[13] and took possession of his treasures, his artillery and his luggage.[14]

"Cha Alem or Bahadour chah[15] reigned at that time and flung himself after him. He was defeated and forced to shut himself up in Talvandi, from where he fled alone on horseback. Talvandi was immediately captured, and all the Sikhs massacred. It was razed in the year 1122 Hejira (1710 CE). Gobindsingue withdrew to the mountains of Jammu, from where he returned to Talvandi in 1129 Hejira in the reign of Farouksiar and rebuilt it under the name of Lohagar at the head of one hundred thousand of his people and ravaged the whole country from there. Three governors of Lahore died during these wars."

In his *Historical Papers on India* (*Papiers historiques sur l'Inde*), M. Gentil reports in greater detail the defeats and progress of the Siks, of Schah aalem (son of Aurengzebe) and of Faroukhsiar. He explicates the year 1121 Hegira, 1709 CE, in this way:

"In the month of *Schawal* he (Schah aalem) marched against the Rana (of Odeipur) to punish him for his lack of faith and his revolt. The Sikhs, followers of the sect of Nanak, pillaged the countryside of Lahor, attacked Vasirkhan, governor of Sarhind, killed him, and took possession of his treasures, his artillery and all his luggage.

"Cha aalem sent orders to all his troops in the region of the province to join together and rush toward the Siks. He himself marched in a great hurry. He rushed against the Rana, who made his peace, and then came back for the Siks.

"At the approach of Cha alem, Gobind, their chief, abandoned all that he had taken and came to Sarhind. Roustouns del khan and Firoz khan, who had been sent to reconnoitre the countryside, encountered the Sikhs, attacked them and defeated them. They left Sarhind and shut themselves up in Talvandi, on the other bank of the Soutladje, which they had fortified. A short time later, Cha aalem invested them and had the place bombarded for fifteen days. Gobind, fearing that he would finally be captured, fled on horseback by a place that was not guarded by the enemy and abandoned his Siks to the mercy of the besiegers. All who stayed in the place were massacred, and Talvandi was demolished."

"In 1129 Hejira (1716 CE), Gobindsingue, leader of the Sikhs, who had withdrawn to the mountains of Djammou, always harassed by the Rajah (who did everything he could to capture him), returned to Talvandi, refortified it and called it Louagar. He assembled all his Siks there, to the number of one hundred thousand, and ravaged the entire countryside. Three governors of Lahor died in this war."

I do not find either Talvandi or Lohagar in modern maps. In Indoustan, the latter name means mountain or town of iron. This place was situated, as we have seen, on the other bank of the Satlage and should not be remote from the Djammou mountains, the continuation to the west of the Kumaon, which is north of Sarhind. It may be the Tulloom of Mr. Rennell's map. Tarvar, Talvar or Talvand, in Indoustan, means sabre; from there perhaps comes the legend "Sabre, etc," which we will see below, engraved on the money that Gobindsingue had minted at Lohagar.

"Abdoussamad Khan," continues Mr. Gentil's summary, "Governor of the province, gathered all his forces there and marched against the rebels. In the space of three months, there were numerous battles, which forced Gobindsingue to shut himself up in his new fortress of Lohagar, which he was besieged and forced to surrender himself with his wife, his son and three hundred Sikhs. They were taken to Dehli. His son and his pregnant wife were delivered into the custody of Darbarkhan, the palace eunuch, and Gobindsingue with his 300 Siks to the Lieutenant of Police, who everyday beheaded ten of them in the middle of the market on their refusal to become Musulmans. All preferred death to changing their religion. Faroukhsiar had the death of Gobindsingue postponed because he wanted to see him and ask him about his alleged divinity. In the end, having had him asked if, in the light of all that had happened to him, he did not see that he was a man and he not having responded at all, his execution was ordained. And he and his son had their heads cut off immediately. The people of Dehli mourned their deaths.

"Gobindsinge had had money minted at Lohagar, on which was engraved in Indian characters 'Sabre and Victory' on one side, and on the other 'Gobind Gourou.'

"After the death of Gobind and during the [period] of Adinabeguekhan,[16] who reduced them completely to a state from which they could not stir, the Siks gathered and again took part in events. The defeated Aabdali and the Mogol governors against whom they had fought many battles for many years, at the end of which they took possession of the whole of the province of Lahor, of which the principal chiefs shared out the districts, and from whence they continually made incursions up to the surroundings of Dehli.

"Djessingue[17] succeeded Gobindsingue and had coinage struck at Lahor, on which were engraved these two Persian verses:

'Siccazad dar djehan ze fasel akal
'tact Ahmad guereft Djessa kalal.

"the weak Djessingue, by the grace of God (the Supreme God, *hak aal*), has taken possession of the throne of Ahmad and has had this coin struck in the world."

The preceding facts, or those that follow the capture and death of Gobinsingue are detailed further in Mr. Gentil's *Historical Papers on India* (*Papiers historiques sur l'Inde*):

"In order to avenge the deaths of his people, Faroukhsiar," this educated traveller says, "sent Abdoussamadkhan[18] to confront the devastations (of the Siks) and instructed the Governor of Sarhind to join him with all his forces. As soon as he had arrived at Lahore, he had a proclamation issued by which he summoned every good Musulman to take arms and join him to make war against Gobinsingue. He gathered approximately five thousand horsemen and ten thousand foot soldiers, with whom he marched against that rebel. Each of the two leaders fortified his camp. Both sides bombarded each other for three months, after which Gobinsingue went back to Louhagar.

"Abdoussamadkhan pursued him and surrounded the place so well that no provisions could enter it. After eleven months of siege, with nothing to live on, Gobinsingue gave himself up with all his family and 300 Siks. The others had died of hunger, or had found a way to save themselves. Abdoussamadkhan had them all taken to Dehli under the escort of his son Zekeriakhan.

"The son and pregnant wife of Gobinsingue were turned over to the eunuch Darbarkhan and Gobinsingue and his 300 Siks to the Cotoual, who had ten of them beheaded in the market every day when they refused to become Musulmans. Almost all preferred death to changing religion. Faroukhsiar had the death of Gobinsingue postponed, because he wanted to see him and question him on his pretended divinity. At the end he had him asked whether he did not understand well that he was a man after all that had happened to him. He made no response. The order was immediately given to chop off his head and in the same manner that of his son. The people of Delhi mourned their deaths.

"Zekeriakhan was made a Sept Azari and named Bahadour Governor of Tatta and Moultan, and his father Abdussamadkhan Governor of Lahor and Cachemire. The Siks stayed quiet until the death of Mohammed Schah. . .

"In 1171 Hegira (1757 AD), in order to occupy the Marates, the Visir Gazi ouddinkhan had them summoned and sent them against Teimour Schah[19] (whom Aabdali, Emperor of the Patanes, his father, had left as ruler of Lahor with Djehankhan as Visir). Adinabegkhan defeated Djehankha, who fell back to Lahor, called the Siks to his aid, took Teimour Schah with him and marched against Adinabegkhan. The latter took Sarhind and made the Governor prisoner: he joined the Marates. First they chased the Siks whom they encountered coming to the help of Djehankhan and afterwards continued their march toward Lahor, which they entered without opposition. Djehankhan having withdrawn to Kateki, the Marates marched in pursuit of him and were defeated two coss from Lahor, where they were forced to retreat. Adinabegkhan immediately dispatched 12,000 horsemen under the command of his deputy Mirazizekhan, who had reached Djehankhan, gave battle to him and defeated him.

"In 1177 Hegira (1763 AD) Aabdali returned to Indoustan up to Jauesser, where he defeated the Siks and subsequently returned to his territories.

"In 1778 Hegira (1764 AD) Gaziouddinkhan allied himself with the Marates, the Djats and the Siks and attacked Najibkhan, who had been appointed by Aabdali, in Dehli. He defended it so well that he forced them to make peace with him.

"Writing in 1768, Mr. Dow gives as general of the Sikh army Jessaritsingue: is this the same leader as Djessingue? He also named Nitehsingues as a person greatly respected among this nation."[20]

Could the town named Jauesser in Mr. Gentil's *Historical Papers* (*Papiers historiques*) be Gaugur, in the south-east near Sarhind, or Ghianaur to the northwest of Dehli, somewhat remote from that town?

"The Siks," Mr. Gentil continues in his summary, "are today quite numerous and admit into their sect or republican society all types of religions, just as the Beraiguis and Saniassis admit in theirs all type of Gentiles."

The Beraguis and the Sanniasis are spirituals orders who renounce all sensual feelings to the world and all pleasures in order to ascend to the contemplation of the Supreme Being and are above all the observances that form the exterior practices of Indian religion. There are true and false Saniassis, and the deceitfulness of the latter gives occasion to people, particularly outsiders, to slander the former.

"When they receive someone into the number of the Siks, the person receiving them, dressed in blue, has brought before him a large bowl filled with water. He washes his feet and cleans [perhaps 'cuts'] his nails there, and makes each person who wishes to become a Sik drink of this water. Each will let his beard and hair grow and never cut them again. After they have been admitted, they cry in a loud voice: long live Jaissingue (principal leader of the Siks), our master! Then the senior Siks give them food to eat, and all that they eat is stirred with the tooth of a wild boar. This latter ceremony is especially done to a Musulman who becomes Sik in order that he no longer feel repugnance towards pork."[21]

The boar's tooth may be a remainder of mythological custom relating to the Boar incarnation of Vischnou.

"At present the Siks are the ramparts of the Mughal empire for preventing the successors of Aabdali from taking possession of Dehli. They are always armed and are masters of the province of Lahore, of Moultan, etc."

Mr. Dow tells us that in case of need they can prepare 60,000 good horsemen.

Reforms in the matter of religion do not all have the same origin as that of those of the Siks; they do not all bring the same advantage to the countries that accept them or those that they border. But in general at some distance from the leader, often in his lifetime, they become customary and maintain themselves by the same means, and they all have their martyrs the Siks have in Gobindsingue and his three hundred followers.

As for the rest it is necessary to observe that when the accounts say that the Siks devastated the whole country it is Mahometans who are speaking, Mogols: just as their writers never refer to the Marates except under the name of Gahnims (looters, thieves).

I like the ending of Gobinsingue: it has an element of the great and the sublime about it. The divinity that the Mogol Emperor did not understand—that he should not have understood—is nothing but identification with the Universal Being, produced before this life, according to the Beids, the forgiving of all needs by the absolute domain in the internal and external sense.

For eleven months, the Ragepoute carried on an obstinate resistance: he saw most of his troops die of hunger. In giving himself up with 300 Siks, he made easier the escape of others and saved the life of his pregnant wife. To see ten of his disciples executed at a time every day seems as much shock as could have been given him.

Gobinsingue's hour arrives. The monarch makes fun of his pretended divinity: the wise man does not answer; one does not reason with the hangman.

The leader of the Siks loses in silence, at the hand of the executioner, the form that the Great Soul gave him to manifest himself in this lower world; and the people of Dehli, who do not share the interests of the Sovereign, see in this important person only the inimitable model of a voluntary deprivation, which they marvel at in mourning his death.

NOTES

1. Susan Gole, *Early Maps of India* (Edinburgh: Skilton, 1978), 71.
2. C.H. Loehlin, *The Granth of Guru Gobind Singh and the Khalsa Brotherhood* (Lucknow: Lucknow Publishing House, 1971), 67.
3. Max Arthur Macauliffe, *The Sikh Religion: Its Gurus, Sacred Writings and Authors*, 6 vols. in 3 (Oxford: Clarendon, 1909. Reprint, Delhi: S. Chand, 1985), 250; Khazan Singh, *History and Philosophy of Sikh Religion* (Lahore: 1914), pt 1, 216.
4. *The Encyclopaedia of Sikhism*, s.v. "Khālsā."
5. Irfan Habib trans., "An Account of the Sikhs, 1808: From Ghulām 'Alī Khān, 'Imādu's Sa'ādat," in *Sikh History from Persian Sources*, ed. J.S. Grewal and Irfan Habib, 213.
6. A corrupt spelling of Amritsar (q.v.), also known as Chakk Rāmdās (q.v.).
7. Phonetic spelling of Chakk (q.v.).
8. Gurū Nānak did not spend time in Amritsar, which was founded by Gurū Rām Dās (q.v.).
9. Sikhs are not idolators since the Sikh faith quite categorically rejects idolatry. The account later contradicts this statement by saying that the Sikhs "do not accept images or sculptures."
10. Gurū Nānak (q.v.) was born in 1469. During his lifetime, the first of the "Great Mughals" Bābur (1483–1530, reigned 1526–1530) was periodically reigning in Northern India.
11. *Colsa* is clearly a reference to Khālsā whereas *Colassa* is a reference to *Khulāsā* (q.v.), a term used for *Sahajdhārīs* (q.v.) in the eighteenth and nineteenth century. W.H. McLeod, *Historical Dictionary of Sikhism* (Lanham, Md. and London: Scarecrow, 1995. Reprinted by Oxford University Press, New Delhi, 2002), 121.
12. Ahmad Shāh Abdālī or Durrānī (q.v.).
13. Wazīr Khān (q.v.).
14. From this point in the account, the author refers to Bandā Bahādur (q.v.) as "Gobindsingue."
15. Emperor Bahadur Shāh (q.v.).
16. Ādīnā Beg Khān (q.v.).
17. Jassā Singh Āhlūvālīā (q.v.), who was the fourth head of the *Buddhā Dal* (q.v.), was born in 1718, two years after the death of Bandā (referred to as "Gobindsingue"), which rules him out as being his immediate successor. The coin inscription given by Gentil is attributed to Jassā Singh and appears to be the same as that mentioned by Browne (see part II, chapter 9). Gentil's translation of the original Persian which he transliterates in the text appears faulty as he refers to Jassā Singh and not Jassā Kalāl. For a fuller discussion of this

coin inscription, see part II, chapter 9. Another inscription on a Sikh coin is given by Wendel (part I, chapter 2) which he says was struck in 1765.

18. 'Abd us-Samad Khān (q.v.).

19. Timur Shāh (q.v.).

20. Muhammad Kasim Ibn Hindu Shāh [Astarabadī Ferishtāh], *The History of Hindostan, from the Earliest Account of Time to the Death of Akbar; Translated from the Persian of Mahummud Casim Ferishtah . . .*, trans. Alexander Dow, 3 vols (London: T. Becket and P.A. de Hondt, 1770–1772). See part VI, chapter 29 for the excerpts relating to the Sikhs.

21. Du Perron has given a rather interesting and unique example of the initiation ceremony which has elements from both *charan amrit* (q.v.) *and khande dī pahul* (q.v.) ceremonies. Variants on the use of a boar's tooth during the ceremony have been noted by other commentators and include the use of boar's tusks, bones and blood in preparing the *amrit* (q.v.) (Polier, part II, chapter 8; Scott, part VI, chapter 34).

PART II

COMPANY MEN

CHAPTER 4

EXECUTION OF BANDĀ SINGH BAHĀDUR
IN DELHI, 1716

Madras Diary and Consultation Book, 1715–1719, 87 Range 239.

The mission lead by John Surman in 1714 to the court of the then Mughal Emperor Farrukh Sīyār (1683–1719) has been described as "the most important step taken by the English in Bengal from the foundation of Calcutta . . . to the conquest of Bengal by Clive."[1] Surman, a bureaucrat in the fledgling East India Company, headed a trade mission to obtain a royal seal in order to allow exclusivity of trade in Bengal. Similar to the monopoly trading rights of Elizabethan England, the cherished imperial *farmān* was the ticket to instant fortune. Drawing on over a hundred years of trading knowledge in India, the embassy's role was to flatter, ingratiate, and bribe their way through to the emperor and buy his favor for the much-needed imperial signature.

After a considerable period of indecision, it was finally settled that the men to be nominated to the embassy were John Surman—chief, Khwajah Sarhad—second, Edward Stephenson—third, and Hugh Barker—secretary and accountant.

For three months from August 1714, Surman's embassy snaked its way from Patnā to Delhi dragging with it 160 bullock wagons, 15 camels, 10 carts, 22 oxen, and an enormous retinue of servants to service the ambassadors and their ever-increasing stock. The mission's servants included a trumpeter, 6 soldiers, a clock maker, 4 smiths, 10 carpenters, 30 spadesmen, and 1,200 porters, besides the wagoners and drivers.[2]

The mission had got off to a good start by securing an imperial escort for the long journey during which any number of bandits would have happily relieved them of their royal gifts. Emperor Farrukh Sīyār was clearly looking forward to receiving this mission and made arrangement for security and travel expenses along the way. The mission that made Surman's name was a

success but not without hitch. Surman's greatest triumph had been hard
won. It was through cunning and guile that they made the unrelenting
Farrukh Sīyār sign the *farmān*, largely by threatening to pull the British
out of Sūrat. Given this mutually unthinkable scenario, the emperor finally
conceded and the *farmān* that the British had waited over a century for, was
signed.

The success of the Surman mission may well have struck an early
diplomatic victory, but it also gives the Sikh historian a window on a figure
in Sikh history who "changed the course of not only Sikh history but also of
the history of Panjab."[3] In Delhi, Surman and Stephenson witnessed the
entry of Bandā Bahādur and hundreds of other captured Sikhs. Bandā, who
had been a thorn in the side of Mughal Punjab since his return from the
Deccan in 1709, was captured after a prolonged siege lasting some eight
months. Bandā and his Sikhs had been pushed up from the plains to the
village of Gurdās-Nangal just six kilometers from the town of Gurdāspur.
There, they were subjected to the gruesome conditions of a medieval siege
prompting the Muslim diarist of the time, Khāfi Khān, to comment "many
died of dysentery and deprivation . . . When all the grass was gone, they
gathered leaves from the trees. When these were consumed, they stripped
the bark and broke off the small shoots, dried them, ground them and
used them instead of flour, thus keeping body and soul together. They collected the bones of small animals and used them in the same way. Some
assert that they saw a few of the Sikhs cut flesh from their own thighs roast
it, and eat it."[4] Despite their considerable resolve, the royal army finally
broke through and captured Bandā Bahādur and the last of the surviving
Sikhs. Before reaching Delhi, they were paraded through the streets of
Lahore. Surman and Stephenson noted their entry into Delhi in a single
sentence of a February 17, 1716 diary note:

> [T]he rebel Gorow arrived from Lahore, making his entry on an elephant in an
> iron cage . . .

The entry of Bandā Bahādur and his Sikhs into Delhi is better articulated
with greater detail by a number of eyewitnesses. One Muslim eyewitness had
gone to see the procession of the Sikh prisoners and recorded what he saw:

> On this day I had gone to see the *tamasha* [spectacle] as far as the Mandavi-i-
> Namak [Salt Market] and had thence accompanied the procession to the
> Qilah-i-Mubarik [Imperial Fort]. There was hardly any one in the city who had
> not come out to see the *tamasha* or to enjoy the show of the extirpation of the
> accused ones [Sikhs]. Such a crowd in the bazaars and lanes had been rarely
> seen. And the Musalman could not contain themselves for joy. But those unfor-
> tunate Sikhs, who had been reduced to this last extremity, were quite happy
> and contented with their fate; not the slightest sign of dejection or humility
> was seen on their faces. In fact, most of them, as they passed along on their
> camels, seemed happy and cheerful, joyfully singing the sacred hymns of their

Scripture. And, if any one from amongst those in the lanes and bazaars called out to them that their own excesses had reduced them to that condition, they quickly retorted saying that it had been so willed by the Almighty and that their capture and misfortune was in accordance with His Will. And, if any one said, "Now you will be killed," they shouted, "Kill us. When were we afraid of death? Had we been afraid of it, how could we have fought so many battles with you? It was merely through starvation and for want of food that we fell into your hands, otherwise you know already what deeds we are capable of."[5]

It was their entry and subsequent execution that was witnessed and noted by the Surman mission. The day book in which the entries of letters, memoirs, and notes, is now preserved as part of the India Office Collections at the British Library. The entire mission's progress is noted in copperplate script from mundane realities of daily life to the final issuance of the precious *farmān*.

Described as "unexciting"[6] John Surman was arguably one of India's best early, unflappable bureaucrats. In an age when the East India Company men bullied, coerced, lied, and bribed their way to personal fortunes, Surman preferred public interests to private and seemed more intent on the establishment of the English trade and the English position in India than personal progression.

A generation before Robert Clive and Warren Hastings, whose moral elasticity defined the opulent lifestyles and ill-gotten gains of the *Nabobs*, John Surman was a man of seeming integrity, strong passions, and a strong will. Unlike some of the men who came after him, Surman was born into a middle class family—the son of John Surman, a London coach maker, and his wife Susanna. The younger John was elected a writer on December 20, 1706. Although the date of his birth is not known it can be well assumed that the young Surman was the usual age of seventeen for this profession. He set sail for Bengal in February 1707 arriving there some six months later. By 1710, he was sent to Patnā, an important East India Company entrepôt. Here, he seems to have excelled and by 1712, though not out of his writership; Surman was taken into the council at Patnā as being "very sufficiently qualified to give his advice and every way fit to assist in these troublesome times."[7] He certainly seems to have lived up to the glowing praise.

After the monumental success of the embassy to Delhi, Surman was rightfully triumphant and his future should have been assured. Sadly, however, he died shortly afterward, a commentator noting obliquely that "the directors and a lady's cruelty in England hastened his death."

Of Khwajah Sarhad, little is known other than his Armenian roots and his role as principal merchant in the settlement in Calcutta.[8] He was deputized to the embassy to act as principal agent and interpreter. The diary describes at length the awards that would be made to Sarhad should he succeed in procuring the trading rights they so desired; with the holy grail of the custom free trade arrangement at Sūrat he was to be rewarded with Rs. 100,000.

The third in the negotiation, Edward Stephenson, was a character in the mould of those administrators that followed him. Diplomatically described by C.R. Wilson as "without that conspicuous ability and zeal for the public service which distinguish John Surman he was content to do his duty and get rich quietly. Consequently he succeeded in satisfying his masters."[9]

Born in Cumberland in 1691, his father was Edward Stephenson of Keswick; his mother, Rebecca was connected with the Winders of Lorton and of the City of London. Like Surman, he joined the Company at seventeen as a writer in 1708, landing in Bengal two years later. His career accelerated in India; a succession of promotions brought him to the post of a supporting role to the chief of the Surman embassy at the time of this important trade mission. India must have treated him well as he retired to England well-off and highly respected, living until the age of seventy-two.

The secretary, Hugh Barker, was the antithesis of John Surman's quiet, competent, and honorable administration. His career in the East India Company was dogged by scandal and incompetence but he dodged any serious setback by calling on his connections and influence with the court of directors. He was unflatteringly described as "an unprofitable servant of the Company, neglectful of its interests, using whatever abilities and opportunities he had solely for his own advantage."[10] Like most young men who foresaw their fortune in India, Barker petitioned the Company for a post as a writer aged just seventeen. His arrival in Bengal was just a year after Stephenson's, landing in 1711. His role in the embassy to Delhi was apparently acceptable and he is said to have discharged his duties satisfactorily under the supervision of Surman and Stephenson. It was only later in Patnā that he was dismissed from the service on moral grounds, only to be restored through plying some influence on the directors.

The letter remains the only British eyewitness account of the event of Bandā's death in Delhi. There exist a number of valuable Persian accounts from diarists, news writers, and imperial officials. The most notable of these Persian accounts being: Mirzā Muhammad, 'Ibratnāma; Muhammad Hādī Kāmwar Khān, Tazkiratu's Salātīn Chaghatā; Khāfī Khān, Muntakhabu'l Lubāb; and Muhammad Shafi' "Warid," Mir'āt-i Wāridāt. All of these accounts are to be found translated into English with notes in J.S. Grewal and Irfan Habib ed., Sikh History from Persian Sources (New Delhi: Tulika, 2001).

This was not the Englishmen's first encounter with the Sikhs. The British historiographer, Robert Orme, noted in 1778 that "these procrastination had already led the embassy to the month of April 1716, when the emperor took the field, and marched towards Lahore against the Sykes, a nation of Indians lately reared to power, and bearing mortal enmity to the Mohamedans. The ambassadors followed the camp. The campaign was tedious though successful."[11]

The short account from Surman and Stephenson should be noted in the context of their only knowledge of Sikhs as an imperial frustration. Despite this, they give an unemotional account even noting some admiration of the Sikhs as they met their fate at the hands of the Mughal executioner.

LETTER XII

The Honourable Robert Hedges Esq.,
President & Governor of Fort William, & Council in Bengal.
Honourable Sirs, etc.,
We wrote your Honour on the 7th ultimo since which we have received no letters.

The great Rebel Gooroo[12] who has been for these 20 years so troublesome in the Subaship of Lahore is at length taken with all his family and attendance by Abd-us-Samad Cawn[13] the Suba of that province. Some days ago they entered the city laden with fetters, his whole attendants which were left alive being about seven hundred and eighty all severally mounted on camels which were sent out of the City for that purpose, besides about two thousand heads stuck upon poles, being those who died by the sword in battle. He was carried into the presence of the King, and from thence to a close prison. He at present has his life prolonged with most of his mutsuddys[14] in the hope to get an Account of his treasure in the several parts of his Kingdom, and of those that assisted him, when afterwards he will be executed, for the rest there are 100 each day beheaded.[15] It is not a little remarkable with what patience they undergo their fate,[16] and to the last it has not been found that one apostatised from his new formed Religion.

We are,
Honourable Sir & Sirs,
Your most obedient humble servants,
John Surman,
Edward Stephenson.
Cojee Seerhaud assenting.
Hugh Barker, Secretary.
Dilly March the 10th, 1716

NOTES

1. C.R. Wilson, *The Early Annals of the English in Bengal* (London: 1895), vol. 2, part 2, chapter 1.i.
2. *Madras Diary and Consultation Book*, 1715–1719, 87 Range 239, 7, 8, 275.
3. Gupta, *History of the Sikhs*, 2: 35.
4. Khāfī Khān, *Muntakhabu'l Lubāb*, quoted in *The Encyclopaedia of Sikhism*, s.v. "Bandā Singh Bahadur."
5. Mirzā Muhammad Harisi, *Ibrāt Nāmā*, 52b–53a, quoted in Ganda Singh, *Life of Banda Singh Bahadur* (Patiala: Punjabi University, 1999), 148.
6. John Keay, *India: A History* (London: Harper Collins, 2000), 374.
7. Wilson, *Early Annals*, vol. 2, part 2, xii.
8. Robert Orme, *A History of the Military Transactions of the British Nation in Indostan* (London: 1778), vol. 2, book 4, 19.
9. Wilson, *Early Annals*, vol. 2, part 2, xii.
10. Ibid., xii.
11. Orme, *Military Transactions*, 22.

12. A reference to Bandā Singh Bahādur (1670–1716) (q.v.) who was frequently viewed by non-Sikh writers of the eighteenth century as the spiritual successor of Gurū Gobind Singh.

13. 'Abd-us-Samad Khān (d. 1737) (q.v.). He was appointed by Farrukh-Sīyār (q.v.) with the intention of exterminating the Sikhs. According to the *Akhbār-i-Darbār-i-Mu'allā*, 'Abd us-Samad Khān marched from Lahore at the head of 12,000 horsemen and an equal number of infantry, as well as a large artillery force, and closed in upon Bandā Singh as he was preparing for battle near village Batālā. Bandā made a determined stand against the Imperial force but evacuated Batālā and took shelter in the *havelī*, or fortress, in Gurdās-Nangal. 'Abd us-Samad Khān laid a tight siege that lasted eight months. Bhagat Singh, trans. and ed., *Akhbār-i-Darbār-i-Mu'allā*, Patiala, 1984, quoted in *The Encyclopaedia of Sikhism*, s.v. " 'Abd us-Samad Khān."

14. An accountant.

15. Bandā Singh and the other Sikh prisoners were conducted to Delhi on February 27, 1716. On March 5, the executions of one hundred Sikhs per day commenced and continued unabated for a week. By the tenth of the same month, the date of the mission's letter, some 600 Sikhs had been executed. On June 19, some four months after he had first arrived as a prisoner in Delhi, Bandā Singh was himself executed, after witnessing the hacking to death of his four-year-old son.

16. Sayyed Muhammad, the author of the *Tabsīrat-un-Nazirin*, was also present during this historic occasion. "At that time I addressed one of them by signs that that was the result of their arrogance and insolence. He put his hand on his forehead to express that it was predestined. The expression of his meaning at that time pleased me very much." Singh, *Life of Banda Singh Bahadur*, 148–9.

CHAPTER 5

OMĪCHAND, THE PLASSEY
PROTAGONIST, 1757

Robert Orme, *A History of the Military Transactions of the British Nation in Indostan, from the year MDCCXLV [1745]*, 2 vols. (London: Printed for John Nourse, 1780), 2: 50–1, 182–3.

Early British consciousness of Sikhs would have been principally formed by any contact between the English East India Company and those Sikhs in Bengal rather than the Punjab. Over a thousand miles from the Punjab, those few Sikhs who were in Bengal were largely Punjabi traders, many of whom managed to acquire immense wealth and influence in Muslim-administered Bengal. These Punjabi traders came from the community of merchants par excellence, the *Khatrīs*, a community made up of a Hindu majority but with a sizeable Sikh population. A phenomenon peculiar to the *Khatrī* Sikhs of the Punjab was their reluctance to join the Khālsā *panth* (community) and remain wedded to the teachings of Gurū Nānak.[1] *Khatrī* Sikhs shaped the majority of the *Nānakpanthī* community who formed a significant proportion of the Sikh community of the eighteenth century.

In their incessant pursuit of trade, the eighteenth century Punjabi *Khatrīs* found rich pickings in eastern India with the growing influence of the British and, more importantly, a fabulously rich and exploding new export trade. A measure of their growing influence was a shift from a financial to a growing political power, exemplified in the Mahārājās of Burdwān, Kishenbabū, Ghanshyām, Krishnārām, Jagatrām, Kirtīchand, and Chitrāsen who ruled in the last phase of the seventeenth century and belonged to the *Khatrī* caste of the Punjab.

In the important trading city of Murshīdābad, one of the most important of the moneymen was the great "Sikh trader"[2] commonly known as Omīchand. His real name was more likely Amīrchand. Omīchand refers to himself only once in the extant records of the time, and in that case writes

"Amirchandrajir." Variant spellings in early European accounts refer to him as Umichand but more commonly Omīchand. He is quite frequently described as a *Nānakpanthī* or a Sikh; presumably, this distinction was made by contemporary commentators because of the inability to categorize him as either Hindu or Muslim. Of Omīchand's early life little is known; he seems to have come to Calcutta from Azimabād in Patnā. His reference to himself as "Agrawallah" as early as 1742[3] may indicate that he had also identified himself as being from Agra as some historians have suggested. Others have interpreted his signature as "Umichand Agarwal"[4] which would indicate a caste affiliation to the *Bānīās*—the elite of the Punjabi trading community. Early chroniclers were more concerned with Omīchand's role as chief trading intermediary with the East India Company than of Omīchand's background or origins.

The primary business of the East India Company was to purchase materials from India through a variety of agents to trade to willing markets in the West. The go-betweens in these transactions were the *dādnī* merchants who were made staggeringly wealthy as a result. *Dādnī* was a term used to describe an advance given to craftsmen. In the context of the trading community in Calcutta, it is a term used to describe the merchants who would advance payments to suppliers before selling the goods onward to the English to furnish their contracts. Omīchand made his early fortune as an associate, and later a partner, of the premier Calcutta trading house, the Seths. He soon tired of the partnership and struck out alone. By the 1730s, he had established himself as a leading merchant in his own right in the area. Despite being seen as a corrupting influence on English trade—he was actively involved in monopolizing the *dādnī* contracts through a series of false names—the Company thought it best to retain his services rather than risk him switching allegiances to the Dutch or the French. It also earned him a reputation as "immensely rich and infinitely slimy."[5]

The favorable terms that gave him his first foothold would no doubt have left only a little profit had his produce not "deteriorated in quality and increased in price."[6] Despite these regressions, it seems clear that by 1747 his reputation was assured. During a spat between council members who were reviewing Omīchand's proposal to supply a significant proportion of the Company's contracts, one of the council members noted that "his natural and acquired capacity for business, his extraordinary knowledge of the Inland trade and his greater command of money all which qualities I think render him a proper person to deal with for ready money."[7] With this endorsement, Omīchand's trade and accompanying wealth outstripped that of his old associates and now his rivals. In 1750, the Company owed him more than Rs. 1.6 million; he owned Calcutta's finest houses and had a retinue of 300 men.

The British historiographer of the East India Company, Robert Orme, writes:

pp. 50–1
[1756] Amongst the Gentoo merchants established in Calcutta was one named Omicund, a man of great sagacity and understanding, which he had employed

for forty years with unceasing diligence to increase his fortune. The presidency had long permitted him to provide much more of the company's investment than the share allowed to any other contractor; by which, and other indulgences, he was to become the most opulent inhabitant in the colony. The extent of his habitation, divided into various departments; the number of his servants continually employed in various occupations, and a retinue of armed men in constant pay resembled more the state of a prince than the condition of a merchant. His commerce extended to all parts of Bengal and Behar, and by presents and services he had acquired so much influence with the principal officers of the government of Muxadavad, that the presidency in times of difficulty used to employ his mediation with the Nabob. This pre-eminence, however, did not fail to render him the object of much envy: the manufactures provided for the company having every year since the first irruption of the Morattoes decreased in quality and increased in price, much of this detriment was imputed to the avarice and iniquity of Omichund; and the company determining, if possible, to restore their investment to the former condition of price and quality, relinquished in the year 1753, their usual method of contracting with merchants, and sent *Gomastahs*, or Gentoo factors in their own pay, to provide the investment at different *Aurangs*,[8] or cloth markets in the province. From this time Omichund was excluded from any participation in the company's affairs, which, diminishing his commercial advantages, vexed his avarice, although possessed of four millions of rupees. However, he still continued the trade, which he used to carry on independent of the investment, and redoubled his attention to maintain his importance at Muxadavad; in consequence of which Rajah-bullub at this time requested his good offices to his son Kissendas, whom Omichund received on his arrival with much hospitality, and lodged the family in a convenient habitation.

The trading community in Calcutta, including Omīchand, traded in almost everything, although Omīchand's specialty was in saltpeter and opium, which was sourced (as the British later found out to their utter shock) through an unlawful agreement with the *faujdār* of Rungpure. The relationship that the wily Omīchand later used to his great advantage was his close association at the court of Ālīvardī Khān and later his grandson Siraj ud-Daulā. This connection served both parties well, as the court became rich on the English trade through Omīchand, and the *Khatrī* trader used the influence of court to bail him out. When in 1734 Omīchand was struck off the list of the Company's *dādnī* merchants, the Khān's brother made an impassioned plea for his reinstatement, even going so far as standing for security for the sums advanced to him.[9]

His checkered career as principal merchant to the English acquired him a vast fortune, and he was known to own the finest residences in Calcutta, but he was also its worst landlord. In one of the earliest records of Omīchand, he is mentioned in the judicial records of 1755 where the following representation was made: ". . . the jurors for our sovereign Lord the King present that Omichand of this place inhabitant, having been frequently presented to the court by several grand Jury for neglecting to repair his houses so great in number in this town which he is possessed of, several of which are quite untenable . . . remain still in a ruinous and untenable condition . . . the Jurors therefore do say that the accused's neglect is a great nuisance to the town in general and to the inhabitants thereof . . . the said nuisance still remain to the hazard of the lives of many inhabitants who are obliged to rent the said houses for want of others as likewise passengers passing by and endangering neighbouring houses by their fall."[10]

However, Omīchand's place in history, which is undoubted, was not as an unscrupulous trader and appalling landlord but as a central protagonist in the events surrounding the Battle of Plassey. A battle of military insignificance that won Clive of India his epithet and allowed the Company's directors the "power to be as great as you please in the kingdom of Bengal."[11]

Over a period of a century, ever since the first British merchants had landed in Bengal, the dependence on the consent of the local *nawāb*, chief, or even the emperor was unquestioned. Often, however, the chieftains were not quite as benign as the traders would have liked. Simultaneously, traders grew in confidence, security, and authority while Mughal power waned under its own incompetence, nepotism, and internal struggles. In the fractious and volatile courts and local dominions, the East India Company became kingmaker and power broker. However, all that was needed was an instance of heavy-handed intervention and that delicate role would turn eventually into annexation and governance. Plassey was that event. Following the conclusion of the Battle of Plassey in 1757, the British confidently and aggressively pursued political domination over increasing sections of the subcontinent in the name of protecting the trade of the East India Company. In the vacuum of governance that followed the end of the reign of the great Mughals, the pursuit of trade rapidly turned into the outright domination of the country.

In Bengal, where the East India Company were a dominant force in the principal trading towns of Calcutta, a problem was brewing under the stewardship of a young, inexperienced, and hot-headed *nawāb*. Siraj ud-Daulā was the grandson of the venerable Ālīvardī Khān who ruled over Bengal, Orīssā, and Bihār during the disintegration of Mughal power. He was an independent sovereign paying only nominal acquiesces to a remote and distracted emperor in Delhi. His grandson was destined to become *nawāb* on his death in 1756 and his son-in-law, Mīr Jafar, to become the new *nawāb*'s military general and paymaster.

Like his grandfather, Siraj shared a distrust and anxiety at the growing influence of the British. However, unlike his grandfather, the young monarch was noted more for his "ignorance and indecision."[12] In spite of this, his sovereignty was assured, largely due to the lack of outright hostility toward the British. Despite this apparent security, he signed his own death warrant by publicly and quite sickeningly insulting the Seth brothers, powerful Hindu moneymen who bankrolled much of the business of Bengal.[13] Enraged, they flexed their muscles by exploiting their unique position as business partners of both the Company and the court. Preferring Christian overlords to brutish Muslim ones, the genesis of a *coup d'état* was developing.

To stoke the flames further, the Seths and their fellow conspirators inflamed English–Mughal relations through a series of miscommunications, rumors, and outright lies; a once cordial relationship disintegrated in a matter of months. The gang now comprised of Omīchand, Manik Chand, the minister and general Rāi Durlābh, and most significantly, Mīr Jafar, the most powerful figure in the Muslim military aristocracy and new leader of this confederation of grandees.[14]

Omīchand's role was central. He was, it appears, chief instigator in the plot against the *nawāb*. Omīchand, as the favored go-between in the relationship between the Company and the court, was in the privileged and unique position of having the ear of both parties. This was a power that he knew only too well, and a power that he was keen to leverage.

With Robert Clive, then governor of Fort Saint David, successfully embroiled in the plot against the *nawāb*, Omīchand shamelessly double-crossed the plotters, threatening to expose the entire conspiracy to the young king. Omīchand was hardly a man in need but despite this, his price for silence was enormous—enough to catapult him far beyond the wealth of the Bengalī Bankers. What followed has been described as a "victory of guile over greed."[15] Clive, anxious to silence Omīchand and equally desperate not to pay over a quarter of the haul promised to the Europeans to his old adversary, drew up two identical treaties—one false treaty acceding to Omīchand's demands and a real one that would suit Clive and the other conspirators. To make the sham treaty even more compelling, Clive would mischievously bargain Omīchand down a peg or two and have it signed by Mīr Jafar and the British. In a final act of deceit, Clive even went so far as to forge the signature of a second witness. Both these acts would see an incredulous Robert Clive facing parliament, answering for the nature by which he conducted business in Bengal.

When the relationship had finally and irrecoverably broken down, the pieces were in place for a battle. Unknown to Siraj ud-Daulā, his cards were stacked against him. He was fighting against a well-armed adversary and, unknown to him, against many of his own men. Plassey was by all accounts nothing more than a very messy skirmish. The *nawāb*'s troops bungled the use of their own field guns, blowing their own powder reserves and frightening their war elephants, vital powerhouses to maneuver their artillery. Even Mīr Jafar's defection, the subject of the most intricate planning and delicate negotiations, was chaotic. In the pandemonium of fire, Jafar's messenger refused to cross the lines and his men were accidentally bombarded by Clive's forces. Ironically, it did not matter as the *nawāb*'s troops crumbled and fled the battleground. Siraj lead the way but was captured and killed by his successor's henchmen. This ugly and seemingly insignificant battle did eventually mark a critical point in British and Indian history as it signified the point at which the British turned kingmaker, and the balance of power swung from the Mughals to the Company and simultaneously marginalized the growing influence of the French in India. With the campaign at Plassey complete, it was time to reap the rewards. Mīr Jafar got his throne, the European Community in Calcutta received £550,000, the Hindus £220,000, the Armenians £77,000, and the army and navy £275,000. Clive as Commander-in-Chief of the Company's land forces would, therefore, rake in the lion's share of the loot; in addition to personal gifts from Mīr Jafar this amounted to £275,000. Omīchand, who had tried to extract a heavy price, some 5 percent of the *nawāb*'s money and one-quarter of the jewels, an estimated one million sterling, would receive nothing. His "great financial gamble failed miserably"[16] and it was the job of Clive and Scrafton (Watts' political assistant in the *nawāb's* court) to break the bad news. According to Robert Orme, a member of the council at Madras, and historiographer to the Company (from 1769 to 1801) who witnessed this occasion:

pp. 182–3

[1757] The conference being ended, Clive and Scrafton went towards Omichund, who was waiting in full assurance of hearing the glad tidings of his good fortune; when Clive said, "It is now time to undeceive Omichund:" on which, Scrafton said to him in the Indostan language, "Omichund, the red paper is a trick; "you are to have nothing." These words overpowered him like a blast of sulphur; he sunk back, fainting, and would have fallen to the ground, had not one of his attendants caught him in his arms; they carried him to his palankin, in which they conveyed him to his house, where he remained many hours in stupid melancholy, and began to show some symptoms of insanity. Some days after, he visited Colonel Clive, who advised him to make a pilgrimage to some pagoda; which he accordingly did soon after, to a famous one near Maulada: he went, and returned insane his mind every day more and more approaching to idiotism and, contrary to the usual manners of old age in Indostan, still more to the former excellence of his understanding, he delighted in being continually dressed in the richest garments, and ornamented with the most costly jewels. In this state of imbecility, he died about a year and a half after the shock of his disappointment. Grounded on his importance, by knowing the secret, he held out the terror of betraying it, to secure his own advantages. Whether he would have betrayed it, if refused, is uncertain: for part of his fortune was in the power of the English, and he had the utmost vengeance of Jaffier and his confederates to fear. However, the experiment was not to be tried. But, on the other hand, as his tales and artifices prevented Surajah Dowlah from believing the representation of his most trusty servants, who early suspected, and at length were convinced, that the English were confederated with Jaffier; the 2,000,000 of rupees he expected should have been paid him, and he left to enjoy them in oblivion and contempt.

The writer of these words, Robert Orme, started his career in the East India Company like many others, as a fifteen-year-old writer. It ended as anything but ordinary with the soldier-historian becoming a close personal friend of Robert Clive and member of the Council at Madras. He was one of the few people privy to the goings-on during the planning and execution of the Plassey battle and committed to paper his observations of the *Nānakpanthī* trader Omīchand. In 1759, two years after Plassey, he was dramatically captured by the French in Mauritius on his way home. Released in 1760, he returned to England where he published his great work *A History of the Military Transactions of the British Nation in Indostan from the Year 1745* and *Historical Fragments of the Mogul Empire, of the Morattoes, and of the English Concerns in Indostan from the Year 1659*. The former was published in three volumes in 1763–1778 and 1781; the latter was published in 1782. He also left an important collection of manuscripts under the heading "Orme Collection" that is now preserved in the Oriental and India Office Collection at the British Library. It is from this collection of miscellany that a number of accounts with pertinent references to the Sikhs have been reproduced elsewhere in this book (Wendel, part I, chapter 2; Anon, part II, chapter 6; Polier, part II, chapter 8). He died in Great Ealing aged seventy-three years on January 13, 1801.[17]

Robert Clive had played his hand masterfully. His deception of Omīchand was a master-stroke in corruption that set the tone for early British rule over India. In another note of early imperialism, Clive makes a patronizing memorandum note on Omīchand: "Omichand had merited well while acting in concert with Mr. Watts, but I had reason to think his intriguing disposition was carrying him too far in the pursuit of his private interest, therefore recommend him to a visit of devotion to Malda. He is a person capable of rendering you great service while properly restrained, therefore not to be wholly discarded. Records of Government August 6, 1757."[18]

According to Orme, who otherwise rarely descends into polemics, Omīchand, overwhelmed by the shock of the deception, lapsed into a mental illness that finally killed him. The story that Omīchand lost his mind is fanciful. This is endorsed by the documentary evidence of the time. Following his death, a lengthy family quarrel and litigation ensued. At no time during these proceedings was his mental health even questioned or raised. It is also clear that his business dealings with the English continued after the Plassey incident. In fact, Omīchand was still dealing saltpeter to the English until 1758, when the Company appropriated itself the monopoly right to trade in the commodity from the puppet *nawāb* Mīr Jafar.[19] Omīchand may well have been aggrieved at the treatment that he received from the English. However, he was being overly naive as he had been a victim of his own ruse. Early in his career, whilst still the partner of Bostom Das Seth, he convinced the ailing Seth to mortgage his entire property to himself in order to stave off creditors who would try to make a claim on the property when Seth finally died. Omīchand concocted a fake mortgage, which allowed him to fend off creditors, and gradually sell parts of the property, pay back some of the creditors, and make a tidy profit. Although it is unlikely that he went insane, he must certainly have been enraged by the outcome. Clive certainly would have had reason not to cross his path, and in the only known visual representation of Omīchand (see illustration 2) there is a depiction of the trader's ghost haunting a terrified Clive. There is evidence that he developed a religious turn in the period following Plassey. He talked, it is noted, of taking a pilgrimage to Amritsar, and in his will he asked to leave a substantial amount as a donation to *Sree Gobind Nanakji*. His legacy, of course, was vast, some Rs. 4.4 million, of which only Rs. 160,000 was identified as going to his family, the rest to the donation. *Sree Gobind Nanakji* is thought to be a reference to the *takht* at Nānded or Patnā. However, there ensued a lengthy litigation battle following his death between Hīrā Singh (heir of Omīchand's brother-in-law Hazūrī Mal) and Bulākī Singh (nephew of Diachand, Omīchand's *pālak bettā*, or adopted son). The quarrel between these two helped to ruin the trust property of their ancestor. The original executor of the will was Hazūrī Mal. It is commonly thought that Omīchand bequeathed a substantial sum to the Magdalen and Foundling charities in England, however, this is not borne out in the text of his will. Later researches have pointed out that the source of the donation was Hazūrī Māl, who made the payments in the name of Omīchand as a gesture of goodwill to the British.[20]

The names of the protagonists in the litigation do shed some light on the nature of their relationship to their faith. Omīchand and his adopted son and some of the other family members (including his brothers Gulābchand, Kisshanchand, and Deepachand) were not Singhs of the Khālsā. However, within two generations, Hīrā Singh and Bulākī Singh were fighting out the remnants of Omīchand's inheritance; by that stage they had certainly started to identify themselves as Khālsā Sikhs or Sikhs of Gurū Gobind Singh.

During his career as the chief trading partner of the English, Omīchand made a great play of his loyalty to the Company and its employees. This, of course, was a complete facade, and the English knew it. He was no more loyal to them than they were to him. In an ironic early account of Omīchand, dated just months before the great fraud at Plassey, Watts writes from Murshīdābad: "Omichand told the Nabob that he had lived under the English protection for these forty years and never knew them once to be guilty of breaking their word—to the truth of which he took his oath by touching a Brahmin's foot—and that if a lie could be proved in England on any one they were to spit upon and never trusted."[21]

NOTES

1. Jeevan Deol, "Eighteenth-Century Khalsa Identity: Discourse, Praxis and Narrative," in *Sikh Religion, Culture and Ethnicity*, ed. Christopher Shackle, Gurharpal Singh, and Arvindpal Singh Mandair (Richmond: Curzon, 2000), 27.
2. Narendra Krishna Sinha, *The Economic History of Bengal: From Plassey to the Permanent Settlement*, 3rd ed. (Calcutta: Firma K.L. Mukhopadhyay, 1981–1984), 241.
3. Sushil Chaudhury, *From Prosperity to Decline: Eighteenth Century Bengal* (Delhi: Manohar, 1995), 116, quoting from Factory Records, Patna, vol. 2, April 3, 1742.
4. Chaudhury, *From Prosperity to Decline*, 267.
5. Mark Bence-Jones, *Clive of India* (London: Constable, 1974), 110.
6. J. Tallboys Wheeler, *Early Records of British India* (London: Trubner & Co, 1878), 225.

7. John Forster quoted from BPC, vol. 20, f. 109–9vo, August 15, 1747 in Chaudhury, *From Prosperity to Decline*, 117.

8. *Gomastas* were local agents deputised by the Company to provide investments at provincial cloth markets, known as *Aurungs*.

9. Chaudhury, *From Prosperity to Decline*, 118.

10. Sinha, *Economic History*, 243.

11. Fort William-India House Correspondence, vol. 2, 250, quoted in Lawrence James, *Raj: The Making and Unmaking of British India* (London: Little Brown, 1997), 36.

12. Philip Mason, abridged ed. *The Men Who Ruled India* (London: J. Cape, 1985), 32.

13. Of Siraj ud-Daulā, Lawrence James writes "He was ill-equipped for the task: resolute by starts, he was easily disheartened and his fickle vindictiveness lost him friends among his courtiers and more powerful subjects. He did not, for instance, help himself by threatening forcibly to convert and circumcise leading members of the Hindu banking oligarchy." James, *Raj*, 31.

14. Mason, *The Men Who Ruled India*, 35–38.

15. James, *Raj*, 34.

16. Sinha, *Economic History*, 241.

17. *Dictionary of Indian Biography*, s.v. "Orme, Robert"; *Biographical Dictionary of South Asia*, s.v. "Orme, Robert"; *The Cyclopaedia of India and of Eastern and Southern Asia*, s.v. "Orme, Robert."

18. Revd. J. Long, *Selections from Unpublished Records of Government for the Years 1748–1767 Inclusive*, ed. Mahadevaprasad Saha (Calcutta: Firma K.L. Mukhopadhyay, 1973), 139.

19. Chaudhury, *From Prosperity to Decline*, 270.

20. Sinha, *Economic History*, 246.

21. Long, *Selections*, 109.

CHAPTER 6

OF THE SEIKH'S OR SIKHAN, C. 1760

Eur Mss OV173, part 10, 175–7, Orme Collection MSS, Oriental and Indian Office Collection, British Library, London.

This rather brief sketch of the Sikhs is found within a much larger collection of manuscripts gathered by Robert Orme in preparation of his *History of the Military Transactions of the British Nation in Indostan from the Year 1745*, three volumes (London: 1763–1778). Orme, who was the East India Company's historiographer from 1769 to his death in 1801, bequeathed his large collection of papers to his friend, John Roberts, who presented them to the Company. They are now deposited in the Oriental and Indian Office Collection at the British Library in London.[1] Other papers from the Orme collection that have been reproduced elsewhere in this book (Wendel, part I, chapter 2; Polier, part II, chapter 8). Also, a discussion of Orme in the context of his role in the Omīchand affair has been given in part II, chapter 5.

This short, anonymous, and undated account contains many errors and omissions throughout. It is not know for whom it was written or the sources it relied upon. In fact, the opening sentence places the birth of Gurū Nānak in the late fourteenth century, almost a century too early. This is the first of the many mistakes that follow.

The final line stands out as an unobvious conclusion to a rather sketchy account. Its recommendation of commencing a correspondence with the chiefs of these "Hoords of People called Seikhs" (some of whom appear to have been named) is intriguing in that it appears to be aimed at a reader in a quasi-official position with the ability or, possibly, the inclination to commence such a correspondence. Alas, no further clues are available to understand the exact context that gave rise to this note "Of the Seikh's or Sikhan."

About Four hundred Years ago[2] in the mountainous parts of the Provinces of Punjaab lived Nanek Shah, a Hindoo Phaquire, he was much esteemed both by his own Cast and the Musselmen who knew him.

In the Reign of Allum Guire[3] lived Tegue Bahadar[4] Seikh. [W]hile this Monarch was in the Deccan, Two Children extreamly beautiful said to be great grand Sons or of the race of Nanek Shah were seized by Bazed Khaan[5] Phouzdar of Sirhind, & detained for the Vilest purposes. He in the mean time fearing a complaint at the presence against him by the whole Cast, cut off the two Children, and wrote to his Master that he had been obliged to destroy two of the most hardened unbelievers in his dominions, of a Sect of the most dangerous to their Prophets Religion.[6]

Tegue Bahadar being reported at the Presence as dangerous, wether from an apprehension that he might resent this abuse or because he was said to have four or five Thousand of his Cast about him, was sent for to Court, and put under closs confinement in the Fortress of Gwaliar[7] where he afterwards suffered death. [U]pon this occasion the Seikh's vowed revenge upon the Musselmen.

In the Reign of Bahadar Shah, Nabob Sheikh[8] made his appearance & having collected a number of his brethren together, openly declared his intentions of Rebellion. Bahadar Shah set out in person against them with his Army to Lahore & after a Bloody Engagement defeated them & took numbers of Prisoners.

In Pherukhseers[9] Reign, Bundeh[10] Seikh collected One hundred Thousand Horse & Foot, & possessed himself of the Country as far as Paneput within four Munsells[11] of Delhi. At this time Abdal Summid Khaan[12] was Subadar of Kashmire, the King immediately sent him Sunnuds[13] for Lahore, with orders to proceed against the Seikh's with all his Forces, & that he in person was also on the Road with his Army. The Seikhs maintained themselves for a Year & a half, at last the remains of them were forced to shut themselves up in the Kellah[14] of Gaurdaspaura otherwise BundaGurr[15] where after many hardships they agreed to surrender themselves but were contrary to agreement betwixt them mostly all cut off by Abdall Summid Khaan. This Man was the father of Zekeriah Khaan[16] who succeeded him in the Subahdarry of Lahore & for near forty years of their Gouvernment in that Province there were no Seikhs that is the Cast who never cut off their Hair, were obliged to Shave their beards, in order to hide themselves from their resentment.[17]

While Mean al Mulk[18] the Son of Khemar al der Khaan was Subah of Lahore the Seikhs became again powerful and dangerous.

Jessa Sing, Khera Sing, Nath Sing & Gaajen Sing.[19]

The opposition which the Hoords of People called Seikhs have at different times given Achmed Shah Durannie as well as the former Kings of Hindoostan & to the Governors of Lahore is worthy of observation & above all Western connections a correspondence ought to [be] supported & kept up amongst them—for they have no standing Chief.[20]

NOTES

1. S.C. Sutton, *A Guide to the India Office Library* (London: H.M.S.O., 1967), 21.
2. This paper is a part of the Orme Collection in the British Library which means that it can be dated no later than 1801, the year Orme died, but more likely in the 1760s when Orme was working on his *Military Transactions*. Thus, the author places Gurū Nānak's birth between 1360 and 1400, almost a whole century too early.
3. Emperor Aurangzeb (q.v.).
4. Gurū Tegh Bahādur (q.v.).
5. It was actually Wazīr Khān (q.v.).

6. The author has confused Gurū Tegh Bahādur for Gurū Gobind Singh (q.v.), whose two younger sons were captured by Wazīr Khān, the *faujdār* (commander) of Sirhind and executed.

7. The author has confused Gurū Tegh Bahādur for his father, Gurū Hargobind, who was imprisoned in Gwalior fort by Emperor Jahāngīr.

8. This appears to be a reference to Bandā Bahādur (q.v.) but the name used is confusing. In the next paragraph Bandā is actually mentioned specifically so the identity of "Nabob Sheikh" is not clear.

9. Farrukh Sīyār (q.v.).

10. Bandā Bahādur (q.v.).

11. The place for resting after a march, so here means four days march away.

12. 'Abd us-Samad Khān (q.v.).

13. A diploma, patent or deed of grant by the government of office, privilege, or right.

14. *Qilā* or fort.

15. Literally the "fort of Bandā."

16. Zakarīyā Khān (q.v.).

17. This policy was only really effective amongst the urban classes who were in the employment of the Mughals as administrators. In 1710, a precautionary measure was taken by Bahādur Shāh to stem the tide of support that he felt was being given to Bandā from the community of *Khatrī* Sikhs in Delhi. "[There was] an order for all Hindus employed in the imperial offices to shave off their beards. As the Sikhs had many well-wishers among the Khatri clerks, these men were thus forced to choose between losing their appointments, or committing an act that excluded them from the Sikh sect. The order was carried out, it seems, in a very harsh manner. Petty officers perambulated the streets and bazars of the camp, followed by barbers bearing dirty water in a scavenger's vessel. Whenever a Hindu was met wearing a beard, he was seized and his beard shaved off. The clerks in the imperial offices hid in their quarters, and did not appear again in public, until they had been shaved." William Irvine, *Later Mughals*, ed. Jadunath Sarker, 2 vols. (Calcutta: M.C. Sarkar & Sons; London: Luzac & Co., 1922, Reprinted New Delhi, 1971), 1: 105–6.

18. Mu'īn ul-Mulk, also known as Mīr Mannū (q.v.).

19. This appears to be a list of Sikh leaders that were prominent either when the "Seikhs became again powerful and dangerous" or when the account was written.

20. See Browne (part II, chapter 9) for references to the British corresponding with various Sikh chiefs toward the end of the eighteenth century.

CHAPTER 7

WARREN HASTINGS'S MEMORANDUM ON
THE THREAT OF THE SIKHS, 1784

Forrest, *Selections*, III, 1123–5, National Archives of India, New Delhi, Secret Proceedings, December 14, 1784, pp. 537–44.

The image of the respectable late-Victorian Englishman in India, defending the virtue of the natives, himself, and the *memsahibs*, and simultaneously working nobly to earn a living and possibly his fortune in India, was in sharp contrast to the earlier age of Company men. In the heady days of early empire building, fortunes were made as a result of moral flexibility and judicious wit as well as favorable trading conditions.

The epitome of the early Company man or *nabob* was Warren Hastings whose policies and example generated a gold rush mentality that populated the subcontinent with eager young men who wanted to break from class-ridden English society to seek their fortune in India.

These pioneers of Indian administration aggressively defended their right to trade. Trade required products and markets but also political clout. The politics of the old country were as important as those of the subcontinent. In both these countries the early Company men worked assiduously in controlling local politics; Robert Clive would cause a force majeur on a local *rājā* or *nawāb*, subduing him with the Company army and being paid a handsome personal tribute. At home, the Company's leading lights would acquire the ultimate in social status symbols—a seat in the House of Commons. With this, even the government of the United Kingdom was slowly brought into line with Company policy.

Men like Warren Hastings were the early empire builders, although motivated largely by personal gain rather than national loyalty. With the natural concentration of trade around the port cities of Madras, Bengal, and Calcutta, few of the *nabobs* dared or even needed to visit the north of the country—areas occupied by the Sikhs. A limited number of Sikhs—*Nānakpanthīs*—were resident in the trading cities, and these were predominately *Khatrī* traders. As *Nānakpanthīs*, little would have distinguished them from the Hindu majority. The accounts that originate from the early empire builders concern themselves largely with the character of the Sikh people that they encountered.

This, then, is the context in which Warren Hastings, desperate to control any interlopers into the growing influence of the Company, wrote a memo[1] on the increasing incursions of the Sikhs. His response was typical Warren Hastings, patient but cautious. John MacPherson, who was later to become the governor-general after the expulsion of Hastings and the nemesis of James Brown (part II, chapter 9), had a more bombastic approach to the Sikhs. He noted ". . . should the Sikhs invade the Vizier's countries we must repel them, and the Shahzada with Scindia's support might be of use on the occasion, but until such invasion I am for my part averse to commence any hostilities against them though I believe they may become in time a formidable power."[2]

One aspect of Hastings's memo that merits attention is his remark about two Sikh officers stationed in the vegetable market or "Subzee Mundee" in the Imperial capital. These were men attached to Baghel Singh—of the Karorasinghīā *misl*—who had entered Delhi with his forces in March 1783. He was unchallenged in his advance and the fearful Mughal emperor, Shāh Ālum II, quickly sought to agree terms of his stay. Incredibly, the Mughal allowed Baghel Singh to commence building seven *gurdwārās* connected with the Sikh *Gurūs* and to collect 37.5 percent of all octroi duties in the city. Baghel Singh and his 4,000 troops remained stationed at Delhi until November 1783.

I have already said that there is now no power which can be properly so called in that part of Hindustan which borders on the dominions of the Company and their ally the Nabob Vizier. But this affirmation, though strictly true with relation to the question of present danger, must be taken solely in that restrictive application of it. A new source of serious contemplation has arisen from a nearer quarter, namely, that of the Sikhs, a people who from a mean sect of religious schismatics have rapidly grown into the masters of a dominion extending from the most western branch of the Attock to the walls of Dehli. Its present state is too contemptible to be an object of apprehension to any force which could be opposed to it, but the King, who derives as much of his present weakness from their encroachments, as from the usurpations of his own servants, which have excited them. They are by their bodily frame and habits of life eminently suited to the military profession; but this propensity is qualified by a spirit of independence which is a great check to its exertion. Every village has its separate and distinct ruler acknowledging no control, but that of the people of his own immediate community, who in their turn yield him little more than nominal submission.

For some years past the Sikhs quitting their predatory incursions have fixed themselves in the lands which submitted to them, appointing collectors of their revenues, and officers for their Government. No opposition was made to them. The only instance in which it was attempted was in the year 1779, when the Minister Mudjed-ul-Dowlah marched from Dehli with an army of 30,000 men to attack them, and without the sight of an enemy purchased an ignominious retreat. They obtained quiet possession of the *purgana* of Sheaumlee, one of the King's personal domains lying within 30 *coss* of Dehli; while I was at Lucknow, they carried their depredations to the very suburbs of Dehli, where two of their officers actually reside in a quarter called Subzee Mundee, which is chiefly occupied by shroffs and shopkeepers, for the double purpose of levying their *rauky* (which is the name given to that species of contribution) and of protecting the inhabitants from the marauders of their own nation.

We are too apt to despise the danger which we have not experienced, and to conclude that what has not happened in the ordinary course of events never will happen. On such a presumption my conclusions may expose me to the ridicule of those who may deem them the mere effusions of a wild imagination. I am willing to submit to this consequence if the events which I have foreboded shall be prevented by reasonable means of opposition; but I trust to time, and that not distant, for verifying my prediction if this people is permitted to grow into maturity without interruption.

I now proceed to shew the present means by which this interruption may be effected, and another point of some consequence attained with it.

I have mentioned in my report of the 1st instant that it was one part of the Prince's plan to offer his services to the King to be employed against the Sikhs. The battalions which the Nabob Vizier has allowed for his escort cannot attend him beyond the Nabob's own frontier. If he carries them further he must provide their pay and subsistence, as their place must of course in that case be supplied by other levies, for which there is no other provision than that which is allotted to his actual establishment. This condition is in effect an insuperable bar to their employment, nor would it be prudent to trust his fortune on the first trial of it to the rabble of his father's army, unpaid and accustomed to disregard command. If the station at Futtyghur must be continued the detachment cannot be better employed either in whole or part than on service with the Prince. It will more effectually keep the Sikhs at a distance, by advancing with such an influence to attack them, than by waiting within its own sphere of defence to repel them. I must here inform the Board that the Prince repeatedly and earnestly solicited me to endeavour to obtain their authority, for he knew the extent of my own, for an employment of the detachment. I discouraged the expectation but promised to communicate his requisition.

I will confess that the apprehension of his return upon our protection, the desire of executing the arduous task which the Board were pleased to assign me, and a yet stronger impulse arising from the hope of blasting the growth of a generation whose strength might become fatal to our own, strongly pleaded in my mind for supporting his wishes. But to these I opposed the more urgent consideration of the Company's distresses, and their solemn call upon us to relieve them, and I had resolved to report to the Board the Prince's request, but at the same time to state my objections to it, which in my judgment outweighed the advantages that might arise from a compliance with it.

I choose in this place to observe that the actual expense of the detachment is 1,88,705 current rupees per month, or 22,64,466 per annum, of which 81,030 current rupees per month or 9,72,360 per annum, are the extra expenses of the staff, field *batta*, and contingencies which belong to it as a detached corps, and which would cease with its reduction, besides that it would facilitate the reduction of the strength of the army.

But if the expense is to be continued it may surely be better continued for some useful purpose than to keep up the parade of a great military corps designed merely to be inactive in its quarters.

On this ground, therefore, and on the supposition promised, I revert to my original sentiments in favour of the Prince's plan, but as this will require some qualification in the execution of it, I will state my recommendation of it in the terms of a proposition, *viz.*, that if it shall be the resolution of the Board to continue the detachment now under the command of Colonel Sir John Cumming at Furruckabad, and if the Prince Mirza Jehandar Shah shall apply with the authority of the King and the concurrence of Mahadajee Sindia for the assistance of an English military force to act in conjunction with him to expel the Sikhs from the territories of which they have lately possessed themselves in the neighbourhood of Dehli, it may be granted, and such a portion of the said detachment allotted to that service as shall be hereafter judged adequate to it.

NOTES

1. Forrest, *Selections*, III, 1123–5; N.A.I., Secret Proceedings, December 14, 1784, 537–4. Gupta, *History of the Sikhs* 3: 192–5.
2. Forrest, *Selections*, III, 1125 in ibid., 3: 192–5.

CHAPTER 8

THE WRITINGS OF COLONEL POLIER
ON THE SIKHS, 1776–1802

One of the most prolific early commentators on the Sikhs was an unlikely Swiss soldier-trader, Antoine-Louis Henri Polier (1741–1795), who acquired the Mughal title *Arsalān-i-Jang*.[1] A member of a distinguished Swiss-Protestant family, Polier followed his clan's fortunes to India where, in a succession of chameleon-like career changes, and in the employ of figures as diverse and notable as Warren Hastings and Shāh Ālum II, Polier witnessed and commentated on the late eighteenth-century Sikhs. Polier left four works that make mention of the Sikhs: *History of the Seeks*: A paper read before the Asiatic Society of Bengal, December 20, 1787; *Extract of a Letter from Major Polier at Delhi to Colonel Ironside at Belgram*, May 22, 1776, Asiatic Annual Review for the year 1800 (London: 1801); *Shah Alam II and his Court. A Narrative of the Transactions at the Court of Delhy from the Year 1771 to the Present Time*; and finally *A Character of the Sieks, from the Observations of Colonel Polier and Mr Forster*, Asiatic Annual Review for the year 1802 (London: 1803). Further brief comments in his collection of letters, the *I'jāz-i Arsalānī*, literally the wonder of *Arsalānī*,[2] make mention of Sikhs but not in any significant volume or with any substantially new information to require further commentary.

The Sikhs that Polier encountered are portrayed as annoyances to trade and the political status quo. They are also viewed as rustic guerrilla fighters who regularly upset his own sense of propriety. Polier's account must be read in the context of his personal history and that of his position and aspirations in the India of the day.

Polier arrived in India in 1757, seemingly poised to make a mark. His paternal uncle, Paul Philippe Polier, was already in the employ of the East India Company in Madras. Polier's early career in the Company was as a Madras cadet under Robert Clive, fighting against the French. There seems to have been no crisis of conscience about taking up arms against a country that was once his ancestral home. Whether this was due to hostile Protestant–Catholic sentiment in France, his Swiss self-identification, or whether it was simple political expediency on Polier's part, is unknown. However, it served him very well. He rose quickly in prominence and in 1761, was posted to Bengal where he met Clive's ultimate successor, Warren Hastings, and began what was to become a long-lasting friendship. Polier was to spend many years of his life in India under some suspicion from the deeply xenophobic East India Company and from Warren Hastings's own enemies. Despite this, he was successively promoted to the rank of captain lieutenant in the army in the post of chief engineer responsible for the construction of Fort William. Plagued by his detractors, but sponsored by Hastings, Polier found himself simultaneously demoted from his post as chief engineer but promoted to the rank of major. By 1766, however, he had hit the bureaucratic glass ceiling, which faced most foreigners in the eighteenth century. Still a major in the East India Company Army but now resentful of the Company's reluctance to advance his career further, Polier was given permission to obtain a secondment into the Survey Department of Shujā-ud-Daulā, the *nawāb* of Awadh (or Oudh). Polier became an effective double agent, loyal ally to the *nawāb*, and fabulously wealthy private trader during his sojourn in the *nawāb's* employ. His time in Awadh was marked publicly by his support of the *nawāb's* conflict against the Jats including the infamous siege of Agra Fort. The *nawāb* was fond of European mercenaries and Polier found himself in the company of mercenaries, other double agents, and budding *nabobs*. Chief amongst these was the famous eighteenth-century Jesuit Padre, Wendel. Padre Wendel's association with Polier extended from friendship to supplying political information to his spymaster, Polier (see part I, chapter 2 for Wendel's comments on the Sikhs).

Whether it was his success as a private trader, his foreignness in the eyes of the British, or his ostensible support for Shujā-ud-Daulā's actions, something serious served to create opponents in the Company. Compounding this, those that simultaneously opposed Polier's long time friend and sponsor, Warren Hastings, publicly asserted that Polier's dual role was untenable. In October 1775, Polier tendered his resignation from Company service and the embattled Hastings accepted. For most men, facing life without the employment and the substantial support of the East India Company, resignation also meant returning to England. However, by 1775 Polier had effectively installed himself economically and socially within Indian high society. By the time of his resignation, Polier possessed extensive residences in Lucknow and Faizabad, two Indian wives, children, and a sophisticated taste in Indo-Persian culture, ranging from food, clothing, and habits, to a rapidly increasing collection of manuscripts and paintings.

In 1776, just a year after his break with the Company, he joined the service with the Mughal Emperor Shāh Ālum II in Delhi as engineer, agent, and general counsel. This apparent promotion in Mughal society had earlier caused Polier some degree of financial hardship, as the *jagīr* that accompanied his position was never fully realized due to political intrigue within the emperor's court. Further friction with the court mandarins restricted Polier's ability to trade freely with the support of a private army as he had originally wished. From his new home of Delhi, Polier was keen to please the emperor and report on the various local groups who were making capital as Mughal power faded and crumbled throughout Northern India. It was in Delhi that Polier naturally came to comment on the Sikhs. It was also from the period of Polier's stay in the emperor's court that he based his *History of Shah Alam II.* The difficulties in court proved too much, and by 1781, Polier was lobbying his old friend Warren Hastings to be restored into Company service. The political landscape had changed and with Hastings's intervention, Polier was allowed back into the Company's fold with the long-awaited promotion to the rank of lieutenant colonel. He shifted back to Lucknow and developed an increasing interest in indigenous arts, specifically collecting manuscripts and paintings, to the extent of commissioning numerous works from a local artist. Soldier-engineer turned philanthropist, Polier also organized selections of the *Mahābhārata* to be translated into Persian for the British orientalist Richard Johnson, then a resident of the city. This may have piqued Polier's interest in the Hindu religion as shortly afterward Polier sent volumes of the *Vedas*, which he had acquired from the Rājā of Jaipur, to William Jones of the British Library. This was no mean feat; the manuscript was acquired only after giving assurances that it would only be bound in silks and velvet and with the assistance of his friend and fellow European in the Mughal courts, Khiradmand Khān Don Pedros (the Rājā's Portuguese physician Don Pedro de Silva). In 1784, Polier who was rapidly reinventing himself into an orientalist was appointed a member of the Asiatic Society of Bengal.

After thirty-two years in India, Polier returned to Switzerland via England. Notwithstanding his two wives in India, in 1791 he married Anne Rose Marie Louis Berthoudt—daughter of Jacob, Baron von Berchem. With his European wife, Polier fathered another two sons. Polier was to spend only four years in Europe reaping the rewards of his Indian fortune, throwing lavish Asian style parties at his home in Lausanne. Throughout his life in Europe, Polier maintained his household in Faizābad, his two wives Bībī Jugnū Begam, and Bībī Zinat Begum and his two sons Bābā Anthony and Bābājān. However, despite his enormous wealth, or maybe because of it, he met a mysterious and bloody end. In 1795, he was attacked and killed by unknown assailants, apparently robbers. To his son and heir by his European wife, rather than his eldest son in India, he left the majority of his fine collection of Indian manuscripts, paintings, and other fine art as well as the title of *Comte de Polier*. To students of Sikh history, Polier left three major articles on the Sikhs and an influence which informed many of the other writers on Sikhs of his time. *The Siques,* written around 1780, was presented to the Asiatic Society of Bengal in 1787; an extract of a letter to Colonel Ironside dated May 22, 1776, written prior to the paper but published later, illustrates that there is little appreciable change in Polier's view or his observations on the Sikhs. Polier's *Shah Alum II and his Court*[3] contains a few disconnected notes on the Sikhs. A further published account titled *A Character of the Sieks, from the Observations of Colonel Polier and Mr Forster* remains anonymous but undoubtedly has influences from the writings of both men. The paper titled *The Siques* was on account of the evidence presented therein written around 1780 and was therefore, the first "connected account of the Sikh people written by a European."[4] At times, the language that he employs in *The Siques* is reminiscent of the other contemporary Muslim commentators. When Polier writes, "For the Siques not only destroyed the mosques and profaned the places of worship, but also compelled many Musulmen to embrace their sect, which boasts of violent hatred to that of Mohammed," it is almost identical to extracts from the *Muntakhabu'l Lubāb*[5] "Wherever they found a mosque, a tomb, or a gravestone of a respected Musulman, they broke it to pieces, dug it up, and made no sin of scattering the bones of the dead." This closeness to the Islamic view of the early Khālsā is explained in the familiarity of Polier's position within the Shāh's court just four years earlier. The works should also be read in context of Polier's own comments on his knowledge of the non-Islamic world in India. Although an avid collector of Indian manuscripts, fine arts, and Vedic scripture, in his preface to *Le Mahābhārata* he betrays his own shortcomings as an expert on Hindu India. "As the course of my researches on this matter [namely the Sikhs] brought me in due time to the Indous [Hindus], and to the religion of this people that is indigenous to India, I found myself embarrassed on a great number of points, and greatly astonished that after such a long stay in India (where I had spent more time with the natives of the land than with the Europeans), I still knew so little, and so poorly, the basis of their primitive mythology."[6] For Polier, the Sikh religion would have been even more inaccessible, and no doubt he relied heavily on Islamic sources for information on the Sikhs and their practices.

Like many European commentators, Polier sometimes presents a confused picture in his inferences. For the most part, he confuses Banda Bahādur with Gurū Gobind Singh. The reign of Farrukh-Sīyār saw the final campaigns against Bandā Bahādur, not Gurū Gobind Singh as Polier asserts in the opening section. It is, however, the political commentary in *The Siques* that is worthy of note and contains valuable details. Polier links the lifting of the siege of Rām Raonī by Mīr Mannū to corruption on the part of Kaurā Mall—a trusted officer in the employ of the Mughals. Dīwān Kaurā Mall is more likely to have assisted the Sikhs due to a shared kinship or even political expediency rather than a bribe. George Forster prefers the former explanation, noting "the preservation of the Sicques from the effect of Meer Munno's success appears to have been largely promoted by the interference of his minister Korah Mul, who, being himself a Sicque, naturally became a trusty advocate of the sect."[7] Kaurā Mall did successfully negotiate both the settlement of the siege and indeed Sikh support against the Afghānī invasions. It is likely, therefore, that a beleaguered Mīr Mannū used this act of leniency to gain Sikh leverage against Ahmad Shāh Durrānī who was preparing to invade India through the Punjab for the second time in November 1748. It is not unsurprising that as a result of the compromise, 10,000 Sikhs under the leadership of Jassā Singh Āhlūvālīā helped Kaurā Mall win the final battle (October 1749) against Shāh Nawaz Khān in the conquest of the province of Multān.[8] Polier also writes with some insight into the mercenary nature of the Sikhs *misls* and the internal politics that dogged intra-*misl* politics during times of relative peace. "When out of their country, the Siques will indifferently fight for whoever pays them best, and their chiefs will engage some on each side of the question without the smallest hesitation or scruple." Polier's was not an isolated or inaccurate observation. In October 1765, a body of the Sikhs invaded the dominions of the Rohīllā Afghān, Najīb ud-Daulā, but were repulsed by Rājā Amar Singh of Patiālā who came to his aid.[9] This spirit of division among the Sikh chiefs was also well known to the Marāthās, especially when Mahādjī Scindiā tried negotiating a treaty with them. His deputy, Ambaji Ingle, met the Sikhs in March 1785 while they were encamped near Sonīpat. He wrote to Scindiā: "The Sikhs are gathered in a large body; but they are disunited. Some of their chiefs command 5,000 horse each, some 1,000 and others 2,000. They are hostile to one another. The Sikhs of Lahore are not on good terms with the Sikhs of Pānipāt side. The latter numbering about 15,000 have offered to join us in fighting the Lahore Sikhs." Mahādjī replied: "Beware, they are all at one. They will deceive us at the time of battle, when they will go over to their brethren."[10] *The Siques* ends with a predictive note, which when written in 1780 must have sounded absurd. The Sikhs, a guerrilla people in the ascendancy of power would, according to the prophecy quoted by Polier, "after remaining sometime the terror of India would at last be finally destroyed by white men coming from the westward." Polier's confident assertion of the triumph of the Company over the Sikhs would have to wait until 1849 to be partially validated. The letter to Colonel Ironside is dated earlier than the paper titled *The Siques* but was published some time later. In just a few words, Polier betrays his own prejudices against the Sikhs who he clearly regards with derision. Praise and contempt is heaped in equal measure as he regards the superior quality of the Sikh horseman but despises their tactics and the effect that they were having on the Mughal ruling classes. Polier's own fortune was inextricably linked to the fortunes of the Mughal court and as an insatiable trader and moneymaker, his motives are quite clear. *A Character of the Sieks*, by an anonymous writer but citing Forster and Polier as sources presents an altogether more balanced view of the Sikhs, no doubt an influence from the intensely curious and open-minded Forster. The account is sufficiently detailed to provide a picture of the Sikhs as rigorous, earthy people. Drawing on the military Sikhs that Forster and Polier encountered, picture of an adventurous and hardy people emerge. Nestled within this quite short passage is a reference to the Sikh banker and central protagonist to the conspiracy at Plassey, Omīchand (see part II, chapter 5). Here, the two writers present the early contemporary written reference to Omīchand's son.[11] They also make mention of Mahā Singh Sukkarchakkīā, a prominent *misl* leader and father of Mahārājā Ranjīt Singh (1780–1839). In closing this note, the writer states that "we may see some ambitious chief, led on by his genius and success, and absorbing the power of his associates, display from the ruins of their commonwealth the standard of monarchy. . . . I have little hesitation in saying, that the Sieks would be soon advanced to the first rank amongst the native princes of Hindustan, and would become a terror to the surrounding states." Unknown to the author of these words, the son of the aforementioned Mahā Singh, Ranjīt Singh, would eventually prove the prophecy true and become ruler of a sovereign state.

The final text ascribed to Polier is an English manuscript in the library of the Royal Asiatic Society of Bengal titled *A Narrative of the Transactions at the Court of Delhy*. The time frame covered by the entire manuscript is years from 1771 to 1779 and is marked as being completed on August 15, 1779, coinciding with 'Abd ul-Ahad Khān's campaign against the Sikhs which commenced in July 1779. Latterly published, and ascribed by Sir Jadunath Sarkar to Polier,[12] the text contains a number of references to the relationship of the court of Shāh Ālum II and the Sikhs, a relationship marked by pursuit and conflict. The central Sikh protagonist was the then Rājā of Patiālā, Amar Singh, of whom there is some contemporary detail in this account.

"A SNAKE WITH MANY HEADS": POLIER'S WARNING TO THE ENGLISH, 1776
Antoine Louis Henri Polier, "Extract of a letter from Major Polier at Delhi to Colonel Ironside at Belgram," May 22, 1776, *Asiatic Annual Review for the Year 1800* (London: 1801), pp. 32–5.

The king's dominions are bounded on the north, NW. and WNW. by the Siques: to the NE. and within the Doab Zabita Chan[13] possess a large tract of country which heretofore belonged to the king, but is now, by the late treaty, finally made over to him.

As for the Seikhs, that formidable aristocratic republick, I may safely say, it is only so to a weak defenceless state, such as this is. It is properly the snake with many heads. Each zamindar who from the Attock to Hansey Issar,[14] and to the gates of Delhi lets his beard grow, cries wah gorow,[15] eats pork, wears an iron bracelet,[16] drinks bang, abominates the smoking of tobacco and can command from ten followers on horseback to upwards, sets up immediately for a Seik Sirdar, and as far as is in his power aggrandizes himself at the expense of his weaker neighbours; if Hindu or Mussulman so much the better; if not, even amongst his own fraternity will he seek to extend his influence and power; only with this difference, in their intestine divisions, from what is seen everywhere else, that the husbandman and the labourer, in their own districts, are perfectly safe and unmolested, let what will happen around them.

From this small sketch it may be easily conceived that the Seiks are much less formidable than they are represented. It is true that they join together when invaded as was the case when Abdallah[17] passed through their country. But notwithstanding they had assembled an immense body of cavalry, extremely well mounted, yet they never presumed to make a single charge on the Durrany army, or even on detachments, and considering their irregularity and want of discipline and subordination, it was well for them, I think, they did not. They satisfied themselves in making a kind of hussar war of it, cutting off stragglers and intercepting provisions. In this they excel. To say the truth, they are indefatigable, mounted on the best horses that India can afford, each carries a matchlock of a large bore, which they handle dexterously enough, and with they annoy considerably, avoiding, at the same time, going in large bodies or approaching too near. Such is their way of making war, which can only appear dangerous to the wretched Hindustani troops of these quarters, who tremble as much at the name of a Seik, as people used to do, not so long ago, at the mention of Mahrattas. But what is more to be admired is that those Seik Sirdars, whose territories border on the King's were but very lately of the Jauts and of their caste and tribe, under which domination had they remained, no one would have thought of them; but now that they have put on their iron bracelet, fifty of them are enough to keep at bay a whole battalion of the King's forces, such as they are. This shows the force of prejudice and the value of military reputation. Such are the immediate neighbours of the King.

Five hundred of Nujhaf Khan's horses dare not encounter fifty Seik horsemen; and yet the last are as despicable a set of creatures as any that can be imagined! On the whole, was it not Sombre's[18] party, and Letafet's[19] forces, Nujhaf Khan would not be able to stand his ground half an hour; and yet this is The Mighty Chief!

POLIER'S MUGHAL MEMOIRS ON THE SIKH INCURSIONS, 1776
Antoine Louis Henri Polier, *Shah Alam II and his Court: A Narrative of the Transactions at the Court of Delhy from the Year 1771 to the Present Time.* Ed. Pratul C. Gupta. (Calcutta: S.C. Sarkar and sons, 1947), pp. 46–8; 56–60; 62–3.

pp. 46–8

. . . in the beginning of 1776, Rhaimdat Khan soon reduced his four purgunnahs, and in consequence of his *carte blanche* increased his troops, from numbers of straggling Rohillas who resorted to him from all sides. He then extended himself, and soon seized on all the country adjoining to him the greatest part of which belonged to Najhaf Khan who being then busy with the siege of Dig could not spare troops to oppose him. He also defeated some bodies of Siques who pretended to face him and in a couple of months overrun a vast extent of country, with a vigour and resolution unequalled. He wrested from Najhaf Khan the fine provinces of Hansy and Hissar and defeated in a surprise Mahomed Bochir Khan then in Najhaf Khan's service, whom he stripped of all he had. In short Rhaimdat Khan was successful every where, and did Najhaf Khan an infinite mischief.

He attacked also Amer Sing, a powerful Zemindar, bordering on the Siques,[20] and who had himself adopted their sect[21] and overrun his country, taking many rich towns, and making an immense booty. He thus went on, and it is hard to say where he would have stopped, had not fortune interfered and removed from Najhaf Khan, the most dangerous enemy he ever had. Rhaimdat Khan had just surrounded Gind the capital place of a petty Zemindar, by name Gujheput Sing and related to Amer Sing,[22] and was treating with the garrison for a surrender of the place, and the payment of a sum of money. His troops loaded with plunder, unsuspecting any enemy in the field, unprepared and dispersed up and down in different parts, were on sudden attacked early in the morning by a party of about 5,000 Siques who had reached Gind in the night to save the place if possible. Rhaimdat Khan with the few people he could immediately [collect?] and [?] soon drove them off; but advancing close to the walls of the place in the pursuit, he was mortally wounded by 3 balls in the head and body. With the Chief the spirit of the party sunk. The Rohillas were immediately put in confusion, and such as stood cut to pieces. The defeat was as compleat as could be, all the plunder they had before collected, was taken from them, and such as escaped with life, were stript naked, and otherwise ill used, not only by the Siques, but also by the country people, who in such cases always turn on the conqueror's side, but who besides were glad to revenge the ills they had been made to suffer before, from the Rohillas, who are in general a very mercyless people. Thus fell Rhaimdat Khan a Chief of the greatest intrepidity, and at the same time it is said, a man of principles, true to his word, and a religious strict partizan of the Mahomedan faith.

Amer Sing joined by the Siques immediately possessed himself of all Rhaimdat Khan's conquests; which he kept, until Najhaf Khan, after taking of Dig, was enabled to send Najhaf Couly Khan with a considerable force in that quarter; when after some conferences Amer Sing gave up all that had heretofore belonged to Najhaf Khan, as for the King's purgunnahs they were also delivered up, on some concessions made by the minister, in favour of Amer Sing and his relation. Rhaimdat Khan's defeat happened in May 1776, so that the Court of Delhy met almost at the same time with two considerable checks.

Najhaf Khan had been highly exasperated at many of the proceedings of the minister, who tho: he kept up the most friendly appearances, with him, was consequently endeavouring to throw obstacles in his way, and encourage his enemies underhand. The bad success his machinations had met with, made Abdulahd Khan think of making up matters with Najhaf Khan now grown by the capture of Dig powerful and at liberty to take his revenge. All the blame was laid on Rhaimdat Khan, and the best colouring put on all that had passed that the things would admit of.

pp. 56–60

To say precisely what is the minister's [Abdulahd Khan] real intention in this expedition is not an easy matter. Great doings were to follow if the publick reports and his own declarations were to be credited. Some disputes had arisen betwixt Amer Sing (a powerful Zemindar bordering on the Siques, and himself a follower of their sect) and some of the neighbouring Chiefs of the Siques. They fought, and Amer Sing was defeated. He then solicited help from the Court of Delhy. It was promised to him on stipulating a valuable consideration. However, the succour was delayed so long, and appeared so precarious, that Amer Sing thought it most prudent to make his peace with his brethren. Matters were therefore compromised betwixt them at an expence of about two lacks of rupees, before the minister had marched from Delhy. However, it did not prevent him from setting out on his favourite expedition and he now further gave out he meant to bring to reason, the purgunnahs of Sonput, Panniput, etc., part of the domains, which lay in his way to Amer Sing and did not pay the rents as they ought.

The army marched, sometimes it was given out, that Amer Sing was to join with all his forces, and the Siques were to be drove back from all the country on this side of Sirhind, at other times it was said the Siques were to join the army and an attack to be made jointly with them on Amer Sing, who was to be dispossessed of his country, which the minister and Siques were to divide. That the minister had both those projects in view, I doubt not, and would willingly have put one of them into execution. But neither the Siques or Amer Sing will be so unwise, as to coincide with him. Amer Sing kept aloof, and he has not yet thought proper to come to the presence, tho: strongly solicited, and invited in the most friendly manner, on the contrary, he has gone to near Lahore on pretence of a marriage, at the same time he has declared he had no more differences with the Siques, and that everything was accommodated betwixt them.

The Siques have also notwithstanding they had already began hostilities against the army's foraging parties, been invited to come and take service. They have not declined it, but insisted on the discharge of some arrears they claim, regular and punctual payments for the future, and stipulate it is said, not to fight against either Amer Sing, Najhaf Khan or Zabeta Khan. In this state stand the conferences at present.

The army is near Panniput, and it is evident it is not meant to act against the Siques, since several of their Chiefs have already been entertained in the minister's service to the number of above 3,000. As for Amer Sing, I believe it is meant to make him pay more money which in all likelyhood he will do. But as to reducing of him, I imagine it is more than what the minister's army can do by itself, tho: numerous enough, if the Siques continue in their resolution of not joining in the attack. In the interim a design is formed by the minister against a petty Zemindar bordering on the Siques and on the purgunnahs of Panniput who possesess a small territory of about 4 lacks of rupees per annum, and who seems equally on bad in terms with Amer Sing and the Siques. For that purpose the army had moved towards him, but so slowly and cautiously, that I judge that business will also end in some pecuniary compromise.

There has been also for some time past a report spread that the minister has strongly solicited Zabeta Khan to join him with all his forces, and both together assisted by a number of Sique auxiliaries were to fall on the territory of Pattergurh across the Ganges (now in the hands of Asef al dowlah) and that Zabeeta Khan had assented to the proposal provided Najhaf Khan to whom he was to write approved of it. I will in no shape vouch for the truth of this report, at the same time ridicule of the intended attempt, is no reason whatever to set aside the likelyhood of the minister's having at least talked of such a scheme or of having proposed it to Zabeeta Khan; however, be it as it will, the minister who with his army is not far from the Jumnah on the eastern banks of which Zabeta Khan is encamped, has ordered boats to be collected from all parts to form a bridge to cross his army; such a step would intimate that all his schemes and projects against the Siques are at an end and that he has now other views. It may also be no more than a feint to cover another game. But whatever it is, I am convinced the old adage of *mons parturienns nascitur ridiculus mus* [sic] will be applicable to him and his manoeuvres.

Perhaps the minister has intentions of recovering from Najhaf Khan those purugunnahs the latter farms from the King, and for which he has not been very punctual in the payments; as they are all situate in the Doab, it may be the true cause of the present movement and that the report above related has only been spread by the minister, with a view, of raising his own reputation with his own people, occasioning some remonstrances on the part of Asef al dowlah and afterwards showing his condescension in desisting from an enterprise, he is after all, too wise I think, to have ever thought of in earnest, or at least on cool reflexion intended to execute. If such is his design, he is to be commended for at last exerting himself in putting the royal domains on a proper footing which ought to be done previously to the undertaking anything outwards. But even this point, which is not very great in itself, I question whether he will dare put in execution, for notwithstanding the hatred he bears to Najhaf Khan he has been constantly very cautious hitherto, of breaking openly with him, which in all likelyhood would happen, was the minister to resume the purgunnahs farmed by Najhaf Khan against the latter's consent.

On the otherhand it must be said that the minster has a difficult game to play: that both Najhaf Khan and Zabeta Khaan instead of joining him and acting in concert against the Siques, have refused to come under various pretences, and on the contrary encourage the Siques underhand to oppose him. That besides they constantly counteract all the minister's schemes for the publick good, and whatever may tend to the honour and welfare of the King, whom they do all in their power to keep in as dependent a state as possible, barely leaving him wherewith to subsist, and that thus situated it is not to be wonder'd at, if as a last resource, the minister has in the end, thought of raising forces and endeavouring amongst so many independent rebellious neighbours to secure some of the ancient domains of the empire. Such are Abdulahd Khan's plans and general reasons for this expedition, but tho: they are plausible and not without some foundation, yet I am not mistaken, some secret motives, had also their due shares in engaging him to raise such considerable forces, and in undertaking an enterprise which considering the powerful neighbours he is surrounded with, does not promise him much success. Those motives I will endeavour to develop.

pp. 62–3

Such I verily believe have been the motives which have influenced the minister, to raise the forces he has. For however sanguine he may be in his expectations of conquest and hope of imitating and rivalling Najhaf Khan, he cannot I think be so blinded as not to see how vastly different times and circumstances are at present, from those which were so favourable to Najhaf Khan, setting intirely aside the personal qualifications which in Najhaf Khan are those of a hardly soldier and a bold adventurer, but in Abdulahd Khan are only those of a cabinet politician. Besides which motives, as there is some reason to think Najhaf Khan will soon be able to compromise matters one way or another with the Matchery Rajah, and that in such a case he proposes to fall immediately on the Siques with all his forces. It is not improbable that the minister wishes to have it in his power then, to join himself with him and come in for a share in the territories which will be recovered from those plunderers, and which he could neither obtain or keep afterwards, without a considerable force. All those causes have no doubt coincided in bringing the minister to act as he has.

Abdulahd Khan has now with him in the field near six Battns, of seapoys, four of which are compleat, and the two others made up of detached Companies, about 7, or 8,000 foot more and 6,000 horse, exclusive of the mercenary Siques and the allies. He has also a considerable train of artillery, tho: none of the best, and he is daily increasing it. This force which I have put down much lower than the publick reports make it, it is far greater than all the revenues of the domains in present possession everything included could defray. It must therefore be a matter of surprise how the minister can find means to subsist such an army, and at the same time be able to answer the demands and necessary charges of the King's household, etc. It is true the troops are ill-paid and much in arrears, and as for the King's immediate servants they are happy if in a year they can get 4 or even 2 months' pay. Nevertheless the real expensces are still far beyond the full revenues, and the minister must have had recourse to his private treasury to be able to maintain such a force. As for the King, however wiling Abdulahd Khan may be to make him bear a share in the extraordinary expence, I am convinced he will not of his own accord or without force be brought to pay for it out of his private coffers which if fame is to credited are said not to be empty.

The King's possessions are confined mostly to the environs of Delhy and the whole may amount to about 70 purgunnahs great and small; the full revenues of which, were they duly settled, carefully managed and secured from the ravages of the Siques, would not amount to less than 50 lacks of rupees and perhaps to 60 per annum. But they are very far from being brought to the point of culture or safety, and I believe if I state the real revenue from those purgunnahs at 20 lacks it is the utmost the King has received for some years past out of them. It is true this sum is exclusive of the jaguirs granted to the princes, the minister and some of the Omrahs of the court, which tho: they are not considerable, still they all together make a sum of at least twelve lacks more. In that number of 70 purgunnahs are included several which Najhaf Khan had appropriated to himself and for which he pays little or nothing, also the others in the Doab in a fine situation which are farmed by Affrasiab Khan in Najhaf Khan's name at little more than half their real value and yet it is not without difficult and some discounts the amount is paid.

A Treatise on the History, Religion and Culture of the Sikhs, 1787
Antoine Louis Henri Polier, "The Siques," *History of the Seeks: A Paper read before the Asiatic Society of Bengal December 20, 1787*, Orme Collection MSS, Oriental and India Office Collection, British Library, London, XIX, pp. 73–83.

The Siques date the Origin of their Sect as far back as the reign of Ackbar,[23] at which time lived in the Environs of Lahore a reputed Saint named *Gorou Nanack*. (In their language, *Gorou* signifies Master or Leader, and *Sique* a Disciple.) This Man had many followers, who embraced his Doctrine, and acknowledged him at the head of a new Sect, which, however, during that reign and the three succeeding ones did not encrease much, or at least never attempted to rise against the lawful Authority. It was not till the Reign of Bahardur Shah that they began to appear in Arms[24] and endeavoured to shake off their Allegiance, at which time under the Direction of a new Saint one *Gorou Govind* they laid the foundation of a kind of Republic, which might prove very formidable to its neighbours, and overwhelm them in the End, did not at the same time their disunion, intestine Divisions of Jealousies prevent them from extending their power so far as they might otherwise.

Originally and in general the Siques are Zemindars or Cultivators of Land, and of that tribe called *Jatts*, which in this part of India, are reckoned the best and most laborious Tillers, tho' at the same time they are also noted for being of an unquiet and turbulent Disposition. This tribe of the *Jatts* one of the lowest amongst the Hindoos, is very numerous and dispersed in all the Country from the *Attek* to the *Sind* and to the Southward far beyond Agra; and tho' in that Extent, it be intermixed with some others, nevertheless in those provinces, it is by far the most considerable Tribe.

The troubles and rebellions, which disturbed the Empire during the tumultous reign of *Bahadur Shah*, gave the Siques an Opportunity of rising in Arms, and shaking off the Royal Authority: This however, they did by degrees; they fortified themselves at a place called *Ramrowry*, about 20 Cosses this Side of Lahore, and there established their principal place of worship, which is at a large Tank called *Ambar Sar*,[25] or *Chak*.

The Siques then began to encrease greatly in numbers, many proselites were made, some from fear, others from a love of novelty and Independence; All that came, tho' from the lowest and most abject Casts were received, contrary to the Hindoo Customs, which admit of no Change of Cast, and even Musulmen were in the number of the Converts. The fame of *Gorou Govind* who then made his appearance[26] and of whom many prodigies were related, contributed greatly to establish this Sect. This reputed Saint soon found himself at the head of a numerous force, and began to make Excursions and Converts sword in hand. He exerted himself so successfully, that at last he drew the Attention of Government towards him. Farockseer was then on the throne. An Army was formed in or about 1715 under the command of *Abdul Somad Khan*[27] Subadar of Lahore, and he had orders to exterminate the Sect. It was not an easy task, however after many marches and pursuits he came up with their main body, which he totally defeated.[28] He had even the good Luck to take *Gorou Govind*[29] himself Prisoner. The Gorou was sent to Delhi, shut up in an iron Cage, and afterwards put to Death, and his Disciples wherever they could be caught, were on their refusal of turning Mohamedans, immediately executed. The Chace became so hot after them, and was carried on with so much spirit, and so unrelenting a vigour, that the very name seemed extinct, and those few who still remained, were obliged by shaving off their beard, and hair, to deny their Sect and Leader.[30] After this, for many years, no more mention is made of the Siques, and it was not until some time after Nadir Shah's Invasion[31] that they began to show their head again. However the gallant Mir Monnow then Subadar of the provinces of Lahore and Multan, attacked them briskly, and gave them little time to get Strength; Indeed he might have crushed them entirely, had he not at the Instigation of *Coranmul*[32] his Naib or Deputy in the Subadary of Multan, accepted a Sum of Money to save their Capital *Ramrowny* which he had surrounded, and was on the point of taking. This false Step Coranmul engaged him to take, to lessen the merit, it is said of *Adina beg Khan*, a brave and valiant Officer (in whom Mir Momnou placed great Confidence) who had conducted the Expedition against the Siques, and who of Course must have gained much glory had they been entirely reduced. However from whatever Motives it might be, the Siques escaped total Destruction; they paid largely for it, and Mir Momnou who had other work on his hand, was no sooner at a distance, than they began to strengthen themselves anew. It is true for some time and while *Coranmul* lived,[33] they were by his Influence over them kept in tolerable Order, and obliged to remain quite; and moreover Mir Momnou's Orders to convert them to Musulmanism or destroy them, wherever they could be found stroling in Arms, were also during his life strictly and vigorously executed.

But the Anarchy and Confusion which ensued after Mir Momnou's Death,[34] in the provinces of Lahore and Multan, from the different Competitors for the Subadary, and the intrigues of his Widow, who wanted to retain the Government in her hands, and actually was for a considerable time in possession of it, prevented that Attention from being paid to the Siques, which their Spirit and rebellious Principles required; It was then they began to grow formidable and to assume a real Independence. They formed themselves into a kind of Republic, and in the Course of a few years possessed themselves of the full Government of the provinces of Lahore and Multan.

About that time they attracted the notice of Ahmed Shah *Abdally*, the *Durany* king, whose Country extends to the River *Attek*, the northern Boundary of the Subah of Lahore. Those Durany's are very strict Musulmen; tho' at the same time perhaps, the most lawless bloody minded barbarians on the face of the Earth. They saw with Rage the progress of the Siques, and particularly the manner in which they proceeded towards the Islam or Mohammedan Religion. For the Siques not only destroyed the Mosques and profaned the places of worship, but also compelled many Musulmen to embrace their Sect, which boasts of violent hatred to that of Mahomed.[35] The Siques besides had at different times while *Ahmed Shah Abdally* passed thro their Country in his Excursions towards Indostan, severely molested him in his marches, and never failed cutting off their straggling parties, and laying hold of every Opportunity of distressing him.[36] All those reasons engaged *Ahmed Shah* to think of chastizing them in earnest. He was then, by having jointly with all the Mohammedans (Amrahs of this part of Indostan) defeated the Mahrattas,[37] and drove them away to the Decan, at liberty to turn his Arms towards them; Accordingly he entered their Country with a powerful Army. The Siques were in no shape able to face him; they were defeated wherever they presented themselves, and pursued with all the Violence and Spirit of religious Enthusiasm.[38] They were forced to fly with their Effects, Families and Cattle into the Jungles and impervious Woods with which the Country abounds, and to abandon all the rest to the Durany's. They, however, still hovered round them at some distance with their Cavalry, and lost no Opportunity of cutting off their Stragglers and otherwise distressing them. *Ahmed Shah Abdally* in the meantime took their famous place of Worship, which was immediately razed to the Ground.[39] The holy Tank was filled up, and a price set on the Siques. Many Pyramids were made of their heads, both at Lahore and other places,[40] and in short it is certain that had *Ahmed Shah Abdally* remained 3 or 4 years in those parts, the Sect would have been at an End; tho' perhaps the Country would have been depopulated by it, so very keen were the Duranies in their pursuit of them. Ahmed Shah however desirous he might be to retain those fine provinces in his possession, could not it seems spare so much time to reduce them effectually. The vast Interest of his Dominions which extended from the Caspian Sea, to the Gulph of Sind (and to which he had no other right but from his Sword and good fortune) joined to his long absence from home, made it necessary for him to return to quell some Revolts which threatened his upper provinces. He therefore contented himself with appointing different Governors to rule thro' the Country, and having left a Garrison of 4 or 5000 Men in Lahore he recrossed the Attek and continued his March towards Balk, where some Chiefs had thrown off their allegiance. The Siques immediately began to avail themselves of his absence, which many Circumstances rendered much longer than he at first intended. They rose in arms every where and fell on the Duranies on all Sides. They surrounded Lahore and after some time obliged the Garrison to surrender at Discretion. They now retorted amply on the Duranies. The Mosques which had been rebuilt were demolished with every mark of indignity, and washed with Hog's Blood. The Duranies changed were forced with their own hands to dig and restore the famous tank of *Ambar Sar*, which was soon brought to its antient State, and newly adorned with Buildings. In short the Siques were now absolute Masters,[41] and having fully established their Religion and national Councils, they began to extend themselves to the Southward and Westward amongst their Neighbours, most of whom they brought under Contribution From that time till *Ahmed Shah Abdally's* death, which happened about 8 or nine years ago. The Siques had several times to encounter with his forces, but Ahmed Shah never had it in his power to spare so much time as was necessary to reduce them compleatly, and was soon forced to relinquish that Object.

Since his Death and the Accession of Timur Shah[42] his Son, the Siques have been but little molested from that Quarter. They have been emboldened to take from him the City of Multan, which they possessed some time; Tho' they have been forced to relinquish it lately, they have nevertheless retained the greatest part of that Subah, and *Timur Shah* seems either too indolent, or too much employed at home, to think of beginning a Contest with them in earnest.

Such has been the rise and progress of the Siques to this Day which must be attributed, not so much to their bravery, Conduct or military knowledge, as to the Anarchy and Confusion that has desolated the Empire one may say for these 60 or 70 years past, that is ever since the Death of that great Aurangzeb but more particularly from the weak Government during the reigns of *Mahomed Sha, Ahmed Shah*, and *Allumguir Sany* the last of which may be cited as an Example of the weakest & most wretched that ever was.

In their military Capacity the Siques are far from being so formidable as they are generally represented, or as they might be. It is true they are in general exceedingly well mounted, that their horses and themselves will undergo much fatigue, and perform very expeditious marches, and that they have excellent match locks which carry a good way and which they manage on horse back with tolerable Execution; All that must be allowed them, and also that they are very abstemious and satisfied with what no other Horsemen in India perhaps would put up with; but when it is considered in what disorderly manner the fights, that they know not what it is to be in close Order, or to charge Sword in hand, and that they never could yet be brought to face the Duranies, tho' 3 or 4 to one; It must be acknowledged that at best they are but the *Croates* of India, and indeed they resemble them very much, in more than one point.

As for the Government of the Siques, it is properly an Aristocracy, in which no preeminence is allowed except that which power and force naturally gives, otherwise all the Chiefs, great or small, and even the poorest and most abject Sique, look on themselves as perfectly equal, in all the public Concerns, and in the greatest Council or *Goormotta* of the Nation, held annually either at *Ambarsar, Lahore* or some other place everything is decided by the plurality of Votes taken indifferently from all who chuse to be present at it. In this Council or Diet all the public Affairs are debated such as alliances, Wars and the Excursions intended to be made in the ensuing year. The Contributions collected in the last Expedition are also duly accounted for, and retributed among the Chiefs in proportion to their forces, who, on their Side, must take Care to satisfy their Dependants in their full proportion, who would was it otherwise, soon quit them and address themselves to others. The Chiefs are extremely numerous, and some of them have at their Command as far as 10– or 12000 Horses, however the generality are very inferior; many have only 15 or 20 Horses, and from that number up to 1000 or 2000. It is computed that their whole force if joined together would amount to nearly 200 thousand Horse, a power which would be truly formidable did it act under one Chief or one Order. But divided as it is, amongst 4 or 500 Chiefs who all look on themselves as independent of each other, whose Interests and views are almost all different, and perpetually jarring, it is much weakened thereby.[43] It is true in Case of an Invasion or foreign Attack, they are bound to support one another as much as lays in their power, however the Spirit of Independence is such that it is not without difficulty they can be prevailed on to act in Concert, even for the public good. For in the War against *Ahmed Shah Abdally* it was but seldom that a greater force than 60,000 Men could be brought together to oppose him; tho' certainly the Occasion called for their most strenuous Exertions; but in such times those only present themselves who have a great deal to lose. When out of their Country the Siques will indifferently fight for whoever pays them best, and their Chiefs will engage, some on each Side of the Question without the smallest hesitation or scruple. But when they are not retained in service, or are unemployed at home in Disputes amongst themselves, they, particularly those on the Borders, set off generally after the Rains, and make excursions in Bodies of 10,000 Horses or more, on the neighbours. They plunder all they can lay their hands on, burn the Town and Villages, and do infinite Mischief. It is true they seldom kill in cold blood, or make Slaves, however when they meet with handsome male Children, and robustly made, they carry them away and adopt them.[44] The Cattle is their principal Aim, they carry them off in vast numbers, and send them into their own Country, depriving by that means the wretched Labourer and Husbandman from the Capacity of doing anything for himself afterwards. Thus they ruin and depopulate the finest provinces. To obviate those Evils there is no other way expect agreeing with one of their Chiefs for a certain yearly tribute which they call *Racky*, in general a trifle will satisfy them, from two to five p.cent on the Revenues, particularly if at a distance, and provided this is regularly paid; it is said no further hindrance or molestation will be received from them; On the contrary the Chief to whom the Tribute or *Racky* is paid, takes the District under his protection, and is ready to fight against any of Brethren who might think of disturbing it. This Method has been adopted by most of the Zemindars bordering on them; who at the same time not to trust implicitly to the good faith of those free Booters have taken care to fortify their towns and put themselves on a defensive footing, without that, whole Provinces would be a Desart. The Siques possess an immediate tract of Country, the whole Soubah of Lahore, the greatest part of that of Multan and part of that of Delhi, including all the country called *Penjab*. They also carry their Excursions thro' every part of the last *Soubah*, and through part of Agra. Their own immediate possessions, are exceedingly well cultivated, populous and rich; The Revenues in general taken in kind throughout and not in Money, which is very favourable to the Tiller. In short few Countries can vie with theirs, particularly in this part of India.

The Siques are in general strong and well made, accustomed from their Infancy to the most labourious Life and hardest fare, they make marches and undergo fatigues that will appear really astonishing. In their Excursions they carry no tents or baggage with them, except perhaps a small tent for the principal Chief; the rest Shelter themselves under a Blanket, which serves them also in the cold Weather, to wrap themselves in, and which in a March covers their Saddles. They have mostly two horses a piece, and some three; their horses are middle sized, but exceeding good, strong and high spirited, and mild tempered;[45] The Provinces of Lahore and Multan, noted for producing the best Horses in Indostan, supply them amply, and indeed they take the greatest Care to encrease their numbers by all means in their power; and tho' they make merry in the Demise of one of their Brethren,[46] they condole and lament the Death of a Horse, thus shewing their Value for an animal so necessary to them in their Excursions.[47]

As for the food of the Siques it is the coarsest, and such as the poorest People in Hindostan use from necessity. Bread baked in Ashes, soaked afterwards in a Mash made of different kinds of pulse, is their best Dish, and such as they seldom indulge themselves with, except when at full Leisure; otherwise Vetches or Grains hastily parched are all they care for. They abhor smoking of Tobacco, for what Reason I cannot find, but intoxicate themselves freely either with Spirits or Bang; A Cup of the last they seldom fail taking at night after a fatigue. Their Dress is extremely scanty, a pair of blue Drawers, a kind of chequered Plaid worn partly round the middle and partly over the shoulder with a mean blue Turban forms all their Equipage. Their Chiefs are distinguished by having some heavy gold Bracelets on their Wrists and sometimes a Chain of the same Metal round their Turbans and by being mounted on better Horses, otherwise no distinction appears amongst them.

The Sect of the Siques has a strong taint of the Gentoo[48] Religion, they venerate the Cow, and abstain piously from killing or feeding on it, and they also pay some Respect to the *Devtas* or Idols.[49] But their great object of worship is with them their own saints, or those whom they have honoured with the name of Gorou. Those they invoke continually, and they seem to look on them as everything. Wah Gorou repeated several times is their only Simbol, from which the Musulmen have (not without Reason) taxed them with being downright Atheists. Their mode of initiating their Converts, is by making them drink out of a Pan in which the feet of those present have been washed[50] meaning by that, I presume, to abolish all those Distinctions of Casts which so much encumber the Gentoos; they also steep in it, particularly for a Musulman the tusks or Bones of a Boar and add some of the Blood of that Animal to it. This with repeating the Simbol to *Wah Gorou* wearing an Iron Bracelet on one

Arm, and letting the Hair of the head and beard grow forms the whole Mystery of their Religion, if such a filthy beastly Ceremony, can be dignified with that name. They have also stated Pilgrimages both to the Ganges[51] and their famous Tank at *Ambarsar* where at fixed times they wash and perform some trifling Ceremonies, invoking at the same time their *Gorou*.

Such are the Siques the terror and Plague of this part of India, a Nation and power well calculated for doing Mischief and encouraging Rebellion in the Zemindars or Cultivators, who often follow the Steps, at first with a View of saving themselves and afterwards from the pleasure of Independence, and indeed it is that, which makes them so troublesome for they begin to have Connections in almost all the parts they visit in their Excursions, and if they are not attacked, soon in their own proper Provinces, it is much too be feared their tenets and Manners will be adopted by all the Zemindars of the *Soubah* of *Delhi*, and part of *Agra*. It is however imagined that so soon as Najhaf Khan is clear of the Matchery Rajah,[52] he means to turn all his forces towards the Siques, and at least to drive them from this Side of Sirhind, which he may I think easily do, tho perhaps it would not be safe for him to go farther, except Timur Shah should on his Side attack them also across the *Attek*, then indeed and by remaining a few years in the Centre of their Country they might be effectually reduced. The Siques make no Account of Infantry except for the Defence of their forts, and have no Artillery their rapid motions will not allow of their having any with them, tho' they are not ignorant of the Effect of it, when well served, which they take Care to avoid as much as possible. I have nothing more to add to this Account except a pretended Prophecy which the Siques say has been delivered down by some of their *Gorou*. That the Siques after remaining sometime the terror of India would at last be finally destroyed by white Men coming from the Westward. Who are to be those white Men, time must discover, but the Siques themselves think the Europeans will fulfill the Prophecy, and are meant by it.

A CHARACTER OF THE SIKHS, 1802
"A Character of the Sieks, from the observations of Colonel Polier and Mr Forster," *Asiatic Annual Review for the year 1802* (London: 1803), pp. 9–12.

The Sieks are in general strong and well made; accustomed from their infancy to the most laborious life, and hardest fare, they make marches and undergo fatigues that really appear astonishing. In their excursions they carry no tents or baggage, except perhaps a small tent for the principal officer: the rest shelter themselves under blankets, which serve them also in the cold weather to wrap themselves in, and which, on a march, cover their saddles. They have commonly two, some of them three horses each, of the middle size, strong, active, and mild tempered. The provinces of Lahore and Moultan, noted for a breed of the best horses in Hindustan, afford them an ample supply; and indeed they take the greatest care to increase it by all means in their power. Though they make merry on the demise of any of their brethren, they mourn for the death of a horse: thus shewing their love of an animal so necessary to them in their professional capacity. The food of the Sieks is of the coarsest kind, and such as the poorest people in Hindustan use from necessity. Bread baked in ashes, and soaked in a mash made of different sorts of pulse, is the best dish, and such as they never indulge in but when at full leisure; otherwise vetches and tares, hastily parched, is all they care for. They abhor smoking tobacco, for what reason I cannot discover; but intoxicate themselves freely with spirits of their own country manufacture: a cup of the last they never fail taking after a fatigue at night. Their dress is extremely scanty; a pair of long blue drawers, and a kind of chequered plaid, a part of which is fastened round the waist, and the other thrown over the shoulder, with a mean turban, form their clothing and equipage. The chiefs are distinguished by wearing some heavy gold bracelets on their wrists, and sometimes a chain of the same metal bound round their turbans, and by being mounted on better horses: otherwise, no distinction appears amongst them—The chiefs are numerous, some of whom have the command of ten or twelve thousand cavalry; but this power is confined to a small number, the inferior officers maintaining from one to two thousand, and many not more than twenty or thirty horses, a certain quota of which is furnished by the chief, the greater part being the individual property of the horsemen. From the spirit of independence so invariably infused amongst them, their mutual jealousy, and rapacious roving temper, the Sieks at this day are seldom seen co-operating in national concert; but actuated by the influence of an individual ambition or private distrust, they pursue such plans only as coincide with these motives. An example of their forces being engaged in opposite interests, has been noticed in the case of Mhah Sing,[53] who succoured the rajah of Jumbo, against the Siek party who had invaded his country. Before the chiefs of the mountaineers country, at the head of the Panjab, were reduced to a tributary state, severe depredations were committed on them by the Sieks, who plundered and destroyed their habitations, carried off the cattle, and, if strong and well formed, the male children, who were made converts to the faith of Nanock. But since the payment of a fixed tribute has been stipulated, which does not amount to more than five per cent. on the revenue, the mountaineers are little molested, except when the Sieks have been called in to adjust their domestic quarrels. The extensive and fertile territories of the Sieks, and their attachment and application, in the midst of warfare, to the occupations of agriculture, must evidently produce a large revenue. The districts dependant on Lahore, in the reign of Aurungzebe,[54] produced, according to Mr Bernier, a revenue of two hundred forty-six lacks and ninety-five thousand rupees; and we are naturally led to suppose, from the industrious skill of the Sieks in the various branches of cultivation, that no great decrease of that amount can have taken place since the Panjab has fallen into their possession.

An extensive and valuable commerce is also maintained in their country, which has been extended to distant quarters of India, particularly to the provinces of Bengal and Bahar, where many Siek merchants of opulence at this time reside. The Omichund, who took so active, though unfortunate, a share in the revolution which the English effected in Bengal, was a Siek, as is his adopted son, who is now an inhabitant of Calcutta. Merchants of every nation or sect, who may introduce a traffic into their territories, or are established under their government, experience a full protection, and enjoy commercial privileges in common with their own subjects. At the same time it must be noticed, that such immunities are granted only to those who remain amongst them, or import wares for the immediate supply of the Siek markets. But the foreign traders, or even travellers, who attempt to pass through the Panjab, are often plundered and usually ill-treated: in the event of no molestation being offered to people of this description, the escape is ever spoken of with a degree of joyful surprise, and a thanksgiving is offered to Providence for the singular escape. This conduct, inimical to the progress of civilization, and an impediment to the influx of wealth, proceeds from an extreme jealousy of strangers, added to a rapacity of temper, which make them averse to the encouragement of any scheme in whose success they do not immediately participate.

The Sieks are not rigorous in their stipulations with the Mahommedan proselytes, who, if they abstain from beef's flesh, (which is held in equal abhorrence by the Sieks as by the Hindus,) and perform the more ostensible duties, as burning their dead, and preserving the hair of the head, an indulgent latitude is granted in all the other articles of the creed of Nanock. The Mahommedans who reside in the Panjab are subject to occasional oppression, and often to the insult of the lower classes of the people; among who it is not an uncommon practice to defile the places of worship, by throwing in the carcasses of hogs and other things held impure by the Mussulman law. The Mahommedans are also prohibited from announcing their stated time of prayer, which, conformably to their usage, is proclaimed in a loud tone of voice. A Siek who in the chase shall have slain a wild hog, is frequently known to compel the first Mahommedan he meets to carry to his home the body of the animal; and, on being initiated into the rites of their religion, the Sieks will sometimes require a Mahommedan convert to bind on his arm the tusk of a boar, that by this act of national impurity he may the more avowedly testify a renunciation and contempt of his former faith. These facts will sufficiently mark the haughty and insulting demeanour, which, with few deviations, forms a prominent feature in the character of the military Sieks: but we may also ascribe a certain portion of their severe and contumelious treatment of the Mahommedans, to a remembrance of recent injuries.

The discordant interests which agitate the Siek nation, and the constitutional genius of the people, must incapacitate them, during the existence of these causes, from becoming a formidable, defensive power; nor are they invested with that species of executive strength which is necessary to advance and establish a distant conquest. In the defence and recovery of their country, the Sieks displayed a courage of the most obstinate kind, and manifested a perseverance, under the pressure of calamities, which bear an ample testimony of native resource, when the common danger had roused them to action, and gave but one impulse to their spirit. Should any future cause call for the combined efforts of the Sieks to maintain the existence of empire and religion, we may see some ambitious chief, led on by his genius and success, and absorbing the power of his associates, display from the ruins of their commonwealth the standard of monarchy. The page of history is filled with the like effects, springing from the like causes. Under such a form of government, I have little hesitation in saying, that the Sieks would be soon advanced to the first rank amongst the native princes of Hindustan, and would become a terror to the surrounding states.

NOTES

1. Polier's Mughal title, literally "the lion of the battle" was conferred upon him by Shāh Ālum II during his time in the royal court.
2. Published as Muzaffar Alam and Seema Alavi ed., *A European Experience of the Mughal Orient, The I'jaz-I Arsalani (Persian Letters, 1773–1779) of Antoine-Louis Henri Polier* (New Delhi: Oxford University Press, 2001).
3. Antoine-Louis Henri Polier, *Shah Alam II and his Court*, ed. Pratul C. Gupta (Calcutta: S.C. Sarkar and sons, 1947), 46–63.
4. Singh, *Early European Accounts of the Sikhs*, 189.
5. Sir Henry M. Elliot, *History of India as Told by its own Historians; the Mohameddan Period*, 8 vols., ed. Prof. John Dawson (London: Trubner and Co, 1867–1877), 415.
6. Alam Alavi ed., *The I'jaz-I Arsalani*, 65.
7. George Forster, *A Journey from Bengal to England*, 2 vols. (London: R. Faulder, 1798), 1: 272–3; 284–5. See part III, chapter 12.

8. Ganda Singh, *Mahārājā Kaurā Mall Bahādur* (Amritsar: Khalsa College, 1942), 73–82.

9. Gupta, *History of the Sikhs*, 3: 381.

10. Ibid., 3: 207.

11. George Williamson, subsecretary to the Council during the years 1757 to 1761, commented, under oath in court proceedings in 1793 that: "I have seen Omichand and Dialchand (Diachand) together during Omichand's life. The first time I ever saw them was at Mr. Drake's, the Governor. I did not then know who either of them were but Omichand was leading Dialchand by the hand into the council room which must have been just after the capture of Calcutta, by his going up and embracing each member of the Council among whom Colonel Clive was sitting as Commander-in-Chief of the army. Omichand introduced Dialchand to each of them as his *palak betta* (adopted son)." Sinha, *Economic History*, 243–4.

12. Polier, *Shah Alam II and his Court*, 1.

13. Zābitā Khān (q.v.) ruled territory in the Yamunā-Gangetic Doāb. His father, Najīb ud-Daulā (q.v.), had been frustrated by the Karorasinghīā *misl* who had captured key villages and extracted large tributes. In 1776, Zābitā Khān had joined with his father's nemesis Baghel Singh Karorasinghīā (q.v.), Rāi Singh Bhangī, and Tārā Singh Ghaibā to loot the areas around present day New Delhi. Polier was writing just a few years after Karam Singh, leader of the Shahīd clan of Sandhū Jats, had overrun a large tract of land belonging to Zābitā Khān in the upper Gangetic Doāb. Gupta, *History of the Sikhs*, 3: 78.

14. Hansī and Hissār in present day Haryānā.

15. Vāhigurū (q.v.).

16. Karā (q.v.).

17. Ahmad Shāh Abdālī (q.v.).

18. Walter Reinhardt, a German mercenary who served with the Jats and then with Najaf Khān (q.v.). He employed western methods of warfare for training sepoys.

19. Letāfat Alī Khān, a eunuch general and formerly in the service of Oudh who held much influence over Najaf Khān.

20. Rājā Amar Singh of Patiālā (q.v.). It is interesting to note that Polier ascribes Patiālā as an area bordering on the Sikhs. Patiālā—a Sikh state in its own right—remained distinct from Punjab of the *misl* leaders.

21. Amar Singh was fifth generation Sikh, his ancestor Bābā Phūl (d. 1652) had been blessed by Gurū Hargobind, and his grandfather Bābā Ālā Singh who founded the Patiālā State took *pahul* at the hands of Nawāb Kapūr Singh, third leader of the *Buddhā Dal*.

22. The rulers of Jīnd and Patiālā trace their descendancy from a common ancestor, Bābā Phul. Phul's eldest son, Tilok Singh, was the ancestor of the Jīnd State and the younger son, Ramā, ancestor of the rulers of the Patiālā State.

23. Gurū Nānak (q.v.) was born in 1469 during the reign of the first Lodī king, Bahol Khān (1450–1488). During the Gurū's lifetime the first of the "Great Mughals" Bābur (1483–1530, reigned 1526–1530) (q.v.) was periodically reigning in Northern India. Gurū Nānak died in 1539 during the reign of the second Mughal emperor, Humāyūn (1508–1556, reigned 1530–1540).

24. The sixth Gurū Hargobind (1606–1644) did "appear in arms" during the reigns of the emperors Jahāngīr (1569–1627, reigned 1605–1627) (q.v.) and Shāh Jahān (1592–1666, reigned 1627–1658). However, this comment is

likely to be a reference to Bandā Bahādur (q.v.), whose prominence coincided with the reign of Bahādur Shāh (1643–1712, reigned 1707–1712) (q.v.).

25. Amritsar (q.v.), the city that includes the Harimandar Sāhib Temple complex, was not established at Rām-Rāonī (q.v.) as stated by Polier which is nearby. Amritsar, pronounced *Ambarsar* by unlettered rural dialects of Punjab, was founded by Gurū Rāmdās (q.v.) in 1574, 174 years before the Rām-Rāonī came into existence. The town had earlier been called Rāmdāspur, Chakk Rāmdās, or simply Chakk Gurū (q.v.), and was marked as such in eighteenth century maps of the area.

26. Polier confuses Gurū Gobind Singh with Bandā Bahādur.

27. 'Abd us-Samad Khān (q.v.)

28. An eight-month siege took place at the village of Gurdās-Nangal, near Gurdāspur. Conditions became extremely severe for the besieged and they were finally defeated on December 7, 1715.

29. It was Bandā Bahādur who was taken prisoner (part II chapter 4), not Gurū Gobind Singh who died on October 7, 1708.

30. This alludes to the edicts issued by Emperor Bahādur Shāh (q.v.) and later by his grandson (by his second son 'Azim al-Shan) Farrukh-Sīyār (q.v.) ordering extermination of the Sikhs wherever they were to be found. In 1710, Bahādur Shāh ordered Bakhshī-ul-Mumālik Mahābat Khān to write to the *faujdārs* of the territories of Shāhjahānabad to kill the Sikhs wherever found in their territories. This order was repeated during the reign of Farrukh-Sīyār saying: "wherever found, the followers of this sect should be unhesitatingly killed," *Miftāh-ut-Tawārīkh*, 398.

31. This happened in the year 1739.

32. Kaurā Mall (q.v.).

33. He died in 1752.

34. Mīr Mannū (q.v.) died in November 1753.

35. It is worth considering this contemporary comment which touches upon the reason why the Sikhs felt the way they did toward the invading Muslims: ". . . we may also ascribe a certain portion of their severe and contumelious treatment of the Mahommedans, to a remembrance of recent injuries." *A Character of the Sieks, from the Observations of Colonel Polier and Mr Forster*, Annual Asiatic Review for the year 1802 (1803), 9–12.

36. For tactics and combat method of the Sikhs the reader is advised to consult Arjan Dass Malik, *An Indian Guerrilla War: The Sikh Peoples War 1699–1768* (New Dehli: Wiley Eastern Ltd, 1975), later published as Arjan Dass Malik, *The Sword of the Khalsa* (New Delhi: Manohar Publishers and Distributors, 1999).

37. The Marāthās were engaged and defeated at the Battle of Pānīpat fought on January 14, 1761.

38. This took place on February 5, 1762, where the Sikhs suffered between 20,000 and 30,000 casualties (mainly non-combatants) in a single day. This event is known by Sikh historians as *waddā ghalūghārā* or the great holocaust.

39. The Harimandar Sāhib (q.v.) at Amritsar, popularly known as the Golden Temple, which was blown up with gunpowder and the tank defiled by Ahmad Shāh Durrānī on April 10, 1762.

40. The early Mughals were fond of noticeable displays of their ability to put down rebellion. In 1632, Peter Mundy, an Englishmen traveling in Mughal India was compelled to write and even sketch a tower of heads of "rebels and

theeves" that was composed of "heads mortared and plaistered in, leavineinge out nothing but their verie face." Peter Mundy, *Travels in Europe and Asia, 1608–1667*, ed. Sir R.C. Temple, 5 vols (Cambridge: Hakluyt Society, 1907–1936), 2: 90.

41. Lahore was occupied by the Sikhs on April 16, 1765 with Sirdār Gujar Singh Bhangī and Lahinā Singh at the head. Kābulī Mall was then the governor of the province on behalf of Ahmad Shāh and his nephew Amīr Singh, in the absence of the governor at Jammū, was compelled to surrender to the Sikhs.

42. Ahmad Shāh Durrānī died on October 16, 1772. Timur Shāh (q.v.) conquered Multān from the Sikhs in February 1780.

43. The lack of unity among the Sikh chiefs was also commented on to the court of directors on February 5, 1794: "There is the greatest enmity among them and continual war about disputed boundary. They have no union whatever. Everyone wishes the destruction of his neighbour and seeks to extirpate him. The old chiefs, who were experienced in war and had fought against Ahmad Shah are all dead, and their children are untried." Gupta, *History of the Sikhs*, 4: 457. For further details on the internecine warfare among the Sikhs, see ibid., 3: 124–5, and Bhagat Singh, *History of the Sikh Misals* (Patiala: Punjabi University, 1993), 341–57.

44. The making of slaves by Sikhs was noted by William Francklin, *The History of the Reign of Shah Alum* (part IV, chapter 16). Kidnapping is less commonly referred to but was an observed practice in eighteenth century Punjab. It is commonly known that the Persian and Afghān invaders gained materially from kidnapping and slavery, for which the most attractive and strong children were at greatest risk of being abducted.

45. The best horses were those specially bred and imported from Peshāwar, Afghānistān, and Seistān through merchants and agents. By the nineteenth century, Sohan Lal Suri in *Umdat-ut-Tawarikh* tells us that Sikhs were extensive breeders of their own horses and depended very little on imports. Fauja Singh Bajwa, *Military System of the Sikh*, (Delhi: Motilal Banarsidass, 1964), 208.

46. This is a common description that can also be found in Balthazar Solvyns, *Les Hindoûs*, 4 vols. (Paris: Chez L'Auteur, 1808–1812). See part III, chapter 15. It is likely to originate in the offerings made to villagers and family at the death of an older family member in memory and in celebration of a long-lived life (*barra*).

47. The respect shown to a horse by a Sikh warrior of the eighteenth century is typified by the vernacular term for a horse as *jān bhāī*, or life brother.

48. *Gentoo* is a pejorative form for Hindu.

49. This could be a reference to the various characters called *Avtārs* or incarnations of Vishnū, mentioned throughout the *Dasam Granth* scriptures of Gurū Gobind Singh, and revered by the Hindu masses as Gods. Alternatively, Polier may have based this comment on meeting Sikhs (e.g. the *Udāsīs* and *Nirmalās*) who were not averse to utilizing idols in their capacity as *simritī*, or tools for remembering God, as opposed to worshipping the idol itself (a subtle distinction that is all too easy to misinterpret).

50. In mainstream Khālsā Sikh practice, the *charan amrit* (q.v.) initiation method was replaced in 1699 by the *khande dī pahul* (q.v.) method but appears to have continued according to Polier. It could have been that Polier received his information from Sikhs belonging to the *Udāsī, Sevā Panthī* or *Nirmalā* traditions who still continue *charan amrit* as a way of initiating new adherents.

51. At the time this account was written, Haridvār, famous for its huge annual gathering (see Thomas Hardwicke's account part III, chapter 14), was under the rule of Rāi Singh of Jagādharī, a prominent member of the Bhangī *misl*.

52. References to Mirzā Najaf Khān, the Mughal *mīr bakhshī*, and his campaign against Rāo Rājā Pratāp Singh of Macherī.

53. Mahā Singh (q.v.), father of Ranjīt Singh (q.v.).

54. See also A.C. Banerjee, "Aurangzeb and the Sikh Gurus," in *Punjab Past and Present: Essays in Honour of Dr Ganda Singh*, ed. Harbans Singh and N. Gerald Barrier (Patiala: Punjabi University, 1976), 119–43.

CHAPTER 9

BROWNE'S TREATISE ON
THE SIKHS, 1788

Lt.-Col. James Browne, *India Tracts: Containing a Description of the Jungle Terry Districts, Their Revenues, Trade, and Government: With a Plan for the Improvement of Them. Also an History of the Origin and Progress of the Sicks* (Logographic Press, Printing-House Square, Black-Friars, 1788), pp. 1–30.

Military man, failed ambassador, and linguist, James Browne entered the service of the East India Company in 1765 aged twenty-one. He rose from cadet to captain in six years, attracting the attention of the venerable Warren Hastings with whom Browne's own fortune would be tied for the rest of his life. Hastings, then governor-general, appointed Browne as his aide-de-camp. He was appointed collector of the Jungleterry districts in 1773. However, he encountered great difficulty in administering the country and settling disturbances. Becoming acutely aware of the nuisance created by the Sikhs in the Punjab, he was sent by the council on an embassy to Shāh Ālum II at Delhi to negotiate with him for assistance against the Sikhs.

A power struggle in the waning court of Shāh Ālum II in Delhi created an opportunity for the marauding Sikhs and Marāthās and a headache for Warren Hastings, who relied on imperial patronage to carry on the trade of the Company. Political machinations were inevitable, but safeguarding the Company interest was paramount; Hastings needed a trustworthy agent in the royal capital to keep abreast of the rapidly changing situation. James Browne, now a major, was selected for the job. It was during this time, as the official resident in the imperial city of Delhi, that Browne came to translate the manuscript that forms the bulk of his treatise on the Sikhs.

Browne's tenure was a disaster; he disregarded his impartiality and constantly threw his lot behind a succession of claimants to the throne, even contemplating inviting the Mughals and the British to join forces against the undesirable Marāthās. His impunity ended when Warren Hastings left for

England in 1785 and he too was recalled. In London, he evidently used his enforced retirement to complete this treatise, submitting it in September 1787. September was to prove a busy month for Browne who also challenged his nemesis, Sir John MacPherson, to a duel in Hyde Park to settle his grievance against MacPherson's refusal to publicly apologize to him following his treatment after the Delhi debacle. Neither was hurt.

His *Indian Tracts*, which he says were written by the order of Warren Hastings, describing the Jungleterry districts, and giving an account of the Sikhs was published in 1788.

Four years before his death in 1792, Browne returned to India. In Calcutta he married, fathered a son, and died aged just forty-eight.

Whilst Brown's account is widely lauded as the "first regular treatise on the Sikhs"[1] the work is not entirely his own. The account itself is in two distinct parts with an attached map which is not reproduced here. The bulk of the text is a translation of an abridged Persian manuscript. The original text was the *Risālā-i-Nānak* by Budh Singh Arorā and Lālā Ajāib Singh Sūraj. The latter was a servant of James Browne. Preceding the translation is a short introduction in Browne's own words where he discusses "the manners and customs of the Sicks." Here, he was aided by his personal interactions with Sikhs. He notes that he had "conversed with several Sicks, who were sent to me by different chiefs on complimentary messages." We know of some of the messengers that Browne met while corresponding with the Sikh chiefs. Baghel Singh Karorasinghīā's *vakīl* (agent), Lakhpat Rāi, communicated frequently with Browne in 1783 and his letters were delivered by Khushāl Singh and Mangal Sain. Replying to one of Browne's letters, he wrote that notable chiefs such as Jassā Singh Āhlūvālīā "who is the highest and greatest and in that country called Badshah [King] Singh," and Baghel Singh including many others were willing to establish friendly relations with the British government. Lakhpat Rāi sent another letter enclosed with the epistles from Jassā Singh Āhlūvālīā, Lahinā Singh, Baghel Singh, and Sāhib Singh of Patiālā expressing declarations of mutual goodwill and cooperation. Another prominent Sikh who corresponded with Browne was Karam Singh Shāhīd who had sent his letter via his son, Kalyān Singh.[2]

In the introduction, Browne gives a hint to the motivation for the work. As the personal agent of Warren Hastings, governor-general of India, it was his role to gather intelligence on the strength, resources, and capability of potential enemies. It was in this capacity that Browne took an active interest in Sikhs, stating that "the first and most important object which presented itself was the great irregular Aristocracy of the Sikhs, a sect which, from a small beginning in the neighborhood of Lahore, has established itself in a complete possession of all the country between the Attock and the Sutledge and levies contribution to the very frontier of the Vizir's dominions." The Persian manuscript belonging to the two Sikhs that Browne had encountered seemed to give him a sufficient starting point to use as a political overview for his master.

James Browne is one of the earliest western writers to comment on the discordant nature of Sikh–Mughal relationship that was such a defining feature during the formation of the Khālsā. He points to the Mughal–Sikh relationship under Aurangzeb as the source of this conflict, missing entirely the earlier troubles that the Sikh Gurūs faced.

A unique feature of Browne's text is his comments on Sikh coinage, which have been the subject of some debate by both Sikh historians and numisticians. Browne claims that the Sikhs, upon entering Lahore, struck a coin in the name of their leader Jassā Singh Āhlūvālīā. The Sikhs did capture Lahore and mint coins in November 1761 according to Hari Ram Gupta[3] although this is subject to some conjecture from other writers. While no example of this coin survives, it is claimed by Browne that the Sikhs struck a coin bearing the inscription "coin struck in the world by the Grace of God, in the country of Ahmed captured by Jassā Kelāl." There exists little physical evidence to support the claim, and only circumstantial evidence against this thesis. The inscription, which is virtually the same as that given by Du Perron (see part I, chapter 3), is odd, most notably for the use of Jassā Kelāl (not Jassā Singh) and also for breaking from the precedent of Bandā Bahādur who claimed victory in the name of the Gurū rather than himself when he struck coins after the sacking of Sirhind. Ganesh Dās, in *Risālā-e-Sāhib Numa* asserts that these coins were minted by the mullahs of Lahore in order to incite their co-religionists in Kābul to rise up and avenge the Sikhs in memory of Ahmad Shāh Abdālī. Discounting this theory, it seems that the Sikhs struck a coin first in the name of Jassā Singh and soon afterward in the names of Gurū Nānak and Gurū Gobind Singh.

Despite Browne's knowledge of urban Sikhs, including the two Sikhs who provided the manuscript that he studied, he appears to be describing rustic Akālī Nihang Sikhs in his final descriptive paragraphs. The differentiation of the *Nānakpanthī*, non-Khālsā urban Sikhs, and the Khālsā warriors was a more pronounced distinction than would be found today. The description of blue clad, *bhang*-drinking, martially orientated Sikhs would indicate the traditions of the Akālī Nihangs.

The text is notable also for an early reference to the *karā*, one of the *pañj kakār*, external symbols that define the outward appearance of the initiated Khālsā Sikh. The *karā* as a *kakār* is subject to some conjecture with some debate on the exact point at which it entered the Sikh uniform. Sikh tradition maintains that the *karā* was one of the five original symbols inculcated by Gurū Gobind Singh when the Khālsā was created in 1699. Some historians assert that the *karā* was a nineteenth century innovation.[4] Of the five outward symbols, the *karā* and the *kangā* are two that are rarely referred to in the older textual traditions of the Khālsā. The reference to *treh mudrā,* or three adornments, is more common. Given the problematic nature of much of the early liturgy of the Khālsā, this issue is not conclusive, but Browne's reference does give some further early evidence to the pre-Tatt Khālsā adoption of the *karā* as one of the *kakārs*.

As Browne's own introduction comes to a conclusion, he commences a competent translation of the Persian text. Despite the fact that two Sikhs furnished the original text, it is not without errors. The text states that Gurū Gobind Singh died in Patnā rather than Nanded. The events described in the subsequent paragraph, including the evacuation of Anandpur Sāhib in December 1704 and the battle at Chamkaur a few days later, all occurred in the lifetime of Gurū Gobind Singh who was present throughout and not after his death as asserted by the authors. A contemporary letter to Wazīr Khān, the *faujdār* of Sirhind, from the secretary of Emperor Aurangzeb confirms this: "His (the addressee's) letter has been received, containing news of the encampment of Gobind, the Nanak devotee, at twelve *kurohs* from Sahrind; of that Commander's despatch of seven hundred cavalry with a park of artillery; of that person's taking refuge in the house of the *zemindar* of the village of Chamkaur; and of his two sons and other companions being killed, and one son and his mother being captured; and other matters. Since His Excellency's petition, comprising an account of these matters, has already been seen by the Emperor, and His Highness Mirza 'Ali Yar Beg has already conveyed his details to His Majesty, the contents of the letter [now received] have not been conveyed to His Majesty."[5]

The text contains some considerable detail on Bandā Bahādur, a figure whose exploits after the death of the tenth Gurū defined the early Khālsā in the eyes of the Mughal authorities and curious Europeans alike. The text notes that Bandā Bahādur "enrolled himself in the fraternity of the Sicks." There is little question that Bandā became a Sikh of Gurū Gobind Singh. There is some contention over whether he took *khande dī pahul* and became a Khālsā Sikh. Hari Ram Gupta is strongly of the opinion that Bandā was not baptized into the Khālsā fraternity.[6] Citing largely political reasons as the motivator, Gupta quotes from Ratan Singh Bhangū's *Prachīn Panth Prakāsh* and Giānī Giān Singh's *Navīn Panth Prakāsh*. Equally eminent historians, such as Dr Ganda Singh argue the opposite case.[7]

Given the Sikh origins of the original Persian text, it is unusual in repeating a claim that during the sacking of Sirhind, the Sikhs "destroyed all the mosques and tombs belonging to the Mussulmans." There are a number of accounts that point to general atrocities committed by Bandā's troops on the Muslim community and their vassals in Sirhind. However, it is worthwhile to note that the mausoleum of Shaikh Ahmad Mujāddid Alif Sanī, the most significant of the tombs in the entire region, is still standing as it did before the battle. Sikh accounts do not make any mention of any atrocities. Sikh sources do make mention of the digging up of a grave of Bībī Anūp Kaur who, at the threat of being kidnapped by Sher Muhammad Khān, had committed suicide. The Sikhs dug out her body and cremated it.[8] Whether these atrocities were committed or not remains unclear, however, the impact of the Sikhs striking the heart of Mughal Punjab would have been conspicuous. The effect was so dramatic that it even contributed to the increase in Sikh numbers amongst Hindu and Muslim Punjabis. A contemporary Persian account notes that "The authority of that deluded sect [of the Sikhs] extended to such an extent that many Hindus and Muhammadans, finding no alternative to obedience and submission adopted their faith and rituals. And their chief [Bandā Singh] captivated the hearts of all towards his inclinations, and, whether a Hindu or a Muhammadan whosoever came in contact with him, he [Bandā Singh] addressed him by the title of Singh. Accordingly Dindar Khan, a powerful ruler of the neighborhood, was named Dindar Singh, and Mir Nasir-ud-Din, the news-writer of Sirhind, became Mir Nasir Singh. In the same way, a large number of Muhammadans abandoned Islam and followed the misguided path [of Sikhism], and took solemn oaths and firm pledges to stand by him."[9]

To JOHN MOTTEUX, ESQ. Chairman of the Honourable Court of Directors, for the Affairs of the Honourable United East India Company.

SIR,

CONFORMABLY to the wish which you were pleased to express, that I should furnish you with an account of the rise and present state of the tribe of people called Sicks; I now beg leave to submit to your perusal, the following translation which I have made of a Persian manuscript, written by my desire while I resided at the Court of Dehly;[10] to which I have added, all the information which I have by other channels acquired, respecting that people; and I have accompanied the whole with a map, specifying the extent of their territories, the names of their chiefs, together with the places of their respective residence, and the number of their forces.—I shall be very happy, if this tract is thought in any degree worthy of your attention, and beg leave to subscribe myself, with great truth and respect,

Your most obliged humble Servant,

JAMES BROWNE

HARLEY-STREET,

Sept. 17, 1787.

INTRODUCTION

During the time of my residence as the English Minister, at the court of his Majesty Shah Alum, I took every opportunity to acquire a knowledge of the strength, resources, disposition, and constitution of the several states bordering on the province of Agra and Dehly, by seeking out, and cultivating a personal intimacy with the best informed men of those several subjects.—In the course of these researches, the first and most important object which presented itself, was the great irregular Aristocracy of the *Sicks*; a sect, which from a small beginning in the neighbourhood of Lahore, has established itself in the complete possession of all the country between the Attock and the Sutledge, and levies contributions to the very frontier of the Vizier's dominions.

Having met with two Hindoos of considerable knowledge, who were natives of Lahore, where they had resided the greater part of their lives, and who had in their possession, accounts of the rise and progress of the Sicks, written in the *Nuggary*[11] (or common Hindoo) character, I persuaded them to let me have a translation of one of them in the Persian language,[12] abridging it as much as they could do, without injuring the essential purpose of information.—After all, I found it extremely defective in a regular continuation of dates, and therefore not deserving the name of a history: however, the dates of the principal events are clearly determined; future opportunities and greater leisure than I possessed while at Delhy, may ascertain those which are at present unknown.—This Persian sketch of an history, I have translated in English, and now beg leave to offer it to my honourable masters, as I am persuaded, that the rapid progress of this sect, will hereafter render a knowledge of them, their strength, and government, very important to the administration of Bengal.—But as in the Persian manuscript very little is said of the manners and customs of the Sicks, I shall insert in this introduction, all that I have been able to discover on those heads.

The people known by the name of *Sicks*, were originally the common inhabitants of the provinces of Lahore and Multan, and mostly of the *Jaut* tribe; the doctrine on which their sect is founded, was introduced by *Gooroo Nanuck*, about two hundred and fifty years ago; and appears to bear that kind of relation to the Hindoo religion, which the Protestant does to the Romish, retaining all the essential principles, but being abridged of most of its ceremonies, as well as of the subordinate objects of veneration.—At first, the sect was merely speculative, quiet, inoffensive, and unarmed; they were first persecuted by the barbarous bigotry of Amungzebe; and persecution, as will ever be the case, gave strength to that which is meant to destroy; the Sicks from necessity confederated together, and finding that their peaceable deportment did not secure them from oppression, they took up arms to defend themselves against a tyrannical government; and as will always happen where the common rights of humanity are violated, a hero arose, whose courage and ability directed the efforts of his inured followers, to a just, though severe revenge.—As the progress of these events is related in the history, I shall only say at present, that as the Mogul government declined, the Sicks in spite of repeated attempts to suppress them, continued to acquire strength.—They made the distinction of their sect, a political as much as a religious principle, rendering the admission into it easy to all, and the immediate temporal advantages of protection and independance, as great and as evident as possible; while they at the same time levied contributions upon all their neighbours, who refused to come into their fraternity.

As to their government, it is aristocratical, but very irregular and imperfect; for the body of the people is divided under a number of chiefs,[13] who possess portions of country, either by former right as Zemindars, or by usurpation.—These chiefs enjoy distinct authority in their respective districts, uncontrolled by any superior power; and only assemble together on particular occasions[14] for the purposes of depredation, or of defence; when in a tumultuous Diet, they choose by majority of votes, a leader to command their joint forces during the expedition; generally from among those chiefs, whose Zemindaries are most considerable; his authority, is however but ill obeyed by so many other chiefs, who though possessed of smaller territories, yet as leaders of the fraternity of Sicks, think themselves perfectly his equals, and barely allow him, during his temporary elevation, the dignity of *Primus inter Pares.*

About thirty years ago, one Jessa Sing Kelal,[15] a chief of considerable weight and abilities, having been chosen commander of their grand army, when it expelled the Aumils of Ahmed Shah Durrany from the city, and Subah of Lahore, became so popular, that he ventured to strike rupees at the mint of Lahore in his own name, with an inscription in Persian to this effect, "Jessa Kelal conquered the country of Ahmed, and struck this coin by the grace of God:"—but after they had been current about fifteen years, the grand Diet of the Sick chiefs, (called *Goormutta*) determined to call in all those rupees, and to strike them in the names of *Gooroo Nanuck*, and *Gooroo Gobind Sing*, the first and the last of their *Gooroos*, or religious leaders; the latter of whom directed them to take up arms against the Mussulmans, and rendered general a kind of feast to be celebrated at the grand Diet, or Goormutta, at which feast they use large dishes called in Persian *Daig*, which I mention to explain the Persian inscription used on their coin from that time, which is as follows, "*Gooroo Gobind Sing*, received from *Nanuck* the *Daig*, the Sword, and rapid Victory."[16]

The city of Lahore is at present divided among the three most powerful chiefs, who share the revenue arising from all imports and duties, &c. within the city, including the mint; the names of the present possessors are, Gujer Sing, Subah Sing, and Laina Sing.[17]

The Diets of the Sicks are held at the holy *Tank* (bason of water) of *Amrutsur*, about twenty coss north by east from Lahore, which was appointed for that purpose by their Gooroo.[18]—Here as I said before, the commander for the campaign is chosen, and their expeditions for the season planned.

The plunder collected during these expeditions, is divided among the chiefs according to the number of their followers, to whom each chief makes his own distribution.

In the districts not reduced to their absolute subjection, but into which they make occasional incursions, they levy a tribute which they call *Raukey*,[19] and which is about one fifth, (as the Marhatta Chout is one fourth) of the annual rent; whenever a Zemindar has agreed to pay this tribute to any Sick chief, that chief not only himself, refrains from plundering him, but will protect him from all others; and this protection is by general consent held so far sacred, that even if the grand army passes through a Zemindary where the safe guards of the lowest Sick chief are stationed, it will not violate them.

Since the Sicks became powerful, and confederated for the purpose of conquest, they have called their confederacy *Khalsa Gee*, or the State, and their grand army *Dull Khalsa Gee*, or the Army of the State.

As the extent of their possessions is clearly expressed in the accompanying map as well as the names of their chiefs, and the number of their forces from the best authorities, I shall only observe, that the country is said to be in a state of high cultivation, which I believe, because they carry into it all the cattle fit for tillage, which come into their possession by plunder, collect a very moderate rent, and that mostly in kind, and during any intestine disputes, their soldiery never molest the husbandman.

Trade however, is in a low state, owing to the insecurity of merchants going backward and forwards through the territories of so many independant chiefs.

Of their manufactures, the principal are very fine cloth, which they make at Lahore, as also the best arms in Hindostan.[20]

Their cavalry is remarkably good, the men being very hardy and well armed with sabres and excellent matchlocks, which they use with great dexterity; the horses bred in their country are of one of the best breeds in the empire, owing to the use formerly made there of Arabian and Persian stallions, and something in the temperature of the air and water of that country. Most of these soldiers have two or three horses each, by which means their incursions are made with great rapidity, their armies marching from fifty to one hundred and twenty miles a day:—their dress is dark blue, as ordered by *Gooroo Gobind*, and gives them, when collected in large bodies together, a very dismal appearance.

The chiefs are only distinguishable from their followers, by finer horses and arms.

I have conversed with several Sicks, who were sent to me by different chiefs on complimentary messages; and I perceived a manly boldness in their manner and conversation, very unlike the other inhabitants of Hindostan, owing no doubt to the freedom of their government.

In their camps they use no tents, even the chiefs are sheltered by nothing more than small *Numgheras* (square canopies of coarse cotton cloth) supported on four slender poles—the common soldiers pitch a blanket on two sticks, and fasten the corners down to the ground with wooden pins, so that they encamp or decamp in a few minutes.

Among their customs, the following are remarkable:

They will not use tobacco, though its use is universal to all the inhabitants of Hindostan, yet they drink spirits and smoke *Bang* (the leaves of hemp) to the greatest excess of intoxication.

In admitting a proselyte, they make him drink Sherbet out of a large cup, with certain ceremonies, as will be seen hereafter, and which are designed to signify, that every distinction is abolished, except that of being a Sick, even a Mussulman may become a Sick on these conditions.—From the time that he is admitted into the fraternity, he wears a steel ring round one of his wrists,[21] lets his hair and beard grow to full length, and calls on the name of the Gooroo in confirmation of all engagements.

These are all the circumstances respecting this Sect, which are not specifically mentioned in the history: to which I will add, that a sect which contained in its original principles so much internal vigour, as sustained it against the bloody persecution of a great government, determined and interested to suppress it, raised it up again with fresh strength on every opportunity which occurred; and at length enabled it so far to subdue all opposition, as to acquire an entire and undisturbed dominion over some of the finest provinces of the empire, from whence it makes incursions into others, holding out protection to all who join, and destruction to all who oppose it; a sect, which makes religion and politics unite in its aggrandizement, and renders the entrance into it so easy to all who desire to become members of it, cannot fail to extend itself very far, and in the end to be exceedingly formidable to all its neighbours.

Respecting the map which accompanies this history, it was laid down from a Persian map of Punjab which I procured at Agra; and was put into its present shape by Lieutenant James Nathaniel Rind, of the Bengal establishment, who commanded the escorte which accompanied me while resident at the Shah's court, and whom I must here beg leave to mention as a very deserving officer.—The map, however, is designed principally as a political chart, to shew the extent of the dominions of the Sicks, and the places where the chiefs reside: on points of Geographical knowledge, I have to just an opinion of Major Rennell's abilities, to attempt an improvement of any work of his; and I therefore give this explanation of the design of the accompanying map, that no other may be imputed to me.

HISTORY OF THE ORIGIN AND PROGRESS OF THE SICKS[22]

(AH 963/ AD 1529) In the latter end of the reign of Sultan Baber, *Nanuck Shah*, a Dervish, by tribe a *Ketteree*,[23] lived in the village of Shoderah,[24] situated about seven crores (or coss) east of the river Chenab; as he was a man of a most exemplary life, and eminent for his piety, charity, and abstinence, he became famous throughout Hindostan, and wherever he went teaching his doctrine, he made a great number of proselytes; he wrote several books upon the nature and institutions of his order; such as the *Purraun Sunkely*,[25] &c. which he distributed for the regulation of the worship of his followers.—He took the title of *Gooroo*, or religious Teacher, and called his followers in general *Sicks*, which signifies followers of a Sect, but his immediate disciples, whom he instructed in the mysteries of his doctrine, he called *Murids*, or Disciples; these terms are often confounded, but they are properly very distinct.

After the death of Gooroo Nanuck, his successors were in the following order

1. Gooroo Ankud
2. Gooroo Amerdad
3. Gooroo Ramdas

4. Gooroo Arjun who wrote the Gurhunt, now generally followed as the rule of discipline.
5. Gooroo Ramroy.
6. Gooroo Hur Roy.
7. Gooroo Hurry Siri Kirsen, these upon an average to have exercised their office about twenty-two years each.

(AH 1073/ AD 1662) In the year of the Hegira, 1073, Aurungzebe being on the throne, a son was borne to Gooroo Hurry Siri Kirshen, to whom they gave the name of Taigh Bahadur, when his son came to the age of puberty,—being remarkable for his piety and abstinence—his followers conceived a superstitious veneration for him and used among themselves, to call him the true King; he on his part, whatever he received in presents, or offerings from his disciples, or the Sicks in general, he laid out in provisions, which he publicly distributed to all who chose to receive them; this brought great numbers to participate of his bounty.

The news writers of Lahore, soon transmitted an account of these circumstances to Aurungzebe, who was then engaged in the war of the Deckan; and his Majesty being very particular in his examination of all persons who pretended to extraordinary sanctity, he sent some Yessawils (Ushers) to bring Taigh Behader to his presence, who on their arrival at the place of his residence immediately set out with them, and soon arrived the court.

(AH 1096/ AD 1684) Aurungzebe having called him into his presence, examined him very strictly respecting the revelations and miracles to which he supposed that he pretended; to which Taigh Behader replied, "that he was a Dervish; that he subsisted on the alms of the charitable, and passed his life in the contemplation and adoration of God; but that he neither pretended to revelations nor miracles". The Shah again said, "they call you the True King, and Taigh Behader (which was a military title), what presumption is this?"-to which Taigh Behader replied, "whatever is, is from God; Dervishes have nothing to do with titles or honours". The Shah preceiving that he could discover nothing of the revelations or miracles attributed to this Dervish, gave orders for putting him to death immediately. At that time, a Bramin of the name of Murdanch, who stood by, said to Taigh Behader, "If you will give me permission, I will imprecate curses on these persecutors, and justice of God, you shall see them instantly destroyed". But Taigh Behader, according to the counsel given to him at parting by father, to preserve the secret of the sect, though it should cost him his life, replied, "The time is not yet come, God himself will punish them, and raise up a hero, who will exact ample vengeance for my blood."

He was accordingly put to death,[i] and upon the spot where he suffered Martyrdom, a monument has been erected, which is still in being, and offerings are made at it.[26]

(AH 1116/ AD 1704) Soon after this, the widow of Taigh Behader, having been left with child, was delivered of a son, to whom they gave the name of *Gobind Sing*,[27] who growing up, and being about twenty years of age, conceived an ardent desire to revenge the death of his father; but either finding his party too weak, or wanting

---

[i] Aurungzebe seems on this, as well as on many other occasions, to have made religion a veil to cover his political tyranny; the real motive of this cruelty to Taigh Behader, was most probably, resentment for his having allowed his followers to call him the true King; and his having used a military title, which was not granted by Royal Patent, agreeably to the customs of that Government, of all which he was exceeding jealous.

resolution in his own mind to attempt so dangerous an enterprize, he[ii] by the advice of the Bramins, performed a number of superstitious rites, in expectation, that some manifestation of the Divine pleasure would appear in his favour; at length a voice was said to have been heard from heaven, declaring the revenge he sought for, should not be attained by him, but by his disciples after his death; and that his sect should at last arrive at the highest point of strength and dominion.

The mind of Gooroo Gobind Sing, seems to have become disordered by the influence of these superstitious reveries, and to have remained for some time in that state; but at length having recovered his reason, he put on a dress of dark blue, let his hair and beard grow to their full length, and instructed his sect to follow his example in these points.—He also directed them to arm themselves in expectation of the hour, when the prophecy should be fulfilled.

(AH 1118/ AD 1706) From this time, the Sicks animated with enthusiasm, began to collect together from all parts of the Empire, and multitudes of new proselytes were daily enrolled in the sect, which was rendered important by the martyrdom of Taigh Behader.—Gooroo Gobind Sing, established a ceremony to be used on the reception of new proselytes, which ceremony is called *Poil*, and consists of making them drink Sherbet out of a cup, stirring it round with a dagger, and pronouncing a certain incantation[iii] at the same time.

(AH 1118/ AD 1706) Advice being conveyed to Aurungzebe of all these particulars, he sent orders to the Navab Vizier Khan, who was then Foujdar of Sirhind, to take the requisite steps for suppressing this threatening insurrection; but before this order was received, Gooroo Gobind, having gone to collect his followers from the eastern provinces, died at the city of Patna;[28] and his wife having died sometime before,[29] two children whom he had, the one about six, the other about five years old,[30] were left under the care of his mother, (the widow of Taigh Behader) who hearing of the Shah's orders to Vizier Khan, attempted to fly with her two grand children from *Amrutsur* to *Macowal*; which was her native place.—Many of Gooroo Gobind's followers accompanied, in order to escort them safe to the place of their destination.—By the time they had got to the village of *Chumkore*, which was seven coss from Sirhind, the Navab Vizier Khan, according to the Shah's orders, sent a body of troops commanded by Khizzer Kahn Malnere, together with the Buckshy of his own army, to take Gooroo Gobind's family prisoners, and bring them to Sirhind.—Khizzer Khan having overtaken them at that place, the Sicks who accompanied the Gooroo's family, defended them with the greatest resolution; many of the Shah's people were killed, as well as of the Sicks; but as the former were vastly superior in number, the two children, together with their grandmother, were taken prisoners, and all their wealth and property, which they were carrying away with them was plundered;—the few Sicks who survived, escaped by flight.—Khizzer Khan brought his prisoners to the Navab Vizier Khan at Sirhind, who put them in confinement, and advised Aurungzebe of it.

(AH 1118/ AD 1706) They say, that Vizier Khan, who had been forty years Foujdar of Sirhind, had never oppressed any person under his authority, but was distinguished for his justice and humanity; and from the natural goodness of his disposition, he

---

[ii] I have omitted the detail of these superstitions, which would but tire the enlightened European reader; their object was no doubt, to impress the common people with a belief that their cause was supported by divine favour and protection.

[iii] This incantation I could never get the words of, though I took some pains to do so.—It seems to be among the Arcana of this sect.

conceived a regard for these children of Gooroo Gobind, often sent for them, and shewed them kindness.—It happened one day, that he was asking them in a jesting manner, how much they had been plundered of, to which the eldest of the children innocently replied, "that the wealth of Dervishes was too great to be counted."— *Suchanund,*[31] a *Kettery,* who was *Dewan* to the Navab Vizier Khan, said to him, "perhaps these children may give the same kind of answer if they are examined by the Shah; if so, what will become of us all, and who shall satisfy his Majesty? It would be safer to put the children to death, which is the only way of securing ourselves from the Shah's rapacity."

Vizier Kahn, being unwilling to destroy these innocent children, hesitated a long time; but at length his dread of the Shah's displeasure,[iv] should he suspect him of having secreted the treasure plundered from Gooroo Gobind's family, getting the better of every other consideration, he said to Khizzer Khan, "Many of your friends and followers were killed by the Sicks, who escorted these children, you ought to retaliate by killing the children, as the cause of the death of so many of the faithful."[v]— Khizzer Khan, however, rejected the proposal with horror, and nobly replied, "both I and my followers are soldiers, and whoever oppose us in open war, we either kill them, or are killed ourselves; but what you propose, is the business of the executioner." However, the destined period of the childrens lives being come, one Kurruckchy Beg, a Mogul in the Shah's service, undertook to perpetrate this barbarous murder, and went to the prison where the innocent victims were confined; the children clung round the neck of their grandmother to save themselves, but the villain tore them away, and cut their throats with a knife,[32] in the presence of this miserable woman, who, unable longer to bear such a load of calamity, her husband, Taigh Behader, having been murdered before, (as was related) and her grand children now butchered before her eyes, sunk under the violence of grief and horror, excited by this last scene, and divine mercy by an immediate death, released her from further sufferings.[vi]

(AH 1118/ AD 1706) One *Bundah,*[33] a *Biragee Fakeer,* and the native of a village called Pundory, in the *Doab* of Beit Jalinder, had been for many years the intimate friend of Gooroo Gobind; and hearing of the destruction of his defenceless family, he gave way to the deepest impressions of grief and resentment, which at length settled into a fixed determination to seek revenge; for this purpose, he went to all the most powerful and zealous of the Sicks, who had been the followers of Gooroo Gobind, and having excited in them the same spirit with which he himself was actuated, and enrolled himself in the fraternity of the Sicks, he, with surprising diligence and activity, and aided by uncommon abilities, collected the sect together in arms from all quarters, and inspired them with the most ardent spirit of revenge.

(AH 1119/ AD 1707) Fortunately for the execution of Bundah's design, about this time, Aurungzebe died in the Deckan, and the succession to the throne being

---

[iv] This is a striking instance of the tyranny of Aurungzebe's Government, and indeed of the horrid effect of despotism, on the characters of those who live under its influence; when we here behold a man naturally mild and compassionate, committing the most atrocious crime, from dread of the consequence which would have attended his acting conformably to his conscience, and the dictates of humanity.

[v] Retaliation for blood called in the Koran Kussaus, is considered by the Mussulmans, as a moral and religious duty to the next in connection.

[vi] Of all the instances of cruelty exercised on the propagators of new doctrines, this is the most barbarous and outrageous;—Defenceless women and children, have usually escaped, even from religious fury.—No wonder, then, that the vengeance of the Sicks was so severe.

disputed between his sons, (as is well known to those who are conversant in the history of Hindostan,) great confusion arose in all parts of the empire.—Bundah taking advantage of this opportunity, and having collected together a large, though irregular army of Sicks, marched to attack Navab Vizier Khan, who was then at Sirhind, the seat of his government.—Vizier Khan came out to give them battle with all the troops he had, and the armies coming to action near *Alwan Siray*, the Sicks, inspired by enthusiasm and revenge, gave the Mussulmans a total defeat: Vizier Khan was killed upon the spot, and the greater part of his army was cut in pieces. Proceeding to the town of Sirhind, the Sicks put to death all the family of Vizier Khan, and every dependant and servant belonging to him:—Suchanund the Dewan, by whose advice the children of Gooroo Gobind had been murdered, was torn to pieces, with every circumstance of cruelty which savage cruelty could dictate. After which, they destroyed all the mosques and tombs belonging to the Mussulmans; and such was the terror which their severity and fury excited, that neither Hindoos nor Mussulmans found any means of safety, but in acknowledging and submitting to their authority, and professing to belong to their sect; which disposition, Bundah, who was a man of great art and address, encouraged by every means, with a view to encrease his force: treating those with the most flattering kindness who came into the sect, and those who refused with unrelenting severity:—so that in a short time, all the districts from Paniput to near Lahore, acknowledged the authority of the Sicks; and Behader Shah[34] being then in the Deckan, with the Imperial Army, there was no force in the provinces of Lahore, Dehly or Agra, able to undertake the reduction of the insurgents.

(AH 1120/ AD 1708) Behader Shah, having defeated his brother Kâm Bucksh, was desirous of remaining some time longer in that part of his dominions, in order to make a complete settlement of all the *Soubah's* (or provinces) of the Deckan; but when the advices arrived of Bundah's insurrection, and Vizier Khan's defeat and death, the danger appeared too pressing to admit of delay: he therefore determined to move with his whole force towards Sirhind, sending before him an advanced army of cavalry and artillery, under the command of Sultan Kouly Khan, nephew of Rustum dil Khan; to which he joined all the Mussulmans who had fled from Sirhind and other parts, to avoid the fury of the Sicks. His Majesty ordered Sultan Kouly Khan to march by way of Dehly, and thereby stop the progress of the Sicks on that side;—protecting the inhabitants as much as possible,—to prevent the insurrection from spreading,—and to put every man to the sword that he should find with his hair and beard at full length;—that being the characteristic external of the Sicks.

(AH 1120/ AD 1708) Sultan Kouly Khan, with the zeal of a faithful servant, marched as expeditiously as possible, and having passed by way of Dehly, he came to Paniput; resolved to attack the Sicks, though his army was exceedingly weak, when compared with the prodigious force now got together under the enemy's standard. The Sicks on their part, being flushed with victory, and confident in their numbers, were no less willing to come to action. The battle began, in which there was great slaughter on both sides, but especially on that of the Sicks; who being destitute of discipline, and unprovided with artillery, suffered very severely; when Kisury Sing Buckshy,[35] to whom Bundah had given the command of this division of his army, being killed by an arrow, the Sicks began to give way, were at length totally defeated, and the remainder of their army fled to join Bundah, who had remained with the rest of his forces at Sirhind. The next day, Sultan Kouly Khan being joined by a reinforcement sent after him by the Shah, under the command of the Vizier Khan Khanan, marched to Sirhind: Bundah drew up his army, which consisted of between forty and fifty thousand horse and foot, to receive the Mussulmans:—the battle was long and bloody;—but at length, the royal army making a desperate charge upon one part of the enemy's front, broke through, and a general defeat ensued, with terrible slaughter of the Sicks. Bundah being unable to rally his disheartened troops, fled with as many as he could collect together, and took refuge in a strong fort called *Loaghur*,[vii] which stood near Macawal;[36] whither the royal army pursued them, and surrounding the fort began to lay siege to it.

In the mean time the Shah, hearing that Loaghur was invested, marched on as expeditiously as possible, and without halting, at Dehly, joined the camp of the Vizier and Sultan Kouly Khan, before Loaghur. By the time that the siege had lasted a month, the besieged finding their provisions and ammunition fail them, and being determined to sell their lives as dear as possible, they sallied out of the fort sword in hand.—A desperate, but unequally conflict ensued; the greater part of the Sicks were cut in pieces on the spot; many were taken prisoners, in which number was their leader Bundah,[37] who was confined in an iron cage, and together with the other prisoners was sent to Dehly, where they were all publickly executed, after having been offered their lives on condition of embracing the Mussulman faith, which they rejected with contempt. The few remaining Sicks fled to the mountains, where they concealed themselves; and the Zemindars and Riots of the country who had joined them during their insurrection, partly to secure themselves, and partly for the sake of plunder, now cut off their beards and hair,[38] and returned to their original occupations.

From this time, during the reigns of Behader Shah, Jehander Shah, Ferocksir, and the short reigns of Rafi al Dirjat, and his brother, Abdul Summud Khan being Subadar of Lahore, none of this sect ever ventured to appear in arms; but concealed themselves by every means for near twelve years.

(AH 1131/ AD 1718) In the year of the Hegira 1131, Mahammud Shah being on the throne, and Zekariah Khan being Subadar of Lahore, the Sicks, though unable to appear in any considerable force, began to plunder, and carry on a kind of predatory war in the skirts of the mountains, as if to try the temper of government; and this practice they continued with little variation for twenty years.

(AH 1151/ AD 1738) In the year of Hegira 1151, Nadir Shah the King of Persia, invaded Hindostan, and as his army committed dreadful ravages wherever they went, the inhabitants fled to the hills for safety; while the Subadars of the Provinces, being unable to resist, submitted to the invader.

On this occasion, the Sicks collecting together, began to commit depredations on all sides, possessing themselves of the property of the inhabitants who had fled to avoid the Persians, and plundering every place in their reach.—At the same time they fortified themselves near a village called *Dullival*,[39] on the banks of the *Ravy*, where they were joined by many Zemindars, who had secretly favoured their sect, and now rejoiced to see it once more in a condition to declare itself.

Some time after this, Nadir Shah returned to Persia, having plundered at Dehly, wealth to an almost incredible amount, and having bestowed the Empire of Hindostan on Mahummud Shah, as his own free gift,—He left behind him Nasir Khan, to collect the Subah of Cabul, and four Mahls, (districts) belonging to the Subah of Lahore; (being parts of the Empire of Hindostan, made over to him by the treaty with Mahummud Shah.) The rest of the Subah of Lahore was continued under

---

[vii] This place as well as some others mentioned in the History, having been totally destroyed, are not inserted in the map.

Zekariah Khan, as Subadar, on the part of Mahummud Shah.—Zekariah Khan appointed Adina Beg Khan to be Foujdar of the *Doab* of *Bary*, with orders to reduce the Sicks to obedience.[40]

The force he had with him was fully equal to the execution of that service; but Adina Beg, considering that if he should entirely put an end to all disturbances in that district, there would remain no necessity for continuing him in so extensive a command, he carried on intrigues with the Chiefs of the Sicks, and secretly encouraged them to continue their depredations; at the same time, pretending to be very desirous of subduing them. From this management, the Sicks became daily more powerful, and seized upon several places in the distant parts of the Subah of Lahore. They also began again to perform publick pilgrimages to the Holy Tank at *Amrutsur*, without molestation.

About this time, Zekariah Khan died,[41] leaving two sons, the elder of whom was by the Shah appointed to succeed his father, as Subadar of Lahore; but disputes arising between the two brothers, the affairs of the Province became greatly neglected, and the Sicks increased in strength.

(AH 1151/ AD 1738) Some time before this, Nadir Shah having been assassinated in Persia,[42] Almud Khan Durranny, one of his principal officers, established himself at Kandahar, and seized upon that Province, in which he had considerable family connections; at the same time laying claim to the other[viii] Provinces of Hindostan, which had been ceded to Nadir Shah by the treaty before mentioned, and assuming the title of Shah or King.

Soon after which, he seized upon Nasir Khan, whom Nadir Shah had left Subadar of Cabul, (as said before) together with the treasure which he had collected from the time of Nadir Shah's return to Persia, being above a *crore* of rupees. He also demanded his daughter from him in marriage.—Nasir Khan being then entirely in his power, consented, and obtained liberty to go to his followers who were in *Paishawir*, under pretence of making the necessary preparations:—he was obliged, however, to leave his son as hostage; but as soon as he was at liberty, he considered the giving his daughter to a man of a different tribe, as a disgrace not to be submitted to, and therefore began to collect forces for his own defence. Yet some time after, Almud Shah Durranny, approaching him, though with a very inferior army, his followers dispersed, and Nasir Khan fled towards Dehly, which furnished Ahmud Shah Durranny with a plea for his first invasion of Hindostan. He accordingly passed the Attock, Jelum, and Chenab, and came to Lahore.[43]

(AH 1159/ AD 1746) Shah Nevaz Khan, (one of the sons of Zekariah Khan) who was then Subadar of Lahore, immediately submitted; and the Durranny Shah entering the city of Lahore, seized upon the treasury and the armoury there, and proclaimed himself master of that Province also.

(AH 1160/ AD 1747) It is foreign from the design of this history, to enter into a detail of these events, which are all related in the general history of the empire; suffice it to say, that the Durranny Shah was at length obliged to return to Kandahar; and that in the year of the Hegira 1160, Mahummud Shah having died, was succeeded by his son Ahmed Shah, who nominated *Mir Munnoo*, called *Moin ul Mullock*, son to the late Vizier *Kummer ul dien Khan*, to the Subadary of Lahore and Multan.

During these troubles, the Sick Chiefs Jessa Sing Kelal, Chirsah Sing, Tokah Sing, and Kirwar Sing,[44] had got together about 5000 horse; to which army they (for the

---

[viii] These were Cabul, Paishawar, and Tatta: in a word, every thing west of the Attock, or Indus.

first time) gave the title of *Dul Khalsah Gee*,[45] or the Army of the State, and with which they made themselves masters of the *Doab of Bary.*—Moin ul Mullock again appointed Adina Beg Khan to the Foujdary of that Doab; who marching thither, began as formerly to intrigue with the Sicks, and took no effectual means to suppress them. In one action indeed, he defeated them, and killed about 600 Sicks; but as the confusion prevailing in the empire, had reduced thousands of people to distress, they were daily joining the Sicks for the sake of plunder took the *Poil*, and let their hair grow, upon which they were inrolled in the *Dul*, which now began to encrease with surprising rapidity.[ix]

(AH 1163/ AD 1750) About three years after this, Ahmed Shah Durranny, again invaded Hindostan,[46] and having defeated Moin ul Mullock, seized on Lahore, levied a very heavy contribution from it, and afterwards appointed Moin ul Mullock to be Subadar on his part of Lahore and Multan, having given the daughter of Moin ul Mullock in marriage to his own son, the Prince Timur Shah: after this, the Durranny Shah returned to Kandahar.

During this war, Adina beg Khan having joined Moin ul Mullock with all his forces, the Sicks had nothing left to oppose them, and therefore they daily became more formidable. They cut off the royal garrison in the Fort of Tanniser, destroyed the fort, and plundered all the neighbouring districts.

After the departure of the Durranny Shah, Moin ul Mullock again sent Adina Beg Khan against the Sicks, who seemed now to be inclined to discharge his duty with fidelity, for having received intelligence that they were assembled near Macowal, to celebrate the festival of the *Hooly*,[47] he, by a forced march, surprised them, and put so many of them to death, that the remainder were obliged to disperse for a while, but soon began to plunder again in small parties.

(AH 1165/ AD 1752) In the year of the Hegira 1165, Moin ul Mullock died,[48] and his widow appointed one Beckary Khan, to manage the government of her deceased husband, as Naib (or deputy) on her part; but having detected him in a design to seize on her person, and usurp the government himself, she caused him to be strangled: and appointed *Syed Jumeil ul dien Khan* to the office of her Naib.

A short time after this, the troubles arising at Dehly, which ended in the Vizier Ghazi ul dien Khan's deposing Ahmed Shah, and raising to the throne Alumgire Sani, the reins of government became entirely relaxed, and the Sicks gathered new strengths.

(AH 1169/ AD 1755) In the year of the Hegira 1169, Ahmed Shah Durranny again invaded Hindostan, and came to Lahore.[49]—By this time, the Sicks were become very numerous, and their *Dul* was in the neighbourhood of Lahore; but they were afraid to attack the Durranny army: however, they plundered all people who straggled from the camp, and cut off provisions going to it.—But the Durranny Shah being desirous of getting as soon as possible to Dehly, took no notice of these insults.

After plundering Dehly, Muttra, and all the circumjacent towns and villages, and exercising unheard of barbarities, the Durranny Shah marched back to Kandahar; leaving a chief of the name of Ahmed Khan, to command in Sirhind, and his own son, the Prince Timur Shah, with an army under the command of Jehan Khan, one of his best officers, to collect the Subahs of Lahore and Multan.

(AH 1169/ AD 1755) Jehan Khan from a principle of religious zeal, destroyed the places of worship belonging to the Sicks at *Amrutsur*,[50] and filled up the sacred Tank, which they so highly venerate: upon which the Sicks collected together under their

---

[ix] This naturally accounts for the rapid rise of the Sicks, which commenced about this time.

chiefs from all quarters, and blockading the city of Lahore, collected the revenues of the country all round for their own use. Jehan Khan with the Prince, marched out to give them battle; but after several actions, finding the Sicks too numerous for him to contend with, he retreated to Kandahar.

Upon this occasion, Jessa Sing Kelal, who was at the time commander in chief of the *Dul*, struck rupees in his own name, at the royal mint at Lahore, with the following inscription, "Jessa Kelal conquered the country of Ahmed, and struck this coin by the Grace of God."

After the retreat of Jehan Khan, the Court of Dehly appointed Adina Beg Khan to be Subadar of Lahore; but the force with which he was furnished by so weak a government, was not equal to encountering the Sicks: he was therefore obliged to stop at Sirhind; and finding that he could not obtain any assistance from the administration at Dehly, he applied to the Marhatta chief Rogonaut Row, who at that time commanded a large army in the Province of Agra, and offered to assist him in reducing Punjab; to which the Marhatta chief agreed, and marched to Sirhind; where he was joined by Adina Beg Khan with his own army, and some of the inferior Sick chiefs, whom he had brought over by great promises.

(AH 1169/ AD 1755) The first operation was to expel and plunder Ahmed Khan, whom the Durranny Shah had left to command in Sirhind.—On this occasion the Sick chiefs, who had joined Adina Beg Khan, plundered the town of Sirhind; which gave great offence to the Marhatta chiefs, who projected falling upon the Sicks, and plundering them in return: which coming to the knowledge of Adina Beg Khan, by whose influence these Sicks had been induced to join the Marhattas, he gave them immediate notice of the design which was formed against them, upon which, they marched away in the night.

The Sick leaders who were in possession of Lahore, did not think their army a match for the Marhattas, when reinforced by Adina Beg Khan, they therefore drew off to the skirts of the mountains; and the Marhattas established garrisons in Lahore, Multan, &c. But their government was of short duration, for soon after this, attempting to expel the Rohillas from their possessions, *Nujeab ul Doulah*, the principal Rohilla chief, applied to the Durranny Shah for assistance:—alledging, that being his subjects,[x] they could apply to no one else for redress; and that, therefore, they entreated he would support them against the infidels.

Ahmed Shah Durranny accordingly left Kundahar,[51] with his whole force; and as soon as it was known that he had crossed the Attock, all the Marhatta garrisons in Lahore and Multan, fled without waiting for his nearer approach.

(AH 1172/ AD 1758) The Vizier Ghazi ul dien Khan, who kept his Majesty Alumgire Sani as a prisoner in his own palace, expecting that the Durranny Shah would call him to a severe account, if Alumgire Sani should complain to him; in a transport of rage and despair he put him to death: and after placing another of the royal line upon the throne, by the title of Shah Jehan Sani, he left Dehly with all his forces, and joined the Marhatta army, which was then besieging the Rohillas at *Sukertall*.

The events of this campaign are foreign to our subject, it is only necessary to say, that the Durranny Shah having raised the siege of Sukertall, and defeated the Marhatta chiefs Junkoo and Mulhar Row in several actions, in one of which, Dattea Pateel (the elder brother of Mahado Row Sindea) was killed; and being joined by all

---

[x] All the Rohilla tribes come from the country belonging to the Durranny Shāh, and those settled in Hindostan, still call him their King.

the Rohilla chiefs, as also by the Navab Shuja ul Dowla, cantoned for the rainy season near *Coel* in the Doab, between the Ganges and the Jumna.

(AH 1173/ AD 1759) While Ahmed Shah Durranny remained at Coel, he received advice, that Adina Beg Khan, whom he had once more appointed, Subadar of Lahore, was dead,[52] and that the Sicks taking advantage of that event, had assembled in great numbers, attacked and defeated *Sumbu das*, the Dewan of Adina Beg Khan, who after his master's death had attempted to keep things in order.—On this intelligence, the Durranny Shah appointed Zien Khan to be Foujdar of Sirhind, and Bullund Khan to be Subadar of Lahore, and dispatched them to their stations with an army of 10,000 horse.

The conclusion of the rains was followed by that famous campaign, which put to final trial the grand question of EMPIRE between the Mussulmans, and Marhattas; and ending by the fatal battle of *Paniput*, which was fought on the 20th of Jemad ul Sani 1174, decided it in favour of the Mussulmans, and gave a blow to the Marhatta power, which it has not entirely recovered yet.

After this, Ahmed Shah Durranny, having settled the government at Dehly in the hands of Nujeib ul Doula, and placed *Mirza Jewan Buckt* on the throne, as representative of his father *Shah Alum*, who was then in Bengal, he marched back towards Kandahar.

As soon as he had passed the Suttedge, the Sicks began to plunder the stragglers from his camp, which he forebore to resent at that time, his army being loaded with plunder; however, to secure his camp from insult, he every night threw up a slight work round it, and in this manner he continued his march to the Attock, the Sicks following him all the way.

When the Durranny army had passed the Attock, the Sicks returned, and having blockaded Lahore, they compelled Bullund Khan to retreat with his garrison, upon which they took possession of that city, and all the country from the Attock to Sirhind.

However, Zein Khan, whom the Durranny Shah had left as Foujdare of Sirhind, being assisted by Hinghun Khan, a pattan chief, of the district of Malnair (south west from Sirhind) still supported himself against them.

(AH 1175/ AD 1761) The following year, the Sicks to the number of about forty thousand horse, ravaged the whole territory of Malnair, in revenge for the assistance given by Hinghun Khan to the Durranny Aumil; but soon after Ahmed Shah Durranny having marched to Lahore to punish the Sicks, for having expelled Bullund Khan, Hinghun Khan contrived in the night to escape, and fled to the Duranny camp for protection.—The Durranny Shah sent thirty thousand horse under his conduct, who marching seventy crores (one hundred and forty miles) almost without[xi] intermission, suprized the army of the Sicks, at a place called *Barnala*, and put great numbers to the sword;[53] the rest as usual, dispersed for a time; after which, the Shah proceeded to Sirhind, where he was met by Nujeib ul Dowla, and the other principal *Omrahs*; and having received their compliments, returned back to Kandahar, leaving Saudet yab Khan, one of his officers, with a large detachment in the Doab of Beit Jalinder, and Rajah *Cabully Mul*, as Subadar of Lahore.

(AH 1176/ AD 1762) The beginning of the following year, the Sicks assembling again, drove Rajah Cabully Mul out of Lahore, and Saudet yab Khan, from the Doab

---

[xi] The horses used by the Durrannies, are of the breed called Turki; they are not large, but the most useful, quiet and best bottomed horses, that are I believe in the world.—They live to a great age, so that I have seen horses in the use of common troopers, that they have declared to be near forty years old.

of Beit Jalinder, establishing themselves in both those places; after which they invaded Malnair, defeated and killed Hinghun Khan, a man of great courage and ability, who had long been a considerable check to their progress in that quarter.

They next attacked Sirhind, and coming to action with Zien Khan, the Durranny Foujdar, near Rajah Seray, defeated and killed him also; after which they plundered and burnt Sirhind, having a particular enthusiastick hatred to that place, on account of the murder of Gooroo Gobind's children, which was perpetrated there. By these successes, the whole country form the Attock to Karnal, acknowledged the authority of the Sicks.[54]

(AH 1177/ AD 1763) The following year Nujeib ul Dowla being engaged in a war with *Surujh Mul*, the Rajah of the Jauts, the Sick chiefs, Koshial Sing, Bugheil Sing, Sahib Sing, Baug Sing, Kurrum Sing, and Roy Sing,[55] crossed the Jumna with their forces, and plundered the district of Saharunpoor belonging to Nujeib ul Dowla; upon which that chief immediately marched to protect his own country, and partly by force, partly by negociation, got the Sicks to repass the Jumna.

(AH 1178/ AD 1764) The next year *Jewar Sing*, the son and successor of *Surujh Mul*, in order to revenge the death of his father, who had been killed the year before in battle against Nujeib ul Dowla, collected together all his own followers, and being reinforced by thirty thousand Marhattas under Mulhar Row, and twenty-five thousand Sicks under several different chiefs,[56] laid siege to the city of Dehly.—The siege lasted three months; in which time Nujeib ul Dowla, having written advice of his situation to Almed Shah Duranny, and solicited his aid, his Majesty immediately marched from Cabul where he then was, and to avoid any interruption from the Sicks, he proceeded along the skirts of the mountains, and had reached as far as *Gurry Kotanah*, when a peace was concluded between Nujeib ul Dowla and Jewar Sing, through the mediation of Mulhar Row, and the siege of Dehly was raised. Nujeib ul Dowla immediately sent intelligence of this to the Duranny Shah, and after expressing his gratitude for the ready assistance his Majesty had afforded him, he entreated him to return from the place which he was then at, least the arrival of his army in the neighbourhood of Dehly, should renew the calamities of that unhappy city.—The Durranny Shah, according to this address, repassed the Sutledge, and marched back towards his own country by the Lahore road.

In the mean time, the Sick chiefs, determined to revenge the defeat they had suffered at Barnala,—assembled their whole force at Amrutsur, to the number of sixty thousand horse and foot; and took an oath to exert every effort to cut off the Shah's army. Almed Shah Durranny receiving advice of this, sent a person to the Sick leaders in quality of Ambassador, to negociate a peace with them, and prevent that effusion of blood, which their desperate determination threatened to produce;—but on the arrival of this person in the camp of the Sicks, instead of listening to his proposals, they plundered him and his followers, and drove them away.—Almed Shah Durranny finding all accommodation impossible, marched immediately to give battle to the Sicks; and coming to Amrutsur in the evening, encamped close to the enemy. In the morning the Sicks drew up their army on foot, and immediately proceeded to attack the Durrannies sword in hand; and the Durrannies, with equal resolution, received their attack on foot also. The battle was long and bloody,[57] and the loss so great on both sides, that at length both armies drew off to their respective camps; the next morning neither party was inclined to renew the conflict, and the Shah resumed his march without any further interruption.[xii]

[xii] It is to be supposed, that in a battle thus disputed, both sides claimed the victory; the Durrannies bring in proof, their having marched on unmolested; the Sicks, that the Durranny Shāh never again returned to Lahore.

Some time after this, Ahmed Shah Durranny died, and was succeeded by his son the Prince Timur Shah, who has been too much employed on the side of Persia in keeping possession of the provinces usurped by his father from that empire, to have leisure for attempting to reduce the power of the Sicks.—Nor has any Potentate yet appeared on the side of Hindostan, equal to such a task:—some feeble attempts have been made, which have only confirmed the strength of the Sicks Government, as a little water thrown on a fire, does but increase its heat: so that for twenty years past, they have employed themselves in completely reducing the whole country from Attock to Karnal, and dividing it among their own sect.

(AH 1178/ AD 1764) Soon after the last expulsion of the Aumils of the Durranny Shah, the Sicks held a general Diet at Amrutsur, in which they determined to call in the rupees which were struck in the name of Jessa Kelal, and to strike them for the future in the name of their *Gooroos*, with an inscription to this effect, "*Gooroo Gobind Sing*, received from *Nanuck*, the *Daig*,[xiii] the sword and rapid victory," which coin is current throughout their dominions to this day.

Thus has the Divine pleasure notified to Gooroo Gobind, been at length fulfilled; and thus has Providence raised up this sect in consideration of the piety and charity of Gooroo Nanuck its founder, that mankind beholding the reward of virtue, may learn to practise it.

THUS far the Persian manuscript extends;[58] to which I beg leave to add, that the Sicks are the only one of the many powers who have enriched themselves out of the spoils of the Mogul Empire, which fairly and openly avows its independence.—They will not suffer the name of his Majesty Shah Alum to appear upon their coin; but have substituted that of their Gooroo; and instead of the year of the King's reign, and of the Hegira, which is the established date on all the coin throughout the empire, they use the era of *Bickermajeet*, called the *Sumbut*.[59]

1779: After Ahmed Shah Durranny returned to Kandahar in 1764, as has been related, though the Sicks possessed themselves of the town and province of Lahore, and of all the open country of Multan, yet the Durranny garrison of Multan still remained in that fortress till the death of Ahmed Shah Durranny: soon after which, the Sicks compelled them to retire, and placed a garrison of their own there;—But in the year 1779, Timur Shah (the successor to Ahmed Shah Duranny) came from Cabul, with a large army, and laying siege to Multan, took it, after defeating the army sent by the Sicks to raise the siege: when he returned to Cabul, leaving a garrison in Multan, which has remained there ever since.

1785: Since the complete settlement of the Sicks in their present possessions, which was not entirely effected till near the year 1770, the chiefs to the westward of the Sutledge, who are the most powerful, have not been engaged in any important expedition, till the year 1785, when they invaded the Rajah of Jumboo, and compelled him to pay them tribute.

The incursions which are made annually into the territories lately belonging to Zabita Khan, are merely effected by a temporary confederacy of the chiefs between the Sutledge and the Jumna.

These incursions are sometimes carried across the Ganges,[xiv] into the Vizier's territories, as happened in March 1785; when a large body of Sicks passed over, and remained in that country several days, plundering to an immense amount, and

---

[xiii] This has been explained in the Introduction, I have several of these rupees in my possession.

[xiv] From the middle of March till June, the Ganges is fordable in several places between the falls at Hurdwar, and the town of Ferockabad.

burning and destroying the villages without opposition; though repeated advice had been received beforehand of their designs. But these insults may always be prevented, by common attention in the Vizier's administration; and by sending proper detachments to the several fords of the Ganges during the dry season.

In 1785, Mahajee Scindea (having before seized on the Shah's person, and the entire administration of his affairs) entered into an alliance with the leaders of the Sicks, between the Sutledge and the Jumna, both offensive and defensive: one of the articles of which treaty expressly says as follows;—"Besides the royal lands, whatever shall be acquired by either party (Scindea or the Sicks) with mutual consent, *on either side the Jumna*, from Hindoos or Mussulmans, one third thereof shall belong to the *Khalsah Gee*—" (the Sick State.) This clearly points at the Vizier's country.

As soon as this treaty was framed, I obtained a copy of it, which I transmitted to Mr. Macpherson,[60] then acting as Governor General, April the 9th. What use he made of the information, I cannot tell: but surely a confederacy of two such formidable powers as the Sicks and Marhattas, close to the Vizier's frontier, must afford matter for very serious apprehension, to every person who is anxious for the safety of the Company's possessions in India; which are so intimately connected with those of the Vizier, that prosperity or calamity must be in common to them both.[61]

In this point of view, I beg leave to conclude this sketch, with my earnest recommendation of that circumstance to the attention of the Company's administration:— for even admitting all that the advocates for Scindea can say of his sincerity, he is but mortal; and with him will expire all that security which has been supposed to arise from his personal character.

NOTES

1. Singh, *Early European Accounts*, 535.
2. Gupta, *History of the Sikhs*, 3: 172–3, 186.
3. Ibid., 2: 173–8.
4. McLeod, *Historical Dictionary of Sikhism*, 81.
5. Irfan Habib trans., Inayatullah Khan, "Documents on the Sikhs and Gurū Gobind Singh: From *Ahkam-I Ālamgīri*, 1703–7," in *Sikh History from Persian Sources*, ed. J.S. Grewal and Irfan Habib, 97.
6. Gupta, *History of the Sikhs*, 2: 4–6; Khushwant Singh, *A History of the Sikhs*, 2 vols. (Princeton, NJ: Princeton University Press, 1963, 1966. Revised edition, Delhi: Oxford University Press, 1991), 2: 4–6.
7. Singh, *Life of Banda Singh Bahadur*, 10–14.
8. Surjit Singh Gandhi, *Sikhs in the Eighteenth Century* (Amritsar: Singh Bros., 1999), 33.
9. Dastur-ul-Insha, 6a; Ruqat-I-Nawāb Amin-ud-Daulā, Rupa No. 3 quoted in Singh, *Life of Banda Singh Bahadur*, 49–50.
10. The Persian document that Browne refers to is a Persian translation of the *Risālā-i-Nānak* by Budh Singh Arorā and Lālā Ajāib Singh Sūraj.
11. *Devanāgrī* or Sanskrit script.
12. The Persian translation of this manuscript is now lodged at the British Museum, London.
13. Browne alludes to the confederations or *misls* (q.v.) that formed Sikh governance over Punjab periodically throughout the latter half of the eighteenth century. At the time of his writing this account (1785), the leaders of the major *misls* would have been Bhāg Singh of the Āhlūvālīā *misl* (see illustration 7),

Tārā Singh Ghaibā of the Dallevālīā *misl* (see illustration 6), Khushāl Singh of the Singhpurīā *misl*, Baghel Singh of the Karorasinghīā *misl*, Mohar Singh of the Nishānānvālī *misl*, Karam Singh of the Shahīdī *misl*, Gulāb Singh of the Bhangī *misl*, Jai Singh of the Kanhaiyā *misl* (see illustration 4), Jassā Singh Rāmgharīā of the Rāmgharīā *misl*, Mahā Singh of the Sukkarchakkīā *misl*, Sāhib Singh of Patiālā, Gajpat Singh of Jīnd, and Hamīr Singh of Nābhā.

14. *Gurmatā* (q.v.). During the eighteenth century, *Gurmatās* were regularly held at the times of the two main festivals, *Baisākhī* and *Divālī*.

15. Jassā Singh Āhlūvālīā (q.v.).

16. Known in numismatic circles as the *Gobind Shāhi*, the coin bears the inscription from the seals, *hukamnāmās*, and *farmāns* of Gurū Gobind Singh and later, Bandā Bahādur. The couplet used on the Gobind Shāhi coins was "*Deg Teg O Fateh Nusrat Be-dirang, Yaft Az Nānak Gurū Gobind Singh.*" Jyoti Rai, "The Divine Coinage of the Sikhs," *The Sikh Messenger* (April 1999), 39–43.

17. These men were all associated with the powerful Bhangī *misl*.

18. Most *Gurmatās* did take place at the Akāl Takht (q.v.) in Amritsar. This was largely for logistical reasons as it was the place where, twice a year on *Baisākhī* and *Divālī* the Sikh *misaldārs* would meet, so a *Gurmatā* would be inevitable.

19. *Rākhī* (q.v.).

20. There is a peculiar section of the Sikh community called *Siklīgar* Sikhs. They are ironsmiths who have specialized in the craft of constructing and polishing weapons. The *Siklīgars* first came into contact with Sikhism in the early seventeenth century when they were drafted in by Gurū Hargobind to meet his ever increasing military requirements.

21. *Karā* (q.v.).

22. What follows is the English rendering of the Persian translation of *Risālā-i-Nānak* that was prepared for Browne by Budh Singh Arorā and Lālā Ajāib Singh Sūraj.

23. Gurū Nānak was born into a Bedī family, a subcaste of the *Khatrīs*. The word *Khatrī* is a prakritized form of the Sanskrit *kashatrīyā*, which is the warrior caste in Hindu society; this is the likely cause of confusion in this case. *The Encyclopaedia of Sikhism*, s.v. "Bedī"; Denzil Ibbetson, *Punjab Castes* (Lahore: 1916, reprint Lahore: Sang-e-Meel Publications, 1994), 247.

24. Gurū Nānak was born and lived throughout most of his life in the village of Talwandī Rāi Bhoe, now named Nankānā Sāhib and situated about forty miles from Lahore. Khushwant Singh, *A History of the Sikhs*, 1: 30.

25. The *Prān Sanglī*, literally the chain of breath or vital air, is often attributed to Gurū Nānak but is more likely apocryphal, concerning itself largely with yogic practices, particularly breath control. An eclectic collection of writings that run to some eighty chapters, it is structured as a series of expositions of Gurū Nānak as a response to a question posed by Rājā Shivnabh of Sanglādīp (Sri Lanka), where the *Prān Sanglī* is said to have been composed. Liturgical tradition testifies that Gurū Arjan despatched Bhāi Pairā Mokhā to Sanglādīp to procure a copy of the manuscript during the time of the compilation of the Ādi Granth. On scrutiny by the Gurū it was deemed unauthentic. *The Encyclopaedia of Sikhism*, s.v. "Prān Sanglī."

26. This is an early reference to *gurdwārā* Sīs Ganj in the Chāndnī Chowk area of Old Delhi. In March 1783, and with the full agreement of the Mughal emperor, Shāh Ālum II, Baghel Singh Karorasinghīā entered Delhi and commenced building seven *gurdwārās* connected with the Sikh Gurūs.

Baghel Singh did not know the exact location where Gurū Tegh Bahādur had been beheaded though he was aware that it was near a mosque in Chāndnī Chowk. Fortunately, an aged Muslim water-carrier woman informed him that her father, who had washed the place after the Gurū's execution, had told her that the Gurū sat on a wooden *chaukī* (seat) facing east inside the compound wall of the mosque, and his head had fallen in front of him. Accordingly a portion of the wall was pulled down and the *gurdwārā* was built in the compound. Gupta, *History of the Sikhs*, 3: 169.

27. The Gurū was nine years old when his father was executed in 1675, and was then known as Gobind Rāi, the name Singh being taken in 1699 on the establishment of the Khālsā.

28. Browne does not correct the mistakes about the Gurū's place of death, which was in 1708 at Nānded in the present day state of Mahārāshtrā, some three years after the death of the two younger sons mentioned later in the account.

29. Gurū Gobind Singh's first wife, Mātā Jīto, died in 1700 but his other two wives, Mātā Sundarī (d. 1747) and Mātā Sāhib Devā (died between 1734 and 1747), both survived their husband.

30. The *Sāhibzādās* (Princes), which was the title all the Gurūs' sons were known by, were Zorāwar Singh and Fateh Singh, aged nine and six respectively, when they were captured.

31. Suchānand (d. 1710) was a *Khatrī* official in the court of Nawāb Wazīr Khān. Macauliffe (*The Sikh Religion*, 196) states that Suchānand was the official who uttered the fatal words "the progeny of a serpent shall grow up as serpents, and therefore should not be spared" at the wavering Wazīr Khān, thus sealing the fate of Zorāwar Singh and Fateh Singh, the two youngest sons of Gurū Gobind Singh. *The Encyclopaedia of Sikhism*, s.v. "Suchchānand."

32. Ganda Singh and Teja Sigh, *A Short History of the Sikhs* (Bombay: Orient Longmans, 1950. Reprint, Patiālā: Punjabi University, 1989), 69 n. 1 notes that Kesar Singh Chhibbar's *Bansāvalīnāmā Dasān Padshāhīān dā* (1780) and Sukhā Singh's *Gurbilās Pādshāhī Dasvīn* (1797), two early Sikh historical narratives on the life of the tenth Gurū, state that the method of execution was actually bricking alive followed by beheading.

33. Bandā Bahādur (q.v.) was a follower of *Bairāgī* Rām Dās before he met Gurū Gobind Singh. *Bairāgīs* or *Vairāgīs* are a sect of Hindu ascetics, eschewing colour or passion and detached from all worldly attachments. Founded in the twelfth century, the sect comprises of a class of itinerant penitents living a secluded life of extreme poverty, wearing few clothes and living on begging. Ibbetson, *Punjab Castes*, 227.

34. Emperor Bahādur Shāh (q.v.).

35. The term "Buckshy" or *bakhshī* would indicate that Kisury Singh was a paymaster of a military body although there is no recorded information on this individual.

36. Mākhowāl is the original name for Anāndpur Sāhib, the main residence of Gurū Gobind Singh.

37. Bandā Bahādur actually evaded capture at *Lohgarh* (q.v.), but was captured after an eight-month siege at Gurdās-Nangal near Gurdāspur in December 1715.

38. It is accepted that a large following gathered around Bandā Singh after his entry into the Punjab, many purely for the hope of gaining financially through plunder and pillage. In this light, this statement is likely to be true for these

types of followers. This is in stark contrast to those Sikhs who remained faithful to their cause and suffered the ordeals of imprisonment, torture, and execution with their leader at the hands of the Mughal authorities. See Surman in part II, chapter 4.

39. This was a small mud fort conveniently situated in the centre of a dense forest to the northwest of Amritsar on the bank of the river Rāvī.

40. "They (Sikhs) established themselves in the Bari Doab under the leadership of Bhag Singh Ahluwalia. They stopped the traffic, plundered and raided a large number of villages and towns and exacting heavy tributes from the neighbouring zemindars. Jassa Singh Ahluwalia, the son of Bhag Singh's sister, a handsome and courageous youth, was his uncle's deputy and exercised full authority over matters and things concerning Bhag Singh. The other Sikh chiefs also accepted the leadership of the Ahluwalia Sardar and willingly worked under him. Thus the administration of the whole Doab seemed, at the time, to be passing into the hands of the Sikhs." Sohan Lal Suri, *An Outstanding Original Source of Panjab History: Umdat-ut-Tawarikh*, trans. V.S. Suri (Delhi: S. Chand, 1961), 109.

41. This was in July 1745.

42. This happened in June 1747.

43. Ahmad Shāh Abdālī arrived at Shāhdārā near Lahore in January 1748.

44. Jassā Sing Kelāl is Jassā Singh Āhlūvālīā (q.v.); Chirsah Sing is possibly Charhat Singh Sukkarchakkīā (q.v.); Tokah Sing is likely to be a reference to Jassā Singh Rāmgharīā (q.v.); Kirwar Sing is a name that is not recorded and has no obvious variants, which suggests he was probably the leader of a smaller contingent outside the recognized and well-documented *misl* hierarchy.

45. The collective of all Sikh *misls* (q.v.).

46. Ahmad Shāh's third invasion commenced in December 1751 and lasted for four months. Notably Dīwān Kaurā Mall, Muin's most trusted officer and an ally of the Sikhs, was killed in an engagement following a siege of Lahore by Ahmad Shāh in March 1752.

47. *Holī* was celebrated in force by the Sikhs as *Hollā Mohallā* on the day following the colorful festival.

48. This was in November 1753.

49. In his fourth invasion, Ahmad Shāh arrived at Lahore in December 1756.

50. The date of the Durrānī's desecration of the Harimandar Sāhib is generally given as November 1757 rather than 1755 as stated by Browne. Jahān Khān was the *Wazīr*, or deputy, of Prince Timur, Ahmad Shāh Durrānī's son. The battle preceding this event is described by Tahmās Khān who was present throughout. In his description he makes mention of the five-man group headed by the famous Bābā Dīp Singh who gained the appellation *Shahīd* or martyr, following his fearless exploits in his last battle, at the age of seventy five, protecting the Harimandar Sāhib against the 5,000-strong army of Jahān Khān. "The victorious army closely pursued them [the Sikhs] to Chak Guru [Amritsar]. The Wazir stood at a spot there. Five Sikhs on foot were seen standing at the gate of the Chak. The [Afghān] troops made a sally and killed them. Mir Ni'mat Khan, one of the notables of Lahore, attained martyrdom at that place. The camp of the victorious army was established there." Irfan Habib trans., "Re-emergence of Sikh Power in the Punjab, 1784–64: From Tahmās Khān, *Qissa-i Tahmās-i Miskīn* or *Tahmās Nāma*," in ed. J.S. Grewal

and I. Habib, *Sikh History from Persian Sources* (New Delhi: Tulika, 2001), 176.

51. Ahmad Shāh commenced his fifth invasion in the Autumn of 1759 and reached Lahore in October.

52. Ādīnā Beg Khān actually died in September 1758, almost a year before Ahmad Shāh's fifth invasion.

53. The *waddā ghallūghāra* or great holocaust in which 20,000–30,000 Sikhs were slain by Ahmad Shāh in February 1762.

54. The Sikhs gained their important victory at Sirhind in January 1764.

55. These *Sirdārs* were Khushhāl Singh Singhpuriā (nephew of Nawāb Kapūr Singh of Faizullāpur), Baghel Singh Karorasinghiā, Sāhib Singh Bhangī, Bhāg Singh of Jīnd, Karam Singh Nirmalā, and Rāi Singh Bhangī of Būriā. They all had territories below the Sutlej and went south and east for their incursions into neighboring territories. Tahmās Khān who fought against the Sikhs in these campaigns in the army of Najīb ud-Daulā writes: "The Sikhs after having completed their occupation and settlement of Sirhind district in one year made a further advance. In that year 40,000 of their horsemen crossed the Jamuna and disturbed and looted the Saharanpur and Meerut districts. Nawab Najib Khan, for a month or two, moved in every direction where the Sikhs were reported to be roving, in order to protect the country, and fought and usually defeated them. As they did not make a firm stand anywhere and offer battle, he had to run back after them, but they did not give up their jackal tricks." *Tahmās Nāmā*, Tahmās Khān, as quoted in Gupta, *History of the Sikhs*, 3: 48.

56. The Sikhs arrived in Delhi in January 1765. The biographer of Najīb ud-Daulā was an eyewitness to the fighting methods employed by the Sikhs. "The Rohillas engaged the Sikhs with their matchlocks. The musketry fight continued briskly till two *gharis* after nightfall. Mian Niaz Gul, a *risaldar* of Najib, was wounded with a bullet. The Rohilla infantry plied their muskets well. Najib told his men to fire their rockets wherever the Sikh horsemen were standing crowded in a knot, so that they were scattered by the rockets. At some places fighting took place and many Sikhs were wounded. About the time of sunset, a Sikh who wore silver armour, fell down from his horse and the Sikhs wished to carry his corpse off, while the Rohillas, desiring to seize his property, attempted to detain the body. Here the battle raged furiously; three Rohillas were slain and seven wounded, while many of the Sikhs were also wounded. At last, the Rohillas with drawn swords dragged the corpse away. A pouch was found in his belt, containing gold coins, valued at Rs. 1,000. In this manner fighting with the Sikhs went on for nearly one month." *Tarikh-e-Najīb-ud-daula*, Sayid Nūr-ud-Dīn Hussain Khān, ff. 84b–5a quoted in Gupta, *History of the Sikhs*, 3: 50.

57. It was during the winter of 1764 that Ahmad Shāh Abdālī invaded India for the seventh time. He advanced upon Amritsar and came face to face with Gurbakhsh Singh Nihang of the Shahīdi *misl* (following the death of Dīp Singh in 1757) at the head of only thirty men who had stayed behind in the deserted city to face the invading Afghāns. According to Ratan Singh Bhangū, *Prachīn Panth Prakāsh*, "Bhai Gurbakhsh Singh, with garlands round his neck and sword on his shoulder, dressed himself as a bridegroom, his men forming the marriage party, waiting eagerly to court the bride-death." *The Encyclopaedia of Sikhism*, s.v. "Gurbakhsh Singh, Bhāī."

58. The final paragraphs are endnotes added by Browne and are not part of the original Persian text. The treaty that Browne refers to was between the Marāthās and the Khālsā (represented by *Sirdār* Baghel Singh and others). These treaties, between the Sikhs and Marāthās and the alliance of the Sikhs and the East India Company, proposed in May 1785 never came to fruition.

59. The common system of reckoning dates by chroniclers and historians in North India is called *Bikramī Sammat*. The origins of the *Bikramī* era is generally traced to a Rājā Vikramdityā (or Bikramajīt) of Ujjain and it began some fifty-seven years before the Christian era. *The Encyclopaedia of Sikhism*, s.v. "Sikh Calendar."

60. Sir John McPherson, who became acting governor-general of India after the recall of Warren Hastings.

61. Browne need not have worried as the treaty was soon broken since the Sikhs recommenced their established practice of collecting *rākhī* (protection money) as early as June 1785.

CHAPTER 10

RANJĪT SINGH'S CORRESPONDENCE
WITH THE BRITISH, 1803

The most noble and Marquis of Wellesley, *History of All the Events and Transactions which have Taken Place in India: Containing the Negotiations of the British Government, Relative to the glorious Success of the Late War* (London: J. Stockdale, 1805), pp. 133–4; 184–5.

Despite the brevity of remarks by the Marquis of Wellesley, the then governor-general of India, there is considerable detail on the political intrigues between the various Sikh chiefs and the British response to that politicking. Wellesley (1760–1842), a seasoned politician, was no stranger to these underhand practices. He was born Richard Colley, Marquis of Wellesley, at the ancestral home of Dangen Castle in Meath, Ireland. In his privileged position as the first son of landed gentry, his route through formal education was typical; Harrow, Eton, and Christ Church Oxford. Notwithstanding an Irish peerage, he became the second Earl of Mornington on his father's death in 1781; he was eligible for election to the House of Commons where his political career commenced in 1784. An ambitious, well-connected, and tough politician, he rapidly ascended the political ladder from a member of the Board of Control of India as a privileged and precocious twenty-three-year-old to his appointment as governor-general of India aged just thirty-seven, acquiring the title Baron Wellesley.

Equally concerned with increasing British influence in India as with checking French pretensions on the subcontinent, he set about a successful campaign of active intervention in the affairs of the some of the more powerful and independent Mahārājās. His ensuing military ventures were assisted by the considerable skills of his younger brother Arthur, later the first Duke of Wellington. These conflicts chiefly involved the Mahārājās of Mysore and Hyderābād who were actively pursuing alliances with France and countering the hostilities of the Marāthās and Oude kingdoms, and were otherwise frustrating the terms of trade enjoyed by the East India Company. In 1799, now a Marquis, he defeated and killed Tīpū Sultān, leader of Mysore, and later embarked on the Marāthā War (1803–1805), which untimely succeeded in subduing a substantial threat to British domination in Northern India and put the East India Company just a short step from the Punjab. During his governorship, the regions of Mysore, Tanjore, Sūrat, and Carnātic were made subsidiary to the British Government while the independence of Hyderābād and Oudh were significantly reduced.

The Marquis had every right to be proud of his achievement and added with pride the line "*Super Indos protenit Imperium*" (he extended the Empire over the Indians) to his family's achievement of arms. Despite the "glorious success of the late war [1803–1805]" his aggressive exploits and wild spending on "little wars" was causing considerable concern in England. In 1805, just as Ranjīt Singh was facilitating the peace treaty between the British and the Marāthās, Wellesley was recalled to Britain. He found himself answering to Parliament; the Company's debts were colossal—standing in 1806 at £28.5 million—two-thirds of which stemmed from the Marquis's wars.[1]

In a final act of humiliation, the Marquis's replacement was the ailing and aged Lord Cornwallis, the man he had previously succeeded as governor-general of India. Cornwallis was under a strict brief not to engage in any further wars or make any additional annexations. Wellesley went to Spain as ambassador in 1809. He served as foreign secretary (1810–1812) under Spencer Perceval. A supporter of Catholic Emancipation, Wellesley became Lord Lieutenant of Ireland in 1821. He resigned (1828) when his brother, then an opponent of Catholic Emancipation, became Prime Minister, but he served again as Lord Lieutenant for a brief period (1833–1834) after the issue of Catholic Emancipation had been settled.

In this memoir note, the date of Ranjīt Singh's correspondence with the British is significant. Here, some two years prior to the treaty of Amritsar in 1806 with the British, Ranjīt Singh was making overtures on securing his southern border. In these two short paragraphs, the intentions of Ranjīt Singh become increasingly clear. Fearing the British more than his neighboring Phūlkīān Rājās, Ranjīt Singh was playing a strategy of appeasement by offering to the Company, the states of the Phūlkīān Rājās for the price of a peace treaty. There was some doubt in Wellesley's mind as to the legality of Ranjīt Singh's offer. However, the Mahārājā himself would have considered it entirely legitimate, as he had frequently, and quite successfully, quashed Phūlkīān pretensions in the southern part of his territory and by 1805 the Phūlkīān Rājās all but paid tribute to Ranjīt Singh. Presumably, Ranjīt's offer would have extended no further than to offer nonpartisanship to the Sikh Rājās of Patiālā, Jīnd, and Nābhā rather than active support of the British.

---

pp. 133–4

THE SCHEIKS CHIEFS

392. Besides the numerous measures prescribed the Governor General in his different dispatches to the commander in chief, and which have been already spoken of, his

excellency thought it right to annex thereto new instructions, with the view of obtaining the co-operation of the principal chiefs of the tribe of the Scheiks, in the event of a war against the Mahrattas, and to prevail on the Rajah of Puttcalah[2] to oppose the progress of Gholam-Mohamed-Khan in the Rohilconde.

For the detail of these instructions, the Governor General refers your honorable committee to the minutes noted under date 2nd March, 1804, No. 11.

pp. 184–5

SCHEICKS

554. The 392d and 393d paragraphs of this dispatch contain the instructions given by the Governor-general to his excellency the commander in chief, relative to the means of conciliating the friendship of the principal Scheicks chiefs on the engagements to be concluded with them. The nature of the operations of the commander in chief gave him no opportunity to accomplish the end proposed by those instructions. The principal objects were, in fact, obtained by the neutrality of the Scheicks chiefs during the war, which may in a great degree be attributed to the rapid progress and glorious triumphs of the British arms.

555. The commander in chief, however, as has been already stated to your honorable committee in our dispatches of the 25th September, 1803, received proposals on behalf of Runjeet-Sing, rajah of Lahore, to cede to the British government the territory possessed by some chiefs of the tribe of Scheicks, situate south of the river Sutlege, upon condition of a defensive alliance against the respective enemies of those chiefs, and of the British nation.

556. It was not, however, to the advantage of the British government to possess territory in that part, although the power of disposing of it would have facilitated the arrangements which it might have had to make afterwards; but the Governor-general had doubts of the right of the rajah Runjeet-Sing to transfer that territory; and in all events, the Governor-general was apprehensive, that if he disposed of that territory, it would become necessary, for the attainment of his object, to employ force against those chiefs who would not confirm the arrangement, and likewise to alienate those even that the Governor-general had principally in view to conciliate. His excellency, therefore, thought it sufficient that the amicable dispositions of Runjeet-Sing, manifested by his proposals, were encouraged, without concluding any positive engagement with that chief. The Governor-general also received a letter from the rajah Saheb-Sing, chief of Puttecalah, whereby he testified his friendly dispositions to the British government.

NOTES

1. James, *Raj*, 77.
2. Rājā Sāhib Singh of Patiālā (q.v.).

CHAPTER 11

A STATESMAN'S NOTE FROM THE AFGHĀN FRONTIER, 1809

Mountstuart Elphinstone, *An account of the Kingdom of Caubul and its Dependencies in Persia, Tartary and India* (London: 1815), pp. 75–6.

This short extract from Elphinstone's 1815 published work on his embassy to Kābul contains several interesting observations of the Sikhs, in particular, the Sikhs of the North-West Frontier Province and around the Rāwalpindī area. Elphinstone's mission to Kābul in 1808 was motivated by the British desire to exert greater influence over the Shāh and to try to frustrate the designs of the French. Following the success of the mission, Elphinstone was appointed Resident to Poonā and Governor of Bombay for eight years until his retirement in 1827.

His career in India had started off modestly as a seventeen-year-old writer but with his aristocratic roots (his father was eleventh Baron Elphinstone), he quickly rose through the Company ranks. He was stationed in Benares in 1795 and by 1801 was appointed assistant to the resident at the court of Bajo Rāi, the Peshwā at Poonā and later resident at Nāgpur.

Elphinstone's mission to Kābul and his later residency at Bombay established him as an elder statesman and administrator of India. He took his retirement seriously, twice refusing the coveted position of governor-general of India.[1]

Elphinstone's description of the Sikhs of Rāwalpindī as possessing "rough manners" and a "barbarous language" is redolent of early descriptions of Sikh warriors. A much later nineteenth century description of *Holla Mohallā*, the annual Sikh festival at Anandpur Sāhib, illustrates this: "The dark standard of the Anandpur *Gurdwara*, accompanied by Nihangs clad in dark blue clothes and conical head-dresses encircled with steel quoits, is specially worthy of notice. Many of the Nihangs are mounted and rush wildly about, frantically gesticulating and shouting, and bearing themselves as if engaged in defending their standard against a foe."[2]

Elphinstone's remarks on the "barbarity" of language is possibly a reference to the *gargaj bole* (lit. thunderous utterances) peculiar to the Akālī Nihang warriors. This "barbarous" language is one of defiance and optimism that reflects their martial accoutrements and character. The *gargaj bole* utilizes a special vocabulary of euphemisms that makes light of hardships, even in the harshest of conditions and circumstances. The wooden club is *akal dān* (the dispenser of wisdom); a pair of shoes are *athak savārī* (a tireless mount); to die is *charāī karnā* (to invade or set out on an expedition); a person blind in one eye is *lakh netarā* (one with a 100,000 eyes); when one is empty of provisions, he is *mast* (in ecstasy); and the approach of one Akālī Nihang is hailed as the approach of *savā lakh* (an army of 125,000). Another peculiar aspect of the *gargaj bole* has been attributed to Bandā Singh Bahādur. "By his order all nouns in Hindi and Persian having feminine terminations were changed into the masculine form. For instance, *sawari* (a retinue) and *kachari* (a Court-house or office) were pronounced by him and his Sikhs, *sawara* and *kachara*!"[3]

The military man and historian Lt-Col John Malcolm had a more rudimentary explanation for their way of talking: "Talking aloud is so habitual to a Sikh, that he bawls a secret in your ear . . . [It is fair] to impute this boisterous and rude habit to their living almost constantly in a camp, in which their voice certainly loses that nice modulated tone which distinguishes the more polished inhabitants of cities."[4]

---

4 July 1809

We were received by a party of Siks soon after we passed their frontier; and, from this time, we met with no trace of Dooraunee language or manners among the people. Though pleased with the Siks on the borders, we could not but be struck with the rough manners, the barbarous language, and the naked bodies of the people, among whom we were come; nor was it with any partiality that we perceived an increased resemblance to the customs of Hindoostan. In three marches we reached Rawil Pindee.

. . . The town of Rawil Pindee is large and populous. It is a pretty place, is composed of terraced houses, and is very like a town west of the Indus. The country round is open, scattered with single hills, and tolerably cultivated, We halted here for six days to get Runjeet Sing's leave to advance. We now saw a good deal of the Siks, whom we found to be disposed to be civil, and by no means unpleasing. They were manly in their appearance; and were tall, and thin, though muscular. They wore little clothes, their legs, half their thighs, and generally their arms and bodies, being bare; but they had often large scarfs, thrown loosely over one shoulder.[5] Their turbans were not large, but high, and rather flattened in front. Their beards, and hair on their heads and bodies, are never touched by scissars. They generally carry matchlocks, or bows, the better sort generally bows; and never pay a visit without a fine one in their hand, and an embroidered quiver by their side. They speak Punjaubee, and sometimes attempt Hindoostaunee, but I seldom understood them without an interpreter. Persian was quite unknown. They do not know the name of the Dooraunees, though that tribe has often conquered their country. They either call them by the general name of Khorassaunees,[6] or by the erroneous one of Ghiljee.[7]

Notes

1. *Dictionary of Indian Biography*, s.v. "Elphinstone, Montsuart"; Syed Razi Wasti Ed., *Biographical Dictionary of South Asia* (Lahore: Publishers United, 1980), 159.
2. "Hoshiapur District," in *Punjab Gazetteer* (Government of Punjab, 1883–1884), 49–50.
3. Irvine, *Later Mughals*, 111.
4. Lt. Col. John Malcolm, *Sketch of the Sikhs* (London: John Murray, 1812), 129–30.
5. For an example of the type of dress described, see illustration 9 (from Solvyns, part III, chapter 15).
6. The inhabitants of Khorasān.
7. In *Prachīn Panth Prakāsh*, Ratan Singh Bhangū refers to the Afghān invaders as *gilje*, the Punjabī term for vultures.

PART III

TRAVELERS

CHAPTER 12

"SICQUES, TIGERS, OR THIEVES,"
GEORGE FORSTER, 1783

George Forster, *A Journey from Bengal to England, through the Northern Part of India, Kashmire, Afghanistan, and Persia; and into Russia, by the Caspian Sea*, 2 vols. (London: Printed for R. Faulder, 1798), vol. I: pp. 197–201; 215; 223–35; 248–50; 253–95.

One of the most striking aspects of the East India Company's domination of the subcontinent throughout the latter part of the eighteenth century was the fragility upon which it was based. Massively outnumbered by an often hostile and certainly resentful populace, the officers of the Company defended themselves with the same locals in the form of a native *sepoy* army. Disliked by native princes and merchants, valuable trade agreements were revoked and coercion applied with a "moral elasticity"[1] that pitted rivals against each other. When force was needed, it was defended with indignation in Calcutta and in London.

The internal vulnerability, however, was not the cause of the greatest concern. The greatest threat to British domination of India was Russia. Separated by the largely unknown territories of Afghānistān and central Asia, these two great nations puffed out their respective chests. By the mid-nineteenth century, the question was not if Russia would invade but when and how. Throughout the latter half of the same century, British empire-makers were preoccupied by this single inexorable question.

Central to the British defense of its dominion was military intelligence. This was in part generated through a band of industrious and courageous young men. Most were army officers, skilled in local languages, who would take a land route through Europe and into India in order to chart and classify the terrain and peoples that formed the potent threat to security. When Alexander Burns, an extraordinary linguist and engaging personality, was dispatched in 1831 with the seemingly innocuous mission to deliver a gift of six dapple-gray drayhorses from William IV to Mahārājā Ranjīt Singh, he kept an impressive diary of his travels with an extraordinary eye for military detail. As he sailed up the Indus to Lahore, he noted the path for future British conquest as well as vulnerabilities in potential defenses.

This was a high-risk occupation, but the wheeze of gathering military and logistical intelligence through seemingly innocent travels was a huge draw for young men with steel nerves and a taste for adventure. The Great Game was born.

The phrase "The Great Game" was coined in 1841 by Arthur Connolly (1807–1842), but its practitioners had been "playing" for a great deal longer than that. Some of the earliest pioneers were the late-eighteenth century travelers spurned on by travel and adventure rather than for the purposes of spying. One such man was George Forster (d. 1792). Of his early life very little is known, but what can be ascertained is that by 1782 he was a civil servant in the Madras establishment of the East India Company.[2] An unlikely adventurer, in 1782 he traveled from India through Kashmīr, Afghānistān, Herat, Persia, by the Caspian Sea into Russia. It seems that the Sikh incursions into Delhi and the Ganga *doāb* had sufficiently alarmed the East India Company for them to perceive the Sikhs as a frustration on their designs. The governor-general, Warren Hastings quickly responded with a slew of intelligence gathering exercises, many of which centered on the Sikhs: James Browne (part II, chapter 9), Sayyid Ghulām Hussain (part VI, chapter 32), and George Forster were all charged with studying their history and relaying back to himself and the directors. Forster was dispatched to travel across the Sikh territory disguised as a Muslim horse trader.

Forster's memoirs from that journey were published posthumously in two volumes as *A Journey from Bengal to England through the Northern Part of India, Kashmire, Afghanistan, and Persia; and into Russia, by the Caspian Sea* (London: Printed for R. Faulder, 1798). In 1785, Forster wrote a detailed letter, essentially a draft for the chapter on the Sikhs in *A Journey from Bengal*. This letter was sent to a Mr. Gregory and is marked "Charlotte Street, Portland Place, 9 June 1785." The extract relating to the Sikhs and the Punjab were observations made by Forster between February and April 1783, some nine months after he had left Calcutta.

Soon after the British failed to get the possession of Orīssā from the Marāthās, Warren Hasting's departed his position as governor-general. Lord Cornwallis his successor opened negotiations for defensive alliance with the Marāthā chief by sending George Forster to Nāgpur. Forster's attempt was unsuccessful and it was in Nāgpur during that failed mission that Forster died in 1792.

One of the longest of the accounts to predate Malcolm's *Sketch of the Sikhs* (London: John Murray, 1812), Forster gives an intimate and personal account of his travel and his acquaintance with Sikhs. Unlike many of the empire builders and military men, Forster was courageous enough to share his fears of the unknown with his reader. It is with visible relief that Forster writes that "unhurt by the Sicques, tigers, or thieves, I am safely lodged in

Nourpour" in the opening lines of his letters. This deferential attitude, and his low profile in conducting his travels, allowed Forster to gain an insight into the manners and political machinations of the Sikhs that eluded many of the more ostentatious travelers that followed him.

The extracts reproduced here are from his letters found in volume I in the section called *Abbreviated History of the Rohilahs, Shujah-ud-Dowlah, and the Sicques*. In letters IX and X, Forster is able to shed substantial detail on Sikh activity in the hill states as an eyewitness to Sikh horsemen attached to different *misls*. Arousing little suspicion, Forster was even able to conduct several interviews with some of the Sikhs he met along the way. Letter XI is where the importance of Forster's account becomes apparent. As he states in the opening line: "The frequent introduction of the Sicques to your notice, will have naturally excited a desire to examine the history of this new and extraordinary people, who within a period of twenty years, have conquered a tract of country, extending in certain directions from the Ganges to the Indus." What emerges is a genuine, detailed account, shaped by near-fatal encounters, which progresses from initial prejudice and suspicion to some considerable degree of respect.

---

pp. 197–201
LETTER IX
Bellaspour, 22d February, 1783
DEAR SIR,
ON the 28th, at Dayrah, the residence of the deputy of the Siringnaghur rajah. This small town, which is populous and neatly built, may be called the capital of the lower division[i] of Siringnaghur, which includes a space of level country lying between a chain of scattered hills on the south, and the larger range of northern mountains. The Sicques have an unrestrained access into these parts through the southern hills, which are broken by small valleys; and, fearing no opposition from Zabitah Khan,[3] they can at pleasure penetrate into the lower districts of Siringnaghur. The chief resides at a town bearing the common name of the territory, which lyes, I am informed, about one hundred miles to the north, and by the east of Lall Dong. The inactivity of the present rajah has enabled the Sicques to exact from this country a regular tribute.[ii] Of what superior courage and resource was that chief of Siringnaghur, who, in defiance of Aurungzebe, the most powerful prince of his time, protected the son[iii] of Dara, brother of the emperor, and his deadly foe, regardless of every menace. But he fell to the *sacra sames auri*, the most destructive evil, my friend, which Pandora's box let loose upon the sons of man. It hath often armed the son against the father, hath sown dissention in the marriage bed, and broken the tye of honour, and the bonds of friendship.

TO adjust the account of Siringnaghur customs, the kasilah halted until the 15th, when we proceeded to Kheynsapoor—ten cosses. At this place, I saw two Sicque

---

[i] It is called the *doone*, or low country.
[ii] Said to be four thousand rupees annually.
[iii] See Bernier's account of Sipahi Sheko's retreat into Siringnaghur.

horsemen, who had been sent from their country to receive the Siringnaghur tribute,[4] which is collected from the revenue of certain custom-houses. From the manner in which these men were treated, or rather treated themselves, I frequently wished for the power of migrating into the body of a Sicque for a few weeks—so well did these cavaliers fare. No sooner had they alighted than beds were provided for their repose, and their horses were supplied with green barley pulled out of the field. The Kasilah travellers were contented to lodge on the ground, and expressed their thanks for permission to purchase what they required;—such is the difference between those who were in, and those who were out of power.

ON the 6th of March crossed the Jumna, and halted on the western banks—eight cosses. It flows with a clear stream to the south-east, and has about the same breadth with the Ganges.[iv] Fish abound in this part of the Jumna, as I myself saw; but I believe the adjacent inhabitants do not use any means of catching them. No cultivation is seen in the vicinity of the Jumna, though a spacious plain extends on the western side, and might be watered without much difficulty from the river. The Siringnaghur territory, which here terminates, is bounded on the north and the north-east, by the districts of independent Hindoo Rahahs; on the south by Oude; on the west and north-west by the Jumna; and the south-west by the dominions of the Sicques. From Lall Dong to the Ganges, the country forms with little interruption a continued chain of woody hills. The elephant, which abounds in these forests, but of a size and quality inferior to that found in the Chittagong and Malay quarters, is here only valued for its ivory. From the Ganges to the Jumna, the road lies through an extensive valley, of a good soil, but thinly inhabited, and interspersed with wood. The food of the people is wheaten bread and pease, the latter being usually made into a soup; and, believe me, that in the course of my life I never eat a meal with a higher relish. Vigorous health, indeed, daily labour, and a clear air, will recommend to the appetite worse things than wheaten cakes and pease-soup. The attempt to ascertain the revenue of a country in which I have been so cursory a sojourner, would be presumptuous. I will therefore generally say, that Siringnaghur is computed to give an annual produce of about twenty lacks of rupees. The officer on the western side of the Jumna, taxed me in the sum of two rupees; alledging, that being merely a passenger, and unconnected with any traffic from which an advantage would arise to the country, that I was taxable in myself. The same argument being held as at the Siringnaghur pass, and esteeming myself fortunate at falling under no minuter notice, I paid the fine with pleasure.

ON the 7th, at Karidah—eight cosses: and on the 8th, at Coleroon—seven cosses,—hamlets of a few houses. Here two Kashmirians, a Sunassee,[v] myself and servant, quitted the kasilah, and on the 9th, arrived at Nhan—eight cosses; the residence of the chief of a territory of the same name; and who on the day of our arrival, made a public entry into the town after a long absence. A division of the Nhan country extends to the southward of the head of the Punjab, and bordering the country of the Sicques, they agreeably to a conduct observed with all their weaker neighbours, took possession of it. The Rajah armed himself to recover the districts in question, but after a desultory warfare in which he acquired much military credit, he was obliged to sue for peace; nor were the conquered lands restored until he consented to remit a tribute of two thousand rupees to a certain Sicque chief.[5] This sum you

---

[iv] It is to be noticed, that I crossed these rivers at the season of their lowest ebb.
[v] The name of a Hindoo tribe, chiefly composed of mendicants; though I have seen a Sunassee conducting an extensive commerce.

will doubtless deem trifling, and it is so in your country, where specie is plenty, and the mode of living comfortably luxurious and extravagant. But amongst these mountaineers, whose manners are rude and simple, who seek for little else than the necessaries of life, which are produced to them in great abundance, this amount is important, and to collect it, requires even oppressive exertion.

p. 215

LETTER X

Nourpour, 1783.

DEAR SIR,

ON the 22d of last month, I had the pleasure of describing to you my journey from Lall Dong to Bellaspour, and I can now with pleasure say, that unhurt by the Sicques, tigers, or thieves, I am safely lodged in Nourpour, the principal town of a district of the same name. From the western bank of the Setloud, we proceeded on the 24th of March to the village of Comour Hattee, eight cosses. An Hattee, which in the language of this country signifies retail shop, affords the best accommodation for a traveller, and I always endeavoured to make one my halting place. There I procured wheat, wheat-meal, pease, and ghee,[vi] of which my common fare is composed, and by the applying in civil terms, the shop keeper commonly indulged me with the use of the front part of his shop.

pp. 223–35

. . . We were informed that two hundred Sicques who had been lately entertained in the Kangrah service,[6] would soon appear. Aware of the licentious manners of the disciples of Nanock,[vii] especially when employed in foreign service, I would then willingly have sacrificed a moiety of my property to have had the other secured. There was no other remedy than assuming the look of confidence and ease, which, Heaven knows, ill corresponded with my heart: so pushing my horse into a quick trot, I was speedily conveyed into the midst of this formidable corps, who received me very attentively, but without offering any violence. Imagining our approach to have been that of the enemy, the Sicques were preparing for the fight, to which they loudly exclaimed, in the tone of religious ejaculation, that their prophet had summoned them.[7] In token of respect, I had dismounted, and was leading my horse, when a Sicque, a smart fellow, mounted on a active mare, touched me in passing. The high mettled animal, whether in contempt of me or my horse, perhaps of both, attacked us fiercely from the rear, and in the assault, which was violent, the Sicque fell to the ground. The action having commenced on the top of a hill, he rolled with great rapidity to the bottom of it, and in his way down, left behind him his matchlock, sword, and turban: so compleat a derangement I feared, would have irritated the whole Sicque body, but on evincing the shew of much sorrow for the disaster, and having assiduously assisted in investing the fallen horseman with his scattered appurtenances, I received general thanks.

MY good fortune, which had this day repelled a series of perils, conveyed me in safety to the camp of the Kangrah, or as he is often called, from a more ancient name of his country, the Katochin chief. We regaled ourselves this evening with great joy, having suffered from hunger as well as fatigue, though we had only travelled about sixteen or seventeen miles. A small body, chiefly of horse, was stationed at this camp; the greater part of the forces under the command of the Rajah, being employed in

---

[vi] Butter boiled, in which state it is always used for culinary purposes in India.

[vii] The founder of the Sicques.

the siege of Kote Kangrah. The common road to Jumbo from hence, lay through Nadone, the principal town in the Kangrah country, and through the district of Huriepour; but these places being then overrun by the Sicques, we were obliged to deviate from the usual track, and proceed to the westward. It is to be feared that these turbulent mountaineers, the disturbers of their solitary abode, will stir up such commotions in their land, as to wholly shut up this road, the only secure one from India to Kashmire, or render the passage so precarious, that no advantage will compensate the risk.[viii]

ON the 30th, we moved, and joining the kasilah of the iron merchants again, accompanied it to Sooree—six cosses:—a small village, of which most of the carriers were inhabitants. The halt was made at this village from a desire of the carriers to see their families, for it was at the distance of a full day's journey out of their road. To the eastward of Sooree, which lies in a valley, we crossed a ridge of high and steep mountains.

ON the 31st, at Bompal—four cosses:—a small hamlet situated on an eminence. This day's journey was made short for the accommodation of the iron merchants, who went to the Kangrah camp to attempt the recovery of the property which the Sicques had plundered; but they returned without redress, and now seemed anxious to leave the country; as instead of procuring a restitution or payment, farther demands had been made. All this night, I was exposed to a continued and copious rain—and here let me observe, with sincere thanks for the blessing of a hale constitution, that though I have, in the course of this journey, endured much severity of weather, my health has hitherto received no injury.

A CONTINUANCE of the rain detained us at Bompal until the 2d of April, when we arrived at Chumbah[8]—eight cosses:—a small village, depending on the chiefship of Jessoul. At a short distance from Bompal, we were stopped by the collector of Nadone, who had come three miles from his house, in defiance of the troubled state of the country, to receive from us a toll duty of a few pence. At about mid-way on the right hand side of the road is seen a place of Hindoo worship, at the foot of which runs the Byas Gunge,[ix] with a rapid stream of about one hundred yards broad.[x] A great part of the road from Bompal to Chumbah lay through a valley, watered by the Byas, on the north side of which is seen the level and fertile districts of Huriepour. The territory of Kangrah, or Ktochin, is limited on the north, and north-west by Huriepour; on the east by Chumbay; on the south by Kalour; and on the west by the Punjab. The ordinary revenue, estimated at seven lacks of rupees, has been much diminished by the chief's alliance with the Sicques, who spread destruction wherever they go. These marauders are now acting the part of the man whom fable represents to have been invited by the horse, to aid his contest with the boar; and you know the uses to which the thoughtless horse was applied, when victory was decided in favour of the combined forces.

THIS day, our little party which had been joined in the Bellaspour camp by the Kashmirians, resolved, from a dread of the Sicques, who had invested the common track, to quit the kasilah, and through detached paths endeavour to reach Jumbo. A native trader of India, it is to be observed, holds his time in small estimation, and would rather halt for two or three months, than incur even a common risk.

[viii] This apprehension has been since verified.
[ix] The second of the Punjab rivers from the Eastwards.
[x] The current runs to the left.

ON the 3d, at Dada—ten cosses; dependant on the chief of Sebah. From a stream running through the village, we procured some excellent fish, of the size and something of the taste of trouts. This district, by its approach to the head of the Punjab, lies wholly at the mercy of the Sicques, who are I think the plainest dealers in the world. The fort of Sebah,[xi] standing pleasantly on the brink of a rivulet, lay on our road; and in passing it, I saw two Sicque cavaliers strike a terror into the chief and all his people, though shut up within their fort. They had been sent to collect the tribute which the Sicques had imposed on all the mountain chiefs from the Ganges to Jumbo; and, offended at the delay of the payment, these high spoken men were holding to affrighted Hindoos, that style of language, which one of our provincial magistrates would direct at a gipsy, or sturdy beggar. Indeed, my friend, no ordinary exertion of fortitude, no common share of philanthropy is required, to wield with temper the rod of power; which, from the frailty of his nature, man is every inclined to use with severity. Yet surely when he looks into himself, he will see many a strong reason to qualify its stroke. From a spirit of impatience, which having long actuated me, I am induced to think is innate, I quitted my companions, and going about a mile in front, fell in with a horseman, who had much the appearance of a freebooter; but being well armed, and evidently the stronger man, I do not apprehend any risk from a rencounter. Seeing me a stranger, and from the quality of my equipment, a fit subject for plunder, he stopped me, and in a peremptory manner, asked my occupation, and place of abode. My answers were neither explanatory nor gracious, and my departure abrupt, though he had expressed a strong desire of farther communication; and seemed offended at the unconcern of my deportment. About a quarter of a mile farther on, I met a Sicque horseman, well armed, who was evidently in search of adventure. After reconnoitring me attentively, and apprehending, I imagine, that a contest would be of doubtful event, for my sword was long, and my countenance by the air I had assumed, fierce, he politely saluted me, and passed. The person whom I had first saw, had halted, and on the junction of the Sicque, a council was held by them on the subject of my moveables; the result of which was to return and take them from me. My companions who gave me this information came up while these men of the blade were communing on the plan of attack, and an eclaircissement took place. They discovered that these footmen, four in number, were associates of him, whose property they intended to invade; and naturally concluded, that however decided the odds of two to one might have been, so great an additional strength to our party, would manifestly turn the chances; and, swayed probably by this forcible argument, they gave us no molestation.

ON the 4th at Tulwara,—ten cosses; a village in the district of Dutar, where the Sicque chief[9] has erected a small fort, and holds the adjacent territory. The country to the southward now assumed a level aspect, which to me had an effect inexpressibly pleasing; for my eye had long been disgusted, and, I may say, imprisoned, by mountain piled on mountain, till the highest pierced the clouds. The district of Dutar, or Dutarah, extends on the interior side of the Punjab hills, through which our late southern inclination has penetrated. In this day's journey, our party was reduced to the Kashmirian trader and myself; three Kashmirians, who had joined our party in the Bellaspour Camp, went on before, and my servant lagged behind. In the evening, having reached the bottom of a hill, we observed a body of horsemen

---

[xi] Situate about three cosses to the south-west of Dada, and the only fortified residence I have seen among the mountains. The vicinity of the Punjab has perhaps induced the mountaineers to fortify this place.

descending in our road. The sight of these men, who were immediately known to be Sicques, gave a serious alarm; and on their near approach, I deposited, unnoticed by my companions, my little property of bills and cash in an adjacent bush. But we had formed an unjust opinion of these cavaliers; and I am to think myself singularly fortunate, in being enabled in two instances to place their conduct in a favourable point of view. This party, consisting of about two hundred, many of whom were Mahometans,[10] was then marching into the Hurriepour district. Summoning an affected composure of countenance, we affected to smoke our pipes, from which some of the Mahometans took a whiff *en passant*, and at the same time gave us an assurance of protection against any ill designs of their associates; for notwithstanding the looks we had borrowed, they must have seen much embarrassment in them. After their departure, I took my valuables out of the bush without the observance of my companion, who was transported with joy at the escape, swearing, by his beard, that on reaching our evening quarters, he would offer up to Mahomet, or to his national saint Mucdoom Saib, two-penny worth of brown sugar, in thanksgiving for the extraordinary preservation. We met many of the Sicque stragglers, who are always the most mischievous; these we directed to speedily join their companions, who, we said, had strictly enjoined us to give such directions; and this pretended message gave us some credit; for seeing we had not been plundered by their party, they followed the same meritorious example.

A SHOP-KEEPER accommodated us with a convenient lodging at Tulwara, where, being joined by my servant, who had likewise been involved in the dangers of the day, though he had carefully preserved the remains of the fish that had been procured at Dada, a sumptuous feast was served up, and joyously participated. The truth of this remark will be readily acknowledged by those, who, from the like adventures, have reached in the evening a safe retreat. My friend, who faithfully performed the tenor of his promise, reprobated my insensibility of the providential interposition that had been made in our behalf. It was in vain to urge the merits of internal prayer, or to assert, that I had already offered unfeigned thanks for our escape, which I trusted would not be the less acceptable from the want of sugar. This being a doctrine wholly repugnant to his creed, which existed only in noisy and ostentatious ceremony, I drew on myself a further severe reproach.

ON the 5th at Badpour—seven cosses: a populous village in the Nourpour district. About two cosses to the eastward of Badpour, we crossed at the Rhay Ghaut, or Puttun,[xii] in a ferry-boat, the Byas Gungah, and came into the Jumbo road, which in this quarter has not yet experienced the depredation of the Sicques.

ON the 6th, at Gungatau—ten cosses. In the passage of a rivulet near this village, the horse, in suddenly stopping to drink, threw me headlong into the water, where among the rest of my chattels, a bill on Jumbo was thoroughly drenched: nor was this the first injury it had received.

ON the 7th, at Nourpour; the residence of the chief of a district of the same name. This town situate on the top of a hill, which is ascended by stone steps, has the appearance of opulence and industry. Towards the south-east the country is open and of a pleasant aspect, to which a winding stream of fine water gives additional beauty. Mountains that have already made my eyes ach, contract the view to the west and north; but these have their uses; and having experienced an essential one, not to give it a place would be ungenerous. The heat of the sun now growing intense would have been severely felt, had not the wind which came from the north-west received a cool

---

[xii] The name of a ferry in some parts of the Punjab.

refreshing quality from the snows which on that quarter cover the hills; and had it not been for a like favourable situation, the residence in the Bellaspour camp, the remembrance of which makes me shudder, might have proved fatal to us.

ON a plain adjacent to the town of Nourpour, was encamped a Jumbo kasilah, chiefly the property of Sunassees,[xiii] and consigned to the Dehli market. From these people I learned, that the chief of Jumbo was much embarrassed in his finances, from a destructive war he had entered into with the Sicques: that to raise supplies he had levied a general contribution on the inhabitants of the city, and that his exactions had induced many of the principal merchants to abandon the place. The Sunassees had employed in their service two or three Kashmirians, who are men of an universal occupation, and endowed with unwearied patience and activity in the cause of gain. They told me that I should incur a manifest risk in going to Jumbo, at a time, when the appearance of persons of any property, attracted the notice of government: an information then more alarming, as my business at Jumbo required a personal attendance. Whilst I am writing of Nourpour, it may not be superfluous to mention, that a respectable merchant named Daud Khan, a native of the Punjab, resides in that town. He had lived many years at Jumbo, but having felt the oppression of that government, he has taken refuge in Nourpour, where he enjoys, with a moderate security of property, the benefit of a fine air and a plentiful country, and should any of our countrymen come this way in the Mahometan character, they may be confidently assured of deriving conveniency, from an acquaintance with Daud Khan.

ON the 8th, halted. On the 9th, at the village of Bunguree—eight cosses. My servant, from a cold and a constitutional weakness in his breast, which he said had long afflicted him, was this day scarcely able to walk, I am now fearful that the burthen he was loaded with, was too heavy a one, and I am also to accuse myself of not alleviating its weight, by an exercise of those offices of kindness, which the law of humanity, as well as the usages of servitude, especially in the Asiatic world, obliges a master to shew his servant, the more so if he is a good one; and to say that this follower of my fortunes was not a good servant, would be an unworthy attempt to exculpate, at the expence of his character, my frequent neglect. But should I ever be enabled to recompence his worth, the act shall be classed among those of my best deeds. I used to fortify my occasional dissatisfaction at him, by enlarging too rigorously on the petulance of his temper; but I hold the reason no longer valid, nor will it atone for the compunction I feel, when I recall to my mind the many affectionate services which the honest fellow performed in the course of a laborious journey.

THE districts of Nourpour on the north, are bounded by the river Rawee; on the east by the Chambay[xiv] country; on the west by some small Hindoo districts, lying at the head of the Punjab, and by the river Byas; and on the south by Huriepour. The revenues of Nourpour are calculated at four lacks of rupees, and it would seem that it enjoys a state of more infernal quiet, is lest molested by the Sicques, and governed more equitably than any of the adjacent territories.

ON the 10th, at Plassee—ten cosses:—a small village in the Bissouly district. About eight miles to the north-west of Bunguree, and opposite to the fort of Bissouly, crossed the Rawee,[xv] which is about one hundred and twenty yards in breadth, and

---

[xiii] Though this sect, conformably to the tenets of their doctrine, ought to renounce or never engage in the affairs of the world, yet many of its members have become merchants, soldiers, and statesmen.

[xiv] A mountainous territory of large extent.

[xv] The Rawee is the Central Punjab river, and runs near the city of Lahore.

very rapid. In the ferry-boat were two Sicques going to the fort, of which, a detachment they belonged to, had taken possession, in consequence of being called in to the assistance of the Bissouly chief. Though this be the invariable result of every connection made with the Sicques, the infatuated mountaineers never fail to seek their aid when engaged in war. A bordering chief had invaded the Bissouly districts, plundered the inhabitants, and burned their villages, before any opposition was made. The Sicques were called in to repel the enemy, and defend the fort of Bissouly; but after performing the required service, they became pleased with their new situation, and refused to relinquish it.

A QUICK progress through this country, and avoiding the track of the Sicques, were strongly, though unnecessarily, recommended to us. The boatman at the ferry of Bissouly, though a brother Mahometan, made an exorbitant demand of hire, which was considerably lessened by the interference of the Sicque horsemen, who saw the imposition, and had only to make known their will to effect obedience.

pp. 248–50

. . . IT appears that Jumbo continued to increase its power and commerce until the year 1770, the period of Runzeid Deve's death,[11] when one of his sons, the present chief, contrary to the intention and express will of his father, seized on the government, put to death one of his brothers, the intended successor, and imprisoned another; who having made his escape sought the protection of the Sicques.[12] Pleased in having obtained so favourable a pretext for entering Jumbo, which they attempted in vain during the administration of Runzeid Deve, the Sicques promised to espouse the fugitive's cause with vigour. A small sum had been annually exacted by them from Jumbo, but in a much less proportion than what was levied in the adjacent territories. The Sicques, indeed, aware of the respectable state of the Jumbo force, and the ability of the chief, were contented with the name of tribute. The most valuable division of the Jumbo districts, lay in the plain country, forming part of the northern Punjab; which, under pretence of affording assistance to the person who lately fought their protection, a body of Sicques have laid waste. They are now prosecuting a vigorous war against the present chief, who through the defection of many of his people, driven by oppressions to the party of his brother, became unable to make any effectual stand; and that his ill fortune might be complete, he called into his aid, a party of Sicque mercenaries, commanded by Mhah Sing,[13] a powerful officer in that quarter, who has firmly established his authority at Jumbo, and has erected a fort at the fourth entrance of the principal pass leading into the Punjab. For defraying the expence incurred by the Sicque troops, the Jumbo chief has made rigorous demands on the native inhabitants of the city, and is now throwing an eye on the foreign merchants; who, dreading his disposition and necessities, have taken a general alarm. It was with much pleasure I saw the person on whom my bill was drawn, a man of a fair and honourable character, enjoying, amidst these disorders, a moderate security. He seemed to have procured the favour of Mhah Sing, who, with other officers of the party, supported him against the designs of the Rajah. The person entrusted with the government of the town of Jumbo, during the absence of the chief then in the field, was so exact a counterpart of his master in the system of oppression, that I was advised to a speedy departure, lest I should fall under an inspection. Though much fatigued by an harrassing journey, and the sale of my horse, with other necessary concerns, was to be adjusted, such was the ascendancy of my fears, that on the 16th of the month, I was ready to proceed.

IN laying before you these scattered pieces of intelligence, I must not forget to notice, that the courtezans and female dancers of the Punjab and Kashmire, or rather a mixed breed of both these countries, are beautiful women, and are held in great estimation through all the northern parts of India: the merchants established at Jumbo, often become so fondly attached to a dancing girl, that, neglecting their occupation, they have been known to dissipate, at her will, the whole of their property; and I have seen some of them reduced to a subsistence on charity; for these girls, in the manner of their profession, are profuse and rapacious.

Pp. 253–95

LETTER XI

DEAR SIR,

THE frequent introduction of the Sicques to your notice, will have naturally excited a desire to examine the history of this new and extraordinary people, who within a period of twenty years, have conquered a tract of country, extending in certain directions from the Ganges to the Indus.[14] My knowledge of the subject does not permit me to deduce, on substantial authority, their history from the period in which Nanock their first institutor and law-giver lived, or mark with an order of dates the progress which this people have made, and the varying gradations of their power, until their attainment of their present state of national importance. You who are apprized of the futility of the documents which compose the general texture of Eastern record,[xvi] who have witnessed the irresistible tendency of an Asiatic mind to fiction, and the produce of its ductile fancy, will grant me an indulgent scope, and will, I trust, believe, that though the body of the history be not complete, such parts only will be noticed, as are either founded on received tradition, or on those legends which have the least exceptionable claims to credit.

UNDER shelter of this preliminary, I will proceed to inform you that Nanock,[xvii] the founder of the Sicque nation, was born in the year of the Christian aera, 1469, during the reign of Sultan Beloul,[xviii] at the village of Tulwundy,[xix] about sixty miles to the westward of Lahore. Nanock appears to have possessed qualities happily

---

[xvi] Neither the genius of the people nor the form of their government is feasible to the growth of History, which is rarely seen to flourish on despotic ground. The actions of Asiatic princes are usually recorded by their own scribes; and we know that a large portion of the annals of India was manufactured under imperial inspection. It is, therefore, scarcely within the verge of probability, that a writer, attracted by so powerful an influence, would dared to have thrown the piercing light of History on the reigning monarch, or even to have examined with freedom the actions of his ancestors, who have, for more than two hundred years, maintained an unbroken succession of the Empire of Hindostan. Oriental speech, pregnant with figure, and capable of expressing the wildest flights of fancy, disdains the limits of History. It is better fitted to modulate poetic strains, and describe the wide region of romance; where it can roam without restraint, and happily without the power of committing extensive injuries.

[xvii] He was of the *Chittery* or second cast of Hindoos, and according to a secret belief of the Sicques, a species of secondary incarnation of the Supreme Deity.

[xviii] A Patan king of Delhi, who reigned previous to Baber's conquest of Hindostan.

[xix] This village is now known by the name of Rhaypour. The terms given by the Sicques to their places of worship, are *Sunghut*, *Durmsallah*, and *Dairah*, words signifying, in the Hinduee, an assembly of the people, a charitable or pious foundation, and a house. This last appellation seems to be applied in an eminent sense, as "the house." The Sicques, in commemoration of the place of Nanock's birth, have erected an edifice at Tulwundy, where a grand festival is annually celebrated.

adapted to effect the institution of a new system of religion. He was inflexibly just; he enjoyed from nature a commanding elocution, and was endowed with a calm passive fortitude, which successfully supported him through the long course of a dangerous occupation. The tenets of Nanock forbid the worship of images, and ordain that the places of public prayer shall be of plain construction, and devoid of every exhibition of figure. A book, entitled the *Grunth*, which contains the civil and religious institutes of Nanock, is the only typical object which the Sicques have admitted into their places of worship.[15] Instead of the intermediation of subordinate deities, they are directed to address their prayer to one God, who, without the aid of any delegate, is to be considered the unassociated ruler of the universe.[xx] Though many essential differences exist between the religious code of the Hindoos and that of the Sicques, a large space of their ground-work exhibits strong features of similarity. The article indeed of the admission of proselytes amongst the Sicques, has caused an essential deviation from the Hindoo system, and apparently levelled those barriers which were constructed by Brimha, for the arrangement of the different ranks and professions of his people. Yet this indiscriminate admission, by the qualifications which have been adopted, do not widely infringe on the customs and prejudices of those Hindoos who have embraced the faith of the Sicques. They still preserve the distinctions which originally marked their sects, and perform many of the ancient ceremonies of their nation. They form matrimonial connections only in their own tribes, and adhere implicitly to the rules prescribed by the Hindoo law, in the choice and preparation of their food. The only aliment used in common, by the Sicques at this day, is the *pursaud*,[xxi] or sacred bread, from the participation of which no tribe of class of their people is excluded.

FEW events of historical importance are related of Nanock, the founder of this sect, who possessing neither territory nor wealth, nor aided by the force of arms, preached his doctrine in peace, and manifested, in the countries which he visited, an unaffected simplicity of manners. He journeyed through most of the kingdoms in India, from whence, according to the tradition of the Sicques, he went into Persia and Arabia. In his travels, which with short intervals continued for the space of fifteen years, he was attended by a Mahometan musician, named Murdana, who became his convert, and ever remained faithfully attached to his person. It is said that in one of the expeditions of Baber[xxii] into India, Nanock having been apprehended by some of the soldiers, was brought before that prince, who informed of the sanctity of his character, treated him with respect and indulgence. As no records of the Moghul Empire bear a testimony of the existence of this sect during the period in which Nanock lived, it cannot be supposed that his converts were numerous or powerful. Nanock, according to the Sicque records, died in the month of August, A. D. 1539,[16] aged seventy years, at Dayrah,[17] a village on the banks of the Rawee, about forty miles to the northward of Lahore, where a vast concourse of people annually assemble, to perform certain ceremonies in commemoration of the day of his decease. Nanock,

[xx] When it is noticed that the worship of the Hindoos is loaded with a mass of puerile ceremony, and oftentimes conducted with a ridiculous grimace, it will not seem surprizing that a creed, founded on principles calculated to promote the establishment of a simple uniform religion, and promulgated by a man of distinguished tribe and exemplary manners, should draw to it proselytes even in the bigotted regions of India.

[xxi] The *pursaud* is said to be a composition of flour, butter, and certain spices; this bread after being consecrated by the Bramins, is also used by some sects of Hindoos in the ceremony of administering an oath, particularly in that quarter of the Orissa province, contiguous to the temple of Juggud Nautt.

[xxii] Baber defeated the Patan King of Hindostan, in A.D. 1526.

though he had two sons, devolved the charge of the mission to his favourite disciple Anghut,[xxiii] a Hindoo of the Chittery tribe, to whom he also entrusted the publication[xiv] of the laws and precepts of his doctrine. Anghut, who seems to have passed this time in retirement, died about the year 1542,[18] at the town of Khadour,[xxv] the place of his nativity. He was succeeded by Ammerdass, a native of the Lahore district, who propagated the new doctrine without molestation, and died in the year 1574, at the village of Govindual.[xxvi] Ramdass,[xxvii] who had espoused the daughter of the last preceptor of the Sicques, was then chosen the representative of their sect. This priest lived in the reign of Acbar, and, according to the tradition of the Sicques, experienced some marks of that emperor's favour. Retiring in the latter part of his life to a small district[xxviii] in the vicinity of Lahore, which Acbar had granted to him, he founded the town of Ramdasspour. He repaired also and ornamented a reservoir of water, which had in ancient times been dedicated at that place by the Hindoos to their God *Ram*, and to which he now gave the name of *Amrut Sir*.[xxix] Ramdass made a compilation of the history and precepts of his predecessors, and annexing his own commentaries, ordained that his disciples should form the principles of their faith on the doctrine set forth in the joint collection.[19] Ramdass died at the town he had founded about the year 1581, and was succeeded by his son Arjun, who having incurred the displeasure of a Hindoo[xxx] favoured by Jehanguir, was committed by that prince to the persecution of his enemy; and his death, which happened in the year 1606 at Lahore, was caused it is said by the rigour of confinement.[20] The succession devolved on Hurrgovind, his only son, who actuated by revenge for the cruelties exercised on his father, and strongly supported by the enthusiastic valour of his adherents, he dragged the Hindoo from his house, though within the walls of Lahore, and put him to death.[21] Fearing the effects of the emperor's displeasure, Hurrgovind fled to Hurtarpour, a village founded by his father, where he collected an armed body for the defence of his person, and according to the records of the nation, defeated a force that Jehanguir had sent to punish his rebellion.[22] But the vein of incongruous story which runs through the atchievements of this militant priest, preclude the derivation of any extensive historical use. The only passage deserving a serious notice, represents that an officer of Jehanguir, named Mahobut Khan, effected the Sicque's submission to the emperor, who ordered him to be imprisoned in the fort of Gualior: but that after a short confinement, he was, at the intercession of Mahobut Khan, set at liberty.[23] It is not seen that Hurrgovind disturbed the peace of the Moghul government at a future period, but passing his days in a recluse manner, he died about the year 1644, at Khyrutpour, a village in the Punjab. The Sicques conferred the office of priesthood on Harray, the grandson of Hurrgovind, though four[24] of their late preceptor's sons were alive. No other mention is made of Harray, than that he died in the year 1661 at Khyrutpour. At his death, a violent contest arose for the succession

---

[xxiii] Nanock changed the original name of his successor, which was Lina.

[xxiv] The religious and historical writing of the Sicques, are written in a character called the *Gooroo Mhookee*, or the language of the *Goorooos*, or priests. This letter, which is said to have been invented by Nanock, differs from the various characters in use among the Hindoos.

[xxv] A village in the Punjab, about forty miles to the eastward of Lahore.

[xxvi] Situate on the Byas, the second Punjab river from the eastward.

[xxvii] This Gooroo was born in the city of Lahore.

[xxviii] At the distance of twenty four miles from Lahore.

[xxix] *Amrut*, according to the mythology of the Hindoos, is a water said to bestow immortality on those who drink it; and *Sir*, in certain dialects of the Hinduee, signifies a piece of water.

[xxx] Named Chaundoo.

which was claimed by the respective adherents of his two sons, Ramroy and Hurkishen, then in infancy; but not being enabled to adjust their claims at home, they appealed to the courts of law at Delhi, where the opponents appeared, and set forth their several pretensions. The cause it is said terminated in a permission being granted to the Sicques to nominate their own priest; when, adjusting the contest, they elected Hurkishen, who died at Dehli in 1664, a short time after his investiture.

HURKISHEN was succeeded by Taigh Bhahauder, his uncle,[25] who appears to have been persecuted with inveterate animosity by the adherents of Ramroy; who being supported by some persons of influence at the court of Aurungzebe, an order was obtained for the imprisonment of the new priest. Taigh Bhahauder, after remaining in confinement at Dehli for the space of two years,[26] was released at the intreaty of Jay Sing, the powerful chief of Jaynaghur, who was at that time proceeding to Bengal on the service of government. The Sicque accompanied his patron to Bengal, whence he returned to the city of Patna, which became his usual place of abode. The records of the Sicques say that Ramroy still maintained a claim to the priesthood, and that after a long series of virulent persecution, he accomplished the destruction of Taigh Bhahauder, who was conveyed to Dehli by an order of Court, and in the year 1675, publickly put to death. The formal execution of a person, against whom, the Sicques say, no criminal charge was exhibited, is so repugnant to the character and the actions of Aurungzebe, that we are involuntarily led to charge the Sicques of a wilful misrepresentation of facts, injurious to the memory of the prince, and extravagantly partial to the cause of their priest. No document for the elucidation of this passage appearing in any of the memoirs of Hindostan that have reached my knowledge, I am prevented from discovering the quality of the crime which subjected Taigh Bhahauder to capital punishment.[27]

GOVIND SING, then a youth, and the only son of Taigh Bhahauder, was called to the succession by the largest portion of the Sicque's disciples: but the intelligence of his father's death, and dread of a like fate, had induced him to fly from Patna, whence he retired after a series of various adventures into the territory of Siringnaghur. Though Govind Sing could not then have reached his fifteenth year, he evinced many marks of a haughty and turbulent spirit, which was conspicuously shewn in his conduct to the Siringnaghur chief. On pretence of an insult being offered, he collected his party, which amounted it is said to four or five thousand men, and defeated a body of the Siringnaghur troops;[28] but being worsted in some future action, or, according to the authority of the Sicque, obliged by an order of the emperor to leave the country of Siringnaghur, he proceeded with his adherents to the Punjab, where he was hospitably[xxxi] received by a marauding Hindoo chief of that quarter.[29] Endowed with an active and daring temper, the Sicque assisted his new associate in various expeditions against the bordering landholders, and often in opposing the forces of government. The predatory conduct of Govind Singh rendering him obnoxious to the governor of Sirhend, he was attacked and driven from his place of residence. Being afterwards discovered amongst the hills in the northern parts of the Sirhend districts, he was so vigorously pressed by the imperial troops, that abandoning his family and effects, he was compelled to save himself by speedy flight. Vizier Khan, the governor of Sirhend, sullied the reputation he had acquired in this service, by putting to death, in cold blood, the two younger sons of Govind Sing. A severe vengeance was taken for this act at a future period by the Sicques, who giving a loose to savage and indiscriminate cruelty,

---

[xxxi] The dependencies of Mackaval, through which the river Sutledge runs, were given by this Hindoo to Govind Sing, where he founded certain villages. [Ed. this refers to Anandpur Sahib.]

massacred the Mahometans, of every age and sex, that fell into their hands. After his late disaster, Govind Sing found a secure retreat in the Lacky Jungles,[xxxii] which its natural defence, a scarcity of water, and the valour of its inhabitants,[xxxiii] had rendered at that day impregnable. But when the resentment of government abated, he returned without molestation to his former residence in the Punjab. The Sicques say, he even received marks of favour from Bhahauder Shah,[30] who being apprised of his military abilities, gave him a charge in the army[31] which marched into the Decan to oppose the rebellion of Rambuchsh.[xxxiv] Govind Sing was assassinated during this expedition by a Patan soldier, and he died of his wounds in 1708, at the town of Nandere,[xxxv] without leaving any male issue; and a tradition delivered to the Sicques, limiting their priests to the number of ten, induced them to appoint no successor to Govind Sing. A Sicque disciple, named Bunda, who had attended Govind Sing to the Decan, came, after the death of his chief, into the Punjab; where, claiming a merit from his late connection, he raised a small force, and in various desultory enterprizes, established the character of a brave but cruel soldier. His successes at length drew to his standard the whole body of the Sicque nation, which had now widely deviated from the precepts of their founder.[32] A confidence in their strength, rendered presumptuous by the absence of the emperor, had made them rapacious and daring, and the late persecutions, cruel and enthusiastic. Bunda, after dispersing the parties of the lesser Mahometan chiefs, attacked the forces of Vizier Khan, the governor of Sirhend, who fell in action that was fought with an obstinate valour, but ended in the total defeat of the imperial troops. The Sicques expressed an extraordinary joy at this victory, as it enabled them to satiate their revenge for the death of the sons of Govind Sing. The wife of Vizier Khan, with his children and a vast multitude of the inhabitants of Sirhend were destroyed with every species of wild fury. The mosques were overthrown or polluted, and the dead, torn out of their graves, were exposed to the beasts of prey.[33] A party of Sicques had at the same time penetrated the greater Duab, and seized on the town and certain districts of Saharanpour,[xxxvi] where they slaughtered the inhabitants, or forcibly made them converts to the new faith. Bunda, who had rapidly acquired the possession of an extensive territory, was now deserted by his good fortune. He had crossed the river Sutledge with an intention of carrying his conquests to the westward, but being encountered by Shems Khan, an imperial officer who commanded in that quarter, he was repulsed with a great loss. The Sicque's troops employed in the Duab expedition, had even approached the vicinity of Dehli, but they were defeated by the forces of the empire, and driven back to the districts which still remained subject to Bunda.

SUCH was the situation of the Sicques when Bhahauder Shah finished the Decan campaign, and returned in the year 1710 to Hindostan. Alarmed at the progress, and irritated at the cruelties they had exercised, he marched towards their stations with a determination to crush the sect, and revenge the injuries that had been inflicted on the Mahometan religion. Sultan Rouli Khan, one of his principal officers, advanced with a division of the army, and encountering the Sicques on the plains of Sirhend, put

---

[xxxii] A woody country, situate in the northern part of the Punjab, and famous for a breed of excellent horses, called the Jungle Tazee.

[xxxiii] The Jatts.

[xxxiv] A brother of Bhahauder Shah.

[xxxv] Nandere is situate near the banks of the Godavery, about 100 miles to the north-east of Hyderabad.

[xxxvi] For its situation, see Rennell's map. [Ed. this is a reference to Major James Rennell, *Memoir of a map of Hindoostan*, (London: 1783).]

them to flight after a bloody conflict; and a party of the fugitives who had taken refuge with Bunda, in a strong post, were made prisoners, though not before their chief had escaped. The Sicques who survived this disaster, though compelled to disperse, and their chief to wander about the country in disguise, were not conquered in the reign of Bhahauder Shah. The death[xxxvii] of this prince impeded the success of an active pursuit which had been made after the vanquished sectaries, on whose lives a price was set in every part of the empire. Conformably to the order of the last priest, the disciples of Nanock had permitted the growth of the hair of the head and beard. An edict was therefore issued, compelling the Hindoos of every tribe to cut off their hair.

JEHANDAR SHAH,[xxxviii] who succeeded to the empire, made a feeble effort to accomplish the extirpation of the Sicques, but his short reign being involved in an alternate series of debauchery, and tumultuous defence of his country against the invasion of Furruck Sir, this people were encouraged to emerge from their concealment, and again take up the sword. In the reign of Furruck Sir,[xxxix] the Sicques, who had then collected a large force,[xl] were vigorously attacked by Abdul Sumet Khan, the governor of Lahore, who gave them battle near the fort of Loghur,[xli] and gained a decisive victory. Those who escaped took shelter with Bunda in Loghur, but being closely invested, and reduced to extreme distress from hunger, they surrendered at discretion.[xlii] The captives were conveyed in triumph to Dehli, where being exhibited in an ignominious manner to the inhabitants of the city, they met a deserved fate, for their savage and often unprovoked cruelties. Yet they met it with an undaunted firmness, and died amidst the wondering praise of the populace.[34]

HAVING thus briefly related the origin of the Sicques,[xliii] with a chronological notice of their ten priests, and the issue of Bunda's attempt to establish an independent dominion, I will interrupt the historical narrative at this period, by a summary description of certain domestic ordinances established by Nanock and his successors. The person desirous of becoming a member of the Sicque doctrine, is conducted into the presence of five or more of their people, of any class or profession, assembled for the occasion, when one of them pours into the hollow of his hand a little water, which, being touched by the toe of each of the Sicques,[35] the proselyte swallows, previously repeating the words "*Wah[xliv] gooroojee ka khalsah, wah gooroojee ka futtah*." After the performance of this obligation, a cup filled with sherbet is introduced, out of which he drinks five times, and repeats at intervals the afore-mentioned ejaculation. At the conclusion of this ceremony, the convert is instructed in the use of a prayer of great length, in which the religious, moral, and political duties of a Sicque are set forth, and the observance of them enjoined.

[xxxvii] Bhahauder Shah died about the year 1712.

[xxxviii] This Emperor reigned only a few months.

[xxxix] Furruck Sir's reign continued from 1712–3 to 1719.

[xl] The Sicque forces amounted, it is said, to 20,000 cavalry.

[xli] Situate about one hundred miles to the north-west of Lahore.

[xlii] This event happened in 1714.

[xliii] The Sicques affix to their proper name the word *Sing*, which signifying a lion in the Sanscrit language, the appellation of *Sing* belongs properly to the military order. The civil body of the people, artizans, merchants, and all the lower classes, being denominated *Sicques*, or disciples.

[xliv] These words, composed of the Arabic and Hindoo languages, convey a benediction on the government of the Sicques, and on the memory of their priests. The Sicques salute each other by the expression *Wah Gooroo*, without any inclination of the body, or motion of the hand. The government at large, and their armies, are denominated *Khalsa* and *Khalsajee*.

THE first part of the initiation observed in admitting a proselyte, denotes the equality of the followers of Nanock, and is designed to destroy the fabric of ceremony and form, which the Hindoos are now taught to consider as the essential principle of their religion: but the purpose of the Sicque priests in elevating the new religion on this simple base, has been but partially executed. The military Sicques permit the hair of the head and the beard to grow long; they usually fix an iron bracelet on the left hand, and they are prohibited the use of tobacco. These regulations, which were probably instituted by the law-givers to distinguish them from other nations, are now become duties of a primary class, and seem almost to form the essence of their creed.[xlv] By a law of Nanock, widows are expressly forbidden to destroy themselves at the death of their husbands, and are permitted to renew the ceremonies of marriage. But so strong is yet the adherence of the Sicques who have been converted from the Hindoo tribes, to the ancient customs of their country, that many of their women are seen ascending the funeral pile; nor are they ever induced to enter a second time into the connubial state. The Sicques, after the manner of the Hindoos, bury their dead;[36] and they oblige the Mahometan converts to adopt the like usage. They hold a lamentation for the death of any person criminal, and equally unjust as to be afflicted with grief at the payment of an equitable debt, or the surrender of a trust. Their belief of a future state seems to correspond in most of its parts with the metempsychosis of the Hindoos; and as a sketch of that system has been already given, any further explanation of it is unnecessary.

THE Sicque nation is composed of two distinct sects, or orders of people; those who compose the most ancient one are denominated *Khualasah*,[xlvi] and adhere, with little deviation, to the institutions of Nanock, and the eight succeeding priests; in obedience to which, the Khualasah sect are usually occupied in civil and domestic duties. They cut off the hair of their heads and beards and in their manners and appearance resemble the ordinary classes of the Hindoos.[xlvii]

THE modern order of the Sicques, entitled *Khalsa*, was founded by Govind Sing; who, deviating from the ordinances of his predecessors, imparted a strong military spirit to this adherents, whose zealous attachment enabled him to indulge the bent of a fierce and turbulent temper, and to give scope to an ambition, naturally arising from the power which his popularity had created. Govind Sing is said to have restricted his sectaries from the use of tobacco, and to have enjoined them to permit the growth of the beard, and the hair of the head. The military division of the people is composed of the Khalsa sect, which, from a native harshness of features and haughtiness of deportment, is conspicuously discriminated from that of the Khualasah, and other classes of the foreign converts.

[xlv] This would appear to be an effect naturally produced in the minds of the bulk of mankind, who eagerly fix their attention and their affections on exterior objects; which having been taught to behold, with sentiments of respect and religious enthusiasm they become so strongly attached to them, that a portion of temporal welfare, with the hope of future happiness, seems among many nations to depend on a rigorous observance of form. A conspicuous example of this disposition was evinced in the rage which the Russians manifested on being obliged by Peter to shave their beards. The prince perhaps encountered less danger and difficulty in giving a new form and new manners to the empire, than in accomplishing that change in the persons of his subjects.

[xlvi] *Khualasah* conveys virtually the same meaning in the Arabic, as *Khalsah*, which signifies *pure, genuine*, &c.

[xlvii] I have been informed that matrimonial connections are occasionally formed between the Hindoos, and *Khualasah* Sicques.

FOR the space of seventy years after the death of Nanock, the growth of the Sicques was slow, and their conduct was regulated by a temperate discretion. But when the Moghul empire had received its mortal wound from the commotions which arose amongst the sons and the grandsons of Aurungzebe; when it was no longer guided by the skilful and vigorous hand which had diffused wisdom and spirit throughout its vast machine, the disciples of Nanock issued into the field, and participated in the varying fortunes of the day. The rebellions of the distant provinces, and the factions and intrigues of the court, events which rapidly followed the death of Aurungzebe, gave a powerful aid to the exertions of the Sicques; who improving the favourable occasion, carried their depredations, even in the reign of Bhahauder Shah, to the environs of the capital. The situation[xlviii] of the country where the doctrine of the Sicques had been the most widely promulgated, and where they first formed a military body, contributed to augment their power, as well as afford shelter against a superior force of their enemies. On the skirts of forest and mountains, impervious to cavalry, they enjoyed also the benefits arising from the vicinity of an opulent populous territory, which at once afforded a store of converts and plunder.

The Sicque common-wealth acquired an active strength from the spirit and valour of Bunda, who had inspired them with a zeal, which rendered meritorious every act of cruelty to the enemies of their faith, and gave their attacks, until opposed by the collected force of the empire, an irresistible impulse. The success of this fierce adventurer, had allured to his standard a numerous body of proselytes: some to obtain a protection against the rapacity of the Sicque government, others to take shelter from the oppressions or just demands of the empire: whilst many embraced the new doctrine, from the hope of participating the plunder of the Punjab. The larger portion of the converts were of the tribe of Jatts[xlix] and Goojers; a people who are chiefly seen in the northern parts of India. They are esteemed skilful and active husbandmen, but notorious for a turbulent and restless temper.

THE defeat and death of Bunda effected a total destruction of the power of the Sicques, and, ostensibly, an extirpation of their sect. An edict was issued by Furruck Sir, directing that every Sicque falling into the hands of his officers, should on a refusal of embracing the Mahometan faith, be put to the sword. A valuable reward was also given by the emperor, for the head of every Sicque; and such was the keen spirit that animated the persecution, such the success of the exertions, that the name of a Sicque no longer existed in the Moghul dominion. Those who still adhered to the tenets of Nanock, either fled into the mountains at the head of the Punjab, or cut off their hair, and exteriorly renounced the profession of their religion.

AFTER a period of more than thirty years, the spark that had lain concealed amongst the ruins of the fabrick of Nanock, burst forth, and produced a flame which hath never been extinguished. It is mentioned that the Sicque forces appeared in arms at the period of Nadir Shah's return from Delhi;[l] when the Persian army, encumbered with spoil, and regardless of order, was attacked in the rear by detached predatory parties of Sicque cavalry, who occasionally fell upon the baggage-guards, and acquired a large plunder. During the periods of tumult and distress, which followed the Persian,[li] and the first Afghan invasion, the Sicques emerged more conspicuously from their places of concealment; and collecting a numerous party of promiscuous adventurers,

---

[xlviii] In the vicinity of the Punjab mountains.

[xlix] The Khalsah Sicques have largely originated from these tribes.

[l] 1739.

[li] From the year 1739 to 1746.

they soon rose into military importance. Even at the low ebb to which the Sicques had been reduced by the destruction of their force, the death of their leader, and the proscription of their sect, they had continued to resort secretly to Amrut Sir; and as the attention of the empire became, at subsequent periods, fixed on subjects that demanded an undivided force, the Sicques were not molested in visiting their favourite place of worship, which gradually rose into the capital of their narrow territory. Meer Munnoo,[lii] the governor of Lahore in the reign of Ahmed Shah,[liii] alarmed at an encrease of power, the evils of which had been already manifested by the devastations of the Sicques in his own country, made a vigorous attack on them; and it is supposed that their force would then have been annihilated, had not this people found a strenuous advocate in his minister Korah Mul, who was himself of the Khualasah sect,[37] and diverted Meer Munnoo from reaping the full fruits of the superiority he had gained.

ADINA BEG KHAN, an officer in the service of Meer Munnoo, had been sent with an army into the centre of the Sicque districts, which he over-run; and, encountering their army some time in the year 1749, had defeated it with great slaughter.[liv] A permanent accommodation was ultimately effected through the mediation of Korah Mul, between the Sicques and the governor of Lahore, who being engaged in operations that led to more interesting objects, the Sicques were left at liberty to acquire strength, and enlarge their territory, which extended from the vicinity of Lahore, to the foot of the mountains. Whilst Korah Mul lived, his influence over the Sicques confined them to their own limit, and restrained their depredations. But the death of this officer, who was slain[lv] in an action fought with the Afghans, and the tumult which arose at the decease of Munnoo,[lvi] from the various competitors to the government of Lahore, enabled the Sicques to fix the basis of a power, which, though severely shaken at a subsequent period, has raised them from a lawless banditti to the rank of sovereigns of an extensive dominion. The charm which had so powerfully operated in augmenting and consolidating the spacious empire of the Indian Moghuls, and had in the eastern world proclaimed it invincible, was now broken; and a wide theatre was opened, in which every band of bold adventurers had an ample scope to exercise their courage, and where the most alluring objects were held out to the grasp of ambition and avarice. The southern territories had been dismembered from the empire; and the Persians and Afghans, the Mahrattas and the Sicques, had severally plundered and laid waste the northern provinces, and the capital.

AFTER the death of Meer Munnoo, and a rapid succession of fleeting governors, the government of Lahore devolved on Adina Beg Khan;[lvii] and the court of Dehli, in opposition to the arrangements of the Duranny Ahmed Shah, who had annexed the Lahore province to his dominion, avowedly supported the power which Adina Beg had assumed in the Punjab. The courage and military experience of this officer found an active employment in curbing the turbulent and rapacious spirit of the Sicques: but aware of the advantages that would arise from a confederacy with a people whose depredation, accompanied with every species of rapine, could not be prevented without continued warfare, Adina Beg made an alliance with the

---

[lii] The son of Kummer ud Dein, the vizier of Mahomet Shah.
[liii] This prince succeeded to the empire in 1747, and was deposed in 1753.
[liv] This action was fought near the village of Mackavaul, in the northern districts of the Punjab.
[lv] The death of Korah Mul happened in the year 1751.
[lvi] Meer Munnoo died in the year 1752.
[lvii] The officer who defeated the Sicques at the battle of Mackavaul.

Sicques, founded on a scheme of combined hostilities against the Afghans, whose territories[lviii] he invited them to lay waste, without requiring participation of the booty. Every infringement of the compact being severely resented by Adina Beg, the Sicques were rarely seen interrupting the peace of his government.

THE court of Dehli, having by intrigue and occasional military aids, zealously contributed to promote the successes of the Lahore Chief, Ahmed Shah brought an army in the year 1756 into India, to recover the possession of the Punjab, and to punish Ghaze-ud-Dien, the minister of Alumguir the Second, who had assumed an absolute authority in the capital. Adina Beg, an active supporter of the minister's interests, which were closely united with his own, not having a sufficient force to meet Ahmed Shah Duranny in the field, fled into the adjacent mountains, where he remained in concealment until the departure of the Afghan prince to his northern dominions.

IN the year 1757, or 1758, a numerous army of Mahrattas,[lix] after subduing the adjacent territory, arrived in the city of Dehli, where their chiefs assumed an absolute sway. Adina Beg, aware of the benefits of an alliance with the Mahrattas, represented to their chiefs, that the Punjab garrisons, weakened by the departure of Ahmed Shah, would fall an easy conquest to their arms, which he offered to reinforce with his party, and the influence he possessed in that quarter. The Mahratta army moved without delay into the Punjab, and, expelling the Afghans from Sirhend and Lahore, reduced to their power a tract of country that extended to the river Jaylum.[lx] National commotions calling the principal Mahratta officers into the Decan, they appointed Adina Beg Khan, who had largely promoted their success, the governor of Lahore: but he died early in the following year, at an advanced age, highly celebrated in Upper India for his military and political talents.

THE Sicques, awed by the superiour power of the Mahrattas, and fearful of incurring the resentment of Adina Beg, had not during his government, carried their depredations into the low country. In the course of the several expeditions which the Afghans made into India under Ahmed Shah, they were severely harassed by the Sicques, who cut off many of their detached parties; and evinced, in the various schemes of annoying the Afghans, an indefatigable intrepidity.

AHMED SHAH, having in conjunction with the Mahometan chiefs of Hindostan, routed the combined forces of the Hindoos at the battle of Pannifrett, in the beginning of the year 1761, and driven the Mahrattas from the northern provinces, meditated a full revenge on the Sicques; who, during a small interval of his absence, had in the latter end of the same year, seized on the largest division of the Lahore province. Early in the year 1762, he entered the Punjab which he over-run with a numerous army, dispersing the Sicques wherever they appeared, and diffusing a general terror by the havock which marked his invasion. The Afghan soon became possessed of all the low country, and the Sicques dismayed at his rapid success, and the cruelties exercised by his fierce soldiery, abandoned the plains, and sought a shelter with their families in the skirts of the mountains. A large party of Sicques had retired towards the northern districts[lxi] of Sirhend, which being more than an hundred miles

---

[lviii] The Afghans were at that time possessed of a tract of country, reaching from the Chinnaun river to the Indus.

[lix] They had been invited into Hindostan by Ghaze-ud-Dien, to support an administration which was detested by the people, and opposed by a party at court. Had not the arms of Ahmed Shah the Duranny prevailed over the Mahrattas at the battle of Pannifrett, it is probable that the Mahometan power would have been extinguished in India.

[lx] The fifth Punjab river from the eastward.

[lxi] The village of Goojerwal and Basspour, were at that time in their common places of refuge.

distant from Lahore, the station of the Afghan army, they were not apprehensive of any immediate attack. But the motions and onset of Ahmed Shah were equally rapid and dreadful. He fell suddenly on this body in February 1762, having marched from Lahore in less than two days, and cut to pieces, it is said, twenty-five thousand of their cavalry. The Sicques, in their day of success, having defiled and destroyed the mosques and other sacred places of the Mahometans, compelling also many of them to embrace the faith of Nanock, now felt the savage vengeance of their enemies. Amrut Sir was rased to the ground, and the sacred waters choaked up with its ruins. Pyramids were erected, and covered with the heads of slaughtered Sicques; and it is mentioned, that Ahmed Shah caused the walls of the principal mosques which had been polluted by the Sicques to be washed with their blood, that the contamination might be removed, and the ignominy offered to the religion of Mahomet, expiated. Yet these examples of ferocious rigour did not quell the native courage of the Sicques, who still continued to issue from the fastnesses, to hover on the rear of the Afghan armies, and to cut off their scattered parties.

AHMED SHAH, in the close of the year 1762, returned into Afghānistān, which being composed of provinces recently conquered or acquired, and inhabited by a warlike fierce people, demanded a vigilant personal attention. A body of his troops, commanded by an officer of distinguished rank, had been stationed in the Lahore territory, and in the capital, which was strongly garrisoned. But soon after the march of Ahmed Shah, the Sicques were seen descending from their various holds on the Punjab, which they rapidly laid waste, and after several desultory actions, in which the Afghans were defeated, they besieged, and what seems extraordinary, they took the city of Lahore;[38] where wildly indulging the enmity that had never ceased to inflame them against these severe scourges of their nation, they committed violent outrages. The mosques that had been rebuilt or restored to use by the Mahometans, were demolished with every mark of contempt and indignation; and the Afghans, in chains, washed the foundations with the blood of hogs. They were also compelled to excavate the reservoir at Amrut Sir, which in the preceding year they had filled up. The Sicques, however, keenly actuated by resentment, set a bound to the impulse of revenge; and though the Afghan massacre and persecution must have been deeply imprinted on their minds, they did not, it is said, destroy one prisoner in cold blood.

THE records of the Sicques give a relation of a battle fought with the Afghans, previously to the capture of Lahore: but as its asserted issue does not correspond with the series of success, which conspicuously in India accompanied the Afghan arms under Ahmed Shah, or stand supported by any collatoral proof to which I have had access, I am necessarily led to doubt some parts of the Sicque's relation. This event is said to have happened in October 1762, when the collected body of the Sicque nation, amounting to sixty thousand cavalry, had formed a junction at the ruins of Amrut Sir, for the purpose of performing some appointed ceremony, and where they resolved, expecting the attack, to pledge their national existence on the event of a battle. Ahmed Shah, at that time encamped at Lahore, marched with a strong force to Amrut Sir,[lxii] and immediately engaged the Sicques; who, roused by the fury of a desperate revenge, in sight also of the ground sacred to the founders of their religion, whose monuments had been destroyed by the enemy they were then to combat, displayed, during a bloody contest, which lasted from the morning until night, an enthusiastic and fierce courage, which ultimately forced Ahmed Shah to draw off his army and retire with precipitation to Lahore. The Sicques, it is also said, pursued the

---

lxii This place is about forty miles to the westward of Lahore.

enemy to that city, which they took after a short siege; and that Ahmed Shah, having made his escape before the surrender, crossed the Indus. Any probability of this event can only be reconciled by a supposition, that the army of Ahmed Shah had suffered some extraordinary reductions, previously to the period in which this occurrence[lxiii] is said to have happened. Without a further discussion of this clouded fact, we will proceed to the common annals of the day, where it is seen that the Duranny returned into the Punjab, in the autumn of 1763, when he retook Lahore, and again drove the Sicques from the low country. The success of this prince, though decided at the moment, were not followed by either a benefit to himself or to the country he conquered; and could be only traced by slaughter and rapine; for in the course of the following year, during his short absence, the Sicques ravaged the Punjab, expelled the Afghan garrisons, and pursued their fortune with so vigorous a rapidity, that during the year 1764, they had over-run, and seized on, an extent of territory reaching from the borders of the Indus to the districts of Dehli.

AHMED SHAH, in the three following years, continued to maintain a desultory war with the Sicques; but possessing no treasure in India, fearing also the effects of a remote residence from his native dominion, he must have at length shrunk from the difficulties of conquering a numerous people, who when driven from the plains, possessed impenetrable retreats in forests and mountains; and, what was more dreadful to their enemies, an invincible courage.[39]

AFTER the year 1767, the period of his last campaign in India, Ahmed Shah, seems to have wholly relinquished the design of subduing the Punjab. The Sicques now became the rulers of a large country, in every part of which they established an undivided authority, and raised in it the solid structure of a religion, in the propagation and defence of which, their persevering valour merit a common applause.

TIMUR SHAH, the reigning prince of Afghanistan, the son of Ahmed Shah, had made war on the Sicques with various success. During the interval of his last campaign in India, he wrested from them the city, with a large division of the province of Moultan; which the Sicques, contrary to the spirit of their national character, evacuated after a weak resistance. This surrender might on the first view be termed pusillanimous, especially when the inactive disposition of Timur is considered; but it seems to have been a natural consequence of their eternal divisions, and the fears entertained by the body at large, of the encrease of individual power. The dominions of the Sicques, whose limits are ever in a state of fluctuation, was, in the year 1782, bounded on the north by the chain of mountains that extend in an oblique line across the head of the Punjab; on the east by the possessions of the emperor and his officers, which reach to Pannifrett and Kurrwaul; on the south-east by the Agra districts; on the south by Moultan; and on the west by the Indus, except where the town and independencies of Attock, and some petty chiefships, are interspersed.

THE Sicques have reduced the largest portion of the territory of Zabitah Khan, leaving him little more than the fort of Ghous Ghur, with a very limited domain in its vicinity. This chief, the degenerate son of Najeb-ud-Dowlah, has made no vigorous effort in his defence; but thinking to sooth them, and divert their encroachments, assumed the name of a Sicque, and ostensibly, it is said, became a convert to the faith of Nanock.[lxiv] It is not seen that he derived any benefit from his apostacy; for at the

---

[lxiii] A total eclipse of the sun is said to have happened on the day of action.

[lxiv] Durm Sing, was the name taken by Zabitah Khan. He was succeeded by his son Gholam Bhahauder, in 1785, who, though an active solider, and respected by the Sicques, is not emancipated from their power.

period of my journey through the Duab, the Sicques were investing his fort, and he was reduced to the desperate alternative of calling in a body of their mercenaries to his assistance.

IN the beginning of the year 1783, a part of Sicques traversing the Ghous Ghur districts, approached the Ganges, where it forms the western limit of Rohilcund, with an intention of crossing the river, and invading the country of the vizier.[40] Being at that time in Rohilcund, I witnessed the terror and general alarm which prevailed amongst the inhabitants, who, deserting the open country, had retired into forts and places inaccessible to cavalry. The Sicques, perceiving the difficulty of passing a river in the face of the vizier's troops, which were posted on the eastern bank, receded from their purpose. This fact has been adduced to shew that the Sicques command an uninterrupted passage to the Ganges.[lxv]

THUS have I laid before you, according to the most substantial authorities that I could obtain, the origin of the Sicques; their first territorial establishment, and the outlines of the progress they made, in extending a spacious dominion, and consolidating the power which they at this day possess. We have seen this people, at two different periods, combating the force of the Moghul empire, and so severely depressed by its superior strength, that the existence of their sect was brought to the edge of annihilation. The Afghan war involved them in a series of still more grievous calamity; as they had then laid the foundation of a growing power, and more sensibly felt the ravages of a formidable foe. They were driven from the sanctuary of their religion, and persecuted with a rage which seemed to keep pace with the encreasing strength and inveteracy of their enemy: yet we have seen, that in the lowest ebb of fortune, they retained the spirit of resource; that they boldly seized on every hold which offered support; and, by an invincible perseverance, that they ultimately rose superior in a contest with the most potent prince of his age. Grand auxiliary causes operated also in the formation and final establishment of the Sicques' dominion. It hath already been noticed, that the first efforts of this people commenced at a time when the Moghul empire lost it energy and vigour; when intestine commotions, the intrigues of a luxurious court, and the defection of distant governors, had promoted the increase of individual interests, and a common relaxation of allegiance.

THE decisive superiority obtained over the Sicques, by Meer Munnoo, would, we must believe, with a judicious application of its uses, have removed to a farther distance the rank which this state now maintains in Hindostan. To develope the actions of men, with whose history we are trivially acquainted, would be fabricating too refined a system of speculation; nor would I now investigate so obscure a subject, were it not to generally observe, that the preservation of the Sicques from the effects of Meer Munnoo's success, appears to have been largely promoted by the interference of his minister Khorah Mul, who being himself a Sicque, naturally became a trusty advocate of the sect; and who, it is said, completed his ascendancy over the Mahometan, by a considerable donation. But the distracted state of Ahmed Shah's Afghan and Persian dominion, which urgently called on a personal administration, afforded the Sicques the most favourable occasions of accomplishing the conquest of the Punjab; and it is probable, that, had the Afghan prince been enabled to prolong his campaigns in Hindostan, the Sicques would not, during his life, have attained any extensive degree of national consequence.

[lxv] The Sicque forces assembled again in the beginning of the year 1785, when they entered the province of Rohilcund, and having laid it waste, for the space of one hundred miles, they returned unmolested.

I FIND an embarrassment in applying a distinct term to the form of the Sicque government, which, on the first view, bears an appearance of aristocracy; but a closer examination discovers a large vein of popular power branching through many of its parts. No honorary or titular distinction is conferred on any member[lxvi] of the state, and the chiefs are treated with a deference that would seem to arise only from the military charges they may at the instant be invested with, and from a self-preserving regard to the subordination necessarily required in conducting an armed body. Though orders are issued in a Sicque army, and a species of obedience observed, punishments are rarely inflicted; and chiefs, who often command parties of not more than fifty men, being numerous, its motions are tumultuous and irregular. An equality of rank is maintained in their civil society, which no class of men, however wealthy or powerful, is suffered to break down. At the periods when general councils of the nation were convened, which consisted of the army at large, every member had the privilege of delivering his opinion; and the majority, it is said, decided on the subject in debate. The Khalsah Sicques, even of the lowest order, are turbulent people, and possess a haughtiness of deportment which, in the common occurrences of life, peculiarly marks their character. Examples of this disposition I have myself witnessed, and one of them I think merits a distinct notice. In travelling through the Siringnaghur country, our party was joined by a Sicque horseman, and being desirous of procuring his acquaintance, I studiously offered him the various attentions which men observe to those they court. But the Sicque received my advances with a fixed reserve and disdain, giving me, however, no individual cause of offence; for his department to the other passengers was not less contemptuous. His answer, when I asked him the name of his chief, was wholly conformable to the observations I had made of his nation. He told me (in a tone of voice, and with an expression of countenance, which seemed to revolt at the idea of servitude) that he disdained an earthly superiour, and acknowledge no other master than his prophet!

THE civil and military government of the Sicques, before a common interest had ceased to actuate its operations, was conducted by general and limited assemblies, which presided over the different departments of the state. The grand convention, called in their language *Goorimotta*,[41] was that in which the army met to transact the more important affairs of the nation; as the declaration of war or peace, forming alliances, and detaching parties on the service of the year. The amount of the contributions levied on the public account was reported to this assembly, and divided among the chiefs, proportionably to the number of their troops. They were at the same time obliged to distribute a certain share of this property to their soldiers, who, on any cause of dissatisfaction, made no hesitation in quitting their service, and following a more popular leader. Subordinate officers were established for registering the political correspondence of the state, and for providing warlike stores; and the administration of ecclesiastical affairs was entrusted to a certain society of religeuse, composed chiefly of the descendants of their original priests, but they did not possess any influence in the temporal regulation of the state. These were the principal ordinances enacted by the first chiefs, when the people were united and a common object governed their public conduct. The dominions of the Sicques, now widely extended, have been since divided into numerous states, which pursue an independent interest, without a regard to general policy. The grand assembly is now rarely summoned, nor have the Sicques, since the Afghan war, been embarked in any united cause.

[lxvi] The posterity of the ten priests are occasionally denominated *purgadahs*, that is, descendants of a saint, or prophet.

THEIR military force may be said to consist essentially of cavalry; for though some artillery is maintained, it is auxwardly managed, and its uses ill understood; and their infantry, held in low estimation, usually garrison the forts, and are employed in the meaner duties of the service. A Sicque horseman is armed with a matchlock and sabre of excellent metal, and his horse is strong and well formed. In this matter I speak from a personal knowledge, having in the course of my journey seen two of their parties, each of which amounted to about two hundred horsemen. They were clothed in white vests,[lxvii] and their arms were preserved in good order: the accoutrements, consisting of priming horns and ammunition pouches, were chiefly covered with European scarlet cloth, and ornamented with gold lace. The predilection of the Sicques for the match-lock musquet, and the constant use they make of it, causes a difference in their manner of attack from that of any other Indian cavalry; a party, from forty to fifty, advance in a quick pace to the distance of a carabine shot from the enemy, and then, that the fire may be given with the greater certainty, the horses are drawn up, and their pieces discharged; when, speedily retiring about a hundred paces, they load and repeat the same mode of annoying the enemy. The horses have been so expertly trained to the performance of this operation, that on receiving a stroke of the hand, they stop from a full career. But it is not by this mode of combat that the Sicques have become a formidable people. Their successes and conquests have largely originated from an activity unparalleled by other Indian nations, from their endurance of excessive fatigue, and a keen resentment of injuries.[42] The personal endowments of the Sicques are derived from a temperance of diet, and a forbearance from many of those sensual pleasures, which have enervated the Indian Mahometans. A body of their cavalry has been known to make marches of forty or fifty miles, and to continue the exertion for many successive days.

THE forces of this nation must be numerous, though I am not possessed of any substantial document for ascertaining the amount. A Sicque will confidently say, that his country can furnish three hundred thousand cavalry, and, to authenticate the assertion, affirms that every person, holding even a small property, is provided with a horse, match-lock, and side-arms. But in qualification of this account, if we admit that the Sicques when united can bring two hundred thousand horse into the field, their force in cavalry is greater than that of any other state in Hindostan. A passage which I extracted from a memoir,[lxviii] written at Dehli in 1777, exhibits a lively picture of this people in their military capacity. "The Sicques," it represents, "are in general strong and well made; accustomed from their infancy to the most laborious life, and hardest fare, they make marches, and undergo fatigues that really appear astonishing. In their excursions they carry no tents or baggage, except, perhaps, a small tent for the principal officer: the rest shelter themselves under blankets, which serve them also in the cold weather to wrap themselves in, and which, on a march, cover their saddles. They have commonly two, some of them three, horses each, of the middle size, strong, active, and mild tempered. The provinces of Lahore and Moultan, noted for a breed of the best horses in Hindostan, afford them an ample supply; and indeed they take the greatest care to encrease it by all means in their power. Though they make merry on the demise of any of their brethren, they mourn for the death of a horse: thus shewing their love of an animal so necessary to them in their professional capacity. The food of the Sicques is of the coarsest kind, and such as the poorest people in Hindostan use from necessity. Bread, baked in ashes, and soaked in a

---

[lxvii] A long calico gown, having a close body and sleeves, with a white skirt.

[lxviii] I believe it was written by Colonel Polier. [Ed. see part II chapter 8.]

mash made of different sorts of pulse, is the best dish, and such as they never indulge in but when at full leisure; otherwise, vetches and tares, hastily parched, is all they care for. They abhor smoking tobacco, for what reason I cannot discover; but intoxicate themselves freely with spirits of their own country manufacture. A cup of the last they never fail taking after a fatigue at night. Their dress is extremely scanty: a pair of long blue drawers, and a kind of checkered plaid, a part of which is fastened round the waist, and the other thrown over the shoulder, with a mean turban, form their clothing and equipage. The chiefs are distinguished by wearing some heavy gold bracelets on their wrists, and sometimes a chain of the same metal bound round their turbans, and by being mounted on better horses: otherwise, no distinction appears amongst them. The chiefs are numerous, some of whom have the command of ten or twelve thousand cavalry; but this power is confined to a small number, the inferior officers maintaining from one to two thousand, and many not more than twenty or thirty horses; a certain quota of which is furnished by the chief, the greater part being the individual property of the horsemen."

FROM the spirit of independence so invariably infused amongst them, their mutual jealousy, and a rapacious roving temper, the Sicques at this day are seldom seen co-operating in national concert, but actuated by the influence of an individual ambition, or private distrust, they pursue such plans only as coincide with these motives. An example of their forces being engaged in opposite interests, has been noticed in the case of Mhah Sing, who succoured the Rajah of Jumbo, against the Sicque party, which had invaded his country. Before the chiefs of the Mountaineers country, at the head of the Punjab, were reduced to a tributary state, severe depredations were committed on them by the Sicques, who plundered and destroyed their habitations, carried off the cattle, and, if strong and well formed, the male children, who were made converts to the faith of Nanock. But since the payment of a fixed tribute has been stipulated, which does not amount to more than five per cent on the revenue, the Mountaineers are little molested, except when the Sicques have been called in to adjust their domestic quarrels.

THE extensive and fertile territory of the Sicques, and their attachment and application in the midst of warfare to the occupations of agriculture, must evidently produce a large revenue. The districts dependant on Lahore in the reign of Aurungzebe, produced, according to Mr Bernier, a revenue of two hundred and forty-six lacks and ninety-five thousand rupees;[lxix] and we are naturally led to suppose, from the industrious skill of the Sicques in the various branches of cultivation, that no great decrease of that amount can have taken place since the Punjab has fallen into their possession.

AN extensive and valuable commerce is also maintained in their country, which has been extended to distant quarters of India; particularly to the provinces of Bengal and Bahar, where many Sicque merchants of opulence at this time reside. The Omichund[43] who took so active, though unfortunate, a share in the revolution, which the English effected in Bengal, was a Sicque; as is his adopted son, who is now an inhabitant of Calcutta. Merchants of every nation or sect, who may introduce a traffick into their territories, or are established under their government, experience a full protection, and enjoy commercial privileges in common with their own subjects. At the same time it must be noticed, that such immunities are granted only to those who remain amongst them, or import wares for the immediate supply of the Sicque markets. But the foreign traders, or even travellers, who attempt to pass through the Punjab, are

---

[lxix] Two millions four hundred and sixty-nine thousand five hundred pounds sterling, at two shillings for the rupee.

often plundered and usually ill-treated. In the event of no molestation being offered to people of this description, the escape is ever spoken of with a degree of joyful surprise, and a thanksgiving is offered to Providence for the singular escape. This conduct, inimical to the progress of civilization, and an impediment to the influx of wealth, proceeds from an extreme jealousy of strangers, added to a rapacity of temper, which makes them averse to the encouragement of any scheme in whose success they do not immediately participate.

THE Sicques are not rigorous in their stipulations with the Mahometan proselytes, who, if they abstain from beef's flesh, (which is held in equal abhorrence by the Sicques as by the Hindoos), and perform the more ostensible duties, as burning their dead, and preserving the hair of the head, an indulgent latitude is granted in all the other articles of the creed of Nanock. The Mahometans who reside in the Punjab are subject to occasional oppression, and often to the insult of the lower classes of the people; among whom it is not an uncommon practice to defile the places of worship, by throwing in the carcases of hogs and other things held impure by the Musselman law. The Mahometans are also prohibited from announcing their stated times of prayer, which, conformably to their usage, is proclaimed in a loud tone of voice. A Sicque who in the chace shall have slain a wild hog, is frequently known to compel the first Mahometan he meets to carry to his home the body of the animal; and, on being initiated into the rites of their religion, the Sicques will sometimes require a Mahometan convert to bind on his arm the tusk of a boar, that by this act of national impurity, he may the more avowedly testify a renunciation and contempt of the tenets of his former faith. These facts will sufficiently mark the haughty and insulting demeanor, which, with few deviations, forms a prominent feature in the character of the military Sicques; but we may also ascribe a certain portion of their severe and contumelious treatment of the Mahometans, to a remembrance of recent injuries.

THE discordant interests which agitate the Sicque nation, and the constitutional genius of the people, must incapacitate them, during the existence of these causes, from becoming a formidable offensive power; nor are they invested with that species of executive strength which is necessary to advance and establish a distant conquest. In the defence and recovery of their country, the Sicques displayed a courage of the most obstinate kind, and manifested a perseverance, under the pressure of calamities, which bear an ample testimony of native resource, when the common danger had roused them to action, and gave but one impulse to their spirit. Should any future cause call for the combined efforts of the Sicques to maintain the existence of empire and religion, we may see some ambitious chief led on by his genius and success, and, absorbing the power of his associates, display, from the ruins of their commonwealth, the standard of monarchy.[44] The page of history is filled with the like effects, springing from the like causes. Under such a form of government, I have little hesitation in saying, that the Sicques would be soon advanced to the first rank amongst the native princes of Hindostan; and would become a terror to the surrounding states.[lxx]

I am,

Dear Sir,

Yours, &c.

[lxx] Mhadgee Scindia, a Mahratta chief, by seizing the relics of the Imperial authority and domain, has placed himself in the situation which the Sicques must have been desirous of occupying. This resolution will naturally create a national enmity, perhaps a contest, between the northern branch of the Mahratta empire, and the Sicques.

NOTES

1. James, *Raj*, 44.
2. *Dictionary of Indian Biography*, s.v. "Forster, George."
3. Zābitā Khān (d. 1785) (q.v.) was the Rohīllā chief whose territories bordered on the lower districts of Srīnagar in the state of Garhwāl.
4. The men were sent by the Bhangī *misl* Sirdār, Rāi Singh of Būriā, who collected the tribute from Garhwāl state.
5. A reference to the Karorāsinghīā Sirdār, Bhangā Singh of Thānesar, who held Sirmur state tributary. Its capital is Nahān.
6. The Kāngrā chief, Rājā Sansār Chand (1765–1823), requested the assistance of Jai Singh Kanhaiyā (see illustration 3 for both of their portraits with other hill rājās) in the recovery of the Kāngrā fort, his ancestral home, from Nawāb Saif Alī Khān (an old Mughal officer). The combined forces laid a siege in 1782, and during the following year, the Nawāb died of old age resulting in the surrender of the fort. The siege was still underway when Forster passed through on his travels, and the Sikh horsemen he mentions were most likely men of the Kanhaiyā *misl*. Interestingly, the fort fell into the hands of Jai Singh who held it until 1786, when he was compelled to retire from the hills due to losses in the plains.
7. An example of a battle cry from the eighteenth century that has been kept alive in the oral tradition of the Akālī Nihangs: "Young Nihangs get ready! Taking hold of battle standards they run into battle. Facing the Pathāns they challenge them. Seeing [the Nihangs], the great master-less (i.e. without a Gurū), shaven-headed warriors flee. Says Gurū Gobind Singh, 'Be fearless then you may call yourself a Gurū's Singh. Give your head and say, make me yours.'" We are grateful to Nidar Singh Nihang for providing this information.
8. Jai Singh (d. 1793) was the Kanhaiyā *misl* leader whose authority held sway over the Kāngrā group of states at the time of Forster's travels. He was paid an annual tribute by Rāj Singh (1755–1794), the ruler of Chambā: "In the Kangra Settlement Report, Mr. Barnes refers to a document in his (Jai Singh's) name fixing the amount of tribute payable by Chamba at 4,001 rupees. This document is dated A.D. 1776." *District and State Gazetteers of the Undivided Punjab*, 4 vols. (Delhi: Low Price Publications, 1993. Reprint of 1910 edition), vol. 3, 'Chamba State', 99.
9. This is probably a reference to Jai Singh Kanhaiyā (see illustration 4) who held Datār as a tributary and was active in the Hill States at the time of this account. Sikh military involvement in the Hill States began with Jassā Singh Rāmgharīā who made several states (namely Kāngrā, Nūrpur, and Chambā) tributary in 1770. Five years later, supremacy passed to Jai Singh Kanhaiyā, who retained it until 1785–1786.
10. Forster presents us with a very interesting mixed party of Muslim and Sikh horsemen. It may be that the men were part of an alliance between the Sikhs and their old ally, Zābitā Khān, the Rohīllā chief. A letter dated Lucknow, May 31, 1775, mentions one such Rohīllā–Sikh alliance: "Zabitah Khan who has collected a large number of the Sikhs in the vicinity of the capital is making disturbances there." Calendar of Persian Correspondence, vol. IV, 1815 in Gupta, *History of the Sikhs*, 3: 87, n. 2.
11. Forster is wrong here as Ranjīt Dev died in April 1781, two years before he traveled through the region.

12. Forster's account is slightly confused as he is mixing two events in the history of Jammū. Ranjīt Dev had two sons, Brij Rāj Dev and Dalel Singh. Brij Rāj Dev was overlooked as a successor due to his dissolute character, so he revolted against his father in 1774, seeking the assistance of Charhat Singh Sukkarchakkīā and Jai Singh Kanhaiyā in seizing the throne of Jammū. Ranjīt Dev called on the powerful Bhangī chiefs, Jhandā Singh and Gandā Singh, to whom he had been paying a tribute since 1770. During the campaign, Charhat Singh died when his own gun burst, and Jhandā Singh was murdered at the instigation of Jai Singh. Eventually, both parties retired from the field with heavy losses, and peace was established between Ranjīt Dev and Brij Rāj Dev, who was declared the rightful successor. After the campaign, the son of the late Charhat Singh, the ten-year-old Mahā Singh, exchanged turbans with Brij Rāj Dev as a sign of lifelong friendship. In 1782, Brij Rāj Dev arranged for the murder of his more popular younger brother, Dalel Singh, and one of his sons while they were on a religious tour. Dalel Singh's younger son, Jīt Singh, who was still at Jammū, was imprisoned. He escaped and sought the protection of the Bhangīs. Taking advantage of the enmity that existed between the Bhangī and Kanhaiyā *misls*, Brij Rāj Dev invited Haqīqat Singh Kanhaiyā (a cousin of Jai Singh), with the promise of one lakh rupees, to help in ousting the Bhangīs from the *parganah* of Karianwālā (which Forster calls "the most valuable division of the Jumbo districts"). However, Brij Rāj Dev took possession himself and declined to pay up, with the result that the Bhangī and Kanhaiyā chiefs formed an alliance against him. The latter called on his friend, Mahā Singh, to support his cause. The ensuing campaign is the one that Forster writes about.

13. Mahā Singh (1773–1790) (q.v.) was nineteen years old at the time.

14. The beginnings of Sikh territorial gain started in earnest following the fall of Sirhind, which was captured by them in January 1764. A vast tract of land, 350 km long and 250 km wide, worth an annual revenue of approximately fifty-two lakhs of rupees fell into the hands of the Sikhs, who became the *de facto* rulers of the Punjab. "Tradition still describes how the Sikhs dispersed as soon as the battle was won, and how, riding day and night, each horseman would throw his belt and scabbard, his articles of dress and accoutrement, until he was almost naked, into successive villages to mark them as his." J.D. Cunningham, *A History of the Sikhs* (London: John Murray, 1849. Reprint, New Delhi: S. Chand & Co., 1985), 92–3.

15. At the time of writing this account, weapons were also a strong feature of Sikh worship, having been introduced by the sixth Gurū, Hargobind, and formerly prescribed by the tenth Gurū, Gobind Singh: "We have seen that one great distinguishing feature of their system is that war is made an essential part of religion. To indicate their belief in this doctrine they worship the military weapons of their Gurus." Monier Williams, *Religious Thought and Life in India* (London: 1883), pt. 1, 172.

16. This was actually September 7, 1539. *The Encyclopaedia of Sikhism*, s.v. "Gurū Nānak."

17. This place is known as Derā Bābā Nānak at Kartārpur, and is now in Pakistan.

18. This should be March 29, 1552. *The Encyclopaedia of Sikhism*, s.v. "Angad Dev, Gurū."

19. The compilation of the Sikh scriptures, the Ādi Gurū Granth Sāhib, was undertaken by Gurū Arjan, the son of Gurū Rām Dās, and completed in

1604. The histories of the earlier Gurūs were recorded in the *Janam Sākhīs*, none of which are known to have been written by any of the Gurūs.

20. Refer to part I, chapter 1 for a contemporary account of the execution of Gurū Arjan. Shaikh Ahmad Sirhindī (1564–1624), the most prominent member of the Naqshbandī order in India, derived great satisfaction from the execution. In one of his letters (No. 193 in the *Maktūbāt-i-Imām-i-Rabbānī*, or "Epistles of the Divine Prelate") he writes: "The execution at this time of the accursed Kafir of Goindwall . . . with whatever motive . . . is an act of the highest grace for the followers of Islam." Gupta, *History of the Sikhs*, 1: 153.

21. Sikh tradition holds that Chandū Shāh, a wealthy banker and revenue official of the Mughal court at Lahore, took charge of Gurū Arjan and had him tortured to death (as ordered by Emperor Jahāngīr). Chandū Shāh made a poor gram-parcher, Gurdittā, heat up a large iron plate, upon which the Gurū was seated, and ordered him to pour hot sand over the Gurū. Some years later when Jahāngīr was reconciled to Gurū Hargobind, Chandū Shāh was handed over to the Sikhs. They paraded him through the streets of Lahore and when they passed where Gurdittā practised his trade, out of contempt for the cruel Chandū Shāh, he threw his heavy, hot ladle at him, striking him in the stomach and killing him. *The Encyclopaedia of Sikhism*, s.v. "Gurdittā Bhathiārā."

22. None of the Gurū's battles were fought against Jahāngīr. Rather, several were fought against the Mughal *faujdārs* during the reign of Shāh Jahān. The first occurred in 1628, when Shāh Jahān was hunting in the jungles of Jallo between Lahore and Amritsar. Gurū Hargobind and his Sikhs were also hunting in the same area and a quarrel broke out about the game between the imperial servants and the Sikhs. A skirmish followed in which the imperialists were beaten.

23. A contemporary writer reported the imprisonment of the Gurū as being for a period of twelve years. This appears excessive and most likely included a period of house arrest in the Punjab in addition to time spent in Gwalior fort. "After Arjan Mal, Hargobind also made a claim to succession and sat in his father's seat. He always accompanied the victorious camp of Jahāngīr. He encountered many difficulties. One was [i.e. arose from the fact] that he adopted the style of soldiers, and, contrary to his father's practice, girded the sword, employed servants and took to hunting. His Majesty Jannat Makānī [Jahāngīr] sent Hargobind to Gwalior on account of the demand for the balance of the fine he had imposed on Arjan Mal. He remained in that place for twelve years. He was not allowed salted food. During that period, the *masands* and Sikhs went and knelt down in *sijda* [i.e. with foreheads touching the ground] before the wall of the fort. At last, His Majesty Jannat Makānī, out of kindness, released the *Gurū*." Irfan Habib trans., "Sikhism and the Sikhs 1645–46 from 'Mobad,' *Dabistān-i-Mazāhib*," in *Sikh History from Persian Sources*, ed. J.S. Grewal and I. Habib (New Delhi: Tulika, 2001), 68.

24. Three sons survived the Gurū: Ani Rāi, Sūraj Mall, and Tegh Bahādur.

25. He was actually a granduncle.

26. Forster's comments about the Gurū being imprisoned for two years does not appear correct and has not been generally accepted by Sikh historians. Rājā Jai Singh (1605–1667) of Jaipur is known to have had connections with the seventh and eighth Gurūs (Gurū Har Rāi and Gurū Har Krishan, respectively) but he was sent to the Deccan by Emperor Aurangzeb late in 1664 (the year that Tegh Bahādur became Gurū), where he eventually died some three years later. It is unlikely that he accompanied the Gurū to Bengal, as Forster has claimed. However Jai Singh's son, Rām Singh, was sent by Aurangzeb in

January 1668 on an expedition against the Ahoms of Assām. He is believed
to have met the Gurū at Dhākā, setting off together for Assām at the close of
1668. *The Encyclopaedia of Sikhism*, s.v. "Tegh Bahādur, Gurū."

27. Gurū Gobind Singh provides the reason for his father's execution in his autobiographical composition *Bachitar Nātak*: "My father sacrificed his life, to
protect the religion of the Hindus—their sacred thread and frontal mark. In
this dark Kali age, he performed this supreme act of sacrifice. For the sake of
Dharma [righteousness], he gave away his head, without a sigh on his lips. Lo,
he surrendered his life—but not his resolve." Gopal Singh, *A History of the
Sikh People* (New Delhi: World Book Centre, 1979. Revised and updated New
Delhi: World Book Centre, 1988), 257.

28. The altercation between the young Gurū Gobind Singh and the Srīnagar chief
is not documented in any of the recognized sources.

29. The identity of the "Hindoo chief" mentioned by Forster cannot be identi-
fied for sure. He notes earlier that this chief gave Mākhovāl to Gurū Gobind
Singh which leads to the uncertainty in naming him as it was his father, Gurū
Tegh Bahādur, who purchased the land from the Rājā of Bilāspur. Gurū
Gobind Singh lived there for some time, re-naming it Anandpur Sāhib.

30. A report (*akbhārāt-i-darbār-i-mu'allā*) dated August 4, 1707 from Bahādur
Shāh's court confirms this point: "Gobind the Nānakī came armed, in accordance with orders, and presented himself, making an offering of 100 *ashrafis*
[gold coins]. A robe of honour and *padak* [medallion], set with precious
stones, was given to him, and he was permitted to leave." Irfan Habib trans.,
"Gurū Gobind Singh and the Sikhs of the Khālsa, reports from Bahādur
Shāh's Court, 1707–10" in *Sikh History from Persian Sources*, ed. J.S. Grewal
and Irfan Habib, 2001, 106.

31. The Gurū's movements in the company of the emperor have been misinter-
preted by many early writers. There is no firm evidence of the Gurū ever having taken a military command in the Mughal emperor's army. Given the
Gurū's independent character, it is more probable that he was invited by the
emperor to accompany him while they conducted their diplomatic discussions
over the issues of persecution faced by the Gurū and the Sikhs in the Punjab.
Macauliffe, *The Sikh Religion*, 234–5.

32. The principal points of deviation include the abandoning of blue clothes for
red, the adoption of the new salutation "Fateh Darshan" and abstinence from
eating meat. These points were noted by the grandson of a contemporary to
Bandā Bahādur, Ratan Singh Bhangū, *Prachīn Panth Prakāsh*, 132–3.

33. This is an oft-quoted observation. The evidence to the contrary of this is the
presence of extant Mughal monuments in Sirhind, principally the tomb of
Shaikh Ahmad Sirhindī.

34. Refer to part II, chapter 4 for notes on contemporary accounts of the execution of Bandā Singh Bahādur.

35. Forster is describing the *charan amrit* (q.v.) ceremony which was the method
of initiation used by all of the Gurūs before Gurū Gobind Singh established
khande dī pahul (q.v.). This latter method was used when initiating into the
Khālsā (q.v.) and incorporates an undeniable military ethos. However, even
with the establishment of the Khālsā, the non-military orders within the Sikh
community, mainly the *Udāsīs, Sevā Panthīs*, and *Nirmalās*, continued to use
charan amrit, even to the present day.

36. This is wrong as cremation is the way of dealing with the bodies of the dead.
Forster actually corrects himself later on in his account.

37. Khulāsā (q.v.).

38. Lahore was first occupied in May 1764 by the Bhangī *misl Sirdārs*. A Muslim witness to their presence in the city wrote, "The city had been ruined by the atrocities of the Sikhs. All the people of the place were in trouble and misery. The whole town from inside and its suburbs lay in ruin. Its building had been pulled down and all the mosques were deserted. They were spoiled by the dung and fodder of their horses. The learned peoples, nobles and the Sayyids of the city led a miserable life. When the Dogs [Sikhs] partitioned this land, the city became the *Jagir* of the accursed Jhanda [Singh Bhangī]. They divided the whole country, Sarhind, Lahore, Panjab, Multan, Jhang, Khusab and the Chenab among themselves." Qāzī Nūr Mohammed, *Jang Namah*, Gupta, *History of the Sikhs*, 2: 215. It was then reoccupied by Ahmad Shāh in December 1766, but taken again by the Bhangī *Sirdārs* in July 1767 when Ahmad Shāh returned to his own country. Also see Griffith, part III, chapter 13.

39. Another example of a battle chant from the rich oral tradition of the Akālī Nihangs illustrates this "invincible courage" of the Sikhs: "Seeing the army of locusts [the enemy], the Singhs laugh. They shout out challenges and battle cries. Like tigers, the Singhs roar. Hearing the roar of the Singhs, the hearts of those worthless cowards shudder with fear. They can find no place to hide. They can find no direction to run and escape. In their hearts, they feel like crying. Oh, the Singhs are very powerful and strong. None may subdue them. The Singhs deal mighty blows. No one can suffer their strikes. The Singhs are very war-like. They are always waging war. The Singhs know great technique. With the application of their first technique they subdue and slay. Oh, you pathetic locust, why have you come? Why have you entered the mouth of death? Oh, run, run and hide, hide from your death. Hide crying in your mother's lap. If you resist the Khālsā, you will have your head and face cut. You will have your legs and arms broken. You will have your stomach and entrails ripped out. If you resist the Khālsā, your nose will be split, your neck broken. Into the mouth of death you will fall. Oh, run, run and hide, hide from your death, hide crying in your mother's lap. Or else the Khālsā's staff is about to thunder. Taking your life, I will correct your errant ways." We are grateful to Nidar Singh Nihang for this information.

40. Oudh territory—British protectorate.

41. Though Forster mentions *Gurmatā* (q.v.), he actual means the *Sarbat Khālsā* (q.v.).

42. Tradition relates how Sikh warriors considered the scars inflicted in the thick of battle as medals on their bodies which they happily suffered with resilience. An example of this attitude is to be found in the account of Botā Singh and Garjā Singh who were martyred in 1738 fighting with just their *salotar* (clubs) and stones against a much larger Mughal force, who were mounted and armed with matchlocks and bows: "When the [enemy's] weapons cut their skin or muscle, the [two] Singhs did not acknowledge [the pain]. But when their bones were broken, only then did the Singhs begin to tire. The arrows struck them but the Singhs pulled them out and threw them to the ground. [Taunting the Mughals] the Singhs said, 'Wasted are your arrows. They do not even tear our bodies.'" Bhangū, *Prachīn Panth Prakāsh*, 245.

43. See part II, chapter 5 for more details.

44. This prediction was later fulfilled by Ranjīt Singh of the Sukkarchakkīā *misl*.

CHAPTER 13

"EXTRAORDINARY MODERN PEOPLE":
DOMINIONS OF THE SIKHS, 1794

Mr Griffith to Mr Adamson, Bombay (dated Surat, February 17, 1794),
Containing Information Respecting the Characters of the Inhabitants on the
Banks of the Indus (Home Misc. Series 456b), Oriental and Indian Office
Collection, British Library, London, pp. 625–99.

Little is known of John Griffith, the author of the copperplate script
memorandum now preserved in the India Office library. He was, for some
time, Resident at the Basra factory in Iraq, then the chief of the Surat Factory
in India, followed by a short stint as Governor of Bombay in 1795. It was
from Surat in 1794 that he wrote to Alexander Adamson, an Assistant to
Treasurer and Transfer Master in Bombay, with details of the most important
inhabitants on the banks of the river Indus. His introductory remarks clarify
the rationale for his work: "The Manners and Disposition of the People, who
occupy its [the river Indus's] Banks, are perhaps as various as the face of the
Country, which they inhabit. The slightest information on the subject of its
present Political and Commercial State hitherto, in general but obscurely
known, may be considered not entirely unworthy of Attention." Griffith
begins with an account of Sind and Multān before touching upon the Sikhs.
He ends with a detailed account of Kandahār, which at the time would have
been the principal city for the Durrānīs whose plunderous invasions plagued
the Punjab for almost a century.

It is clear from the nature of the document that Griffith authored that he
was extremely interested in the natural history of the region he wrote about.
His memorandum is preoccupied with the most intimate detail of the flora of
the Punjab, and it would not be unreasonable to assume that the reason for its
instruction was to determine the lay of the land should the British ever wish to
occupy the area from the Punjab to Kandahār in Afghanistan. Many of the

later nineteenth century *Great Gamers* who were to craftily map and plan possible entry routes from Russia into India also took particular note of the flora of the country they traveled through. These notes became vitally important military intelligence as London and Moscow simultaneously assessed the viability of sending tens of thousands of armed men and support systems through the hostile passes between the two countries. If this was the case, and indeed Griffith was an early unsuspecting gamer, then his hand written notes would represent the raw data that the military machine in London would later use in their planning of the Punjab Campaigns. His later counterparts produced watered down, boys-own version of their travels for the general public, whilst retaining the more important revelations for their London spymasters.

Griffith's writings do shed light, in a very detailed manner, on the politics of the Punjab during his travel through the country. A particular feature of the memorandum is the emergence of an important political nexus occurring around Lahore. Specifically mentioned in the text are four *misl* leaders: Lahinā Singh, Gujjar Singh, Dīwān Singh, and Mahā Singh.

Whilst Lahinā Singh and Gujjar Singh can be identified as members of the Bhangī *misl*, they were not directly related to each other. Lahinā Singh was the son of a smallholder from the Jalandhar Doāb. As a young boy he ran away from home arriving at the doorstep of an important *misaldār*, the legendary Gurbakhsh Singh, reputed to be one of Harī Singh Bhangī's best warriors. It is said that they derived their epithet from the copious use of *bhang* by the founder of the *misl*, Chajjā Singh, a contemporary of Bandā Singh Bahādur and Gurū Gobind Singh.

Lahinā Singh became an adopted son, usurping the favored status of Gurbakhsh Singh's eldest nephew, Gujjar Singh. In 1763 when the old *misaldār* died, the two sons violently clashed with each other laying claim to the not-inconsiderable property that Gurbakhsh Singh had amassed during his plundering days under Harī Singh Bhangī.

The dispute finally settled, the warring brothers set their sights northward to the once grand Mughal city of Lahore. Now crumbling in the wake of Mughal decline, an ineffectual and despotic Hindu vassal of Ahmad Shāh Durrānī administered the city. Motivated by the rich pickings and the relative ease with which Lahore could be attained, the brothers mounted an audacious attack. The Governor, Kābulī Mal, quickly realized the futility of resistance and in a final despicable act, plundered the city one last time, leaving his nephew, Amīr Singh, to face the Sikhs. The city was captured with relative ease, and the brothers were joined the next morning by other Bhangī *Sirdār*s and leaders of the Kanhaiyā *misl*. Ultimately the new Sikh rulers of Lahore were joined by a Charhat Singh Sukkarchakkīā whose son, Mahā Singh, would figure prominently in the life of Gujjar Singh, and grandson, Ranjīt Singh, would ultimately capture, hold, and rule a sovereign Punjab kingdom, for forty years until his death in 1839, from Lahore.

With peace, the old squabbles between the brothers reignited. Resolution was found in a pact that split the city three ways between the Bhangī brothers and a prominent Kanhaiyā *misaldār*, Sobhā Singh.

Gujjar Singh, presumably bored by the bureaucracy of peacetime, headed north where he enjoyed considerable success in capturing Gujrāt. He died in 1788 some six years before the date of the memorandum. Judging by his inclusion in Griffith's list of Sikh chiefs of the time, his personality must still have loomed large over the Punjab.

In 1767, two years after taking the city, the newly self-appointed Sikh governors of Lahore beat a hasty retreat as Ahmad Shāh Durrānī made what became his final descent into the Punjab. Within a year, the *Sirdār*s had returned and reinstalled themselves. In 1794 when Griffith wrote the memorandum, Lahinā Singh was an "able and enlightened administrator"[1] of Lahore along with Sobhā Singh Kanhaiyā who rather mysteriously is not warranted a mention in Griffith's account.

Gujjar Singh, who is mentioned, had by that stage headquartered himself in Gujrāt but died in 1788 leaving three sons. Having married his second son Sāhib Singh to the daughter of Charhat Singh Sukkarchakkīā, he had hoped to cement the future of the Bhangī *misl* through marriage. However, he had unwittingly invited a Trojan horse into his family—one that would ultimately and tumultuously lead to the end of Gujjar Singh's beloved Bhangī *misl*.

Sāhib Singh's new brother-in-law was Mahā Singh Sukkarchakkīā. The two quarreled bitterly despite the attempts by Rāj Kaur, sister of Mahā Singh, to reconcile the two *Sirdār*s. Quarrels turned to conflict and in 1792 the two battled. At the age of just thirty-two, Mahā Singh was inexplicably injured, dying some three days late in Gujrānwālā. His son, Ranjīt Singh, was only twelve at the time of the events that led to his father's death.

Ranjīt moved characteristically quickly when he finally acquired power. Having taken Lahore and maneuvered Sāhib Singh out of power, he further marginalized the now debilitated and debauched Sāhib Singh by granting him a subservient *jagīr* within his own territory. In 1810, when Sāhib Singh Bhangī died and Ranjīt Singh had married two of his widows, he finally and irrevocably subsumed the Bhangī *misl*, finally avenging the sanguine events of his father's death and putting an end to one of the most prominent Sikh confederacies of the eighteenth century.

It is likely that Griffith witnessed Sikh warriors as is evidenced in his description of Sikhs. The "capaciously large" turbans, wound with wire and war implements is almost uniquely unusual to the Akālī Nihangs—now a marginalized element of the Sikh *panth* but according to Griffiths the archetypal Sikh warrior of the time. The practice of drinking *bhang*, a sacrament containing dried cannabis leaves, and the unremitting devotion to blue clothing is similarly redolent of the Akālī Nihangs. Griffith also notes the tactics of the Sikhs in engaging with their enemy. In this case, he notes the particular relationship between the Sikh guerrillas and the Durrānī invaders. Describing the Sikh community as a disparate one without a formal organization and later identifying the mode of attack in terms of small groups of men attacking and harassing the enemy, Griffith gives a vivid account of the Sikh peoples' war of the eighteenth century. One veteran of this period summed up the tactic in rustic terms: "Hit the enemy hard enough to kill, run, turn back and hit him again; run again, hit and run until you exasperate the enemy, and then, melt away."[2]

Griffith gives the reader an interesting summary of the character of the Sikhs. Their reputation is that of "being rather mild and benignant than otherwise, in their interior Government." He is also confident enough to give them credit "for many of the good Qualities of Humanity."

In his 1794 account, Griffith makes mention of a prophecy attributed, he says, to the sacred writing of the Sikhs. The prophecy of the pending emergence of the British as a force that would destroy Mughal rule in Delhi is ascribed to the capture and martyrdom of Gurū Tegh Bahādur. Traditional sources are firm in stating that the Emperor Aurangzeb was enraged that the imprisoned Gurū had breached the royal etiquette by gazing southward toward the imperial *zenānā*. Confronted with this further offence, the Gurū is said to have replied, "I was looking in the direction of the Europeans who are coming from beyond the seas to tear down thy *pardas* and destroy thine empire."[3] This prophecy reappeared in subsequent years in different forms finally developing into the prediction of an Anglo-Sikh conquest of Delhi.[4]

The River Sind or Indus is well known to be formed by the confluence of ten subordinate Streams, issuing chiefly from among the Mountains of the greater and lesser Tibet. It traverses a Tract of Country, near six hundred and fifty British Miles in direct length, from the Station of Attok, to it's disemboguement in the Arabian Sea.

The Manners and Disposition of the People, who occupy it's Banks, are perhaps as various as the face of the Country, which they inhabit. The slightest information on the subject of it's present Political and Commercial State hitherto, in general but obscurely known, may be considered not entirely unworthy of Attention.

This is the object of the following Notes.

Unfortunately, the only light we are enabled to throw upon the Business, is derived principally from the verbal relation of Natives, who, from the habit of observing but superficially, things that do not interest them, are sometimes faithful, but seldom accurate in their representations; In one point of view, however, we may venture to give implicit credit to the following circumstances, namely, so far as they relate to Commercial Produce.

Sind, or Sindah
The Province of Sind, comprehending the Delta of the Indus called Tattah, extends along the Sea Coast, from the Confines of Kutch, to the Western Branch of the Sind about 170 Miles, and along that River towards Multan; to Behkker, about 300 Miles. It is at present a Government tributary to Salem Shah, the Son and Successor of Timmur Shah Durrani, King of Kandahar and Kabul, who died about the middle of 1792; Futtah Ally the Surdaar of the Province, and who has held possession near 20 years, resides at Nagure Tattah, in the general defalcation of the Empire of Dehly, he wrested it from Gulaam Shah, the Moghul's Subahdar; But a report is now prevailing that a force is advancing from Kandahar to remove him, and establish a Relation of Gulaam Shah's in his Room.

The Subjects of this Chief are composed of various casts, Mahomedans and Hindoos; Of the latter, are Brahmins, Katries, Banians, Jaats, and Koolis. The Jaats[5] are said to observe some institutions similar to the Seiks, wear their Hair and Beards in the same manner, and are part of the same People, who under Swrudge Mul,[6] &c[a], formerly possessed many of the Countries in the North of India, now in the hands of Scindia and the Mahrattas. Of the Mahomedans, are both Moghuls and Belouhties.[7] These last are that race of Men, commonly known in the middle parts of Hindostan by the name of Sindians; of much estimation in the Indian Armies, warlike, but untractably averse to discipline; They were also formerly well known on the Coast of Mekraan, or rather Laar; to the former, their Country is contiguous, for their thievish, inhospitable, and treacherous disposition to the Voyagers who touched upon that Coast.

The principal places in the Country are as follows; Nagur Tattah, the Capital Heiderabad; Sind an open Town 70 Coss above Tattah; Rhodabad Jurna or the old Rhodabad, Rhodabad nawa, or the new; Rambunder, Shahabad, Ammerkote, probably that marked in the Map, in the Desert of Kutch, Mittakote, Karaly, Bunder, Aomarkote, Hujraat, Shaherabad, and Behkker. This last was formerly a place of some strength and importance, and the Capital of considerable Territory, but is now like most others in this unhappy Country, falling to ruins; the Historian of the first ten years of the Reign of Aurungzebe, mentions the Fort of Bhakur, as a place of strength, into which the accomplished but unfortunate Dara Shegoh threw some of his Women and Treasure, in his distressful flight towards Kutch. Below this Place about 25 Coss, the same Historian says, there is a Road leading towards Kandahar, which the afflicted Prince was inclined to follow, and which probably would have rescued him from the fate, with which he afterwards met, but the entreaties of his Women, terrified with the idea of the difficulties they expected to encounter on that Road, and the fortune of his crafty and victorious Brother prevailing, he continued his Flight down the Indus.

The Country is described at that time to have been for the most part Jungul, or Forest on both Sides the River from Bhakur to Suvestaan, another Port about half way between Bhakur and the Forks of the Indus, which obliged Aurungzebes Generals to relinquish the pursuit; There exists but little reason to suppose that the Country is much improved since that period.

The Manufactures of the Country are all sorts of white and coloured Piece Goods. Here also are bred, excellent Horses for Cavalry, Camels, and Horned Cattle in abundance; the Soil produces Grain of Sorts, Cotton, Indigo, Sugar, Saltpetre, Hing or Assafatida, with fruits of various kinds.

The prevailing Color of Apparel of the Inhabitants is Black or rather dark Blue. They receive in importation from Gujraat &c[a] Silk, Nutmegs, Cloves, Mace, Ambir, Copper, Oil, Teakwood, planks &c[a].

The Surdaar maintains, it is said, a considerable Body of Horse and foot, but of the Revenue, by which he is enabled to support them, no probable estimate can be formed.

At Strikaarpoor, opposite to Behkker, commences a Track of Country Adjacent, to both sides of the River in the hands of the Dadoopootra—a people who form a lawless Banditti, principally Faquiers, have of late years established themselves into a permanent Government, under their Chieftain Bhavel Khawn; Some distance above Behkker, and reckoned midway between Multan and Tattah, is their Capital Bhavilpoor; At this place, the Kabul Merchants are permitted to pass their Horses, and from hence they cross the Desert to Bukaneer, about 70 Coss distance; At this place also, the Gagra, (quere, Kaggar) a River of considerable width and depth, empties itself into the Indus. Strikaarpoor is a very considerable Mart for Horses; The

Country altho' in rather a wild State, is represented to be extremely populous and full of Villages. The Dadoopootra acknowledge themselves tributary to Salem Shah.[8] From the Character of these People, the communication between Multan and the Sea must prove exceedingly precarious, and sometimes totally impracticable, and perhaps this is the best reason that can be offered, why the Merchants in general from the South East of Persia, Cabul, &c[a], to refer to fatiguing and circuitous land Journey by Jaudpoor &c[a] in their way to the West of India, and relinquish the advantage of a noble River, navigable for Vessels of 20 and 50 Tons, nearly as high up as it's confluence with the Sutlooje.[9] We have reason to conclude this Country the least explored by the English, of any in India.

Multan

Proceeding up the Indus from Bhavilpoor, we pass through the same difficult Country on both sides the River, and the Bone of Continual Contention between the Officers of Salem Shah, the Dadoopootra, and the Seick, to Sidpoor,[10] in the possession of the latter, about 40 Coss below the City of Multan.

The City of Multan with the principal part of the Peninsula of Outch, was taken from the Seick about 15 years ago by Timmur Shah the Durrani, to whose Son and Successor Salam Shah, it is still subject. It is estimated about 500 Coss from Dehly, and 250 from Lahore; It is situated about 3 Coss from the Chunnah or Chunnaab;[11] The Fort, garrisoned by Salem Shah's Patans, is said to be washed by that River when flooded. The City is falling fast to Ruins, inhabited by Mahommedans and Hindoos, and Seeck, which last it would appear are daily gaining ground in this part of India.

The Manufacturers are Piece Goods, white Cloths, and Chintz of all sorts. The adjacent Country produces various kinds of Grain, also Cotton and Indigo, and fruits, &c[a].

It receives by Importation, Pearl, Kincobs,[12] Gold Thread, Elephants Teeth, Broad Cloths, Nutmegs, Cloves, Mace, Copper, Vermilion &c[a], and Drugs.

Dominians of the Seeck

This extraordinary modern People is in possession of nearly the whole of the fertile Country of the Punjaab, with the Territory South Eastward of the Sutlooje as far as Karnaal, the Scene of Nadir Shah's decisive Victory over the Armies of Mahommed Shah of Dehly, being in extent, from Attok to Karnaal, about 420 Miles, and from Rotass Gur (belonging to Salem Shah) to the Scene of their Contests with the Dadoopootra on the Indus, (excepting the Territory of Outch) about 300 Miles.

Their Capital is the celebrated City of Lahore on the Raavee; Their principal Chiefs, if they can be said to acknowledge any, are four, namely; Lana Sing, Goojer Sing, Diwan Sing,[13] and Maha Sing. It may not perhaps be deemed amiss, to offer in this place, what circumstances we have been able to collect, relating to this eccentric Class of Mankind.

They are said to have received their Tenets from a Hindoo of the Kutree cast, of the name of Nanuk, a Fanatic in the reign of the Emperor Aurungzebe. This Man having long led the Life of an Ascetic,[14] pretended to have received a divine revelation to the following effect;

"Baba Nanuk eici horon jeici Nunne doo"

that is nearly expressing,

"Nanuk, have the same Dependence on the
"Creator, as the tender blade of Grass,
"which receives its nourishment from the
 "dew of heaven".

This he looked upon as an order to divest himself of obedience to all human Authority, and was consequently an object of long persecution to that Emperor, who had him confined in a strong Cage.[15] This had the ordinary effect of persecution, tho increasing the number of his followers. The Seick, in the performance of the religious Ceremonies, always invoke the name of their Founder Baba Nanuk, whom they also call their Guru, and frequently reiterate the Word Bhalden.[16] The Tenets of Nanuk have been collected into a Book, which they call their Ghiruntejee, and guard as a sacred Deposit, or rather Oracle, at a place called Amber Ser, two and twenty Coss in the Dehly side of Lahore; Here they assemble in great numbers (150, or 200,000 Men) at two fixed periods of the year, about October and April, to consult upon their Warlike Operations;[17] The Decisions of the Oracle, whether for War or Peace, they invariably adhere to. Their Book, they declare contains a prediction that "the Europeans will one day be in possession of Dehly."[18] This probably the Oracle, or rather the Interpreter of the Oracle, has suggested to keep suspicion awake.

The Seiks receive Proselytes of almost every Cast, a point in which they differ most materially from the Hindoos. To initiate Mahommedans into their mysteries, the pre-pare a Dish of Hogs legs, which the Converts are obliged to partake of, previous to admission. They have forbid absolutely the use of the Hookah, but they are as liberal in the use of Bang, and Ophiam, as their Neighbours. They are not prohibited the use of Animal food of any kind, excepting Beef, which they are rigidly scrupulous in abstaining from. They never shave either Head or Beard; They sometimes wear yel-low, but the prevailing Colour of their Cloaths is deep blue; They make their Turbans capaciously large, over which they frequently wear a piece of pliable Iron Chain or Net work.[19]

They are in general excellently mounted, and have a Body of thirty or forty thou-sand chosen Horse, always stationed along the Attok, to frustrate the Attempts of the Durranies or Abdallis, to whom they are inveterate Enemies, and by whom on two sides they are surrounded. The remainder of the Nation is dispersed all over their Dominions, without Order or Restraint. Their mode of making War is desultory, sel-dom attacking in large Bodies, and to sum up all we can at present learn concerning this strange people, they have the Character of being rather mild and benignant than otherwise, in their interior Government, and if it be true, what hath been confidently asserted, that the fundamental principle of their Religion is the Worship of the one Supreme God of the Universe, we may safely venture to give them credit for many of the good Qualities of Humanity.

Their places of greatest consideration, after the Capital Lahore, are said to be as follows; Amberser, their place of Religious visitation as mentioned above;

Kalanoor[20] butala,[21] among the Hills South East of Lahore;
Sersamaana;[22]

Jwalajee,[23] a place of pilgrimage of the Hindoos, 150 Coss from Dehly among the Hills, where there is a subterranean fire, and from which Aurungzebe thought to have procured Sulphur;
Shahdowla Gujraat, 40 Coss from Lahore, famous for a Manufacture of excellent Sword blades, and Matchlock pieces;
Jalendurr;
Puttealah;
Pehooah;
Kwlehittur, &c; and,
Karnaal, 40 Coss from Dehly.
They have a considerable Military Station at Attok, but it is said, unfortified.

The principle Manufactures of Lahore, are Kilmaans, a kind of coarse, or blanket Shawls, made of the Wool of the Tails of certain Sheep, White Cloths fine and coarse, Piece Goods. The Punjaab produces Grains of all sorts known in India, Cotton, Indigo, Jaggree and a variety of Fruits.

They receive in importation from Gujraat Pearl, Kincobs Gold thread, Cutnic, Elephants Teeth, Broad Cloths, Nutmegs, Cloves, Mace, Cardamums, Amber, Dry dates, Iron, Lead, Copper Vermilion, Coconuts, &c^a and Drugs.

Kandahar or the Dominian of the Durranies

The left Bank of the Indus, coming from the Sea Coast, as high up as the parallel of Kashmeer, is almost entirely in the hands of Salem Shah Durrani, and the Chiefs tributary to him, and Eastward of the Attok he skirts the Seick Nation to some distance beyond the Territory of Jamboo. A reference to Major Rennel's incomparable Map[24] will afford a pretty clear idea of the importance of this Frontier, to whatever Power may be in possession of it.

This formidable Kingdom was founded about forty eight years ago by Ahmed Khawn abdalli, one of Nader Shah's principal Officers.

Mirza Mehadi relates in his History of Nader Shah, that in the confusion which followed the Murder of that Prince (Hiz,–1160) the Afghan and Oozbek Troops assembled together from the different Quarters of the Camp, under Ahmed Khawn, who from the warmth of his Attachment to the House of his deceased Master, determined to avenge his Death, but being repulsed by the Assharians and consequently frustrated in his design, he drew off the Afghans, and retreated to the Fortress of Kandahar, where embracing the opportunity offered by the troubles which afterwards desolated Persia, he assumed the Chuttur, or Ensign of Royalty, under the name of Ahmed Shah, well known from the dreadful overthrow he gave the united powers of the Mahratta Empire about 28 years ago, on the Plains of Paniput.[25]

He was succeeded about 3 years after that Battle by his Son Timmur Shah,[26] who assumed the Title of Durra Durrani,[27] or Pearl of the Durranies; the latter is the name by which he distinguished a Corps of Household Troops, which consisted originally of Abyssinian Slaves, raised by contribution among his Subjects, and probably constituted on the same principles with the Mamluks of Egypt. From an Ornament which they wore in their Ears, they received the Appellation of Durrani.[28] They at first amounted to no more than two or three thousand, but latterly they were augmented to twelve and even twenty thousand Men, the Flower of the Shah's Armies, and particularly intrusted with the Guard of the Royal Person. Timmer Shah died about the middle of 1792.

A younger Brother[29] was preparing to dispute the Sovereign Authority with Salem Shah, the present Monarch, but by the timely mediation of some of the Moghul Chieftains, the matter was prudently compromised, without having recourse to the Sword; Salem Shah was placed upon his Father's Throne, and his Brother was satisfied with the Government of Kabul, where he resides.

Salem Shah is in possession of Guezni, Kabul, Pecshour, Kandahaar, and some Territories on the Persian Side, being a considerable part of the Dominions of the celebrated and victorious Mahmud Subuktegnim.[30]

On the South East Side of the Attok, he possesses the delicious and wealthy Province of Kashmeer, the Paradise of India, and the only Country in the World where the universally admired Shawl is manufactured. This inimitable Article is, it is said, produced from the Fleece of an Animal called Bhera, or a Species of Sheep or Goat, subsisting on the Mountain Fruits peculiar to the Country. On that side also, he is Master of the rich Territory of Jamboo, described as nearly as inaccessible as

Kashmeer; In this quarter he is also in possession of the important Fortress of Rotass Gur,[31] with most of the strong holds on the Hilly Frontier of the Seicks, with whom he is in a state of perpetual Hostility. The Revenues he collects at this day from the two Provinces of Kashmeer and Jamboo only, amount, it is said, to two or three Million Sterling.

Salem Shah Durrani resides alternately at Kandahar & Kabul, at the former in the Heats, and the latter in the cold Season, when the Mountains are covered with Snow.

His Military Establishment consists chiefly of Horse, to the number, it is said, of about 150,000; His Foot he does not hold in much esteem, only employing them to garrison his Fortresses; And very happily, we do not hear that his Equipment of Artillery is by any means respectable.

His Cavalry are all excellently mounted, incomparably superior to any that can be brought to oppose them from Hindoostan. The impression of Terror left on the minds of the Mahrattas, by the fatal Carnage at Paniput, is so indelible, that it is pretty generally believed they will hardly, if ever, be again prevailed upon to sustain the charge of the Abdallis; among many instances of the prevalence of this sentiment of dread it is related, a Mahratta is not ashamed, if his horse should happen to start when drinking water, to exclaim, "dost thou see the Shadow of an Abdalli"?

In fact, (it is far from an unreasonable conjecture,) this is the real cause, to which we are to attribute the unremitting attention paid by Scindia, of late years, to the improvement of his Artillery and Infantry, for the Alarm, that the Shah is advancing, is as regular at Dehly, as the Revolutions of the Seasons, and it would appear from recent Accounts, that the period is not very distant, when that will certainly come to pass. A Son of Shah Alum, the present Shadow of the Moghul Emperors, has disappeared for some years past; it is now confidently reported, that he has found an Assylum with the Durrani. There is scarce a single dissenting opinion among the Natives, but whenever Salem Shah actually puts his Armies in motion towards Dehly, that unfortunate City will once more be abandoned to it's fate, and not improbably the greatest portion of the North of India.

It perhaps interests us materially to reflect, that if this Prince knew how to reap the advantages, which he might derive from his resources, from the warlike and intrepid Characters of his Subjects, from the opening of a safe Port in the Indus, for the Importation of Arms and Military Stores, we may have solid reasons, for apprehending another inundation of Tartars; Happy for our Settlements in Bengal, that they have the Ganges to oppose to them!

The Province of Kabul is esteemed peculiarly productive; it's breed of Horses is perhaps equal to any in the World, for the purpose of Cavalry; As an instance of the celerity and expedition, with which they can travel, it is said, that after the Capture of Dehly, Ahmed Shah marched a Body of his Horses, from Bultun Gur[32] (15 Coss from Dehly) to Mutha, a distance of about 50 Coss, in one Night; in consequence of which rapid March, the wretched City was surprised, and left to the Mercy of a barbarous Soldiery.

The Inhabitants of Salem Shahs Dominions are principally Mahomedans, with some Hindoos, who have adopted the Institutions of Baba Manuk, and are called Katri.

The Manufactures are, Shawls, Kelmaans or Blanket Shawls, Woollen Cloths, and Blankets.

The Soil produces Grain, and various sorts of Fruit, excellent in their kind, particularly Melons and Pomegranates. Their Horses are exported in considerable Numbers, by Joudpoor, Jesselmee, and Bickanear, as mentioned above, to different parts of India.

They receive in return, from Gujraat, &c, Pearl, Indigo, Nutmegs, Cloves, Saffron, Pepper, Bettlenut, Copper, Lead, Drugs, &c. &c.

N.B. The Coss are calculated at nearly one and a half English Miles each.

NOTES

1. Khushwant Singh, *A History of the Sikhs*, 1: 161.
2. Bhangū, *Prachīn Panth Prakāsh*, 303 quoted in Malik, *Indian Guerrilla Warfare*, 81.
3. Macauliffe, *The Sikh Religion*, 4: 381.
4. Ramesh Chander Dogra and Gobind Singh Mansukhani ed., *Encyclopaedia of Sikh Religion and Culture* (New Delhi: Vikas, 1995), 423–4.
5. Jats (q.v.).
6. Sūraj Mall (s.v.).
7. Belūchīs, people of Belūchīstān.
8. Salem Shāh may be a reference to Zemān Shāh (q.v.) as later in the work he is referred to as a successor to Timur (q.v.).
9. The Sutlej or Satluj, ancient Studrī is one of Punjab's five rivers. The Sutlej dissects Punjab forming the boundary between the southern Malwā districts and the Jalandhar Doāb.
10. Sītpur (Seetpore), a small town in the Muzaffargarh district of the Punjab now in Pakistan.
11. The Chenāb is one of the five principle rivers that gives Punjab its name. The Chenāb, now in Pakistan, separates the Rachnā Doāb from the Chaj Doāb.
12. *Kimkhāb* or *kamkhāb* is embroidered cloth.
13. *Diwan Sing* or Dīwān Singh Lundah Dallevālīā, who took possession of Sikandrā, Saran, Akālgarh, and Bara in the Ambālā District. His headquarters were in Sikandrā and he is sometimes referred to as Dīvān Singh Sikandrā although he was from Bastī near Amritsar. He was one of the prominent Dallevālīā *Sirdārs* subordinate to the *misl* leader Tārā Singh Dallevālīā (1710–1807) (see Illustration 6). Ghandi, *Sikhs in the Eighteenth Century*, 531; Gupta, *History of the Sikhs*, 4: 66.
14. Gurū Nānak was a contemporary of Bābur (q.v.) and not Aurangzeb (q.v.). Furthermore Gurū Nānak rejected the ascetic lifestyle for that of a house-holder, shown by the fact that the Gurū was a married man and had two sons, Srī Chand (q.v.) and Lakhmī Chand (q.v.).
15. Gurū Nānak could not have been imprisoned by Aurangzeb. This could be a reference to the apocryphal story of Gurū Nānak's imprisonment by a previous Mughal emperor, Bābur. There are several other examples of the Sikh Gurūs being imprisoned by Mughal emperors. Jahāngīr imprisoned and ultimately martyred Gurū Arjan in 1606. Some ten years later Gurū Hargobind was also imprisoned by Jahāngīr at Gwalior. During the reign of Aurangzeb, Gurū Tegh Bahādur was imprisoned in Delhi before being publicly executed in 1675.
16. It is not known what the word "Bhalden" means in this context.
17. The months of October and April represent the festivals of *Divālī* and *Baisākhī* respectively, the regular times in the annual calendar when the Sikhs met to discuss matters of state. See *Gurmatā* (q.v.) and Sarbat Khālsā (q.v.).
18. There is no such prophecy in the Gurū Granth Sāhib. There is a story ascribed to Gurū Tegh Bahādur, the ninth Gurū. This prophetic statement is repeated by James Browne (see part II chapter 9).

19. This is an early reference to the Sikh turban known as *dastār būngā* or the turban fortress. The iron chain was used mainly as a device to keep the turban tightly bound. It was also a way of securing small but very sharp weapons which acted as a deterrent to opponents from grabbing the turban, and made it particularly effective as a weapon for close-quarter combat. If required it could be taken off and used either as a lasso or for the tying up of a prisoner. The iron chain could also refer to the practice of wearing sections of chain mail armor in the turban. Both of these practices still exist amongst some of the Akālī Nihangs of the *Buddhā Dal* (q.v.).

20. Kalānaur, a town in the district of Gurdāspur, Punjab, is best known as the place where Emperor Akbar received the news of his father's death. He promptly had himself installed on a throne where he assumed leadership. Hardly a principal location for Sikhs, the only tenuous link is that Kalānaur was on Bandā Bahādur's plundering route through Punjab.

21. Batālā in the Gurdāspur district of Punjab is a town sacred to Gurū Nānak who was married here in 1487. Gurū Hargobind's eldest son, Bābā Gurdittā, was also married in Batālā. The town houses three *gurdwārās* to commemorate these events.

22. This may be a reference to Samānā to the south-west of Patiālā. A historic town, it was visited by Gurū Tegh Bahādur while being pursued by imperial soldiers. A Sūfī local called Mohammed Bach afforded him asylum in Garhī Nazir nearby. The Nihangs constructed a small *gurdwārā* there. Despite this, it isn't regarded as a principal city of the Sikhs.

23. Jwālāmukhī in the district of Kāngrā.

24. Major James Rennell, *Memoir of a Map of Hindoostan* (London: Printed by M. Brown for the author, 1793).

25. The Battle of Pānīpat was fought on January 14, 1761, thirty-three years before the date of this letter.

26. Timur Shāh came to the throne of Afghānistān in 1772 following the death of his father, Ahmad Shāh Durrānī, eleven years after the battle of Pānīpat.

27. The title *Durrānī* was, to begin with, adopted by Timur Shāh's father, Ahmad Shāh, on his being raised to the throne of Afghānistān in 1747.

28. The appellation was given to Ahmad Shāh by his patron-saint Nādir Shāh who called him *Durri-i-Durrān*, the pearl of pearls.

29. Prince Mahmūd.

30. Mahmūd of Ghaznī (997–1030) was the son of Nasir-ud-Dīn-Sabuktgin (977–997).

31. The fort of Rohtas in the district of Jhelum, now in Pakistan.

32. Garh Muktesar in the Hapur tahsīl of Meerut district in Utter Pradesh.

CHAPTER 14

MASSACRE OF FAKĪRS, HARDWICKE, 1796

Thomas Hardwicke, "Narrative of a Journey to Sirinagur" *Asiatick Researches*, vol. VI (London, 1799), pp. 309–19.

The author of this travelog, which winds through Northern India, was Captain Thomas Hardwicke of the Bengal Artillery. By 1823 and at the end of his military career, Hardwicke had risen to the rank of a distinguished major-general. Hardwicke's career started like many as a cadet in the Bengal Artillery in 1778 and rose steadily through the ranks, seeing action in the second Mysore War (1780–1784), Vellore and Cuddalore, and the third Mysore War (1790–1792). In 1793, he returned to the Bengal establishment and took part in the action during the second Rohīllā war. Hardwicke commanded ordnance at Cawnpore and Furlough and later became Commandant before retiring in 1823. He was an enthusiastic supporter of the Asiatic Society of Bengal, becoming its Vice-President from 1820 to 1822. He took a particular interest in the study of flora and fauna and commissioned Indian and English artists to make drawings for him.

One of his publications in the journal of the society, *Asiatick Researches*, contains a fascinating account of a massacre of fakīrs in the pilgrimage town of Haridvār by Sikhs from Patiālā. The event took place in 1796 and Hardwicke had it published in the 1799 volume of the journal.

Haridvār remains a place of pilgrimage for Hindus, but in the eighteenth century the site also attracted Sikhs, a practice that is now almost extinct; contemporary accounts make mention of prominent Sikhs visiting the annual fair there.[1] A short account in a later travelogue by a Mrs A. Deane dated 1812 noted the presence of a unique gathering of Sikh principals at Haridvār:[2] "The following morning some of our party, myself among the number, made an excursion to the celebrated bathing-place of *Hurdoar*, where we fell in with a party of *Sieks* of high rank: they consisted of the *Ranee Mutaab Kour*, wife of Rajah Rungeet Sing; Rajah *Sahib Sing*, of

Patialah, and his wife; Rajahs *Bodge Sing* and *Burgwaan Sing*. These people paid us every mark of respect and politeness: they were attended by a numerous retinue". The practice of Sikhs visiting Haridvār continued well into the nineteenth century. The Māhārājā of Nābhā, Hīra Singh (1843–1911), visited the fair in the 1870s: "August 15, 1874—Arrived at Hardwar on 5th and halted there for three days during which he [Hīra Singh] bathed twice at Kushabarth and once at Hardwar, distributed alms liberally and received benedictions from Brahmans."[3]

The incident that forms the central relevant portion of this account was reported several years later (with inaccuracies) in The Times newspaper in 1801: "We have received a Private Letter by the late Overland Dispatch from Bombay, by which we are informed that the Seiks threaten the whole tribe of Fakeers with immediate hostility, in consequence of some supposed transgression on the part of the Fakeers." This report has been reproduced in part V, chapter 27.

Apparently, a similar altercation occurred during the Kumbh fair at Haridvār in 1819, when a party of *Udāsīs* were attacked by a group of *Bairāgīs* who resented the former marching out in a ceremonial procession with the *Gurū Granth Sāhib* amidst it. The head of the *Udāsīs*, Mahant Pritam Dās (1752–1831), enlisted the help of some Sikh chiefs who were attending the fair and had the *Bairāgīs* suitably punished.[4]

A roughly contemporaneous, but unrelated, account in James Duncan Phillips, *Salem and the Indies* (Boston: Houghton Mifflin Co., 1947), 364 recounts the memoirs of Captain Stephen Phillips, an eighteenth century trader. James Duncan Phillips notes that after the captain's retirement he "brought back [to Salem] a tall, black-bearded Sikh who stalked around town in the turban and white woolen coat and red sash of his sect." This 1799 account is the earliest recorded instance of a Sikh traveler in the west and provides and intriguing counterpoint to early European travelers to India, like Hardwicke, who commentated on the Sikhs.

HAVING sometime ago visited the mountainous country of *Sirinagur*; I hope a succinct detail of some of the most remarkable circumstances, which occurred in that journey, will not be unacceptable to the *Asiatick* Society.

ON the 3d of *March* 1796, I commenced the journey, from *Futtehghur* in company with Mr. HUNTER; and we arrived; on the 19th of the same month, at *Anoopsheher* our route was circuitous, for the purpose of visiting the several indigo plantations, established by *European* gentlemen, in this part of *Dooab*. Here were conspicuously displayed, the effects of skill, of industry, and of a spirit of commercial enterprize, in beautifying and enriching a country, which, in other parts exhibiting only waste and forest, supplies, indeed, matter to gratify the curiosity of a naturalist, but suggests to the philanthropic mind the most gloomy reflections.

AT *Anoopsheher* I recruited the necessary supplies for the prosecution of my journey, and on the 23d, continued my march alone; for my fellow traveller was under the necessity of returning, from this place, to attend the residency with DOWLUT ROW SINDEAH, on a visit to the *Marhatta* camp.

ON the 30th of *March*, I arrived at *Nejeebabad*: the town is about six furlongs in length; with some regular streets, broad, and enclosed by barriers at different distances, forming distinct bazars. In the neighbourhood, are the remains of many considerable buildings. Near the south-west end of the town is a large garden, called *Sultan Bagh*, containing in the center a spacious square building, erected by one of the sons of NEJEEB-UD-DOWLAH.

ON the north-east side of this garden, and at the distance of 300 yards, is another, in which lies buried NEJEEB-UD-DOWLAH: his grave is without ornament, raised on a terrace, a few feet from the ground, in an area of about eighty yards, surrounded by a square building, formed into apartments and offices, for the accommodation of the servants, appointed to perform the usual ceremonies, for the benefit of departed souls.

A CONSIDERABLE traffic is carried on here, in wood, bamboos, iron, copper and tincal, brought from the hills. It is also the center of an extensive trade from *Lahore, Cabul*, and *Cashmir*, to the east and south-east part of *Hindustan*.

AT the distance of ten miles and six and a half furlongs, from *Nejeebabad*, on the road to *Hurdwar*, is *Subbul-gurh*, a very extensive line of fortification, enclosing the town; both of which exhibit little more than naked walls, falling to decay. Much of the ground, within the fort, is in cultivation. In the south-east curtain, or face of the fort, is a lofty brick-built gateway. The high road leads close past the north-east bastion, and continues along the north face, the whole length, within thirty or forty yards of the ditch.

ON the 1st of *April*, I arrived at *Unjennee Ghat*, about three miles below *Hurdwar*, on the eastern side of the river. The town of *Hurdwar* occupies a very small spot, consisting of a few buildings of brick, the property of eminent *Goosseyns*.[5] It is situated on the point of land at the base of the hills, on the western side of the river.

THE stream here divides itself into three channels, the principal of which is on the eastern side, and running along a pleasant bank called *Chandnee Ghat*, meets the base of the hill, which gives this name to the *Ghat* below. The deepest channel at present is in some places about fifteen feet, a depth not long continued; and near the termination of each reach of the river, the stream breaks, with rapidity, over beds of large loose stones, sometimes with no more water than sufficient to give passage to large unloaded boats. The points of the islands, several of which are formed in the bed of the river, are principally of loose pebbles and sand; but the rest of the land, between the different channels is covered with the *Mimosa Catechu*.

THE ascent of the hill, called *Chandnee*, commences at a little distance from *Unjennee*, from which, to the top of the hill, I consider about two miles and a quarter. Some part of this distance, however, is a long and elevated level bank. The ascent to the high part of the hill, is very steep; the path narrow, and requiring much attention and exertion, to prevent accidents in stepping, from the looseness of the stones and earth.

ON the top of this hill is a *Tersool* or trident, about fourteen feet high, of stone, supported by a small square base of mason work: the base of the forks is ornamented, on the east side, with figures of the sun and moon, between which, upon the shaft, is the figure of GANÉSA.

NEAR the base of the shaft, are the figures of KAAL-KA DÉVI, and HANUMAN, the former on the east, the latter west. The space on the summit of this hill, is not twice larger than the square of the pedestal of the trident: from this, a narrow ridge leads to another hill, something higher: and in this manner, the hills here are mostly connected; the highest being generally of a conical form. They are very thinly clad with vegetable productions: the trees are few, and small; and the grass, at this season of the year, parched up. In some parts of the hills, however, where the aspect is more northerly, the grass is more abundant, finer, and seemingly much liked by the cattle.

ON the top of *Chandnee*, a *Brahmen* is stationed to receive contributions from visitors during the continuance of the *Mela*: the produce, he says, upon an average, is, for that time, about ten rupees per day.

THIS *Mela*, or fair, is an annual assemblage of *Hindus*, to bathe, for a certain number of days, in the waters of the *Ganges*, at this consecrated spot. The period of ablution is that of the Sun's entering Aries; which, according to the *Hindu* computation, being reckoned from a fixed point, now happens about twenty days later than the vernal equinox. It accordingly fell on the evening of the 8th of *April*. But every twelfth year, when Jupiter is in Aquarius, at the time of the Sun's entering Aries, the concourse of people is greatly augmented. The present is one of those periods, and the multitude collected here, on this occasion, may, I think, with moderation, be computed at two and a half millions of souls.[i] Although the performance of a religious duty is their primary object, yet, many avail themselves of the occasion, to transact business, and carry on an extensive annual commerce. In this concourse of nations, it is a matter of no small amusement to a curious observer, to trace the dress, features, manners, &c. which characterize the people of the different countries of *Cabul*, *Cashmir*, *Lahore*, *Butaan*, *Sirinagur*, *Cummmow*, and the plains of *Hindustan*. From some of these very distant countries, whole families, men, women and children, undertake the journey, some travelling on foot, some on horseback, and many, particularly women and children, in long heavy carts, railed, and covered with sloping matted roofs, to defend them against the sun and wet weather: and during the continuance of the fair, these serve also as habitations.

AMONG the natives of countries so distant from all intercourse with people of our colour, it is natural to suppose that the faces, dress and equipage of the gentlemen who were then at *Hurdwar*, were looked upon by many as objects of great curiosity: indeed it exceeded all my ideas before on the subject, and as often as we passed through the crowd in our palanquins, we were followed by numbers, of both women and men, eager to keep pace, and admiring, with evident astonishment, every thing which met their eyes. Elderly women, in particular, salaamed with the greatest reverence; many shewed an eagerness to touch some part of our dress, which being permitted, they generally retired with a salaam, and apparently much satisfied.

AT our tents, parties succeeded parties throughout the day, where they would take their stand for hours together, silently surveying every thing they saw.

SOMETIMES more inquisitive visitors approached even to the doors of the tent, and finding they were not repelled, though venturing within, they generally retired, with additional gratification; and frequently returned, as introductors to new visitors, whose expectations they had raised, by the relation of what themselves had seen.

THE most troublesome guests were the *Goosseyns*, who being the first here in point of numbers and power, thought it warrantable to take more freedoms than others

---

[i] THIS estimation may appear enormous; and it therefore becomes necessary to give some account of the grounds on which it was formed. Small sums are paid by all, at the different watering places; and the collectors at each of these, in rendering their accounts to the Mehunts, who regulate the police, are obliged to form as exact a register, as a place of so much bustle will admit of. From the principal of these offices, the number of the multitude is found out, probably within a few thousands. The Goosseyn, on whose information the calculation was formed, had access to these records; and the result, as delivered above, was thought more likely to be under, than over, the truth.

did: and it was no easy matter to be, at any time, free from their company: it was, however, politically prudent, to tolerate them; for, by being allowed to take possession of every spot round the tents, even within ropes, they might be considered as a kind of safe guard, against visitors of worse descriptions; in fact, they made a shew of being our protectors.

IN the early part of the *Mela*, or fair, this sect of *Fakeers* erected the standard of superiority, and proclaimed themselves regulators of the police.

APPREHENDING opposition, in assuming this authority, they published an edict, prohibiting all other tribes from entering the place with their swords, or arms of any other description. This was ill received at first, and for some days it was expected force must have decided the matter; however the *Byraagees*, who were the next powerful sect, gave up the point, and the rest followed their example. Thus the *Goosseyns* paraded with their swords and shields, while every other tribe carried only bamboos through the fair.

THE ruling power was consequently held by the priests of the *Goosseyns*, distinguished by the appellation of *Mehunts*, and during the continuance of the *Mela*, the police was under their authority, and all the duties levied and collected by them. For *Hurdwar*, though immediately connected with the *Mahratta* government, and, at all other seasons, under the rule and controul of that state, is, on these occasions, usurped, by that party of the *Fakeers*, who prove themselves most powerful; and though the collections made upon pilgrims, cattle, and all species of merchandize, amount to a very considerable sum; yet no part is remitted to the treasury of the *Mahratta* state.

THESE *Mehunts* meet in council daily: hear and decide upon all complaints brought before them, either against individuals, or of a nature tending to disturb the public tranquillity, and the well management of this immense multitude.

AS one of these assemblies was on the high road near our tents, we had frequent opportunities of noticing their meetings; and one of our sepoys, having occasion to appear before it, in a cause of some consequence, it gave us an opportunity of learning some thing of the nature of their proceeding.

THE sepoy, it seems, on leaving the station, where his battalion was doing duty, was entrusted, by one of the native officers, with fifty rupees, and a commission to purchase a camel. With the intention of executing this trust, he mixed with a crowd, where some camels were exposed for sale; and while endeavouring to cheapen one to the limits of his purse; shewing the money, and tempting the camel merchant to accept, for his beast, the fifty rupees, he drew the attention of a party of *Marwar* men, who were mediating a plan to get it from him. Five or six of those men, separating from the crowd, got round him, said, they (or one of them) had lost his money, to the amount of fifty rupees; that he, the sepoy, was the man who had it; and, with much clamour and force, they got the money from him. Fortunately, the sepoy's comrades were near; he ran towards them and communicated the alarm, and got assistance, before the fellows had time to make off, or secrete the money; they, however, assumed a great deal of effrontery, and demanded that the matter should be submitted to the decision of the *Mehunts*: before this tribunal the cause was consequently brought, and an accusation laid against the sepoy, by these men of *Marwar*: the money was produced, and lodged in court, and the cause on both sides, heard the deliberation. Unluckily for the *Marwarees*, they had neither opportunity to examine or change the money; and knew not what species of coin made up this sum: which circumstance led to their conviction; for being enjoined by the *Mehunts*, to describe the money they had lost, they named coin very different from what the purse contained: but when the sepoy was called upon to answer the same question, he specified the money exactly. The judges immediately gave a decision, in favour of the sepoy, and restored him his money: the *Marwars* were fined each in the sum of five rupees, and sentenced to receive each fifty stripes, upon their bare backs with the *Korah*.

THE *Goosseyns* maintained an uncontested authority, till the arrival of about 12 or 14,000 *Seek* horsemen, with their families, &c. who encamped on the plains about *Jualapore*.[6] Their errand here was avowed to be bathing; and soon after their arrival they sent OODASSEE,[7] their principal priest or *Gooroo*, to make choice of a situation on the river side, where he erected the distinguishing flag of their sect, for the guidance and direction of its followers, to the spot. It appeared however, that no compliments or intimation of their intentions, had been made to the ruling power; and the *Goosseyns*, not willing to admit of any infringement of their authority, pulled down the flag, and drove out of the place those who accompanied it. Some slight resistance was shewn by the *Seeks*, in support of their priest, and the dignity of their flag, but was repelled with much violence, and the *Goosseyns*, not content with driving them away, abused and plundered the whole party, to a considerable amount.

THE old priest OODASSEE, on his return to the *Seek* camp, complained to Rajah SAHEB SING,[8] their chief, in the name of the body collective, of the insult and violence they had met with from the *Goosseyns*.

A CONSULTATION was immediately held by the three chiefs of the *Seek* forces, viz. Rajah SAHEB SING of *Puteealah*, and ROY SING and SHERE SING of *Booreah*,[9] who silenced the complaints by promising to demand redress and restitution for what they had been plundered of.

A VAKEEL was immediately despatched, with a representation, from the *Seeks* to the *Mehunts*, or priests of the *Goosseyns*, pointing out the right, they conceived they possessed, in common with all other nations, to have access to the river; and complaining of the wanton insults they had met with, from their tribes, when in the peaceable execution of their duty: however, as they had no remedy, to make amends for some part of the ill treatment they met with, yet they demanded an immediate retribution of all they had been plundered of, and free access to the river or place of bathing.

THE *Mehunts* heard their complaints, expressed concern at what had happened, and promised their assistance, in obtaining the redress sought for: and the matter, for the present, rested here; the *Goosseyns* giving back, to the *Seeks*, all the plunder they had taken, and admitting of their free ingress and egress to the river.

ALL was pretty quiet, during the few remaining days of bathing; but on the morning of the 10th of *April*, (which day concluded the *Mela*) a scene of much confusion and bloodshed ensued. About eight o'clock on that morning, the *Seeks* (having previously deposited their women, children, and property in a village, at some distance from *Hurdwar*) assembled in force, and proceeded to the different watering places, where they attacked, with swords, spears, and fire-arms, every tribe of *Fakeers* that came in their way. These people made some resistance, but being all on foot, and few, if any, having fire-arms, the contest was unequal: and the *Seeks*, who were all mounted, drove the poor *Sannyassees*, *Byraagees*, *Goosseyns*, *Naagees*, &c. before them, with irresistible fury. Having discharged their pieces within a few paces, they rushed upon those unfortunate pilgrims with their swords, and having slaughtered a great number, pursued the remainder, until, by flight to the hills, or by swimming the river, they escaped the revenge of their pursuers.

THE confusion, spread among other descriptions of people, was inconceivable; and every one, thinking himself equally an object of their resentment, sought every means of safety that offered: many took to the river, and in the attempt to swim across, several were drowned: of those who endeavoured to escape to the heights, numbers were plundered, but none who had not the habit of a *Fakeer* was in the least hurt: many parties of straggling horsemen now ranged the island, between *Hurdwar* and *Unjinnee gaut*; plundering the people to the very water's-edge, immediately opposite to us; fortunately for thousands, who crowded to this *gaut*, the greatest part of one of the vizeer's battalions, with two six-pounders were stationed here; two companies of which with an addition of a few of our own sepoys, and a native officer, whom Captain MURRAY very judiciously sent across the river, kept the approach of the horse in check. Finding they could not attack the crowd on the water's-edge, without receiving a smart fire, from the sepoys, as well as exposing themselves to the fire of the guns, they drew off, and by about three o'clock in the afternoon, all was again quiet.

AT this time, the cause of such an attack, or the future intentions of this body of *Seeks*, was all a mystery to us; and popular report favoured the conjecture, that they intended to profit from the present occasion, and by crossing the river, at a few miles lower down, return, and plunder the myriads of travellers who crowded the roads through *Rohilcund*. However, the next morning discovered they had no such intentions; as from the adjacent heights, we saw them take their departure, in three divisions, bending their march in a westerly course, or directly from us. The number which had crowded to the river side, opposite to our tents, was too great to be ferried over in the course of the night, and consequently remained in that situation: fearful of the approach of day, and in dreadful alarm from the expectation of another visit from the *Seeks*, but by eight o'clock, their minds were more at ease, and they offered up their prayers for the *English* gentlemen, whose presence, they universally believed, had been the means of dispersing the enemy.

FROM the various information we had now collected, we concluded this hostile conduct of the *Seeks* was purely in revenge against the tribes of *Fakeers*: many of the wounded came to our camp to solicit chirurgical assistance and they all seemed very sensible, that they only were the objects of the enemy's fury.[10]

ACCOUNTS agree that the *Fakeers* lost about five hundred men killed, among whom was one of their *Mehunts*, or priests named MAUNPOOREE; and they had many wounded: of the *Seeks* about twenty were killed, but the number of wounded not known.

NOTES

1. See also Tour to Lahore (part IV, chapter 19).
2. Deane, *A Tour Through Upper Provinces of Hindustan*, 190.
3. S. Rangaiyar, *Diary of the Late Maharaja of Nabha: A Biography Based on the Maharaja's Diary*, (Lucknow: Indian Daily Telegraph, 1924), 6.
4. *The Encyclopaedia of Sikhism*, s.v. "Prītam Dās, Mahant (1752–1831)."
5. "Roughly speaking, [Gosain] denotes an ascetic of any order, but it further connotes that he is of some standing and influence. Strictly speaking, however, the Gosains form a distinct order, which differs both from the Bairagis and the Sanniasis, though they are often entitled Gosains, and often the Brahmans alone are considered privileged to be so styled." H.A. Rose, *A Glossary of the Tribes and Castes of the Punjab and North-West Frontier Province*, 2 vols (Lahore: Civil and Military Gazette, 1911. Reprint New Delhi: Asian Educational Services, 1990), 2: 303.

6. Jawālāpur was held by Rāi Singh and Sher Singh, two of the key figures who appear later on in the account.

7. In the groundbreaking anthropological work *The People of India*, 6 vols, ed. J. Forbes Watson and Sir John Kaye (London: W.H. Allen and Co., 1868–1872), vol. IV, 196, s.v. "Oodassee," Philip Meadows Taylor had this to say about the 'Oodassee' (*Udāsī*): "The word 'oodas' signifies 'unsettled', 'melancholy', or 'sad', and has been adopted by these devotees to distinguish their class or sect. What the Bairagees are to the Hindoo class, the Oodassees are to the Sikhs. They are followers of Nanuk, the great Sikh teacher and founder of the national Sikh faith, and observe his doctrines and precepts . . . Oodassees visit Hindu shrines as pilgrims and follow Sikhs in their established localities. Thus they are found all over the Punjab and North-West Provinces, and as far south as Hyderabad, in the Deccan; where, as also at Nandair, on the Godavery, there are colonies of military Sikhs in the service of the Nizam's government . . . They have usually the title of Bawa, or Father, and the 'Oodassee Bawa' is often a welcome guest in Sikh or Hindu villages or families, reciting his sacred texts, or telling to the wondering ears of listening matrons and children the marvellous scenes of large religious fairs and gatherings, of gorgeous Hindu and Sikh ceremonies, and his own personal adventures . . . Such are Oodassess; thrown up, as it were, from, in many respects, the purest monotheistic faith in India; the only one which has had the effect of exciting patriotism, and creating a national spiritual dominion; a tribute, as it were, to the Hinduism from which it emerged, and of which it could not be entirely divested."

8. The Mahārājā of Patiālā (1773–1813).

9. Rāi Singh Bhangī of Jagādhrī and Sher Singh of Būrīā held Jawālāpur in their estates, which was effectively the entrance to Haridvār. Hence, it brought them a significant income from the visiting pilgrims. However, as Hardwicke notes, the share from Haridvār itself went to the Gosains.

10. G.R.C. Williams, while concluding the account of this episode several decades later, remarks: "The Sikhs are, let me remind the reader, like all Asiatics, by nature prone to treachery and exceedingly vindictive. When their passions are roused, they perhaps, surpass others as much in perfidy and cruelty as they unquestionably do in endurance and bravery. The representative Singh, frank and open-hearted, straightforward and chivalrous, is a creature of imagination. Indeed such qualities are book-makers, viewing him from a distance, love to attribute to him, rarely exist in a barbarian, however valorous he may be. At all events, a fine or a flogging could not wipe out the insults above described, in the estimation of a haughty Sirdar of the last century, nor was it likely that the greedy freebooters of Jugadree and Booreea, having once got what they considered a good excuse for inflicting reprisals, would calmly witness the appropriation of dues, the collection of which they had themselves once enjoyed. Under the circumstances, an explosion was inevitable. The cesses imposed upon the pockets probably, when they held pilgrims at one time went into their Joualapore in *jaedad* [territory assigned for the support of troops]." *Calcutta Review*, vol. LXI, 1875, 46 in Gupta, *History of the Sikhs*, 3: 285.

CHAPTER 15

AN ARTIST'S IMPRESSIONS OF THE
SIKHS, BALT SOLVYNS, 1796

Balthazar Solvyns, *A Collection of Two Hundred and Fifty Colored Etchings: Descriptive of the Manners, Customs, Character, Dress, and Religious Ceremonies of the Hindoos* (Calcutta: 1796, 1799), section I, number 9 "A Sic"; section VII number 8 "Naunuck Punthy"; and Balthazar Solvyns, *Les Hindoûs*, 4 vols. (Paris: Chez L'Auteur, 1808–12), vol. I, section 8, number 5 "Sics, A Hindoo Tribe"; vol. II, section 4, number 6 "Nanuck-punthy."

It was in the unlikely location of Calcutta, over a thousand miles from Punjab, that an unlucky Flemish artist gave the world the first known published image of a Khālsā Sikh by a European. In spite of the figure of the *Nānakpanthī* Omīchand (see part II, chapter 5) looming large over the trading community of Calcutta in the early eighteenth century, by the nineteenth century, only a handful of locals described themselves as Sikhs.

Notwithstanding the paucity of Sikhs, Francois Balthazar Solvyns[1] managed to capture in his encyclopedic works, two Sikh figures, one that could be catagorized in the Khālsā mould of today and an altogether more baffling image, which he titled *Nānakpanthī* or "follower of the path of Nānak."

Like many of his contemporaries, Solvyns headed east to seek his fortune but unlike many of his contemporaries, he was an artist rather than a military man or budding Company trader. However, work was seen to be plentiful in Bengal, with English artists being rewarded handsomely for rendering the exotic and romantic for locals and expatriates. Celebrated portrait artists readily found a market in the patronage of "nawabs and nabobs alike."[2] Solvyns arrived in Calcutta in 1791 at the age of 31, one of the more mature journeymen to enter India. His earliest successes were not in the commissions of Calcutta's gentry but in the more humble pursuit of decorating coaches and palanquins as an itinerant artist. Over the next three years, this commercial work provided him with an income and the ability to indulge his real passion of sketching life as he saw it around him. In 1794, having secured the necessary subscribers for a private publication, he announced his intention to publish "a collection of two hundred and fifty coloured etchings: descriptive of the manners, customs and dresses of the Hindoos."[3] In two editions in 1796 and 1799, both published in Calcutta, Solvyns's vast work endeavored to capture the castes, servants, costumes, means of transport, modes of smoking, fakīrs, musical instruments, and festivals of the people he saw in late-eighteenth-century Calcutta.

"A Sic" is among the sixty-six prints in the first of these twelve sections, depicting "Hindoo castes, with their professions." In the seventh section titled "faquirs and holy mendicants," Solvyns captures the image of what he titles a "Nanauk Panthy." Solvyns displays an almost ethnographic angle to his work. He assiduously catalogs the vast diversity that he saw around him.

Described as "rather crudely done; the forms and settings were monotonous; and the colors were of somber hue,"[4] Solvyns's work was a commercial failure. Whether it was the quality of the work, the physical size, or the price, the books stayed on the shelves with his expected market steadfastly refusing to purchase.

Solvyns suffered a further setback after the failure of his effort. In an act of blatant plagiarism, London publisher Edward Orme published a slimmer sixty-print version titled *The Costumes of Indoostan* (London: Edward Orme, 1804, 1807) noting only that it was "after Solvyns." Redrawn and re-presented, Orme's edition proved fantastically successful. Solvyns gained neither financially nor in fame.

Solvyns stood firm. He left India, returned to Paris, married into money, and set about re-publishing his work. With almost missionary zeal, Solvyns berated the inaccuracy of Orientalist study in India and sought in his giant four-volume *Les Hindoûs* to correct his situation in words and pictures.

In 288 plates and published in Paris over four years from 1808 to 1812, this edition was altogether finer in execution and better suited for the market. In the changes that the artist made, he provided some further information and left some further tantalizing questions. The Paris edition contained sketches of a group of "Sics" and a "Nanuk-Panthy" with some expanded descriptive text accompanying each print (see illustrations 9 and 10). A victim of misfortune once again, Solvyns's latest project failed to succeed. This time it was international politics and the economy of Europe that conspired against him. The fall out from the Napoleonic wars led his wealthy collectors and libraries to abandon him. The edition was not only enormously complex and riddled with problems, it was an expensive affair that resulted in another financial disaster for Solvyns. He left Paris in 1814 to spend the last six years of his life in Antwerp, the city of his birth, where he was appointed Captain of the Port of Antwerp in the newly formed Kingdom of the Netherlands. He died on October 10, 1824.[5]

In dress and description, Solvyns's "Sics" are redolent of the contemporary Khālsā Sikh ideal. With flowing beards, *kachchh*, and *karā*, Solvyns captured perfectly the outward essence of the Khālsā. In the accompanying text, he alludes to the lure of the guerrilla lifestyle for the Sikh warriors of the eighteenth century. He further mentions the military tactics and strategy that defined early Khālsā guerilla warfare.[6] The mode of attack can be summarized into the single strategy of *dhaī phat* or two and a half strikes. This has been noted by numerous writers of the time, including Polier (part II, chapter 8) and Griffith (part III, chapter 13). Solvyns notes that the weakness of the Sikhs' favorite harassment tactic is its inability to sustain itself against a strongly fought counterattack.

The claim that Gurū Nānak was in some way related to Timur (or Tamarlane) and became a Hindu is absurd and mars an otherwise accurate and insightful account.

The only other comment is a perplexing social one. Solvyns notes that Sikhs mourn the birth of a child and rejoice a death. He also notes the wearing of white at funerary occasions, which is a common practice amongst Hindus and Sikhs. It is also not uncommon to celebrate the life of a respected elder on their death with an almost festive funeral service (*bibān*) followed by a village feast (*barra*); a life long-lived is cause for a remembrance *akhand pāth* (nonstop reading of the Gurū Granth Sāhib) and the distribution of sweets. There are few explanations for mourning when a child is born, rather the opposite, although it may be that Solvyns had stumbled across the unpalatable response to the birth of a female child in a largely paternalistic society.

The two reference works that Solvyns mentions in his first account of the "Sics" are also reproduced later in this book in part VI (chapters 30 and 32).

The commentary that accompanies the *Nānakpanthī* engraving is an altogether more problematic description. The most notable attributes are a single whisker and a single shoe. He further notes a pair of sticks and a religious fraud perpetuated by them on passersby. The description does not fit into any known or observed definition of a *Nānakpanthī*, although unlike the Khālsā Sikhs who were prescribed a religious uniform, no such uniform was prescribed for the various *Sahajdhārī* groups that existed. The only components of the description that are reminiscent of any known branches of the Sikh *Panth* are the two sticks that Solvyns describe. A nineteenth century description of the *Suthrāshāhī* paints a surprisingly comparable picture 'They make a perpendicular black streak down the forehead, and carry two small black sticks about half a yard in length, which they clash together when they solicit alms. They lead a vagabond life, begging and singing songs in the Punjabi and other dialects, mostly of a moral or mystic tendency. They are held in great disrepute, however, and are not infrequently gamblers, drunkards, and thieves. They look up to TEGH BAHADER, the father of GURU GOVIND, as their founder.'[7] An early representation of a *Suthrāshāhī* is shown in illustration 14.

"A Sic"
Calcutta edition: Section I, Number 9.

A Sic in his family dress—the back ground represents them armed as Soldiers. The History and origin of this curious Tribe, are to be met with in Hadgee Mustafah's Translate of Golaum Housain Khaun's Seir Mutaquirean;[8] and an account of them by Mr. Wilkins, is inserted in lst Volume of the Transactions of the Asiatic Society.[9]

"Sics, a Hindoo Tribe."
Paris edition: Volume I, Section 8, Number 5.

These Hindoos form also a people with independent laws and customs. There are persons who hesitate to rank them among the Hindoos. But it is certain that their tribe was founded by Nanuck-Shah, a descendant of Timur's, who through expiations and money was allowed to become a Hindoo. The first volume of the Transactions of the Asiatic Society of Calcutta may be consulted upon this subject.[10]

The Sics never quit their families but for military service. They are brave, and acquit themselves well in battle; but all their force is in their first charge: if that is resisted, their defeat soon follows.

It is worthy of observation, that among them a family goes into mourning on the birth of a child, and rejoices and puts on white clothes when death carries off one of its members. This custom, which has been remarked among other nations, proceeds from an opinion perhaps too well founded, that this world is a vale of tears and misery, from which it is always a happiness to be delivered.

The Sic who forms the principal figure in this engraving, is in his ordinary costume, which is black, or oftener very dark blue. The back ground of the plate gives a view of the mountainous country which these Hindoos inhabit, with a group of their warriors near a tent, which is their ordinary abode.

"A Naunuk Punthy"
Calcutta edition: Section VII, Number 8.

A Nanuk-Punthy,—a sectary formed by Nanuk, and are remarkable for wearing one shoe only and shaving one mustache,—he is represented setting in Durnah, a religious fraud, an account of which is given in the 3d volume of the Asiatic Researches, in Article 22, on some extraordinary Facts, Customs, and Practices of the Hindoos.[11]

"Nanuk-Punthy"
Paris edition: Volume II, Section 4, Number 6.

The Faquirs who go by the name of *Nanuk-Punthys* are very different, and much more peaceable than those of which we have just been speaking. Their outward appearance offers something striking, not to be met with among any of the other Faquirs; which is caused by their wearing only one whisker and one shoe. The origin of so strange a custom still remains unknown to me, notwithstanding all my endeavours to discover it. Every Faquir of this class has his turban covered with a sort of network of wire, of which also he wears a kind of cord as a collar round his neck. To the left side of the turban, above the ear, are fastened two little bells of silver. The *Nanuk-Punthy* carries besides in each hand a stick which he is continually striking together, reciting at the same time, with a most extraordinary volubility of tongue, a *Durnah* or text of the Hindoo legend. There is a pretty ample description of this *Durnah* or text in the third volume of the Memoirs of the Society of Calcutta. These Faquirs are persuaded that this pious trick gives them an incontestable claim upon the charity and beneficence of all those upon whom they intrude their endless declamations; to which, as often as they are disappointed, curses and reproaches succeed with equal volubility. They pretend to have a warrant for this in the precepts of their sect; and we must remember that the Hindoos feel more hurt by reviling language than by any other sort of ill treatment.

Some of the *Nanuck-Punthys* choose the markets and public places for the theatre of their perpetual harangues: others go from house to house, from shop to shop, striking their sticks together and pouring forth their declamations, untired and incessant, excess in the well filled intervals of scolding. This is their trade, the profession they have embraced for life. They are in other respects quiet in their demeanour, and are even treated with some degree of respect, especially among the Sics and the Mahrattas.

NOTES

1. For a detailed biographical study of Balt Solvyns, see Robert Hardgrave, *Boats of Bengal: Eighteenth Century Portraits by Balthazar Solvyns* (New Delhi: Manohar, 2001).

2. Robert L Hardgrave, "An Early Portrayal of the Sikhs: Two 18th Century Etchings by Baltazard Solvyns," *International Journal of Punjab Studies*, 3 (1996): 213–27.

3. Balt Solvyns, *A Collection of Two Hundred and Fifty Coloured Etchings: Descriptive of the Manners, Customs, and Dresses of the Hindoos* (Calcutta: 1796, 1799).

4. Hardgrave, "An Early Portrayal of the Sikhs," 213–27.

5. *Dictionary of Indian Biography*, s.v. "Solvyns, Francois Balthazar."

6. The strategy and tactics are fully discussed in Arjan Dass Malik, *An Indian Guerrilla War: The Sikh Peoples War 1699–1768*, Wiley Eastern Ltd, 1975 (later published as *The Sword of the Khalsa*, Manohar Publishers and Distributors, 1999).

7. Asiatic Researches, vol. 42 (Calcutta: 1832), 236.

8. See part VI, chapter 32 for this account.

9. See part VI, chapter 30 for this account.

10. The only article discussing the Sikhs in this volume is Charles Wilkins's account cited in note 9 above. It makes no reference to Gurū Nānak being a descendant of Timur.

11. The article, which appeared in volume 4 and not 3 as mentioned by Solvyns, makes no mention of *Nānakpanthīs*. It describes the "Durnah" as a form of extortion where the supplicant "sets down in *Dherna*" before somebody's house and threatens them with suicide or engages in a fast until satisfaction is obtained. Sir John Shore, "On Some Extraordinary Facts, Customs and Practices of the Hindus," Article 22, *Asiatic Researches* (Calcutta: 1795), 4: 330–1.

PART IV

MILITARY MEN

CHAPTER 16

FRANCKLIN'S HISTORY OF THE REIGN
OF SHĀH ĀLUM, 1798

William Francklin, *The History of the Reign of Shah-Aulum, the Present Emperor of Hindostaun* (London: Printed for the author, by Cooper and Graham; and sold by R. Faulder, etc., 1798), pp. 71–8; 86–90.

William Francklin was a regular contributor of translations, literary papers, and other scholarly works to the Asiatic Society of Bengal including *Observations Made on a Tour from Bengal to Persia*, in the years 1786–1787 (London: T. Cadell, 1790). He became a member of the council and a librarian to the society during his retirement, but it was not as a scholar or orientalist that he was trained. He was born to a wealthy family in 1763 and educated at Westminster and Trinity College, Cambridge. Joining the East India Company's Bengal Native Infantry in 1783, he rose successively in the military ranks to a Lt. Colonel in 1814 and its regulating officer in 1815. In 1825 Francklin retired from service, choosing to remain in India where he died fourteen years later in 1839.

The account of the Sikhs taken from *The History of the Reign of Shah-Aulum* has been previously published in a much abridged form in Ganda Singh ed., *Early European Accounts of the Sikhs* (New Delhi: Today & Tomorrow's Printers & Publishers, 1974). For such a late account (1798), there is a preponderance of mistakes. For example, Francklin notes that Gurū Nānak lies buried in Amritsar; he lists the Gurūs but excludes Gurū Gobind Singh, and not un-typically confuses Bandā Bahādur as one of the Gurūs. These errors and omission are all the more surprising given the sources that Francklin used, including some Sikhs associated with a principal Sikh confederacy—the Karorasinghīā *misl*.

Dulchā Singh (also called Dulha Singh or Dulja Singh) was a prominent member of the Karorasinghīā *misl* in the late eighteenth century and, as Francklin acknowledges, he gathered most of his information about the

Sikhs from Dulchā Singh's brother. Dulchā Singh is known to have accompanied Baghel Singh, the head of the *misl*, to Delhi in 1783 where the latter undertook the task of constructing seven historically important *gurd-wārās*. On May 9, 1785, Dulchā Singh along with Mohar Singh of the Nishānānvālī *misl* made treaties of friendship with Mahādjī Scindiā, the regent of the Mughal Empire, and received robes of honor, necklaces of pearls, and horses from the Marāthās. This arrangement helps explain the reason why the body of Sikhs Francklin met in Pānīpat were said to be in the service of Scindiā. In April 1789, Scindiā also granted a large *jagīr* to Baghel Singh in order to restrain other Sikhs from plundering imperial territories.[1]

By his own estimation, his account is flawed, and he notes modestly that he "has to apologise for giving a sketch so imperfect, though he is happy to learn there is another and far better account already before the public from the late Colonel James Browne, of the Bengal establishment, but which account the author has not seen. The account here given stands merely on his own researches." By 1803 when he published an account of the Irish adventurer, George Thomas (part IV, chapter 17), Francklin had corrected many of his previous errors.

One of Francklin's more significant errors, especially since he writes primarily as a military man, was estimating the size of the Sikh military force. Francklin relies solely on the Sikh chief he met in Pānīpat in 1793–1794 for his estimation of the Sikh forces in Punjab. Here he is able to give valuable insight into the disparate military leaders of the Sikh *misls* (published in the table given in note ii). However, Francklin's estimate of the total Sikh fighting force under the Sikh *Sirdārs* is in the order of 248,000 men, the foremost leaders being the young Ranjīt Singh (70,000 men) and Harī Singh (40,000 men) of the Bhangī *misl* (a confederacy that Ranjīt finally subsumed in 1810). To George Thomas, who was interviewed later by Francklin, this was a fabrication on the part of the Sikhs: "The number of cavalry, which it is supposed, this nation was able to assemble, has been considerably over-rated, in consequence of a custom, which formerly obtained among the Seiks, of forming an association of their forces, under a particular chief. From this association of their forces, they had the general interests of the community in view. To those who were ignorant of the secret causes of the association, this junction of forces, was frequently mistaken for the army of an individual; and this error, was perhaps increased by the natural partiality of the Seiks themselves, to magnify the force, and enhance the character of their own nation."

Francklin was well-qualified to paint a vivid picture of the geopolitics of his time—the waning years of Mughal rule in northern India. He was not so astute in his assessment of the Sikhs as a faith group with a distinct philosophy, traditions, and lifecycle rituals. He notes that "In this recluse state, aided by the effusions of a fervid imagination, Nanick framed a system of religion, composed from the speculative and contemplative theories of Mussulman divinity, which he delivered to his numerous followers as of divine origin." Francklin makes this interesting, albeit brief, point regarding the basis of the Sikh faith. However, as was the case with the majority of commentators of the Sikhs in the eighteenth century, very few managed to appreciate the subtleties of a relatively new and unknown faith.

---

pp. 71–8

[A.D. 1776] The conquest of the Jauts being now complete, Nujuff Khan directed his attention to the collection of the revenues, and in reforming the abuses which had prevailed during the war. But in the midst of his arrangements, he was suddenly called off by letters received from Delhi, which required his immediate presence at that city. Zabita Khan, whose success, as already related, had inflamed his resentment and excited his ambition, was resolved to persist in his rebellion, and actually threatened Delhi with a siege. Previous, however, to proceeding to open hostilities, he augmented his army, and took into his pay large bodies of *Seiks*.

He formed, moreover, connections with some of the principal chiefs of that nation; and in order to render this alliance the more effectual, he embraced the tenets of this extraordinary sect, and became a convert to their faith.[2] The part which the Seiks have borne in the transactions of later times in the upper parts of Hindostaun, justify an attempt to describe their origin and progressive advancement to authority in the empire.

During the reigns of Akbar, Jehanguire, Shah Jehan and Aurengzeeb, the annals of Hindostaun exhibit a series of events and brilliant actions which raised the empire to the first station in the history of Asia. Emulating the conduct of their founder the great Timoor, those princes whilst they trod in his steps rendered their dominions flourishing and their people happy, and the power of that august family appeared established on so solid a basis as to bid defiance to the fluctuating and capricious changes of fortune; but the seeds of dissolution and decay were internally generated even in the height of their prosperity; and the indolence, folly and effeminacy, of the princes of later times, overthrew the fabrick of power, and buried the authority of the house of Timoor under its ruins. Out of the shipwreck of its former grandeur, several new and independent states arose. To the *Seiks*, among others, may be assigned an interesting station; obscure in their origin, in a remote part of the province of Lahoor, this tribe had nothing but novelty to recommend itself or attract notice.

In the reign of the Emperor Baber, *Nanick Shah*, founder of the tribe, was born at a small village named Tulbindee, in the province of Lahoor; at an early period of life, this extraordinary person, who possessed a good capacity and amiable manners, forsook the world, and devoted himself to a life of religious austerity. In this recluse state, aided by the effusions of a fervid imagination, Nanick framed a system of religion, composed from the speculative and contemplative theories of Mussulman divinity, which he delivered to his numerous followers as of divine origin. This book he termed Gurrunt, which, in the Punjabee dialect, implies scriptural. Nanick, after reaching his nintieth year, expired peaceably, and was buried at Amrit Seer,[3] where his tomb to the present day attracts the attention, and animates the piety of his numerous disciples. He left two children, Lucsmi Doss and Sree Chund.[4]

At this death, Nanick Shah, with a view to render permanent his new system, ordained that the succession should be elective and not hereditary, an ordination which, as it precluded the supreme authority from remaining in one family, placed the benevolent and disinterested views of the founder in a light truly amiable. Sree Chund, who found means to secure his election, presided over the tribe for several years, and, at his death, Angajee succeeded.[5] But this custom, though it obtained for some time, was at length set aside, and Gooroo Ram was the first who established an hereditary succession.

The tribe continuing to increase by vast number of converts which it had acquired, had not hitherto attracted the notice of the neighbouring powers; occupied in paying a scrupulous adherence to the laws and ordinations of their founder, the Seiks were looked upon as harmless, inoffensive devotees; but the period was at hand when they were to act a different part, and to contend with vigour against imperial authority. Teigh Behadur, whose actions and misfortunes render his name memorable, was the first who took up arms against the officers of Aurengzeeb, till after many bloody encounters with the king's troops, he was at length overcome, taken prisoner, and put to death.[6] His successors, animated by revenge, continued a predatory war with the descendants of Aurengzeeb, and, during the struggle, the Seiks acquired a considerable addition of territory. Among the most memorable of these chiefs, was Bundah, who, after a long and severe contest, was taken prisoner, carried to Delhi, and there suffered with heroic fortitude an ignominious death.[i]

In the reign of Ahumud Shah the tribe became very formidable. Profiting by the disturbances which then prevailed in every part of the empire, the Seiks again made head against the government, and with far better success. They conquered the whole of the Punjab, (or country included within the five rivers which fall into the Indus) and even pushed their arms beyond it.

In the last reign (Aulum Geer the Second) their dominions were bounded on the west by the country of Cabul, and extended eastward to the vicinity of Delhi, north by a range of high mountains, and to the southwest they embraced the province of Moultan and the city of Tatta, situated on the banks of the Indus. Lahoor, the capital of Punjab, was selected as their chief city of residence,[7] and as such has since continued. They possess many large towns, and among the principal are those of Puttiali, Hurrial, Loeh Ghur, Serhind, Shahabad, and Tanasser. The Seik territories are said to contain prodigious quantities of cattle, horses, oxen, cows, and sheep; and grain of various kinds is produced in abundance. The precious metals are very scarce; and their trade is for that reason chiefly carried on by barter, especially in the manufacturing towns.

At Pattiali they make excellent cloth, and fire arms superior to most parts of Hindostaun. The collected force of the Seiks is immense, they being able to bring into the field an army of 250,000[ii] men, a force apparently terrific, but, from want of

---

[i] See a particular account of this enterprising chief in Captain Scott's second volume of the History of Deccan. Article Furrok Seer. [Ed. see part VI, chapter 34.]

[ii] The following table, which was delivered to the author by a Seik chief when at Pannepat in 1793–4, will exhibit the situation of the different chiefs at that period.

	Men
Beejee Sing	12,000
Tanah Sing	22,000
Jessah Sing	14,000
Kurrun Sing (of Shahabad)	12,000
Jessah Sing (of Ramghur)	12,000
Jundut Sing (of Amrit Seer)	24,000
Khosal Sing (of Fuzoolah Pore)	22,000
Herri Sing (on the confines of Moultan)	40,000
Runjet Sing (of Loeh Ghur)	70,000
Shahur Sing (of Pattiali), Loll Sing, Jufwaunt Sing (of Nawbeh), Gujput Sing (of Chunda), and other chiefs	20,000
Total	248,000

union among themselves, not much to be dreaded by their neighbours. Divided into distinct districts, each chief rules over the portion appropriated to him with uncontroled sway; and tenacious of his authority, and jealous of his brethren, it seldom happens that this nation makes an united effort[iii].

The Seiks are armed with a spear, scymetar, and excellent matchlock. Their horses are strong, very patient under hardship, and undergo incredible fatigue. The men are accustomed to charge on full gallop, on a sudden they stop, discharge their pieces with a deliberate aim, when suddenly wheeling about, after performing three or four turns, they renew the attack. The shock is impressive when offered only to infantry, but against artillery they cannot stand. It is a fact well known and established, that a few field pieces is sufficient to keep in check their most numerous bodies. Inured from their infancy to the hardships of a military life, the Seiks are addicted to predatory warfare, in a manner peculiar to themselves alone. When determined to invade a neighbouring province, they assemble at first in small numbers on the frontier, when having first demanded the *raki* or tribute, if it be complied with, they retire peaceably; but when this is denied, hostilities commence, and the Seiks, in their progress, are accustomed to lay waste the country on all sides, carrying along with them as many of the inhabitants as they can take prisoners, and all the cattle. The prisoners are detained as slaves, unless redeemed by a pecuniary compensation.[8]—But though fond of plunder, the Seiks, in the interior parts of their country, preserve good order, and a regular government: and the cultivation of their lands is attended with much assiduity. Their revenues are collected at two stated periods of six months each; and by an equitable adjustment between the proprietor and cultivator, the latter is allowed a fifth part as the reward of his labour.

Of their religion much information has not as yet been acquired; but it has been remarked by an ingenious and spirited historian, that in the act of receiving proselytes, they compel them to the performance of an act equally abhorrent to the principles of the Hindoo or Mahommedan faith.[iv] Yet, notwithstanding the nature of their ceremonies, it is certain they continue to gain numerous converts.

The Seiks, in their persons, are tall, and of a manly erect deportment; their aspect is ferocious, their eyes piercing and animated; and in tracing their features a striking resemblance is observable to the *Arabs* who inhabit the banks of the Euphrates. The dress of the males consists of a coarse cloth of blue cotton, thrown loosely over the shoulders, and coming down between the legs, is confined round the waist by a belt of cotton. An ample turban of blue cloth covers the head, and over this is frequently wore a sash of silk and cotton mixed, resembling both in colour and pattern a *Scotch*

[iii] The alarm once excited in the British government of the formidable power of this nation, might be obviated by observing, that the discordant and clashing interests of the respective Seik chiefs prevent almost the possibility of a general union; and even if disposed to attack the territory of our ally, the vizir, they would be necessitated to keep a watchful eye over their own territories, which would be left open to invasion from the north. It is well known that Zemaun Shah, the king of Cabul, is desirous of sharing in the fertile province of Punjab, and especially of getting possession of Lahoor, emphatically termed the key of Hindostaun. His late attack at the end of 1796, is a proof of this assertion.

[iv] By obliging the Mussulmaun to drink water, in which some Seiks have washed their feet, mixed with hog's blood, and the Hindoo with that of a cow. See Captain Scott, Vol.II. article Furrok Seer. [Ed. see part VI, chapter 34.]

Tartan. They speak the Aufghaun or Pooshto language, with prolific additions of Persian, Arabic, and Hindoovee.[v]

pp. 86–90

[A.D. 1779] . . . During the remainder of the current year, little occurs at Delhi worthy of notice; but the ensuing season exhibited a new scene of action, and occasioned a considerable alteration on the face of affairs at court. The Seiks, who for several years had confined themselves to their own territories, now suddenly appeared in great numbers on the frontiers. A great force under different leaders having assembled, entered the king's territories, and commenced their usual course of plunder and devastation. They soon penetrated as far as Carnal, a large city 100 miles north of the capital. Of this they took possession, and dispersed their parties in various directions to overrun the province of Delhi. To repel this daring invasion, Mujud Al Dowla,[9] accompanied by Furkhinda Bukht, a prince of the royal family, were ordered to take the field.[10] Twenty thousand men, with a respectable train of artillery, were soon ready to march. Advancing by easy marches along the western bank of the river Jumna, the royal army reached Carnal without interruption. At this place Runjeet Sing and Deo Sing, two of the principal leaders of the Seiks, dispatched a vakeel to camp with offers of submission. They promised a puishcush of three lacks of rupees, and to recal their associates from their predatory incursions. Mujud Al Dowla acquiescing in the proposal, those chiefs were directed to attend the royal army in its future progress.[11] Accordingly having evacuated the town of Carnal, they joined the minister. From Carnal, Mujud Al Dowla advanced to Puttiali, a town 60 coses north of the latter, and situated on the Seik frontier. That place was defended by Amur Sing, who with a numerous garrison, and abundance of provisions, resolved to sustain a siege. Amur Sing had, however, other motives for resistance; he was aware that a large reinforcement of Seiks had left Lahore,[12] and might shortly be expected at Puttiali; nor was he without hope that even in the event of their non-arrival, and the town being hard pressed, but that he should be able to gain over the minister to his views, by the aid of all-powerful gold. However this might have been, Mujud Al Dowla besieged the place in form; but many days had not elapsed, when it was announced to the army, that a negociation for peace was in train. Amur Singh consenting to become tributary, commissioners were appointed on both sides to draw up an amicable treaty. The conferences accordingly commenced; but an act of treachery on the part of the Seiks, and in which it was suspected the minister had a considerable share, suddenly dissolved the meeting. To relate with precision the circumstances which led to this breach of faith, we must recollect that the Seik chieftains, who had submitted at Carnal, were still in the royal camp. They having received advice of the expected reinforcement of their countrymen being near at hand, sent notification of it to Amar

---

[v] In the year 1793–4, the author was at Panneput in company with Major Charles Reynolds, of the Bombay establishment, employed by the British Government on a survey through the Doo Ab; the result of which, when communicated to the public, will no doubt prove a valuable addition to the geography already acquired. At that time he saw a body of Seiks then in the service of the great Sindiah; they were about one thousand in number, under the command of Doolchee Sing, from whose brother most of the information above mentioned was received. The author has to apologise for giving a sketch so imperfect, though he is happy to learn there is another and far better account already before the public from the late Colonel James Browne [Ed. see part II, chapter 9], of the Bengal establishment, but which account the author has not seen. The account here given stands merely on his own researches.

Sing; at the same time advising that chief by some means or other to break off the treaty then pending.[13]

Agreeably to this information, Amar Sing exhibited to the commissioners many shuffling evasions and pretexts; and to this was added an haughty and contemptuous behaviour, which could not be mistaken. Rajah Daieram, the chief commissioner, perceiving his drift, quitted the town of Pattiali, and with his associates returned to camp.

Meanwhile the traitors there endeavoured by studied respect to preclude all suspicion of their fidelity in the mind of the minister. Mujud Al Dowla said nothing; and his shameful supineness on this occasion in suffering the insults sustained by the royal commissioners at Pattiali to pass unnoticed, afforded additional proofs of his collusion in the disgraceful scene. Early on the following morning, Runjeet Sing and his associate suddenly left the camp: a party was directed to go in pursuit of them; this party had scarcely cleared the advanced posts of the army, when they discovered the van guard of an immense host of Seiks, who by forced marches had advanced thus far unnoticed. At the same instant Amar Sing, of Pattiali, issuing out of the fort, covered the retreat of the traitors, and with them shortly after joined the troops from Lahoor. The Seiks now made a violent attack on all sides: accustomed to a desultory mode of warfare, they charged the line in several parts at once, and by the fierceness of their onset, threw the king's troops into confusion. The whole army would now have been sacrificed had not the officer who commanded in the rear, by a well-directed fire of his artillery, given a timely check to the enemy. The kings' troops were, however, compelled to retire; and for four days made a disgraceful and disorderly retreat. On the fifth day, the army reached Panniput, under the walls of which they encamped. Here the Seiks quitted them; and unsatiated with success, and fiercely thirsting for plunder, they divided into separate columns, and crossing the Jumna, spread themselves over the upper parts of the Doo Ab, committing every where acts of cruelty, devastation, and death.

The late disgraceful scenes had excited in the army universal indignation against Mujud Al Dowla. On him the eyes of all men were bent; and numbers scrupled not openly to accuse him of having been bribed by the Seiks to betray the king's interests, and devote his army to utter ruin.[14] If, indeed, it be considered that a finer and better appointed army never marched from Delhi, that they were flushed with recent successes, and animated by the preference of a prince of the blood; that this army should be incompetent to sustain the shock of a tumultuous rabble, appeared incredible in the eyes of all men, and proved the reproaches thrown on the minister to be strictly merited. Even after the enemy had retired, instead of remaining on the frontier to recover his soldiers from their late depression, he, as if panic struck, marched precipitately to the capital, thereby leaving the whole country exposed in his rear, and the wretched inhabitants a prey to the ravages of those barbarous invaders. But he was soon to receive a punishment adequate to his deserts.

Intelligence of this disastrous event arriving at Delhi, consternation and dismay seized on all. The king was highly incensed at the base conduct of Mujud Al Dowla; and to prevent farther ill consequences, required the immediate attendance of the captain general. It was indeed high time for some effectual interference. On one hand the Seiks were filling the Doo Ab with outrage and devastation, while on the other several of the Zemindars, availing themselves of the confusion of the times, rose in arms in many parts of the country.

The minister, who by this time had reached Delhi, on his arrival laboured incessantly to remove from the king's mind all suspicion of his fidelity. He entered into a long defence of his conduct, wherein he attempted to prove that the late disaster was imputable not to his want of attachment, but to the common accidents of war; that for himself he had ever been one of the foremost in seal and exertion for his majesty's service.

NOTES

1. Gupta, *History of the Sikhs*, 4: 93–103; Singh, *A History of the Sikh Misals*, 280.
2. Around 1775 the Sikhs under the leadership of Rāi Singh Bhangī, Baghel Singh Karorasinghīā, and Tārā Singh Ghaibā of the Dallevālīā *misl* (see illustration 6) raided the territory of Zābitā Khān in the Gangā Doāb. An embattled Zābitā Khān, still reeling from a dispute with Shāh Ālum II, avoided a conflict with a pay-off of Rs. 50,000 and an understanding of friendly alliance against the emperor. Two years later following the defeat of Zābitā Khān with his Rohīllā–Sikh force against the Imperial army he sought shelter in the Sikh camp. In a state of desperation and to further cement the alliance, he publicly declared himself a Sikh convert and took the name Dharam Singh. This event led to the following saying which is still current in the Sahāranpur district: "Ek Gurū ka do chelā, adhā Sikh adhā Rohīllā" (The Gurū's one disciple was half Sikh and half Rohīllā.). Gupta, *History of the Sikhs*, 3: 83–99.
3. Gurū Nānak was seventy-years-old when he passed away in 1539. He was cremated at Kartārpur and not, as Francklin asserts, buried at Amritsar.
4. Bābā Lakhmī Dās (1497–1555) and Bābā Srī Chand (1494–1629).
5. It is generally accepted that Gurū Nānak nominated his successor, Gurū Angad, during his own lifetime, and that Bābā Srī Chand did not occupy the *Gurgaddī* (spiritual seat of the Gurū) after his father.
6. Francklin is confused regarding the events of Gurū Tegh Bahādur's life as, according to the traditionally accepted account, he did not fight any "bloody encounters" with Aurangzeb. Francklin may have meant to apply this statement to Gurū Gobind Singh who did engage militarily against the Mughal Empire during the reign of Aurangzeb.
7. Lahore was occupied by the Sikhs in November 1761. Gupta, *History of the Sikhs*, 2: 173–8.
8. Examples of the Sikhs taking prisoners are not uncommon. In 1762, captured Afghān soldiers were taken to Amritsar and made to excavate the *sarovar* (tank) that had been filled with the rubble of the Harimandar Sāhib, blown up by Ahmad Shāh. More unusual are the instances of where Sikhs have kidnapped the finest children and raised them as their own. For instance, Hari Ram Gupta records the family tradition of the Usmānī Shaikhs: after the capture of Deoband by Rāi Singh Bhangī in 1775, he kidnapped a handsome boy called Qalandar Bakhsh who had not reached his tenth year. He was "converted" to Sikhism and only returned to the family after his maternal grandfather paid over a large sum of money. Gupta, *History of the Sikhs*, 3: 86. Polier also mentions the kidnapping of the most handsome and robustly made children they came across (see part II, chapter 8).
9. 'Abd ul-Ahad Khān (q.v.).
10. The expedition left Delhi in June 1779.
11. At Karnāl many Sikh chiefs including Sāhib Singh Khondāh, Diwān Singh, Baghel Singh, and Karam Singh Nirmalā waited upon Nawāb 'Abd ul-Ahad Khān. It is not clear who the chiefs mentioned by Francklin were, but they may be Gajpat Singh of Jīnd and Desū Singh of Kaithal. The chronicler,

Tahmas Khān Miskīn, who was present in the campaign states: "Gajpat Singh [of Jīnd] who had been in charge of the administration of the Karnal District for twenty years presented himself in the camp. Having taken responsibility for all the affairs of the neighbourhood, he became the Nawab's chief confidant and sole adviser in all the business of the government. The Nawab regulated his march, according to his instruction and guidance. He enlisted every Sikh who came in search of service. Every Sikh chief who interviewed him received elephants, aigrettes, etc., according to his rank. He appointed Sikh military posts in places where the inhabitants had fled away in fear of the royal troops. Abdul Ahad Khan was a very wise and experienced old man, and was in the habit of studying books of history and literature. But as he had fallen a victim to misfortune he lost all of his sagacity. He avoided his own companions, gave entire confidence in public as well as in private affairs to the Sikhs; and whenever he undertook any expedition, it was done at their advice. He did not take this fact into consideration that they were non-Muslims, and however attached outwardly they were to him, they would deceive him just in the critical hour." Gupta, *History of the Sikhs*, 3: 107.

12. When 'Abd ul-Ahad Khān commenced his expedition into Sikh territory in June 1779, Amar Singh notified the Mājhā Sikhs, under the leadership of Jassā Singh Āhlūvālīā, of the impending danger. According to the biographical *Jassā Singh Binod*, they responded thus: "Jassa Singh was at Batala. When he got the news, he immediately wrote to the Sikh that they should not delay any longer, as Abdul Ahad had marched from Delhi into their country. Jai Singh, Hakikat Singh, Trilok Singh, Amar Singh Bagha, Amar Singh Kingra and other Kahnaiya Sardārs came to the same place and the camp was fixed at Achal. Rāmgharīās fought with them and two of their places were taken." Gupta, *History of the Sikhs*, 3: 117.

13. About the fight that later ensued, Miskīn noted: "After Tara Singh Ghaiba [of the Dallevālīā *misl*] had joined Amar Singh, most of the Sikh Sardars lately engaged by the Nawab ['Abd ul-Ahad Khān] suddenly deserted him." Gupta, *History of the Sikhs*, 3: 116.

14. It is believed that 'Abd ul-Ahad Khān was advised by Baghel Singh to bribe the Mājhā Sikh chiefs, thereby avoiding the disaster of the Sikhs plundering him as he retreated to Delhi. The advice was taken and payments were made but Jassā Singh Āhlūvālīā commanded his men to make the most of the Khān's flight: "I have heard that the Nawab is about to retreat. If he does so, you should give him no quarter." *Jassā Singh Binod* in Gupta, *History of the Sikhs*, 3: 117.

CHAPTER 17

MEMOIRS OF AN IRISH MAHĀRĀJĀ, 1803

William Francklin, *Military Memoirs of Mr. George Thomas; Who, by Extraordinary Talents and Enterprize, Rose from an Obscure Situation to the Rank of a General, in the Service of the Native Powers in the North-West of India, etc. Compiled and Arranged from Mr. Thomas's Original Documents* (Calcutta: 1803. Reprint, London: John Stockdale, 1805), pp. 100–14; 343–4; 352; 355; 369–70.

William Francklin's background has been mentioned earlier in the introduction to his other work, *The Reign of Shah-Aulum* (chapter 16). The subject for his next book were the military memoirs of Mr. George Thomas, the adventurer from Tipperary, whom he met in 1802. This was shortly after Thomas surrendered at his fort of Georgegarh in the district of Jhajjar to an allied force of Sikhs and Marāthās (lead by a French officer, Louis Bourquien). Speaking of his surrender, Thomas summarized it thus: "Considering, therefore (concludes Mr Thomas) that I had entirely lost my party, and with it the hopes of at present subduing my enemies, the Sikhs and the powers in the French interests; that I had no expectation of succour from any quarter, Luckwa having gone to Joudpore; that if hostilities continued, my resource in money would have failed; in this situation I agreed to evacuate the fort; and, the necessary arrangements being completed, I stipulated for a battalion of Sepoys to escort me to the English frontier, where I arrived in the middle of January 1802."[1]

Thomas was exiled to British-controlled territory and en route to Calcutta, he met the then Captain Francklin, "an assiduous chronicler of the contemporary Moghul scene."[2] Francklin persuaded Thomas to tell his story, "although he at first protested that he would prefer to do it in Persian or Hindustani as his English was so rusty."[3] Francklin managed to interview Thomas in detail before he died in Berhāmpor, West Bengal, on August 22, 1802. He noted his battles, plots, and marches but unfortunately gave no information about his early years and missed several years in Thomas's later life. Aside from Francklin's account, details of Thomas's adventurous life as a mercenary soldier turned provincial ruler have been given in a newspaper report (part V, chapter 28), as well as by William Thorn in his *Memoir of the War in India* (part IV, chapter 18).

Thomas's observations of the Sikhs are incredibly useful, especially given the level of direct contact he had as a result of his many campaigns against them in the latter part of the eighteenth century and in the years leading up to his death in 1802. He cherished dreams of conquering the Punjab, and fought one of his best campaigns against the Sikh chiefs.

Some of the most fascinating observations in Thomas's memoirs are his recollections of the Sikhs' preparation for battle, their methods of fighting, love of weapons and horses, incredible powers of endurance, and hard lifestyle. These facets are related in true eyewitness fashion with an outstanding eye for the smallest detail. From reading his comments, it would seem that the Sikhs were Thomas's enemy of choice, and he actually enjoyed the many engagements he had with them over his eventful military career. His observations on the incessant infighting that plagued intra-Sikh relationships in his days are revealing, as is the fact that he considers this a fairly new phenomenon. It seems true that the lack of a powerful single common enemy threatening the whole community in the Punjab such as the Persian, Nādir Shāh, or the Afghān, Ahmad Shāh Abdalī, left a power vacuum which the Sikhs themselves stepped into, establishing independent kingdoms throughout the land. The Sikh historian, Giānī Gian Singh, writing in the late nineteenth century, explains why the Sikhs began establishing kingdoms: "First the Khālsā only punished offenders. Whenever they heard of rulers committing atrocities and injustice, they quickly went there [to punish them]. That is why they spent a day in one place and the night some where else. Then the people, tired of the atrocities inflicted by their rulers, pleaded strongly with the Sikh *Sirdārs*, 'Until you do not take the lands for yourself, the people will not live in peace nor can they be freed from injustice. This is why you should punish those rulers who tyrannise us, take the administration off their lands into your own hands and save the populace from these daily injustices.' "[4] The process of establishing Sikh kingdoms inevitably led to conflicts between the Sikhs themselves, with one *misl* vying for the territory of another. What is apparent is that the Sikhs whom Thomas encountered were different, especially in terms of mutual cooperation, from previous generations who had fought side by side in the life and death struggles of the early- to mid-eighteenth century.

In the memoirs, Ranjīt Singh gets a special mention as being the "chief of most consequence" who had "acquired a decided ascendancy over the other chiefs, though he be frequently in a state of warfare with his neighbours." This young man, then only in his early twenties, already stood out as the most powerful of the Sikh *Sirdārs*, and Thomas's comments—specifically about him—tend to suggest that he knew his memoirs would be utilized by key decision makers in British India. In naming Ranjīt Singh, he was indicating the principal protagonist that the British would have to acquaint themselves with in their dealings with the Punjab. This is exactly what happened in 1805 when Lord Lake's army entered the Punjab hot on the heels of the fleeing Marāthā, Holkār Rāo (part IV, chapter 18). Viewed in this light, Thomas's comments on the actual size of the combined Sikh force are understandably of utmost importance and he puts forward a novel reason, based on his own unique experiences, for why he considers previous estimates to have considerably inflated the figure (this was even done by Francklin in his *Shāh-Aulum* in chapter 16).

Thomas is one of the few commentators to mention Sikh women. Even though he remarks that they were not treated well by their husbands, he makes it a point to mention their bravery where they had "actually taken up arms to defend their habitations, from the desultory attacks of the enemy, and throughout the contest, behaved themselves with an intrepidity of spirit, highly praiseworthy." History is not kind in naming such women but examples are occasionally found in Sikh history books. Giānī Giān Singh notes one such example. In the 1720s, Zakriyā Khān, the governor of the Punjab, established fast-moving patrols under the direct command of his deputy, Moman Khān, to subdue Sikh highwaymen who were causing havoc in his administration. One well-known highwayman was Bahādur Singh of village Chavandā. He and his band of highwaymen always managed to evade capture by the Mughal patrols. It so happened that Bahādur Singh's son was to marry, and on the appointed day, all the men folk of Chavandā left to accompany the wedding party. A Jat spy of a neighboring village brought news of this development to Moman Khān. Realizing that only Bahādur Singh's wife and other women were left in the village, Moman Khān quickly marched to Chavandā with a large force. The Sikh women somehow heard of the approaching Mughal army. The wife of Bahādur Singh, whose name history does not record, realized she had no time to send a message to her husband so she decided to organize the other Sikh women and their Jat women relatives to defend the village. These brave women, wielding clubs and swords, managed to batter and repulse Moman Khān and his troops. Giānī Giān Singh writes: "Hearing of the success of the women of Chavandā, the Singhnīā in the Punjab were happy. Taking courage [and inspired by this example] many times did the Singhnīā fight the Turks. They knew well how to protect their honour, religion and their homes."[5]

Shortly after the book was first published in Calcutta in 1803, Francklin presented a signed copy to Henry Wellesley,[6] a member of the famous family who played a critical role in the expansion of British territories in India. His elder brother, the Marquis Wellesley, was governor-general of India from 1798 to 1805. During this time, he pursued his "forward policy" with conviction, annexing regions[7] with a view to increasing the Company's rule, elevating the British government to the position of paramount power in India, and the utilization of Indian resources in the resistance of what was considered the menace of Napoleon's worldwide ambition. Henry initially acted as personal secretary to his elder brother, the governor-general, but was later promoted by him to the appointment of lieutenant-governor of the ceded districts of Oudh in 1801. Their younger brother, Sir Arthur Wellesley (future Duke of Wellington), was a major-general, instrumental in defeating the Marāthās at the battle of Assaye in September 1803, which paved the way for British domination in Delhi. It was shortly after the victory at Assaye that Henry received his copy of the book from Francklin. What makes this Calcutta edition remarkable are two pages which do not make an appearance in the London edition published two years later in 1805. The relevant extracts from those two pages are reproduced below and speak of the pro-expansionist opinions of George Thomas in relation to the Punjab. Thomas's concluding thoughts to Francklin on his section on the Sikhs on pages 77–8[8] reads: "In their moral character, the Sikhs are alike faithless to friends and foes; Unable or unwilling to look forward to futurity, present advantage is the sole ruler of their proceeding, this renders them eager to embrace the first offers for forming a foreign connection. Considered as a nation their alliance can be of no service in a political point of view, while the mode of government, their habits and prejudices, utterly preclude the hope of their ever becoming real friends. It is however, Mr. Thomas's opinion that by wresting from them the possessions they have usurped, and by the establishment of a respectable force, in the north west frontier, the expences of which might be defrayed out of the revenues of the province, the British government would not only derive essential advantages, from securing their own possessions form future incursions from the north, but likewise contributable in a very high degree to establish the permanency and the tranquility of their southern and western neighbours."

On this revealing note, Mr Thomas concludes his remarks on the Sikhs, his favorite enemies.

---

pp. 100–14

THE extensive and fertile country described by Arrian and other ancient historians, as comprehended within the five great rivers, the Hydaspes, the Hydraötes, the Acesines, the Hyphasis, and the Sutledge, is, by modern geographers, denominated Punjab.

On the north it is bounded by the mountains inhabited by the tribe Yoosuf Zey; on the east by the mountains of Naun,[9] Serinnaghur and Jumbo; on the west by the river Sind or Attock;[i] and on the south by the districts of Panniput, and the province of Harrianah. It is two hundred and fifty cosses from the north to south, and nearly one hundred from east to west. Notwithstanding the state of warfare in which the chiefs of Punjab are constantly involved, the country is in a state of high cultivation; and though the population be great, grain is cheaper than in any other part of India. This advantage in a great measure is derived from the numerous rivers by which it is watered. Advancing from the south, a traveller meets in rapid succession the Sersooty, the Cugger, the Chowah, and the Sutledge.

---

[i] This river above the city of Attock is called by the Natives Aba Seen.

The Sersooty, after passing the towns of Moostufabad, Shahabad, and Tehnasser, and overflowing the country on each of its banks, joins itself to the Cugger to the north-west of Kaythul.

The Cugger, on the contrary, after passing the towns of Bunnoor, Seyfabad, Puttialah, Jowhana, and Jomalpore, enters the country of the Batties at the town of Arwah, formerly the capital of the district. The Chowah, in like manner, after passing through an extensive tract of country which it fertilizes and enriches, is finally lost in the sands of Sonaum.

The Punjab yields to no part of India in fertility of soil; it produces in the greatest abundance, sugar-cane, wheat, barley, rice, pulse of all sorts, tobacco, and various fruits; and it is also well supplied with cattle. The principal manufactures of this country are swords, match-locks, cotton cloths, and silks both coarse and fine.[10]

This nation, if united, could bring into the field from fifty to sixty thousand cavalry, but it is Mr. Thomas's opinion that they will never unite or be so formidable to their neighbours as they have heretofore been. Internal commotions and civil strife have of late years generated a spirit of revenge and disunion among the chiefs, which it will take a long time to overcome.

The number of cavalry which it is supposed this nation was able to assemble has been considerably over-rated, in consequence of a custom which formerly obtained among the Seiks, of forming an association of their forces under a particular chief. From this association of their forces they had the general interests of the community in view. To those who were ignorant of the secret causes of the association, this junction of forces was frequently mistaken for the army of an individual; and this error was perhaps increased by the natural partiality of the Seiks themselves to magnify the force and enhance the character of their own nation.[11]

It has been remarked, that the Seiks are able to collect from fifty to sixty thousand horse; but, to render this number effective, those who do not take the field, or who remain at home to guard possessions, must be included.

Estimating the force of the different districts the aggregate will be seen in the subjoined schedule.[ii]

By this statement it will appear that the entire force of this nation, exclusive of the district held by Zemaun Shah, eastward of the Attock,[iii] can amount to no more than sixty-four thousand men, and those two-thirds might probably take the field, were a chief of experience and enterprize to appear amongst them; but this in Mr. Thomas's opinion is highly improbable. The chief of most consequence at present is Runjeet

[ii]

	Cavalry
The districts south of the Sutledge,	15,000
The Dooab, or country between the Sutledge and Beyah,	8,000
Between the Beyah and Rowee,	11,000
Force of Bugheel Sing, chief of Pattialah,	12,000
The countries above Lahore, the inhabitants of which are chiefly under the influence of Runjeet Sing,	11,000
To which may be added the force of Nizamuddeen Khan	5,000
Roy Elias	1,300
Other Patan chiefs, in pay of the Seiks	800
Grand total	64,100

[iii] These districts are computed to reach Sirhind to the banks of that river.

Sing: he, having possession of Lahore, which may be termed the capital of the Punjab, has acquired a decided ascendancy over the other chiefs, though he be frequently in a state of warfare with his neighbours who inhabit that part of the country situated between the Beyah and the Rawee. This chief is deemed by the natives as the most powerful among then. He possesses one thousand horse, which are his own property.

The repeated invasion of the Punjab by small armies of late years, affords a convincing proof that the national force of the Seiks cannot be so formidable as has been represented. Several instances occur in support of this assertion. Not many years since, Dara Row Scindia invaded it at the head of ten thousand men; though not more than six thousand of that number deserved the name of troops, the remainder being a despicable rabble. Though joined on his march by two chiefs, Buggeel Sing and Kurrum Sing, he was at length opposed by Sahib Sing, the chief of Fyzealpore. That chief was encamped under the walls of Kussoor,[iv] having the river Cuggur in his front; was defeated in an engagement, and the ensuing day the fort surrendered. Sahib Sing then agreed to pay the Mahrattas a sum of money, and most of the chiefs south of the Sutledge having by this time submitted to Dara Row, opposition was at an end.[12]

It was successively invaded by the armies of Ambajee, Bala Row, and Nana Furkhia, who drove the seiks repeatedly before them.

In 1800 Mr. Thomas himself entered their country at the head of five thousand troops and sixty pieces of artillery; and though by the instigation of enemies, who promised them assistance, the chiefs south of the Sutledge and in the Dooab (or country between the two rivers[v]) combined against him, yet he penetrated as far as the Sutledge. During that campaign he never saw more than ten thousand Seiks in one army: he remained in their country six months, two of which were passed without competition, and he finally compelled them to purchase peace.

Of late years the rajah of Serinnagur has likewise made some conquests in Punjab, chiefly between the Beyah and the Sutledge; and Nizamuddeen Khan, the patan before mentioned, has also acquired territory yielding a revenue of three lacks of rupees per annum.

The Seiks, though united, have never made any considerable opposition against the force of Zemaun Shah, who has frequently attacked them; but it may be urged, that a great difference is to be expected from a formidable army of sixty thousand men, led on by the Shah in person, and the princes the blood, compared with the detached bodies already described. Hence it would appear that this nation is not so formidable as they have been represented, and in all probability they never will be formidable when opposed by regular troops.[13]

The Seiks are armed with a spear, matchlock, and scymetar. Their method of fighting, as described by Mr. Thomas, is singular: after performing the requisite duties of their religion by ablution and prayer, they comb their hair and beards with peculiar care; then mounting their horses, ride forth towards the enemy, with whom they engage in a continued skirmish, advancing and retreating until man and horse become equally fatigued. They then draw off to some distance from the enemy, and, meeting with cultivated ground, they permit their horses to graze of their own accord, while they parch a little gram for themselves; and after satisfying nature by this frugal repast, if the enemy be near, they renew the skirmishing. Should he have

---

[iv] Kussor, a fort south of the river Sutledge.
[v] The Beyah and the Sutledge.

retreated they provide forage for their cattle, and endeavor to procure a meal for themselves.

Seldom indulging in the comforts of a tent, whilst in the enemy's country, the repast of a seik cannot be supposed to be either sumptuous or elegant. Seated on the ground with a mat spread before them, a bramin,[14] appointed for the purpose, serves out a portion of food to each individual, the cakes of flour which they eat during the meal serving them in the room of dishes and plates.[vi]

The seiks are remarkably fond of the flesh of the jungle hog, which they kill in chace: this food is allowable by their law. They likewise eat of mutton and fish; but these being deemed unlawful the bramins will not partake, leaving those who chuse to transgress their institutes to answer for themselves. In the city or in the field the seiks never smoke tobacco: they are not, however, averse to drinking spirituous liquors, in which they sometimes indulge to an immoderate excess; and they likewise freely take opium, bang, and other intoxicating drugs. In their convivial parties each man is compelled to drink out of his own vessel.

Accustomed from their earliest infancy to a life of hardship and difficulty, the seiks despise the comforts of a tent; in lieu of this, each horseman if furnished with two blankets, one for himself and the other for his horse. These blankets, which are placed beneath the saddle, with a gram bag and heel ropes, comprize, in time of war, the baggage of a seik. Their cooking utensils are carried on tattoos.[15] Considering this mode of life, and the extraordinary rapidity of their movements, it cannot be matter of wonder if they perform marches, which, to those who are only accustomed to European warfare, must appear almost incredible.

The Seiks, among other customs singular in their nature, never suffer their hair or beards to be cut: consequently, when mounted on horseback, their flowing locks and half naked-bodies, which are formed in the stoutest and most athletic mould, the glittering of their arms, and the size and speed of their horses, render their appearance imposing and formidable, and superior to most of the cavalry in Hindoostan.

In use of their arms, especially the matchlock, and sabre, they are uncommonly expert; some use bows and arrows. In addition to the articles of dress which have been described in recent publications[vii] of the times, Mr. Thomas mentions that the arms and wrists of the Seiks are decorated with bangles of gold, silver, brass, and iron, according to the circumstances of the wearers; but among the chiefs, of the respective tribes, the horse-furniture, in which they take the greatest pride (and which, with the exception of the inlaying of their fire-arms, is their luxury), is uncommonly splendid; for, though a seik will scruple to expend the most trifling sum on his food or clothing, he will spare no expence in endeavouring to excel his comrades in the furniture of his horse and in the richness and brightness of his armour, a circumstance,

---

[vi] Does not this circumstances recall our ideas to the situation of Æneas and his companions, shortly after their landing on the coast of Italy? The condition of Æneas exhibits a specimen of primeval simplicity of manners among the Romans, no less singular than the coincidence of customs existing in Punjab at the present day appears strikingly interesting.

Consumtis hic forte aliis, ut vertere morsus
Exiguam in Cererem penuria adegit edendi,
Et violare manu malisq. audacibus orbem
Fatilis crusti, patulis nec parcere quadris,
Heus! etiam mensas consumimus, inquit Iulus.

                             Virg. Æn. Lib. 7.

[vii] Consult the *History of the Shah Aulum.*

which appears to bear no inconsiderable resemblance to the customs of the ancient Spartans.[viii]

Considerable similarity in their general customs may be traced with those of the Jauts. Though these in some districts apparently vary, the difference is not material; and their permitting an interchange of marriages with the Jauts of the Dooab and Harrianah amounts almost to a conclusive proof of their affinity of origin.

The Seiks allow foreigners of every description to join their standard, to sit in their company, and to shave their beards; but, excepting in the instance of the Jauts, they will not consent to intermarriages; nor will they eat or drink from the hands of an alien, except he be a bramin, and for this cast they always profess the highest veneration.[16]

If, indeed, some regulations which are in their nature purely military, and which were introduced by their founder Nanick, be excepted, it will be found that the Seiks are neither more or less than Jauts in their primitive state.

Thus far, says Mr. Thomas, we have seen the fair side of the picture; let us now consider the reverse.—The Seiks are false, sanguinary, and faithless; they are addicted to plunder, and the acquirement of wealth by any means, however nefarious. Instances have occurred of a child's arm being raised against his parent, and of brothers destroying each other.

Women amongst them are held in little estimation, and though ill treated by their husbands, and prohibited from accompanying them in their wars, these unhappy females nevertheless attend to their domestic concerns with a diligence and sedulousness deserving of a better fate.

Instances, indeed, have not unfrequently occurred, in which they have actually taken up arms to defend their habitations from the desultory attacks of the enemy, and throughout the contest behaved themselves with an intrepidity of spirit highly praiseworthy.[17]

In the seik army, the modes of payments are various: but the most common is at the time of harvest, when every soldier receives the amount of his pay in grain and other articles, the produce of the country; to some is given money in small sums, and to others lands are allotted for their maintenance. Three–fifths of the horses in the Punjab are the property of the different chieftains: the remainder belong to the peasantry who have become settlers.

A Seik soldier has also his portion of the plunder acquired in the course of a campaign: this is set aside as a reward for his services; and in addition to it, he sometimes increases his gains by secreting part of the public plunder.[18]

The nature of the seik government is singular, and probably had its origin in the unsettled state of the tribe when first established in their possessions. Within his own domains each chief is lord paramount. He exerts an exclusive authority over his vassals, even to the power of life and death; and to increase the population of his districts, he proffers a ready and hospitable asylum to fugitives from all parts of India. Hence, in the seik territories, though the government be arbitrary, there exists much less cause for oppression than in many of the neighbouring states; and hence likewise, the cultivator of the soil being liable to frequent change of masters, by the numerous revolutions that are perpetually occurring, may be considered as one of the causes of the fluctuation of the national force.[ix]

[viii] See Cornelius Nepos, and Pausanias.

[ix] In the above sketch of the situation and resources of the seik nation, Mr Thomas does not include the territories of Zemaun Shah lying east of the Attock; part of which were, during the reigns of the emperors, included in the Punjab, and may therefore be considered as belonging to it.

pp. 343–4
Appendix I.
Of the trade in general carried on in the countries to the North–West of Delhi.
I. PUNJAB. An open trade with this country from every part of Hindoostan has long since ceased; but petty merchants, by applying for passports from the respective chiefs of the Seik territories, previous to entering their boundaries, are generally supplied with them, and by this means still continue a trifling commercial intercourse.

Their exports to the countries west of the Attock, consist of sugar, rice, indigo, wheat, and white cloth. Their imports from those countries are swords, horses, fruit, lead and spices. The exports to Cashmere may be considered nearly the same as into Persia; their imports from Cashmere are shawls, and a variety of cloths, saffron, and fruit.

With the inhabitants of the mountains they exchange cloths, matchlocks, and horses, for iron, and other inferior commodities. From the Deckan are imported sulfur, indigo, salt, lead, iron, Europe coarse cloth, and spices: their exports are horses, camels, sugar, rice, white cloth, matchlocks, swords, and bows and arrows.

This trade is not carried on by any particular route, but depends on the character of the chiefs of those districts through which they pass. The most considerable part of the trade is, however, carried on from Amrut Seer, by way of Machaywara to Duttyala; southward by way of Hansi, Rauge Ghur, and Oreecha, into the western part of the Rajepoot country by way of Kythul, Jeind, and Dadery, and finally by Karnaul towards Delhi and the Ganges.

p. 352
Appendix II.
PROSPECTUS
Having been appointed in 1792 to accompany an escort ordered to attend captain Reynolds, of the Bombay establishment, on a survey through the Dooab and the adjoining countries, it appears to me that in the course of this expedition, much information may be gained on subjects hitherto sufficiently investigated and developed; what I conceive to be most useful in the researches above alluded to, may be reduced under the following headings:

p. 355
THE SEIKS
8th. This nation, so obscure as hardly to be mentioned even as a tribe, at the beginning of the present century, have, within these last thirty years, raised themselves in such reputation as not only to attract the notice, but excite the alarm of their neighbours on both sides of their government.

They possess the whole of the Punjaub, and it is very probable will one day or other have an eye to a participation of the Viziers provinces.[19] I propose, therefore, to obtain every possible information of their tribe, manners, customs, and spirit of government, and, should we be able, to penetrate Punjaub, to describe the face of that country, and the natural and commercial productions.[x]

pp. 369–70
Appendix IV.
A general Abstract of the Countries, and their Inhabitants in the north-west parts of the Peninsula of Hindoostan; with the Distance of the capital Cities from Delhi in British Miles.

---

[x] See the *History of Shah Aulum*, and present work.

1st. THE Punjab or country of the Seiks, is composed of the province of Lahore, and the chukla or division called Sirhind. The inhabitants in general are Seiks, though the cultivators of the soil are many of them Jauts.

Force Cavalry 60,000, Artillery 40 pieces.
Infantry 5,000, Revenue 5 crores.
Capital, Lahore, N. W. by N. three hundred Miles.

2d. The Hurrianah country is included in the Sirkar of Hissar; it is called in the map the Lesser Baloochistaun. The inhabitants are chiefly Jauts, with the exception of a few Rajepoot, and Rungur villages, which last application is given to such of the Rajpoots who have embraced the Mahomedan religion. Does not Rungur imply coloured, or stained, or of mixed blood?

Capital Hissar, W. N. W. one hundred and eight miles.

3d. The country called Thanessar, consists of the western parts of Tahnessar, Karnaul, Kythul, Panniput, Sefeedoo, Jeind, Kosohan, and Dehatarut. The inhabitants are chiefly Jauts, though some have become Seiks, and a few are Rajepoots, but of a low caste.

No particular capital.

Notes

1. William Francklin, *Military Memoirs of Mr. George Thomas*. (London: 1805), 244.
2. Shelford Bidwell, *Swords for Hire: European Mercenaries in Eighteenth-Century India* (John Murray, 1981), 211.
3. Ibid., 211.
4. Giānī Giān Singh, *Twārīkh Gurū Khālsā*, 3 vols. (Sialkot: 1891–1894. Reprint Bhāsha Vibāgh, Punjab, 1970), 2 vols., 2: 226.
5. Giānī Giān Singh, *Navīn Panth Prakāsh* (Amritsar: 1880. Reprint Punjab: Bhāsha Vibāgh, 1987), 578–9.
6. The note at the beginning of this copy reads: "The Honourable Henry Wellesley with the author's best compliments, Calcutta October 21st 1803."
7. The five annexations effected by the close of 1801 were Mysore, the Carnātic, Tanjore, Surat, and a large portion of Oudh. Vincent A. Smith, *The Oxford History of India* (Oxford: 1920), 589.
8. The only copy known to exist with these pages intact is now in a private collection.
9. Nahan.
10. It is noteworthy that this list comprises the most important items required by a Sikh warrior: "In spite of the simplicity of his habits, he took a pardonable pride in the adornment of his person and the proper maintenance of his accoutrements. Like the ancient Spartan, he never failed to carefully comb out and adjust his long hair and beard before the battle, and his white vest contrasting with his scarlet trappings made a fair show as he rode along gallantly to the fight." *Calcutta Review*, vol. LX, 1875, 29, as quoted in Gupta, *History of the Sikhs*, 3: 66.
11. In *The History of the Reign of Shah-Aulum* (part IV, chapter 16), Francklin estimates the force under Ranjīt Singh alone as 70,000 men, which is more than the entire number of all the Sikh chiefs according to George Thomas. This may well be the result of the overestimation mentioned by Thomas.

12. Following the succession in 1781 of the eight-year-old Sāhib Singh (1773–1813) as the ruler of Patiālā, disturbances continually broke out throughout the state. His *Dīwān* (Minister), Nānū Mall proved critical in suppressing these rebellions, and it was he who called in Dhārā Rāo, the Marāthā leader, in 1789 to protect Patiālā from the encroachment of neighbouring *Sirdārs*. Baghel Singh, leader of the Karorasinghīā *misl*, arranged matters with the Marāthā, who agreed at the price of two lakhs of rupees. The combined Marāthā–Sikh force succeeded in subduing the neighboring chiefs. They also marched against, and captured, Banur (of which half share belonged to Patiālā who assisted in capturing it in 1763), which was then in the possession of Khushāl Singh (not Sāhib Singh as stated), leader of the Singhpurīā *misl*. Lepel Griffin, *The Rajas of the Punjab*, 59–61; Gupta, *History of the Sikhs*, 4: 170.

13. This assertion, though considered to be generally true at the time of writing, was later to be proved erroneous. When Mahārājā Ranjīt Singh introduced a European style of training for his army, the result were some of the closest contests the British forces ever encountered in India, namely at Mudkī, Ferozeshāh, and Sobrāon in 1845–1846.

14. The presence of Brahmins to serve food for the Sikhs is an interesting observation but one that is not reported widely in other contemporary accounts, nor is it considered an orthodox practice today. It may be that the Sikhs observed by Thomas (mainly those of the Phūlkīān states: Patiālā, Nābhā, Jīnd, Kaithal, and Farīdkot) were not averse to maintaining the position of those of the higher caste in Hinduism, in exchange for their services in matters of state, which were deemed their hereditary positions.

15. Ponies.

16. As mentioned earlier, there are few contemporary instances of the Sikhs observing the higher caste distinction of the Brahmins. In all likelihood, it was the persistence of Brahmin influence in the courts of some of the Sikh chiefs that lead to George Thomas making this observation.

17. Thomas may have been recalling his encounters with Sāhib Kaur (1771–1801), the older and very able sister of the Mahārājā of Patiālā, Sāhib Singh (1773–1813), when recording his thoughts on Sikh women in battle: "Next, he [Thomas] embarked on an unprofitable raid on Patiala which turned out badly, as did an attempt to capture the city of Jhind just outside his borders and which would have made a valuable addition to his domain. Sahib Singh Phulkiani of Patiala was, for a Sikh, a spiritless creature; but his sister Kunur had the unusual distinction of 'seeing off' Thomas. She rallied the Sikh troops, forced him to raise the siege of Jhind, and encouraged the country folk to rise up all round him and harass him. Although Thomas when he met the Sikhs in the field gave them, as usual, a good beating or two, due to her efforts he ended up back in Hariana with nothing to show for his trouble except one or two empty victories and some casualties he could ill-afford. He bore Kunur no ill-will and in the next year was to rescue her from her brother's evil intentions, they having fallen out. (Perhaps he should have married her. It could have had the most intriguing political and genetic consequences.)" Bidwell, *Swords for Hire*, 149–50.

18. When the Sikhs, under the leadership of Jassā Singh Āhlūvālīā and Baghel Singh, marched in a body of 60,000 towards Ghāzīābad, twenty kilometres south of Delhi, they acquired substantial quantities of booty. Giānī Giān Singh comments on how the Sikhs viewed plunder in his *Navīn Panth*

Prakāsh : "When the Sikhs entered this town, the people fled away. The Sikhs caught the rich men of the place, tied them to pillars and by severely beating them compelled them to disclose the places of their hidden treasures. When the Sikhs had looted the town, Baghel Singh and Jassa Singh spread a cloth, and asked the chiefs to give away one-tenth of their booty in cash for the service of the Guru. The sum collected amounted to a lakh of rupees. This money was spent on Hari Mandar at Amritsar." Gupta, *History of the Sikhs*, 3: 163–4.

19. A reference to the Wazīr of Oudh, virtually a British protectorate controlled through the Residency at Lucknow. The Anglo–Sikh treaty of 1806, which followed the flight of Jasvant Rāo Holkar from the British into the Punjab in 1805, brought the powerful Sikh chief, Ranjīt Singh, into direct contact with the British government. The articles of the treaty effectively bound the Sikhs from invading British territories, including Oudh. For more on the treaty, see Thorn, part IV, chapter 18.

Illustration 1 "Mardānā and Nānak Shāh," c. 1780. From a set of 64 paintings of the Hindu gods, the incarnations of Vishnū, and of minor divinities and the planets. The paintings, in the Lucknow style, were commissioned by Colonel Antoine Polier who wrote several papers on the Sikhs (see part II, chapter 8). This is the earliest known painting of Gurū Nānak commissioned by a European.

Illustration 2 The ghost of Omīchand, 1773. This rare satirical print from the Westminster Magazine shows a startled Lord Clive (held by the arms) coming face-to-face with an apparition of Omīchand, the Sikh who was the principal merchant to the English in Calcutta. Clive had tricked him out of his share of an immense fortune in the run up to the Battle of Plassey in 1757 (see part II, chapter 5).

Illustration 3 A conference in the Punjab Hills, c. 1775. The main figure is Khālsā Jai Singh Kanhaiyā (top right, dressed in white) with two "Khālsā (A)kālbūngīā" (dressed in dark clothes) meeting with tributary hill chiefs. These include Sansār Chand of Kāngrā (center, and anticlockwise in an arc from top), Rājā Rāj Singh of Chambā, Rājā Pragās Chand of Guler, Rājā Jagrūp Singh of Jassoāl, and Rājā Narain Singh of Sībā, accompanied by their ministers. The nature of the relationship between the hill states and the Sikhs was witnessed firsthand by the traveler, George Forster (part II, chapter 12).

Illustration 4   Jai Singh Kanhaiyā with attendant, mid–late eighteenth century. One of the most prominent of the Sikh *misl* leaders, he was initiated into the Khālsā by the famous Nawāb Kapūr Singh and joined the ranks of the itinerant warriors under Amar Singh Kingrā. He died in 1793, at the age of 81, having taken part in many of the historical events of his time that witnessed the transformation of the Sikhs from fugitives with a price on their heads to the rulers of a vast and rich territory.

Illustration 5 Gurbakhsh Singh Kanhaiyā on horseback with armed attendant, mid–late eighteenth century. The son of Jai Singh Kanhaiyā, it was his death in an internecine Sikh battle in 1785 that brought about an alliance between the Kanhaiyā and Sukkarchākkīā *misls* in the form of a matrimonial tie. The late Gurbakhsh Singh's daughter was betrothed to the five-year-old Ranjīt Singh who later became the outright ruler of the Punjab with the support of Gurbakhsh Singh's influential widow, Sadā Kaur.

Illustration 6 Tārā Singh Ghaibā, head of the Dallevālīā *misl*, with attendant and an armed youth, mid–late eighteenth century. He was born in 1717, the year after the first attempt at independent Sikh rule ended with the execution of Bandā Bahādur in Delhi (see part II, chapter 4). He lived to the age of ninety, fighting against successive Persian, Afghān, and Mahrātā incursions into the Punjab to see Sikh rule re-established once again in 1799.

Illustration 7 Bhāg Singh Āhluvālīā, mid–late eighteenth century. He was a cousin of the great Sikh commander Jassā Sikh Āhlūvālīā, the fourth leader of the Buddhā Dal. His son, Fateh Singh Āhlūvālīā, played a key role in the first treaty signed between the Sikhs and the British in 1806.

Illustration 8 Amar Singh (Kingrā?) with attendant, mid–late eighteenth century. An elderly Sikh *misldār* with a heavily pock-marked face. The distinctive manner in which he has wound his large turban has been clearly depicted by the artist.

Illustration 9
"Sics. A Hindoo tribe."

Illustration 10
"Nānuk-Punthy."

Illustrations 9 and 10 are from *Les Hindous*, by Balthazar Solvyns (Paris, 1808–1812). The detailed descriptions that accompany these early images are given in part III, chapter 15.

Illustration 11 A horseman of Mahārājā Ranjīt Singh, c. 1814. This fine illustration captures perfectly the typical Sikh cavalryman of the *misl* period. The sparsely dressed warrior with flowing beard, armed with matchlock gun, sword, dagger, bow, arrows, and shield mounted on a finely decorated and powerful steed fits perfectly with the description given by George Thomas, the long-time adversary of the Sikhs popularly known as the "Irish Maharaja" (part IV, chapter 17).

Illustration 12 "A Seik." By the Patnā artist, Jai Rām Dās, c. 1815. Patnā was the birthplace of Gurū Gobind Singh and had a large Sikh population. The scholar, Charles Wilkins, arrived in the city in 1781. His valuable notes of his visit to one of the *gurdwārās* and his discussion with some of the Patnā Sikhs there is reproduced in part VI, chapter 30.

Illustration 13
Nāngā nānakshāhī (*Nagga naunuckshahy*).

Illustration 14
Suthrāshāhī (*Sootrasahee*).

Illustrations 13–15 are from an album of 80 paintings by a Patnā artist depicting the *Avtārs* of Vishnū and a series of paintings of ascetics and fakīrs, c. 1818. The individuals shown all belong to orders within the broad *Udāsī* Sikh tradition established by Bābā Srī Chand, the eldest son of Gurū Nānak. Thomas Hardwicke (part III, chapter 14) describes the central role of an *Udāsī* amongst a party of Sikhs at the Haridvār fair in 1796.

Illustration 15
Nānakshāhī (*Nanucksahee*).

Illustration 16 Sikh.

Illustration 17 Nānapanthī.

Illustration 18 Akālī.

Illustrations 16–18 are from *Tashrīh al-akvām,* a Persian manuscript by Colonel James Skinner, c. 1825, containing notes on the origins and occupations of the castes, tribes, and sects of the Punjab.

Illustration 19   Ranjīt Singh, Mahārājā of Punjab.

Illustrations 19–22 are from the *Tazkirat al-umarā*, a Persian manuscript written by Colonel James Skinner sometime prior to 1830. The work contains historical notes on princely families of Rājputānā and the Punjab. Of the latter, details and portraits of twelve Sikh families are given including two of the most important Sikh chiefs of their day, Ranjīt Singh and Fateh Singh. In 1806, these men in their early twenties negotiated the first treaty between the Sikhs and the British. William Thorn, also then in his twenties, was present at his historic juncture in the Anglo–Sikh relationship and gave his version in his memoirs (part IV, chapter 18).

Illustration 20   Rājā Fateh Singh Āhlūvālīā of Kapūrthalā.

Illustration 21   Mahārājā Karam Singh of Patiālā.

Illustration 22   The Rānī of the late Rūp Singh of Radaur.

CHAPTER 18

STANDOFF IN RANJĪT SINGH'S
PUNJAB, 1806

William Thorn, *Memoir of the War in India Conducted by General Lord Lake and Sir Arthur Wellesley from its Commencement in 1803 to its Termination in 1806, on the Banks of the Hyphasis with Historical Sketches, Topographical Descriptions and Statistical Observations, Illustrated by maps and plans of operations* (London: 1818), pp. 478–503, 506–7.

Sir William Thorn's (1781–1843) published memoirs contain his recollections from the years 1803 to 1806. The section relating specifically to the Sikhs dates from the latter part of that period. At just twenty-four when he encountered the Sikhs, Thorn had acquired a considerable knowledge of the military system of the early colonials, which he refers to in his account.

Thorn joined the 29th Light Dragoons in India in 1799, the year that Mahārājā Ranjīt Singh had entered and secured Lahore. He served under Lord Lake during the Marāthā War in 1803 and at Laswārī toward the end of that same year. The extract relates to his memoirs of the pursuit of Holkār Rāo into the Punjab, which occurred in 1805, prior to which Thorn had served at Delhi and Dīg in 1804.

An avowed military man and a constant traveler, he was witness to some of the most important campaigns in early British Empire building in southeast Asia. He was later to serve in the capture of Mauritius in 1810, followed by Java in 1811, and Palembang in Sumatra. At the age of thirty-three, he returned to England where he busied himself in writing his memoirs, authoring *Memoirs of the Conquest of Java, etc.* in 1815 and *A Memoir of the Late War in India, 1803–1806*—from which this extract is taken—in 1818.

His entry into the establishment was secure when he was appointed Brevet-Lt-Colonel and later in 1832, a knight of the Royal Hanoverian Guelphic order. He died on November 29, 1843.

Thorn's account reads like a travelog through the southern part of the Punjab. The purpose of his memoir was to recount the latter part of Lord Lake's campaign against the Marāthā chief, Jasvant Holkār Rāo. The wily Marāthā, having been totally routed at Fatehgarh and Dīg by Generals Lake and Fraser, retreated deep into Ranjīt Singh's Punjab hoping, no doubt, to drag the Sikhs into his battle. Ranjīt Singh was politically an altogether different character from the minor Sikh *rājās* and *misldārs* who had previously supported the Marāthās. He would have recognized the folly of allowing the Punjab to become a battleground for two foreign nations let alone risking his Khālsā forces in a battle from which he had little to gain. They had just taken Multān leaving a large portion of Muslim Punjab within his grasp. The presence of the Marāthās and the British was an infuriating distraction. However, Rāo's continued company in Amritsar was unnerving and Lake, with his army now provocatively camped at Jalālābād, was an even more menacing problem. Lord Lake's saber rattling just 35 kilometers from Amritsar had shaken the Mahārājā and ultimately had the desired effect. Ranjīt Singh and Fateh Singh Āhlūvālīā (see illustration 20) called grand council (*Sarbat Khālsā*) to formulate a response. The resolution was a unanimous one. Ranjīt Singh would act as mediator, thus avoiding a partisan role, and would eject the warring factions from his land. By January 1806, a peace treaty was signed; the Marāthās retreated and renounced all their possession in Northern India. Suddenly, Ranjīt Singh had a new neighbor.

Thorn's travels took him through the Phūlkīān States and into the Punjab, hot on the heels of the fleeing Jasvant Holkar Rāo. The account opens with a recollection of the exploits of the mercenary and personal empire builder, George Thomas, with specific reference to his interaction with the ruling family of Patiālā (see also part IV, chapter 17 for more on Thomas). The then Rāja of Patiālā, Sāhib Singh (1773–1813), ascended to the throne at the age of just eight after his father, Amar Singh, died in 1781. In his minority, power passed to his grandmother, Rānī Hukman, his father's Prime Minister, Dīwān Nānū Mall, his father's first cousin, Rājinder Kaur, and his brilliant older sister, Rānī Sāhib Kaur. Thomas's 1799 attack on Jīnd drew fire from the neighboring principalities of Patiālā, Kaithal, Lādvā, Thānesar, as well as the state of Jīnd. At the head of nine thousand troops, Sāhib Kaur was instrumental in dislodging Thomas and negotiating the settlement between the Sikh chiefs and their adversary. She signed the agreement on behalf of her brother, Rāja Sāhib Singh. The Rāja viewed the settlement by his sister as usurping his own authority; coupled with his ambitious wife and a newly born heir (Karam Singh), Sāhib Singh used this event to harass his sister. She was hounded from her fort in Ubhevāl (near Sunām) and imprisoned in Patiālā. It is said that the Rānī successfully petitioned George Thomas to aid in her release.[1] When she finally executed an escape from the fort she was captured again; this time she was allowed to return to her fortress town of Ubhevāl where she died in 1801 aged just thirty.[2]

Thorn's travelog through the Punjab traces a route from the royal city of Nābhā to Ludhiānā and then crossing the Sutlej into Jalandhar. Inasmuch as the ascendancy of the Kingdom of Lahore is evidenced in his writing on Ranjīt Singh, it is also clear that by that time Nābhā had lost its preeminent position within the Phūlkīān family of states. The Nābhā chiefs claim precedence over the other Phūlkīān houses on account of their descent from the eldest branch of the family. The common ancestor of the Phūlkīān Rājās, Phūl, is said to have had two sons, Gurdittā and Sukhchain; the Nābhā branch traces its ancestry through the elder brother, with Sukhchain the founder of the house of Jīnd.

Thorn then commences a treatise on the Sikhs after he mentions that Holkār Rāo was camped at Amritsar at the time of writing. His chronology continues apace through the early Gurū period and through the period of Mughal decline and Sikh ascendancy as political masters of the Punjab. Thorn then gives an important and detailed account on the negotiations that took place between the British party headed by Lord Lake, representatives of the young Ranjīt Singh, and Holkār Rāo Scindiā. Interestingly, he does not give credence to, or even mentions, a story that Ranjīt Singh would later tell visitors of his going in disguise into the British camp to negotiate directly with Lake.

Later, Thorn gives a detailed eyewitness account of the Sikh troop formations. These are likely to have been drilled and inspired by European deserters from the East India Company's army, later to be improved to the highest standards seen in India by the mercenary Napoleonic generals that Ranjīt Singh began to employ in the 1820s. Although the account is not clear as to which Sikh chief was the architect of the parade, the description of troop columns does imply a formality that was only really known by Ranjīt Singh. His description of Sikh cavalry is reminiscent of the description of Akālī Nihang Sikhs, clothed in blue and keen on the use of the *chakara*, the fabled steel quoit. Thorn is also able to identify a singular deficiency in the early arsenal of Ranjīt Singh—the weakness of the artillery. Thorn was not alone in recognizing this deficiency. Ranjīt Singh, too, was at pains to upgrade this section of his armory. On the face of it, the adoption of artillery by the Sikhs appears haphazard even though Ranjīt Singh readily appreciated the crucial function of artillery in modern warfare. He established a workshop for the repair and casting of guns as early as 1807. In 1809, he exploited the good relations established with the British by producing mortars based on models sent for from Ludhiānā. The East India Company seemed happy at first for the Sikhs to learn from them.

Ranjīt Singh was apparently a keen collector of artillery. Sir Charles Metcalfe, envoy to the court of Ranjīt Singh in 1809, commented dryly that: "The Raja's attachment to his guns and his opinion of their weight, are both so great that he would never miss an opportunity of obtaining a gun. If he learns that there is a gun in any fort, he cannot rest until he has taken the fort to get at the gun or until the gun has been given to him to save the fort. He immediately dismounts the gun from the wall and drags it after him as an addition to his field train."[3]

A prominent engineer, Mīan Qādir Bakhsh, was granted full access to study the British military workshops at Ludhiānā. He later wrote a gunnery manual in Persian. Ranjīt Singh also employed skilled workmen imported from neighboring British-controlled regions at an early stage. By 1814, he had employed thirty skilled Delhi craftsmen for all manner of tasks.

As early as 1810, a pair of horse drawn artillery pieces was made by Gopāl Singh Jamadār imitating the East India Company's own designs, and by 1831, Ranjīt Singh had a hundred such guns. As the artillery arm expanded, it was periodically reorganized, at first into separate batteries, according to size and the type of draft animals used (1814), and later into fully fledged brigades combined with the infantry and cavalry (1822–1823). A considerable industrial base developed to support this growing arm. Six foundries and probably twice as many workshops making all manner of components, shot and shell, carriages, harness, and gunpowder were in operation.

It would seem that in the early days, Ranjīt Singh was keen to obtain artillery by whatever means he could, through diplomacy, conquest, or trade. While many of these guns may have been retired from active duty or even recast as more modern pieces were developed in the 1820s, many of the more prestigious guns were held in such respect that they were used alongside second or perhaps even third generation cannons in the Anglo-Sikh wars of 1845–1846 and 1848–1849.

Thorn is also able to furnish a fine description of Holkār Rāo. Describing him variously as a "a good-looking, lively man" and "savagely inhuman." In doing so, he gives a valuable insight into the British view on one of their greatest threats to imperial dominance in Northern India. The account ends as Thorn and the party of Lord Lake leave the Punjab through Patiālā via Sirhind. He adds a final cursory note on Bandā Bahādur and the events of the destruction of Sirhind in 1710. In his account, Thorn makes mention of Colonel John Malcolm who became familiar with the Sikhs during his role as interpreter during the treaty negotiations. He later gave his own eyewitness account of the Sikhs in *Asiatick Researches* in 1810 which was later published as a book in his famous *Sketch of the Sikhs*.

---

pp. 478–503

In the mean time, Jeswunt Row Holkar, who, after his flight from Hindoostan, retreated into the Joodpore and Rajepoot country, had succeeded in collecting some artillery and a number of followers, with the determination of marching to the northward, in search of plunder and conquest. According to his own phraseology, he was now destitute of any other estate or property than what he carried upon the saddle of his horse; and therefore, as an adventurer, he was resolved to seek both, either among friends or enemies. After eluding the division of Major-General Jones, who marched from Rampoorah, to intercept him on his line of route; and that of Colonel Ball, in the Rewary hills, Holkar proceeded through the provinces to the north-west of Delhi, at the head of a numerous rabble, and having with him sixty pieces of canon, of which last, though half were unserviceable, they were calculated to impress awe upon the Seiks; into whose country he now entered. Lord Lake, upon this, judged it expedient to put the British force instantly in motion, to prevent the Seiks from declaring for the Mahratta chieftain, or, in case they should already have done so, to destroy, in the bud, the new coalition.[4] Accordingly, the troops stationed at Agra and Secundra marched towards Mutra, on the tenth of October; while a strong detachment, consisting of the tenth regiment, and the first battalions of the twenty-second and fourth regiments of native infantry, with a proportion of artillery, under the command of Major-General Dowdeswell, was ordered to Sehranpoor, for the protection of the northern part of the Dooab. Lord Lake himself marched towards Delhi on the twenty-eighth, with the remaining corps, formed in brigades, as follows:

Cavalry.

6th Nat. Cav. H.M. 25th Drgs. H.M. 24th Drgs.   3rd Nat. Cav. H.M. 8th Drgs.
1st Brigade.   2nd Brigade.
Brigadier General Need commanding   Brigadier General Wood commanding.

Reserve.

1st B. 9th Nat. I. 1st B.11th Nat. I Company's European Regt. H.M.22nd Foot.
Brigadier General Mercer commanding.

Park.   Horse Artillery.
Captain Pennington.   Captain Brown.

On the twenty-ninth, we met the British garrison of Deeg, at Chattah, after their evacuation of that fortress, which was restored to the Bhurtpoor rajah; and continuing our route, we arrived on the seventh of November at Delhi; in the afternoon of which day Lord Lake paid a visit to the emperor, attended by his staff, and all the brigadiers in camp.

The day following, the army continued its march to the northward, moving by easy stages to Tarpoliah, Allipore, Beronteka Serai, and on the eleventh, to Souniput, a small, town thirty miles north-west from Delhi. The whole of this country, which was formerly fertilized, by a canal dug by Ali Merdan Khan, is now overgrown with jungle, and is generally in a very desolate state. Souniput belonged to the lately established but short-lived principality of George Thomas,[5] a native of Ireland, who, in the year 1782, came to India, in the situation of a boatswain on board of a ship of war. This singular man, whose adventures have a romantic cast, after residing some years with the Polygars, and traversing the whole peninsula of India, entered into the service of the Begum Somroo, who, perceiving his talents, gave him at length the command of her troops. But through the influence of his enemies, he lost her favour; on which he went over to Appakanda Row, a Mahratta chieftain, by whom he was readily employed, and who afterwards, in consideration of his fidelity and valour, adopted him as his son, with a considerable grant of lands in the Mewattie district. Mr Thomas, however, had still to struggle with the machinations of his secret enemies; but the energy of his character gained him a complete triumph; and of his generosity he gave a striking proof, in saving the life of his former mistress, the Begum, and restoring her to the musnud, after she had been dethroned by her step-son.

The fame of our adventurer received additional lustre from his exploits against the Seiks;[6] in consequence of which the Mahratta states, who considered him as their bulwark on the side of these marauders, conferred on him the districts of Souniput, Panniput, and Carnawl, yielding a revenue of ten lacs of rupees, for the support of two thousand infantry, and sixteen pieces of cannon. Having thus obtained the distinction of a chieftain, George Thomas formed the resolution of founding an independent sovereignty upon an extensive scale in the country of Hurrianah, which had been for many years without any fixed authority. In this object he succeeded; and after an arduous contest with the Rajah of Pattealah,[7] and other chiefs of the Seiks, he established his power as far as the river Caugger, and fixed his residence at Hansy, about ninety miles north-west of Delhi. Intending this place for the capital of his newly-acquired dominions, of which it was the centre, he repaired the fortifications, and gave considerable encouragements to strangers to induce them to become settlers. He also formed a mint; and wisely judging that force of arms alone could maintain him in the principality which he had founded, he made the best preparations for carrying on offensive and defensive war, by manufacturing muskets, matchlocks, and gunpowder. By these means, and a prudent exercise of his power, combined with unremitting activity, he gave to his territory a consolidation which promised such an extension of empire and civilization, as would have immortalized his name, had the enlarged views which he entertained been carried into effect.

One favourable object with him, after settling his capital, and securing his estates, was that of attempting the conquest of the Punjab, and having the honour of planting the British standard on the banks of the Attock. But this patriotic ambition he was unable to gratify; for though in a manner unparalleled, he had, without any foreign assistance, and in the front of a vigorous opposition, maintained his little sovereignty from the year 1798 to the close of 1801, his enemies increased; and, through the treachery of his own officers, instigated by the French, they succeeded in undermining his authority, so that he was compelled to seek an asylum in the territories of his natural sovereign, where, on the twenty-second of August, 1802, in the prime of life, he closed his eventful and romantic career in his way to Calcutta. His death was much regretted by those who knew him, on account of the amiable private virtues which he possessed, no less than for the vigorous energy of his character, and his unshaken loyalty, of which last he gave a striking proof, when, in tendering his dominions and conquests to his country, he said: "I wish to give them to my king, and to serve him the remainder of my days, which I can only do as a soldier in this part of the world."

From this historic sketch of a remarkable person, who in a remoter age might have ranked with Lycurgus, Numa Pompilius, or Manco Capac, we must now turn to the progress of our army in quest of an adventurer of a different description. After a halt of three days near Gonour, on the seventeenth of November we reached Panniput, distant fifty-nine miles north-west from Delhi, and famous only for the number of battles fought in its neighbourhood. The last remarkable one was in the year 1761, between the Mussulmans under Ahmed Shah, the Abdalli, Sovereign of Cabul, and the combined Mahrattas, which ended after a most obstinate conflict in the total defeat of the latter, who lost their whole army, with two hundred pieces of artillery, and their camp equipage of every kind. Of five hundred thousand souls, including women and children, who were in the field with the Mahrattas, very few escaped alive: and the bigotted victors carried their ferocious spirit so far as to murder their helpless prisoners in cold blood; for which they alleged this excuse, that when they left their own country, their mothers, sisters, and wives, desired them, whenever they should defeat the unbelievers, to kill a few of them on their account, that they also might obtain merit in the sight of God. In this manner thousands were destroyed, and the camp of the conquerors after the battle exhibited the shocking spectacle of heaps of human heads piled up before the doors of the tents.

On this occasion the flower of the Mahratta chiefs fell, among whom were Sadasiva Row Bhow, the actual general, and Biswas Row, the eldest son of the Paishwah Bala

Row, who, as such, though but seventeen years of age, was the nominal commander-in-chief. When the body of this youth was brought to the tent of Shah Ahmed, the whole of the camp thronged to see it, every one expressing his admiration at the beauty of the appearance; till at length some of the infuriated tribe exclaimed: "This is the body of the king of the unbelievers: we will have it dried and stuffed, that it may be carried home to Cabul." But this barbarity was prevented by the interposition of Shujah ul Dowlah, Nawaub of Oude, who represented to the Shah that enmity should be carried no further than death; on which the body was ordered to be burnt, together with that of the general, Sadasiva Row, which was found under a heap of slain, and recognized, says a writer who was in the battle, by many curious marks.

The town of Panniput, which was once a place of great consequence, covering the space of twenty-four miles, is now in a decayed condition; and has nothing worthy of observation within its ruinous walls except the tomb of a Mahommedan saint, or Kalindar, named Boo Ally.

Pursuing our route by Chourah, we came on the twentieth to Carnawl,[8] the northern boundary of the district of Delhi, and bordering on the Seik dominions, into which we were now entering; and passing by Azinabad and Tannassar, we came on the twenty-third to the Sursooty river, which we crossed over a fine stone bridge at a little neat town named Phoait. The next day the army encamped one hundred and fifty-four miles from Delhi, near Pattealah, or Pattyalaya, the capital of the Seik chief of this part of the country.[9] This town, which is the most flourishing in the district of Sirhind, is surrounded by a strong mud wall, and has within side a square citadel,[10] the residence of the rajah; which chief, in a visit to our camp, informed Lord Lake that Holkar had endeavoured, without effect, to prevail on the Seiks in these parts either to join him with their forces, or to supply him with money.[11] The indifferent reception which he met with, however, was owing, no doubt, to the precipitancy of his movements, in consequence of our close pursuit, which obliged him to make the best of his way for the Sutledge; in crossing which river lay his only chance of security.

After halting on the twenty-seventh at Nabeh, which is a very pretty town, we came the day following to Amirghur; thus marching nearly in the tract of Peer Mahmoud, the general of Timur Khan, and on the skirts of the great sandy desert, which stretches from the shores of the Indus to within one hundred miles of Delhi. On our left appeared sand hills in endless succession, like the waves of the ocean, desolate and dreary to an immense extent, and scantily interspersed with the Baubool, or *Mimosa Arabica*; while to the front and right of these immense wastes, the eye was deceived by those illusions, so frequent on the wild plains of Africa and Asia, known by the French term of "mirage," and in Persian, "Sirraub." These optical deceptions exhibited the representations of spacious lakes and rivers, with trees and other objects, in such a lively manner, as almost to cheat the senses of persons familiarly acquainted with the phenomenon; while they who were oppressed by excessive heat and parched with thirst, cheered themselves in the hope of being soon refreshed with water from the friendly tank or cooling stream, of which they thought they had so clear a prospect. Often were we thus agitated between expectancy and disappointment, flattering our imaginations with a speedy indulgence; when just as the delightful vision appeared on the point of being realized, like the cup of Tantalus, the whole vanished, and left us nothing to rest upon but arid plains of glittering and burning sands.

On the twenty-ninth we formed at Rawseeanah a junction with Colonel Burn's[12] detachment, consisting of four battalions of sepoys, two Tallinkas, and one of

Nujeebs, besides Skinner's and Murray's independent cavalry. This force had been despatched some time before from Panniput, with the view of seizing the guns of Holkar, or of cutting off his retreat in the event of his attempting to get back by the way of the desert, on being prevented from crossing the Sutledge.

The commander-in-chief having inspected these troops, and expressed his satisfaction at their appearance, re-inforced his own little army with the two bodies of independent cavalry, and three of the sepoy corps; the second battalion of the fourteenth; the first battalion of the twenty-first; and the second battalion of the seventeenth regiments, forming the second brigade under Colonel Burn; while the first battalion of the twenty-fourth native infantry, with the two Tallinka battalions, and one of Nujeebs, were detached for the protection of our supplies.

On the second of December, we reached Ludheana, situated on an outlet of the Sutledge, which here forms an island; but the town itself had been deserted on our approach. After halting here two days, we proceeded on the fifth to the banks of that river, the ancient Hesudrus, and immediately a battalion of sepoys crossed over in boats, to secure the Ghaut, or ford, for the passage of the rest of the army, the whole of whom, with the exception of two other battalions of sepoys, who were left in charge of the baggage and carts, followed the next morning; the river here being about breast deep, and its breadth near a mile from bank to bank. After passing the night close to Keranah, a walled town on the north side, we continued our pursuit on the seventh through the Punjab or the country of the five rivers, the fields of which were now in the richest state of cultivation, abounding on all sides with wheat, barley, rice, Indian corn, sugar-cane, tobacco, cotton, and the various esculent vegetables of Europe. We also passed in our route mulberry, walnut, chestnut, and apple trees.

During our march, the most scrupulous regard was paid to the property of the inhabitants, as well that which was exposed, as that which they had in their dwellings; and where any injury happened unavoidably to be committed, a liberal compensation in money soon prevented complaint, or restored confidence.

Thus our route through this remote part of India, and amongst a people naturally fierce and jealous, was pursued not only without opposition, but with cordiality on both sides. As all supplies were punctually paid for, we wanted nothing that the country could produce; which accommodating reciprocation begat a cheerful intercourse, that increased as we proceeded. The general satisfaction we felt at the conduct of the Seiks was heightened by the report of this day, that Holkar had been disappointed in his attempt to cross the Beyah river, which gave us hopes that the capture of his guns at least would now reward our laborious exertions. After a very long march we encamped, with orders to be ready at a moment's notice, at Jumshire, on the Bine rivulet; where we passed a very disagreeable night. The rain poured down in torrents, accompanied with thunder and lightning: in the midst of which confusion of the elements, a number of horses belonging to the cavalry broke loose from their picquets, galloping about with the utmost fury after the mare ponies through the bazaars, where they attacked, like tigers, all persons indiscriminately; so that several persons lost lives, and others received serious injury from these vicious animals of the Jungle Tawsey breed. The alarm thus excited was aggravated by rumours that enemies were approaching, which made us all hail the dawn of the morning with gladness, when we resumed our march, and after passing Jallindar, a large and populous town, about midway between the Sutledge and Beyah, we reached the banks of the Caly rivulet. Here a party of Skinner's horse was detached in advance to the Beyah, where they arrived just time enough to have a glimpse of Holkar's rear-guard; the whole army of that chief having passed the river the preceding day.

A spectacle of lively interest was exhibited on the ninth of December, when the British standard waved with majestic dignity on the banks of the Beyah, the ancient Hyphasis, opposite the Rajpoor Gaut; which impressive scene was heightened in effect by the picturesque view that presented itself to the multitude of admiring observers. In the extreme distance from north to east arose the snowy ridge of old Imaus, or the modern Himalaya mountains, whose loftiest peak, Dhawala-giri, exceeds Chimboraço, the highest of the Andes by more than six thousand feet. The fleecy softness of this faint and irregular outline appeared to great advantage, in resting upon immense masses of nearer elevations, whose rocky eminences in chaotic confusion were most beautifully contrasted with pine-clad hills, still closer to the view, and these again relieved to the eye by the prospect of a fine undulating country of hill and dale, covered with luxuriant vegetation, and enlivened by numerous villages, temples, and ruins, to the extent of thirty miles, bounded by the noble river, which, flowing in majestic grandeur immediately before us, brought to our recollection that we were standing, as it were, upon classic ground.

Holkar at this time lay encamped at Amrutsir, at about an equal distance from our camp and Lahore, the capital of the Seiks on the ancient Hydraotes, now the Rauvee river.

Amrutsir, or Ambertsir, which signifies the water of immortality, derives its name from a famous tank or reservoir at this place, and is farther noted for the tomb of the celebrated Nauik Shah, the founder of the Seik nation.[13] He was a Hindoo of the military tribe; but being of a contemplative disposition, he devoted himself when young to the most austere exercises of his religion; till at length his mind beginning to waver between Brahminism and Islamism, his doubts ended in a resolution to attempt something like a reconciliation of the two systems, and the formation of a new sect, consisting of proselytes from both persuasions. The design was bold; and considering the superstition of the Hindoos, and the bigotry of the Mohammedans, it would almost appear to have been an impracticable one; but the reformer succeeded to a degree little, if at all, inferior to that which marked the early course of the prophet of Arabia, which was the more extraordinary, considering the terms he required of converts; those laid upon Mussulmans being the renunciation of circumcision, and the eating of swine's flesh. While the prejudices of the Hindoos, on the other hand, were shocked by the abolition of the distinction of casts, and the adoption of every kind of animal food except that of cows. Nanick affected also the sacred and legislative character, by drawing up articles of belief, and a code of laws for his followers: the former he reduced to the simplest principles of theism, in admitting the unity of the divine essence, and a future state of rewards and punishments; the latter inculcating universal philanthropy, in the exercise of hospitality to strangers, and the forbearance from all injuries against each other. This creed and body of precepts Nanick reduced into verse, for more easy remembrance, and familiar instruction of his disciples, who regard the work as sacred, by the title of "Goorrunt," and the author as a person gifted with inspiration. The name Seik signifies, imperatively, "to learn;" and being the first word of each commandment in their scriptures, it became the characteristic appellation of every new convert.[14] For some years these people were looked upon as mere harmless devotees, from whose increase no danger was to be apprehended; but, toward the close of the reign of Aurungzebe, their numbers and strength emboldened them to wage war against the imperial armies, in which they were often successful.[15]

In proportion as the Mogul state declined, the Seiks advanced both in power and enterprize; and availing themselves of the disturbances which prevailed in the reign of Ahmed Shah, they conquered the whole of the Punjab, and pushed their arms almost to the gates of Delhi. At a more recent period they excited some alarm in the British government; but fortunately the want of union between their several chiefs prevented such a co-operation as might have rendered them formidable enemies. Of the weakness arising from this discordance the proof was apparent, in the rapidity with which Holkar and his pursuers passed through their country, which both parties found unprepared for resistance.

It is probable, however, that Holkar had received some assurances of succour from the Seiks before he ventured to commit himself, as it were, to their mercy; since it certainly was in their power to have harassed him very much in his flight. That no opposition was made to this fugitive chief, more than implied an inclination to favour his cause, in the hope of sharing the immense spoils of our territories; and that the Seiks did not actually join Holkar for the attainment of that object, can only be ascribed to the promptitude of Lord Lake, in driving the Mahratta army before him quite through the heart of the Punjab, thereby impressing the inhabitants with a dread of our power, and convincing their chiefs of the folly of contending with it.

Such was the effect of our presence, that in a grand Gooroo Mata, or national council, held at Amrutsir, the assembled heads of the Seiks unanimously agreed to withhold all aid from Holkar; while at the same time, as the most effectual means of getting rid of both parties, they came to a resolution of interposing in the character of mediators. Accordingly, Futty Sing, as the vakeel of Runjeet Sing, chief of Lahore, and of the Seik confederacy, came to the British camp on the nineteenth of December, and was received with every mark of respect. The next day Bala Ram Seit, the vakeel of Holkar, being introduced in form, the conferences began, and terminated four days afterwards in a treaty[16] on the terms dictated by Lord Lake, according to the instructions given by the supreme government, by which that chief was reinstated in dominions to which he never had any right, and which, even if he had, he deserved to have forfeited.

These pacific transactions were also distinguished by negotiations on the part of Scindiah, carried on between his vakeel the Moonshee Karul Nyne, who accompanied our army, and Colonel Malcolm, the political agent of the Company, under the immediate direction of Lord Lake, which conference also ended amicably in a treaty of alliance, confirming generally that made on the part of the British government by Sir Arthur Wellesley, at Surjee Anjengaum, but with this exception, that the Company explicitly refused to acknowledge the right of Scindiah to any claims upon Gwalior and Gohud, under the preceding treaty, though, from friendly considerations, it was agreed to cede to him the former, and such parts of the latter territory as were described in a schedule annexed. Scindiah on the other hand relinquished all claim to pensions that had been granted to some of his officers by that treaty, to the annual amount of fifteen lacs of rupees.

After providing an indemnification for the injury done to the British resident, and stopping the pensions forfeited by Bappoo Scindiah and Sudashe Row, on account of their treacherous conduct and defection, the insulted honour of our government was further vindicated by a pledge on the part of Scindiah that he would thenceforward never admit his father-in-law, Surjee Row Gautka, to his councils. The reason for marking this man so pointedly was the fact that the violence committed upon the person and property of our resident originated with him; besides which robbery, he had been guilty of so many other flagitious acts, as to be declared a public enemy to the British government.

Though the Chumbul marked the boundary line on the north between the two states, extending from the limits of Gohud on the east, to Kotta on the west, the small and unproductive districts of Bhadeck and Sooseperarah only were ceded to the Company, as being on the banks of the Jumna, and preserving the communication between Agra and Bundelcund. On the other hand, the Company with extraordinary liberality granted Scindiah personally the annual sum of four lacs of rupees; and assigned within their territories in Hindoostan a jaghire, to the amount of two lacs more to his wife, and one lac to his daughter. The Company further engaged not to interfere with any settlement which Scindiah might make with the Rajahs of Oudepoor, Joudpoor, Kotta, or other tributary chiefs of Malwa, Meywar, or Marwar, nor in any arrangements he might be pleased to enter into with Jeswunt Row Holkar, or his family, respecting claims to tribute or territory north of the river Taptie, and south of the Chumbul.

The ratification of this treaty arrived on the morning of the twenty-fifth of December, 1805, when two royal salutes were fired, one in celebration of the sacred and joyful event commemorated on this day, which was now for the first time announced on the banks of the Hyphasis; and the other in honour of the general peace just established throughout India.

On the last day of the year, the Seik chiefs, who had brought their camp near the river, opposite to our's, were gratified with a show of European tactics, in compliance with their repeated wishes to that effect. For this purpose a brigade of cavalry, with one of infantry, composed of the twenty-second regiment of foot, and two battalions of sepoys, paraded at three o'clock in the afternoon on the right of our camp, where they received Lord Lake, who was accompanied by the chiefs, with a general salute. Having passed along the line, his lordship placed himself opposite the centre, where also stood the Seiks, with Colonel Malcolm as their interpreter, mounted on elephants. The troops now began their manoeuvres: the infantry, after forming into close columns of regiments, separately moved up, and deployed into line close to the reviewing party, and went through the motions of loading and firing; but there being no blank ammunition in camp, the native spectators were deprived of the effect which that mode of firing would have produced: and as they could not understand the nature of the platoon motions, unless they saw the flash and heard the report, they were incapable of perceiving the advantages which the disciplined solider has with his firelock over their raw matchlock men. The line next changed front, throwing back the left; which was succeeded by the square; and a general charge closed the day. The horse artillery on this occasion fired a few rounds, whilst the cavalry moved with rapidity through the intervals of the infantry up to the charge; and the instant they were halted, the guns were again heard firing in advance of the line, which produced much astonishment among the natives, who whispered to one another, "thank God that we did not go to war with the English."

After the lapse of several days, Holkar's vakeel returned; when it appeared, that instead of presenting the intended ratification of the treaty on the part of his master, he had recourse to objections and evasions; in consequence of which he was ordered to quit the camp immediately, as all intercourse was at an end. On hearing this, the ambassador pulled out a paper in the hand-writing of Holkar, instructing him to get better terms if he could, but if not to accept those which were offered. The authenticity of the document being questioned, the order was repeated, and the vakeel was told that the army would march to the Ghaut on the following day; and that if the papers were not presented duly signed within two days afterwards, the passage of the river would immediately ensue. In pursuance of this determination, the army marched down the left bank of the river to Gogorwal Ghaut, on the fifth of January; and in the afternoon of the seventh the treaty was presented to Lord Lake with great ceremony.

On the right of his lordship were seated several of the Seik chiefs, whose joy at the event was visibly marked in their countenances; and on his left were Colonel Malcolm and the vakeels of Holkar. A silk bag was first presented, containing a letter from Holkar, expressive of his pacific disposition, the sincerity of his professions, and his desire to live in amity with the English government. After the reading of this, the treaty itself, signed and sealed by Holkar, was delivered to the general, at which instant a royal salute was fired; and his lordship, in a short speech to the ambassadors present, told them that as the British government never violated any of its engagements, the continuance of the peace would depend upon themselves.

The only cession made on the part of Holkar in this agreement that materially affected his interests, or his pride, was the total renunciation of all claim upon the districts of Tonk Rampoorah, Boondie, Lakharie, Sumeydee, Bhamungaum, Daee, and other places north of the Boondie hills. A temporary relinquishment, indeed, of the fortress of Chandore, and some other parts of the hereditary estates of Holkar in the Deccan, was stipulated; but this was no more than a conditional measure, adopted as a security for his good behaviour during the period of eighteen months. In other respects the treaty varied very little from that which had been entered into with Scinidiah; and upon the whole both were much more favourable to those chiefs than they had any right to expect after the repeated aggressions which they had committed.

Holkar himself, a short time previous to this settlement, evidently despaired of ever being again restored to any part of his family estate, since, according to his own emphatic language, his whole country lay upon the bow of his saddle. Notwithstanding this, and the obvious necessity confirmed by recent experience, of abridging the power of these restless characters, on whose good faith no reliance could be placed, Lord Lake had the mortification of seeing the only effectual bond of security which he had provided in the treaty with Holkar destroyed by Sir George Barlow, who delivered back, without any indemnification, those valuable districts which had been retained more for the protection of the petty states, who had adhered faithfully to the British government, than for our own advantage. His lordship reasoned with eloquence, and remonstrated with firmness, upon the imprudence of thus early at least relinquishing what had been so lately acquired; but his arguments and persuasions proved alike unavailing: the alliances formed with the rajah of Jeypoor, and other Rajpoot princes, were abrogated. Of these last, the most to be pitied was the Boondee Rajah, whose integrity and attachment had been displayed in a very remarkable manner, particularly during the disastrous retreat of Colonel Monson, who experienced from this loyal chief the readiest assistance, and an asylum when he was hard pressed by the ferocious Holkar.

But to return to the proceedings connected with the confirmation of the treaty:— on the day after its public delivery at our camp, Mr Metcalf, escorted by two battalions of sepoys, proceeded to that of Holkar, where the whole army were so elated at the restoration of peace, that they celebrated it with rejoicings for several days together. Mr Metcalf was received by the chief himself with every mark of distinction in full durbar; and all present seemed to view in expressions of satisfaction and respect on the occasion, except Meer Khan, whose chagrin at not having been included in the negotiations, and rewarded with a jaghire, broke through the bounds of all decorum; and he actually refused to attend the durbar till he was in a manner compelled to it by the mandate of Holkar; but even then he behaved with sullen reserve, and appeared as if meditating how he should carry into effect the declaration made by himself, upon his disappointment, that "a fly could torment an elephant."

This man arose from the situation of a common private, or Pindaree, to the command of a banditti, which, in such a perturbed country, gave him considerable advantages, so long as he could keep his people together by plunder; and by engaging in the service of those contending powers from whom most was to be obtained. During the present negotiations, he presumed, though no better than a brigand, or adventurer, to set up claims to remuneration, as an independent chief; and he even went the length of demanding his native city of Sumbul, in the province of Rohilcund, but without meeting with the slightest attention.

Meer Khan, however, has continued in the service of Holkar ever since; and on the mental derangement of that chief, occasioned by excessive drinking, he has obtained the sole management of his affairs, which he administers in the name of Holkar's wife.

At the period of these transactions, Jeswunt Row Holkar was a good-looking, lively man; and though he had but one eye, his countenance might on the whole be termed handsome. There was also a pleasantness in his manners and conversation that but ill comported with the abominable cruelties of which he was guilty to the prisoners, however wounded and helpless, whom the chance of war threw into his hands; yet this was only a part of capricious disposition, which continually transported him to extremes; for sometimes he would assume the most stately deportment, and array himself in gorgeous apparel, covered with pearls and diamonds; all of which he as suddenly cast aside, and with only a clout round his middle, would gallop on a bareridged poney throughout his camp. In the same spirit he was generous to his followers, though savagely inhuman to his enemies; but neither his liberality nor his cruelty had any bounds: all was the effect of immediate impulse and passion, which of course gave a strange colour to his actions. It has been said, however, that amidst this extravagance, bordering on madness, which was heightened by the immoderate drinking of brandy, he had a mind more quick of conception and fertile in resources than any of the other Mahratta chiefs, which made him a dangerous foe, and rendered the repression of his power an indispensable measure, at a time when the British dominions in the east were perilously situated.

The predatory system of warfare also adopted by Holkar, and the manner in which it was carried on, threatened such serious consequences to our provinces, and to the friendly states under our protection, as to call for immediate and vigorous measures to prevent the extension of the mischief. What, therefore, some men would have despised, Lord Lake judiciously considered as an incipient evil, that might be crushed in its infancy by energetic operations, but which, if neglected, would increase in strength, and become more difficult of suppression. Happily for the British interests, the promptitude with which his lordship acted in pursuing the fugitive, without allowing him any resting place, had the desired effect of preventing him from gaining such an access of auxiliary support, as would have enabled him to roll back with the impetuosity of a torrent over the plains of Hindoostan. The termination of the war, therefore, was peculiarly glorious; and it received additional lustre from the consideration, that where Alexander erected twelve massy altars as the memorial of the pride of conquest, there the power of a hyperborean nation, whom he would have designated as barbarous, had, after the lapse of many ages, made the same river witness to the settlement of an honourable union, embracing the interests of the principal states in India, and laying the foundation of an enlightened system, which only requires to be followed up in the same spirit, to prove equally advantageous to the innumerable tribes scattered over this immense region, and to the great foreign power under whose fostering care alone they can keep the blessings of peace and civilization.

Having accomplished the arduous object in which it had been employed, at the distance of near three hundred miles from Delhi, and where no European force had ever before been seen, the British army began to retrace its steps on the ninth of January, 1806.

Our departure was very satisfactory to the Seiks, who, notwithstanding their friendly professions, could hardly help feeling some apprehensions for their beautiful country from the presence of a formidable array, against which they were conscious how difficult it would have been to have made any effectual stand. The military strength of these people consists chiefly of horsemen, of whom they might probably, if united, bring about one hundred thousand into field; but the want of cordiality among the several chiefs, who are absolute in their respective districts, and the jealousy with which they view each other, must ever render them, as long as they are so discordant, too weak to disturb the general tranquillity of India. They are well mounted, expert in the use of the spear and the matchlock, and generally allowed to be excellent marksmen. Being accompanied by several bodies of them on our march, we had frequent opportunities of observing their peculiar tactics. At one time they would come up full gallop, and making a sudden stop, fire with deliberate aim; and at another, without halting, they would, with the same quickness, take a sudden wheel round, and discharge their pieces over their right shoulders, or behind their backs, as they returned. Besides the matchlock, spear, and scimitar, which are all excellent in their kinds, some of the Seiks are armed with a very singular weapon, which they use with great and destructive effect against cavalry. It consists of a hollow circle, made of finely tempered steel, with an exceeding sharp edge, about a foot in diameter, and an inch in breadth on the inner side. This instrument the horseman poises on his fore-finger, and after giving it two or three swift motions, to accelerate its velocity, sends it from him to the distance of some hundreds of yards, the ring cutting and maiming, most dreadfully, every living object that may chance to be in its way.[17] Rockets are also in use among these people; but their artillery is of the very worst description; and so little knowledge have they of the proper direction and management of carriage guns, that in their visits to our camp, they asked, with great simplicity, whether every ball had not its destined object, and particularly whether we had not one expressly intended for Runjeet Sing, the head of the Seik confederacy.

Though inured to predatory warfare almost from infancy, and of course habitually disposed to plunder their neighbours, the Seiks observe the greatest order at home, where their industry is manifest in the highly cultivated state of the country. In their persons they are generally tall, erect, and of a manly open deportment; animated in their countenances, and of a very inquisitive disposition. They differ from the rest of the Hindoos in the article of dress no otherwise than by giving the preference to blue cotton cloths, and silks of the same colour. The soldiery have, however, a custom of suffering the hair of the head, as well as the beard, to grow to an immoderate length, conformably to the injunction of Gooroo Govind, one of their military priests, who flourished in the time of Aurungzebe, and who distinguished himself by giving his nation a warlike character, and changing its name from Seiks to Singh, which appellative signifying a lion, had before been exclusively acquired by the Rajepoot tribes. So great was the fame acquired by this innovator, that while Nanick is considered as the author or their religion, the Seiks revere Gooroo Govind as the founder of their political greatness.

The climate of the Punjab is uncommonly mild; and though in the thirty-second degree of north latitude, we experienced sharp frosts during the night: the days were exceedingly delightful. Ice, which is gathered on the neighbouring hills, may here be had all the year round.

On the ninth of January, the British army marched to Burrua, and the next day passed the town of Jallindar, ninety-two miles S. E. from Lahore, and formerly a place of great magnitude, but at present almost dilapidated. Our route was now continued through an extensive Dhaka jungle to Raipoor, on the Bine rivulet, seventeen miles from our last ground; the road being for the most part a deep sand, and narrow; the country open, and partially cultivated.

After halting a day, we proceeded to Phogwara, a walled village; and on the thirteenth to Keranaghaut, on the Sutledge, where we rested five days, during which we enjoyed much sport in hunting tigers, of whom several were killed not far from the camp.

On the eighteenth we re-crossed the Sutledge, which has since become the north-western boundary of the British empire in India, by an agreement entered into with Runjeet Sing, chief of Lahore. This measure had before been contemplated by Lord Lake, as very desirable to the security of our territories; but the proposition not being agreeable to the neutralizing policy then adopted, both in England and the east, was at that time rejected. Under the administration of Lord Minto, however, in 1809, it was revived, and carried into full effect, much to the satisfaction of the Seik inhabitants on the southern side of the river, who were too sensible of the advantages arising from an equitable government not to rejoice in being placed under British protection.[18] By this settlement, Ludheana has obtained the distinction of being the most advanced military station belonging to the English on the Indian continent; and its importance may be estimated from the consideration that the position effectually guards, with comparatively a small garrison, the only assailable quarter in the north, from whence Hindoostan has hitherto been invaded and conquered. To the eastward of this post lies the great sandy desert, extending as far as the Indus, and the awful appearance of which so appalled the troops of Alexander, that they refused to proceed any farther through a country replete with such formidable dangers. On the east a rocky barrier presents itself equally terrific, in the vast mountains of Sewalik and Tibet, while to the north the Sutledge, guarded as it now is by British Troops, defends the passage into Hindoostan from Persia and Tartary.

pp. 506–7

. . . From this digression, which it is hoped will find an excuse in the importance of the subject, it is now time to return to our army at Ludheana. The temperature of the climate here, though in the latitude of thirty degrees fifty-three minutes north, alternates to the very opposite extremes at different periods of the year. During four or five months, the weather is intensely cold, and in the summer season the heat is intolerable, being aggravated by the violent winds which blow from the desert, and bring with them immense clouds of burning sand. Much inconvenience is also occasionally experienced here from the rains, which fall in great abundance, and with considerable violence.

On the nineteenth of January our army continued its march by Sanaval, Laskary-Khan-Serai, and Bouglah, through a well cultivated country, to Sirhind, distant one hundred and fifty-five miles N. W. from Delhi. This city was formerly the capital of the province which still bears its name, but the place has gone rapidly to decay since the chief has fixed his residence at Pattealah. According to Abul Fazel, who wrote his geography of India in 1582, Sirhind was then in a most flourishing state, containing splendid buildings and delightful gardens; but in 1707 the Seik chief, Bairaggee Bandar, ravaged the city and levelled all the public structures to the ground, so that it now exhibits hardly any thing but a melancholy mass of extensive ruins.[19] The immediate neighbourhood abounds with mango groves, and tanks of excellent water; though the latter is scarce, and the country barren, in that part of the province which lies on the side of Hausi, Hissar and Carnawl, where scarcely any other vegetation is to be seen than underwood. To remedy this evil, Feroze the third, in the year 1357, cut canals from the Jumna and Sutledge, by which means of irrigation the soil was fertilized: but these useful works falling into decay through neglect, the natural aridity has returned. As this was formerly the great route which the Persians and Tartars took for the invasion of Hindoostan, that circumstance will account in some measure for the decline of a town so much exposed to those merciless depredators. Having halted here four days, the army renewed its course on the twenty-seventh, by Pindarsi and Buttowleah, two insignificant places, marching along bad roads, and through jungles of Dhaka and grass to Umballa, which it reached on the twenty-ninth. This is a fine town, situated south of a branch of the Caggar river, which falls into the Sursooty near Mouneck. Formerly there were two good bridges at this place, but they are now fallen down, and the water near them was at this time very deep; but where we crossed, about midway between the two, it was no higher than the knee. On the thirtieth we came to Lunida-Lundee, a walled town, in a well cultivated country, the chief productions of which are rice and sugar-canes. Game, hereabouts, is very plentiful, particularly wild hogs, one of which was killed within our lines. On the thirty-first we passed the large town of Shahabad, formerly, as its name imports, a royal residence; and after resting during the night near Kutlary, a small but walled village, the next day we reached Tannassar, where we re-entered our first route.

Tannassar, with the exception of Pattealah, is the largest town in this district, and is held in great veneration among the Hindoos, who resort to it as a place of peculiar sanctity, for the purpose of performing their ablutions in the holy river Saraswaty, or Sursooty.

Notes

1. Ghandi, *Sikhs in the Eighteenth Century*, 506.
2. Lepel Griffin, *Rajas of Punjab*, 85; Charles Grey, *European Adventurers of Northern India, 1785 to 1849*, ed. H.L.O. Garrett (Lahore: The Punjab Printing Co. Goverment, 1870. Reprint, New Delhi: Manu Publications, 1977), 34–58; *The Encyclopaedia of Sikhism*, s.v. "Sāhib Kaur, Bībī (1771–1801)."
3. George Bruce, *Six Battles for India: The Anglo Sikh Wars, 1845–6, 1848–9* (London: Arthur Baker Ltd, 1969), 41.
4. Lake had no cause for concern from Ranjīt Singh who had no intentions of joining with the Marāthā leader. However, Latif notes that minor Sikh chiefs of the trans-Sutlej such as Gurdit Singh Lādwā and Bhangā Singh of Thānesar had already pledged their allegiance to Holkār. Furthermore, he had received considerable contributions from Rājā Sāhib Singh and Rānī Ās Kaur of Patiālā. Syad Muhammad Latif, *History of the Panjab from the Remotest Antiquity to the Present Time* (Calcutta: Central Press, 1891. Reprint, New Delhi: Kalyani Publishers, 1997), 362.

5. See also part V, chapter 28 for a contemporary newspaper account of the life of George Thomas.

6. See part IV, chapter 17 for Francklin's *Military Memoirs of George Thomas.*

7. Rājā Sāhib Singh of Patiālā (1773–1813) (q.v.).

8. Karnāl, a district town now in Haryana situated on the Grand Trunk Road 123 km north of Delhi. His mode of transport is described as a *chourah* but it is not known what this means.

9. Rājā Sāhib Singh (q.v.).

10. *Qilā Mubārak*, Patiālā. Construction of the fort was started by Bābā Ālā Singh (1691–1765), the founder of the Phūlkīān house of Patiālā. The site he chose was on the ruined mound of an earlier habitation known as Patānvālā Theh, from which the name of the city is said to have been derived. Initially, a mud fortress (*kachchī garhī*) known as *Sodhīān dī Garhī* was sited close to the current location of Qilā Mubārak. In 1763, Ālā Singh laid the foundation stone for the new fort and named this Qilā Mubārak, literally, the great fort. *The Encyclopaedia of Sikhism*, s.v. "Patiālā."

11. Secondary accounts state otherwise, noting that "during his stay in Patiala he had obtained large contributions from Rājā Sāhib Singh and Rānī Aus Kaur" Latif, *History of the Panjab*, 362.

12. In 1804, Lt. Col. Burn, commander of the British detachment at Deoband (now in Utter Pradesh), led an expedition against the cis-Sutlej chiefs, Gurdit Singh of Lādwā and Karnāl Singh and Sher Singh of Būriā, Rāi Singh of Jagādhrī, Jodh Singh of Kālsīā, and Mehtāb Singh of Thānesar, who had joined forces with the Marāthās against the British in 1803. Burn's troops defeated the Sikhs in December 1804 at Sharanpur. The Sikh chiefs were all granted amnesty with the exception of Gurdit Singh. Burn arrived in Karnāl and secured from him the surrender of the town. *The Encyclopaedia of Sikhism*, s.v. "Burn, Lt-Col.," Griffin, *Rajas of Punjab*, 90.

13. Amritsar certainly does not contain a tomb to Gurū Nānak although this is an oft-repeated error in early European narrative on the town (see this part, chapter 16, where a similar comment is also made by William Francklin). Tradition holds that toward the end of the Gurū's life, he spoke to settle the argument as to whether his body should be buried according to Muslim custom or cremated according to Hindu custom. The issue was to be settled by each community placing flowers next to him as he went sleep. The community's flowers that remained fresh the next day would win through. The next morning, both sets of flowers were still fresh and the Gurū's body had disappeared. This story is probably apocryphal as a similar version is given of the death of Kabīr.

14. It is not entirely clear what Thomas means by this statement. The *shabads* or spiritual verses in the Gurū Granth Sāhib do not all begin with the word "Seik".

15. Gurū Gobind Singh (1666–1708) led his Sikhs in a number of actions against imperial forces. Following an action in Bhangānī against Rājā Fateh Chand in 1688, the Gurū and his Sikhs were involved in a battle with a Mughal commander, Alif Khān, at Nadaun in March 1691. Later skirmishes against imperial forces included the Hussainī battle against Hussain Khān in 1696 which concluded with a resounding victory for the Sikhs. However, not all engagements with Mughal forces proved to be so successful. In 1705, the *faujdār* of Sirhind lay siege to Anandpur which ended some eight months later when

the Gurū, with a small number of Sikhs, was able to make it to the village of Chamkaur with imperial troops close on their heels. At the resulting battle, the Gurū's two eldest sons were killed along with most of the Sikh contingent that had accompanied him from Anandpur. At the behest of the five remaining Sikhs, the Gurū again escaped into the wilderness.

16. This is known as the Anglo-Sikh treaty of 1806. *The Encyclopaedia of Sikhism*, s.v. "Anglo–Sikh Treaty (1806)."

17. *Chakkar* (q.v.).

18. This agreement was concluded in the Anglo-Sikh treaty of 1809. *The Encyclopaedia of Sikhism*, s.v. "Anglo-Sikh Treaty."

19. Sirhind was sacked by Bandā Bahādur in response to the role of the *faujdār*, Nawāb Wazīr Khān, in ordering to death the two youngest sons of Gurū Gobind Singh. The main battle was fought at Chappar-Chirī near Sirhind on May 12, 1710, where the Mughal army were routed and Nawāb Wazīr Khān killed. Bhāī Bāj Singh was appointed governor, although the town was retaken by imperial troops soon after. *The Encyclopaedia of Sikhism*, s.v. "Sirhind;" *Imperial Gazetteer of India: Provincial Series Punjab*, 2 vols. (Calcutta, nd), 2: 309.

CHAPTER 19

A FAILED SPYING MISSION TO
LAHORE, 1808

"Tour to Lahore. From the manuscript notes of an officer of the Bengal army, made from actual observation, during a late tour through the Punjab to Lahore; and affording, among much valuable matter, some illustrations of the character and manners of Sik'hs," *The Asiatic Annual Register*, vol. XI—for the Year 1809 (London: Printed for T. Cadell and W. Davies, etc., 1811), pp. 421–40.

The pages of *The Asiatic Annual Register* for the year 1809 include an intriguingly detailed account of a most extraordinary travelog, from the relative security of Company-controlled lands into the heart of Ranjīt Singh's capital city, Lahore. For any westerner to dare to travel though the Punjab was quite uncommon, and brave to the point of foolhardy. Ranjīt Singh, then ruler of Lahore, maintained a simple foreign policy: foreigners were not to be permitted within the boundaries of his country. It was an effective and uncomplicated method of resisting foreign spies, and as far as desisting white-skinned European travelers was concerned, relatively straightforward to police. Even as late as 1838, when Lord Auckland, the then Governor-General of India, requested to travel to Shimlā from Calcutta, passing through the Punjab, there commenced a lengthy negotiation period. Clearly, the thought of an official British mission was more troubling than a single traveler, but nonetheless the policy was quite clear.

The author of this memoir was, according to Hari Ram Gupta, most probably Captain Matthews, Deputy Commissary of Ordnance at Fatehgarh, who traveled through the Punjab in 1808 in an unofficial capacity and ostensibly for "private amusement."[1] The real reason was not quite so mundane. Matthews was in fact a military spy dispatched by the then commander in chief of the British army[2] to survey the power and military resource of

Ranjīt Singh. Matthews's strategy was to pose as a British tourist en-route to Kashmīr. He quickly ingratiated himself into the entourage of Ranjīt Singh's first wife, Mehtāb Kaur, in order to make easy his entry into the citadel at Lahore. The masquerade was a flimsy one, and the wily Mahārājā saw right through it, intercepting the Captain at Amritsar where he dispatched Rama Nand, the Chief Banker at Amritsar, to receive Matthews when he arrived. Arūr Mall, another close confident, was entrusted with the role of escort to Lahore. There, Ranjīt Singh entertained Matthews but kept a close eye on him with a special tent pitched within earshot of the palace.

There were few pretensions of Matthews's supposed tour to Kashmīr. Within a few days, the Mahārājā had given the Captain a rare audience and quickly used the occasion to hand him a letter to impart on the British Governor-General. In the letter, received in Calcutta on July 6, 1808, the Mahārājā referred to the warnings given by Rājās Bhāg Singh of Jīnd, Jaswant Singh of Nābhā, Bhāī Lāl Singh of Kaithal, and Chain Singh on behalf of Rājā Sāhib Singh of Patiālā, and Ratan Kaur, the widow of Tārā Singh Ghaibā, that the British government were making preparations for a war against him. Ranjīt Singh further cleverly suggested that, "the best way of further cementing the friendship between the two governments would be to form a defensive and offensive alliance on the following conditions: (1) That the country on the Western side of the river Jamuna with the exception of the Stations occupied by the English being subject to his authority, let it remain so. (2) Whoever is my enemy shall be the enemy of the English and whoever is the enemy of the English shall be the enemy of my government Sarkar Khalsa Jeo. (3) The reports of interested persons, untill duly investigated shall produce no misunderstanding between the English government and myself. (4) Whoever shall be all enemy of this State and of the British Government shall be expelled by the Joint endevours of both States and so on."[3]

The cunning Ranjīt Singh may well have been playing the British at their own game. The response was dramatic and predictable—the British in Calcutta were thoroughly embarrassed and swiftly withdrew Matthews from Lahore and desperately tried to minimize the diplomatic blunder with the court of directors lamenting that, "such valuable information would have been acquired through the agency of the persons actually employed in a political capacity to save the British Government unnecessary embarrassment."[4]

Matthews's short stay in the Punjab had seemingly ruffled feathers in Lahore as well as Calcutta. He was accused of refusing to remove his shoes on entering the Harimandar Sāhib, where it was also said that he pestered female pilgrims at the temple. However, his own account is upbeat and he commented that "My first visit to the temple cost me 200 rupees, which I bestowed with pleasure, and returned much gratified by the reception I met with from the priests, who prayed, at parting, for everlasting friendship with the English, and a common expression of the Singhs here and elsewhere is, 'Gooroo Bukshaga, raj.'—'May Gooroogobind give you the country.' "

This statement is in sharp contract to the attitude of the Akālīs just a year later in March 1809. The very same Akālī priests (led by Akālī Phūlā Singh, the head of the *Buddhā Dal* and the Akāl Takht) were involved in a skirmish with the Muslim escort of Sir Charles Metcalfe, the British envoy to the court of Lahore, during Mohurram celebrations. Lives were lost on both sides and a difficult diplomatic situation arose for Ranjīt Singh who expressed his apologies for the behavior of the Akālīs. A contemporary account of the incident, published in the same volume as Matthews's account, is as follows: "*Extract of a letter from Major-General St. Leger's army, 7th March, 1809.* You have no doubt heard of the awkward dispute between the sepoys of Mr. Metcalfe's escort and the Seiks; but, as you may not perhaps have heard correct particulars, I will give them to you.—You must know that Imrutsir (the place where our envoy and Runjeit Sing at present are,) is considered by the Seiks as most holy; their prophet Nanock Shah being there buried,—and that they hold all Mussulmans in the utmost abhorrence. Mr. Metcalfe's guard consists of two companies of infantry under captain Popham: and, the Mussulmans of the detachment were, according to annual custom, celebrating the Mohurrum. The Seik fanatics could not brook this, and resolved to put them all to death. Luckily, however, captain Popham and Mr. Metcalfe had intelligence of their intention. At this time, they were at some distance from Runjeit Sing's camp, and the sepoys were drawn up on parade; when, all of a sudden, the gates of the town were thrown open, and out came about 4 or 500 armed men, with drums beating and colours flying, and took post behind a small bank a little in front of the sepoys, whence they commenced an irregular fire. Popham did not stir until one of his men and lieutenant Ferguson were wounded, he then ordered his party to advance, and, on getting near, to fire a volley and charge,—which they did, and pursued the Seiks to the ditch of the town; when Runjeit himself came down and behaved very well, took our party away and sent a force to protect them. They say, that he is totally blameless in the business, and behaved most handsomely. Our loss was 17 wounded, and that of the Seiks 5 killed and 25 wounded."[5]

On the 15th April last, I crossed the Jumna, at Rejenore Ghaut, seven coss from Saharanpore, in company with a large kasila[6] of Sik'hs, returning from the Hardoar Mela; and arrived at the town of Borea,[7] situated in the Doab, that part of the frontier so called from lying between the rivers Jumna and Sutledge. I was much gratified with the general appearance of the country, then in a high state of cultivation, affording satisfactory proof of the fertility of the soil, and industry of the people. I was no less pleased with the kind reception I experienced from the inhabitants of the town of Borea; who all assembled near my tent, to gratify their curiosity with the novel and extraordinary sight of an European. Many of the Jautnee ladies, wives of the royuts, begged leave to be introduced to my presence, and every look and gesture testified their surprise. They stood near me, laughed heartily at my appearance, and made a multitude of inquiries. They asked me if I did not wear a hat; if ever I ventured to expose my face to the sun, or if I always staid within doors, or moved about under cover? whether the table which was placed in my tent, was that I slept upon? (although my cot was close beside it, but with the curtains down.) They took a particular survey of the cot, looked at the bed clothes and curtains: they then examined the lining of the tent, &c. &c. at all which they seemed greatly surprised and delighted. Curiosity is one of the strongest passions of the fair sex, whether in Europe or in India; and you may judge how much the Jautnee ladies were gratified on this occasion, by their exclamation, that God had been very kind in indulging them with so wonderful a sight as an European, which they considered as equal to the two other great gifts of heaven, namely, the sun and moon. This ludicrous comparison, the ladies probably intended as a compliment to me; though it must be ascribed, in some measure, to their fondness for hyperbole, which I had frequent opportunities to remark. They were all of pleasing appearance, with mild, regular features, and olive complexion, agreeably contrasted by beautiful, well-arranged, white teeth; for which all the natives of the Punjab, both men and women, are remarkable. Neither pawn nor the beetle nut grow in any part of this country; and the lips and teeth of the natives are unstained by the use of these luxuries, which give so disgusting an appearance to the mouths of many other Asiatics.

The people were well dressed, and bore every appearance of health, ease, and contentment; the effects of a just and good government, to which the inhabitants of those districts are happily subject; and, in proof of this observation, I may mention that, during the whole course of my inquiries, I heard not one cause of complaint. The cultivators are assessed to the amount of one half of the produce of their crops, which is paid in kind to the chief,[8] as money currency is very limited throughout the Punjab. Although that is the general rate of assessment, yet every allowance is made to the cultivator for unfavourable seasons, and every species of oppression carefully guarded against by the chief, who, although he is absolute, rules with such moderation and justice, that he is beloved and revered by his people, whose happiness he studies to promote. Though vested with uncontrolled power, his administration of justice is mild and equitable. He seldom dooms to death even for murder: so lenient is the system of polity, that crimes of that heinous nature are punished by the temporary imprisonment of the criminal, by corporal chastisement, and confiscation of property of every denomination, which the chief converts to his own use. All offences, whether murder or the slightest misdemeanour, are under the cognizance of the kotewall, who submits a detail of all the cases that come before him to the chief, by whom alone punishments are awarded, agreeable to his will. This system of judicial administration seems to have a happy effect, insomuch that capital crimes are rarely perpetrated, and the police in the different towns is so well regulated that persons of all nations enter them with confidence, and meet with no molestation while they remain. The same attention is shewn to an English gentleman as in our own territory, by the kotewall, who readily sends the usual supplies of provision, and for which he will receive no payment. He also furnishes a guard of Chokeedars at night.

The town of Borea and the adjoining districts were independent of rajah Runjeit Sing, at the time I allude to. The inhabitants of that tract of country are both Singhs and Sik'hs. The Singhs, or Lions, are proselytes of Gooroogobind Singh, a reputed saint, who lived in the reign of Alum-gheer[9] and declared himself to the world as the converter of men into lions. They are all soldiers; but Gooroogobind Singh was not a Singh himself.[10] Neither the time nor manner of his death is noticed in any record, nor in any traditional account.[11]

A Sik'h wishing to become a Singh, finds no difficulty in accomplishing his proselytism. He goes to the Akalees, or priests of the sect, at Amrutsur, who ask him if he wishes to become a convert to their persuasion, and if so, to produce proofs of his determination; upon which the convert breaks with his own hands, the zunar, the small thread, or cord, worn across the shoulders by most of the Hindoo sects, and after the performance of certain ceremonies,[12] he is given to drink a sherbet made of sugar and water, from the hand of an Akalee. After this initiation, he never shaves his beard, nor cuts his hair, and ought not, according to a rigorous observance of the doctrines, to pair his nails, but that is dispensed with, though contrary to the rules of the lawgiver. Now become a Singh, he is heterodox, and distinct from the Hindoos, by whom he is considered as an apostate. He is not restricted in his diet, but is allowed, by the tenets of his new religion, to devour whatever food his appetite may prompt, excepting beef. He is allowed also to drink every kind of liquor, such as the Singhs. The Sik'hs are those, who (if originally Hindoos,) together with the peculiar tenets and observances prescribed to the sect by its founder, Nanuk, retain firmly the institutions of their faith, in strict conformity to the doctrines of Brahma.

Both the Sik'hs and Singhs marry one wife, and in the event of her death may marry again; but if the husband die, the widow cannot again enter the nuptial state, but the widow of a Jaut is allowed to marry a second or third husband.[13] Widows rarely declare themselves Suttees[i] in any part of the Punjab; but in the city of Jumoo, a contrary practice prevails. There it is generally practised, and is indeed considered as an indispensable sacrifice to the names of the deceased husband; and, if the widow does not voluntarily attend the corpse of her husband, and consign herself with it to the flames, the rajeepoots consider it their duty, in such cases, to put the widows to death, and to cast their bodes into the fire, to be burnt with her husband's. So horrible a custom as this, does, I believe, no where else prevail. However frequent the instances of widows devoting themselves to death on the pile with their deceased husbands, yet in all these cases, excepting in the city of Jumoo, if it be not in every instance voluntary, there is no where else, that it is ever urged or enforced by any measure of compulsion.

A Sik'h will neither eat nor drink with a Singh, after the abjuration of his faith, and rejection of the doctrines of Brahma, nor have any further intercourse or connection with him, than if he were a christian. Many Jauts become Singhs, and the wives of both, that is both of Singhs and Jauts, are not immured, and shut up like the Sik'h women, but go abroad unveiled and at pleasure; and the women of both sects bear the general reputation of chastity.

I arrived, on the 18th of April, at Mulana, where I found the weather piercingly cold during the nights, and till 8 o'clock in the morning. My route lay through a fine level open country, with a delightful view of the distant hills, passing Mustafabad, a pretty large town, walled in; but it may be noted that every town, and even villages, are surrounded by a wall, in this part of the country, as a defence against the attacks of parties of predatory horse from the Punjab. Mustafabad has a citadel in its interior, built of burnt bricks, with curtains, round towers of the angles, and a cavalier in which the chief resides. He exercises the functions both of prince and judge. The town of Mustafabad and four villages are dependent upon him. This part of the country is so completely divided and sub-divided into small independencies, that many of the villages, according to the information I obtained, are governed by two chieftains, one exercising independent jurisdiction over one portion of the inhabitants, and the other over the remainder; each being entirely independent of the other; and this is pretty nearly the state of government throughout the country extending to the Sutledge.

---

[i] Widow who devotes herself to death on the funeral pile of her husband.

Mulana is a small town, walled in, and has a citadel in the centre. Here I conversed with a sturdy, veteran Singh, who was present at the battle of Buxar,[14] and had visited Calcutta at that time. He mentioned that the people in the Doab generally live to 80, 90, and 100 years, an account to which I could readily assent, from the appearance of the country, which is very open, dry, free from jungle, and well cultivated. He told me that he never recollected such a season as the present, which has been remarkable for frequent showers of rain at short intervals, since the beginning of March, and which have had the effect of keeping off the hot winds, that usually prevail in this part of the country during that month, though only in a moderate degree.

Mango groves are as numerous in the country between the Jumna and Sutledge, as in our own provinces, and the chief difference that I could perceive, was in the nature of the soil, which here is a fine brown marl, producing wheat, barley, gram, and other grains, and capable of great extension in its cultivation. The different chiefs are too jealous of each other to admit of any general combination for the public good. They are chiefly occupied with selfish, narrow views, anxious as to the means of maintaining their own independence, to repress the encroachments, or to take advantage of a rival chieftain. In this state the country has remained for a long series of years.

From what I had hitherto experienced, I was convinced, that during my journeying in this country, I should be regarded as an object of rare and singular curiosity; and every day gave fresh proof of the fact. No sooner was my tent pitched, than it was surrounded by all the inhabitants of the neighbourhood. Wherever I came, the curiosity of the people was excited. Men, women, and children, on horseback and on foot, assembled from every quarter of the vicinity; and never quitted me till the darkness of night deprived them of so marvellous a sight as a white man without a beard.

On the 19th I arrived at Umballa, passing Bimball in my course, a town like most others in this part of the country, walled in, and having a large citadel, much resembling in appearance those ancient English castles, formerly the strong holds of the feudal barons. Mulana, and all the country lying between it and Umbala, are dependencies of Dia Cour and Roop Coar,[15] relics of Goorbukhsh Singh and Lal Singh,[16] the deceased zemindars of those districts. They can bring into the field between 7 and 8,000 fighting men, horse and foot. Their families reside in a well built citadel, surrounded by a brick wall with round bastions. The town is large and populous, the houses are mostly built of burnt bricks. The streets are so very narrow, as scarcely to afford room for the passage of an elephant. The country between Mulana and Umbala, appears fertile, and is extremely well cultivated. Having enquired why the more powerful zemindars did not reduce the weaker to their subjection, I was told that they had no desire to extend their possessions, or to cause commotions by such acts of injustice, and that they were content with the territory that they already possessed.

At Umbala I met the usual kind attention. On my arrival, I had a visit from the Dewan, deputed on the part of the ladies of the citadel, politely requesting to know, if I would allow them to order dinner to be prepared for me. The inhabitants throughout this country, and as far as the Sutledge, bear a high character for hospitality and kindness to strangers. Their benevolence is not narrowed by bigotry or prejudice, and disclaims the distinctions of religion or complexion. They are particularly attentive to travellers of all casts or countries. The chief of every town makes a point of subsisting all poor and needy travellers, from his own funds, a part of which are set aside for that purpose, and when that falls short, from an increased number of indigent claimants, their wants are supplied by a subscription made from the principal inhabitants of the place. It is very pleasing to travel through the town and villages of this country. The inhabitants receive the stranger with an air of welcome that prepossesses him in their favour. They are, at the same time, courteous and respectful, contrary to what the traveller experiences in Mussulman towns; where he is looked upon with contempt, and regarded as an unwelcome intruder. The character of the Sik'hs had been represented to me in a very favourable light, and my own observations confirmed all that I had heard in their favour. They are just and amiable in their social intercourse, and affectionate in their domestic relations. One quality particularly raises the character of the Sik'hs above all other Asiatics; and that is, their higher veneration for truth. Both as a people and as individuals, they may be considered as much less addicted to the low artifices of evasion, lying, or dissimulation, than any other race of Asiatics. Implicit dependence may be placed upon their promise, in all matters either of public or private concern; and if a Sik'h declares himself your friend, he will not disappoint your confidence; if, on the other hand, he bears enmity to any one, he declares it without reserve.—Upon the whole, they are a plain, manly, hospitable, and industrious people, and by far the best race I have ever met in India. They have all the essential qualities of a good soldier:—in their persons they are hardy and athletic; of active habits, patient, faithful, and brave. They are strongly attached to their chiefs, and will never desert them, while they are well treated.

On the 20th of April, I march to Patala, in a southerly direction.—The country continues open and pretty well cultivated, but without mango trees; there are, however, large peepul[ii] trees about the different villages, and also hedges of the jow, growing to middling-sized trees, which to European eye, have a novel and pretty appearance. These hedges are cut by the natives, and commonly used for fuel.

Although the soil of this part of the country is so favourable to the production of grain, the crops were by no means so full and luxuriant as in the company's territories. From inattention on the part of the landholders, together with the unorganized state of the country, which being held in petty independencies, and beyond the Sutledge, in jageer and jeedad, is only partially cultivated. The royuts raise no more than sufficient for home consumption; whereas under proper management, a large surplus might be raised for exportation. The country, though fertile, is uncommonly dry, and irrigation becomes necessary to ensure a plentiful harvest; yet wells are only seen near towns and villages, where they water their crops; but the distant fields, when ploughed and sown, are left to take their chance of the weather, notwithstanding the simple and ingenious method they employ to draw their water, and consequently they produce low and scanty crops. The water is drawn up from the wells by what we call the Persian wheel. Why this piece of mechanism is so named, I know not; and here, where it is in very general use, the natives do not assign its invention to the Persians, but claim it as their own;—they call it rahutt. One of these rahutts I examined particularly; it was worked by two bullocks, and gave a constant supply of water. It was constructed with three wheels, two of which were placed vertically, and the third horizontally. The former were fixed on an axle, over which the governing, or horizontal wheel was turned by the passage of the bullocks; it had 42 pots, each holding 5 1/2 quarts of water, all fastened to a circular cordage close to each other; these descending two or three cubits into the water, were filled in succession; and on passing their horizontal direction, at the top of the well, emptied themselves into a wooden receiver; whence the water was conducted by a trough to the different channels of divergence. In some places two rahutts are worked at the same time, on opposite sides of the well; and in this way, they water a considerable space in a short time.

[ii] Ficus religiosa

The receiver is placed within the wheel, but has no connection with it. Water is found throughout this country, at a depth of from 10 to 15 cubits from the surface.

Pateata[17] is a place of considerable extent, surrounded by a mud wall and ditch, but neither affording any great defence. The rajah Sahib Singh[18] was strengthening the former by an additional wall of unburnt brick, three feet thick, to guard against the attacks of his enemies. His place of residence is within the town, in a citadel of shewy and lofty appearance.[19] It is a square fort built of burnt brick, with curtains and round bastions, in which I am told he has 3 or 4 guns. At this place there are several little monuments of deceased Sik'hs,[20] some of them bearing inscriptions of the name, age, &c of the deceased, which do not here denote the person interred to have been a self-devoted Suttee, as is generally the case where such monuments appear in other parts. That practice does not prevail in this part of the country. These monuments are built over a small part of the body, after reducing it to ashes, and the remainder is thrown into the nearest river, to the margin of which Hindoo bodies are carried to be burnt. The bodies are never thrown into the river, without the previous ceremony of burning, in any part of the Punjab. A Christian musician, named Paris, late master of the band in the 4th Native regiment, was this day killed by two Sik'hs in an affray, originating about a prostitute of the town. He was what is called a half cast man, and had deserted from his corps, on account of debt. He was here called captain Paris, and had the command of a small body of foot, in the rajah's service. The two men who killed him, were immediately confined, and their property confiscated. Paris, however, was the aggressor, he had not only given the first abuse, but wounded one of the Sik'hs. Confiscation of property and imprisonment is in general, as before noted, the only punishment inflicted for wilful murder. This, perhaps, in most countries, might render crimes of that sanguinary nature more frequent; here it does by no means appear to have that effect; and the penalty is found to be sufficient; for murders I believe, are far less frequent than in any country equally populous; which I think a convincing proof of the good fellowship, subsisting among the inhabitants of these countries, and of the general character they bear for moderation and good manners.

On the 24th, I arrived at Makewara. The direct road from Unbala to this place is by Kajepoor and Shirhand. I was this day informed that Shujah-ul-Mulk, king of Kandahar and Cabul,[21] having marched to the country of Littee, appointed Sheer Mohummud Khan vizier, who taking advantage of his absence, raised to the musnud one of Zemaun Shah's sons, and disclaimed any further obedience to the king's authority; but the son, aware of the vizier's treachery, wrote privately to Sujah-ul-Mulk, pressing his immediate return to prevent the vizier's proclaiming himself king. The king obeyed the summons, came speedily back, and put the vizier to death! Abdallah Khan, son of the vizier, and Subah of Cashmeer, in consequence of his father's murder, resolved to throw off his allegiance to the king, and sent an invitation to rajah Runjeit Singh, to march his army to his support, offering him considerable pecuniary recompence. Makewara is a small town within four miles and a half of the Sutledge, whose course ran under it, about twenty-two years ago, but has since taken a distant and more northerly direction.

On the 25th, I crossed the Sutledge, or as anciently called, Satrudhra, (Rudh, implying blood in Sanscrit,) where a bloody battle was fought, and arrived at Rahoon. This river seems to have its source in the hills, bearing from this, about north-east, and flows in a south-westerly direction, through a fine, open, champaign, country. Its banks are very low, and it bears the appearance of a fine canal running into two channels; the first fordable, and in breadth about one hundred yards, and the second three hundred and fifty yards across; the water is deep but not rapid. There are twenty boats at the ghaut, of rude construction, but well adapted for crossing artillery and cavalry, in one of which both my elephants crossed with ease. They are each capable of containing twenty horses, the men ride into them at once, without dismounting; they resemble in figure what we call an oblong square, with a prow at one end, without which they would look more like tubs than boats, they are thirty feet long, twelve broad, and the sides fourteen inches, with bottoms of six planks thick; each plank one and a half inch. The river, during the rains, is full one and a half mile broad. The distance from the Jumna to the Sutledge is six stages; being sixty of their coss, each measuring 2,600 ordinary paces.

On the 26th April, I marched to Mukoondpoor, distant twelve miles; the road very good and the country open. There are no mango trees at this place, nor any other shelter for tents. This village is walled in, and is held in jageer by a person named Sahib Singh Badee,[22] who has prohibited shooting within his demesnes. The present is their harvest season; and although the land is covered with the crop, the rajah's cavalry not only prefer riding through the corn fields, to following the course of the road, but help themselves without ceremony to bundles of ripe corn, to feed their horses at the journey's end. This they do whether in their own country, or their neighbour's; a practice authorised, they say, by their master.

I have lately had occasion to notice some specimens of that insolence for which the head fakeers are generally remarked, and which every European traveller in the Punjab, must be prepared to expect. Yesterday, one of those sainted personages, who travel about the country in fine palkees, with numerous attendants, came in our way. He eyed me, as I passed him upon the road, with a look of the most ineffable contempt. He was clad in a garb of silk, and was accompanied by some horsemen to protect his sacred person, and to declare his dignity. He entered into conversation with my moonshee, and told him that he would write to his friend, in charge of the ghaut at the Beeah river, not to suffer me to cross; and that he would also use his influence with the rajah to turn me out of his country.

On this day's march, my moonshee was accosted by a Kandahar moghull, on his way to Cawnpore, with the following salutation:—"Where are you travelling to I wonder? What! You are the menial of a christian. I can tell you, that you would sooner bite the dust, than dare attempt to go into my country in this style; you think yourselves very great people, but I will teach you that I am as good as you." &c. To all which the moonshee made no reply. This moghull was alone, and mounted on a tattoo. At parting, he scoffed and spit upon the ground as a mark of his contempt, and concluded by adding, that we were a parcel of low, ignorant, wretches. I was all this time in front in my palkee, otherwise I should no doubt have come in for a share of his compliments. The rajah Runjeit Singh has but few Mussulmans either in his service or country, and not one of those in any high situation or place of trust.[23] There are about ten or twelve thousand of them in his army, but they are confined to the lowest ranks, their privileges and indulgences are closely circumscribed, and they are not allowed to call the Azan in a loud voice in any part of the country.

On the 27th, I marched to Phugwara. I observed that the bullocks and sheep, between this place and the Jumna, are small and lean, and it is remarkable that in the Punjab they have neither tame hogs nor ducks, and but very few geese. Fowls of a small breed are procurable.

Phugwara is a large town, walled in, and is the residence of Futteh Singh, Alloowateea's[24] collector, who holds four purgunnahs of Runjeit Singh. This country is so very dry, and so free from jungle, that no kind of game is to be found.

Neither the Arhar,[iii] nor bajera,[iv] are here produced; but wheat, barley, gram,[v] mote,[vi] mongh,[vii] joaar,[viii] oord,[ix] and the sugar cane, grow in great luxuriance, and are all cheap. Wheat flour, 1 maund per rupee; barley, 1 maund 10 seers; gram, 1 maund; mote, 1 maund ; mongh, 35 seers; oord, 35 seers; kund, seah, or goor,[x] 1 maund 15 seers; and rice, 20 seers per rupee. Some coarse kinds of cloth are manufactured in this part of the country.

On the 28th, I marched to Jalunder. The country open and dry, and the road good. The morning very cold. High hills in sight, and distant sixty miles. There is a very large mango grove to the eastward, and another to the south of this town; both are said to produce excellent fruit. We received information today, that about eight miles from this town, at the village of Darowly, sixty horsemen stopped a car belonging to the Rannee, (who was absent) wounded one of her servants, and carried off a horse. My moonshee no sooner received the information, than he girded on his sword, called for his bow and arrows, and set off toward the place of attack, where he met the plunderers, who enquired for the Rannee, the (wife of Runjeit Singh, in whose company I travelled from Hurdooar) and being told that she was gone in front, they went off, saying they had nothing to do with any one else. This attack upon the Rannee's car, was meant in retaliation for some former acts of aggression and plunder, made on them by Runjeit Singh. I must not omit to say, that my little moonshee shewed himself a brave and enterprising character, sallying forth with his father and fifty armed men, to oppose the assailants, whose numbers were reported to be forty; and it was dreaded that they had plundered the moonshee's wife. He declared that a most bloody conflict would have ensued, in spite of the enemy's superiority, had they offered any violence to his family: but fortunately they had not such intention. Had they known the contents of the Rannee's Rutt, they might have obtained and carried off a considerable booty, as all her jewels, to the amount of a lack of rupees; were lodged in that carriage.

Jalunder is a place of great extent, but is now in ruins. It was the former residence of the Afghans, and is now inhabited by their descendants, and by the Sik'hs, who are the principal people here. They construct their habitations, from the materials of the old walls and ruins of the houses, formerly occupied by the Afghans: a striking monument of divine vengeance, over the fallen fortunes of that sanguinary and oppressive people. The houses were all originally built of burnt brick, they were strong and commodious, but have given way to time principally from the want of lime cement. This place is held in jageer by two brothers, now at war with each other.[25] They keep up a constant fire of small arms during the day, and set fire to each others corn fields at night, to the loss and ruin of their respective districts. They have a number of rahutts here, for the purpose of watering their tobacco cultivation, which requires constant moisture, and they find that mode of watering the easiest and less expensive. There are several small tanks of water near the town. The name and fame of lord Lake, whose route on his return from the Sutledge, was by this place, are as

---

[iii] Cytisus Cajan
[iv] Holcus Spicatus
[v] Cicer Arietinum
[vi] Phaseolus Lobarus
[vii] Holcus Sorghum
[viii] Phaseolus Mungo
[ix] Phaseolus Max
[x] Coarse sugar or Jaggry

well known as in our own countries, and the victories, the justice, and moderation, that distinguished his lordship's career, at the head of his army in the Punjab have established the English character, for bravery, liberality, and honour, on the firmest foundation.

When Runjeit Singh reduced this part of the Punjab, it seems to have been more with a view to shew his power, than for any purpose of aggrandizement: since wherever he met no opposition, he restored the towns and their dependencies to their former proprietors, to be held of him in jageer; but where he was opposed by the chieftains, he dispossessed them, and appointed others to succeed as their jageerdars. They are so feudatory as to acknowledge fealty to the rajah, being bound to obey his commands, and join him with their adherents, in all cases requiring it; but they pay him no fixed tribute.

On the 29th, marched to the Chuckvee Ghaut, and was fired upon from a small mud fort on the road, belonging to one of the brothers, mentioned above, who took us for a party belonging to his hostile brother, but no accident happened.

30th, crossed the Beeah or Beeas, anciently called Bapasa, on the same kind of boats as at the Sutledge. The Beeah flows in two branches, the waters of which are deep but not rapid: its western banks are high, and its breadth cannot be less, in rainy seasons, than one mile and a half.

May 1st, marched to Oodamitta; here I found the name of lord Lake much better known than that of Alexander the Great, whose name is totally forgotten, and the people here are ignorant of the name and exploits of that extraordinary hero, as much so indeed, as if he had never visited their country. Singularly strange it must appear, that an event so memorable in the history of the world, and so universally recorded in the countries of Europe, has not left a vestige of itself behind, in the country of its occurrence. It is vain to enquire for the altars raised by Alexander in commemoration of this event, or of the ground where they stood, for the Macedonian visit, and the name of Alexander are as entirely unknown, on the spot on which he encamped, as if they had belonged to another world. The name of Lake is here familiarly known, and as it is cherished with grateful recollection by the people of the present day, the march of the modern hero and his gallant army to the banks of the Beeah, or Hyphasis, bids fair to be much longer perpetuated in the popular recollection of the Punjab, than to the famed visit of antiquity, and perhaps most justly so; for the conduct of the British army and their noble leader, while in this country, was calculated to impress its inhabitants with the highest admiration and respect for the British name and character, nor did it fail in its effect. It has raised a monument in the affections and remembrance of the people, that will probably survive the memorials of art, and eclipse in its duration the altars of Alexander.

The high opinion which the people of these countries have formed of the English, and the terms of admiration in which they express themselves on that topic, are particularly gratifying. Nor is it difficult to explain the cause to which this favourable judgment is to be ascribed. In every previous case of incursion of a foreign force, with which they were acquainted, might have been employed, as if it conferred right; and power, rarely, if ever, was seen to respect any claims of property, that it could invade with impunity. From preconceptions thus founded, the contrast presented by the army of lord Lake, must necessarily have been viewed with surprise and admiration. In a case where all their traditional information, as well as their own experience had prepared them to expect a course of plunder and rapine, and all the concomitant evils of foreign eruption, they found the principles of justice, honour, and all the highest virtues, regulate the conduct of the British army. They saw an irresistible military force, insensible to the fear of an enemy, yet fearful of offering the slightest injury to persons or property within their power. They saw, what to them appeared a phenomenon, power directed only to the attainment of good; and rigidly maintaining, in the midst of its triumph, the rights of persons and property, both public and private. First impressions are usually the strongest, and as the people of the Punjab knew nothing of the English, from experience or personal observation, before the march of Lord Lake's army into that country, their first acquaintance was made under the most favourable auspices; and that it has made a strong and lasting impression, is evinced in the sentiments of veneration and esteem which they now entertain for the British character. Many of them, with whom I have conversed, do not scruple to express their desire to be placed under the English government.[26]

Between the Beeah Ghaut and this place, the clans of Futteh Singh Allowallah and Ramgureea were at open war;[27] and it seldom happens that the country is free from those petty feuds, an evil that is, perhaps, inseparable from the form of government to which these districts are subject. I saw but few mango trees in this part of my route, but the phola tree grows in every part of the country, forming hedges and clumps, which have a pretty effect, and agreeably diversify the face of the country. The trees attain to the size of an ordinary babool,[xi] and are not unlike it in appearance, bearing small leaves of a medicinal virtue, said to be antibilious. I measured a well at this place, and found the water twenty-three cubits from the surface of the earth and six deep, which I was told is the general depth throughout the country; but in some parts it is from thirty to forty cubits before you come to water. The weather is now rainy, very cool and pleasant.

On the 2d, I arrived at Vutala.[28] This is a large town, lying twenty-four miles east of Amrutsur, it stands upon a fine open plain, and the jageer of the Rannee Sada Koowar, mother-in-law of Runjeit Singh, who resides in a lofty citadel within the town, and from whom I received very great kindness and attention. This town is surrounded by groves of mango trees and tanks of water, and it is considered the healthiest place in the Punjab; they have already reaped about half their harvest. The weather is still very cold with rain, almost every day. They have an excellent plum at this place, but no where else, called Aloocha. Their apples are rather larger and of better flavour than in our parts of Hindoostan, having more acid. They have also mulberries and bares,[xii] but no kinds of fruit.

The fakeer, mentioned on the 26th ultimo, actually went to Runjeit Singh, and warned him of all the bad consequences, which he pretended were likely to follow from his allowing me to travel through his territories; he told him, that I should no sooner return to the Doab, than two or three regiments would be sent to deprive him of his country; but the rajah laughed at the fellow's simplicity, told him he was a fool, and to hold his tongue. He ridiculed the idea of alarm from an European travelling through his country; and said that he himself could travel to Calcutta if he wished it, without any personal risk, and should be sure to meet with attention and protection all the way. These fakeers are said to be great incendiaries, but the rajah never gives attention to what they say. They are extremely haughty and disrespectful.

The hills are distant from Vutala about seventy miles; they appear to be covered with snow, and exhibit a grand view, on the declension of the sun.

On the 10th, I arrived at Amrutsur, an open town, about four coss in circumference; the streets are rather narrow, the houses in general good, lofty, and built of

xi Mimosa Arabica
xii Zizyphus Jijuba

burnt brick; but their apartments are very confined; it may claim, however, some little superiority over the other principal towns of Hindoostan in point of architecture. It is the grand emporium of trade for shawls and saffron from Cashmeer, and a variety of other commodities from the Dukkun and eastern parts of India; shawls are twenty-five per cent. cheaper here, than at Furrukabad. The rajah levies an excise on all merchandise sold in the town, according to its value, which is not complained of by the merchants. The exports of this place are very trifling; the inhabitants only manufacturing some coarse kind of cloth and inferior silks. From being the resort of many rich merchants, and the residence of bankers, Amrutsur is considered a place of great wealth and opulence. The rajah has made a new fort there, and called it Runjeit Ghur,[29] and has brought a canal from the Ravee, a distance of thirty four miles. This canal is narrow and cost but little.

14th, the Rubec,[xiii] is now all reaped. To-day I visited, in due ceremony, and without shoes,[30] Amrutsur, (or the pool of immortality) from which the town takes its name; it is a bason of about one hundred and thirty-five paces square, built of burnt brick, in the centre of which stands a pretty temple, dedicated to Gooroogobind Singh, to which you go by a causeway. It is neatly decorated, both within and without, and the rajah is making additional ornamented work to it at his own expense. In this sacred place is lodged, under a silken canopy, the book of laws, as written by Gooroogobind Singh,[31] in the Goormook'hee character. The temple is called Hurmundul,[32] or God's place; there are from five to six hundred akalees, or priests, belonging to it, who have built good houses for themselves out of the voluntary contributions of people visiting it. Holkar made an offering of two thousand rupees, and they receive considerable sums from the rajah, who visits it twice a day, during his stay at Amrutsur, on which occasion the priests generally press him for money, telling him that his country is the gift of Gooroogobind, without whose will he could not hold it. On that account he seldom stays above four or five days, and generally resides at Lahore, which is still considered the metropolis of the Punjab.

A Sik'h wishing to become a Singh, must go through the ceremonies of the institution at this temple.[33] It is, however, only the more indigent description of them who apostatize, and generally those who are fed by the priests. Although no person can visit the temple without paying, on the first admission, a sum of money to the priests, who divide it equally among themselves, yet they are by no means avaricious; the monies so collected, being either expended on their personal wants, given in charity, or laid out in erecting additional buildings; and there is no instance of an akalee's accumulating money for any other purpose. Choirs of singers assemble at three o'clock every morning, and chaunt their canticles by reliefs, during the day, and till late at night, in the temple; and at two or three other sacred spots, and with great solemnity, thus exciting to religious veneration and awe, and raising the soul to heavenly contemplation. Although the priests are held in the greatest reverence, still you are not to suppose that they are entirely exempt from every vice. In many respects they bear a great similarity of character to British sailors, spending their money thoughtlessly and extravagantly, and as fast as they can get it, chiefly too, like our British tars, in the indulgencies of women and liquor, totally improvident of the future. The concourse of fine women who go to bathe at the temple in the morning is prodigious. The individuals composing this groupe of beauty, are far superior in the elegance of their persons, the symmetry of their forms, and the fine traits of countenance, to the generality of the lower Hindoostanees. The Birakees, (or fine singers)

[xiii] The harvest which is reaped in spring; that of Autumn being called Khureef.

as they are here called, are composed of handsome young women, Mooslimas, but are by no means superior either in their singing or dancing to the nautch sets of other parts of Hindoostan; they are, however, much better dressed, and many of them appear decorated with gold and silver ornaments, to a considerable amount. The Singhs being greatly devoted to pleasure, give every encouragement to the nautch girls. Their songs are chiefly in the Punjab dialect, which is performed as being better understood than the Persian or Hindoostanee, but to an European ear, they are by no means so pleasing, being full of discordant, inharmonious tones.

When Akmud Shah[34] came to Amrutsur, he erazed their temple twice, killed cows, and threw them into the water, which to this day is a cause of great abhorrence to the Mussulmans, whom they seldom mention without this imprecation, "mulitch anass," the worst of people, d—n them.

My first visit to the temple cost me 200 rupees, which I bestowed with pleasure, and returned much gratified by the reception I met with from the priests, who prayed, at parting, for everlasting friendship with the English, and a common expression of the Singhs here and elsewhere is, "Gooroo Bukshaga, raj."—"May Gooroogobind give you the country." Many children have died here lately of the small pox. The inhabitants are subject to fevers also, owing in a great measure to the situation and excessive heat of this place, which is greatly exposed to the sun; having few trees in its neighbourhood, and being encompassed by a wide, barren, uncultivated heath. Syphilitic complaints are but very little known in the Punjab.

The Rajah has a mint here, and the different coins are still struck in the name of the greatest saint in their kalendar, namely, Baba Nanuk Shah; who lived in the time of Akber.[35]

On the 15th, I again visited Amrutsur, but I did not find the priests so courteous and attentive, as on the first day, when they offered me an apartment near the temple, and also gave notice that I might ascend to the top of it when I pleased. But now this indulgence is forbidden, and the apartment shut, both offers being revoked from some doubt of their propriety in the minds of a few of the priests, and one dissenting voice is quite sufficient to deter the whole of them from fulfilling a promise, or from the performance of any previous resolution; however, they sent a choir of psalm singers to my tent, who sung a number of psalms, as composed by Baba Nanuk Shah, Gooroogobind Singh, and the other saints, to the tune of the Rubab (four stringed instruments,) Dotara, (two ditto,) Sarinda, or Bebec, and the Tublah, transporting the soul to heavenly musings; and although in so different a language from the songs of David, they strike the ear as compositions of the same kind, and are all in praise of the attributes and unity of God.

When I entered the temple, I took off my hat, a mark of respect that did not escape the notice of the priests, and which pleased them exceedingly;[36] it was talked of the whole day in terms highly pleasing to me. They regarded it as an instance of European respect and humility in presence of the deity, and they did not fail to contrast it with the conduct of many Singhs and others, who go there unceremoniously with their swords on, and forget the respect that is due to the prejudices, customs, and religion of the country.[37] The priests of this temple may justly be considered a most happy set of mortals, as they freely acknowledge themselves to be. They are much employed in prayer, or in sacred songs and heavenly musings, without any of the cares and solicitudes that perplex the busy crowd. All their wants are supplied by the rajah, who has set apart certain lands in Jaedad which alone are amply sufficient to supply the necessaries of life in abundance, to the whole establishment, of the priests of the temple. The names of their ten saints are as follows: Baba Nanuk Shah,

Amerdass Shah, Gooroo Arjun Shah, Gooroo Tegh Bahadur, Gooroo Angut, Gooroo Ram Das, Gooroo Hurgobind, Gooroo Hurkissen, Gooroogobind Singh Sahib.

This part of the Punjab, as well as every other part of it, where the rajah's influence and authority exits, is under a good police, and the country perfectly safe for travellers; capital crimes and robberies seldom occurring, from the severe examples the rajah has lately made by hanging the offenders, in some instances, by confiscating the property, and putting to death all the inhabitants of the towns and villages, near the place where such robberies have been committed; and so salutary, or to speak perhaps more correctly, so effectual have these examples proved, that single persons unguarded, travel now in safety, perfectly secure both in their lives and property.[38]

Good camels are procurable here in great numbers at 50 rupees each. They come down laden with rock salt, from a mine called Noon Mean, about 80 miles to the northward of Lahore. One morning lately, I passed a string of 600 of them all laden with salt, which they carry in slings, a large lump on each side of the camel, resembling in appearance blocks of unwrought marble.

20th, I arrived at Lahore. The name of this capital, I find to be a corruption of Ellahnoor, or God's splendid city; it stands on the east side of the river, which is deep, and about 300 yards across, but its stream is not rapid.

Lahore, 20th of May.—One angle of the fort is within a few yards of the stream, the rajah resides in the fort. It is a place of no strength, without a ditch or any defences for canon, and has more the appearance of a palace, than a place of defence. Its walls are lofty, and decorated on the outside, in the highest style of eastern ornament; but hastening to ruin, as well as almost all the private houses, and all the musjids in the place, exhibiting the effects of the destructive hand of time, in as a great degree as the cities of Delhi and Agra, and already its ruins are fully as extensive as those of the latter city. The present name of the river is a corruption of Ayravutee,[xiv] which name was given to it by the rajah Inder, who lived in the Sutte-yug and was married on its banks, to a lady of that name. Its banks are low, and its course being through a flat country, all the way from it source, the water is constantly muddy, and is not used by the inhabitants, who only drink water from the wells, which here and throughout the Punjab is excellent.

Lahore is still a pretty large town, composed of lofty houses; the streets are very narrow, it has a good bazar, but it is not inhabited by people of any wealth or consequence; Zemaun Shah having, on his coming to this place eight years ago, plundered it of thirty lacks of rupees; since which time the principal bankers and merchants have considered Amrustur the safer place of the two, and reside chiefly at the latter city.

The next river, now called Chenab, was formerly named Chunderbaga[xv] by the same rajah, as mentioned above. Baga, meaning pleasure, (i.e.) the place of pleasure, where he experienced some favourite gratification, and the Jelum, anciently called Inderanee,[xvi] Indran meaning sweet, so called from it salubrious waters, which they say are always clear, and as cold as ice, and very wholesome.

On the 23d, I waited upon the rajah Runjeit Singh, who received me very politely, in a grand, lofty, spacious saloon of the palace, all of marble, and inlaid with red and

---

[xiv] Alravatee means "belonging to Airvaata," which last is the name of Indra's elephants.

[xv] Chandrabhaga is the ancient name of the Chinab in the Purans. The word signifies a part of the moon, from the clearness of its water.

[xvi] Inderanee is the name of Indra's wife. Indra is Jupiter of the Hindoos.

other coloured stones, pretty much resembling that at Agra. It is about 100 feet in length and is called the Aeena Mukul, from the decoration of its roof by small square-shaped pieces of glass, at which the rajah informed me the Singhs used to amuse themselves by firing with their matchlocks, and would soon have destroyed it totally, had he not put a stop to their amusement by making it his chief place of abode. In front of this saloon there was a fountain playing, and, in the centre of it is his hot weather sleeping room, tattied in: his wives and other ladies occupying the greater part of the palace, which is very spacious, and all built of marble.

This palace was originally founded by Akber; additional buildings were given to it by Jehankeer, by Shah Jehan, and by Aurungzebe. Several Eran, Kandahar, and Punjab horses were stationed in front of the palace, all richly caparisoned.

The rajah is about twenty-seven years old, he is blind of his left eye, which he lost in infancy, by the small pox; he is rather below the middle stature, and of very affable unaffected manners, active, and fond of exercise on horseback, which he takes early every morning. He is considered brave and clever in the field, quick in his conceptions and possesses a very good natural understanding. He asked me a number of questions, and first as to my religion; he did not detain me long upon this point of inquiry, but hastened to subjects better suited to his comprehension, and in which he seemed to feel a more lively interest. He particularly inquired what number of cavalry one of our battalions could beat. I told him thirty thousand with ease, which he seemed to think rather too great a number; and after pausing a moment or two, observed that he believed that they were a match for 20,000. He then asked me if I understood the discipline of cavalry and infantry, and if his troops could be made equal to ours? If I could lay a gun well; cast canon, and make small arms, &c. &c.? Almost all his questions were upon military topics.

He is quite the soldier, and regrets that he can get no active clever Europeans into his service; his personal bravery is such, that he frequently leads on his storming parties, and is the first man to enter the breach. Like most Hindus, he is a fatalist which gives additional energy to his natural courage. He says it is vain for a man to attempt to hide himself, since whatever is doomed to be his end must inevitably happen, as pre-ordained.

24th.—Crossed the *Ravee*, and visited Shah Durrah, about two miles north of Lahore. Here stands the celebrated mausoleum of Jehangeer, within a wall of nearly 600 yards square, with gateways formed of redstone. It is a magnificent building, of 66 paces square, with octangular towers, at the angles, and flights of 56 steps to the top. The roof is covered with slabs of white marble, and it is about 14 feet high. The marble tomb in its centre, is larger than Shah Jehan's, at Agra; it is inlaid exactly in the same manner, and is as perfect as the day it was made. The four aisles, or passages to it, are laid with slabs of white and black marble, the Ajoobah and other stones, all very beautiful; and although the ornamental part of the workmanship of the interior is not so profuse as that of the Taje, is at once strikingly elegant, and would appear wonderful to a person, who had not previously visited Agra. I could get no correct account of the cost of this building; one man who pretended to know, said it had cost 3 crores of rupees, which put a stop to any further enquiries, as I was told he was the only person who could give any information on the subject; but I think, it must have cost full half as much as the Taje, the same workmanship and the same hands of the same workmen, are seen in both. This mausoleum is still in good condition, in spite of the lapse of time; some of the marble railing is beginning to fall, as well as parts of the domes of the angular towers; but in general it is in much better repair than any other buildings of the Moghul emperors, either at Delhi or Agra. The rajah spends many of the hottest days of the year under the vaults of these aisles, where, from their being so completely shaded and sheltered from the influence of the sun, it must always be cool. During the night of the same season, he sleeps on the top of the building.

Tavernier has committed a gross mistake in saying that the remains of Jehangeer were interred in a garden between Delhi and Agra. His tomb bears the following inscription in Arabic:

"The resplendent place of sleep of his Majesty. The asylum of pardon. Nooroodeen Mohummud Jehangeer, Badshah, who died in the year 1037 of the Hejera, 186 years ago."[xvii]

"*Translation of the Arabic Inscription*

"In the name of God, the compassionate and the merciful. He is the pardoner of sins. Almighty and blessed God said (say Oh Mohummud!) Oh my servants, ye that have multiplied sins upon yourselves be not hopeless of God's mercy. Verily, God will pardon all sins, he is the pardoner and the merciful; every soul shall taste of death, and ye shall meet your rewards at the day of judgment; and he that shall be brought out of the fire, shall be admitted into paradise and find redemption; for what is the life of the world but deceitful goods. Then, (say Oh Mohummud) my Lord, pardon and be merciful, for thou art the most merciful of the merciful, immaculate cherisher, the cherisher of the west.

"All praise to God, the Lord of the universe."

Near this monument, but in a separate inclosure, stands the mausoleum of the famous Kahjah Ayass, father of the celebrated Noor Jehan, it is of a neat octagon figure, having a dome which is covered with marble slabs; the tomb is of marble, inlaid with flower-work of stone, and bears Arabic inscriptions of the ninety-nine names of God, &c. but what is singular enough, neither the name of the deceased, nor the time of his decease, are noticed: this tomb is neglected and is falling into ruin. To the southward of this, on the open plain, is to be seen the monument of Noor Jehan Begum Ashruffle Nissa; it is a square of 36 paces, low, with a flat roof, the tomb of plain marble, without any kind of inscription and is still in good condition. Close to it is another, said to contain the remains of her favourite waiting maid; the aisles to which are vaulted, but are now in a ruinous state. The wall by which it was enclosed is completely levelled with the ground, and as the rajah pays not attention to it, his Sowari find it a cool convenient place for the accommodation of themselves and their horses. The country on that side of the river is pretty well cultivated, and studded with clumps of mango, jameen, and plane trees, contiguous to the monuments; and, in its wider landscape, presenting to the eye a vast extent of verdant plain. The rajah has a mint here, as well as at Amrutsur, and also a cannon foundery; but his brass guns have been purchased in different parts of India, his workmen seldom succeeding in casting good guns.[39]

25th.—The rajah very kindly offered to solicit of Ata Mohummed Khan, subadar of Cashmeer, permission for my visiting his country, and if leave be obtained, he proposes to furnish me with an escort of horse, the Sharah, or high road, being considered as very unsafe, and travellers liable to be plundered and put to death; the countries lying between the hills of Cashmeer and Punjab, being inhabited by independent hordes, who are neither subject to the rajah nor soubahdar, and who subsist chiefly by plunder.

This morning, the Rajah shewed me his gun practice within the fort, at a marked place 250 yards distant; his gunners fired several rounds from an English iron 12-pounder,

---

[xvii] The year of our Lord 1808, being of the Hejera 1223.

a Dutch brass 5-pounder, and three other brass guns, country-made, and a very fine brass 5-pounder which he took from the Pataula rajah, and which has an iron cylinder like the gun captured at the battle of Dehly, and carries very accurately. The Rajah, who is a capital shot, laid his gun, and hit the centre of the target, the first shot. Their carriages are tolerably good, and one of them was lately made by a carpenter from Dehly,[40] in imitation of ours, though not equally well executed; it is constructed of good, well-seasoned sisso-wood, and cost him 1200 rupees. They have elevating screws, and in good order: his Goolandauze are from Perron's and the Begum Samroo's service. They have been well trained and are very expert. The English gun bears the king's arms, and was brought into this country 50 years ago by Jeind Khan, subahdar of Guzerat. This practice with the guns, and horse-exercise are the favourite amusements of the Rajah, from day-break till 8 o'clock. His gunpowder is of the common kind, as usually manufactured in the country, and is made at Lahore and Amrutsur. He has both brass and ironshot, all heat, and some brass shells, which he fires out of ten-inch mortars, with wooden fuzes, and which his golandauze informed me answered extremely well, seldom bursting before they come in contact with the ground. Three of his golandauze having hit the target in this morning's exercise, received each 100 rupees and a piece of cloth, which kind of reward he never fails to make to any of his soldiers displaying particular bravery or dexterity; an encouragement which, if combined with a regular, good system of discipline, would excite great emulation, and promote perfection, but without which the natural indolence and love of ease of these people, together with the inferiority of their understanding, operate as a bar to that exertion so necessary to attainments. The Rajah is at all times, both feared and beloved by his soldiers, to whom he is kind and just.

May 28th.—I again visited the raja Runjeit Singh, whom I found in the lower apartment of the palace. There were two beautiful Punjabee horses, picketed close to him, saddled, bridled, and all ready to be mounted. In many other parts of that elegant building, were also picketed several other horses, though of inferior note and beauty to the two that I have just noticed.

On the 29th.—I visited the ruins of Lahore, which afford a melancholy picture of fallen splendour. These ruins present a striking view of the influence of time; and of the vicissitude of all sublunary things, the mind is naturally depressed with a crowd of melancholy reflections, in contemplating the extensive scene of dilapidation; the image of the greatness and activity of this city in its former days, rush upon the imagination, and comparing those with the present desolation, the mouldering ruins, the gloom and death-like solitude that now envelope the scene, the contrast oppresses the heart with sorrow, while it mournfully declares the instability of human hopes and projects, and the vanity of all human pursuits. Here the lofty dwellings, and the musjids, which not 50 years ago raised their tops to the skies, and were the pride of a busy and active population, are now crumbling into dust, and in less than half a century more will be levelled with the ground. In going over these ruins, I saw not a human being; all was silence, solitude, and gloom, in perfect accordance with the train of melancholy ideas produced by the surrounding objects. The decay of the musjids and other buildings, is greatly accelerated in consequence of their having been built without the use of any lime cement. This city in the days of its glory must have been most splendid and well deserving the name it bore of Allah Noor.

30th.—On making enquiries respecting the route to the westward, I am informed that the distance from hence to Eeran is no less than 105 days journey; 15 from this to Peshawur crossing on the road the four rivers Ravee, Cheneb, Jalum, and Attock. From thence to Cabul 8 days; and 20 days from thence to Kandahar, and very little water to be met with on the road. From Kandahar to Herat is a journey of 24 days, crossing the two rivers Arkundoo and Almun. From Herat to Mushud is a distance of 16 days journey crossing one river, namely the Goorean, and from Mushud to Eeran 22 days travel. According to the best information that I can obtain, it appears that from Lahore to the Attock there is no danger to be apprehended by travellers, but from thence to Herat there is very great danger, from large gangs of desperate thieves and murderers, who frequent that part of the road; but from Herat to Eeran you travel in perfect safety.

June 4th. To day I visited the rajah's pleasure garden called the Shalamar. It is situated three miles to the eastward of the town of Lahore. It is planned and laid out in the usual manner of all large oriental gardens, with long puckah walks, intersecting each other at right angles, and enclosing parterres of shrubbery and flowers.

The wells here are from 35 to 40 cubits deep; I mean that is the depth of earth which they are obliged to cut before they reach the water.

The rajah Runjeit Singh, within the short period of two years, has reduced to a tributary state all the chiefs who were formerly independent of him, and occupying the countries from the banks of the Jumna to the Scind, and should no attempt be made by his neighbours to check his growing power, a few years more will make him very formidable. Soldiers of fortune are coming into his service from all parts of Hindoostan, from a knowledge of his military views and projects, the high pay he gives, and other encouraging contingencies, that attach to his service.

On the 13th I marched to Sumeen & Kulall, two villages defended by mud forts, delightfully situated, and commanding one of the most finely-diversified prospects that imagination can picture. The plain between these two villages, which is of great extent, and the nearest range of hills, are covered with tall grass, of beautiful verdure, and which affords shelter to game of all kinds. The plain is bounded on the south east by the river Beeak, which winds its meandering stream in a south-westerly direction, through a fine, open, level country. To the east and north-east, are three ranges of hills, the nearest of which is about 7 miles distant, and the farthest 100. These last, which are of great elevation, are either covered with snow or crowned with white-cliffs, exhibiting a grand and captivating prospect, particularly towards the latter part of the day, when the rays of the declining sun tinge their summits with the rosy tints of pink, of azure, of violet, and innumerable hues and shades, blended in endless variety by the pencil of nature; the whole displays a most sublime, beautiful, and majestic landscape, heightened by the contrast of the soft verdure of the plains beneath, and the winding stream of the Beeak, which occasionally opens its course, and occasionally opens its shining bosom to the view. The hills are ranged in the form of an amphitheatre, and tower above each other in majestic grandeur as they recede in the distance. The enjoyment of this delightful scenery is increased by a cool, a serene, and elastic atmosphere. I do not believe that even the beautiful valley of Cashmeer itself can shew a more sublime and pleasing prospect.

The tract of country lying between the Jumna and the Scind, generally speaking, is badly cultivated. Such parts as are cultivated are kept in very good order; but I mean that the proportion of land that is totally neglected is very great, the waste lands exceeding the cultivated by at least as two to one. The rajah cultivates no part of the grounds himself, they are all held by sirdars who pay him tribute, or they are held in jageer[xviii] or jaedad[xix] the latter by the principal part of his army, who subsist

---

[xviii] Land assigned gratuitously, or in consideration of past services, for the personal expenses of an individual, without the express condition of military service in time to come.

[xix] Lands allotted to a chief, for the maintenance of a certain body of troops, which he must have in readiness at all times when required.

themselves in time of peace by the plough, but when called upon for actual service, the rajah not only subsists them, for the time their services are required, but provides them with clothes also. He can call into the field by a signal one hundred thousand fighting men, horse and foot, by collecting all those holding jaedad lands, calling upon the different chiefs for 9–10ths of their force; but his establishment seldom exceeds 14 thousand foot soldiers and 7 thousand horse, whom he pays regularly every six months, partly in grain and partly in money, according to the kind of man and horse (the troopers finding their own horses, match-locks, swords, and arrows, but the Rajah supplies them with ammunition, and a new saddle at the end of every six months.) If the horse be very small, and the rider aged or weak of body, he only gets 100 rupees and 100 maunds of grain; but if of the better kind, he receives 200 rupees and 200 maunds of grain, and if both horse and rider be of the first class, they receive 300 rupees and 300 maunds of grain, for their six months' service. None of the infantry soldiers receive less than 7 rupees per mensem, which he allows to aged and weak-bodied men; but young, stout, handsome men get 8, 9, 10, and 12 rupees, agreeably to the rajah's pleasure, which difference of pay is given to men serving in the same corps. The rajah has a number of good guns and well mounted, which are served by the corps of golandauze formerly mentioned.

Having written to Atah Mohummed Khan, subahdar of Cashmeer, in May last, for permission to visit his country, I got no reply during my residence at Lahore, but two months after my return I received his answer of refusal; in which he says, notwithstanding my application was backed by a recommendation in its favour from the rajah, that he will on no account permit any European to enter his country.

The distance from thence to Lahore, agreeable to my mode of reckoning, of three miles to an hour, amounts to 494 miles, or 30 days journey.

I have made repeated inquiry, but without being able to obtain the slightest information, of Shah Pore, the King Porus of European historians. I have been equally unsuccessful in my inquiries respecting Sickunder Shah, Alexander the Great; nor can I find any trace as to the time when, or by whom, Lahore was founded. They have no records in the country, that I could hear of, and are, in general, a very illiterate people, both the high and lower orders only speaking the Punjab provincial dialect, a language that is still without any written characters,[41] and is a corruption of Hindoostanee and Persian, without any knowledge of books, and few of them can either read or write, though many of them, even the common troopers, speak Persian, Hindoostanee, and Punjabee, without being able to read or write a word of either of these languages.

I must not forget to relate a fact strongly characteristic of the rajah's lenity of disposition: a few months since, a man came into his presence with an intention of putting him to death upon the spot; and having drawn his sword for the purpose of carrying his intention into effect, he was instantly seized, and withheld by the people who were present; but the rajah, instead of punishing him, gave him 50 rupees, and told him, since he would not give him any information respecting the persons who had sent him to commit such a deed, to go about his business, and to profit by the clemency that he had experienced.

I met with one man, a Kutre Hindoo, who pretended to more knowledge than his neighbours, and who is considered by them with a sort of oracular respect. Upon asking him what he understood by Hindoostan, he replied, that country comprising twenty[42] subahdarries, seven of which are in the Dukun, five in Bengal, five in Oude and the Doab, five in the Punjab, 17 of which have been conquered by the English, and the five still independent are the subahs of Lahore, Cashmeer, Moultan, Tattah, and Buter, 200 cosss beyond Moultan and Cabul Hindoostan, extending northerly to Ghuzne and Ghoorbund, both dependencies of Cabul.—In each subah are five chucklas, and in each chuckla 25 purgannahs.

The rajah, Runjeit Singh, informed me, that when Zemaun Shah visited Lahore, about eight years ago, he brought with him three lacks of horsemen, crossed the Ravee, and encamped close under the city, which he plundered of 30 lacks of rupees; at which time the rajah's force did not exceed 40,000, and as he could not venture to give him battle, he took up his position at Amrutsur, but finding the Shah had no inclination to advance further into the country, he stole upon him in a dark night, attacked his lines, and killed a vast number of his people; upon which the Shah recrossed the river next morning, and marched away in great consternation; since which time no attempt has been made by the Afghans to cross the Scind, and they are understood to be greatly in awe of Runjeit Singh's present military strength.[43]

I shall here introduce some remarks which I omitted in their proper places.

I arrived at Hurdoar on the 6th April, and I observed with much satisfaction, every appearance of individual happiness, and of the general prosperity of the country, the greater part of which was in the highest state of cultivation. The inhabitants expressed themselves as content and happy under the protection of the British government, and it is manifest that the security extended to their persons and property, proves a strong incitement to their industry, which, in the course of a few years, has restored their country to prosperity, and raised it to so flourishing a condition, that the name of the Garden of India is much more applicable to it now, than at any former period, even during the government of their favourite Prince, Fyzoola Khan.

The name Hurdoar, or Huridwar, is compounded of Hur or Huri, one of the names of Krishu, and the Shanscrit word dwar, a gate or door, which etymology, with its adjunct, gives Hurs, gate into paradise. This spot was the favourite residence, and place of ablution, of Hur and Runkall. Situated about three miles from Hurdoar, was the residence and bathing place of Ditch perjabut. It is on the same side of the river, and near the place where Dilvellee Singh Saraff of Nujeebabad, and rajah Hera Singh Goojeer, have conjointly with the Gosains, built, within the last seven years, five splendid houses, of strong durable materials, and which are said to have cost no more than thirty-thousand rupees. If these buildings have been raised for so small a sum, they must have been superintended by some extraordinary economy; as upon the lowest European estimate they would amount to a much larger sum. They are constructed of hewn stone and burnt bricks, and are intended for the convenience and accommodation of persons of all descriptions visiting these sacred places.

It would be difficult, and almost impossible to ascertain the actual number of people present at the Mela, but, considering the vast extent of ground they occupy, and they form one continued and uninterrupted crowd, extending not less than three or four coss from Hurdoar down the west side of the river, their number may be estimated at little short of a million. The grand bathing day was on the 11th of April, and the ceremonies were conducted and ended in the most peaceable, quiet, orderly, manner, without the smallest riot on the part of any of the different sects, about the precedency of bathing, which was wont to be a never-failing source of dissension and tumult. In the present instance, every precaution had been previously taken that prudence could suggest. All the pilgrims were carefully disarmed, and a sufficient force, with two guns, were brought near Hurdoar on that day, and so stationed as effectually to over-awe any spirit of riot or disorder. The happy effect of these precautions were remarked by the multitude, and they did not disperse without acknowledging their gratitude and respect to the English government, for those judicious arrangements, which so effectually secured them in the quiet and peaceful performance of their religious ceremonies; and the inhabitants of Multan, Peshawar, Cabul, Kandahar, Cashmeer, and other distant parts of India, who visited Hurdoar on this occasion, will not fail to disseminate through their respective countries, a report highly favourable to the English name; and I can assure you, as a matter of fact, that the pilgrims of these different countries, offer up their prayers and hopes, as they travel along the road, that they may be brought under the English dominion.

A man's curiosity must be great indeed to lead him a second time to witness the Hindoo fair or Mela, for considering the little variety to be expected in the review of people bathing, and the very limited number of commodities offered for sale, suitable to the European taste; the loose sandy ground upon which he is obliged to pitch his tent, without shelter from the sun, although in a jungle of small trees and underwood; the inconvenience experienced from being in the midst of such an immense multitude, create in an aggregate of circumstances sufficient to deter him from placing himself again in so uncomfortable a situation.

The inhabitants of this country are composed of Sik'hs, Singhs, Jauts, Rajeepoots, and other low Hindoo casts. The inhabitants are in the proportion of about one fourth Singhs, who continue to receive converts. The rajah Runjeit is a Singh Punjab. They make good soldiers, are capable of bearing great fatigue, and can march from 40 to 45 miles a day, for a month together. They are not allowed, by the canons of their law-giver, either to cut hair or to shave their beards, or the hair of any other part of their bodies, or even to pare the nails of their hands or feet,[44] but with these orders they find it necessary to dispense.

When I was at Lumeen and Kulal, I received information that the fort of Kongra, situated in the hill, 50 coss to the eastward of the Byass, was besieged by the Napal rajah, with an army of 40,000 men, which had lain before it for two years; and the rajah of that place, Sunsarchud,[45] was in considerable distress, his provision being nearly expended; and it was said that the Napal chieftain meant to extend his conquests in that direction even to Cashmeer, after the reduction of the fort. The Kongra rajah has 50,000 men with him, but he has no guns, except what belong to the fort walls, Ghoolan Mohummud is with him, and two years since a battle was fought there, between the two armies, which ended in a defeat of the Kongra troops, of whom three thousand were slain, and also two thousand Rohillas, commanded by Ghoolan Mohummud in person.

On the 20th of June I left Lahore, arrived at Bhaseen, and encamped under the branches of the largest banyan tree I ever saw. It covers ground sufficient to give shelter to 5000 men and several tents might be pitched under its branches.

On the 26th I crossed the Hyphasis at Bahrawar Ghaut, where there are fifteen passage boats, and arrived at Cupoortool,[46] the residence of Futteh Singh Alowalees, who was absent, but he had given orders for every attention to be paid to me, and I was accordingly received with marks of civility and kindness. Cupoortool is a populous town, but unfavourably situated, upon a barren sandy plain, and without trees to shelter even a single tent.

I marched on the 1st of July to Opra, passing on the road two small villages, one of which is the birthplace of Almass Ali Khan, whose kindred still reside here. On the 2d I marched to Nooneea, crossed the Sutledge, with my attendants and baggage on two boats, at Culiana Ghaut; the river is here narrow and rapid.

On the 5th I marched to Sirhind, which place exhibits a vast extent of ruins, and was in former days a very considerable Afghan city; it now belongs to Burgh Singh;[47] there are numbers of mangoe groves in its vicinity and excellent tanks of water.

From this day I directed my course to Futtyghur; and as I returned by the same route as that I pursued to Lahore, my tour now closed.

NOTES

1. F.S. Aijazuddin, *Lahore: Illustrated views of the 19th Century* (Middlesetown, NJ: Grantha Corp, 1991), 44.

2. M.L. Ahluwalia, *Land Marks in Sikh History, A Fully Researched and Documented History: 1699–1947* (New Delhi: Ashoka International Publishers, 1996), 9.

3. Ibid., 70–1.

4. Ibid., 71.

5. "Extract of a letter from Major-General St. Leger's army, March 7, 1809," *Asiatic Annual Register* Vol. XI—for the Year 1809, 37–8.

6. A caravan.

7. The founders of the Būrīā estate were Nānū Singh and the brothers Bhāg Singh and Rāi Singh, all of them of the Bhangī *misl*. In 1764, they seized the fort of Būrīā from an officer of the Governor of Sirhind. Bhāg Singh later seized more territory (120 villages), which formed the estate of Būrīā, and Rāi Singh acquired eighty-four villages including Jagādhrī. Bhāg Singh died in 1785 and the estate passed to his son, Sher Singh.

8. The chief of Būrīā was either Jaimal Singh or Gulab Singh, the sons of Sher Singh who was killed in 1804 in an engagement with the British at Sahāranpur. Griffin, *The Rajas of the Punjab*, 49.

9. Emperor Aurangzeb (1618–1707) (q.v.).

10. The author makes a distinction between the Khālsā and the non-Khālsā, referring for the former as Singhs and the latter as just Sikhs. His assertion that Gurū Gobind Singh was not a Khālsā Sikh is clearly wrong since the Gurū's name was changed from Gobind Rāi to Gobind Singh after he was initiated by the first five Singhs of the Khālsā fraternity.

11. There are several accounts, both in Persian and in Punjabī that record the time and manner of the death of Gurū Gobind Singh. For example, a Persian newsletter of the Mughal court dated November 10, 1708, states that the Emperor Bahādur Shāh ordered "that the son of Gurū Gobind Rāi Nānakpanthī be given a mourning robe on account of his father's death." Irfan Habib trans., "Gurū Gobind Singh and the Sikhs of the Khālsa, reports from Bahādur Shāh's Court, 1707–10" in *Sikh History from Persian Sources*, ed. J.S. Grewal and Irfan Habib, 2001, 107.

12. It is a shame that the author neglects to mention the "certain ceremonies" since his evidence would have added to the understanding of the early *khande dī pahul* (q.v.) initiation, especially since other early sources vary on key aspects (e.g., the scriptures that were read during the preparation of the *amrit*). A description of how the Akālīs conducted this ceremony would have been particularly revealing, especially as they "have a great interest in maintaining both the religion and government of the Sikhs, as established by Guru Govind" Malcolm, *Sketch of the Sikhs*, 119.

13. Regarding widow remarriage amongst Sikhs, most accounts suggest that the practice seems to have been positively encouraged by the Sikh Gurūs, and that it is not confined to the Jats alone.

14. The Battle of Buxar, which took place on October 23, 1764, was a straight-forward victory for the British against Nawāb Mīr Kasim.

15. Rānī Dayā Kaur was the widow of Gurbakhsh Singh of the Nishānānvālī *misl*. She assumed control over her husband's estate, including the city of Ambālā, on his death in 1786. She was described by Lepel Griffin as "an excellent ruler" and her state as "one of the best managed in the protected territory," Griffin, *Rajas of the Punjab*, 100. By the time that Matthews visited in 1809, Dayā Kaur had lost and regained Ambālā. Ranjīt Singh had captured and divided the property in 1808 only to find the British represented by the agent to the Governor-General, Sir David Ochterlony, supporting Dayā Kaur's claim to the territory. He acceded to the return of Ambālā in the treaty of Amritsar in 1809. Rānī Dayā Kaur administered Ambālā until her death in 1823 when she finally paid the British government back for their intervention some fourteen years earlier. Her territories lapsed into British control. Singh, *A History of the Sikh Misals*, 264.

16. This is presumably Lāl Singh, who with Gurbakhsh Singh acquired Ambālā by deceit and held on to it. Lāl Singh died some years before Gurbakhsh Singh. Griffin, *Rajas of the Punjab*, 99 n.

17. The state of Patiālā.

18. Rājā Sāhib Singh (q.v.).

19. This is the Qila Mubārak which still exists, though in a poor condition given its historical significance. The foundation of the fort was laid in 1763 by Bābā Ālā Singh (1691–1765), the founder of the Patiālā state.

20. These are the *samādhs* of the ancestors of the Patiālā family, including the founding father of the state, Bābā Ālā Singh.

21. Shāh Shujā (1780–1842) or Shujā'ul-Mulk, youngest son of Timur Shāh (q.v.), grandson of Ahmad Shāh Durrānī (q.v.) and younger brother of Zamān Shāh (q.v.).

22. Bābā Sāhib Singh Bedī (1756–1834), tenth in direct descent from Gurū Nānak, was revered for both his spiritual and martial prowess. His chief exploits were the wars against the Afghāns of Malerkotlā in 1794 and the Rājpūts of Rāikot in 1798 (which involved the Irish adventurer, George Thomas). He was held in great esteem by Mahārājā Ranjīt Singh, and at the time of his coronation at Lahore on April 11, 1801, Bābā Sāhib Singh placed the *tilak* or mark of sovereignty on the twenty-year-old's forehead.

23. At the time of writing, Ranjīt Singh's court was well populated with Muslims of high rank. Chief amongst these were three Fakīr brothers. By 1809, Fakīr Azīz ud-Dīn had been promoted from personal physician to effective foreign minister having supported the negotiations with the British envoy Charles Metcalfe (q.v.) and having been present at the signing of the 1809 treaty of Amritsar in Ropar. Nūr ud-Dīn, the youngest brother, was by 1809 a recognized face at court receiving many of the state guests on the Mahārājā's behalf. By 1810, he took Wazīrābād and shortly after was appointed governor of Gujrāt. Imām ud-Dīn, the middle brother, was no less eminent, holding the position of *qilādār* (fort commander) of Gobindgarh at Amritsar. As the repository for the Sikh crown jewels and an important military base, this was a highly responsible position. A notable Muslim military leader in the court of Lahore was Ilāhī Bakhsh who commanded the special artillery wing of the *Fauj-i-Khās* and who participated in most of the Mahārājā's military campaigns, as well as the first Anglo–Sikh war (1845–1846).

24. Fateh Singh Āhlūvālīā (1784–1837) (see illustration 20) was the son of Bhāg Singh (see illustration 7) and grand-nephew of the famed leader of the *Buddhā Dal*, Jassā Singh Āhlūvālīā. Fateh Singh became the leader of the Āhlūvālīā *misl* in 1801 and one of his first acts was to form an alliance with Ranjīt Singh, who had just gained possession of Amritsar. They became close companions and Fateh Singh took part in most of Ranjīt Singh's early campaigns. In 1806, he acted as an agent of Ranjīt Singh and, when Jasvant Rāo Holkar, the Marāthā chief, had sought shelter in the Punjab, he signed the first Anglo-Sikh treaty with Lord Lake. Singh, *History of the Sikh Misals*, 74–83.

25. This appears to be a reference to Budh Singh of Jalandhar who was at the time head of the Singhpurīā *misl*, descendants of the renowned Nawāb Kapūr Singh. The Singhpurīā's territories included Jalandhar. Budh Singh's only brother, Sudh Singh, had died prior to 1795 so it is unclear exactly who Matthews is referring to as the other protagonist. Singh, *History of the Sikh Misals*, 146.

26. The cis-Sutlej Sikh states of Patiālā, Nābhā, Jīnd, Farīdkot, Kaithal, and Kālsīā began negotiations with the rising British power in response to the expansionist policy of Ranjīt Singh. In 1809, they secured their future under British protection in return for pledges of military assistance when required.

27. According to a contemporary commentator, Fateh Singh Āhlūvālīā and Jodh Singh Rāmgharīā (the eldest son of Jassā Singh Rāmgharīā) were old friends. In fact, when the territory of Jodh Singh was seized after his death in 1815 by Ranjīt Singh, Fateh Singh "was not too proud to accept a share of the plunder." Griffin, *The Rajas of the Punjab*, 527.

28. The town of Batālā in Gurdāspur district at the time part of the estates of Rānī Sadā Kaur of the Kanhaiyā *misl*, mother of Ranjīt Singh's first wife, Mehtāb Kaur, and grandmother of Sher Singh (later Mahārājā) and Tārā Singh.

29. This is probably a reference to Gobindgarh fort, which was built by Ranjīt Singh on the ruins of an old fort built by Gujjar Singh Bhangī (d. 1788). It took four years to build (1805–1809) and was named in honor of Gurū Gobind Singh. The fort contained magazines, arsenals, royal stables, and a mint as well as serving as the state treasury.

30. Regarding the wearing of shoes in the Darbar Sāhib, Fanny Eden and her sister, Emily, wrote of their visit to Amritsar with Mahārājā Ranjīt Singh in 1838: "December 14th. Amritsar. Our object was the great Sikh temple, where the book he consults as an oracle is kept. We had all to take off our shoes before we entered even the outer court. Emily and I astutely had our slippers over white satin shoes, and they were quite satisfied when our slippers were taken off." Fanny Eden, *Tigers, Durbars and Kings—Fanny Eden's Indian Journals 1837–1838*, ed. Janet Dunbar (London: John Murray, 1998), 181.

31. Given that Matthews noted the presence of Akālīs at the Darbar Sāhib, it is possible that his observation of a text by Gurū Gobind Singh (either the Dasam Granth or Sarab Loh Granth) is a likely reference to the practice of holding a *dīwān* service in the presence of the three *Granths* (the third being the Gurū Granth Sāhib) as is still done today by the Akālī Nihangs of the *Buddhā Dal*. This is not, however, wholly supported by his remark that only one *Granth* was present.

32. Harimandar Sāhib (q.v.).

33. The actual location where the initiation took place would have been the Akāl Takht (q.v.), which stands opposite the Harimandar Sāhib.
34. A reference to Ahmad Shāh Durrānī who defiled the *sarovar* (tank) in 1757 and who razed the Harimandar Sāhib to the ground in April 1762.
35. Gurū Nānak (1469–1539) lived during the time of Akbar's grandfather, Bābur (1483–1530).
36. This implies that the author went into the Harimandar Sāhib bare-headed, a practice which would offend many Sikhs if it were to happen today. During festivities at Ferozepore organized by Ranjīt Singh in 1838, Fanny Eden did not think it proper to be in the company of Sikhs without a head covering: "I went in a bonnet because though the Sikhs think very ill of us appearing at all, they would think still worse of us if we were to appear with our heads uncovered." Eden, *Tigers, Durbars and Kings*, 174.
37. It seems odd that the priests, who the author states earlier were Akālīs, would complain about weapons in the Harimandar Sāhib. One mid-nineteenth century observer noticed how heavily armed a Sikh priest (also an Akālī) was in another *gurdwārā*: "During my journey, I was encamped for a few days near one of their temples, which afforded me an opportunity of observing their religious exercises . . . The appearance of the Sikh priest is exactly what one might expect in the minister of a war-like people. The tall blue turban, bound with an iron head-piece, the sabre, always close-girded to his side, his shield slung upon his back, and the long beard descending to his breast, give to this warrior-priest a highly picturesque aspect, recalling forcibly to the mind of Europeans the times of the crusaders." Baron Erich Von Schonberg, *Travels in India and Kashmir* (London: 1853), 156.
38. This observation of Ranjīt Singh's attitude towards crime and punishment is not entirely consistent with other accounts of the time. Quoting from William Osborne, *The Court and Camp of Runjeet Sing* (London: H. Colburn, 1840. Reprint Karachi: 1973), 182, George Bruce writes "He ruled with a fist of iron, and while it was said that he never took life, as was a custom then, he sentenced thieves and murderers to have hands, ears or nose cut off, leaving it to chance whether shock, or infection afterwards killed them. 'One blow up of an axe, and then some boiling oil to immerse the stump in, and stop all effusion of blood' writes Osborne, "is all the machinery he requires for his courts of Justice. He is himself accuser, judge, and jury; and five minutes is about the duration of the longest trial at Lahore" Bruce, *Six Battles*, 38.
39. Ranjīt Singh was critically aware of the crucial function of artillery in modern warfare and it would seem that in the early days, Ranjīt Singh was keen to obtain artillery by whatever means he could, through diplomacy, conquest or trade. As Matthews confirms, Ranjīt Singh established a workshop for the repair and casting of guns (as early as 1807). In 1809, he exploited the good relations established with the British by producing mortars based on models sent for from Ludhiānā, and a prominent Sikh engineer, Mīan Qādīr Bakhsh, was granted full access to study the British military workshops there. He later wrote a gunnery manual in Persian titled *Miftā ul Qilā*.
40. Ranjīt Singh employed skilled workmen imported from neighboring British controlled regions at an early stage. By 1814, he had employed 30 skilled Delhi craftsmen for all manner of tasks relating to artillery. We are grateful to Neil Carleton for this information.

41. The author was obviously unaware of the *Gurmukhī* script used for writing Punjabī.

42. The number actually sums to twenty-two and not twenty as stated.

43. Refer to part V, chapter 25 for early newspaper articles mentioning Ranjīt Singh and Zemān Shāh at the end of the eighteenth century.

44. An unusual assertion that is not supported either in Sikh religious code of conduct nor in any other eyewitness accounts.

45. Rājā Sansār Chand (1765–1823). He is depicted in illustration 3.

46. Matthews had reached the city-state of Kapūrthalā, which was the ancestral home of the Āhlūvālīā *misl*, then headed by Fateh Singh Āhlūvālīā (q.v.).

47. The city of Sirhind was part of the principality of Patiālā. Bhurj Singh may well have been the *Sirdār* responsible for the city under the Mahārājā of Patiālā, Sāhib Singh (q.v.).

PART V

NEWS

SIKH TROOP MOVEMENTS IN
PATIĀLĀ, 1784

When, in the second decade of the eighteenth century, John Surman's embassy established itself at Delhi on behalf of the East India Company (see part II, chapter 4), the belief that it would be the beginnings of a sustained flow of news describing the events of the Mughal court were not to be realized. With the political turmoil in the early eighteenth century within Mughal India, the Company began to lose its grip on the information grapevine. Two events in particular that resulted in a steady reduction in news were the decline of the English factory at Agra following the collapse of the indigo trade and the first invasion of Nādir Shāh in 1739.[1] The Company was also poorly informed about the rise of new regional powers, namely the Jats, Marāthās, and Sikhs, who hovered dangerously on the outskirts of Mughal rule.

With the conquest of Bengal following the Battle of Plassey in 1757 and the Company's subsequent management of land-revenue in 1765, there came a control over the land in eastern India which resulted in Europeans traveling and observing more freely. Under the direction of the first Surveyor General of Bengal, James Rennell, British mapping now turned from maritime charts to the recording of inland routeways, towns, and villages, for the three-fold purposes of revenue collection, improved communications, and military campaigns. In 1782, Rennell was able to publish a large map of "Hindoostan," alongside which he published his *Memoir of a Map of Hindoostan; or the Mogul's Empire* (London, 1782). With respect to the Sikh territory, Rennell writes:

> The Seiks are the westernmost nation of Hindoostan: their territories begin at Sirhind, and extend westward to the Indus, the whole course of which from Attock to Sindy, with the low countries on both sides of it, is said to be in their possession: so that their dominions consist generally of the soubahs of Lahore

(or Panjab) Moultan, and Sindy. They are said to consist of a number of small states, independent of each other in their internal government, but connected by a federal union.[2]

As with the Mughals, post and palanquin routes or *dāk* became the lifelines of British India. By 1775, a regular post was established between the three key cities, Calcutta, Patnā, and Banāras, and in the 1780s extensions were made to Lucknow and Hyderabad, with improvements in communication by sea between the Presidencies. Another establishment of Mughal origin that was extensively used for the transmission of information was the *harkārā*, or runner, who also doubled as a spy. The best runners could cover enormous distances with few breaks. There were even claims that some could cover a hundred miles in 24 hours, though half that seems to have been the norm on the hazardous routes between Kābul, Lahore, Delhi, Lucknow, Banāras, and Calcutta.[3]

The British also made intensive use of the Persian newsletter, which was more of a "tolerated espionage system"[4] than an accredited foreign correspondence system. With this strong flow of indigenous intelligence, the Company was placed in a particularly strong position in India compared to other European conquerors in other parts of Asia or Africa. The daily news reports of the rituals, gossip, and proceedings of the court were documents of almost tedious detail when compared with the military reports, which were aimed at military commanders and were, therefore, more perfunctory. These were digests of *harkārā* information with a focus on size, movement, composition, and morale of the force of a potential enemy. This type of report, which was intended to be interpreted in the light of information from other sources, is well illustrated in the first account reproduced here dealing with Sikh troop movements from Patiālā in 1784. This is the earliest known report to be found in an English newspaper that mentions the Sikhs.

It was after 1790 that the Company's India-wide intelligence network began to take shape. While the British stabilized their possessions in eastern India as far as the River Jumnā, the rise of the Sikh state in the Punjab under Ranjīt Singh coupled with the invasion of the Afghān, Zemān Shāh in 1798–1799, continued to cause uneasiness in Calcutta. The Company also feared French and Russian diplomatic activity in the region, leading to several key diplomatic missions at the turn of the nineteenth century. The first was John Malcolm's embassy to Persia of 1801, followed by two missions in 1808–1810: Elphinstone's embassy to Kābul (see part II, chapter 11) and Charles Metcalfe's associated mission to Lahore and Peshāwar (see part IV, introduction to chapter 19).

Details of the land of the Punjab and the nature of the Sikhs were fast moving up Britain's intelligence priority list but their lack of access coupled with complex Punjabi social relationships meant they were not always entirely successful in getting an accurate picture of either:

Up to the beginning of the nineteenth century the Punjab and the Peshawar region possessed no large states that could concentrate and diffuse information.

The rise of the Sikh warbands had cut off and marginalised the Muslim gentry of the small towns which nurtured the administrators and literary men of Hindustan. Lahore was in decline until about 1805, while Amritsar remained a precarious boom town, linked to the cities of Hindustan mainly by the Punjabi shawl merchants settled in Banaras and Patna. The rural Jat society which lay beneath the Sikh, Hindu and Muslim clan groupings were suspicious of the urban elite, and had little concern for the literate Persian culture which had once animated them. Conversely, the Indo-Muslim gentry had only disdain for Jat country life and religion. It is not surprising that the British received only garbled accounts of the rural Sikhs and underestimated the resilience of the Jat clansmen who defeated them at Bharatpur in 1805.[5]

Of these "garbled accounts" which made their way back to British shores, several brief mentions of the Sikhs peppered the reports dealing with the significant events in the north-west regions of India. As would be expected, they are sourced from the main cities where the Company had a presence, including Delhi, Lucknow, Calcutta, and Madras, with information typically coming in via letters and reports from more distant and inaccessible places, for example Kashmīr and Amritsar (see chapter 21).

The delay of reporting from the time of the actual event to the publication in England is in some cases quite significant. From the accounts reproduced here, the quickest reporting is eight months after the event (chapter 20), with the longest taking five years (chapter 27—the newspaper report is actually a summary of the version of the account published two years earlier, with the event occurring three years prior to this first publication). The average time between an event happening in India and the reporting of it in an English newspaper was around ten months.

The newspaper reports provide us with a glimpse of the part played by the Sikhs in the complex web of power struggles, political intrigue, and warfare in the late eighteenth century, highlighting the weakening of the Afghāns, Rohīllās, and Mughals, and the rise of the emerging powers of the Marāthās and Sikhs. One of the key Sikh chiefs, Mahā Singh, the leader of the Sukkarchakkīā *misl*, is named, though no mention is made of his son, Ranjīt Singh, even though he was the most prominent Sikh by the end of the eighteenth century. Some of the events affecting the political scene prior to his taking Lahore in July 1799 are described, including the fourth and fifth invasions of the son of Ahmad Shāh Abdālī, Timur Shāh, and the third and fourth invasions of his son, Zeman Shāh.

Sikh incursions in large numbers into the areas around Delhi also feature in some reports. These "marauding adventurers" were becoming increasingly more of a threat to British designs on Delhi, and it was the governor-general Warren Hastings (see part II, chapter 7) who realized the need for action in protecting Company interests. He was instrumental in the 1780s in gathering information on the Sikhs covering their beliefs, manners, customs, and ambitions, being directly responsible for commissioning the very important accounts written by George Forster (see part II, chapter 12) and Ghulām Hussain Khān (see part VI, chapter 32).

Of the selection of reports reproduced here, the two that must have appeared the most intriguing and unusual to English readers would most certainly have been the accounts depicting the clash between Sikhs and the *Gossain fakīrs* at the Haridvār fair in 1796 (chapter 27), and the letters recounting the life of the Irish adventurer, George Thomas (chapter 28), who encountered the Sikhs in various military engagements and considered them to be his "beloved enemies" (see also his Memoirs, part II, chapter 17).

Significantly, the information in these intriguing newspaper accounts, with their depictions of an exotic people in strange lands and of an Irish sailor "contending with the Mahrattas for the Empire of Hindostan," would undoubtedly have reached a far broader public audience than the more obscure academic journals and reports written for official consumption.

———————

The Morning Post and Daily Advertiser, Tuesday, September 21, 1784 [p. 2, col. 2].

By accounts from Dehli of the 7th Suffer or 1st of January, we learn, that the Seik Sardes have begun their march from Patialy, at the head of 60,000 men, with a declared resolution to exptirpate the Musselmen, and proceed with their devastations.[6] A body of some thousands arrived within seven coss of this yesterday, after a march of 36 coss, which they make nothing of, having no incumbrance of baggage, a Seik being completely furnished and equipped from his saddle bag.[7]

Zenal ab deen Khan, (the brother of the late Mirza Shuffy Khan) finding himself too weak to oppose Afrasiab Khan, the present Ameer ul Omrah, offered terms of accommodation, and he has been received with cordiality and respect by the latter. His troops (a small part excepted, which he is allowed to keep) have joined Afrasiab Khan with their attendants, whose army is now 30,000 strong, including Majif Khooley Khan's division.[8] He has 100 pieces of cannon, and about 200 Europeans, so that he is more than a match for the Seiks, if they attack him. This is not probable they will do, as their main aim is to over-run and plunder the country, which, as they are all horse, and much superior in alertness to the Mogul's, they will hardly be prevented from doing. If however the King's army exerts itself, it can at least keep them from doing much harm between Dehli and Agra.[9]

NOTES

1. C.A. Bayly, *Empire & Information* (Cambridge University Press, 1999), 47.
2. Rennell, *Memoir*, 8–9.
3. Bayly, *Empire & Information*, 64.
4. Ibid., 70.
5. Ibid., 131.
6. In the months before this event, Major James Browne (see part II, chapter 9 for his account of the Sikhs) was informed by Karam Singh Nirmalā (through his son Kalyān Singh) that the Sikhs were to invade Delhi and the Doāb region, but out of regard for the British Government, they had given up the idea of crossing the Gangā into the territory of their ally, the Nawāb of Oudh.

Browne, in a letter dated camp near Shergarh, November 17, 1783, communicated this news to the governor-general, Warren Hastings: "By the two papers which I this day have sent to Major Davy you will perceive the very formidable aspect of the approaching invasion of the Sicks. Their object appears to be no less than the conquest of all the country possessed by the Mussalmans, and the friendly style of their letters to me as the English minister in this part of the country seems calculated to secure our neutrality." Krishna Dayal Bhargava ed., *Browne Correspondence* (Delhi: National Archives of India, 1960), letter no. 55, 114.

7. Refer to Polier (part II, chapter 8) for an insightful account of the endurance capabilities, appearance, and mode of transport of the Sikh horsemen.

8. Mirzā Shafī Khān, the *mukhtār* (regent) and *mīr bakhshī* (paymaster general), was killed in September 1783 in a plot involving Afrasiyab Khān. His younger brother, Mirzā Zain-ul-Abidin Khān, decided to take his revenge by inviting the Sikhs to plunder the Mughal crown lands in the Pānīpat, Sonīpat and Delhi districts in October 1783. On November 19 some Sikhs visiting Zain-ul-Abidin Khān were taken into his service. Shortly afterwards the Mughal emperor, Shāh Ālum II, directed Afrasiyab Khān, the new regent and commander in chief, and Najaf Qulī Khān (second *mīr bakhshī*) to undertake an expedition against the Sikhs and Zain-ul-Abidin Khān. They marched to outside Meerut and commenced talks with Zain-ul-Abidin Khān whom they managed to conciliate. It was agreed that three generals, Afrasiyab Khān, Najaf Qulī Khān, and Zain-ul-Abidin Khān, would work in concert against the Sikhs, as reported in this account. Gupta, *History of the Sikhs*, 3: 182–3.

9. Early in January 1784, a body of 20,000 Sikh cavalry gathered at Būriā on the Jumna. Soon after, a body of 30,000 Sikh horse and foot, headed by Jassā Singh Rāmgharīā and Karam Singh Nirmalā, crossed the Yamunā and commenced their raids in the Doāb region in the neighbourhood of Delhi. The disturbances lasted for several months and by June 1784, the main body of Sikhs retired to their homes, leaving their agents behind to collect *rākhī*, the contribution levied by the Sikhs.

CHAPTER 21

MAHĀ SINGH SUKKARCHAKĪĀ, 1786

The London Chronicle, from Thursday, October 26 to Saturday, October 28, 1786 [p. 414, cols. 2–3].

Extract of a Letter from Delhi, Feb. 19.[1]
"Yesterday advices were received from Cashemire, dated the 3d of January 1786, containing the following particulars:

"The army of Timur Shah, commanded by Muddud Khan, and twenty four other Chiefs, entered the Suba of Cashemire, of which Azad Khan was Subadar on the part of Shah, whose brother, however, he protected against that Prince. Their forces assembled at Sunsor, near Mugassur. Abad, from which place Muddud Khan proceeding by the assistance of the Zemindar of that district, arrived before the city of Khondah (adjacent to Cashemirebad), at two o'clock in the morning, when the gates were shut. His attendants calling out to the people within to open them, the Governor enquired who they were? and was answered, That they were the attendants of Azad Khan; upon which, the centinels throwing open the gates, Muddud Khan, with all his followers, entered the city. When Azad Khan received this intelligence, affirming a brave resolution, he rode with only fifteen attendants to the neighbourhood of Khondah, and standing on the opposite bank of the river which runs under that city, vented his indignation in loud exclamations against Muddud Khan, whom he reproached for his unmanly conduct, in coming concealed like a woman, and entering the city by treachery. Then, quitting the banks of the river, he returned to his army, which was at the distance of twenty coss

"Muddud Khan dispatched 500 horsemen in pursuit of him; but he nevertheless reached his camp in safety with his 15 followers. Then collecting his forces, he marched against Khondah, and began a furious attack, in which 2000 soldiers of Timur Shah's army fell, while the loss on the part of Azad Khan was inconsiderable, the superiority on his side being evident, till Muddud Khan with Meer Babbo (an inhabitant of that district), calling out four succours, all the inhabitant of the city, with sticks and other weapons, flocked together, and issuing forth from the city, fought with so much resolution, that Azad Khan, no longer able to endure the fury of the conflict, fled with 3000 horse to Poonja, where collecting his family and wealth, he fled to the mountains which lie in the district of Khan Bahader.

"It is said, that the son of Muddud Khan is created Nazim (Viceroy) of Cashemire, the capital of which Muddud Khan entered on the 22d of December, and seizing the person of Sucunder Shah (a disaffected brother of Timur Shah), directed the beard of the unhappy Prince to be pulled out with pincers, which is a species of the most ignominious disgrace.

"A letter from Amret Ser, dated Feb. 4, says, that Timur Shah was at Peshawar, where Muddud Khan proposed soon to join him, and to leave his son in charge of the government of Cashemire. It is reported, that Timur Shah intends to proceed to Rhatas.[2] Maha Sing, a considerable chief among the Seiks, is at war with the other leaders of that nation.[3]

"All the advices that have been received from Cashemire are lavish in the praise of Azad Khan, who at the age of 19 years, has displayed such astonishing resolution and conduct."

NOTES

1. On the death of Hājī Karīmdad Khān, the governor of Kashmīr in 1783, his youngest son, Azād Khān, had expelled his two elder brothers, Murtāzā Khān and Zamān Khān, from the government of Kashmīr. These two brothers submitted their claims against their brother to Timur Shāh. He took up their cause and during his fourth invasion of India, which commenced in December 1785, his first objective was to recover Kashmīr. Azād Khān was a forceful young ruler, and employed 3,000 Sikhs to bar Timur's path to Kashmīr at Rāwalpindī. Timur Shāh instigated diplomatic measures to bring about the submission of the young governor but these failed to have the desired effect. A force of 30,000 was sent under Murtāzā Khān and Zamān Khān, the elder brothers of Azād Khān, but the Imperial army was defeated. The Shāh was enraged and sent a larger force under Madad Khān Durrānī and Payendāh Khān. This report describes the battle that followed.

2. Rohtās is a territory in the North West Frontier Province beyond the river Jhelum.

3. Mahā Singh was the leader of the Sukkarchakkīā *misl* and was only twenty-two years old (and father of Ranjīt Singh, then only six years old) when this report was written. A Marathi despatch dated January 18, 1786 states that Mahā Singh Sukkarchakkīā waited on Prince Humāyūn, son of Timur Shāh Durrānī at Hasan Abdal, between Rāwalpindī and Attock, and asked him to place Kashmīr under his control, promising in return a tribute and co-operation of the Sikhs for his advance through Punjab and upon Delhi. It appears that he was not entirely successful in convincing his co-religionists to allow safe passage of the Prince. A Persian newsletter of the court of the Mughal emperor, Shāh Ālum II, dated May 11, 1786 at Kishanpur states: "Timur Shah is encamped at Peshawar. He intended to send Humayun Shah to Delhi, but has given up the idea on account of the opposition of the Sikhs who occupy the intervening road." Gupta, *History of the Sikhs*, 4: 342, 440–2.

CHAPTER 22

SIKHS INVADE DELHI, 1787

The London Chronicle, from Thursday, July 31 to Saturday, August 2, 1787 [p. 109, col. 2].

Extract of a Letter from Bengal.
"The devastations which the Seeks commit near Delhi, the capital of the empire, become daily more unrestrained and extensive; nor is there any Imperial force in this quarter by any means adequate to the defence of the ravaged districts, much less to the expulsion of these marauding adventurers, who have in a great measure over-run the whole country, extending from the borders of Lahore to the neighbourhood of Paniput; but while a perpetual influx of fresh troops, led on by Chiefs[1] who depend solely on the plunder which the country affords for their maintenance, augments the necessity of a speedy adoption of some measures to expel them, it is difficult to say, when the dictates of ambitious policy will yield to the dissuasives of humanity; and when the troops who are requisite for the accomplishment of more favourite objects can be spared for the protection of this almost desolated province."

NOTE

1. This report may be connected to the combined Sikh and Gujar raids in the Imperial territory from Pānīpat to Delhi in January 1786. The Sikhs were keen to realize tributes from *rākhī*, while the Gujars of the neighbourhood of Delhi committed robberies at night. The Sikhs had only the year before entered into a treaty of alliance with the Marāthās, of which a key term was for the Sikhs to desist from levying *rākhī* on any possessions of the Imperial government. However as this report shows the Sikhs did not abide by the treaty for long. Gupta, *History of the Sikhs*, 3: 220.

CHAPTER 23

THE COLLAPSE OF MUGHAL POWER IN LAHORE, 1789

The Diary: or, Woodfall's Register, Thursday, August 20, 1789 [p. 3, col. 2].

Extract of a letter from a gentleman in the East Indies to his friend in Edinburgh.
"Golam Khadir,[1] seeing that the confederates were determined to exterminate him, took post in the fortress of Meraut, opposite to Delhi, entrenched his army round it in the strongest manner, and, in short, took the most vigorous method of defence when too late, as he was strongly invested on all quarters, and his retreat to Ghos Gur totally cut off.

"After some time spent in negotiations, and a desultory kind of war, Golam Khadir, seeing himself so closely invested, and a general storm hourly expected, was determined, with a few chosen friends, to cut his way, under cover of the night, thro' the confederate army, with a view to obtain an asylum in the mountains of Sewallie.

"On the intended night, at twelve o'clock, this daring and cruel regicide, with fifty chosen horsemen, and as much valuable plunder of the royal palace as they could conveniently carry, issued out of one of the gates of Meraut, and cut their way through part of the besieging army; but, being closely followed by a large party of horse under the command of Rajah Hamet Bahadur, and his brother, Ali Bahadur, Golam Khadir's party were entirely cut to pieces.

"Golam Khadir, being wounded in the beginning of the action, and his horse shot under him, attempted to crawl into a hovel by the road side, and endeavoured to bribe two village people to conceal him; but they knowing his rank and consequence, bound him hand and foot, and delivered him over to a party from the confederate army, which arrived at the hovel about this juncture.

"Golam Khadir was conducted to the confederate army with every mark of indignity, and, like another Bajazet, was immediately confined in an iron cage, and carried about as a publick spectacle to the insulting mob. Disputes run high what mode of punishment was to be inflicted on him; but the latest accounts from Delhi mention, that it is now determined that his eyes are to be first scooped from their sockets, with a similar instrument to that with which he caused the unfortunate King's to be extracted. In this situation he is to remain for a certain time, in order that he may himself feel those agonizing and unspeakable sufferings which he had occasioned to another; he is then to be conducted to a place prepared for the occasion, and interred to the middle, in which posture he is to continue to be shot at with poisoned arrows till he expires! His offences, it must be admitted, have been monstrous; his punishment, however, I am sorry to say, though seemingly accommodated to his actions, is a species of refined retribution, which too strongly marks the sanguinary principles, which unfortunately for mankind, still influence certain Eastern states, which have not the happiness (after all that has been said of delinquents) of being under the auspices of a British Government, and of which the natives are more and more convinced every day.

"After the death of Golam Khadir, his army partly dispersed, and partly entered into the service of the confederates, the Royal family was again put in possession of Delhi, and the King's affairs once more wore an appearance of tranquility.

"But Scindia was determined that the King should reap much benefit by the revolution, as he not only took possession of the royal artillery, retaken from Golam Khadir, but also of every thing of value that was found in the camp; and though the King has every respect paid him, merely to give a sanction to Scindia's views, yet in fact his present situation is truly miserable. In short, Scindia does what he pleases, nobody can controul him.

"Timur Shah, King of Caboul, &c. and son to the famous Abdalah, who formerly invaded Hindostan, after many threatenings and preparations has at last marched at the head of 250,000 men, and is now within 100 miles of Lahore, the capital of the Seiks. His declaration is, that he means to exterminate the Seiks,[2] drive the Mahrattahs from this side of India, and to place himself on the throne of Delhi, because the present race are unworthy to sit on it; and says, as he is of the undoubted blood royal, he will never allow the memory of the illustious Timur to be degraded.

"Timur Shah has entered into a treaty with the Rajahs of Jaynagar, Jaypore, and Rewah, who have agreed to join with him their combined forces, on condition that a Seik country (after conquest) is ceded to them. They are powerful and rich Rajahs, so that upon the whole, Timur will have a very formidable army.

Our Government, though they have taken no active part, yet are perfectly on their guard; as the corps at Cawnpore are in orders to hold themselves in readiness to march, and three battalions with a proportion of artillery, have actually marched from Futty Gur (our uppermost military post), and taken post at Anopshere, near Agra, to watch the motions of the combined armies."

"It would be by no means political in us, to allow Timur to attack the Seiks, as, independent of their being on friendly term with us,[3] they form a strong barrier between the Mahrattahs and us, and if ever they are driven out, we shall be engaged in a constant scene of war; besides, Timur has declared himself the enemy of Asoph ul Dowlah,[4] because he, as a Vizir of the empire, did not assist Shah Allum against his enemies."[5]

Notes

1. The Rohīllā chief, Ghulām Qādir (q.v.), was the son of Zābita Khān (q.v.). In an effort to obtain the office of *mīr bakhshī* and title of *amīr-ul-umārā* enjoyed by his father and grandfather, he advanced upon Delhi in August 1787. His negotiations with Baghel Singh of the Karorasinghīā *misl* and other Sikhs to join him were accepted by the former but some Sikhs, namely Bhangā Singh of Thānesar, sided with the Mughal emperor, Shāh Ālum II (q.v.). In September

1787, Ghulām Qādir entered Delhi and forced the terrified emperor to confer upon him the office and title he sought. A year later in August 1788, in an attempt to secure the emperor's secret treasures, he blinded the emperor and committed atrocities on the royal family. By the end of September 1788, the capture of Delhi from the hands of Ghulām Qādir began under the command of the Marāthā Mahādjī Scindiah (the regent plenipotentiary). The account here begins after the Marāthā army had secured the capital on October 2, 1788. Gupta, *History of the Sikhs*, 3: 231–42.

2. Timur Shāh's fifth (and last) invasion of India began when he marched from Peshāwer on November 10, 1788. He crossed the Indus at Attock four days later, advanced toward Multān avoiding Lahore which at the time of writing would have been governed by Lahinā Singh Bhangī and Sobhā Singh Kanhaiyā—see introduction to Griffith (part III, chapter 13)—and headed straight to Bahāwalpur to realize unpaid tribute from the ruling Nawāb. Afterward, he directed his attention towards the Mīrs of Sind, again to realize arrears of tribute, but was compelled to return to Kābul on hearing the news of disturbances in his own frontier by Murād Shāh of Turān. Gupta, *History of the Sikhs* 4: 444.

3. The governor-general, Warren Hastings, deputed Major James Brown as the British Agent to Delhi in 1782. One aspect of his diplomatic mission was to understand better the independent chiefs of states bordering on the territories of the Mughal emperor, Shāh Ālum II. From Agra, Browne contacted Baghel Singh's vakīl Lakhpat Rāi. In reply to one letter, Lakhpat Rāi stated that notable Sikh chiefs such as Jassā Singh Āhlūvālīā "who is the highest and greatest and in that country called Badshah Singh," and Baghel Singh including many others were willing to establish friendly relations with the British Government. Krishna Dayal Bhargava ed., *Browne Correspondence* (New Delhi: National Archives of India, 1960), enclosure 19 to letter no. 41, 74. Browne's reply dated April 27, 1783, held out prospects of "sincere friendship" on the condition of obedience to Shāh Ālum II and laying aside the practice of plundering the Gangā Doāb and the crown lands. The information he collected was compiled into his account for the information of the governor-general called "History of the Origin and Progress of the Sicks" (see part II, chapter 9). Gupta, *History of the Sikhs*, 3: 171–3.

4. Following the British victory at Buxar in 1764, the perpetual right, or *Dīwānship*, over the revenues of certain Oudh territories (namely Bengal, Bihār, and Orīssā) was granted by Shāh Ālum II to the East India Company. By this arrangement, these territories virtually became the property of the Company, and the Nawāb Wazīr of Oudh, Shujā-ud-Daulā, became a close ally of the British. On his death on January 26, 1775, his son, Asaf-ul-Daulā (d. 1797), became the Nawāb.

5. Timur Shāh was married to Shāh Ālum II's sister, hence, they were brothers-in-law.

CHAPTER 24

ZEMĀN SHĀH AND THE SIKHS, 1798

The Times, Monday, February 5, 1798 [p. 4, col. 1].

EAST INDIES. MADRAS, SEPT. 2.
Accounts received within these few days from the upper stations advise us of the prevalence of reports stating that ZEMAUN SHAW had a recent recontre with the principal body of the Seik army, in which he was worsted with considerable loss; and from which he had been compelled to retreat with precipitation.[1]

NOTE

1. Zemān Shāh's third invasion commenced when he left Kābul in October 1796. He halted at Peshāwar for a month and opened negotiations with the Sikh chiefs, including the sixteen-year-old Ranjīt Singh, who had already begun to establish his reputation as a powerful independent chief. The battle reported here took place in Amritsar in January 1797 where approximately 50,000 Sikhs had gathered. A major portion of the Durrānī army was led in person by Zemān Shāh and the two forces commenced fighting early in the morning. The Shāh's camel artillery was pitted against the Sikhs' matchlocks until the afternoon, when the latter gave a signal for an attack, "and agreeable to their mode in close combat, flung away their turbans, let loose their hair, put their beards in their mouths, and dashed into the midst of the Abdallah [Ahamd Shāh Abdālī] army with sword in hand". The Durrānī army eventually gave way and were pursued up to Lahore by the victorious Sikhs. Gupta, *History of the Sikhs*, 4: 474–5.

CHAPTER 25

SUBMISSION TO ZEMĀN SHĀH, 1799

The Times, Friday, July 19, 1799 [p. 3, col. 3].

EAST INDIES. Calcutta, Feb. 11.
Intelligence has been received from Lahore, which states that a number of the Seick Chiefs, had made their submission to *Zemaun Shah*, and that each, in consequence, had received a Khelaut.[1]

Zemaun Shah is said to be employed in settling the territorial revenues of the country, preparatory to proceeding towards Delhi.[2] He expressed a wish that other Seick Chiefs would come in, and make their submission also, in order to receive from him Khelauts.

Juggoo Bappoo has signified his intention to remove from Delhi, in consequence of the expected approach of Zemaun Shah; and, in pursuance of this intention, has directed Mr. *Seton* to muster all his forces, with a view of marching to Acbarabad.

Advices from Delhi mention that *Maha Sing* and *Saib Sing*, two of the Sirdar Seicks, went before Zemaun Shah, and presented a nuzzer of 5 gold mohurs each, and in return received Khelauts.[3] The Shah enquired of them, to whom they paid their collections, and having learnt, directed them in future to pay them to him. Zemaun Shah informed them, if they were dissatisfied they might quit the country; that they had the option of living quietly as his Ryots, or joining the disaffected Seicks, to whom he was resolved to give battle. Intelligence from Jeypour of the 1st states, that the *Vizier* of *Zemaun Shah* had represented to his master that as he was then in safety in the Fort of Lahore, it would be prudent in him to remain there for some days, that he might have an opportunity of settling the affairs of the country; meantime he, the Vizier, would proceed forward to Delhi, and the Shah having consented to the proposition, the Vizier commenced his march, plundering and burning the habitations all the way to the Beyah[4] river, 30 coss on this side Lahore.

Letters have been received, which mention that at two Dustalis of the Shah's troops had marched from Moultan, with an intention of proceeding to Joynagur, and by that route to penetrate to Delhi. The *Jeypour Rajah*, on hearing this news, appeared much alarmed.

Other letters mention, that Juggoo Bappoo had received information from *Scindia*, of Zemaun Shah's having marched from Lahore towards Delhi; and that

Scindia had directed him to take the field, and be upon his guard. Juggoo Bappoo, who was then on his march to Acbarabad, replied to Scindia, that the Ryots had refused to pay the customary tributes—that the country was all in confusion—and that it was therefore necessary that he, *Dowlut Row Scindia*, should march with all his troops to his immediate assistance.

The Merchants of Delhi represented to the Byes, that, as Zemaun Shah was expected at Delhi, they were desirous of obtaining permission so remove their families and effects to a place of safety. Their request was, however, refused; but they were informed, when any certain news was received of the Shah's approach, they should have due notice of it.

On the 21st of January, accounts were received an engagement having taken place between the Seicks and the troops of Zemaun Shah, in which the latter were defeated and driven back to Lahore with great loss. On the 23d the Seicks having recrossed the Beyah river, attacked that part of Zemaun Shah's army which was posted an Umrootsur,[5] and totally defeated it. The Seicks also surprised two important posts of Zemaun Shah's troops on the banks of the Chelum,[6] and put every man of them to the sword.[7]

The Shah has given orders for one part of his army under *Poonde Beg Khan*, to march to Delhi by the route of Putealah.[8]

A person belonging to the Nabob Vizier, who was apprehended in the camp of Zemaun Shah, and who was suspected of having transmitted intelligence from thence, was hung as a spy.

A letter from the Anopsheer, dated the 17th of January, says—The Company's army reached this station on the 28th December, and here we have been encamped ever since: we are full 12,000 effective men, and the number of attendants swells the army to five times that number. We are only three days march from Delhi, but we learn nothing of Zemaun Shah's proceedings or intentions. We are only informed that he has had some skirmishing with the Seicks, and has beaten them.

Notes

1. A dress of honour presented by a superior on ceremonial occasions.
2. Zemān Shāh made his fourth invasion in the autumn of 1798, and it was to be the last foreign invasion from the North-West.
3. The Sikhs, though disunited, were still able to cause havoc in Zemān Shāh's army by employing their guerrilla warfare tactics. On one occasion, they plundered a caravan consisting of merchants with considerable property at the rear of the army. Realizing that his advance to Delhi would be severely disrupted if he did not check the Sikhs, the Shāh began to conciliate them. An agent, Nekī Singh, was despatched to Amritsar in December 1798 to negotiate with the Sikhs for peace. Sāhib Singh Bedī, on behalf of the Sikh chiefs, declined to entertain the proposal but a few days later, the Sikhs decided to act independently with the result that some chiefs began to accept, on the face of things, a peace settlement. Conspicuous amongst these chiefs were Sāhib Singh Bhangī and Ranjīt Singh. The *Maha Sing* mentioned in the article is actually Mohan Singh, who acted on behalf of Ranjīt Singh on this occasion (but it may also be a case of incorrectly identifying Ranjīt Singh by his father's name, Mahā Singh). Gupta, *History of the Sikhs*, 4: 486–509.
4. Beas river.
5. Amritsar (q.v.).

6. Jhelum.
7. These battles actually took place in January 1797, not 1798, and were reported in *The Times*, Monday, February 5, 1798 (see chapter 24). In early January 1798, Zemān Shāh had begun his retreat back to Kābul. His baggage train was protected from attack in the rear by Ranjīt Singh's intervention against other Sikh chiefs who were keen on the idea. He arrived in Peshāwar at the end of January, having been harassed by plundering tribes and suffering the ignominy of losing twelve guns in the river Jhelum. Eight of these guns were later recovered and sent on to the Shāh by Ranjīt Singh in a smart diplomatic move that secured him a royal pleasure and a *farmān* for the capture of Lahore.
8. Patiālā.

CHAPTER 26

SIKHS GATHER TO OPPOSE AFGHĀN RULE, 1800

The English Chronicle, and *Universal Evening Post*, from Saturday, April 19 to Tuesday, April 22, 1800[1] [front page, col. 3].

ZEMAUN SHAH is busied in repairing the fortifications of Lahore, and appears intent on establishing his Government in the Punjub, the Chiefs of which have generally done him homage. The body of Seiks lately assembled at Umrootsur[2] in order to oppose ZEMAUN, have retreated across the Berjah, to resume their respective posts. Two duftahs of the SHAH'S troops lately advanced from Moultan towards Joynagur; but after occasioning general terror, and more especially to the Jeypore Rajah, they have been recalled; in consequence, however, of this circumstance, a considerable number of Delhi merchants, who early in the year 1797 removed with their families and effects to Jeypore, have obtained permission of the Rajah to return. ZEMAUN, it is stated, has abandoned his proposed visit to Delhi; the European troops are, however, as a measure of precaution, to be continued on the frontiers.

NOTES

1. This account appears to be a summary of the report given in *The Times*, Friday, July 19, 1799 (see chapter 25).
2. Amritsar (q.v.).

CHAPTER 27

ATTACK ON FAKĪRS AT HARIDVĀR BY SIKHS, 1801

The Times, Saturday, October 17, 1801 [p. 3, col. 3].

We have received a Private Letter by the late Overland Dispatch from Bombay,[1] by which we are informed, that the Seiks threaten the whole tribe of Fakeers with immediate hostility, in consequence of some supposed transgression on the part of the Fakeers.

It appears that the Seiks had usurped an authority of erecting a flag in Rohilchund, which the Fakeers pulled down, and drove away the little Seik establishment. They maintained peaceable possession of the place till the arrival of about 12 or 14,000 Seik horsemen, when they hoisted the distinguishing flat of their sect. Here they attacked the Fakeers with swords, spears, and fire-arms, and drove them with irresistible fury.

Having discharged their pieces within a few paces, they rushed upon those unfortunate pilgrims that came in their way, and having slaughtered a great number, pursued the remainder, until, by flight to the hills, or by swimming the river, they escaped the revenge of their pursuers. Many were drowned, and of those who endeavored to escape to the heights, numbers were plundered; but none who had not the habit of a Fakeer were in the least hurt.

Accounts agree, that the Fakeers lost about 2000 men killed, among whom was one of their Chiefs, and they had many wounded. The contest was very unequal, for the Seiks were all mounted, and attacked in the night.[2] The Fakeers are bending their march in a westerly course, directly from the Seiks.[3] The number which had crowded to the river side, where they were obliged to remain some time, were fearful of the approach of day, and in dreadful alarm, from the expectation of another visit from the Seiks. The hostile conduct of the Seiks was purely in revenge against the tribes of Fakeers, for disrespect and contempt of their flag.

NOTES

1. This newspaper report was written more than five years after the actual event reported, which took place at the Haridvār fair in April 1796. It was witnessed by Thomas Hardwicke who published his detailed account in *Asiatick Researches* in 1799 (see part III, chapter 14). This report is essentially a summarized version of Hardwicke's account.
2. Not so according to Hardwicke, who says the attack started at eight o'clock in the morning and was over by three o'clock in the afternoon.
3. Hardwicke says it was the Sikhs, and not the fakīrs, who were traveling as described.

CHAPTER 28

AN ACCOUNT OF GEORGE THOMAS, 1802

The Edinburgh Evening Courant, Monday, October 11, 1802 [back page, col. 2].

AN EXTRAORDINARY CHARACTER

Letters from India furnish the following interesting account of an East India adventurer. The first letter on this subject is dated Lucknow, Aug. 20. 1801.—

"George Thomas, an Irishman, ran away from a ship, on which he was the cabin boy, on the Coromandel coast. He found his way to Hyderabad, the capital of the Nizam, where he served as a private soldier. He did not like this service, and spurred on by the spirit of adventure, he crossed the peninsula, and arrived at the Begum of Sumroo's, who has a country about 150 miles N.W. of Delhi. She took him into her service, and he obtained her favour and confidence. She married him to an adopted daughter of her own, and appointed him to the management of a province, the revenues of which he very soon nearly doubled. The expences of his mistress exceeded her income. He felt himself sufficiently established to attempt a reform. She had many Frenchmen in her service, whom she supported at a great expence, and who were entirely useless to her. These Thomas intended to have reduced. The Seiks at this time committing depredations upon the Begum's country, Thomas went to retaliate, which he had often before done with great advantage. During his absence, the Frenchmen found means to make his mistress believe that his plan was to take her country from her, and that for that reason he wished for their dismissal.

"She took the first opportunity of shewing Thomas the change of her sentiments towards him, by insulting his wife, while he was absent. He immediately returned; protected his wife, and left her (the Begum's) service. This was in 1795. He was then at Anopshere. He had not then 500 rupees in the world; a proof of his honesty, for he had been many years collector of a province which at first yielded 70,000 rupees, but which he doubled before he left it. He now went into the service of a Mahratta Chief named Appa Row Cunda. This man ordered him to raise and form some corps, and gave him some districts for the payment of them. The districts were unequal to the payments of his troops, but he managed to support them by the plunder he got during the continual state of warfare in which he was engaged. His Chief was drowned; and being considerably in debt to Thomas, he kept possession, and at last made a property of the districts under his charge. He is a bold determined fellow. He augmented his troops; he formed, in fact, an army for himself; and by conquest he added to his original territory. He has often been called in as an ally by the different contending powers in that quarter. On one occasion he was paid a subsidy of 50,000 rupees a month. His former mistress, some time after he left her, went to ruin, was imprisoned, and treacherously deprived of her country. He marched to her relief, and reinstated her.

"During the last year he has been more bold, and made conquests upon a grander scale than before. His capital, which is one of the strongest places in India, is about 80 miles west of Delhi. It is called Hansee, and is laid down in some of the maps. From this point he entered the Seik country, beat them wherever he could find them, and took possession of a country upon the banks of the Sutledge, yielding near two lacks of rupees per annum. The Sutledge is in all the maps; it is the first of the five rivers which form the country called Punjaub. The Mahrattas could not with indifference view the success of this enterprising adventurer. He was in their neighbourhood. They at first offered to take him and his corps into their service, but they could not settle the terms. They then ordered General Perron, their Commander in Chief, to march against him. The General did not, it would appear, like his antagonist, for he settled with him upon his own terms. Thomas had then in the field 10,000 infantry, 1000 good cavalry, and 50 pieces of cannon, and he was not afraid of the Frenchman. Some friends of mine have been long in the habits of corresponding with him. He has always given them a detail of his different operations; they are wonderful. Our Government cannot assist him; but I know Lord Mornington feels much interested for his success.

"In one of his letters he proposes that we shall attack the Seiks, and he says, very justly, that these people are the enemies of both the Maharattas and the English. All he desires is that our Government will request the Mahrattas not to assist the Seiks. He wants no money, no arms, no troops; and he engages, in three years, to deliver to the Company his whole army, and all that country called the Punjaub, yielding a revenue of two crores of rupees per annum. He will only require to be paid for his cannon. His ambition is to serve his country, and it is by this means he can do it.[1]

The plan may be thought wild and impracticable by those unacquainted with the Seik nation and with Thomas. With the former I have done all I could to get acquainted; the latter I believe to be equal to any thing possible to be performed, and I am fully convinced he will accomplish all he has promised, if the Mahrattas will not interfere. The idea is a grand one. It may give to the nation countries upon the banks of the Indus not less valuable than those they now possess upon the Ganges. It was at Attuck where Alexander first saw and fought the armies of India. It is there where George Thomas proposes to plant the British colours.

"October 1801

George Thomas is now opposing the Mahrattas, and is nearly overpowered by the superiority of their resources; but he struggles hard, and hitherto victory has attended him. If he succeeds in this contest, he will bring about a revolution as extraordinary as any the world has yet seen. The last time I saw him, he was not worth more than 500 rupees, exclusive of his horse. He is now able to contend, and with some success, for no less than the throne of the Mogul. To his own vigorous conduct, to his own exertions and abilities, he owes every thing. He has been assisted by no friend— alone, and always surrounded by enemies. The Frenchman who now opposes him is high in the service of the Mahrattas. A few years ago he was a cook at Calcutta! Such are the distinguished competitors who at present contend for the Imperial Throne of Hindostan!

"February, 1802

"I left George Thomas contending with the Mahrattas for the Empire of Hindostan. He fought several battles with them, in all of which he compelled them to retreat; but they were too numerous for him to gain any thing but a name by the victories he had obtained. Finding that arms would not reduce him, they had recourse to means more certain, though less honourable, and they succeeded, but too well. They bribed his chiefs, and, deserted by his army, he was obliged to fly to his strong fortress. It was distant 100 miles. He reached it in one night, upon one horse. He was soon followed. The few men who remained with him fought bravely for some time, but his enemies subdued them by gold. He found it was in vain, and reluctantly he dictated terms of capitulation. He got 50,000 rupees for giving up his fort, and was besides permitted to carry off his property."[2]

Notes

1. Refer to part IV, introduction to chapter 17 for George Thomas's own words on this subject.
2. It was shortly after this defeat that Thomas met William Francklin who went on to publish his memoirs (see part IV, chapter 17).

PART VI

ORIENTALISTS

CHAPTER 29

FERISHTĀH'S HISTORY OF
HINDŪSTĀN, 1770

Muhammad Kasim Ibn Hindu Shāh [Astarabadī Ferishtāh], *The History of Hindostan, from the Earliest Account of Time to the Death of Akbar; Translated from the Persian of Mahummud Casim Ferishtah . . . Together with a Dissertation Concerning the Religion and Philosophy of the Brahmims*, trans. Alexander Dow, 3 vols. (London: T. Becket and P.A. de Hondt, 1770–1772), 2: 81–3.

Alexander Dow was not an orientalist in the mould of the great scholars that followed him, but an incessantly curious British Company man turned academic. Born in Perthshire, Scotland, he reached Bencoolen (now Benkulu, Indonesia) as a young sailor. He quickly became secretary to the governor and his path through the ranks commenced. He left Indonesia and joined the East India Company military service in 1760, becoming a captain in 1764 and the much-coveted rank of lt.–col. in 1769.

Dow translated much of the work that makes up his *History of the Decline of the Mogul Empire* while he was living in India. During this time, he noted that it was "unpardonable" that Persian literature wasn't well known in the West. This attitude toward Persian literature informed much of Dow's later work and his substantial efforts in bringing to the European consciousness the historiographies of the East. He had previously studied the Persian language in his own personal time when he was an army officer and considered the language "the most polite and learned as well as the most universally understood in Asia."[1] He was to dedicate this particular translation to the betterment of the public. Dow felt passionately that it was important for the English, whose influence was growing in the subcontinent, to understand the history of India, and to that end his collective works attempted to address that issue.

His praise for the language fell short of the scholars themselves. Dow, like many of his contemporaries, poured scorn on the Mughal diarists and chroniclers, who left the only written contemporary Mughal accounts of great events and great men. Local historians, he noted, were too "diffuse and verbose"[2] citing Abdul Faizal, the author of the history of Akbar, as the chief culprit.

Dow uses, for the most part, the works of "Mahummud Casim Ferishta"[3] who is described as a citizen of Delhi during the reign of Jahāngīr (1605–1627) around the early seventeenth century. Dow's intention was to write a canonical history of India of the period in question but before the translation was complete, an injury forced him back to England and he had only completed one volume of his work. Dow wanted to write the complete abridged history, so, before his return to England, he petitioned the Mughal emperor for the necessary source material in manuscript form. However, he was forced to return before any response was forthcoming.

Dow admits that the work, though subtitled the *Present State of Hindostan*, is in reality a history of the Mughal Empire in India, and hardly mentions the Hindus. Ferishtāh, his chief source of information, collected the accounts from various other Persian writers but had little knowledge of Sanskrit; so naturally his history was a jaundiced view.

Perhaps because of this, there are some obvious mistakes in the text, some of which are quite glaring errors. The origins of the faith, the history of Gurū Nānak and the description of the *amrit* ceremony are flawed when compared to either Sikh tradition, current practice, or other contemporary accounts. However, the account is notable for a description of Ahmad Shāh Abdālī, a character who figures prominently, in addition to his chief nemeses, Jassā Singh and Nathā Singh, in the Sikh camps. Both these Sikh leaders are discussed in terms of their standing in the eyes of the common Sikh peasantry and the tactics and battle stratagem they employed.

———

However, Abdalla is, at present, at peace with Kerim, and has taken that favorable opportunity for invading Hindostan.[4] He had, in April 1767, defeated the Seïks in three different actions,[5] and advanced to Sirhind, about forty crores [sic] from Delhi, with an army of fifty thousand horse. It is supposed that Nigib ul Dowla, who, in the name of the present emperor's son, manages the affairs of Delhi, had, as he himself was hard pressed by the Seiks and Jates, called in Abdalla, to take upon him the government. Nigib ul Dowla, by our best intelligence, marched out of the city to meet his ally, with forty thousand men. The armies lay in sight of one another, and they were busy in negotiation, and in settling a plan for their future operations. Abdalla, in the mean time, wrote circular letters to all the princes of India, commanding them to acknowledge him KINGS OF KINGS, and demanding a tribute. Suja ul Dowlat, in particular, had received a very sharp letter from him, upbraiding him for his alliance with INFIDELS,[6] and demanding the imperial revenues, which that suba had converted to his own use for some years back.

Such was the situation of the affairs of Ahmed Abdalla, by our last accounts from Delhi. This prince is brave and active, but he is now in the decline of life. His person is tall and robust, and inclinable to being fat. His face is remarkably broad, his beard very black, and his complexion moderately fair. His appearance, upon the whole, is majestic, and expressive of an uncommon dignity and strength of mind. Though he is not so fierce and cruel as Nadir Shaw, he supports, his authority with no less rigor, and he is by no means less brave than that extraordinary monarch. He, in short, is the most likely person now in India, to restore the ancient power of the empire, should he assume the title of king of Delhi.

The SEIKS border upon the Indian dominions of Abdalla. That nation, it is said, take their name of SEIKS, which signifies DISCIPLES, from their being followers of a certain philosopher of Thibet,[7] who taught the idea of a commonwealth, and the pure doctrine of Deism, without any mixture of either the Mahommedan or Hindoo superstitions. They made their first appearance about the commencement of this century, in the reign of Bahadar Shaw,[8] but were rather reckoned then a particular sect than a nation. Since the empire began to decline, they have prodigiously increased their numbers, by admitting proselytes of all religions, without any other ceremony than an oath, which they tender to them, to oppose monarchy.[9]

The Seiks are, at present divided into several states, which in their internal government are perfectly independent of one another, but they form a powerful alliance against their neighbors. When they are threatened with invasions, an assembly of the states is called, and a general chosen by them, to lead their respective quotas of militia into the field; but, as soon as peace is restored, the power of this kind of dictator ceases, and he returns, in a private capacity, to his own community. The Seiks are now in possession of the whole province of Punjab, the greatest part of Moultan and Sind, both the banks of the Indus from Cashmire to Tatta, and all the country towards Delhi, from Lahore to Sirhind. They have, of late years, been a great check upon the arms of Abdalla; and, though in the course of the last year they have been unsuccessful against that prince in three actions, they are, by no means subdued, but continue a severe clog upon his ambitious views in India.

The chief who leads at present the army of the Seiks, is Jessarit Singh;[10] there is also one Nitteh Singh,[11] who is in great esteem among them. They can, upon an emergency, muster 60,000 good horse; but, though in India they are esteemed brave, they chuse rather to carry on their wars by surprize and stratagem, than by regular operations in the field. By their principles of religion and government, as well as on account of national injuries, they are inveterate enemies of Abdalla, and to the Rohilla powers.[12]

To the east of the dominions of the republic of the Seiks lie the countries which are possessed by the Rohilla Afgans. Nigib ul Dowla, whose history is comprehended in the preceding sections, is, from his power, as well as from the strength of his councils and his own bravery, reckoned their prince. He possesses the city of Delhi, in the name of the family of Timur, together with a considerable territory around it, on both the banks of the Jumna, and his revenues amount to one crore of roupees. He publickly acknowledges the unfortunate Shaw Allum, at Allahabad, king, and allows a pension to his son Jewan Bucht, who, without any power, maintains a kind of regal dignity at Delhi.[13]

Nigib ul Dowla has been known, when hard pressed by his hostile neighbors, to raise 60000 horse; but his revenues are not sufficient to support one tenth of that number. He continues to take the field under the name of buckshi, or captain-general of the Mogul empire; and though he has not the power, or perhaps the inclination, to assist the king, he keeps up a friendly correspondence with him, and, without any necessity, professes obedience and a shew of loyalty.

NOTES

1. Shāh [Astarabadī Firishtāh], *The History of Hindostan*, 1: i.
2. Ibid., 1: ii.
3. See also part VI, chapter 34.
4. Ahmad Shāh Abdālī invaded India for the eighth time in December 1766. His prime minister, Shāh Vālī Khān, wrote to Lord Clive (the British Governor of Calcutta) on April 8,1767, and stated the purpose of this expedition as being "for the extirpation of the ill-fated Sikhs." *Calendar of Persian Correspondence: volume 2 (1767–9)* (Calcutta: Superintendent Government Printing, 1914), letter 284, 2:85.
5. These encounters actually occurred in May 1767, following Sikh incursions into Najīb ud-Daulā's (q.v.) districts of Sāhranpur, Āmbetah, and Nanautāh, followed by an attack on Meerut. He approached Ahmad Shāh and sought his assistance against the Sikhs. Abdālī took up the opportunity with zeal and they defeated the Sikhs in several running battles. One eyewitness estimated the Sikh losses at 9,000 (Miskīn, 267–8, quoted in Gupta, *History of the Sikhs*, 2: 246). However, the Sikhs continued their harassment tactics which, combined with the oppressive burning heat of the Punjab plains that was growing daily, was enough to force Ahmad Shāh to return to Kābul. In the following year, Najīb ud-Daulā admitted his inability to cope with the Sikhs in a letter to the Queen-Mother of Shāh Ālum II: "To this hour her servant has manifested unshaken loyalty to the House of Timur. And his services, however poor or inconsiderable, have yet been zealous and sincere. Hitherto he has preserved the Royal domains, and what he has been able to give, he has given. But now Her Majesty must forgive her servant and not expect what he has no ability to perform. The Sikhs have prevailed and they have written to all the tribes in general to join them, pointing to his weakness and encouraging them to cast him out. Her Majesty will consider him now as unable to provide for his own security here [Delhi]." *Calendar of Persian Correspondence: volume 2 (1767–9)*, letter 847, 2:238–9. Najīb ud-Daulā died soon after in 1770.
6. The "infidels" referred to are the British, who became the close allies of Shujā ud-Daulā, the Nawāb Wazīr of Oudh, who was defeated by them at the battle of Buxar in 1764.
7. This is clearly a mistake though Gurū Nānak did visit Tibet during his third tour lasting from 1515 to 1517.
8. Ferishtāh is apparently oblivious to the origins of the Sikhs, which he has placed after 1707, the year Bahādur Shāh came to the throne.
9. The writer has omitted the details of the traditional ceremony called *khande dī pahul*—an initiation combining a *khandā*, an Indian double-edged sword, sweetened water, and the reading of select scriptural compositions. Oaths regarding obligations and duties would certainly have formed an important aspect of the ceremony. The emphasis given by the writer on the oath to oppose monarchy is likely to have stemmed from the fact that the ruling authorities of the day were the most vehement oppressors of the Sikhs.
10. Jassā Singh Āhlūvālīā (1718–1783), the fourth *Jathedār* (supreme leader) of the *Buddhā Dal* (army of the veterans).
11. This is a possible reference to Natthā Singh, a contemporary of Jassā Singh Āhlūvālīā. Natthā Singh is described as an associate of Bhīmā (also Bhumā) Singh Bhangī, the founder of one of the most prominent and powerful *misls*. Natthā Singh died c. 1750.

12. A despatch written from Calcutta on behalf of Lord Clive to the Nawāb Wazīr of Oudh, dated February 14, 1767, identifies one of the reasons for the enmity between the Sikhs and Ahmad Shāh: "He has received his [the Nawāb's] letter to Lord Clive with the papers of news enclosed. Is extremely glad to know that the Shah's progress has been impeded by the Sikhs. If they continue to cut off his supplies and plunder his baggage, he will be ruined without fighting, and then he will either return to his country or meet with shame and disgrace. As long as he does not defeat the Sikhs or come to terms with them, he cannot penetrate into India. And neither of these events seems probable since the Sikhs have adopted such effective tactics, and since they hate the Shah on his account of his destruction of Chak [Amritsar]." *Calendar of Persian Correspondence: volume 2 (1767–9)*, letter 52, 2:20.

13. The famous poet, Mīr, recorded the following observations while living in Delhi, shortly after the third battle of Pānīpat in 1761: "Two days before his departure Ahmad Shah Abdali nominated Prince Jawan Bakht heir-apparent of Shah Alam, entrusted administration of the city to Najīb ud-Daulā, and then marched away. On the way Zain Khān Afghan, of his own race and tribe, was appointed Subedar of Sarhind. He advanced towards Lahore. As the arrogance of these people had passed beyond limits, God dishonoured them at the hands of the Sikhs. They formed a body of low-born people, weavers, carders, drapers, brokers, grocers, carpenters, highwaymen, peasants, needy, mean, jungle, disgraceful, base and penniless persons. Nearly 40 to 50 thousand Sikhs opposed his grand army. While fighting they were wounded, but they would never turn their back. Sometimes they would disperse and would capture one or two hundred Abdali soldiers and would put them to sword. They would raise a calamity for them in the morning, and in the evening would fall upon them from all four sides. They harassed Abdali's troops so much as they found it difficult to escape. At times they would attack Abdali camps, and at other times they would swoop upon a city and pillage it. With loose beards and hair tied in a knot on the head they would launch an offensive. Hue and cry continued the whole night, and in the day there were frightful screams of lamentation and grumbling. The Sikh infantrymen would strike the Abdali horsemen with a sword. The saddles of their horses were covered with blood. The ordinary Sikh soldiers would drag away Abdali's archers and would inflict upon them all kinds of afflictions. In short these mean people brutalized and disgraced the insincere (Afghans) to such an extent that they lost all prestige in the eyes of chiefs if the neighbourhood. The Durranis could no dare fight them in a pitched battle. To escape with their lives was considered a good fortune. Having entrusted the government to a Hindu they made good their escape. The Sikh army, looting and plundering, pursued them up to the Attock. Having beaten and punished the Abdalis severely they seized this province, worth two crores annually. After a few days the unfortunate Hindu (governor) of Lahore was beheaded, and the Sikhs became the absolute rulers. As there was no other claimant, these mean people divided the country among themselves. They began to bestow favours on their subjects. For want of administrative experience they granted remission in revenues to the cultivators without any hesitation and themselves lived upon booty." *Mir ki Ap Biti* (Urdu), p. 139–41; quoted in Gupta, *History of the Sikhs*, 2: 258–9.

CHAPTER 30

VISIT TO THE TAKHT AT PATNĀ, 1781

Charles Wilkins, "The Sicks and their College at Patna, dated Benares, 1 March 1781," *Transactions of the Asiatick Society*. (Calcutta: 1788), vol. 1, pp. 288–94.

In 1770, a young Charles Wilkins landed in Bengal and started a career as a writer in the East India Company and a vocation that led him to become one of the leading early orientalists. As one of Warren Hastings's "bright young men," Wilkins lived up to his expectations by paving the way for future generations of orientalists, administrators, and ultimately empire builders. The son of Walter Wilkins, Charles was born in 1750. Like many Englishmen of his day, he was interested in the study of oriental languages. He devoted his leisure hours to the study of Sanskrit and was the first Englishman to acquire a thorough knowledge of the language for which he published a grammar in 1779. Under the patronage of the then governor-general, Warren Hastings, he translated the Hindu religious work, the *Bhagavād-gītā*, and deciphered many Sanskrit inscriptions. He prepared the first Bengālī and Persian types and set up printing presses at Calcutta for oriental languages, also assisting the famous orientalist, Sir William Jones, to found the Asiatic Society of Bengal (later the Royal Asiatic Society of Bengal) and establish the well-known series of the *Asiatick Researches*. Wilkins's observations of the Sikhs, therefore, are particularly important as the work of an individual able to contextualize Sikh practice in a comparative context, a point he makes more than once in this letter.

This short letter sent to the Royal Asiatic Society in London reveals a great deal about eighteenth-century Sikhs. Many of the practices described by Wilkins are identical to modern *gurdwārā* traditions. His description of the service consisting of *kīrtan* (devotional singing) followed by an *ardās* (collective prayer) and concluded by the distribution of *prasād* (sacrament) are identical to the practices carried out in the present day. There is little evidence to suggest that the preceding one hundred years were any different. However, his account does hint at some tantalizing gaps and inferences that are different to modern Sikh practice, for example, his reference to the role of the *Dasam Granth* (or writing of the tenth Gurū) in early Sikh traditions.

Enroute to Banāras, Wilkins enters what he calls a "Sikh college" in the center of Patnā.[1] The exact location of this "college" is difficult to assess: the only clue left by Wilkins is its proximity to the Custom House. This would point to the old part of the city. Not unsurprisingly, the five major shrines in the city are situated within the older part of the city, most of them associated with the birth and early life of Guru Gobind Singh. The principal shrine in this area is *Takht Srī Harimandar Sāhib* and the oldest is *Gurdwārā Pahilā Barā Gāi Ghāt*. Both of these shrines would have been in existence at the time of Wilkins's visit, and the *Nirmalā* shrine *Gurdwārā Bāl Līlā Mainī Sangat* near *Takht Harimandar Sāhib* could also have been the "college" Wilkins visited. Indeed, given the *Nirmalās'* primary engagement as preachers, this shrine is a very likely contender. *Gurdwārā Gurū kā Bāgh* and *Gurdwārā Srī Guru Gobind Singh Ghāt* situated in the old part of the city were also likely to have been in existence in 1781.

While Wilkins does not give exact geographical information about the site of the "college," he does give a great deal of detailed architectural information. Unfortunately, every one of the *gurdwārās* mentioned has been replaced by a new building in recent years, so the architectural evidence does not help in establishing which shrine he actually visited. In some cases, the destruction of the old structure was due to ignorance, in others, it was due to the devastating earthquake that struck Bihār in 1934.

Unlike many of his contemporaries, Wilkins writes kindly of the Sikhs. This is probably due to the friendly reception and pleasant manners of the two Sikhs who provided him with much of his information during his visit. All too often, early writers would take a much harsher stance based on incomplete and biased information, invariably obtained from chance meetings with a few militaristic Khālsā Sikhs or worse still, from their enemies.

The information given by Wilkins deviates from modern Sikh practice in two respects. His description of the role of the scripture includes the *Dasam Granth*, while current Sikh practice does not give the text a specific role. His observations are, however, entirely consistent with those of John Malcolm and the contemporary practice of the *Buddhā Dal*, the Sikh warrior collective. He also makes reference to a living Gurū or spiritual guide. Given that this "college" was a centre of teaching and learning, the central role of the Sikh teacher called *Gurdev*, broadly equivalent to *Ustād* and *Achāreyā* in the Muslim and Hindu traditions respectively, may have been confused with the word Gurū.

Wilkins's work on the Sikhs, being one of the earliest accounts that dealt with issues other than military and political, was a long-standing primary source for future writers. He presents an unprejudiced view of the Sikhs and of their practices, so much so that even amongst later missionary activity in India, his influence quite drastically informed views on Christian missionary policy on the Sikhs. In a 1814 article titled "Important Documents Relating to the Seeks in India,"[2] Wilkins's account was quoted along with extracts from the Edinburgh Review of *Sketch of the Sikhs* by Lt. Col. Malcolm. The introduction reads: "To those who wish the propagation of Christianity throughout the world, it must be gratifying to hear of any facts or circumstances favourable to that object." Then follow extensive extracts with the article concluding: "It has not been our object to give a particular history of this sect, which has become a nation in India; but to mention such facts as afford ground to hope that the efforts to introduce Christianity among the natives in that part of the world will not be in vain." It continues further, "The success of Nanac shows that the habits and prejudices of the Hindoos are not so immutably fixed as many in Great Britain have imagined. The pacific character of Nanac, and the approach of his doctrines to those of Christianity, are circumstances remarkable and important; and we need more information on the subject, than we now possess, to account for them without the aid of inspiration. As the dispersion of the Jews facilitated the spread of the gospel among the Gentiles in various parts of the world, so the existence of the Seeks may yet facilitate the spread of the gospel in India. It is devoutly to be desired, that nothing may be done on the part of Christians to introduce their religion among the nations of India, which shall tend to impress a belief that Christianity is less tolerant, mild and pacific, or in any respect less worthy of reception, than the religion of Nanac. Besides, the account we have of the principle doctrines of the Seeks, should excite our gratitude to the common Father of our race, that he has, in one way or another, diffused some correct ideas of himself, more extensively than has been generally known or supposed by Christians."

To
SECRETARY *to the* ASIATICK SOCIETY
S I R,
BEFORE I left *Calcutta*, a Gentleman, with whom I chanced to be discoursing of that sect of people who are distinguished from the worshippers of *Brăhm*, and the followers of MAHOMMED by the appellation Seek, informed me that there was a considerable number of them settled in the city of *Patna*, where they had a College[3] for teaching the tenets of their philosophy. As *Patna* was on my way to *Banaris*, I no sooner arrived there than I inquired after the College, and I was presently conducted to it; and I now request you will please to lay before the Society, the few observations and inquiries which a single visit of about two hours would admit of my making. If, such as they are, they should hereafter be found useful either as a clew to guide another in his researches in the same path, or to add to some future account to render

it more complete, my end in troubling you to lay it before the Society is fully answered.

I have the honor to subscribe myself,

S I R,

Your most obedient humble Servant,

CHARLES WILKINS

Banaris, 1st March 1781.

I FOUND the College of the *Seeks*, situated in one of the narrow streets of *Patna*, at no very considerable distance from the Custom-house. I was permitted to enter the outward gate, but, as soon as I came to the steps which led up into the Chapel, or public hall, I was civilly accosted by two of the Society. I asked them if I might ascend into the hall. They said it was a place of worship open to me and to all men; but, at the same time, intimated that I must take off my shoes.[4] As I consider this ceremony in the same light as uncovering my head upon entering any of our temples dedicated to the Deity, I did not hesitate to comply, and I was then politely conducted into the hall, and seated upon a carpet, in the midst of the assembly, which was so numerous as almost to fill the room. The whole building forms a square of about forty feet, raised from the ground about six or eight steps. The hall is in the center, divided from four other apartments by wooden arches, upon pillars of the same materials, all neatly carved. This room is rather longer than it is broad. The floor was covered with a neat carpet, and furnished with six or seven low desks, on which stood as many of the books of their law; and the walls, above the arches, were hung with Europe looking glasses in gold frames, and pictures of *Mussulman* Princes,[5] and *Hindoo* Deities. A little room, which, as you enter, is situated at the left hand end of the hall, is the chancel, and is furnished with an altar covered with a cloth of gold, upon which was laid a round black shield over a long broad sword, and, on either side, a *chowry* of peacock's feathers, mounted in a silver handle. The altar was raised a little above the ground, in a declining position. Before it stood a low kind of throne plated with silver; but rather too small to be useful; about it were several silver flower pots and rose-water bottles, and on the left hand stood three small *Urns* which appeared to be copper, furnished with notches to receive the donations of the charitable. There stood also near the altar, on a low desk, a great book of a folio size, from which some portions are daily read in their divine service. It was covered over with a blue mantle, on which were printed, in silver letters, some select passages of their law.[6]

AFTER I had had a long conversation with two of the congregation, who had politely seated themselves, on each side of me, on the carpet, and whom I found very intelligent, notice was given, that it was noon and the hour of divine service.[7] The congregation arranged themselves upon the carpet, on each side of the hall, so as to leave a space before the altar from end to end. The great book, desk, and all, was brought, with some little ceremony from the alter, and placed at the opposite extremity of the hall. An old man, with a reverend silver beard, kneeled down before the desk with his face towards the altar; and on one side of him sat a man with a small drum, and two or three with cymbals. The book was now opened, and the old man began to chant to the time of the drum and the cymbals; and, at the conclusion of every verse, most of the congregation joined chorus in a response, with countenances exhibiting great marks of joy. Their tones were by no means harsh; the time was quick; and I learnt that the subject was a Hymn in praise of the unity, the omnipresence, and the omnipotence, of the Deity. I was singularly delighted with the gestures of the old man: I never saw a countenance so expressive of infelt joy, whilst he turned about from one to another, as it were, bespeaking their assents to those truths which his very soul seemed to be engaged in chanting forth. The Hymn being concluded, which consisted of about twenty verses, the whole congregation got up and presented their faces with joined hands towards the altar, in the attitude of prayer. A young man now stood forth; and, with a loud voice and distinct accent, solemnly pronounced a long prayer or kind of liturgy, at certain periods of which all the people joined in a general response, saying *Wā Gooroo!*[8] They prayed against temptation; for grace to do good; for the general good of mankind; and a particular blessing to the *Seeks*: and for the safety of those who at that time were on their travels. This prayer was followed by a short blessing from the old man, and an invitation to the assembly to partake of a friendly feast. The book was then closed and restored to its place at the altar, and the people being seated as before, two men entered bearing a large caldron, called a *Curray*,[9] just taken from the fire, and placed it in the center of the hall upon a low stool. These were followed by others with five of six dishes, some of which were of silver, and a large pile of leaves sewed together with fibres in the form of plates. One of these plates was given to each of the Company without distinction, and the dishes being filled from the caldron, their contents were served out till every one had got his share: myself was not forgotten; and as I was resolved not to give them the smallest occasion for offence, I ate up my portion. It was a kind of sweetmeat, of the consistence of soft brown sugar, composed of flower and sugar mixed up with clarified butter, which is called *Ghee*. Had not the *Ghee* been rancid I should have relished it better. We were next served with a few sugar plums; and here ended the feast and ceremonies of the day. They told me the religious part of the ceremony was daily repeated five times.[10] I now took my leave, inviting some of the principal men amongst them, who were about to return to their own country through *Banaris*, to pay me a visit.

In the course of the conversation I was engaged in with the two *Seeks* before the service, I was able to gather the following circumstances. That the founder of their faith was called *Nāneek Sah*, who flourished about four hundred years ago at *Punjab*, and who, before his apostasy, was a *Hindoo* of the *Kshétry*, or military tribe; and that his body disappeared as the *Hindoos* and the *Mussulmans* were disputing for it; for upon their removing the cloth which covered it, it was gone. That he left behind him a book,[11] composed by himself, in verse and the language of *Punjab*, but a character partly of his own invention; which teaches the doctrines of the faith he had established. That they call this character, in honor of their founder, *Gooroo-Mookhee*:[12] *from the mouth of the preceptor*; that this book, of which that standing near the altar, and several others in the hall, were copies, teaches that there is but one God, omnipotent and omnipresent; filling all space, and pervading all matter; and that he is to be worshipped and invoked. That there will be a day of retribution, when virtue will be rewarded and vice punished, (I forgot to ask in what manner); that it not only commands universal toleration, but forbids disputes with those of another persuasion. That it forbids murder, theft, and such other deeds as are, by the majority of mankind, esteemed crimes, against society; and inculcates the practice of all the virtues, but particularly an universal philanthropy, and a general hospitality to strangers and travellers. This is all my short visit would permit me to learn of this book. It is a folio Volume, containing about four or five hundred pages.[13]

THEY told me further, that some years after this book of *Nāneek Sah* had been promulgated, another made its appearance, now held in almost as much esteem as the former.[14] The name of the author has escaped my memory; but they favored me with an extract from the book itself in praise of the Deity. The passage had struck my ear on my first entering the hall, when the students were all engaged in reading. From the familiarity of the language to the *Hindoovee*, and many *Shanscrit* words, I was able to understand a good deal of it, and I hope, at some future period, to have the honor of laying a translation of it before the Society.[15] They told me I might have copies of both their books, if I would be at the expence of transcribing them.

I NEXT inquired why they were called *Seeks*, and they told me it was a word borrowed from one of the commandments of their founder which signifies "*Learn thou;*" and that it was adopted to distinguish the sect soon after he disappeared. The word, as is well known, has the same import in the *Hindoovee*.

I ASKED them what were the ceremonies used in admitting a proselyte. A person having shewn a sincere inclination to renounce his former opinions, to any five or more *Seeks* assembled together, in any place, as well on the highway as in a house of worship, they send to the first shop where sweetmeats are sold, and procure a small quantity of a particular sort, which is very common, and as I recollect, they call *Batāsā*,[16] and having diluted it in pure water, they sprinkle some of it on the body, and into the eyes of the convert, whilst one of the best instructed repeats to him, in any language with which he is conversant, the chief canons of their faith, exacting from him a solemn promise to abide by them the rest of his life.[17] This is the whole of the ceremony. The new convert may then choose a Gooroo,[18] or preceptor, to teach him the language of their scriptures, who first gives him the alphabet to learn, and so leads him on, by slow degrees, until he wants no further instruction. They offered to admit me into the Society; but I declined the honor; contenting myself with the alphabet which they told me to guard as the apple of my eye, as it was a sacred character. I find it differs but little from the *Dewnagur*. The number, order and powers, of the letters are exactly the same. The language itself is a mixture of *Persian, Arabic*, and some *Shanscrit*, grafted upon the provincial dialect of *Punjab*, which is a kind of *Hindovee*, or, as it is vulgarly called by us, *Moors*.

NOTES

1. Patnā, today in the Indian state of Bihār, remains an important city for Sikhs. It was visited by Gurū Nānak and Gurū Tegh Bahādur and was the birthplace of Gurū Gobind Singh (born on December 22, 1666). A critical centre of commerce and manufacturing, the Patnā of the seventeenth and eighteenth centuries had many diasporic communities including *Nānakpanthīs* at the time of the Gurūs. The city of Patnā has acquired a special status as one of the four *takhts* (spiritual thrones) of the Sikhs, Takht Srī Harimandar Sāhib is located there.

2. *The Christian Disciple*, No. 9, vol. II (September 1814), 269–71. We are grateful to Thomas Belz for providing this information.

3. It is not entirely clear from Wilkins's account whether he visited the original Takht Srī Harimandar Sāhib before it was rebuilt by Mahārājā Ranjīt Singh in the 1830s, or whether he is referring to a Sikh *Dharamsālā*, or *Taksāl*, that also existed in Patnā. Mention is made by L.S.S. O'Malley of the *Dharamsālā* (here called a *sangat*), which was managed by *Nānakpanthīs* or *Nānakshāhīs*. "Patna is famous as being the birth-place of Govind Singh, the great Sikh leader, who was born in 1660, in a house near the Chauk. Ranjīt Singh built or renewed a temple over the spot, and the lane is now called Har Mandir *gali*. It consists of a shrine, a gateway and a residence for the Mahanth [custodian], and in the

centre of the courtyard stands a high flag-staff of *sal* wood presented by Jang Bahādur of Nepal . . . Another *sangat* near the Har Mandir belongs to the Nanakshahi Sikhs; in its garden is a sacred tree, which is believed to have sprung up miraculously from Govind Singh's tooth-pick." L.S.S. O'Malley, *Bengal District Gazetteers: Patna* (Calcutta: Bengal Secretariat Book Depôt, 1907), 211.

4. Wilkins evidently did not display the same level of conceit as Lord Dalhousie, the governor-general of India who oversaw the annexation of the Punjab in 1849. In his diary, he writes of a post-annexation visit to the Golden Temple in Amritsar: "Camp, Lahore, *December 1ˢᵗ*, 1850.They invited me to visit the very shrine itself—the centre of Sikhery—the Holy of Holies of the Gooroo Nanak. I would not go last year, for there is taking off of shoes. I might have walked in with my boots if I had liked; but of course I was not inclined to commit an act of such bad taste and bad policy, and I did not think proper to *take off* my shoes before them as other Europeans do, so I did not go at all. This year they suggested a salvo, and sent me down a pair of grand blue velvet boots, without soles! (for leather is the uncleanliness). These I put on, and we visited the shrine." *Private Letters of the Marquess of Dalhousie*, ed. J.G.A. Baird (London: William Blackwood and Sons, 1911), 146.

5. The 'Mussulman Princes' that Wilkins mentions were probably portraits of the Gurūs painted in the Mughal style. The famous *Nirmalā* scholar, Pandit Tārā Singh Narotam, listed such a portrait of Gurū Gobind Singh in a list of relics conserved in Patnā Sāhib. "10. A picture of Gurū Jī that Bahādur Shāh ordered from an Italian artist and which he delivered at Patnā Sāhib during his passage." Pandit Tārā Singh Narotam, Gurū Tīrath Samgrahi (Kankhāl: Srī Nirmal Panchāyātī Akhārā, 1883), 128. The current whereabouts of this portrait is unknown. We are grateful to Francisco Jose Luis for this information.

6. The following remarks of Monier Williams almost a hundred years later bear a strong similarity to what Wilkins observed. Even though the Akālī guardian that Monier met is conspicuously absent in Wilkins's account, the importance of the traditional weaponry and the *Dasam Granth* in both accounts cannot be overlooked: "The temple dedicated to the tenth Guru Govind, at Patna, was rebuilt by Ranjít Singh about forty years ago. I found it, after some trouble in a side street, hidden from view and approached by a gateway, over which were the images of the first nine Gurus, with Nanak in the centre. The shrine is open on one side. Its guardian had a high-peaked turban encircled by steel rings (cakra), used as weapons. He was evidently an Akali—or 'worshipper of the timeless God'—a term applied to a particular class of Sikh zealots who believe themselves justified in putting every opponent of their religion to the sword . . . On one side, in a small recess—supposed to be the actual room in which Govind was born more than two centuries before—were some of his garments and weapons, and what was once his bed, with other relics, all in a state of decay. On the other side was a kind of low altar, on which were lying under a canopy a beautifully embroidered copy of the Adi-Granth and the Granth of Govind. In the centre, on a raised platform, were a number of sacred swords, which appeared to be as much objects of worship as the sacred books." Williams, *Religious Thought and Life in India*, pt. 1, 174–5.

7. Like most Sikh places of worship, the daily service would be run according to a specific daily, weekly and monthly timetable. Special reverence is not associated with noon, which in this instance may have been a local practice to suit local needs.

8. The congregational prayer, or *ardās*, is normally conducted at the end of each part of the daily service and has remained as such since Wilkins reported it in the latter half of the eighteenth century. An early nineteenth century observer of the Sikhs made the following comments on the *ardās*, laying particular emphasis on the military aspects which Wilkins does not appear to have witnessed. "The Sikhs are not enjoined to observe many forms or prayers. I observed that generally in the evening they offered up a short orison, which, in conformity to the military complexion thrown over all their acts, they repeated, firmly grasping with both hands their swords, and which concluded with a vociferous invocation to their gúrú for victory, and the extension of the faith." Charles Masson [pseud.], *Narrative of Various Journeys in Balochistan, Afghanistan, and the Panjab*, 3 vols. (London: 1842), 1: 424.

9. A *karāhī*, or large iron cauldron.

10. Being the second of the four *takhts*, the daily routine would invariably be spread to cover the whole day and timetabled to accommodate the visiting congregation.

11. Wilkins is probably trying to describe the origins of the *Ādi Gurū Granth Sāhib* (or *Gurū Granth Sāhib*).

12. The *Gurmukhī* script, used for writing the words of the Gurūs, is commonly believed to have been developed by Guru Angad, the second Sikh Gurū. However, there is strong evidence to suggest that Gurū Nānak himself developed the script, which was in existence previously. It has a close relationship to other scripts, e.g. *Landā* and *Tākrī* (a branch of *Shardā* used in Chambā and Kāngrā).

13. The standard printed version of the *Ādi Gurū Granth Sāhib* now has 1,430 pages. There would have been many variations in page length in manuscript copies.

14. This is a reference to the *Dasam Granth*, also known as *Dasam Pātshāh kā Granth* or Book of the Tenth King. This work is a collection of compositions attributed to the Tenth Gurū, Gurū Gobind Singh. According to Kesar Singh Chhibbar in his *Bansāvalīnāmā Dasān Pātshāhīān Kā*, the *Dasam Granth* and the *Ādi Gurū Granth Sāhib* sat in *gurdwārās* separately. Then, in 1698, the Sikhs according to Chhibbar, proposed to Gurū Gobind Singh that the two be bound together in one volume. But the Gurū spoke, "This one is *Ādi-Gurū Granth*, the root book; that one [the *Dasam Granth*] is only for my diversion. Let this be kept in mind, and let the two stay separate." The only Sikhs in modern times who attach any significant importance to the *Dasam Granth* are the Akālī Nihang Singhs of the *Buddhā Dal* (q.v.), whose reputation in relation to safeguarding the tenets of Gurū Gobind Singh have been noted specifically in most historic accounts of the Sikhs.

15. There is no record of Wilkins ever accomplishing this task. According to an article in *The Illustrated London News*, other Europeans did obtain a copy of the *Dasam Granth*: "Sir John Malcolm, while in the Punjaub in 1805, succeeded in procuring a copy of the 'Adi-Gurunth' from a Chief, who sent it to him at night, after having obtained a promise that that he would treat the sacred volume with great respect. A Mr. Colebrook, with persevering assiduity, was able to procure not only the 'Adi-Gurunth,' but the 'Das'ama Padshah Ka Gurunth'—the two most sacred books of the Sikhs." *The Illustrated London News*, April 4, 1846, 221. Sir John Malcolm (1769–1833), the author of *Sketch of the Sikhs*, has reproduced extracts from the *Dasam*

Granth, most notably from the largely autobiographical *Bachitra Nātak* or the "Wonderful Drama." Although he has not named his source, some of the translated passages are remarkably similar to the translation prepared by John Leyden (1775–1811), a British orientalist. His translation of the complete *Bachitra Nātak* (which he calls *Sri Bichetra-Natuk by Guru Govind Sing*) is held in the Mackenzie Collection, Oriental and Indian Office Collection, British Library, Eur Mss Mack XL, part 6. It is possible that Malcolm requested the translation to be used in his *Sketch*, which was first published in *Asiatick Researches* in 1810. Mr Colebrook, who is also mentioned in *The Illustrated London News* article is probably Henry Thomas Colebrook (1765–1837), who presented his collection of 2,749 manuscripts to the British Library in 1819.

16. *Patāsā*—sugar crystals, used in the preparation of the *amrit* ceremony, known as *khande dī pahul*, or sword baptism.

17. The description of the *amrit* ceremony lacks essential details, the most significant being the lack of any mention of a *khandā* (double-edged broad sword) and the recitation of selected passages from both the *Gurū Granth Sāhib* and the *Dasam Granth* by the *Pañj Piāre*, or Five Beloved, in the preparatory stages of the amrit. These omissions are probably due to Wilkins's short visit, being only two hours or so. Nonetheless, it is remarkable that he has obtained what he did, given his unfamiliarity of the subject.

18. Wilkins here appears to be making reference to the *Gurdev*, or teacher, when he mentions *Gooroo*. This would have been a common feature of traditional Indian learning centres, also known as *Dharamsālās* or *Taksāls*. The tradition still continues today.

CHAPTER 31

MEMOIRS OF A MUGHAL
NOBLEMAN, 1786

Irādat Khān, *A Translation of the Memoirs of Eradut Khan, a Nobleman of Hindostan, Containing Interesting Anecdotes of the Emperor Aulumgeer Aurungzebe, and of his successors, Shaw Aulum and Jehaundar Shaw, in which are Displayed the Causes of the Very Precipitate Decline of the Mogul Empire in India*, trans. Jonathan Scott (London: for John Stockdale, 1786), pp. 58–64.

The translator of this work was the talented orientalist and linguist, Jonathan Scott.[1] Arriving in India in 1772, Scott's linguistic talents, primarily in Persian—the language required by aspirants in the diplomatic service in India—lead him to the post of Persian secretary to Warren Hastings, the governor-general of India.

With such luminaries as Sir William Jones, Henry Vansittart, Charles Wilkins, Jonathan Duncan, and others, he founded the *Asiatic Society of Bengal* in January 1784. This event was probably the scholarly highlight of his career in India, as the following year he returned to England. The next twenty years were spent in writing and other academic pursuits. His publications were predominantly translations of Persian works, exploiting his mastery of the language and included a translation of Ferishtāh's *History of the Deccan* (see part VI, chapter 34), and an edition with introduction and additions of the *Arabian Nights*. Between the years 1802 and 1805, he was Professor of Oriental Languages at the RM College and at Haileybury, thereby passing on his talents to generations of Company men, and Indian civil servants to come. Jonathan Scott died in 1829, aged seventy-five.

Scott's translation reproduced here is an abridged version of the *Tārīkh-i-Irādat Khānī*, an undated Persian manuscript in the Oriental Public Library, Patnā, Bihār. Also known as *Maqtal us-Sālatīn*, the manuscript covers the period 1707–1714 during the chaos in the Mughal hierarchy following Emperor Aurangzeb's death.

The memoir's author, Mīr Mubārak Āllāh Irādat Khān, was a high ranking Mughal, well-connected to Aurangzeb's family, and intimately acquainted with Commander Mun'im Khān. His father and grandfather were noblemen of high rank. The former held various offices of importance under the emperor Shah Jahān, and the latter was paymaster general to Jahāngīr. That Irādat Khān was present in the Mughal army at the battle of Lohgarh against Bandā Singh Bahādur makes this account of particular importance.[2]

At this crisis, intelligence arrived that the Siks[i] had risen in rebellion. This sect of infidels,[3] known also by the names of Nannukkea and Gooroh,[4] had long been established in the soubah of Lahore, by a teacher styled Nannuk. Of his descendants was the present chief,[5] to whom had flocked great crowds of all ranks, resigning to his disposal, with blind fidelity, their lives and properties. Thus supported, he excited sedition, and took arms to extend his errors, and overturn the basis of the true faith. He engaged Vizier Khan, the fojedaur of [ii]Sirhind, who was killed in the action, with numbers of his followers; after which the gooroh possessed himself of the town of Sirhind, and many districts of Doaub, as far as[iii] Boreah, Saarunpore, and Shawdouah, on both banks of the river Jumnah, where he committed unlimited excesses, razing all public edifices, as mosques, colleges, mausoleums, and palaces, killing or taking prisoners the faithful of every age and sex, and plundering with the most cruel severity. The oppressions of these wretches were every day increasing, and there was no nobleman daring enough to march from Dhely against them. Asoph ad Dowlah Assud Khan, who governed that capital, shewing great signs of fear, the inhabitants were alarmed and began to fly, with their families and effects, towards the eastern provinces, for shelter from the impending storm. All this being represented to the emperor[6] in the highest colours, his majesty thought it best to march in person against the insurgents: for this reason, he resolved for the present to lay aside the design of totally expelling the rajapootes, and to confirm their allegiance, by winking at their offences, till a more convenient opportunity of punishment. These zemindars had, for generations, been used to obey, and had not, in fact, either fortitude or ability to oppose openly the emperor of Hindostan, whose appearance against them in arms would have been sufficient to curb their insolence; but the khankhanan,[7] alarmed at the insurrection of the Siks, did not properly reflect on that circumstance, and descended to shew the rajapootes such favours as were inconsistent with good policy, as well as the dignity of the sovereign: but he was not alone to blame, as there were other agents in this business. The four princes were constantly intriguing against each other, to obtain influence in the management of public affairs, which occasioned much delay and confusion in business, so that the khankhanan thought it happy to steer his vessel safe through four such [iv]seas; and could not act so independently for the public good as he wished, being obliged to attend to the capricious interests of

---

[i] They now possess the provinces of Lahore, Multan, and part of Dhely, plundering as far south annually as Rohilcund.

[ii] A considerable town, about fifty coss N. of Dhely.

[iii] These districts are now held by Zabtah Khan, a Rohilla chief, who however pays a tribute to the Siks, and it is said has entered into their sect.

[iv] Meaning the power and influence of the four princes.

others, among which he found it difficult to preserve his own. Among the remarkable occurrences of the expedition into Dekkan, was the decline of Jehaun Shaw's influence with his father, and the rise of that of Azeem Ooshawn, of whom till now the emperor had ever been suspicious. The prince Jehaun Shaw was of haughty and independent spirit, ready to take fire on the smallest neglect. This, with the behaviour of his servants, alarmed and displeased the khankhanan, who, for his own safety, watched an opportunity to destroy his influence in public affairs: a task of no great difficulty, to one well acquainted with the disposition of Shaw Aulum, almost equally warm with his son, who had more than once displeased him by his behaviour, so that he had expressed to him his dissatisfaction. The prince, upon this, thought to prove his disinterestedness and independence, by neglecting to frequent the durbar, and engage in business as usual. Azeem Ooshawn, who had reaped experience in office, and was well versed in the intrigues of a court, perceiving coolness taking place between Jehaun Shaw and the khankhanan, paid so much flattering attention to the latter, that by degrees he gained his confidence. This gave still more offence to Jehaun Shaw, who had too much pride to expostulate, but neglected the minister in return. He soon after fell sick, and his indisposition continuing a long time, gave Azeem Ooshawn ample opportunity of acquiring influence over Shaw Aulum, and the favourites whom his majesty trusted with the fullest confidence; while he continued to be pleased with them, but, on the smallest disgust, or in their shortest absence, he forgot them altogether.

Azeem Ooshawn having thus gained the credit he aimed at with his father and the minister, employed it in softening the rigour of government against those who laboured under its displeasure; thinking that, thus obliged by his mediation, they would readily return his favours, by embracing his cause, whenever the death of his father should give him a claim to the empire. It was from this hope, that he advised indulgence to the refractory rajas, and condescended to repair to their camp and conduct them from thence to his father, permitting them to be accompanied by all their troops armed. Such unusual indulgence was far from answering the end expected by the prince, who should have seen, that it could only tend to display publickly the fears of government, and consequently must reflect dishonour on its adviser, and render him weak in the eyes even of those to whom such uncommon honours were allowed. In short, the two rajas, attended by all their followers, paid their respects to his majesty on the line of march, were gratified with his assent to whatever their insolence demanded, and dismissed to their homes with rich presents and assurances of favour.

When this affair was finished, the emperor marched without delay towards Lahore, not even stopping to make an entrance either at Agra or Dhely. In a short time he arrived at Sirhind, which the rebels deserted on his approach, and retired to ᵛDaber, the original residence of their goorroh or chief, where they fortified themselves as strongly as possible.[8] Though this insurrection was not of such importance as to disturb the general repose of the empire, yet his majesty, defender of the faith, hearing that the malice of the rebels was directed at religion, thought it his duty to go against them in person; in this, copying the example of Aulumgeer, who, in the latter part of his reign, appeared at the siege of every fort belonging to unbelievers; otherwise, what ability had a wretched and infatuated rabble to dare the presence of such a glorious monarch? The exertions of one of the principal ameers, or, at all events, of the princes, would have been equal to the extinction of the rebellion, and explosion of the schism.

ᵛ At the entrance of the Sewalic mountains, which connect Hindostan with Thibet.

The imperial army soon arrived within sight of the goorroh's camp, which lay round the walls of Daber on different heights, commanding the passes to that fortress, situated on a summit, surrounded by hollows, craggy rocks, and deep paths. Shaw Aulum had resolved to lie inactive before the enemy for some time, in hopes by this to render them confident, and tempt them to an engagement; on which account he issued positive orders to the princes and all the ameers, not to advance nearer the goorroh's lines on any pretence, however favourable. Some days passed in inactivity, when at length the khankhanan entreated permission of his majesty to advance, with his own followers, to reconnoitre the enemy's position: which was granted, on condition that he should not commence an attack without further orders from the presence. However, when he had arrived within shot of their lines, the enemy began a warm cannonade from their works,[9] while bodies of their infantry on the heights galled him with rockets, musquetry, and arrows. His soldiers, enraged, were not now to be restrained; and the khankhanan, more jealous of his military fame than fearful of the emperor's displeasure, ventured for once to disobey, by giving directions to attack. He dismounted from his horse, and led his brave troops on foot up the most diffi-cult heights, driving the rebels from them with the greatest rapidity and success. This scene passing within sight of the royal camp, the chiefs and soldiers, emulous of glory, waited not for orders, but hastened to join the attack in great numbers; while the emperor and the four princes viewed the sight from the squares of their encamp-ments, with a mixture of anger and satisfaction. At last the enemy were driven from all their works, to the narrow summit round the fort of Daber, where they continued to defend themselves in a desperate manner,[10] but without even the hope of escape from general slaughter; when night coming on, rendered friends and foes undistin-guishable to each other. The khankhanan, sure of having the goorroh in his power, gave orders for his troops to cease the attack, and lie upon their arms in the present position, till the morning should enable him to finish it with success. He had, how-ever, unluckily neglected to block up a narrow path leading from the fort to the hills, either because he had not perceived it, or was satisfied that it could not lead but to where the Imperial troops were posted. The goorroh, a man of great art, generally appeared in the dress and splendor of a prince, when he wished to be public; but, if occasion required privacy, he disguised himself in the habit of [vi] a jogie or synassee, in such a manner, that few, even among his own people, could know him. During the night, he, without acquainting his followers of his intentions,[11] changed his habit, and left the fort undiscovered. The khankhanan, about dawn, renewed the attack, and gained the place, after a short struggle, sword in hand, exulting in the certainty of carrying the goorroh dead or alive to the emperor, whose displeasure at his dis-obedience of orders, would by this service be changed to approbation: but who can relate his weight of grief and disappointment, at finding that his promised prize had escaped, without leaving a trace behind him? The goorroh's speed of foot was uncommon, and he only acquainted with the paths and mazes through the hills that led to the snowy mountains, which he had marked for shelter. The khankhanan lost for an instant almost the use of his faculties, which were absorbed in dread of the emperor's anger, not without reason. As he was, agreeable to custom after an impor-tant victory, beating the march of triumph in his way to the royal tents, orders arrived, commanding him to stop the drums, and not to dare to enter the presence. He retired, drowned in despair, to his own tents; where he had the cruel mortifica-tion of learning every instant, from messengers, that his enemies exulted in his fall

---

[vi] Sects of fakeers, or religious mendicants.

from favour, and openly condemned his conduct with malicious zeal in the presence of his majesty, who was highly enraged against him. But though this did not continue long, and Shaw Aulum, regarding his former services, received him again into favour, after a few days, yet this noble and faithful minister never recovered from the effects of the royal ingratitude. This grief, added to the pain he felt at seeing three of the princes and the ameer al amra using all arts to complete his ruin, stuck like a poisoned arrow in his breast. He lost all satisfaction from worldly enjoyments, the emptiness of which he now so fully experienced, and from the day of his disgrace declined in his health; so that not long after he was reduced to keep his bed, where he lingered a few days, and then resigned his soul to the angel of death; who never, in the uncounted ages of his office, seized on a soul more pure, or less defiled with the frailties of human nature.

NOTES

1. *Dictionary of Indian Biography*, s.v. "Jonathan Scott."
2. *The Encyclopaedia of Sikhism*, s.v. "Tārīkh-i-Irādat Khānī."
3. The term "infidels" is not an uncommon expression used by Muslim writers in early accounts of Sikhs.
4. Possibly a reference to the more common terms *Nānakpanthīs*, the followers of Nānak's way, or *Gur Sikhs*, the Gurū's Sikhs.
5. Bandā Singh Bahādur (q.v.), the military leader of the Sikhs after Gurū Gobind Singh, but neither a Gurū or a descendant of Gurū Nānak.
6. Bahādur Shāh (q.v.).
7. Wazīr Jumlat-ul-Mulk Munim Khān Khān-i-Khānan.
8. In December 1710, the Sikhs retreated towards Lohgarh, in the hills near Sadhaurā, and commenced fortifications in anticipation of an engagement. Writing about the initial skirmishing that took place before the arrival of Bahādur Shāh on December 9, Khāfī Khān lamented, "It is impossible for me to describe the fight which followed. The Sikhs in their fakir dress struck terror into the royal troops. The number of the dead and dying of the Imperialists was so large that, for a time, it seemed they were losing ground." Khāfī Khān, *Muntakhabu'l Lubāb*, 669–70, quoted in Singh, *Life of Banda Singh Bahadur*, 93.
9. The use of artillery was introduced by Gurū Gobind Singh as shown by a *hukamnāmā* (the written orders of the Gurūs) to the Sikh community of Lucknow dated February 19, 1694, which requests them to send him one cannon and ammunition. Loehlin, *The Granth of Guru Gobind Singh*, 66. A visitor to the Punjab almost a century after this account was published notes what may have been the cannon of Gurū Gobind Singh: "In the corridor which divides the two apartments there is an ancient Sikh gun, supposed to be of the time of Govind Singh, the last of their Gurus, or teachers, who died A.D. 1708. In the centre of this gun are two lions, each bestridden by a warrior with a drawn sword in his hand." Mrs J.C. Murray, *Our Visit to Hindostan, Kashmir, and Ladakh* (London: Aynsley, 1879), 61.
10. The battle is described by Khāfī Khān: "Coming out of the fort with all alacrity, enthusiasm and inclination, they raised the cry of '*Fat'h Darshan*,' [and] '*Sachchaa Badshah*,' at the time of battle, and like insects threw themselves madly and bravely upon the fire of artillery and the edge of the sword

and the tips of arrows and spears. They launched rank-shaking assaults on the imperial entrenchments, and everyday many were killed. Some Muslims also earned the eternal merit of martyrdom." Majida Bano trans., "Bandā Bahādur and his Followers: From Khāfī Khān, *Muntakhabu'l Lubāb*" in ed. J.S. Grewal and I. Habib, *Sikh History from Persian Sources* (New Delhi: Tulika, 2001), 156–7.

11. Gulāb Singh Bakhshī, who bore a resemblance to Bandā Bahādur, offered to sacrifice his life for the good of the mission. He dressed himself in the garments of Bandā and seated himself in his place, thereby allowing his leader to effect his escape in the early hours of the day. A similar strategy was employed by Gurū Gobind Singh at the battle of Chamkaur in December 1705, where Sangat Singh assumed the appearance of the Gurū in front of the enemy forces.

CHAPTER 32

A MUSLIM ACCOUNT OF
SIKH HISTORY, 1789

Ghulām Hussain Khān, *A Translation of the Sëir Mutaqharin*, trans.
M. Raymond [Hajee Mustapha, pseud.], 3 vols. (Calcutta: printed by James
White, 1789), pp. 1: 19–20, 22–3, 71–2, 87–97; 3: 137–9, 207–13, 319–27.

The translator, identified as the French Creole, M. Raymond[1] who
assumed the pen name Hajee Mustapha, carried out an incredibly difficult
translation from Persian into English, neither of which was his first language.
Despite this, the translation is a skilled one. He admits in the preface to not
being English, never having been to England and was self-taught in both
English and Persian, the language of Ghulām Hussain. In the early 1780s,
Raymond was the Master of the Eastern Library and of a "cabinet of eastern
curiosities." He further notes that during the period of Warren Hasting's
Governorship (1772–1784), he was asked to curate a collection of Persian
manuscripts, miniatures, and other antiquities largely because he was one of
the few Europeans that understood Persian. His linguistic skills were the
result of private study and he used this new skill to carry out translations and
catalog his rapidly growing collection. However, he lost the entire collection
during the sacking of Jeddah and Mecca in 1770.

At this point, he returned to India and petitioned the English to patron-
ize him. Frustrated at his lost collection, and vowing never to collect again,
he began a new life in some penury in Lucknow. However, during a chance
meeting at a high-society feast, Raymond explains how a decaying book was
thrust toward him. That it contained a Persian language account of the
British Parliament intrigued Raymond, and he quickly broke his earlier vow.
Having procured the other two volumes, he went about completing a translation of the work.

The original author was Mīr Ghulām Hussain Khān, and he notes in the introduction to the original work his lineage and the race he hailed from. Hussain notes that his intention was to furnish to future generations the story of the later Mughals—those kings who sporadically ruled India since the death of the last of the recognized Great Mughals, the Emperor Aurangzeb. Reflecting the contemporary nature of the manuscript (written around 1763), he titled it *Sëir Mutaqherin* or the *Review of Modern Times.*

His account is, in the main, very complimentary towards Gurū Nānak and his teachings but he writes with some derision about the life and times of the other Sikh Gurūs and in doing so betrays his own prejudices. After Gurū Nānak, the narrative jumps to Gurū Tegh Bahādur and covers his execution under the orders of Emperor Aurangzeb. He moves swiftly onto the history of Gurū Gobind Singh but is patchy in his coverage, and includes unconvincing stories that try to explain away the reason for the unshorn hair and blue clothing that distinguish the Khālsā Sikhs.

As one would expect of a courtier of the later Mughals, his treatment of Bandā Singh Bahādur (who he first calls is *Gooroo-govind* then later *Benda*) is quite thorough and contains both praise (for his valor in battle) and slander (for his "infidel" ways and numerous defeats of the Imperial army). He makes it clear that Bandā had instilled fear in the minds of his opponents, and exhibits a palpable sense of relief after his capture and eventual execution in Delhi. These last few days are particularly well written, and are likely to have been based on eyewitness accounts. His report of Bandā's final words before his execution provides a powerful testimony to the nature of the mission of this significant character in Sikh history.

The most unusual and possibly unique aspect of this account is the mention it makes of *Djiven* [Jīvan?] *the Syk* "born at Cabool, of a Catri tribe" who became an accountant in Kashmīr. The writer relates the character and activities of someone who appears to be an important player in eighteenth century Sikh history but surprisingly, no other known account makes mention of this unique character.

The translation also includes the translator's own detailed and often very interesting notes. One in particular that stands out relates to his brief tour inside a *gurdwārā*. His experience is revealing, especially regards the layout of the *gurdwārā*, the *sangat* of Khālsā Sikhs, and the *kīrtan* that he heard. Aside from Charles Wilkins (part VI, chapter 30), this is the only other known eighteenth century European account of a visit to a Sikh place of worship.

The content of the text has been, in many ways, mirrored by the comments in Ferishtāh's *History of the Deccan* (see part VI, chapter 34). The commentary, however historically flawed, is not devoid of value, for the two accounts together do shed light on the nature of Mughal consciousness of the Sikhs in the eighteenth century.

Given that the account reproduced below is not continuous and is taken from various sections and volumes, all of the footnote cues found in the original extract have had to be renumbered (i, ii, etc.) for ease of reference, but with the original cue numbers shown in brackets in the footnotes.

Volume I, section I, pp. 19–20

So much presumption had at last roused the Emperor: He crossed the Nerbedda with intention to chastise the Gentoo Princes, who had so far availed themselves of their distance from court, and the inattention of the times, that they had given battle to the three Sëid Brothers, Ahmed-khan, Hossëin-khan and Qhäiret-khan, who had been all three slain, and all three had on the same day received the palm of martyrdom. This particular had added to the Emperor's indignation, as well as to the apprehensions of those Radjpoots;[i] when an intelligence arrived at court, which made it expedient to temporise with them, and to accept of the submission of those two Princes who payed their homage as the Emperor was passing on his Elephant. He was then indisposed; but the intelligence engaged him to postpone every consideration in order to smother the fire which Gooroo-govind[2] at the head of his Sycks had raised in the mountains.[ii] That incendiary had got himself followed by the Radja and inhabitants of that snowy-country; and he had slain, in battle, Vezir-khan, the Fodjar of Ser-hend. The Emperor, shocked at their ravages; ordered Assed-khan and Zolficar-khan to ascend those mountains, and to blockade, on all sides, the strong hold in which the Gooroo had shut himself up; but in the night, the Radja, who was acquainted with a particular path, found means to elude the enemy's vigilence, and to escape, with all his followers, of whom only a few were intercepted: a neglect that very much affected Assed-khan's character. The Emperor finding that no glory was to be acquired in that country, left Rostem-dil-khan in it, with a body of troops, and turned towards Lahor; and it was in that city that Assed-khan departed this fragile-world. His office of Lieutenant General to the Emperor, was given to Hedäiet-aaly-khan, son to Enaïet-eddin-khan; ard he was installed in it with a rich dress of honor. Qazi-eddin-khan likewise departed his life in his Government of Goodjrat. The Emperor was then encamped on the Banks of the Ravi, the river that flows at Lahor; and it was there that Rostem-dil-khan had the assurance to shew his face at court, after having had the meanness to quit his post, and that too without leave. His impudence met with what it deserved: He was deprived of his grade, command, and Djaghir, and confined in the citadel of Lahor; and Mahmed-amin-khan was sent in his stead.

Volume I, section I, pp. 22–3

Five years had already elapsed since the Emperor's accession to the throne, and it was the third year since he was encamped on the Ravi, close to the city of Lahor, when some alteration was perceived in his mind. It was about the middle of Muharrem, in the year 1124 of the Hedjra. One day he took into his head to give orders for killing all the dogs in camp, as well as all those in the city of Lahor. As such an order, from so sensible a

---

[i] (28) Radj-poots, signify issue of Radja or King. They are the military tribe of India, tall, lean, robust, courageous men, who, very different in that from the Brahmanical race, make no difficulty to eat meat, although living in general upon vegetables.

[ii] (29) This Gooroo-Govind, or Bishop Govind, was then at the head of the Sycks, men, who, after having been Mendicants about three hundred years ago, became soldiers in the sequel, and form now a powerful commonwealth, that has sent more than once sixty thousand horses in the field.

Prince, could not appear but very strange, people were willing to account for it by supposing that some witchcraft or enchantment had been practised upon his person. Such a state of things was the more disagreeable, as the Syks were becoming equally numerous and troublesome: Forbidden from coming in to the city of Lahor, not one of them was to be seen in the day-time; but as soon as it was dark, they never failed to return to the houses of those that used to feed and cherish them; and this manege lasted during the whole night; for at daybreak they would throw themselves in the Ravi,[iii] and after having swam on the other side, they lurked in the neighbouring fields.

THESE manoeuvres of the Syks, as well as the tumult in the Cathedral, I have mentioned upon the faith of a letter which Amin-ed-döoola, of Sambal, had written to his children, and which I have found at length in the papers of his secretary. The latter says, that the Emperor incensed against the Doctors that had excited the tumult which had cost the reader's life, had ordered some of them to be thrown into a prison, and some others to be sent to the fortress of Gooaliar. Sometime after the Emperor having felt a slight indispotion, of which no one suspected any ill, he at once fell into a swoon, in which he suddenly departed from this world, to hasten to a corner of the mansions of eternal mercy. It was the 19th of Muharrem, about two hours before night.

Volume I, section I, pp. 71–2
At last Emir-djemlah and the Emperor with some others who expected great things from him, contrived, or at least thought they had contrived, a scheme for parting the two brothers, whose union and presence had become formidable. It was proposed to Hosseïn-aaly-khan, the youngest, to undertake an expedition against Radja Adjet-sing-rhator, a powerful Hindoo Prince, who since the demise of the Emperor Aorengzib, had assumed great airs of independence, and had been guilty of some unwarrantable actions, such as demolishing Mosques in order to raise idol-temples on their ruins; and all that in the very middle of Oodeïpoor, his capital. Such excesses had necessarily passed unnoticed during the whole reign of Bahadyr-shah, who being eternally involved in civil wars, or busy in destroying the Syks, had no attention to spare for so inferior an object: for the Syks from a fraternity of mendicants, had in his time become a whole army of Bandities, which ruined and desolated the whole province of Lahor.

Volume I, section I, pp. 87–97
In the year one thousand one hundred and twenty-eighth of the Hedjra,[3] that is in the fifth year of Feroh-syür's, a bloody action happened in the plains of the Pendjab, between the Sycs and the Imperialists, in which the latter commanded by Abdol-semed-khan, a famous Viceroy of that province, gave those inhuman free-booters a great defeat in which their General Benda, fell in to the victor's hands. This barbarian, whom nature had formed for a butcher, trusting to the numbers and repeated successes of those other butchers he commanded, had exercised upon the people of God cruelties that exceeded all belief, laying waste the whole province of Lahor: flushed with victories, he had even aspired to a crown; and we shall say something of his history and person. He was a Syc by profession, that is one those men attached to the tenets of Gooroo-govind[iv] and who from their birth or from the moment of their admission,

---

[iii] (30) This circumstance of whole multitudes throwing themselves into a large river, and swimming over, must not surprise the reader. There are so many rivers, lakes; ponds, and waters in India, that every man knows how to swim; and in Bengal, all swim, from the oldest women to the children of four years old.

[iv] (79) The words Gooroo-govind may be rightly translated by those of Bishop Govind. The Gentoos without coming to any particulars, make however a kind of confession on visiting their Gooroo, and this always is done by prostrating the whole body at full length on the ground, with the hands joined and stretched behind the head.

never cut or shave either their beard or whiskers or any hair whatever of their body. They form a particular society as well as a sect, which distinguishes itself by wearing almost always blue cloaths,[v] and going armed at all times. These, when once admitted into that fraternity, never make any difficulty of mixing or communicating with one another, of whatever tribe or clan or race they may have been hitherto; nor do they ever betray anything of those scruples, precautions, and antipathies and customs[vi] so deeply rooted in the Gentoo mind, whatever diversity or opposition there may have hitherto been in their tenets, principles, or common way of life. This sect or fraternity, which spread itself far and near about the latter part of Aorengzib's reign, reckons for its insti- tutor a Gooroo-govind, one of the successors of Nanec-shah, the patriarch of the sect; and here is what we know of this Nanec-shah. He was son to a grain-merchant of the Catri tribe; and in his youth he had been as remarkable for a good conduct and a laud- able character, as well as for the beauty of his face, and the sensibleness of his repar- tees[vii]: Nor was he destitute of money. There was then in those parts a Fakir or religious of note, called Sëid-hassen,[4] a man of eloquence as well as wealth, who having no chil- dren of his own, and being smitten with the beauty of young Nanec, upon whom chanced to cast his eyes, conceived an affection for him, and charged himself with his education. As the young man was early introduced to the knowledge of the most esteemed writings of the Musulmen, and early initiated in the principles of their most approved sophies[viii] and contemplatives, he improved so much in learning, and became so fond of his books, that he made it a practise in his leisure hours, to translate literally or virtually, as his mind prompted him, such of those maxims, as made the deepest

---

[v] (80) It is true that they wear only a short blue jacket, and blue longdraws: but they use likewise the yellow and the white in their turbans, as well as the blue, although by the by the latter is the general colour.

[vi] (81) These scruples and antipathies are so rooted, that even those that become christians at Pondichery and elsewhere, are not to be reasoned with on that head. A Gentoo will abstain not only from any thing prepared or even touched by an European, but even from his water- pot, his knife, his cloaths; and likewise from any thing prepared or touched by any person of a different tribe, or even by a person they are not familiar with, be he of their own tribe. The Brahmans alone or the Levitical tribe are out of this rule. They eat nothing but what they have themselves prepared, but every other tribe deem it an honor and blessing to receive it at their hands; and hence the reason why Brahman cooks are in such high repute.

[vii] (82) The Musulmen, and probably it is the descendants of those so inhumanly used by the Syc's, tell strange things of this surprising beauty of young Nanec's, and of the affection it kin- dled in his tutor's breast; and these things although so very incredible in England, would have nothing surprising in India. The Sycs are silent on that head, and bring Nanec at once from the age of twelve to that of thirty, at which time he had followers. There is another religion, of very great pretentions in this world and of still greater ones in the other, which very prudently leaps from the first year of its Patriarch to his twelfth, and then again, takes another mighty jump up to his fiftieth year, where his history is closed: so important it is that the particulars of the spring, and summer, and even of the autum of a legislator's life should be concealed by a venerable cloud of impenetrable obscurity, Of all the patriarchs, none has ever had his whole life written with any detail but Confu-tse or Confucius, and Mahomet; this last, in the most circumstantial detail that has ever existed.

[viii] (83) The word Sophi from which the Greeks have made Sophos, has at all times, signified a wise man, contemplatif and virtuous; but as these people made it a point to wear nothing but woollen stuffs or camblets, called sofss all over Turkey and Persia, it is not impossible but the garment should have communicated its name to the men. Hence there are in English such words as black-friars and white-friars; this much is certain, that one of the first, bravest, and most virtuous Emperors of the Turks, was called or surnamed, sofi because he wore nothing but sof. It was Soltan-Morad, the first.

impression upon his heart. This was in the idiom of Pendjab[ix], his maternal language. Little by little he strung together these loose sentences, reduced them into some order, and put them in verses; and by this time he had so far shaken off those prejudices of Gentilism which he had imbibed with his milk, that he was become quite another man. His collection becoming numerous, it took the form of a book, which was entitled Grent, and became so famous in the times of Soltan Babr, as to give celebrity to its author, who from that day was followed by multitudes of spectators or well wishers. This book is to this day held in so much veneration and esteem amongst the Sycs, that they never touch or read it, without putting on a respectful air and posture. And in reality, as it is a compound of what he had found most valuable in those books which he had been perusing, and it is written with warmth and eloquence; it has necessarily all the merits and attractions peculiar to truth and sound sense.

In times of yore, the religious persons of that fraternity, Could not be distinguished either in their garb or their usages from the Musulmen fakirs; nor is the difference easily perceptible even to this day. They live in communities both in villages and towns; and their habitations are called Sangats[x] where we always see some one that presides over all the rest. Nanec, their Patriarch left only two children, one of whom when grown-up, used to amuse himself with hunting and all the other pleasures of high life; and in this he has been imitated by his descendents to this day, all of whom are reputed heirs and partakers of his authority. The other son, having addicted himself to a religious life, and taken up the garb of it, his followers have done the same, and look to all intents and purposes like so many Musulmen Fakirs.[5] But what is strange, Nanec-shah had not for his immediate successor either the one or the other of his children, but only a servant of his, called Angad, who sat on the patriarch's carpet with full authority[xi]. The ninth in succession from this Angad was one Tygh-bahadyr,[xii] who was of such an extraordinary character, as drew multitudes after him, all which as well their leader went always armed. This man finding himself at the head of so many thousands of people, became aspiring; and he united his concerns with one Hafyz-aadem, a Musulman Fakir, and one of those that stiled themselves of Sheh-ahmed-serhindi's fraternity. These two men no sooner saw themselves followed by multitudes, implicitly addicted to their chief's will, than forsaking every honest calling, they fell a subsisting by plunder and rapine, laying waste the whole province of Pendjab: for whilst Tygh-bahadyr was levying contributions upon the Hindoos, Hafyz-aadem was doing the same upon the Musulmen. Such excesses having soon attracted the notice of the crown-officers, gazetteers and intelligencers, they wrote to the Emperor Aorengzib that these two men made it a practice to live by plunder and

---

[ix] (84) The Pendjebi is a dialect of the Hindostany, but like all the languages of Hindostan, sonorous, soft and melodious.

[x] (85) The word Sangat, signifies, together and also fraternity: It comes from sang which signifies with, as well as sat.

[xi] (86) This right of siting upon another's carpet implies the right of succeding to his rights and authority; and this ceremony and expression is spread all over the East, from whence it has been brought to the confines of Europe, where we see the Crim-tartars using the same ceremony. As the Khans of the Crim-tartars, as well as all the Tartarian Princes, deduce their pedigree from the famous conqueror Djenghis-khan, we see that when they intend to acknowledge a new Khan or King, they make him sit upon a small carpet which has served to that ancestor of their's, and four men raising the carpet and the new king as high as they can shout out in the middle of the Coorooltäy or assembly: Choc-yasha: live long. A shout that is, echoed by the rest, but as a carpet four hundred years old would not stand such a test, it is always placed upon a new one.

[xii] (87) Tygh-bahadyr signifies a valiant blade.

sac: in answer to such an advice, the Emperor commanded the Viceroy of Pendjab, residing at Lahor, to seize these two miscreants, and to send the Musulman to the country of Afghans, quite up to the last limits of Hindostan, beyond the Atec,[xiii] with defense to him to cross it again under pain of death. Tygh-bahadyr, the other free-booter, he was to send prisoner to the castle of Gooaliar. The Governor executed his orders punctually. Some days after there came an order to the Governor of Gooaliar, to put Tygh-bahadyr to death, to cut his body into four quarters, and to hang them at the four-gates of the fortress: a sentence which was literally executed.[6] But this execution was followed by mournful consequences. Hitherto the Sycs had always worn the Religious garb without any kind of arm or weapon at all: but Gooroo-govind having succeeded to his father, distributed his numerous followers by troops, which he put under the command of his best friends, to whom be gave orders to provide themselves with arms and horses. As soon as he saw them accoutred and mounted, he commenced plundering the country, and raising contributions. But he did not go long unpunished; the Fodjdars of the province joining together, fell upon those free-booters, and soon dispersed them; but Gooroo-govind's two sons having fallen alive in their hands, were put to death. The father's situation was now become full as dangerous: hunted down every where like a wild beast, he retired to a strong hold which secured his person for the present, but at the same time, precluded his escaping to his country and family beyond Serhend; the country betwixt being full of troops and garrisons. The man prompted by his critical situation, applied to the Afghan-mountaineers that live behind Serhend, and he promised them a large sum of money, if they could contrive to carry him to a place of safety. A number of these accepted the bargain, and coming down from their mountains, they engaged him to let grow his beard, whiskers, and every other hair of his body; and when they saw it of a proper length, they put upon him a short blue garb like that used among those highlanders, brought him out of his strong hold amongst themselves, and made him traverse the whole country, not only with perfect safety, but also with honour. For whenever any one put any question about this man which they payed so much respect to, they would answer, that he was a Pir-zada or Holy-man of their's, the Pir-zada of Ootch. Gooroo-govind having been so lucky as to extricate himself out of so great danger, conserved the Afghan garb in memory of that event; and he even made it henceforward the distinctive garb of his followers, no one of which could be admitted into it, unless his hair and beard proved of the proper length, and his garb of the proper pattern. But the loss of his children had made so deep an impression on his heart, that he lost his mind, fell in demence, and shortly after died of grief and sorrow;[7] he was succeeded by Benda, that butcher-like man, of whom we have spoken above. This infernal man having assembled multitudes of desperate fellows, all as enthusiasts, and all as thirsty of revenge as himself, commenced ravaging the country with such a barbarity as had never had an example in India. They spared no Musulman; whether man or woman or child. Pregnant women had their bellies ripped open, and their children dashed against their faces or against the walls. The Emperor, (and it was the mild Bahadyr-shaw) shuddered on hearing of such atrocious deeds. He was obliged to send against those barbarians not only the troops of the province, but entire

---

[xiii] (88) This river, the Indus of the ancient is the same as the Sind which passes at Bacar, and Tatta, and empties itself by two mouths into these, one of which is that of Divel. It bears the name of Atec only in these parts where it serves as boundary to the Empire of Hindostan: for to-day as well as two thousand years ago none could be ferried over without a pass from the Governor of a Fort, Hence called Atec from the verb Atecna to stop or to be stopped.

armies, and these too, commanded by Generals of Importance, such as the Lord of Lords, Munaam-qhan, who at the head of thirty thousand horses enclosed that scelerate in the fort of Loohgar, where he besieged him. The man after having defended himself for some time, contrived to give him the slip by an expedient in which he shewed as much sagacity and wisdom as animal courage and prowess. Nevertheless being still pursued, he was encircled again by three Generals that had joined their troops together: it was Mahmed-amin-qhan, Aghyr-qhan, and Rostem-dil-qhan; but his genius fertile in expedients, extricated himself again: Not that he made any stand before the Imperial troops; he hardly gave them an opportunity to see him: Perpetually on the wing, he kept out of their way, when having given them the slip, he suddenly sallied forth at an opposite side, like some savage escaped from the hunter's nets, and then he put every thing to fire and sword, massacreing every Musulman, and destroying every temple and every Sepulchre of their's, which he could find; in so much that his ravages and barbarities seemed to go on encreasing; and such was the state of things, when Bahadyr-shah departed his life. His children, occupied in disputes about the throne, had no attention to spare for Benda, so that his power became formidable at last. On Feroh-syür's accession to the throne, Eslem-khan, Viceroy of Lahor, received orders to destroy those free-booters; but those free-booters defeated him totally in a pitched battle; and that Viceroy after losing the greatest part of his men, retired within Lahor with his full measure of shame. Benda elated by so unexpected a success, recommenced his barbarities with more fury than ever. It was some time after this battle that Bayezid-khan, Fodjdar of Serhend, hearing of Benda's approach, thought it better to meet him half way; and he was encamped without the walls, when in the evening he retired to a private tent where with a small congregation he was performing the afternoon prayers, when a Syc, as desperate doubtless as any of Hassan-saba's devoted young-men,[xiv] having crept under the wall of the tent, gave him a mortal stab as he was prostrating himself; and in the confusion and surprise which ensued, he retired to his brethren without receiving any hurt. This piece of intelligence having soon reached the capital, the Emperor commanded Abdol-semed-khan, a Tooranian Viceroy of Cashmir, who entertained several thousands of his Country-men, to march against those scelarates; and to encourage him in that expedition, the Emperor sent the patent of the government of Lahor for his son, Zecariah-khan. This General, who since became so famous, had with him several thousand troopers of his nation with several commanders of the highest distinction, such as Kamer-eddin-khan whom we shall fee Vezir-aazem in the sequel, Mahmed-amin-khan and Aghyr-khan: they were at the head of their own troops to which the Emperor added several bodies of his own guards, such as the Vala-shahies, and the Ahedians.[xv]

With such reinforcements Abdol-semed-khan, who waited only for a train of artillery, set out for Lahor, after having appointed for his Lieutenant at Cashmir, his

---

[xiv] (89) Hassan Sirnamed Saba is the man known in the crusades under the name of the old man of the mountains which is a bungling translate of the words Sheh-el-Djebal, the Prince of the hilly country. And as his devoted young men were called its Arabic Hassanin or the Hassanians, this word has given birth to the word Hassasin or Assassin, that signifies a murderer, in six or seven languages of Europe.

[xv] (90) The Emperor's household amounts to forty thousand men, all cavalry, but serving on foot in the citadel in the palace. It consists of several corps such as the Sorqh-poshes or Red-wearers; the Soltanies, or Royals; the Vala-shahies, or high Imperials; the Camul-pushes or Cuirass-wearers; the Ahedians, or Serving single, because these last have the Emperor for their immediate Colonel.

own slave Aref-khan; and taking with him the troops be found encamped at that city, he marched in quest of the barbarians. As he had a good army in which were several thousands of his own country men, these troops fell with such fury upon those wild beasts, and they repeated their attacks with so uninterrupted a perseverance, that they crushed them to atoms; nor did the General give over the pursuit, until he had made an end of them. That miscreant of Benda stood his ground to the amazement of all, and in the first engagement he fought so heroically, that he was very near giving a compleat defeat to the Imperial General; for although beaten and vigorously pursued, he retired from post to post, like a savage of the wilderness from thicket to thicket, losing endlessly his men, and occasioning losses to his pursuers. At last worn down by such an incessant pursuit, he retired to Goordas-poor, the native country of most of those Barbarians, and where their chief had long ago built a strong castle,[8] in which they kept their wives and families with the booty they used to make in their courses. The Imperial General blockaded it immediately, nor was the place unfurnished with provisions; but the multitudes that had successively retired thither were so considerable; and the besiegers kept so watchful a guard, that not a blade of grass, nor a grain of corn could find its way to the fort; and the magazines within being at last emptied of their contents, as the blockade drew to a length, a famine commenced it's ravage amongst the besiegers, who fell a eating any thing that came in their way: asses, horses, and even oxen became food, and what is incredible, cows were devoured. Nevertheless such was the animosity of those wild beasts, and such their consciousness of what they had deserved, that not one of them would talk of a surrender. But every thing within, even to the most venerable, as well as to the most loathsome, having already been turned into food and devoured: and this having produced a bloody flux that swept them by shoals, the survivors asked for quarter and offered to open their gates. The Imperial General ordered them to repair to an eminence, where they would see a pair of colours planted, and where they were to depose their arms and clothes, after which they might repair to his camps. The famished wretches obliged to comply with an order which foreboded nothing good, obeyed punctually; like beasts reduced to their last shift; and having been made fast hand and foot, they were made over to his Moguls or Tartars, who had orders to carry them close to the river that ran under their walls, and there to throw the bodies, after having beheaded them all. The officers and principal men were put in irons, and ordered to march in a body, mounted upon lame, worn-down, mangy asses and camels, with each of them a paper-cap upon his head; and it was with such a cortege that the General entered the city of Lahor, which he reached in few days. It happened that Bayazid-khan's mother, an old Tooranian woman, lived in that city; and hearing what had happened, and that her son's murderer was amongst the prisoners, she requested her attendants to point him to her: For, the man having acquired a character amongst his brethren by such a daring action, had been nick-named Baz-sing[9] by them[xvi], and had been promoted to a considerable office. The old women having got upon a terrace that overlooked the street, lifted up a large stone which she had

---

[xvi] (91) The Falcon-Lion, or Lion with the rapidity of a Falcon. These Titles are common all over India, amongst the Gentoos; but specially in Decan, where, any one that has killed a Tyger, without shooting him, is henceforwards surnamed, Matsa. In Hindostan, he that had killed a Lyon with a sabre, pike, or poinard, assumed the Title of Sing, or Lyon; and it is this institution which the Mahometans had in view, when on their making conquests in India, they perceived so many Generals with the Title of Sing. This institution they copied, by giving to their bravest chiefs, the Title of Djung which implies some remarkable character in war and battle: For those of Döoola and Mulk have been copyed from the Qhalifat, or Arabian monarchy.

provided, and being directed by the sound, (for she was blind) she let it fall so luck-ily, that she killed him outright: and the old lady, after this action said, that she would now die satisfied, and revenged. But this action having, as a signal, roused the peo-ple of that city; and the General conceiving that he might lose all his prisoners through the fury of the mob, ordered them to be conveyed to a place of safety amongst the baggage, where they were covered with trappings of elephants, and every thing that could conceal them from the people's eyes. The next day, he set out of the city at day-break, and with the same precaution; his intention being to present them alive to the Emperor: For further precaution, they were put under the care of Camer-eddin-khan, and his own son, Zacariah-khan; and forwarded to the capital; under a strong escort. As soon as they had arrived in the out-skirts of the city, the Emperor sent out Mahmed-amin-khan, with orders to bring them in, mounted as they were; but preceded by a number of heads fixed upon pikes, amongst which should be seen Benda, with his face besmeared with black, and a wooden-cap on his head. That wretched himself, having been brought before the Emperor, was ordered to the castle, where he was to be shut up, with his son, and two or three of his Chief Commanders. The others were carried by a hundred at a time every day, to the Cotvals tribunal, where they were beheaded; until the whole number of them was completed; but what is singular, these people, not only behaved quietly during the execution, but they would dispute and wrangle with each other, who should be executed first; and they made interest with the executioner for that very purpose. In this manner the whole number of these wretched being told over, and every one of them having received what he had so long deserved, Benda himself was produced; and his son being placed on his lap, the father was ordered to cut his throat, which he did with-out uttering one word: Being then brought nearer to the Magistrate's tribunal, the latter ordered his flesh to be torn off with red-hot pincers; and it was in those tor-ments that he expired, his black soul taking its flight by one of those holes towards the regions for which it seemed so well fitted. It is reported, that Mahmed-amin-khan, having had the curiosity to come close, and to look at the man, was surprised at the nobleness of his features. Struck with such an appearance, he could not help speaking to the wretch. "It is surprising, said he, that one that shews so much accute-ness in his features and so much abilities in his conduct, should have accumulated upon his head a multitude of horrid crimes that would ruin him infallibly in this world as well as the other; crimes that had brought him at last to so excruciating an end." The man with the greatest composure, answered in these terms: "I will tell you, my lord. Whenever men become so corrupt and wicked, as to relinquish the path of equity and to abandon themselves to all kinds of excesses, then it happens in all coun-tries and in all Religions, that providence never fails to suscite such a murderer as me, whose only office is to chastise a race become totally criminal; but when the measure of punishment has been filled, then the butcher's office ceases, and his mission is over: and then that same providence never fails to suscite such a mighty man as you, whose mission is to lay hold of the Barbarian, and to consign him to condign pun-ishment."

"Why should this oppressor's haughtiness and violence last so long?
Is it because God Almighty's scourge strikes without a sound?"

After having been carried thus far by a digression which we thought we owed our readers upon the Sycs, it is but natural that we should revert to the thread of our his-tory, especially as the dissentions at Court carried a most threatening aspect, and seemed to presage infinite ills to the whole Empire.

Volume III, section II, pp. 137–9

We have left Mir-Mannoo nearly absolute Viceroy of both Mooltan and Pendjab. He resided at Lahor, where having mounted his horse to take an airing, he went out of the city, and put his horse on a gallop; when he was suddenly seized by a fit of apoplexy, which ended at once in a palsy, that stopped him short; so that all he could do was to continue his voyage into eternity. This event is recounted in a different manner by a person in his service, who was very familiar with him: he says that Mir-Mannoo was encamped, and that he took horse to look at the troops of one of his commanders, encamped within a short distance, where he sat down to a dinner. The entertainment proving sumptuous, and consisting of a great variety of precious dishes, he tasted of every one; in the evening, he got upon his horse to go home, and put it to a gallop; and he was actually galloping, when finding something that pained him within, he alighted, stretched himself upon the ground, and in a few moments expired. The Abdali king hearing of this sudden death, conferred the government on Mir-Moomen, son to the deceased; and as he as yet a child, he recommended him to his mother together with the whole country. It must be observed that the deceased governor, keeping always a great army on foot; and being engaged besides in a variety of heavy expences, which the revenues of the country could no support; he had betaken himself to the expedient of oppressing and squeezing the body of farmers, as well as the people in general. But his credit was so strong at court, that there was no carrying any complaint against him; and on the other hand, it being a standing rule amongst the Syks to support each other at all events, numbers of people who could find no redress any where, and were driven to so much despair, as to cry *famine, famine,* about the streets, very naturally recurred to that fraternity where they were sure of finding some resource. The whole business of admission seemed to consist in putting on a blue coat, letting the hair grow all over the body, and repairing in shoals to Gooroo-Govind; from that moment they became Syks, and were intitled to the protection of the whole body, and looked like men freed from all their miseries. In this manner this sect or fraternity, which was already in vogue, having turned out to be a sure resource against oppression, it grew to an immense number; especially at this time, when the government of a country involved in troubles was to be managed by a woman: and as that sex is destitute of strength of mind, the disorders and troubles continued to increase. Her ministers commonly availed themselves of her retired life and immured circumstances, to render such an account of their respective departments, each in his own way, as served only to perplex and confound her understanding: hence the tenants and farmers became more oppressed than ever; and shoals of people flocking to the Syks, these people grew exceedingly numerous, and commenced talking high to the officers of government. The nobility and principal men of the country, who looked at these desertions with both amazement and disdain, made it a point to stand aloof; whilst the eunuchs, the freed men of the seraglio, and a variety of homely born vile men, took possession of all the affairs. Things were in such a state, when the young Mir-Moomen departed his life; and then the government fell into the hands of Qhadja-Moosa-Ohrari, his brother-in-law. But as Becari-Qhan, who had acted as prime minister under the deceased Viceroy, wanted to render himself master of the government, and he had been intriguing with that view, the governess, who was informed of his intentions; and was already incensed against him, commanded his attendance within the seraglio or sanctuary; and as soon as he was within the gate, she got him surrounded by a number of stout women, who put him to the cudgel so severely that he expired under the operation. A short time had elapsed since this event, when Qhoadja-Abdollah-Qhan, son to Abdol-semed-Qhan, that ancient victorious of Lahor, having found means to seize and confine the governess, contrived likewise to obtain from the Abdali king, the patents of the two governments. But Feraman-Qhan, who had brought those patents to Lahor, having commenced acting with authority, and plundered and ruined numbers of people; the new Viceroy who did not like his presence, and was also seized by the troops, who became clamorous for their arrears, found it was out of his power to satisfy their demands: so that to save his life and honor he fled from Lahor, to the disgrace of all government. In such a confusion of all order, the governess found means to re-assume the command; and having been in a little time put under confinement by Qhoadja-mirza-Qhan, who had been one of the principal commanders in her husband's army, the troubles at last subsided, and a compromise took place between her and that officer.

Volume III, section III, pp. 207–13

The Syks, those people whom we have represented as nearly destroyed under Feroh-Syur, and who in the sequel had availed themselves of Mir-Manoo's neglect, and of the extortionary administration of his officers, to associate with their Sect a great number of farmers, commenced now to raise their heads. Grown exceedingly numerous, and sensible of the weakness of the present government,- as well as little intimidated by the name of the Abdali king, whom they know to be very far off,-they assembled in battle-array, and, falling upon the Abdali governor left at Lahor, they killed him, took possession of the city; and, not yet satisfied, they proclaimed a certain Chinta;[10] a man from among themselves, Emperor; they made him sit upon a throne, struck money in his name, overran the whole province of Lahor, took possession of it, and made it a point to torment the Musselmen by every means in their power. Intelligence of this revolution having been transmitted to Candahar, the Abdali king resolved to make another expedition into Hindostan; and this was his seventh and last: it took place in the year 1175. But as the territory of Lahor was known to be the spot where the Abdalies first of all landed in their expeditions towards Hindostan, the Syks thought proper to evacuate it entirely; and repairing to the country of Rohy, a district of very difficult access, they took possession of a very strong fort in it, and assembled there from all parts, to the number of two lacs of men, cavalry and infantry. But this did not deter the Abdali King; informed of their retreat, as well as of their numbers, he measured ninety cosses of ground in two days;[xvii] and falling upon those free-boaters the moment he was least expected, he drew smoak from their breasts. About twenty thousand of them became food to his famished and thirsty sabre;[11] but the booty was immense, and beyond all computation. After this victory, seeing no enemy in the field, he put every thing to fire and sword in that country, which had associated with those miscreants; and marching back, he planted his victorious standards in the territory of Lahor, where he employed his time in quieting and regulating that country. Mean while he dispatched an Abdali, called Noor-eddin-Qhan, a near relation of his Vizir, towards Cashmir, with orders to bring the Sycks of that country into order and submission. That country was then in the hands of Djiven the Syk.[12] This man, born at Cabool, of a Catri tribe, had been a writer and an accountant in some office under Shah-Veli-Qhan, Vizir to the Abdali king, who sent him sometime after to enforce a payment due by Mir-Mannoo, governor of Lahor; it was in the year 1167. But Abdollah-Qhan having been ordered to repair to Cashmir to take possession of that country, which still acknowledged the authority of Alemghir the Second, Emperor of Hindostan, that general who succeeded in this expedition, dismissed the Indian

---

[xvii] (1) About two hundred and twenty common miles of a thousand paces each.

governor, and appointed in his stead, Qjhodja-Cootchec; giving at the same time the management of the revenue to the Syk Djiven who thereby became Divan or Intendant of the province. After these regulations, he left the new governor a body of Afghans, and returned to his master. But hardly was he departed when troubles arose in Cashmir; in which Djiven the Syk having been deeply concerned, he commenced by killing the commander of the Afghan troops, after which he confined, and then banished from Cashmir, Qhodja Cotchec himself; at the same time he applied to the Vizir of Hindostan, Umad-el-Mulk, requesting to have the patents of the government of Cashmir in his own name; and these being granted without difficulty, the new governor re-establislied every where the Hindostany government ordered money to be coined, and the Qhoodah to be pronounced, in the name of Alemghir the Second. After this he took possession of the revenue office, sent his collectors everywhere, confiscated all the lands possessed in Djaghir by the grandees of the court, and bore an absolute sway in the country.

Such a revolution could not have been brought about, but by a man of abilities; he was besides a well-looking handsome man, naturally good, and of an obliging disposition; and although a Syk, he seemed in his belief and practice much inclined to Masulmanism; for he used to set apart a sum of money for repairing the monuments of the saints of Cashmir, and for putting in order the gardens and seats that surrounded them, and served for public walks. He made it a practice every day to give dressed victuals to two hundred musulmen; and twice in the month he sent qhoans or tables covered with a variety of dishes to a number of persons abroad: naturally beneficent, he gave to every suitor that applied, but always according to his station or necessities. Every week he had a day set apart for hearing and entertaining the Poets of Cashmir. Amongst these he set apart five of the most learned ones to write the history of that country, from the first period in which it received inhabitants down to his time.[xviii]

... The Abdaly king having set a part a body of Abdalies, and two other bodies composed of Ailats of Qhorassan and of Cuzzel-bashes of Herat, gave them to Nooreddin-Qhan, with orders to the bring the Cashmir to a submission; and he directed the Radja of Djamboo to assist the expedition with a body of his troops, who might serve as guides to the others. This Radja had made it a practice whenever any army passed through his territory, to quit the plains, and to retire to a mountainous difficult country, where he eluded every pursuit, some times indeed submitting to send a present in money; and as it was impossible to penetrate into Cashmir without Cashmirians or other guides; and the Syk Djiven had shut up the passage, and placed Cashmirian troops to guard them;[xix] it became impracticable even to approach that country, without the assistance of people accustomed to those mountains. It was with reason, therefore, that the Abdali-king made an application to the Radja of Jamboo for his assistance, and he desired to see him at his court: this request had been made by the channel of Shah-Veli-Qhan the Abdali's Vizir, and the Radja's particular friend; but the Gentoo Prince would not listen to the proposal. At last the Vizir having sent him his own son to be kept in hostage, until he should return safe into his own country, the Radja became easy in his mind, and he gave the information wanted, and added a body of his own troops to serve as guides, throughout those mountainous tracts. The only passage from the Radja's country into Cashmir is by crossing the Chenav, a river that rushes betwixt two abrupt cliffy shores with so much

---

[xviii] (2) There is an history of Cashmir extant, written by a Cashmirian, but different from these five learned men, which reaches four thousand years back.

[xix] (5) Cashmir is a very strong country, and of difficult access.

rapidity and such depth of water that neither man nor animal can pretend to abide it's fury. Across this rapid river the Vizir Shah-veli Qhan, by the Radjah's advice, ordered a number of tall-trees to be stretched from cliff to cliff; to serve as a bridge, whereon the army might pass; and the whole passed accordingly; after which the Radja with his troops retired to his own country. There remained a narrow mountainous passage in which the Syk Djiven had thrown his best troops; and these having been driven away at last after many actions and much bloodshed, the passage was cleared. Noor-eddin-Qhan having persued the run-aways, made a massacre of them; and without allowing them time to take breath, he arrived with them at the city of Cashmir. Here he was opposed by Djiven himself at the head of what force he could collect; but after a slight action, the citizens fled, he fled with them, and in his flight, he was taken prisoner, with the principal men of the country. The king informed of this success of Noor-eddin-Qhan, appointed him Deputy-governor of the whole province; and in the year 1177 he resolved to return to Candahar: quitting therefore the neighbourhood of Lahor, he marched to Cabool; and this is the last time he came into Hindostan, the present being his seventh expedition into that country; for the troubles that had arisen in his absence in Qhorassan, proved so very serious, that he found no time to destroy the Syks and to establish his government in Lahor and Mooltan upon a sure footing; so that these two provinces, as well as the Tatta, being nearly abandoned, and without a military force, they were invaded again by the Syks who returned and established themselves firmly in those tracts. Not but that Prince, as well as his son and successor (Timur-Shah), used sometimes to send bodies of horses into those countries; but it was rather with a view to procure plunder and to raise contributions, than for any solid purpose; and in fact we see, that to this day, which is in the year 1195, those countries have remained unsubdued by the Abdalies; nor is their authority acknowledged there. On the contrary the Syks, become more numerous and more powerful than ever, have established their collectors in every district of those three provinces; and they seem to make no account of any enemies whatever. But then they are no more those Barbarians we have heard of: sensible of the advantages of good government, they have put themselves upon the footing of using the husbandman and farmer with the utmost regard and tenderness; so that those countries are now in the highest degree of culture and population. Nevertheless the mighty city of Lahor has ceased to be what it was: it has lost its populousness and its beauty. Those crouds of nobility and gentry, with all those learned men that[xx] adorned it, have forsaken its walls, and have preferred exile and distress to the dominion of strangers; whilst those that have bowed to the times, and submitted to that humiliation, and to its concomitants, want of employment and want of subsistence, live lurking in the ruins of their tottering habitations; It appears now, (and. I am writing in the year 1195[13]) that the forces of that flaming sword of the state, the Valiant Mirza-Nedjef-Qhan[xxi] Prince of Princes have penetrated into those countries, and engaged the Syks in many actions, and made them feel his consequence. However it is time alone that can determine how these new broils are likely to end.

Volume III, section IV, pp. 319–27

Nedjaf-Qhan, after the conquest of Acber-bad and the fortress of big, had now become a sovereign Prince: intent only on whatever could establish and increase his

---

[xx] (6) Lahor has been one of the Musulman universities of Hindostan; and its title in the imperial Diplomas and registers is Dar-el-Ylm, the habitation of science.

[xxi] (7) These words answer to the Persian words Zulficar-eddöoolah; Mirza Nedjef Khan-Bahadyr, Emir-ul-umrah.

power, his army which he was augmenting incessantly became so numerous, that there is hardly mentioning its numbers without seeming to deal in exaggerations. His two favorite commanders alone, that is Nedjef-Cooly-Qhan and Afrasiab-Qban, were at the head of two corps that could not amount to less than ten or twelve thousand cavalry and as much infantry. It is true they had both been his slave-boys; but it must be acknowledged that their personal prowess and their military talents were such as warranted all that elevation: the former, especially, who bears a distinguished character for a headlong courage, and an irresistible impetuosity; insomuch that it has been more than once observed, that leaving all the other Generals behind, he seemed intent upon equalling his master him-self. Another valorous commander of Nedjef-Qhan's army and as good a soldier as himself, was Mahmed-Beg-Qhan, the Hamadanian, a general who, by the nobility of his race and the frankness of his character, seemed another Nedjef-Qhan: two qualifications in which he was superior to all the commanders of the army, and especially to the two persons just mentioned. There were several other officers of character in that army, most of them being those that had served with honor under Shudjah-eddöoolah, and had fled from his son's capital or from his camp: for instance, the two Ghossäins, who had under their commands a body of six or seven thousand Fakyrs, as brave as themselves. Morteza-Qhan, son to Mustepha-Qhan, that famous general who had cut so great a figure in Bengal, served also in Nedjef-Qhan's army at the head of five thousand men; and one could see in that camp most of Abool-Mansoor-Qhan's descendants: all men of distinction, who tired with the inattention and vile behaviour of Assef-eddöoolah, had fled from that court, and taken shelter in Nedjef-Qhan's army, where they were promoted to commands, every one according to his merit and abilities. To insure the payment of all these numerous troops, Nedjef-Qhan divided his dominions and conquests into so many parts, the revenues of which were assigned to each commander's management. With such an army, Nedjef-Qhan was always in motion, constantly busy in making conquests upon Radja Dehi-Sing-Seväi, and Radja Dehiradj-Seväi, on one hand; and on the other, upon the Radjpoot Princes of Kedjvaha: he beat these Princes in several engagements, and made himself dreaded far and near, about the outskirts of the provinces of Shah-Djehan-abad and Acber-abad. But although he was so successful in the field, he had enemies at court; and these were Abdool-Ahed-Qhan, the Cashmirian, prime minister, and all the grandees of that dastardly court, who were all timorous and all cowardly; but who possessed so far the Emperor's ear, that he did just as they bid. All these, unable to bear Nedjef-Qhan's influence and prosperity, were exciting Zabeta-Qhan to a revolt. It was the same Zabeta-Qhan, who after the death of Hafyz-Rahmet and the ruin of his nation, had become the head of it, the Rohilahs and Afghans flocking to him from all parts, impressed with a sense of respect for his illustrious pedigree, and a warm admiration for his personal character. He is the same man who had been requested from Shudja-eddöoolah by Nedjef-Qhan, and the same who had owed the highest obligations to that conqueror's partiality and patronage; but there was too much of the Afghan in him, not to set all those ties at nought the most distant prospect. In a moment he forgot how highly he was indebted to Nedjef-Qhan; and listening only to the suggestions of Abdol-ahed-Qhan and his confederates, all men as cowardly and as envious as that minister, he parted from his friend and benefactor; and marched off at the head of his national troops, which were considerable.

Nedjaf-Qhan, amazed at his defection, thought his honor concerned in punishing it immediately: the two armies met: a bloody battle ensued, in which the two parties fought with the utmost bravery; and numbers of brave men fell on both fides, after exhibiting feats of valor and prowess: at last the zephir of divine assistance blowing

directly over Nedjef-Qhan's standards, unfurled their folds, and stretched them open
on the gale of victory. A vast number of Rohilahs were put to the sword, with a very
small loss to the victorious; and Zabeta-Qhan[14] with the remains of his troops, which
even now did not amount to less than thirty thousand men, fled to Ghöus-gur, and
shut himself up in that fortress. From thence he wrote to the principal rulers amongst
the Sycks to request their assistance: he even concluded a treaty with them, by which
he subscribed to such tricks, and entered into such close connections with those
people, that a report spread every where, as if he had forsaken the Musulmanism[xxii]
and made himself a member of their community. Whilst he was connecting himself
by such odious ties with these people, Nedjef-Qhan was advancing upon him: that
general, after giving some repose to his victorious troops, besieged him in Ghöus-gur.
The Rohilas had fortified an intrenched camp under the walls of the fortress; and now
sure of a retreat, they for a whole month together kept Nedjef-Qhan at bay, sallying
out every day to skirmish, and even coming several times to a general engagement.
It is true that they were always beaten, but as true that they always made good their
retreat within their intrenchments. By this time, however, their numbers were so
thinned, that Zabeta-Qhan thought proper to submit, and to propose terms. He
received some officers for hostages, and sent to visit Nedjef-Qhan; but the latter having declined the proposals he had brought, the other asked leave to return, which
being granted immediately, he returned to his camp: there he assembled his own
commanders as well as those of the Sycks that had just come to his assistance, and he
informed them of his being resolved to perish rather than to submit. This declaration
having been received with applause, and with promises of standing by him with their
lives, the next morning, he came out of his camp, preceded by his artillery and a body
of men armed with such rockets and such other missiles as remained to him. Nedjef-
Qhan on his side, glad to see them coming to a fair engagement, arranged his troops,
and taking a body to which he trusted, he pushed before the rest and charged the
enemy, himself the foremost. This appearance intimidated the Rohilahs, who being
valorously charged every where, lost their wonted courage, and were mowed down
by thousands; insomuch that this battle became similar to that famous one, at
Panipoot, where the Abdalies put an end to the Marhatta power, and destroyed their
numerous army. Nedjef-Qhan's soldiers, as much incensed as their master at the perfidy and ingratitude of the Afghans, followed them every where; resolved to make an
end of the enemy. The engagement lasted, without interruption, the whole of that
day: Nedjef-Qhan killed several men with his own hand, and seemed to contend for

---

[xxii] (1) The Sycks are Deists in the strictest sense of the word, and of course, perfectly tolerant and harmless; although as soldiers, they are, like the Marhattas, merciless plunderers, and
incessant skirmishers. The ceremony of the reception of a Proselyte consists in no more than
these two articles: to put on a short dress, of a blue colour, from head to foot; and to let one's
hair grow from head to foot, without ever cutting or clipping or shaving it. One day I got within
one of their temples, invited thereto by the tingling of the cymbals: on appearing within the
door, an old venerable man bid me leave my slippers, as none could enter, but bare-footed. This
admonition I obeyed, and went into a hall covered with carpets, at the northern part of which,
there were several cushions covered with a yellow veil, under which, I was told, lay Nanec-Shah's
book, who is their legislator. At the southern end of the hall, there were fifteen or twenty men
all in blue, and with long beards, sitting, some armed and some not. At the eastern side, but
very near to it, two old men with a small drum and a pair of cymbals, were singing some maxims of morality out of that Book, and this they did with a deal of enthusiasm and contortion.
On getting within the hall, I saluted the company, which returned the salute, and returned it
again when I came out.

the palm of personal prowess with his most forward commanders. This day having put an end to the power of Zabeta-Qhan, as well as to the courage of his new allies, the latter retired to their homes; and Zabeta-Qhan took shelter in the fortress, with all those who had escaped by favour of the darkness. The next morning he sent to camp an humble message, in which he supplicated Nedjef-Qhan's forgiveness; the latter granted it, but would treat no more, and commanded his attendance. Zabeta-Qhan, having no other party left, put on an humble dress, and presenting himself before Nedjef-Qhan in a supplicating posture, he obtained his pardon. Sending then for his people from the fortress, and for his family, he lived a long time in the conqueror's army, entirely unnoticed. In the sequel, he found means to betroth one of his daughters to Nedjef-Cooly-Qhan, who had become Nedjef-Qhan's adoptive son, and acted as his lieutenant-general: and this alliance having facilitated another, he likewise engaged Nedjef-Qhan himself to accept his sister, by which means he came into favour again, and was complimented with the fodjdary of Soharen-poor-booria.

All this while Abdool-Ahed-Qhan was so far master of the Emperor's heart and mind, that he governed the houshold and the court with a single nod of his head; but his main business seemed to be to demolish Nedjef-Qhan's power and influence. He was perpetually upon the watch to hurt him, like a serpent rolled upon itself; but the late victory entirely damped his ardour. As soon as he heard of this total defeat of Zabeta-Qhan, a man on whose pride and prowess, as well as that of his national troops, he had so much relied for humbling Nedjef-Qhan to dust, he concluded that it was preposterous in him to contend any more with so successful a rival: but, as at the same time this defeat of the Rohilahs had also greatly weakened the Sycks, their new allies, he resolved to avail himself of this event; and he concluded that the best party he could take would be to put himself, with the young Shahzadah, at the head of an army, with which he might, by marching up to Ser-hend, subdue a power that seemed to be already in distress: for he reckoned that after having brought them to terms of submission, he might join their forces to his victorious troops, and then fall at once upon his odious rival. This design having been approved by Shah-Aalem, that prince ordered his elder son, Djuvan-Baqht, and his younger son, Ecber-Shah, to join the minister; and the latter was already encamped in the out-skirts of the city, when he published, that "whoever was a soldier would find service in his camp, and ought to come to his standard." The city being full of military men, who breathed nothing but war, his camp was soon filled with a mighty army; and as soon as it was known that there was a perfect concert between the Emperor and him, several commanders who resided in the country, and some others who had a character, but were accustomed to live by war, came from far and near, and joined his troops; so that the encamped army received daily additions. The Emperor, at the same time, having laid his commands on Nedjef-Qhan, the latter sent a body of his own troops to join the Imperial prince; and by such a step, he gave the expedition an air of concert which in reality it had not. The minister having by these means furnished himself with feathers and wings, pushed forwards; and in emulation of Nedjef-Qhan's boldness he advanced beyond Serhend; where, instead of seeking the enemy, he commenced a negotiation with the principal of the Syck rulers;[15] he made a muster of his power, and exhorted him to a timely submission; but all this while he had not minded the poet's advice:

"A wooden sword, engaging like one of steel,
is not likely to support the comparison;

The Syck observing that the minister spent his time in negotiation, soon guessed the temper of the man he was to deal with; and breaking at once the conferences, he prepared to fall upon his enemy; accordingly he attacked the next day. Some skirmishes took place, but nothing like a general engagement; and yet this was enough to damp Abdol-ahed-Qhan's spirits at once: without having suffered any loss or even any check, he took fright at the sight of unsheathed sabres; and his cowardly timorous nature informing him internally that he would never stand the brunt of a battle, he took the Shah-zadah with him and fled without once turning about to look behind on those numerous troops of his, where not a single man had yet moved a foot from his post. After this flight, the troops retired of course, arid Nedjef-Qhan's corps was amongst the first that retreated; but it was in so good order, that no one would chuse to approach it. Some other commanders followed, and retiring in good order, marched off unpursued: numbers of the bravest of the other corps joining together, retired at slow pace likewise; but numbers of others, after having, through their own ill conduct, or the incapacity of their chiefs, roamed about for some time, dispersed at last, and were then set upon one after another by the enemies, who despoiled them of both arms and horses, as well as clothes: it was in such a dismal condition that they fled to their homes, and most of them to the capital; but not without undergoing a variety of hardships: such as compleat disgrace was enough to humble the minister; but it served moreover to demolish him totally.

Nedjaf-Qhan thought of making his profit of it; he had all along stood still like a mark to be shot at by Abdol-ahed-Qhan and his party; and he had all along put up with the daily injuries he received from him; but thinking now that his concerns were blended with those of an incensed public, that cried for vengeance, and concluding that there was no safety for him as well as for the public, but in the removal of that man from all power and influence, he supplicated the Emperor to remove that disturber of the public repose from all his offices and employments, and to send him into condign confinement. The Emperor, who is a strange fort of a man indeed, and of a character that borders upon foolishness and imbecility, made haste to obey his general's mandate; and the latter without losing time, made haste to send a number of trusty officers to the minister's house, where they seized and confined his person, and confiscated his whole fortune: out of all that wealth, the general took nothing for himself but his library, and his Pharmacy, and collection of drugs and fossiles, which really contained great curiosities; but he sent to the Emperor the money, furniture, and jewels; three articles that amounted to a great number of lacs. After this operation Nedjef-Qhan sent several commanders of his own, who repulsed the Sycks, and drove them back to their homes; and these officers exhibited in other respects so much bravery and conduct, that the Sycks acknowledged Nedjef-Qhan's superiority, and behaved submissively to him; although those mendicants turned soldiers, had been during all these troubles receiving such continual additions, that they now reckoned their numbers by lacs. Nedjef-Qhan, having now confirmed his power by that act of authority, has seen his name become an object of dread and respect all over the provinces of Dehli and Acber-abad, where he lives with the utmost splendor and dignity. His character now commenced spreading abroad, and making impression even on the English; a nation acute, provident, and that sees deep into futurity; and he that had been left hitherto, unnoticed and unminded, now received an Envoy from General Coote, who happened to be in that neighbourhood: this envoy was Mr. Massac[xxiii] who delivered a message full of complaints, mixed with some threats, in which he mentionned how much the English had hitherto borne and forborne. Nedjef-Qhan

---

[xxiii] (2) Mr. Massac being born in Aleppo, spoke good Arabic, and was become a proficient in the Persian, which is full of Arabic words, and even whole phrazes.

returned a firm answer, and such as was calculated to impose silence, and to quash all further discussion; but many dangerous troubles having arisen at this very time in the south of India, a stop was put to all further discussions with that rising conqueror: otherwise there is no doubt, but the disputes would have grown warmer between the two parties, and that the respective pretensions would have been supported by armies: so that it is highly probable, that Nedjaf-Qhan would have appeared in the field against the English. We must wait to see what may be the subsequent events; and in whose behalf the divine protection shall be pleased to declare itself: what nation shall prevail by the superiority of it's fortune in the contest; and on whose standards the gale of divine Providence shall be pleased to blow.

"Let us wait till we see which of the two parties, the prevalence of" fate,
Shall raise to the skies, or depress and crush for ever."

NOTES

1. This attribution has been cited in note 12 of Robert L. Hardgrave, Jr., 'An Early Portrayal of the Sikhs: Two 18th Century Etchings by Baltazard Solvyns', originally published in *International Journal of Punjab Studies*, vol. 3, No. 2 (1996), 213–27.

2. The author here makes the common error of mistaking Bandā Bahādur (q.v.) for Gurū Gobind Singh (q.v.).

3. 1128 AH or 1716 CE. Bandā was executed in Delhi in March 1716.

4. Sëid Hassan does not appear as a recorded figure in the life of Gurū Nānak in any of the main *Janam Sākhīs* (life histories) of the Gurū.

5. Gurū Nānak's two sons were Bābā Lakhmī Chand (q.v.) and Bābā Srī Chand (q.v.), the latter referred to as being "addicted to a religious life."

6. This uncommon and wholly erroneous explanation for the reasons behind Gurū Tegh Bahādur's martyrdom which actually took place in Delhi is not corroborated by any other evidence. It is most likely an attempt to conceal the real reasons that the Gurū was martyred. The emperor Aurangzeb's well-developed policy against the Sikhs was already in place, and the Gurū's demise was at the hands of that very policy. Sir Jadunath Sarkar, *History of Aurangzib: Mainly Based on Persian Sources*, 4 vols. (Calcutta: M.C. Sarkar & Sons, 1912–1919), vol. 3, 267, gives an account of the repressive measures taken by the state against non-Muslims. He quotes Khāfī Khān to the effect that "Aurangzib ordered the temples and the Sikhs to be destroyed and the Gurū's agents [masands], for collecting the tithes and presents of the faithful, to be expelled from the cities."

7. Gurū Gobind Singh died in Nānded, in 1708, some three years after the death of his sons. It was certainly not precipitated by the murder of his two youngest sons at the hands of Wazīr Khān. In a defiant message to Emperor Aurangzeb following the tragedy that befell his family, the Gurū wrote "What, if you have killed my four sons? Remember, the coiled snake is still alive. By putting out a few sparks, you have quenched not the fire thereby." *Zafarnāmāh* (78) in Gopal Singh, *A History of the Sikh People 1469–1988* (New Delhi: World Book Centre, 1979. Revised and updated edition New Delhi: World Book Centre, 1988), 311.

8. The siege was within a fortress *havelī* in the village of Gurdās-Nangal.

9. Feristāh (part VI, chapter 34) calls him Tārā Singh.

10. 1175 Hijah, 1762 AD. This is a likely reference to the capture of Lahore and the minting of money by the *Dal Khālsā* under the leadership of Jassā Singh

Āhlūvālīā (q.v.). The name "*Chinta*" is not one that can be ascribed to any Sikh leader of that period and may simply be a mistake on the part of the writer.

11. The *waddā ghallūghārā* (the great massacre) occurred in February 1762 during the seventh invasion of Ahmad Shāh Abdālī into India.

12. Although "*Djiven the Syk*" is referred to a number of times in this account, his identity remains unknown.

13. 1195 Hijah or 1781 AD.

14. The embattled Zābitā Khān (q.v.), desperate for allies, took *khande dī pahul* (q.v.) to become a Sikh, changing his name to Dharam Singh. This was a short lived conversion, reverting back to Islam when it was politically expedient to do so and even married his daughter to his avowed enemy Najaf Khān (q.v.).

15. The Sikh chiefs would have been those that were at the time threatening to overrun Delhi headed by Zābitā Khān (now Dharam Singh). At the time of their initial alliance, Zābitā Khān had enlisted the support of Desū Singh of Kaithal, Rāi Singh, Dulhā Singh, Dīwān Singh, Bhāg Singh, Sāhib Singh Kondhah, Baghel Singh, and Hardukam Singh.

CHAPTER 33

AFGHĀN RETREAT SIGNALS SIKH
PROSPERITY, 1790

Quintin Craufurd, *Sketches Chiefly Relating to the History, Religion, Learning, and Manners, of the Hindoos: With a Concise Account of the Present State of the Native Powers of Hindostan.* (London: printed for T. Cadell, 1790), pp. 356–70.

Quintin Craufurd (1743–1819), best known as a British author and pre-revolutionary Francophile, was born at Kilwinnock on September 22, 1743. It was in his early life that he went to India, where like many well-bred Englishmen he entered the service of the East India Company to seek his fortune. This he did with some degree of success, and by his forties had settled in France, where he concentrated his efforts in the refined tastes of Parisian life. There, he built up an impressive collection of books, antiquities, coins, and fine arts. Craufurd was intimate with the French court, in particular with Marie Antoinette, and he was one of those who arranged the flight to Varennes. He spent a turbulent time after the revolution between England, Belgium, and finally in France where he died on November 23, 1819.

He authored a number of quite diverse works, all inspired by his own life experiences, including: *Sketches Chiefly Relating to the History, Religion, Learning, and Manners, of the Hindoos* (1790), *History of the Bastille* (1798), *Essay on Swift and his Influence on the British Government* (1808), *Researches Concerning the Laws, Theology, Learning and Commerce of Ancient and Modern India* (1817), and *Secret History of the King of France and his Escape from Paris* (first published in 1885).

Craufurd's account in his first work *Sketches Chiefly Relating to the History, Religion, Learning, and Manners, of the Hindoos* deals primarily with the period of the ascendancy of the Afghān chief, Ahmad Shāh Abdālī. The date of this account, in addition to the relative impartiality of the author, gives some considerable insight into one of the most brutal but ironically fortuitous periods in Sikh history.

Craufurd gives a detailed account of the rise of Ahmad Shāh from a prisoner to the scion of Nādir Shāh's Afghān forces. As Ahmad Shāh's future career as invader and plunderer of the imperial Mughal capital and marauder of Punjab was unfolding, the two principal antagonists of the Shāh's designs begin to make their presence felt. These were of course the Sikhs and the Marāthās. Both of these peoples were products of the previous 300 years of Mughal rule and domination by Muslim aristocracy and both these communities were fervent nationalists and ambitiously coveted the Punjab. The only reasonable threat to their ascendancy was the continual invasions by the Afghāns headed by Ahmad Shāh.

Ahmad Shāh dealt with the Sikhs and the Marāthās with characteristic brutality. In 1746 and 1762, the Sikhs faced two colossal losses at the hands of the Afghāns, virtually wiping out the local populace whose support they required for the guerrilla tactics that they were engaging in. The Marāthās suffered no less; sandwiched in 1761 at Pānīpat between the Punjab and Delhi, Ahmad Shāh dealt them a crippling blow. By this time, the Shāh was old and exhausted—a shadow of his former self—and as with most eastern dynasties, lacking a credible successor.

With the Marāthās beaten and the Mughal administration weakened by continual invasions, a political vacuum was developing, which would spread to include the greater part of the Punjab and within which the battle hardened and popular bands of Sikh guerrillas could take advantage. All that was needed was strong and credible leadership and the desire and resilience to unite. That leadership was ably provided by the most powerful of the Sikh guerrilla leaders, Jassā Singh Āhlūvālīā, Harī Singh Bhangī, and Charhat Singh Sukkarchakīā. The genesis of a political nexus was born, unified through a common belief system and a common threat.

This loose confederation of *misls* was to last through most of the latter part of the eighteenth century until the grandson of Charhat Singh Sukkarchakīā, the ambitious Ranjīt Singh, methodically and finally subsumed each *misl* under his own.

In the latter end of 1762,[1] he [Ahmad Shāh Abdālī] again crossed the Attuck, in order to attack the Seiks, whose power having greatly increased, their incursions had become more frequent and dangerous. But his intention seems rather to have been to extirpate than to conquer them. He defeated their army, composed of the troops of their different chiefs; and forced them to take refuge within their woods and strong holds.[2] All who were taken were put to death; and having set a price on the heads of all those who professed their tenets, it is said that heaps of them were frequently to be seen piled up in the market places of the principal towns. Hearing that they had assembled in considerable numbers to celebrate an annual festival at Anbertser, he endeavoured to surprise them. But their chiefs had marched thither with all their forces, and were prepared to receive him. He nevertheless attacked them with great impetuosity. During the battle, there happened an eclipse of the sun, which, whilst interpreted as a favourable omen by the Seiks, dismayed the Mahomedans. Ahmed, after a bloody conflict, was obliged to retreat with precipitation.[3] Soon after, he retired to his northern dominions; but returning the year following, retook several places that had been lost during his absence, and drove the Seiks from the open country. But as soon as he quitted Hindostan, they again came forth; and this kind of warfare seems to have been often repeated.[4]

Ahmed, after being long afflicted with an ulcer in his face,[5] died on the 15th of July 1773,[6] at Kohtoba, a place situated amongst the mountains of Kandahar, whither he had retired for the sake of coolness. He was succeeded by his son Timur, who, though represented as a man of no mean abilities, does not seem to possess the active and enterprising genius of his father. His dominions to the north of the Attuck, form a very extensive kingdom, inhabited by a hardy and warlike people; but he has lost all that he possessed in Hindostan, except the province of Kashmire.

On crossing the Attuck, we enter the territories of the Seiks,[i] a people who owe their religious origin to a Hindoo, named Nanuck, of the Khatry or Rajah cast. His father, Baba Caloo,[7] possessed a small district in the province of Lahore, named Telvandi, where Nanuck was born in the year of Christ 1470.[8] Many stories are told of wonderful indications given by him, in his infancy, of uncommon wisdom and sagacity. He seems to have possessed strong powers, but which received no further cultivation beyond the usual education of the young men of his cast, consisting in little more than learning reading, writing, and arithmetic; and hearing the Shastras, or dissertations on the laws and religion of their country.

According to the custom of the Hindoos, he was married in his early years to one of his own tribe, by whom he had two sons.

It appears that he soon became an admirer of the Narganey worship,[9] and used to declaim against the folly of idols, and the impiety of offering adoration to any but the Supreme Being.

Having often expressed a desire to travel, at the age of about twenty-five years, he quitted his family, and visited Bengal and most of the eastern provinces of Hindostan. In a second excursion he went to the south, it is said, as far as the island of Ceyloan: and, in a third, he went into Persia and Arabia. Those different journies seem to have taken up about fifteen years. But on his return from the third, he declared his intention of not quitting his native country any more;[10] and having expressed a wish of fixing his retreat on the border of some river, at a distance from any town, the Rajah of Calanore, who had become one of his disciples, granted him a piece of land on the banks of the Ravy,[11] about eighty miles north-eastward from the city of Lahore. Here Nanuck established his abode for the rest of his days, in a convenient dwelling that was erected by the Rajah's care: and as he chose to be free from the cares of this world, his wife and children dwelt at Calanore, coming occasionally to visit him. Having acquired great reputation for knowledge, wisdom, and piety, persons of all persuasions went to see him, and the Seiks say, that in his presence they forget that there was any religion but one. He died about the age of seventy.[12] The place of his abode was called Kartarpour, but since his death it has been named Dihra Daira,[13] or the place of worship.

His eldest son, Serik-chund, was the founder of a set of devotees, named Nanuck Shoiy.[14] The second, called Letchimidan,[15] married and had several children. On account of the oppressions of the Mahomedan governors, he altogether forsook

---

[i] Seik is said to mean disciple.

Televandy, the estate of his ancestors, and settled at Kartarpour, which is still in the possession of his descendants. But though they are respected by the Seiks, as being the posterity of Nanuck, yet they are not held in any sacred veneration, nor considered as the heads of their religion or tribe.[16]

Nanuck, when on his death-bed, passing by his children and relations, named his successor to teach his doctrine a favourite disciple, named Lhina, but whom he then called Angud, which is said to signify similar. Angud was likewise of the Khatry cast, and of a respectable family in the same province where Nanuck was born. To him he entrusted the care of collecting his precepts, which he accordingly did, in a work called Pothy,[17] or the book: and in another work, called Jenum Sakky, he gave a history of Nanuck's life.[18] These are written in the Punjab dialect, but in a particular character called Gour Mouekty, said to have been invented by Nanuck himself, for the purpose of writing his doctrines.[ii]

Angud, following the example of Nanuck, named to succeed him as Gourou, or holy master, his disciple Amerdoss; and this mode seems to have been practised, as long as the custom of obeying one supreme chief was observed.

The Seiks appear to have lived for many years in perfect peace and with the rest of mankind; and, being inoffensive in their manners, obtained the protection and goodwill of the Mahomedan court.[19] During this time, the number of their disciples constantly increased; their possessions were considerably extended, some of the neighbouring Rajahs were converted to their religion, and some woody and uncultivated lands were granted to them by the government. But in proportion as their power augmented, they seem to have quitted their meek and humble character, and at last, instead of appearing as suppliants, stood forth in arms. The first military leader of distinction we hear of was Taigh.[20] The next was the tenth and last Gourou, Govand Sing, who, after being engaged in hostilities against the government, made his peace, and even attended the emperor Bahauder Shaw in person.[21] From some private motive of resentment he was assassinated by a Petan soldier,[22] though the Seiks were not without suspicion, that he was killed by the secret order of the emperor. Having neglected to name a successor, or, as some say, declined it out of respect to a prophecy that there would only be ten Gourous, the Seiks chose for their chief a person named Banda.[23] Being of a bold and active disposition, he soon began to make incursions into the neighbouring countries, and maintained a depredatory war with the Soubadar of Lahore for several years. He was at last surprised and taken, and with his family and many of his countrymen sent to Delhi, where they were put to an ignominious death.[24] The blood that was spilt on that occasion, sealed that revenge which the Seiks then swore, and the invincible aversion they have ever since manifested to the Mahomedans. They continued their warfare with the Mogul government for some time, with various success; but taking advantage of the intestine troubles which succeeded the invasion of Nadir Shaw, they subdued several districts. Wherever they conquered, they threw down the mosques; and as they admitted proselytes to their religion, all were obliged to quit their country who did not choose to embrace their doctrine.[25]

Having, as already related, drawn on themselves the vengeance of Ahmed Shaw, he attacked them with his usual vigour. They were now under several chiefs, some of them descendants of their Gourous,[26] and others of Hindoo nobles, who had adopted their faith, and united themselves with the nation. The war with the Affghans lasted several years, during which the Seiks retired into strong holds, or acted offensively in the field, according as they found themselves in force. But in the end they entirely

---

[ii] Colonel Polier [Ed. see part II, chapter 8 for accounts of the Sikhs by Polier].

expelled these northern invaders; and not only conquered all the extensive province of Lahore,[27] but are now in possession of the greatest part of Moultan, and several districts towards Delhi, including in their territories the whole of that rich country, called the Panjab.[iii]

Nanuck having stripped the religion of Brimha of its mythology, the Seiks adore God alone, without image or intermediation; and though they venerate the memory of their founder, as well as of some of their Gourous, whose names they often repeat, yet they neither offer them divine worship, nor apply to them to intercede in their behalf.

They eat any sort of meat, excepting beef; retaining the same regard for the ox as the other Hindoos, and probably from the same cause, its utility. But the meat which is very generally eaten, is pork; perhaps, because forbidden to the Mahomedans.

Blue, which is generally considered as an inauspicious colour by the Hindoos, distinguishes the dress of the Seiks; as if Nanuck meant to show by this, the weakness and absurdity of superstitious prejudices. Their dress commonly consists in blue trowsers of cotton cloth; a sort of plaid generally checkered with blue, which is thrown over the right shoulder, and a blue turban.

The national government is composed of an assembly of their different chiefs,[28] but who individually are independent of each other, and masters of their respective territories. In this assembly every thing that regards the safety of the state, the quota of troops to be furnished by each chief in time of war, the operations of their armies, and the choice of a person to command them, is agitated; and resolved on by the plurality of voices. This assembly meets annually, or as occasion may require, at Anbertser,[29] a place held in a kind of religious veneration, where there is a large tank, which is said to be beautifully ornamented, lined with granit, and surrounded by buildings.[30]

The whole force of the different chiefs collectively may amount to about two hundred thousand horse.[31] But they seldom can be brought to act in concert, unless the nation be threatened with general danger; in which case they never fail to unite.

Besides a sabre, most of their soldiers carry a matchlock gun, which seems a very uncouth weapon for a horseman, but in the use of it they are extremely expert, and are in general excellent marksmen.[32] It carries a larger ball than an English musket to a greater distance; and it is often employed by them with success before the enemy be near enough to use the sword.

They are naturally a strong race of men, and, by their hardy manner of living, are capable of enduring much fatigue. In the field, none but the principal officers have tents, and these extremely small, so that they may be struck and transported with quickness and facility. In cold weather the solider wraps himself, in the night in a coarse blanket, which, when he marches, is folded and carried on his horse.

Of late years almost all the neighbouring countries have been laid under contributions by them; and, to avoid their incursions, several petty chiefs have consented to pay them a small annual tribute, and put themselves under their protection.

Their country is well cultivated; full of inhabitants, and abounds with cattle. The horses of Lahore are supposed to be much superior to those bred in any other part of Hindostan.[iv]

[iii] A tract of country so named, on account of five rivers, which, descending from the northern mountains, enclose and intersect it. They afterwards run into the Snide or Indus.

[iv] The country of Lahore being thought favourable for breeding horses, and producing plenty of excellent forage, studs were established at different places on account of the Mughal emperor. Persian and Arabian stallions were sent to them, and there was a fixed order at all the royal stables, to send to the studs in Lahore all such Arabian and Persian horses as by any accident should be rendered unfit for mounting. Hence perhaps it arose, that the present breed of horses there, is superior to the horses that are bred in other provinces.

It is said that they have a sort of superstitious respect for their sword.[33] It was by it they obtained their independence and power; and by it they preserve them. A Seik, though in other respects infinitely less scrupulous than any other Hindoo, before he will eat with any one of another religion, draws his sword, and passing it over the victuals, repeats some words of prayer, after which he will freely partake of them.[v]

Contrary to the practice of all the other inhabitants of Hindostan, they have an aversion to smoking tobacco. But many of the people smoak and chew bang, so as sometimes to produce a degree of intoxication.[vi]

[v] Mr Stuart [Ed. On the morning of 3 January 1791, a British officer, Lieutenant-Colonel Robert Stuart, was captured in Anūpshahar by a band of robbers who were quickly relieved of their prisoner by some adventurous Sikh horsemen. Their leader, *Sirdār* Bhangā Singh of Thānesar, demanded a ransom for his release, which was eventually paid to the amount of Rs. 60,000. He was set free on 24 October 1791. Whether this is the same Mr Stuart referred to is not known but since Crauford's account was published in 1790, Lt.-Col. Stuart's experiences and observations of 1791 could not have been incorporated in this sketch].

[vi] Colonel Polier.

Notes

1. It was actually the latter end of 1761 when Ahmad Shāh Abdālī set off on his sixth invasion of India. The contemporary author of *Khazānā-e-Amīrā* explains his motives for doing so: "The Sikh people of the Panjab, from the earliest of times, have been a source of mischief and sedition. They are bigoted enemies of the Mussalmans. In spite of the fact that the Shah had so many times over-run India, owing to the want of foresight, they raised the standard of rebellion and disturbance, and killed his viceroy at Lahore. They raised a person named Jassa Singh [Āhlūvālīā] from among themselves to the status of a king, and like the demon, they made him sit on the throne of Jamshid, and blackened the face of the coin with his name. Having taken possession of the city of Lahore and its vicinity, they molested God's creatures in general and the Muslims in particular. Hearing this news, Shah Durrani, according to his established practice, again moved towards India." Ghulām Alī Azād Bilgramo, *Khazānā-e-Amīrā*, 1762–1763 (Cawnpore: 1871), 114, quoted in Gupta, *History of the Sikhs*, 2: 176.

2. The w*addā ghallūghārā*, or the major holocaust that occurred at Kup Rahīrā on February 5, 1762, is how this event is remembered in Sikh history. The Sikhs were severely disadvantaged in that they had to protect their slow-moving baggage train (*vahīr*), which included women, children, old men, and other non-combatants. According to Ratan Singh Bhangū, the Sikh army was "fighting while moving and moving while fighting, and they kept the baggage train marching, covering it as a hen covers its chicks under its wings." Reliable estimates of the losses of the Sikhs range from 25,000 (Tahmas Khān Miskīn, a Muslim chronicler and personal attendant of Muin-ul-mulk, the governor of Punjab, who was present at the battle) to 30,000 (Ratan Singh Bhangū, whose relatives were present).

3. Following the *waddā ghallūghārā*, Ahmad Shāh proceeded to Amritsar in April 1762 and blew up the Harimandar Sāhib (q.v.) with gunpowder. The Sikhs healed their wounds quickly, creating chaos through their continuing disturbances. They gathered in large numbers to celebrate *Divālī* at Amritsar where the battle mentioned in the account occurred on October 17, 1762.

4. To deal with the Afghān invader, the Sikh *misls* (confederacies) developed the following harassment tactics: "The Khalsa created great difficulties for Ahmed Shah by dealing great blows to him. One *misl* would get up early in the morning and go to battle, then another would go at midday. When one returned from the fight, the second would take its place. When the second returned, a third would take its place. The Akālī Singhs would never give up. If one died amongst them, the others would say he had been successful. If the enemy became too strong, they would disengage. When the pursuing enemy turned back, the Singhs could be seen returning behind them. The Afghans tried their utmost to engage them. With eyes wide open, they stood and faced the Khālsā. Covered in armour, they and their horses would stand waiting. They desired to fight with swords but the Singhs preferred to shoot at them from a distance with their muskets. That was how they annoyed Ahmad Shāh, who reached Kābul with great difficulty." Bhangū, *Prachīn Panth Prakāsh*, 431.

5. Sikh tradition holds that the Afghān king was struck on the nose by a flying brick from the Harimandar Sāhib when it was blown up. This caused the ulcer which then became cancerous.

6. Ahmad Shāh actually died on April 14, 1772, the very day the Sikhs crossed the Indus and plundered Peshāwar. *Delhi Chronicle* or *Waqa-e Shah Alam Sani*, Anonymous, 250. Gupta, *History of the Sikhs*, 2:250.

7. Bābā Nānak's father was Mehtā Kaliān Dās Bedī, an accountant in the village of Talwandī Rāi Bhoe, forty miles from Lahore.

8. This should be 1469.

9. This would be contested by most commentators of the Sikh religion today.

10. Before his tour to Persia and Arabia, Gurū Nānak also journeyed into the Himālayās.

11. A well-wisher, Dīwān Kaurā Māll, is thought to have offered Gurū Nānak some land, which later became known as Kartārpur.

12. Gurū Nānak passed away on September 7, 1539.

13. The word *Derā* can refer to a place of abode, house, or habitation. In this context, the word carries the connotation of a temple or memorial over a cremation site. Indeed, Gurū Nānak's ashes were buried near Kartārpur, and a monument was raised over them. This monument was later washed away by a flood in the river. The Gurū's eldest son, Bābā Srī Chand (q.v.), recovered the urn containing the ashes and reburied them nearby (near a well where the Gurū had once rested). This place came to be called Derā Bābā Nānak. The phrase "Dihra Daira" possibly means the village (Persian *deh*) that contains the *Derā*.

14. Bābā Srī Chand (1494–1629) (q.v.) is believed to have established the *Udāsī* order rather than the *Nānakshāhi* order mentioned by Craufurd. However, these and other terms appear to have been used interchangeably: "The term Nanak-panthi, as well as those of Sikh and Hindu, are applied in common parlance in a very loose and confused way. The followers of Nanak returned themselves under various appellations; such as Nanak Shahi, Nanak-dasi, Sikh Nanak-dasi, Sewak Guru Nanak, Nanak-math, Nanak-padri, Baba-panthi, etc. Possibly some of those returned as Adpanthis may really belong to the same sect; the term implying an adherence to the 'original' faith." Rose, *Tribes and Castes of the Punjab*, 3: 155.

15. Bābā Lakhmī Chand (1497–1555) (q.v.).

16. The descendants are referred to as the Bedīs (the caste that Gurū Nānak was born into). Two important personalities from amongst the family were Sāhib

Singh Bedī (1756–1834), the revered contemporary of Mahārājā Ranjīt Singh, and Bābā Sir Khem Singh Bedī (1832–1905), one of the founding members of the Singh Sabha movement in 1873.

17. The *Pothī* of Gurū Nānak is mentioned in the *Purātan Janam Sākhī* (see next note). Bhāī Gurdās (1551–1636) mentions Gurū Nānak having a *kitāb*, or book, when he traveled to Meccā (Var 1, 32). During his stay there, he was asked by the *qāzīs* and *maulvīs* to open his book and tell them whether it says who was better, the Hindu or the Muslim (Var 1, 33).

18. The author of the *Purātan Janam Sākhī*, which is believed to have been written in the late sixteenth or early seventeenth century, is not known with any certainty. It is unlikely to have been written by any of the Gurūs.

19. The Emperor Akbar visited Gurū Arjan at Goindvāl on November 24, 1598. Akbar remitted a portion of the year's revenue to the *zemindārs*, whose hardships were brought to his notice by the Gurū: "When His Majesty (Akbar) left Lahore and reached the neighbourhood of Batala, he came to know that a fight had taken place in the house of Achal between Musalman faqirs and a group of Hindu sanyasis. The Muslim faqirs prevailed and by way of retaliation they demolished the temples of the place. His Majesty King Akbar to do justice against the excesses committed put many of them into prison, and ordered that the demolished temples should be built anew. From there he crossed the river Beas and visited the dwelling place of Gurū Arjan, successor of Bābā Nānak, who was famous for divine love. The Emperor was highly pleased to meet him and with his recitation of the hymns of Bābā Nānak in praise of God. Gurū Arjan offered him a suitable present out of regard for his visit. He represented that during the stay of the imperial army in Panjab the price of grain had gone up, and the revenues of parganahs had been increased. Now on the departure of royal troops the price of corn would come down. It would be difficult for the subjects to pay the enhanced revenue. The Emperor acceded to his request and issued orders to his Chief Diwan to reduce the revenue by one-sixth. He instructed that the revenue must be charged according to the concession granted and nothing more should be demanded." Sujan Rai Bhandari, *Khulasat-ut-Tawarikh*, 1696, quoted by Gupta, *History of the Sikhs*, 1: 134.

20. It was Gurū Hargobind, the father of Gurū Tegh Bahādur, who established military training amongst the Sikhs. Bhāī Gurdās says of him: "The destroyer of the enemies' ranks, the brave, heroic Gurū is yet a lover of mankind." (*Vār* i, 48), Teja Singh and Ganda Singh, *A Short History of the Sikhs*, 1: 37 n. 1.

21. The *Tārikh-i-Bahādurshāhī* says that "Guru Gobind, one of the descendants of Nanak, had come into these districts to travel and accompanied the royal camp. He was in the habit of constantly addressing assemblies of worldly persons, religious fanatics and all sorts of people." Ibid., 1: 73 n.

22. According to an early eighteenth century *Udāsī* account, it was the Pathān's grandfather, Paindā Khān, who was killed in battle by Gurū Hargobind (the grandfather of Gurū Gobind Singh). *Episodes from Lives of the Gurus, Parchian Sewadas*, trans. with commentary by Kharak Singh and Gurtej Singh (Chandigarh: Institute of Sikh Studies, 1995), 87–8.

23. Tradition holds that Bandā Singh Bahādur (q.v.) was chosen by Gurū Gobind Singh to continue the struggle against the oppressive Mughal regime in the Punjab and North India generally.

24. See part II, chapter 4 for an eyewitness account of the entry of the captured Bandā and his companions into Delhi.

25. Even during the height of foreign aggression and invasion, examples can be found of Sikh tolerance to the majority Muslim populous. Ahmad Shāh arrived at Lahore on December 22, 1766 during his eighth invasion of India. The city fathers waited upon him and told him that Lahinā Singh, the Sikh ruler of Lahore who had retired to Kasūr on hearing of Ahmad Shāh's arrival, was a sympathetic ruler who made no difference between Hindu and Muslim citizens. Indeed, on the festivals of Id-uz-zuha he bestowed turbans on the qāzīs, the muftīs and the imāms of mosques. Ahmad Shāh expressed his satisfaction and sent a letter to Lahinā Singh offering him the governorship of Lahore together with a present of the dry fruits of Kābul. The latter declined the invitation on the grounds that by obeying him he would fall in the eyes of his co-religionists. Lahinā Singh returned his fruits and sent him a quantity of an inferior kind of grain, stating that the fruits were the food of kings, while he lived on simple grain. Khushwaqt Rāi, 129; Ali-ud-Dīn, 130a, Gupta, *History of the Sikhs*, 2: 239.

26. It is known that Bandā Singh Bahādur had several important Sikhs with him who were related to the Gurūs. For example, Binod Singh, his son Kāhan Singh and grandson Mīrī Singh were descendants of Gurū Angad, and Bāj Singh and his brother Rām Singh were descended from the third Gurū, Amar Dās. However, during the period of Ahmad Shāh Abdālī's invasions from 1747 to 1769, the majority of the Sikh leaders were not descended from the Sikh Gurūs.

27. The capture of Lahore occurred in November 1761 following a *Gurmatā* (q.v.), a counsel adopted by the Sikhs at an assembly at Amritsar, in October 1761.

28. This is the *Sarbat Khālsā* (q.v.) which has been described in detail by Malcolm, *Sketch of the Sikhs*, 120.

29. Amritsar (q.v.).

30. It is interesting note that the modern term "Golden Temple" is not referred to by the author. At the time this account was written, the upper storey of the *Harimandar Sāhib* would not have been covered in gold leaf.

31. See part IV, chapter 17 for a contemporary breakdown of the Khālsā army.

32. A source of inspiration and knowledge of weaponry for the eighteenth century Sikh warrior, the *Dasam Granth* composition *Shaster Nām Mālā* (The Rosary of the Names of Weapons) devotes the largest number of pages to the praises of the *tupak* or the matchlock rifle.

33. Malcolm, *Sketch of the Sikhs*, 182, notes the Sikh's spiritual devotion to his sword: "The goddess of courage, Bhavani Durga, represented in the Dasama Padshah ka Grant'h, or book of kings of Gurū Govind, as the soul of arms, or tutelary goddess of war, and is addressed thus: 'Thou art the edge of the sword, thou art the arrow, the sword, the knife, and the dagger.'" History provides other examples of devotion to the sword. During the surrender of the Sikh army to the British forces at Rāwalpindī in 1849, one veteran remarked: "Many an old Sikh did I see with his long, white beard, betokening in his soldierly bearing and carriage the pride won in the days of Runjeet, lay his sword on the heap with as much tenderness as a mother would lay her child in its cradle, and then stepping back with tearful eyes bow his head in reverence, and pay it a last farewell. It was a sight which those who saw will never forget." Major H. Daly, *Memoirs of General Sir Henry Dermot Daly* (London: John Murray, 1905), 84–5.

CHAPTER 34

FERISHTĀH'S HISTORY OF
THE DECCAN, 1794

Muhammad Kasim Ibn Hindu Shāh [Astarabadī Ferishtāh], *Ferishta's History of Dekkan from the First Mahummedan Conquests: With a continuation from Other Native Writers of the Events in that Part of India, to the Reduction of its Last Monarchs by the Emperor Aulumgeer Aurungzebe: Also, the Reigns of his Successors in the Empire of Hindoostan to the Present Day: and the History of Bengal, from the Accession of Aliverdee Khan to the Year 1780,* 2 vols., trans., Johnathan Scott (Shrewsbury: Printed for the Editor by J. and W. Eddowes, 1794), 2: 142–6, 236–7, 268–70.

Ferishtāh's far-reaching history of the Deccan details the role that Bandā Bahādur played in the context of Mughal rule in India. The detail with which he covers the period of Bandā's insurrection in Sirhind and the eventual capture and execution of the Sikh chief go some way in underlining the gravity of the revolution that Bandā lead. Subsequent events in India were to reveal that the Sikh revolt in Punjab was only the first to start the destabilization of the Mughal power and would eventually lead to the subservience of the Mughals to the British.

The translator of the original Persian was Jonathan Scott, whose translation of Irādat Khān's *A Translation of the Memoirs of Eradut Khan, a Nobleman of Hindostan* (see part VI, chapter 31) also treats the Sikhs in much the same light as Ferishtāh. In the preface of part V, *Continuation of the History of Aurungzebe's Successors*, from which the extracts reproduced below have been taken, Scott states that he is indebted to certain Persian manuscripts and from "much conversation with many principal and well informed natives on the subject of their history, I can assert the received authenticity of the facts related." It is probable that he used the library and knowledge of his "friend Lieutenant Colonel Polier, whose life long residence and connections at the court of Dhely enabled him to obtain the best information of public and private transactions," in connection with the "present emperor, Shaw Aulum, from 1771 to 1779."

Ferishtāh specifically acknowledges the work of Ghulām Hussain Khān (part VI, chapter 32) who he has used as a source for much of his writings. Indeed, in the detail and in the errors that he repeats, it is obvious that he has been singularly and heavily influenced by it.

----

pp. 142–6

During this year, by the well conducted valour of Abd al Summud Khan, Bunda, chief of the Siks, who had pretended to royalty, and committed great depredations in the province of Lahore, was taken prisoner, and received the just reward of his crimes. He was [i]lineally descended from an adopted son of Nannuk Shaw, the founder of the religion of the Siks, in the reign of the emperor Baber.[1] Nannuk was the son of a Hindoo grain merchant of the Kuttree tribe, and being a youth of good capacity and pleasing manners, engaged the notice of Syed Houssun, a celebrated dirvesh, by whose instructions he made great progress in learning, and became an admirer of the systems of speculative and contemplative divinity of the mussulmaun devotees. Having selected some of their tenets, he translated them into the Punjaubee dialect, with additions of his own, and called the composition Kirrunt,[2] which became the guide of his disciples, who at first formed only a religious sect, without laying claim to political consequence. Nannuk left two sons, but neither of them assumed the supremacy of their order, which was given by election to Angud, one of their father's followers, who held it thirteen years. He, having no son, was succeeded by a disciple, who presided over the order twenty two years, and though he had sons, he placed Ramdass, his son in law, in the direction. Ramdass lived only seven years, and was succeeded by his son Goorroh Arjun, whose son Hir Govind inherited his dignity. Hir Govind's eldest son dying,[3] he was succeeded by his grandson, Hir Roy, who after seventeen years left this world, and was succeeded by his infant son Hir Kishen. He having no issue, his uncle Teeghe Bahadur,[4] younger son of Hir Govind, was elected, but was put to death as a dangerous heretic in the seventeenth year of Aulumgeer's reign,[5] he having collected his followers, and levied contributions from the inhabitants of his neighbourhood, in conjunction with Hafiz Adam, a mussulmaun devotee, and his votaries. Some time after the death of Teeghe Bahadur, his son Goorroh Govind, having collected his followers, gave them arms and horses, which till his time they had never used, and began to commit depredations; but he was soon obliged to fly, and two of his sons, being taken prisoners, were put to death. Being desirous of returning to his home, he prevailed on some Afghauns to conduct him, disguised as one of their devotees, through the army stationed at Sirhind; and for, the remainder of his life kept himself retired, having lost his faculties in grief for his sons. He ordered his disciples to wear blue, and leave their beards and the hair of their heads unshaved, which they do to this day.[ii] He was succeeded by Bunda, one of his followers, who

----

[i] This is contradicted by other writers, who say he was of obscure parentage but the Siks believe this account of his descent, or affect to do so.

[ii] The Siks admit proselytes from any sect. They profess deism. Their ceremonies I am not informed of. They mourn at a birth, and rejoice at death. It is said, every proselyte is obliged to drink the water, in which some Siks have washed their feet, mixed with hog's blood; a horrid abomination to a pious mussulmaun. Hindoo proselytes drink water, in which a few drops of a cow's blood have been mingled.

was also called Goorroh Govind.[6] This man obtained great power; and while Shaw Aulum was in Dekkan against Kaum Bukhsh, collected his followers, to revenge the death of his predecessor's sons. He committed the greatest cruelties on the mussulmauns, in every advantage shewing no quarter to age or sex, and even ripping up women with child. The emperor Shaw Aulum found it necessary to march in person against him, and he was besieged in the fortress of Loeh Ghur, which was taken, but Bunda found means to escape, and raise new insurrections.

The death of Shaw Aulum, the disputes of his sons, and the unsettled state of Jehaundar Shaw's government, prevented means being taken for the extirpation of the heresy; and Bunda, taking advantage of the distraction of the times, acquired an alarming degree of power. Upon the accession of Ferokhsere, Iflaum Khan, Soubadar of Lahore, was sent against him, but defeated with great slaughter; upon which Bazeed Khaun, fojedaur of Sirhind, was commanded to punish him, and took the field. He was assassinated in his tent, when alone at evening prayers, by a Sik, commissioned for that purpose by Bunda, and the murderer escaped unhurt.[7] Abd al Summud Khan, governor of Kashmeer, was now promoted to the Soubadary of Lahore, and sent against the rebels with a great army. After many severe engagements, he forced Bunda to take refuge in a fortress, which was blockaded so effectually, as to cut off every supply. The garrison was reduced to the necessity of eating cows, horses, asses, and other animals forbidden by their laws; when at length, having no provision of any sort left, and being reduced to the extremity of famine and disease, they begged for quarter. Abd al Summud Khan, having planted a standard on the plain, commanded them to come out and lay their arms under it, which they did. He then divided the meaner sort among his chiefs, who cut off their heads, and threw their bodies into a river near the fortress. The chiefs and persons of rank he put in chains, and placed them upon camels and asses, with caps of paper on their heads, and proceeded with them to Lahore in this manner, to excite the derision and insults of the populace. The mother of Bazeed Khan, whose murderer had been rewarded by the Siks, and distinguished by the title of Tara Sing, upon his being pointed out to her in the procession, threw down a heavy stone from the roof of her house as he passed, and killed him on the spot, in revenge for the death of her son. After some days, Bunda and the other captives were sent to Dhely; through which he was carried in an iron cage' upon an elephant, dressed in a robe of gold brocade, and upon his head a red turban, embroidered with gold. Behind him sat a soldier with a drawn sabre. Preceding him were borne by persons mounted on elephants numberless heads of his disciples on long poles, also a cat upon a staff, to denote that not an animal belonging to him was spared from slaughter. After his elephant came, tied two and two upon camels, seven hundred and forty prisoners, having each a hand bound to his neck. Upon their heads were fantastic caps, and they wore habits of sheep skins, with the wool outwards. The Siks bore the insults of the populace with the greatest firmness, and steadily refused the emperor's offers of life if they would embrace the Mahummedan faith. They were put to death, an hundred each day, on the ensuing seven days. On the eighth, Bunda and his son, with their remaining friends, were executed without the city. They were carried to the place of execution in ridiculous procession. A dagger was put into the hands of the chief, who was commanded to kill his infant son; but refusing, the child was slain by the executioner,[8] his heart torn out, and forced into the father's mouth. Bunda was then put to death, by the tearing of his flesh with red hot pincers and other tortures, which he bore with the greatest constancy; and had he not inflicted similar cruelties on others, he might be regarded as a martyr to his faith. It is said, he made the following reply to Mahummud Ameen Khan, who had remonstrated with him on his conduit: "When the sins of a people become excessive, the divine Avenger sends forth among them a tyrant, like myself, to punish their crimes; but when the measure of justice is filled, commits him to the hands of one more powerful, that he may receive the reward of his actions. What are the cruelties and oppressions of the wicked, if they shew not the rod of the Almighty!"[iii]

pp. 236–7

. . . When Ahmed Shaw Abdallee, left his son Timur Shaw with Jehaun Khan at Lahore, that chief thought it prudent to bestow a considerable tract of country in farm on Adeena Beg Khan, the general of the late Meer Munnoo, who was at the head of a considerable body of troops. Adeena Beg accepted his offer, and for same time remained faithful in his employment; but, being at length suspicious of Jehaun Khan's intentions towards him, he quitted his office, and retired to the hills with his followers; where he excited the Siks to rebellion, and, in conjunction with them, overran the country between the rivers Rawee and Suttulludge. Jehaun Khan sent against him Moraud Khan, who was defeated, and the Durannies driven from several places. At this time, Ragonaut Raow, Shumsheer Bahadur, and Holkar, had reached the vicinity of Dhely with an army of Mharattas, to whom Adeena Beg Khan dispatched frequent invitations to invade Lahore, which they accepted. At Sirhind they were opposed by the governor, whom they defeated and took prisoner; after which they proceeded to Lahore by forced marches. Jehaun Khan, after some skirmishing, found himself unequal to defence against such superior numbers, and flying with Timur Shaw in the greatest haste, evacuated the country. His retreat put the victors in possession of the provinces of Lahore and Multaun; the former of which they conferred upon Adeena Beg Khan, on his agreeing to pay them annually the sum of [iv]seventy five lacks of rupees, and retreated to Dhely. On the rains approaching, they marched back to Dekkan, but left a body of troops under Junko, as Soubahdar of Ajmere, to protect their conquests.

pp. 268–70

. . . [A.D. 1779] The royal army had scarce returned to Dhely, when the minister again resolved to take the field, and prevailed on the emperor to send with him his second son, the prince [v]Ferkhundeh Akhter. Great preparations were made, which took up several months, and excited the attention of the public. Various were the reports of his intentions. At one time, it was supposed he had entered into negotiations of alliance with the Mharattas, who had defeated the English army from Bombay, and threatened to attack them in Oude and Bengal. At another, it was rumoured that the royal army was to be joined by the Siks, and to fall on Nujeef Khan for his neglect of the emperor. At length, in the month of June 1779, Mujd ad Dowlah with his royal pupil moved from Dhely, and advanced to Panniput, with six battalions of sepoys armed in the European manner, a considerable train of artillery,

---

[iii] The Siks now possess the provinces of Lahor, Pungjaub, and Moultaun, with great part of Dhely, and bands of them have more than once made inroads on the navob vizier's dominions, but have been as often easily repelled by the approach of our army. They have a tradition among them, from their founder Nannuk, that their order and power will be destroyed by white men from the west; and they regard Europeans as the people destined to fulfil the prophecy. Nannuk is said also to have told the emperor Baber, that his descendants would fill the throne of Dhely for ten generations, and no longer. If so, this prophecy may be regarded as nearly verified, Shaw Aulum being the tenth in descent; and it is more than probable, that after him an emperor will cease to be acknowledged in Hindoostan. At present he is merely nominal.

[iv] Seven hundred thousand pounds.

[v] Of auspicious stars.

six thousand horse, eight thousand irregular infantry, and some bands of mercenary Siks[9]; so that, in point of numbers, his army was formidable, and, with conduct on his part, equal to the conquests of the petty chiefs in his route, whom he might chuse to attack. On his march he seized a zemindar, named Daissoo Sing,[10] from whom he exacted about two lacks of rupees, and then proceeded towards Puttiala, the residence of Amer Sing, ninety coss north-west of Dhely, who had usurped a considerable territory. He was commanded to join the royal army, and pay a compensation for the revenue of the country, which at first he promised, and a negotiation was begun to settle the sum; but the wily zemindar was insincere, and only wanted to gain time, till he should be assisted by the Siks from the province of Lahore,[11] who had promised to protect him, as his reduction would have exposed them to invasion from the royal army. After some days, Amer Sing, joined by many of his allies, threw off the mask, and the Siks in the service of the minister deserted to him, not chusing to fight against their brethren. Mujd ad Dowlah, instead of acting with resolution, would not try the event of persistance in his demands, but began his retreat towards Panniput; to which place he was followed by Amer Sing and the Siks, who harassed his line of march daily, and plundered his baggage, but could make no impression on the main body of his army; a proof that had he acted vigorously, a different fate would have attended his expedition.

The emperor, alarmed at the retreat of his minister, and dreading the event of the army coming to Dhely and demanding their arrears of pay, wrote pressingly to Nujeef Khan, imploring his assistance, and desiring him to take the administration of affairs upon himself. Nujeef Khan, who had long wished for such an opportunity of ruining the minister, and had, it is said, privately negotiated with the Siks and Amer Sing, hastened to Dhely with his army. Mujd ad Dowlah, upon his arrival at the capital, was disgraced and committed to the custody of his rival, who confiscated the greatest part of his effects, a share of which he gave up to the emperor.

NOTES

1. Bandā Bahādur (q.v.) was born in 1670, during the reign of the Emperor Aurangzeb. He was the son of Rām Dev—a Rājpūt of the Bhardwaj clan. Singh, *Life of Banda Bahadur*, 1.
2. The Gurū Granth Sāhib (q.v.).
3. The Gurū's eldest son, Bābā Gurdittā (1613–1638), died in his father's lifetime. Gurū Hargobind was succeeded by Bābā Gurdittā's eldest son, Har Rāi.
4. Actually a granduncle.
5. The accepted year of Gurū Tegh Bahādur's martyrdom in Delhi is 1675, which was the seventeenth year of Aurangzeb's reign.
6. Bandā Bahādur was certainly not called Gurū Gobind. It is believed that he had a similar appearance to Gurū Gobind Singh and that he had coins minted in the name of the tenth Gurū when Sirhind was taken—this may be the origins of the confusion.
7. Ganda Singh states that Bayzid Khān was killed in battle against Bāj Singh and Fateh Singh. Singh, *Life of Banda Bahadur*, 111; this is confirmed by *Ahwal-i-Salatin-i-Hind*, 39a.
8. Here Ferishtāh deviates from Ghulām Hussain who says that Bandā unhesitatingly killed his own son.
9. At Karnāl, many Sikh *Sirdārs*, including Sāhib Singh Khondāh and Gajpat Singh of Jīnd, presented themselves to Nawāb 'Abd ul-Ahad Khān and offered

their assistance in return for pay. "Gajpat Singh became Abdul Ahad's chief confidant and factotum for all government business in that region. By his advice the Khān advanced and enlisted every Sikh *sardār* who interviewed him, elephants, aigrettes, etc., according to his rank. He planted Sikh *thānahs* wherever the ryots had fled away from the villages in fear of the royal troops." Tahmas Khān Miskīn, *Memoirs*, 340, quoted in Jadunath Sarkar, *Fall of the Mughal Empire* (Hyderabad: Longman, 4th ed, 1999), 3: 106.

10. The Sikh Rājā of Kaithal.
11. Included amongst these leaders from beyond the Sutlej was Tārā Singh Ghaibā (see illustration 6) who arrived in a strong body of 15,000 horsemen.

CHAPTER 35

A MODERN HISTORY OF
HINDŪSTĀN, 1803

Thomas Maurice, *The Modern History of Hindostan: Comprehending that of the Greek Empire of Bactria, and Other Great Asiatic Kingdoms, Bordering on its Western Frontier: Commencing at the Period of the Death of Alexander, and Intended to be Brought down to the Close of the Eighteenth Century* (London: Printed for the author, by W. Bulmer and co., 1802–1803), pp. 508–12; 526; 617–20.

Thomas Maurice[1] was born in 1754 and educated at Christ's Hospital, Ealing and Bath, and later at St. John's and University Colleges, Oxford. His ordination in 1774–1778 was followed by several curacies and a vicarage in 1798. He was one of the first scholars to popularize knowledge of the history and religions of the East and as assistant-keeper of manuscripts in the British Museum, he was an early pioneer of the study of these subjects. A spiritual leader, scholar, and historian, his publications included *The History of Hindustan*, 1795; *A Dissertation on the Oriental Trinities*, 1800; *Indian Antiquities*, 1806; *Modern History of Hindustan*, 1802–1810; he also wrote poems. Thomas was still the assistant-keeper of manuscripts at the British Library when he died on March 30, 1824.

There appear to be three main sources of Maurice's account of the Sikhs, all of which have been reproduced earlier. Two that have been named by Maurice in the footnotes are also by orientalists; Charles Wilkins's *Sicks and their College at Patna* (part VI, chapter 30) and Jonathan Scott's *Memoirs of Eradut Khan* (part VI, chapter 31). The third source is not named but has obvious similarities in content with William Francklin's *History of the Reign of Shah-Aulum the Present Emperor of Hindostaun* (part IV, chapter 16). Given the lack of much new information furnished by Maurice, the reader is referred to the relevant introductions of these accounts for significant points relating to the material that follows.

---

pp. 508–12

... [A.D. 1708.] Intelligence about this time arrived that the SEIKS had risen in the north in great force and were ravaging without controul the whole country from the Indus to the Jumna. Of this SECT and NATION, which about this period first began to be formidable, the following summary account from an authentic source[2] may be acceptable to the reader.

The SEIKS are a tribe of Hindoos, who profess to worship one Invisible Being, omnipotent, omnipresent, and whom they consider as degraded by any similitude or images. In truth, both in theory and practice, they are pure theists. They are descended from one NANEEK of the Kattry[3] or war-cast, who flourished in the province of Lahore towards the close of the 15th century, and who from his eminent piety, and superior talents, was reverenced as a sort of prophet among them. Their GOOROOS, or chiefs, of which they enumerate a long succession, seem also to have been invested with a character both sacred and military, as was anciently the case among many eastern people; at once priests and soldiers. Like the present Hindoos, they are perfectly tolerant in matters of faith; though unlike them the Seiks admit of proselytes, which is doubtless one reason of their rapid increase as a people; since proselytes are made without any other ceremony than an oath, binding them to civil and religious obedience. They abhor, however, the multiplicity of idols displayed in their temples, even though attempted to be apologized for under the mild denomination *of the attributes of the deity personified.* The sacred volumes that contain their theological doctrines are written part in Sanscreet,[4] and partly in a character invented by Naneek himself.[i]

[A.D. 1709.] For a long period, equally inoffensive in their tenets and blameless in their manners, they remained undisturbed by the Mahommedan governors of Lahore and Multan, where they principally abounded; but their numbers vastly increasing, especially during the latter period of the reign of Aurungzeb, and with their *numbers* their *power*, during the long absence in Deccan of the imperial army; in short, a religious sect becoming gradually converted into a nation of warriors, hardy from their climate, mounted on fleet horses, and panting for independence, it was absolutely necessary to adopt the most instantaneous and vigorous measures for their reduction. Under their present Gooroo[5] or chief, they had extended their ravages on both banks of the Jumna, and the inhabitants of Delhi itself were struck with consternation. Filled with implacable hatred against the Mahommedans,[6] and with detestation of their religious principles, they every where insulted and plundered them; levelling their mosques and burning their palaces. The governor of Sirhind at the head of the provincial troops had marched against the marauders, but had been defeated and killed.[7] Their wide devastations and cruel excesses, the result of both political and religious rancour, were only to be checked by the Emperor in person, and therefore, for the present, compromising matters in the best manner possible with the Rajapout chiefs, and having conferred on Zoolfeccar the vice-royalty of Deccan, who governed it by deputy, he hastened northward with all his forces. Passing by Agra and Delhi, without entering either of those capitals, he in a short time arrived at Sirhind, where

---

[i] See Mr Wilkins's account of the SEIKS in Asiatic Researches, vol.i. p. 289. Calcutta edition. [Ed.: part VI, chapter 30].

the rebels were collected in great force. On the approach, however, of the imperial army they retired to Daber, the original residence of their chief, where they fortified themselves as strongly as possible. Daber is situated on the summit of a rocky mountain, and round it, at different heights, the greatest part of the rebel army had encamped, secure as they thought amidst its rugged precipices and frightful cavities that seemed to forbid the approach an enemy. The Emperor stationed his army around the foot of the mountain, and resolved to lie inactive for some time before the enemy, in the hope of rendering them confident, and tempting them to risque an engagement. The ardour of the Mogul troops frustrated his intention, for the Vizier having obtained permission with a considerable detachment to reconnoitre the enemy's position, although positively forbidden to make an assault, yet being extremely galled by the fire from the cannon of the fort, as well as by the discharge of rockets and musquetry, both general and soldiers became to the last degree irritated, rushed on impetuously to the attack, clambered up the most difficult heights, penetrated the deepest defiles, and drove the astonished enemy before them with the greatest rapidity under the very walls of the fort. Here, firmly concentrated, the rebel bands made a desperate resistance, and night coming on only suspended, but did not terminate the contest. It was renewed with the earliest dawn; and the remainder of the army having now, by exertions equally laborious, joined their valiant comrades, a dreadful and general slaughter commenced, no mercy being shewn to wretches who had evinced none. They were cut off to a man. The fort was afterwards taken by storm, and all within it also put to death; but the wily Gooroo, who knew the intricate windings of the hills among which Daber is situated, disguised like a Yogee, had made his escape in the night and fled by a secret path to the snowy mountains. The Vizier who had vowed to bring him dead or alive, to the Emperor, as some atonement for his disobedience of orders, was so mortified by the disappointment as well as by the cold reception of his sovereign, after deeds of valour that deserved so warm an one, that he shortly after fell ill, and is supposed to have died of a broken heart.[ii]

[A.D. 1712.] The terrible example thus made of so large a portion of their nation seems not to have had the effect of reducing the Seiks to entire obedience, since, though the resolution of Bahadar to extirpate the Rajapouts remained still unshaken, and he had not yet visited either of his capitals Agra or Delhi, we find him residing at Lahore, most probably to overawe them, and settle the affairs of the northern provinces, in general, till the time of his death, which took place suddenly, and not without suspicion of poison, in 1712. From the vigour with which his reign commenced, from his acknowledged abilities, and the general excellence of his character, if that reign had been prolonged, Bahadur would probably have fixed the empire upon a solid basis, and rendered its glory permanent; but now a dreadful scene of destruction is to take place, and royal blood to flow in still deeper currents. Imperial fratricide, blood-stained Fakeer! look up from thy tomb of affected humility, and view the long train of disasters which thy crimes have entailed on thy miserable descendants!

p. 526

... [A.D. 1715.] Towards the close of this year, the Seiks, who during the late public disturbances, had multiplied considerably, and become very formidable, again appeared in arms. The governors of Lahore and Sirhind[iii] were successively sent

---

[ii] Memoirs of Eradut Khan, p. 64.

[iii] "The Seiks now possess the provinces of Lahore, Panjab, and Multan, with great part of Delhi, and bands of them have more than once made inroads into the Nabob Vizier's dominions, but have been as often easily repelled by the approach of a British army." Note by Captain Scott, 1794.

against them, but the former was defeated with great slaughter, and the latter basely assassinated in his tent by a Seik,[8] sent for the purpose by Bunda, their chief, the same who had escaped by night when the fortress of Daber was invested by Bahadur. The governor of Cashmere now took the field, at the head of an army quadrupled in number, and was successful. They were exterminated without mercy, and Bunda himself being taken, and refusing to turn Mahommedan, first had his infant child butchered before his face, and its palpitating heart forced (horrible atrocity!) into the wretched father's mouth; and was himself afterwards put to death, by having his flesh torn from his bones with red hot pincers, and other exquisite tortures; all which he bore with undaunted firmness.[9] It may here be remarked, that from the rooted hatred borne by this sect towards the Mahommedans, their stern oppressors, the wars between them have ever been carried on with the most unrelenting barbarity.

pp. 617–20

. . . [A.D. 1777.] Next to Nudjuff himself, but far below him (in real dignity and consequence) the most prominent actor on the scene at this time was a crafty, venal, and unprincipled omrah named Mujud al Dowlah, the emperor's minister for civil affairs, highly in favour with his master, but a determined enemy of that commander, and as far as he dared, a resolute opposer of his ambitious projects. The captain-general, however, superior in genius, and commanding the army, looked down with supreme contempt both on the king and his minister. After long abusing the emperor's unlimited confidence, a circumstance arose which at once proved the deep duplicity of his heart, and his utter incapacity to conduct the affairs of a great empire. The SEIKS, whose efforts to become an independent state in Lahore, during the reign of Bahadur Shah, have been already noticed, and who during the late distractions of the empire had become extremely numerous and powerful, about this time[10] made an irruption into the province of Delhi, and extended their devastations to the very shores of the Jumna. To obviate a danger so near and so alarming, and drive the marauders back into their own territories, an army of 20,000 men was immediately raised, and in the absence of Nudjuff, Mujud al Dowlah, accompanied by one of the princes of the blood, was appointed to the command of it. It was attended by a formidable train of artillery, and was considered as a force perfectly adequate to the reduction of the enemy.

[A.D. 1779.] The royal army having advanced as far as Carnaul, near that city fell in with the first detachment of Seiks, which, however, being very inferior in point of numbers avoided an engagement by proposals of submission, and bought their peace by a peishcush of three lacks, and the promise of an annual tribute. They were ordered to attend the march of the imperial troops, which now pursued its progress towards the Seik frontiers, and encamped before Puttiali, a town sixty coss north of the latter, strongly fortified, and commanded by a daring chief, named Amur Sing, who, having a numerous garrison, and abundance of provisions, was resolved to sustain a siege. To this resistance he was further instigated by intelligence of the approach of a large army of Seiks from Lahore, and by his emissaries he contrived to keep up a strict communication with the chieftains of the battalions of his countrymen, attendant in the train of the royal army. By this means he became intimately acquainted with all their plans and movements; and receiving information of the venal character of the minister, he determined to turn it to his advantage, and, to carry on the delusion more effectually, affected to enter into a negociation with the latter, making him costly presents, and still more splendid promises. Commissioners were in consequence mutually appointed to settle the terms of surrender, but those on the part of Amur

Sing were directed as much as possible to procrastinate the final adjustment of matters. At length having received advice of the near approach of the army from Lahore, Amur Sing suddenly broke off the treaty, and, the Seik chieftains having previously lulled suspicion asleep in the mind of the minister, made their escape at the head of their troops, and joined their comrades. The shameful supineness and inaction of Mujud al Dowlah, during these transactions, corroborated the strong suspicions that prevailed throughout the army of his having been bribed to betray the royal cause; but, whether or not he was guilty of actual collusion with the enemy, the result was the same. The immense host of Seiks that had marched from Lahore having been joined by the fugitive battalions, and the troops that composed the garrison of Puttiali, formed together an irresistible army, and at the first onset the king's troops being overpowered by numbers, and the impetuosity of their attack, were thrown into irretrievable confusion, and every where dispersed and put to the rout. The powerful and well-directed fire of the artillery, stationed in the rear, alone saved them from total destruction.

[A.D. 1780.] When intelligence of this fatal disaster reached Delhi, the whole city was thrown into the utmost consternation, and more especially so when it was found that the triumphant enemy, following up their victory, had crossed the Jumna, and in their usual ferocious manner were plundering the northern districts of the Dooab. Messengers were instantly dispatched by the terrified emperor to Nudjuff Khan at Agra, urging the necessity of his immediate return with the army under his command to Delhi, and the summons was cheerfully obeyed by a chief sufficiently confident in his own merit, and who had now a fair opportunity of crushing for ever his inveterate enemy. Mujud al Dowlah, in the mean time, with the remnant of his discomfited army, had returned to the capital amidst the execrations of the people, and in vain endeavoured, by a multitude of fallacious statements, to justify himself to his insulted sovereign. That sovereign heard him with deep but silent indignation, as his palace was surrounded by his troops, and himself wholly at his mercy. On the approach of the captain-general to Delhi, Mujud al Dowlah, and one of the princes of the blood, under the pretence of doing him honour, were ordered to march a few coss to meet him, and conduct him to the presence. The minister, though warned by his friends that treachery was designed him, confidently marched out to meet his rival. On entering his tent, however, he was arrested and sent back under a strong guard to Delhi; and shortly after his whole fortune, amounting to twenty lacks of rupees was seized, and confiscated to the use of the captain-general. That distinguished chief himself was received by the emperor with marks of the highest respect, and under his direction early in the following year an army, ably commanded, was dispatched against the Seiks, who were defeated with great slaughter under the walls of Meerut, and the honour of the imperial army amply vindicated. From this period to his death, Nudjuff Khan resided constantly at Delhi, but became in his conduct more haughty and arrogant than ever, and left the humiliated emperor in the enjoyment of few privileges beyond that of granting empty titles, and the ratification of the acts of his imperious minister. From what he has just read, the reader will perceive that to enter, with any minuteness, into the transactions of this period of the Mogul annals would be only to record the rise and fall of ministers and favourites—to enumerate the struggles of grasping avarice and unprincipled ambition for the spoils of an expiring empire, and is unworthy the province of History. Let us hasten, therefore, to the close of this distressful scene, and contemplate, with due commiseration, the final catastrophe of this distinguished dynasty, and of this once potent empire.

NOTES

1. *Dictionary of Indian Biography*, s.v. "Maurice,Thomas."
2. This authentic source, mentioned in a later footnote, is Scott's translation of Irādat Khān's memoirs (see part VI, chapter 31).
3. *Khatrī* (q.v.).
4. The Gurū Granth Sāhib (q.v.) is written in the *Gurmukhī*, and not Sanskrit, characters. *Gurmukhī*, literally "from the mouth of the Gurū", is traditionally ascribed as an invention of Gurū Angad (1504–1552). As a character set called *Brahmī*, it was a script widely used by *Khatrī* traders and, therefore, would have been known to the early Gurūs in their professional lives. The innovation that Gurū Angad brought was to rearrange certain letters and modified some of the characters giving it a precision and accuracy that was used to render the language of the *Gurū Granth Sāhib*, *Dasam Granth*, and subsequent Punjabī literature, language and cultural expression. *The Encyclopaedia of Sikhism*, s.v. "Gurmukhī."
5. Thomas is making the common mistake of confusing Bandā Bahādur with Gurū Gobind Singh.
6. Other Persian writers have expressed the same sentiment regarding hatred of Muslims, but one writer, Khāfī Khān, doesn't regard the enmity against the Muslims as exclusively Sikh. Rather, those who chose to stand in the way of their mission and on the side of the empire were recognized as the potential enemy: "Although from the lower castes of Hindus, countless people like ants and locusts had gathered round him [Bandā] and lost no time in getting killed or coming into battle for his sake, yet, they did not harm such Hindus of high status as *Khatrīs* of the Punjab, who were colluding in the plans and designs of that rebel [Bandā] or the Jāts, famous for their bravery, who were supporting and joining the army of that doomed one. All remaining Hindus, along with the Muslims, they regarded as deserving to be killed." Majida Bano trans., "Bandā Bahādur and his Followers: From Khāfī Khān, *Muntakhabu'l Lubāb*" in ed. J.S. Grewal, I. Habib, *Sikh History from Persian Sources* (New Delhi: Tulika, 2001), 157.
7. This was Wazīr Khān (d. 1710) (q.v.).
8. The majority of other accounts agree that Wazīr Khān died during the battle of Chappar Chīrī in May 1710. Singh, *Life of Banda Singh Bahadur*, 43–5.
9. For a more detailed account of the entry of Bandā and his companions into Delhi, see part II, chapter 4.
10. These events occurred around the year 1779 and are also described in William Francklin, *The History of the Reign of Shah-Aulum* (see part IV, chapter 16).

GLOSSARY OF NAMES

'Abd us-Samad Khān (d. 1737). Governor of Lahore from 1713–1726. He served at the court of Aurangzeb and then Farrukh-Sīyār. Most notably, Samad Khān was charged with the capture of Bandā Bahādur (q.v.), which he succeeded in doing. Descended from a notable family of Samarkand, his son was Zakarīyā Khān (q.v.).

'Abd ul-Ahad Khān. The deputy *wazīr* (minister) of the Mughal empire in 1773, appointed by Mirzā Najaf Khān, the grand *wazīr*. He was the second *mīr bakhshī* (paymaster general), since the first paymaster general, Zābitā Khān, was generally absent from the royal court.

Ādīnā Beg Khān (d. 1758). Appointed *nazīm* (administrator) of the Jalandhar Doāb in 1739 by Zakarīyā Khān (q.v.), then governor of Lahore. He later became *faujdār* (military leader) of Jalandhar under Mu'in ul-Mulk (q.v.). When Ahmad Shāh Durrānī (q.v.) plundered the Punjab for the third time, he directed Ādīnā Beg to direct his energies towards wiping out the Sikhs who were frustrating Ahmad Shāh's baggage trains. Throughout his career, Ādīnā Beg had a paradoxical relationship with the Sikhs, killing large numbers of Sikh pilgrims at Anandpur Sāhib in 1753 and later admitting Jassā Singh Rāmgarhīā (q.v.) into his army.

Ahmad Shāh Abdālī, Ahmad Shāh Durrānī (1722–1772, reigned 1747–1772). Ahmad Khān was a distinguished combatant in Nādir Shāh's (q.v.) army, rising to the rank of commander of Nādir's *Abdālī* contingent. After the Shāh's death in 1747, Abdālī took advantage of the power vacuum and assumed leadership of the Afghāns and earned the appellation "Shāh". From his base in Kandahar and as tacit heir to Nādir Shāh's eastern dominions, he invaded India nine times between 1747 and 1769. The Shāh's sixth invasion of 1762, was directed toward the Sikhs who had for years been attacking his lines of communication and baggage caravans. On his return from Punjab, the Shāh took out his final revenge on the Harimandar Sāhib, blowing it up and defiling the *sarovar* (tank). His eighth invasion was once again directed at the Sikhs, this one even more frustrating than the last as the days of Sikh guerrilla warfare were at their zenith.

Alumgīr II, Muhammad Aizuddīn (1699–1759, reigned 1754–1759). One of the lesser Mughals to sit on the throne of Delhi. The son of Jahāndār Shāh, he was placed on the throne by Wazīr Ghāzī-ud-dīn Imād-ul-mulk. He adopted the same title as the Emperor Aurangzeb, and called himself Ālumgīr II. An impotent ruler who was sub-servient to the rule of a *wazīr*-kingmaker within his own court, his attempt to assert himself resulted in his ruin, and lead to his gruesome death at the hands of the *wazīr*.

Amar Singh, Rājā (1748–1782). Rājā of Patiālā succeeded Āla Singh, founder of the royal house of Patiālā. Amar Singh's father, Sardūl Singh, died before his grandfather Āla Singh and, thus, Amar Singh became regent. Aged just nineteen when Ahmad

Shāh Durrānī invaded the country, Amar Singh played deft politics with the Abdālī king and secured the governorship of Sirhind with the title *Rājā-i-Rājgān*. With his credentials established, Amar Singh expanded Patiālā to make it the most powerful state of its day between the Yamunā and the Sutlej.

Angad, Guru (1504–1552, Gurūship 1539–1552). Second Gurū of the Sikhs. His name before he became Gurū was Lahinā but was changed to Angad (limb) by Gurū Nānak (q.v.) at the time of his succession in 1539. On the advice of Gurū Nānak, Gurū Angad moved to Khadūr. He started a regular system of collecting offerings to meet the expenses of *langar* (q.v.). He was a keen promoter of physical fitness amongst the growing Sikh community. At the time of his demise, he nominated a seventy-three year old disciple, Amar Dās, to succeed him as the third Gurū.

Arjan, Guru (1563–1606, Gurūship 1581–1606). Fifth Gurū of the Sikhs and son of Gurū Rām Dās (q.v.). His first task as the Gurū was the establishment of the Harimandar Sāhib (often referred to as the Golden Temple) in Chak Rām Dās, the original name of Amritsar. For this, he asked all Sikhs to donate a tenth of their income. Amritsar came to be the premier spiritual and commercial centre of the Punjab. In 1604, he was responsible for compiling the spiritual writings of all the earlier Gurūs and renowned Hindu and Muslim holy men in the *Gurū Granth Sāhib* (q.v.), the present Gurū of the Sikhs. The Mughal Emperor Akbar (q.v.) visited Gurū Arjan in 1598, and was persuaded to remit the annual peasants of the district who had been hard hit by the failure of the monsoon. But Akbar's death in 1605 brought a sudden reversal in the attitude of the Mughals. His son and successor, Jahāngīr (q.v.), put an end to the growing popularity of Gurū Arjan by charging him with treason and torturing him to death.

Aurangzeb, Emperor (1618–1707, reigned 1658–1707). The third son of Emperor Shāh Jahān, he was originally named Muhī-ud-Dīn Muhammad 'Ālumgīr, but was given the name Aurangzeb "Ornament of the Throne" while still a prince. Following a bloody struggle for the succession with his brother, he ascended the throne in 1658, adopting the title Ālumgīr "conqueror of the world." Conflict and martyrdom dominate interactions between the Sikhs and Aurangzeb. It was during the reign of Aurangzeb that Gurū Har Rāi was summoned to the royal court. Gurū Har Krishan's investiture did not suit the emperor and he too was summoned to Delhi. Struck down with smallpox, the eight-year-old Gurū died. His successor, Gurū Tegh Bahādur (q.v.), also suffered at the hands of Aurangzeb's policy of religious persecution. The Gurū was arrested and executed in Delhi. The tenth Gurū, Gobind Singh (q.v.), was continually harassed by imperial troops although there is little evidence that the two ever met. After the fiercest encounter in 1705, which was marked by the duplicity of the Mughal leadership in rescinding a settlement, the Gurū wrote a letter to the Emperor titled *Zafarnāmah* (epistle of victory). The emperor responded with a *farmān* to the deputy governor of Lahore to make peace and a request for a personal meeting between the Gurū and the emperor (*Ahkam-i-Ālamgīrī*). Aurangzeb died on February 20, 1707 before this could take place.

Bābar, Emperor (1483–1530, reigned 1526–1530). A contemporary of Gurū Nānak (q.v.), his full name was Zahīr ud-Dīn Muhammad, the founder of the Mughal empire of India and descendant of Timur (Tamerlane) and of Jenghīz Khān. Responding to an invitation in 1525 from the governor of the Punjab to overthrow the Sultan of Delhi, Bābur began his raids into India. He launched an invasion and defeated the Sultan at Pānīpat in 1526, capturing Agra and Delhi. Later, he conquered nearly all of North India. He was succeeded by his son, Humāyūn.

Baghel Singh Karorasinghīā (1730–1802). Leader of Karorasinghīā *misl* in 1765, at the head of 12,000 men. Renowned for being a good soldier and political negotiator, he was able to win over the Mughals, the Rohīllās, the Marāthās, and British, who all sought his friendship. In 1764, Sikhs in a body of 40,000 under the command of Baghel Singh, overran the territory of Najīb ud-Daulā (q.v.), the Rohīllā chief. In 1775, Baghel Singh with two other *Sirdārs* crossed the Yamunā to occupy that country, then ruled by Zābitā Khān (q.v.) who in desperation offered Baghel Singh large sums of money and proposed an alliance to plunder the crown-lands. The following year, Baghel Singh's forces defeated the Imperial Mughal Army near Muzāffarnagar, leaving the entire Yamunā–Gangetic Doāb at their mercy. In 1783, the Sikhs entered the Red Fort in Delhi. The fearful Mughal emperor, Shāh Ālum II (q.v.), had no choice but to agree to Baghel Singh's plans to raise *gurdwārās* (q.v.) on Sikh historical sites.

Bahādur Shāh, Emperor (1643–1712, reigned 1707–1712). The son and successor of Aurangzeb (q.v.). Born Prince Muhammad Mu'azzām but also known as Shāh Ālum I, he was governor of Kābul when his father died and fought a bloody succession battle with his brother. Mu'azzām ascended the throne under the title of Bahādur Shāh when he was sixty-four years old and died five years later. During his lifetime, the empire was already falling to pieces through internal dissensions.

Bandā Bahādur (1670–1716). The military successor to Gurū Gobind Singh who exacted revenge on Wazīr Khān and was executed in Delhi in 1716. Sikh tradition maintains that Bandā Bahādur was born into a Rajput family in northern Punjab. Although some accounts refer to him meeting Gurū Gobind Singh in the Punjab, it is more likely that the first meeting took place in the Deccan in 1708, shortly before the Gurū died. Bandā assumed the role of military leader of the Khālsā and sought revenge against those who had executed the Gurū's two younger sons. By 1710, Bandā had gathered a peasant army and reached Samān and Sashaurā from the Deccan, sacked them and confronted Wazīr Khān (q.v.) near Sirhind. Here, he fought his most decisive battle, killing Wazīr Khān, sacking the town, and minting coins in the names of the Gurūs. The next five years were a series of running battles between the Khālsā and the Mughals. The governor of Lahore, 'Abd us-Samad Khān (q.v.), succeeded in cornering him and then laying siege for eight months before capturing him alive and transporting him to Delhi where he and the surviving Sikhs were executed.

Charhat Singh Sukkarchakkīā (d. 1770). Born into the Faizullāpurīā *misl*, the eldest of the four sons of *Sirdār* Naudh Singh, Charhat Singh was to make a new name for himself from the name of his ancestral village, Sukerchakk. He was trained at an early age in the art of Sikh guerrilla warfare, seeing action in the opportunistic skirmishes against the Afghan invader, Ahmad Shāh Durrānī (q.v.). His military exploits at the head of the newly formed Sukkarchakkīā *misl* were marked by victory over Emīnābād, Wazīrābād, and Siālkot. Charhat Singh was chief at the time of the rapid rise to power of the Sikh *misls*; he was opportunistic, courageous, reckless, and at times brutal—a perfect mix that propelled the Sukkarchakkīā *misl* to the very zenith of his Sikh contemporaries and paved the way for the ultimate rule of the Punjab by his own progeny. Charhat Singh was killed in battle, at a young age when his own gun burst in the pitch of a characteristic skirmish. His son, Mahā Singh (q.v.), followed by his grandson, Ranjīt Singh (q.v.) led the *misl* after his death.

Clive, Lord Robert (1725–1774). Known to his admirers as the "conqueror of India," he is credited with laying the foundations of the British Empire in India. Clive first arrived in India in 1743 as a civil servant of the East India Company, later transferring to the military service of the Company. In 1756, he secured the British forces in Madras. He then moved to Calcutta, which had been captured by the Nawāb of Bengal, Sīrāj-ud-Daulā, and early in 1757, he recaptured Bengal. Later that year, he defeated the Nawāb at the famous Battle of Plassey. Returning to England in 1760, he was given an Irish peerage and the title Baron Clive of Plassey. In 1765, back in India, he was instrumental in securing the *diwānī* (chief financial management) of the provinces of Bengal, Bihar, and Orīssā from the Mughal emperor. As governor of Bengal, his assumption of the right to collect the revenues of those states involved the Company in the complexities of wide territorial administration, which it was ill-equipped to handle. After his return to England, Clive was bitterly attacked by politicians and others and was accused by Parliament of theft. He was acquitted in 1773 after a long investigation, but, broken in health, he committed suicide.

Daulat Rāo Scindiā, Mahārājā Scindiā of Gwalior (1779–1827). Son of *Sirdār* Anand Rāo Madajī Scindiā Sāhib, he succeeded on the death of his great uncle and adopted father in February 1794. He renounced his sovereignty over a large number of forts to the East India Company, his overlordship over Rajputānā and Gohad, and any interference in the affairs of Delhi, by the treaty of Sarjī Anjangaon on December 30, 1803. The Mahārājā established his capital at Lashkar in 1810.

Farrukh Sīyār, Emperor (1683–1719, reigned 1713–1719). Born Jalāluddīn Muhammad. After the ubiquitous struggle to power, Farrukh Sīyār ascended to the throne at Delhi in 1713. Almost immediately he launched a campaign against the Sikhs who, led by Bandā Bahādur (q.v.), were ravaging the southern boundary of Punjab. Bandā was captured and killed under Farrukh Sīyār's orders and throughout the Punjab a price was put on the head of any Sikh.

Fateh Singh Āhlūvālīā (d. 1836). Grand nephew of Jassā Singh Āhlūvālīā (q.v.) and successor to the Āhlūvālīā chieftainship. Fateh Singh was a close companion of Mahārājā Ranjīt Singh (q.v.) throughout his life, and was present at most of his early successes. Throughout the 1820s, the Āhlūvālīā chief felt threatened by Ranjīt Singh's ambitions on his neighbors, including his own territory and promptly fled to the south of Ranjīt Singh's border and sought protection under the British. The rift was soon repaired and Fateh Singh returned to Lahore and was honorably received by Ranjīt Singh in 1827.

Ghulām Qādir (d. 1789). The son of Zābitā Khān (q.v.) and grandson of Najīb ud-Daulā (q.v.), the Rohīllā chief who had invited Ahmad Shāh Abdālī (q.v.) to come to India and punish the Marāthās which he did in 1761 at the third battle of Pānīpat. In retaliation to this defeat, the Marāthās led an expedition in 1772 with the help of the Mughal Emperor Shāh Ālum II (q.v.) against Zābitā Khān. The entire family of Zābitā Khān and other Rohīllā leaders were arrested and severely humiliated. Among them was Zābitā's son, Ghulām Qādir, who was castrated and made to serve as a page in the palace. In 1787, Ghulām Qādir routed the Marāthā forces and forced the emperor to appoint him as *mīr bakhshī* and regent, the positions held by his father.

After leaving Delhi due to differences with the emperor, he returned the next year and took his revenge. He blinded Shāh Ālum II with great cruelty and subjected the inmates of the palace, princes and princesses to severe hardship and humiliation.

Gobind Singh, Gurū (1666–1708, Gurūship 1675–1708). Tenth Gurū of the Sikhs. Born Gobind Rāi, he was only nine years old when his father, Gurū Tegh Bahādur (q.v.) was executed by Emperor Aurangzeb (q.v.). In his childhood, the Gurū learnt the art of riding, shooting, warfare, and hunting. He studied Persian, Sanskrit, Hindī, and Punjabī. During his life, he was engaged in numerous battles against the Mughals and Hill Rājās. He abolished the system of *masands*—the deputies who had traditionally collected contributions from geographically scattered Sikh communities—due to their high level of corruption. Linked to this was the establishment of the Khālsā (q.v.) in 1699, those Sikhs initiated in a ceremony using the *khandā* (q.v.) or double-edged sword. All four of his sons were killed in a bloody campaign fought him by against the combined forces of the Mughals and Hill Rājās. He traveled to the southern districts of India to discuss with the new Mughal Emperor Bahādur Shāh (q.v.) the persecution he had faced in the Punjab. Whilst in Nanded, a town on the banks of the Godāvrī river, he was stabbed by a Pathān in the stomach in an assassination attempt. The Gurū died sometime after this event, and directed the Sikhs to consider the Gurū Granth Sāhib as their Gurū in the place of a human guide.

Gurdittā, Bābā (1613–1638). Eldest son of Gurū Hargobind who was appointed by Udāsi Bābā Srī Chand (q.v.) to establish four *dhūāns* or *Udāsī* (q.v.) preaching centres. Bābā Gurdittā had two sons, Dhīr Mall and Har Rāi. The latter succeeded Gurū Hargobind as Gurū in 1644.

Hastings, Warren (1732–1818). The first Governor-General of British India. He started as a clerk in the East India Company in 1750, and soon became the manager of a trading post in Bengal. When Calcutta was captured in 1756 by Siraj ud-Daulā, Hastings was taken prisoner but soon released. In 1757, the city was recaptured by the British, and he was made British resident at Murshīdabad. He left India for England in 1764, disgusted with administrative corruption in Bengal, but returned in 1769, becoming governor of Bengal in 1772 and Governor-General of India two years later. Hastings resigned in 1784 and returned to England, and was made a privy councilor in 1814.

Jahāngīr, Emperor (1569–1627, reigned 1605–1627). Mughal emperor of India and son of Akbar (q.v.). He continued his father's policy of expansion. In 1611, Jahāngīr married a Persian widow, Nūr Jahān, and she and her relatives soon dominated the political sphere of the empire, while Jahāngīr devoted himself to cultivation of the arts, especially miniature painting. He welcomed foreign visitors to his court, granting trading privileges first to the Portuguese and then to the English East India Company. He was responsible for the death of Gurū Arjan (q.v.) and maintained a close eye on his son, Gurū Hargobind. Shāh Jahān, his son, succeeded him.

Jai Singh Kanhaiyā (1712–1793). A Sandhū Jat who was initiated into the Khālsā fold by the legendary leader of the *Buddhā Dal* (q.v.), Nawāb Kapūr Singh. He later founded the Kanhaiyā *misl* which rose to prominence as one most powerful of the Sikh confederacies in the late eighteenth century. Jai Singh made territorial gains in conjuction with Jassā Singh Rāmgharīā (q.v.) to subdue many of the hill states to tributary status. However, in 1778, he fought against Jassā Singh Rāmgharīā with the assistance of Mahā Singh Sukkarchakkīā (q.v.) and Jassā Singh Āhlūvālīā (q.v.), the two most significant Sikh chiefs of the day. In another change of fortune a few years later, Jai Singh's son, Gurbakhsh Singh, was killed during a territorial battle against the Sukkarchakkīā *misl*. In a gesture of reconciliation, the warring factions decided on a betrothal between the late Gurbakhsh Singh's daughter, Mehtāb Kaur, and the heir to the Sukkarchakkīā leadership, Ranjīt Singh (q.v.). After Jai Singh's death, Sadā Kaur, the astute wife of Gurbakhsh Singh, took over control of the Kanhaiyā *misl* until it was finally subsumed by Ranjīt Singh in his successful bid to become outright ruler of the Punjab.

Jassā Singh Āhlūvālīā (1718–1783). Born into the family of Badar Singh Kelāl, their hereditary profession would have been distilling and dealing in spirits. He founded the village of Āhlū, seven miles from Lahore, from which the more common appellation of Āhlūvālīā was created. A commander of the *Dal Khālsā* who proclaimed the sovereignty of the Sikhs in 1761, Jassā Singh had initially served under the legendary Nawāb Kapūr Singh and was active when Ahmad Shāh Durrānī (q.v.) made his invasions into the Punjab. In 1748, a *Sarbat Khālsā* (q.v.) at Amritsar resolved to consolidate the sixty-five roving Sikh *jathās* into one command called *Dal Khālsā* (q.v.) under Jassā Singh. Āhlūvālīā was to lead the *Dal Khālsā* at its most precarious times, with the fragile union of Sikh *jathās* and the cruelest persecution under Mīr Mannū (q.v.). When Punjab was plunged into chaos after the 1753 death of Mīr Mannū, Jassā Singh commenced a policy of seizing villages in the Punjab and established the system of *rākhī* (q.v.). Jassā Singh's military accomplishments as leader of the *Dal Khālsā* were marked by the routing of Afghān forces laying siege to Amritsar in April 1754, a rearguard attack on Timur Shāh (q.v.) in 1757, and the attack and capture of Lahore in 1758 to install Ādīnā Beg (q.v.) as governor. An ebullient Sikh army lead by Jassā Singh burst into Lahore in September 1761 chasing the Afghān governor out of the city walls. Jassā Singh Āhlūvālīā was proclaimed king of Lahore with the title of Sultān ul-Qaum (king of the nation). Victory was short lived, as the Duranni Shāh returned and for the next four years Sikhs and the Afghāns skirmished in a war of attrition in Punjab. Jassā Singh died on October 20, 1783 at the age of sixty-five.

Jassā Singh Rāmgharīā (1723–1803). Born into an artisan family in the village of Īchogill near Amritsar. The family's traditional profession was that of *tharkhān* or carpenter. The pejorative *Tokhā* is occasionally used to denote a *tharkhān* caste. Jassā Singh is known as Jassā Singh Tokha in some early references, later and for a short period, Jassā Singh Īchogill and later still, as Jassā Singh Rāmgharīā on account of his rebuilding of the *Rām Raonī* (q.v.) fort, later named *Rāmgarh*. Jassā Singh was the founder of the Rāmgharīā chiefship and one of the most prominent Sikh military leaders in the second half of the eighteenth century. Born into a rich Sikh martial tradition, the young Jassā Singh greatly annoyed the Sikh populace by accepting office under the wily *faujdār* Ādīnā Beg Khān (q.v.) for a short period but redeemed himself by successfully negotiating the lifting of siege of *Rām Raonī*. It was a factious *Dal Khālsā* within which Jassā Singh Rāmgharīā was a major player with the powerful Āhlūvālīā and Kanhaiyā *misls* pitted mercilessly against him. Finally and inevitably, the Rāmgharīā *Sirdār* fled the Punjab to find relative success as a soldier of fortune in and around Delhi. It was only after the death of Jassā Singh. Āhlūvālīā in 1783 and with the support of the Sukkarchakkīā *misl* that Jassā Singh finally returned to Punjab. He reclaimed his ancestral lands after having defeated his old enemy, Jai Singh Kanhaiyā (q.v.), killing his son and heir.

Jasvant Rāo Holkār (d. 1811). A guerilla leader who became the leader of the Holkār Marāthās in 1798. After defeating the Scindiās of Gwalior in 1803, he took on the British forces and defeated Colonel William Monson and besieged Delhi. He was, however, defeated by General Gerard (Lord) Lake (q.v.) at Dīg and Farrukhābād in 1804, and was compelled to make peace a year later after his attempts to rally Mahārājā Ranjīt Singh (q.v.) against the British failed. Soon after, he became insane and died in 1811.

Kaurā Mall, Dīwān (d. 1752). Installed as the ministerof Lahore and Multān during the reign of Muin ul-Mulk (d. 1753), the Mughal governor of the Punjab. Kaurā Mall was a *Khatrī Nānakpanthī* (q.v.) who did not become a Khālsā Sikh but did support the Sikhs and the Khālsā greatly during some of the harshest treatment at the hands of Muin ul-Mulk (q.v.). In recognition of the assistance he rendered at vital times, the Sikhs renamed him Mitta Mal (the name *Kaurā*, or "bitter" in Punjabi, was changed to *Mitta*, or "sweet").

Lake, Lord Gerard (1744–1808). A British general. He entered the foot guards in 1758, becoming a major-general in 1790. After seeing action in the continent and in Ireland, Lake returned to England in 1799, and soon afterward became the commander in chief in India. He applied himself to the improvement of the British Indian army, especially in the direction of making all arms, infantry, cavalry and artillery more mobile and more manageable. In 1802, he was made a full general and in the following year, defeated the Marāthās, took Delhi and Agra, thereby laying down the foundation of British supremacy in India. In 1805, Lake pursued the Marāthā leader, Jasvant Rāo Holkār (q.v.), into the Punjab and compelled him to surrender at Amritsar in December 1805. The British also signed their first treaty with Ranjīt Singh (q.v.) a month later.

Lakhmī Chand, Bābā (1497–1555). Second son of Gurū Nānak (q.v.) born in Sultānpur Lodhī.

Mahā Singh Sukkarchakkīā (d. 1790). Son of Charhat Singh Sukkarchakkīā (q.v.), he married a daughter of Gajpat Singh, the chief of Jīnd, thereby strengthening his own position among the chief *misls* (q.v.). He launched upon a career of conquest and expansion of territory. He captured Rasūlnagar from a Muslim tribe, the *Chatthās*, and renamed it Rāmnagar. In 1782, he proceeded to Jammū whose Dogrā ruler fled leaving the rich city to the mercy of his men. With the loot of Jammū, he raised the Sukkarchakkīā *misl* from a position of comparative obscurity to that of being one of the most prominent. He died in 1790, leaving his only son, Ranjīt Singh (q.v.), to continue what he had started.

Malcolm, Lt.-Col. Sir John (1769–1833). Soldier, diplomat, administrator, and author. At the age of twelve, he received a cadetship in the Indian army, and in 1783 he landed at Madrās. An accomplished Persian interpreter, he distinguished himself in several sensitive diplomatic situations. At the close of the Marāthā War, in 1804, and again in 1805, he negotiated important treaties with the Marāthās, including Jasvant Rāo Holkār (q.v.) and Ranjīt Singh (q.v.). In 1810, he submitted the groundbreaking *Sketch of the Sikhs* for publication in the journal *Asiatick Researches*. He sailed for England in 1811, and shortly after his arrival in the following year was knighted. He devoted his spare time to literary work, publishing *Sketch of the Sikhs* in book-form in 1812.

Mātā Gūjarī (1624–1705). Married to Gurū Tegh Bahādur (q.v.) in 1633, after a betrothal some four years earlier. On the death of Gurū Hargobind, Tegh Bahādur's father, the couple moved from Kīratpur in the Śivālik foothills to Bakālā near Amritsar. After Tegh Bahādur was installed as Gurū in 1644, the family moved east to Mākhovāl near Kīratpur, founding Chakk Nānakī sometime in 1665; this town was later renamed Anandpur Sāhib. In 1666, Mātā Gūjarī gave birth to a son, Gobind Rāi, in Patnā. The Gurū had started the long journey east earlier in 1666. After a prolonged period in the east of the country, the family ultimately moved back to Chakk Nānakī in 1670. In 1675, the Gurū was arrested in Delhi by the Mughals where he was executed. The task of managing the affairs of Chakk Nānakī fell on Mātā Gūjarī's shoulders and she managed them with the assistance of her younger brother, Kirpāl Chand. Mātā Gūjarī died on December 11, 1705, a prisoner of Wazīr Khān (q.v.), *faujdār* of Sirhind.

Metcalfe, Sir Charles Theophilus (1785–1846). Indian and colonial administrator. After studying Oriental languages as the first student at Lord Wellesley's College of Fort William, at the age of nineteen, he was appointed political assistant to General Lake (q.v.), who was then conducting the final campaign of the Marāthā War against Jasvant Rāo Holkār (q.v.). In 1808, aged twenty-three, he was selected by Lord Minto for the important post of envoy to the court of Ranjīt Singh (q.v.) at Lahore. In 1809, he concluded the important treaty securing the independence of the Sikh states between the Sutlej and the Yamunā, thereby establishing the boundary between the dominions of British India and Ranjīt Singh.

Mīr Mannū, Mu'in ul-Mulk (d. 1753). Mughal governor of the Punjab (1748–1753). He took charge of the province after he had defeated the Afghān invader, Ahmad Shāh Durrānī (q.v.), in the battle fought at Mānūpur near Sirhind. As governor of the Punjab, Mīr Mannū proved a worse foe of the Sikhs than his predecessors 'Abd us-Samad Khān (q.v.), Zakarīyā Khān (q.v.), and Yāhīyā Khān (1745–1747), and continued the witch hunt with greater severity. His policy of apprehending Sikhs and forcibly making them shave their heads and beards drove the Sikhs to seek refuge in the mountains and jungles. Under the influence of his *Khatrī* minister, Kaurā Mall (q.v.), he made peace with the Sikhs in order to use their force against the threat of Ahmad Shāh Durrānī. The death of Kaurā Mall in battle against Ahmad Shāh snapped the only link between Mīr Mannū and the Sikh *Sirdārs*. The Sikhs had used the advantage to occupy large parts of his territory, so Mannū now resumed his policy of repression. Prices were again placed on their heads and strict orders were passed against giving refuge to them anywhere. This continued until Mannū's death, from a fall from his horse, in 1753.

Nādir Shāh (1688–1747, Shāh of Iran 1736–1747). He was a member of the Afshar tribe and as a child was taken prisoner by the Uzbeks but escaped and entered the service of the governor of Khorasān. There he earned a reputation for bravery. He then entered the service of the Persians, who were asserting their claims against the Afghāns who had usurped the Persian throne. Nādir proceeded to win a series of battles against the Afghāns. Decisively beaten, they retired to Kandahār. Nādir, however, deposed the last of the Safāvid rulers in 1736 and proclaimed himself as Shāh. During 1738–1739, Nādir Shāh invaded Mughal India, returning to his homeland after taking and sacking Delhi and Lahore and carrying off vast quantities of treasures, including the Koh-i-nūr diamond and the Peacock Throne. It was during Nādir's invasion that the Sikhs were able to replenish their depleted stores after years in a protracted guerilla war under the tenure of the governor of Lahore, Zakarīyā Khān (q.v.). As Nādir Shāh returned home with his immense booty, bands of Sikh fighters relieved him of his treasures. In 1747, during a campaign against rebellious Kurds, Nādir Shāh was assassinated by officers of his own guard. Although the Afshar dynasty he founded was short-lived (1736–1749), Nādir is generally regarded as one of the greatest of all rulers of Persia.

Najaf Khān, Mirzā. Iranian nobleman who became the grand *wazīr*, or prime minister, of the Mughal Empire during the reign of Shāh Alum II.

Najīb ud-Daulā (d. 1770). Born Najīb Khān, he started life as a foot soldier under Alī Muhammad, the first chief of the Rohīllās—an Afghān tribe from Roh in the North-West Frontier region—who made themselves masters of the land called Rohilkhand between the river Ganges and the Kumaon hills in the eighteenth century. Rising quickly through the ranks, he received the title of Najīb ud-Daulā from the Mughal emperor, Ālumgīr II (q.v.). He was later appointed *mīr bakhshī* or paymaster of the army by Ahmad Shāh Durrānī (q.v.) and was to act as his *mukhtār* or agent plenipotentiary. Being an ally of the Durrānī Shāh, he was not in favor with the Sikhs and was continually in conflict with them. The Sikhs frequently made raids into his territories and skirmishes with the Rohīllās continued until his death in 1770. He was succeeded by his son, Zābita Khān (q.v.).

Nānak, Guru (1469–1539, Guruship 1469–1539). First Guru of the Sikhs. He began discussions with holy men of both Hindu and Islamic beliefs at a very early age. For sometime, Guru Nānak worked as a book-keeper of Nawāb Daulat Khān Lodhī, the Afghān chief, at Sultānpur. There he reinstated his childhood association with Mardānā, a Muslim family servant. When Guru Nānak composed his spiritual verses, Mardānā, a *rebec* player, gave them the soul of music. It was at Sultānpur that Guru Nānak had his first vision of "The One God Whose Name Is True," in which he was ordered to preach truth to mankind. He went on four extensive journeys throughout India, Tibet, and Mecca. After many years thus traveling, he finally settled down with his family at Kartārpur, a township on the banks of the river Rāvī. During his lifetime, he nominated his most faithful Sikh, Lahinā, whom he renamed (Guru) Angad (q.v.), as the successor to his spiritual seat.

Omīchand (d. 1767). A Sikh merchant whose name is indelibly associated with the treaty negotiated by Robert Clive (q.v.) before the Battle of Plassey in 1757. His real name was probably Amir Chand. He had long been resident at Calcutta, where he had acquired a large fortune by providing the investment for the Company, and also by acting as intermediary between the English and the native court at Murshīdabad.

Rām Dās, Guru (1534–1581, Guruship 1574–81). Fourth Guru of the Sikhs. Soon after his nomination as the Guru, Rām Dās established a small town for the Sikhs around a constructed tank known as *Guru ka Chak* or *Chak Rām Dās*. He encouraged tradesmen and merchants to establish businesses in the town and with the revenues collected, spread his activities to different parts of the country. Like his predecessors, Guru Rām Dās composed spiritual verses which were later incorporated into the *Guru Granth Sāhib* (q.v.). His youngest son, (Guru) Arjan (q.v.), succeeded him as Guru.

Ranjīt Singh, Māhārājā (1780–1839, reigned 1801–1839). Son of Mahā Singh (q.v.), whom he succeeded in 1792 as head of the Sukkarchakkīā *misl* (q.v.). At the age of 19, he forced from Zamān Shāh (q.v.), the king of Afghānistān, a grant of

Lahore, which he seized by force of arms in 1799. Subsequently, he attacked and annexed Amritsar in 1802, thus becoming master of the two major cities of the Punjab. By 1805, acute difficulties arose between him and the British as to the cis-Sutlej portion of the Punjab. The differences proceeded almost to the point of war; but at the last moment Ranjīt Singh gave way, and for the future, faithfully observed his engagements with the British. He organized a powerful force, which was trained by French and Italian officers, such as Generals Ventura, Allard, and Avitabile, and thus forged the formidable fighting instrument of the Khālsā army. In 1810, he captured Multān after many assaults and a long siege, and in 1820 had consolidated the whole of the Punjab between the Sutlej and the Indus under his dominion. In 1823, the city and province of Peshāwar became tributary to him. Known as *The Lion of the Punjab*, Ranjīt Singh had a genius for command and was the only man in the nineteenth century the Sikhs ever produced strong enough to bind them together. His power was a military aristocracy resting on the personal qualities of its founder, and after his death following a period of paralysis in 1839; the Sikh kingdom fell to pieces through sheer want of leadership.

Sāhib Singh, Rājā (1773–1813, reigned 1781–1813). After the death of his father Amar Singh, Rājā Sāhib Singh, who was six years old, was made the ruler of Patiālā, with the affairs of the state managed by Dīwān Nānū Mall. Sāhib Singh was a very weak figure and was frequently guided and helped by his sister, Sāhib Kaur, who helped save the state in 1794 from usurpation by the Marāthās. It was during his rule that the state came under British protection. He was succeeded by his son, Karam Singh.

Shāh Ālum I. See **Bahādur Shāh, Emperor** (q.v.).

Shāh Ālum II, Emperor (1728–1806, reigned 1759–1806). The son and the successor of Ālumgīr II, originally known as the Shāhzāda Alī Gohar. Proclaimed a rebel by his father, he fled to Shujā-ud-Daulā, *wazīr* of Oudh, and on the death of his father in 1759, assumed the name of Shāh Alum. He joined Shujā-ud-Daulā against the British, but after his defeat at the Battle of Buxar, he sought British protection. In 1765, he granted the *diwanī* (superintendence of the revenue) of Bengal to Lord Clive on behalf of the East India Company. In 1788, the Rohīllā chief Ghulām Qādir (q.v.) seized Delhi and blinded Shāh Ālum. Sindhia restored him to the throne, and after the Marāthā War of 1803 he was again taken under British protection and died in their protection as a pensioner in 1806.

Skinner, James (1778–1841). Eurasian military adventurer in India, son of Lt.-Col. Hercules Skinner, his mother being a Rajput lady. At the age of eighteen, he entered the Marāthā army, where he showed signs of military talent. He remained in the same service until 1803, but on the outbreak of the Marāthā War, he refused to serve against his countrymen and joined Lord Lake (q.v.). He raised a regiment of irregular cavalry called Skinner's Horse. He had an intimate knowledge of the character of the Indian peoples, and his advice was highly valued by successive governor-generals and commanders in chief.

Srī Chand, Bābā (1494–1629). The eldest son of Gurū Nānak (q.v.) who founded the order of *Udāsīs*—holy men who spread the message of the Gurūs all over Asia. Bābā Srī Chand lived to see six of the Gurūs and had close relationships with all of them.

Sūraj Mal (d. 1763). Son of Thākur Badan Singh, the Jat founder of the house of Bhāratpur.

Tegh Bahādur, Gurū (1621–1675, Gurūship 1664–1675). Ninth Gurū of the Sikhs. The youngest son of Gurū Hargobind and brother of Bābā Gurditta (q.v.), on his accession to the status of Gurū, he was constantly persecuted by the many contenders for the same position. Some, such as Dhīr Mall, a disaffected nephew, went as far as employing assassins to kill him but failed in their endeavor. He established the town of Anandpur Sāhib, originally known as Mākhovāl in the Śivālik foothills in the Himāliyās. Whilst on a preaching tour to eastern India, a son was born in 1666 in Patnā. He was named Gobind Rāi, and later became Gurū Gobind Singh (q.v.), the tenth Gurū of the Sikhs. Gurū Tegh Bahādur toured the Punjab extensively and gathered a significant following. After hearing of the religious persecution faced by the Kashmīrī *pandits*, he agreed to help protect their religious freedom against the Mughal regime. Emperor Aurangzeb (q.v.) had the Gurū summoned to Delhi, where he was sentenced to death and executed on November 11, 1675.

Timur Shāh (1746–1793, reigned 1772–1793). The second son of Ahmad Shāh Abdālī (q.v.) who became the ruler of the Afghāns after his father's death. Previously, he was the governor of Herat. He was unable to hold the vast empire created by his father together. As a result, he moved his capital from Kandahār to Kābul in 1776 for security reasons.

Wazīr Khān, Nawāb (d. 1710). Born c. 1630 and a resident for most of his life in Kunjpurā, near Karnāl (now in Haryānā), he rose to the rank of *faujdār* of Sirhind, an administrative area that took in Anandpur Sāhib. He was directly responsible for hostilities against Gurū Gobind Singh (q.v.) and ordered his two youngest sons to be killed while in his custody. He was killed in a battle against Bandā Bahādur (q.v.).

Wellesely, Sir Arthur (1769–1852). British general, also first Duke of Wellington, best known for his victory over Napoleon at the famous Battle of Waterloo in 1814. A leader of the Tory party in the British Parliament as well as a soldier, Wellington was known as the *Iron Duke* for his steadfastness. In 1796, Wellesley, holding the rank of colonel in the army, went to India, where he subsequently received his first independent command. Richard Colley Wellesley, his brother, was appointed governor-general of India in 1797. Arthur took part in several military campaigns; in the Battle of Assāye in 1803, he subdued the Marāthās, an event that saw the British take Delhi and firmly establish themselves as rulers of much of North India. Returning to England in 1805, he was rewarded with a knighthood and was elected to the British Parliament.

Zābitā Khān (d. 1785). The son of Najīb ud-Daulā (q.v.) and leader of the Rohīllā Afghāns of Rohilkhand. He succeeded his father as the *mīr bakhshī* of the Mughal Empire in 1770 but lost most of his territory in 1774 to the Nawāb of Oudh assisted by a British force. He came to terms with the Sikhs, conceding to them the right to collect *rākhī* or protection levy. The Sikhs became his allies when he attempted to take control of Mughal territories and assisted him for several months of onslaught. He was finally defeated in 1777 and fled to the Sikh camp where he strengthened his relationship by officially becoming a Sikh with the name Dharam Singh. He later came back into favor with the Mughal emperor, after which the Sikhs recommenced their raids into his territories. He was succeeded by his son, Ghulām Qādir (q.v.).

Zakarīyā Khān (d. 1745). The son of 'Abd us-Samad Khān (q.v.) and successor to his father as the governor of Lahore from 1726. He had earlier taken part in the Lahore government's operations against Bandā Singh Bahādur (q.v.). He launched a severe policy against the Sikhs, establishing a graded scale of rewards in an attempt to exterminate them from the region. These included a blanket for cutting off a Sikh's hair, ten rupees for information about the whereabouts of a Sikh, and fifty rupees for a Sikh scalp. Even with these measures, he remained unsuccessful in eliminating them and died dispirited in 1745.

Zemān Shāh (d.1801, reigned 1793–1800). Fifth son of Timur Shāh (q.v.) who seized the throne after his father's death in 1793, with the help of *Sirdār* Payendā Khān, a chief of the Barakzay. Zemān Shāh then turned to India with the object of repeating the exploits of his grandfather, Ahmad Shāh (q.v.). He made several incursions into India but the Durrānī Empire had already begun to disintegrate. In 1799, Zemān Shāh was forced to appoint Ranjīt Singh (q.v.) as his governor of Lahore due to pressure from the Sikhs. He hurried back to Afghānistān when he discovered one of his brothers, Mahmūd, was threatening his power in Kandahār. He was captured on his return, blinded, imprisoned in 1800, and died the following year.

GLOSSARY OF TERMS

Ādi Gurū Granth Sāhib. The foremost sacred scriptures of the Sikhs and their Gurū. Normally referred to as the Gurū Granth Sāhib.

Akālī. The original Sikh warriors raised by Gurū Hargobind at the *Akāl Takht* (q.v.), the word *Akālī* means "immortals". They are also known as *Akālī Nihangs* (q.v.) and were distinguishable by their blue dress, weaponry, and bravado language, the *gar gaj bole* (q.v.), all preserved in memory of Gurū Gobind Singh (q.v.).

Akāl Takht/Akāl Būngā (the throne of the Immortal Being). The second most revered Sikh religious establishment after the Harimandar Sāhib, it was built at the instigation of Gurū Arjan Dev (q.v.) by his son, Gurū Hargobind, opposite the Harimandar Sāhib (q.v.).

Amrit (ambrosial nectar). The sweetened water prepared during the Khālsā (q.v.) initiation rite called *khande dī pahul* (q.v.).

Amritsar. The religious capital of the Sikhs. Founded by Gurū Rām Dās (q.v.) and originally known as Chakk Gurū or Chakk Rāmdās, both the Harimandar Sāhib (q.v.) and Akāl Takht (q.v.) are located here.

Ardās. Collective prayer used to conclude most Sikh services. Derived from the Persian ʻarz-dāsht (a written petition) the term is used as a form of deferential address.

Bābā. Term of respect preceding the name of a holy or elderly person.

Bhāī (brother). A term of respect conferred on male Sikhs of piety and learning. This title is also used in the context of a reader of Sikh scriptures.

Bhang. The Punjabī word for cannabis. One of the ingredients in a drink called *sukkhā* (q.v.).

Buddhā Dal (army of veterans). A *gurmatā* (q.v.) in the 1730s decided that the Dal Khālsā (q.v.) should split itself between the younger army, Tarunā Dal (q.v.), and the Army of Veterans, the Buddhā Dal. The Buddhā Dal contained the more experienced of the Khālsā, and retains that position within the order of Akālī Nihangs to this day. Oral traditions also speak of the Buddhā Dal being the army of Bābā Buddhā, one of the most respected Sikhs who lived during the first six Gurūs. He was responsible for training a small standing army that resided at the Akāl Takht (q.v.), which became the core of the Khālsā (q.v.).

Būngā. Tower, residence or fortress.

Chakk Gurū, Chakk Rāmdās. The old name for what became the city of Amritsar.

Chakkar. An iron quoit, usually worn around the turban, used by Akālī Nihang Sikhs as a projectile weapon. The use of the *chakkar* as a weapon is peculiarly Sikh although its roots are in Hindu mythology where it is often portrayed as the favorite weapon of Vishnū.

Charan Amrit. Initiation by water touched by the master's foot. *Charan amrit* or *pagpahul* was a custom prevalent at the time of Gurū Nānak (q.v.). Where the Gurū was not present, a *masand* (q.v.) would lead the baptism by dipping his foot in the baptismal waters. In mainstream Sikh practice, this was replaced in 1699 by the *khande dī pahul* (q.v.).

Coss. See **Koh**.

Dal. Army.

Dal Khālsā. The collective of the fighting forces of Sikh fighting *jathās* (q.v.) or *misls* (q.v.) during the eighteenth century. Formerly split into the Buddhā Dal (q.v.) and the Tarunā Dal (q.v.) in the 1730s.

Dasam Granth. Book of the tenth Gurū. The collected works of Gurū Gobind Singh, compiled by his companion, Bhāī Manī Singh, after his death.

Farmān. An order, patent, or passport.

Faujdār. A military commander or a military governor of a district.

Gar Gaj Bole (words that thunder). Bravado language of the Akālī Nihang Singhs (q.v.). Also referred to as *Nihang Singh de bole* and *Khālsā de bole*.

Granth (book). Used as impious shorthand for, and of, the Sikh sacred texts.

Gurdwārā (the Gurū's gate). A Sikh place of worship, which always houses the Ādi Gurū Granth Sāhib (q.v.), and historically, the Dasam Granth (q.v.).

Gurmatā. The binding decision made at the *Sarbat Khālsā* (q.v.) at the Akāl Takht (q.v.) or any secure place.

Gurū. Literally means from darkness (gu) to light (rū). Teacher, spiritual preceptor, or guide who takes the student from a state of ignorance to knowledge.

Gurū Granth Sāhib. See **Ādi Gurū Granth Sāhib**.

Harimandar Sāhib. The premier Sikh place of worship in Amritsar, built under the supervision of Gurū Arjan (q.v.). Known in the western world as the Golden Temple after the upper storey was gilded during Mahārājā Ranjīt Singh's (q.v.) reign.

Jagīr. Fife, estate, rent-free land grant, regular cash grant for services to the state.

Jang Nāmā. A war ballad.

Jat. An agrarian caste group found throughout northern India, but concentrated largely in the Punjab. Jats have settled and now dominate the culture, politics, and traditions of the Punjab.

Jathā. Group, gathering, squadron.

Jathedār. Leader of a *jathā* (q.v.).

Jalandhar. A major city in the Punjab, situated within the Jalandhar Doāb between the rivers Sutlej and Beās.

Karā. War bracelet made from iron. One of the five Ks that form the uniform of a Khālsā (q.v.) Sikh.

Kachchh. Knee length draws worn specifically for a military life. One of the five K's that form the uniform of a Khālsā (q.v.) Sikh.

Kes. Uncut hair of a Sikh. One of the five K's that form the uniform of a Khālsā (q.v.) Sikh.

Khālsā (crownlands). Signifying the direct and unbroken link between the Gurū and the Sikh. Initiated with a ceremony called *khande dī pahul* (q.v.).

Khandā. Straight, double-edged, broad sword.

Khande dī Pahul. The ceremony that forms the Sikh initiation rite; specific texts are read as the *amrit* (q.v.) is prepared.

Khatrī. Largely to be found in mercantile professions, the *Khatrī* caste is divided into four subgroups; these are further divided into 92 castes.

Khulāsā. A non-Khālsā Sikh.

Koh. An Indian distance varying much in different localities, ranging from two to four miles.

Lakh. One hundred thousand.

Lohgarh (iron fort). Bandā Singh Bahādur (q.v.) was besieged in this fort near Sadhaurā.

Ludhīānā. A large industrial city in the Malwā region of Punjab.

Masand. A group of local community leaders who initially acted as intermediaries between the Gurū and the widely spread *sangats* (q.v.), but who were later removed by Gurū Gobind Singh (q.v.) following corruption in their practices.

Misl (confederacy). On the occasion of Baisakhi in 1734, the supreme leader of the Sikhs, Nawāb Kapūr Singh, organized the sixty-five distinct *jathās*, or groups, of Sikh fighting bands into eleven main *misls*, or divisions. They were further divided into two broad groups, the Buddha Dal (q.v.) and Taruna Dal (q.v.). Each *misl* had a distinguishing title and battle standard, and were of varying strength.

Nānakpanthī (followers of Nanak). Early adopters of Sikhism during the time of the Gurūs were usually referred to as Nānakpanthīs. This remains a generic term for Sikhs who follow the path of the Gurūs but do not take up the Khālsā's call for arms.

Nihang. Traditionally, a term synonymous with the Akālīs (q.v.) but this actually relates to those warrior Khālsā Singhs who ranked directly below them within their order. The word has various meanings such as alligator, lion, sword, unattached to the world, without care for life or death, without taint, pure, beloved solider of the Gurū.

Omrah. A lord or grandee of the Mughal court.

Pahul. See **Khande dī Pahul**.

Pañj Piāre. Five Sikhs of great learning and service to the Sikh religion and nation representing the original five Khālsā (q.v.). Such a body of Khālsā Sikhs is the sanctioning voice of the Gurū.

Panth. The Sikh community composed of Khālsā (q.v.) and non-Khālsā Sikhs called Khulāsā (q.v).

Phūlkīān. Clan name of the house of Phūl based mainly in Patiālā.

Purgunnah. A subdivision of a district.

Rackhī (protection, to protect the life and property of the people). The *rākhī* was a levy, usually of one-fifth of the revenue assessment of a territory, as a fee for the guarantee of peace and protection. This was normally paid twice a year in May and October coinciding with the end of each harvest.

Rām-Rāonī (encloser of Rām). A small, mud-walled enclosure located near Amritsar and raised by the Sikhs in April 1748, it was named the Rām-Rāonī after the fourth Gurū, Rāmdās (q.v.), the founder of Amritsar. As one of the few fortified permanent structures in Mughal Punjab, it became a rallying point for the disparate Sikh communities of the eighteenth century. It faced a siege at the hands of Mīr Mannū (q.v.) which was ultimately lifted after the intervention of Jassā Singh Rāmghariā (q.v.). The fort was rebuilt and renamed Ramgarh, which Jassā Singh used as a base for future operations.

Sahajdhārī. Non-Khālsā Sikh. See **Khulāsā**.

Sangat. The term given to the Sikh congregation, either locally or nationally.

Sarbat Khālsā. Traditionally, a gathering of all Khālsā (q.v.) representatives at the behest of Buddhā Dal's Jathedār (q.v.) of Akāl Takht (q.v.), held there or any secure place. Traditionally, convened during the two main festivals of Baisākhī (April) and Divālī (October).

Sirdār. Traditionally applied to a Khālsā (q.v.) Sikh chief, but later used to denote Sikh nobles and today to a Khālsā Sikh.

Sirhind. Literally the "head of India," this city lies along the Grand Trunk Road, midway between Ambālā and Ludhiānā (q.v.). Sirhind was vitally important Mughal city and one that enjoyed considerable commercial and artistic success. After a series of battles with the *faujdār* (q.v.) of Sirhind in which Gurū Gobind Singh (q.v.) lost two of his sons, Nawāb Wazīr Khān (q.v.) had the two youngest sons captured and executed in Sirhind. In 1710, Bandā Bahādur (q.v.) routed the Mughal army of Wazīr Khān and occupied Sirhind. Over the next forty years, the town changed hands frequently between Sikhs, Mughals, and Afghān invaders as Mughal power disintegrated in Punjab.

Sukkhā (comfort giver). A concoction which includes bhang (q.v.) that was—and still is—used as a sacrament, predominantly by Akālī (q.v.) Sikhs.

Tarunā Dal. The army of the young. See **Buddhā Dal**.

Udāsī. Literally "sad" or "detached." The order of Sikhs established by Gurū Nānak's (q.v.) eldest son, Bābā Srī Chand (q.v.), known for their ascetic ways and achievements in spreading Sikhism throughout the Indian subcontinent. Also refers to the long journeys undertaken by Gurū Nānak before he settled to a life as a householder in Kartārpur.

Vāhigurū (wonderous dispeller of ignorance). The foremost Sikh *mantrā* and designation for the One Creator, Preserver and Destroyer.

Vār. Ballad.

Bibliography

Books in English

Ahluwalia, M.L. *Land Marks in Sikh History, A Fully Researched and Documented History: 1699–1947*. New Delhi: Ashoka International Publishers, 1996.

Ahmed, Zulfiqar, ed. *Selections from the Journal of the Punjab Historical Society: 1 Lahore and the Punjab*. Lahore: Sang-e-Meel Publications, 1982.

Ahmed, Zulfiqar, ed. *Selections from the Journal of the Punjab Historical Society: 2 Punjab*. Lahore: Sang-e-Meel Publications, 1982.

Ahmed, Zulfiqar, ed. *Selections from the Journal of the Punjab Historical Society: 3 Mughal India*. Lahore: Sang-e-Meel Publications, 1982.

Aijazuddin, F.S. *Lahore: Illustrated Views of the 19th Century*. Middlesetown, NJ: Grantha Corp, 1991.

Alam, Muzaffar. *The Crisis of Empire in Mughal North India: Awadh and the Punjab 1707–1748*. Delhi: Oxford University Press, 1986.

Alam, Muzaffar and Sanjay Subrahmanyam, eds. *The Mughal State, 1526–1750*. Delhi; Oxford; New York: Oxford University Press, 1998.

Alam, Muzaffar and Seema Alavi, eds. *A European Experience of the Mughal Orient, The I'jaz-I Arsalani (Persian Letters, 1773–1779) of Antoine-Louis Henri Polier*. New Delhi: Oxford University Press, 2001.

Archer, Edward Caulfield. *Tours In Upper India and in Parts of The Himalaya Mountains; With Accounts of the Courts of The Native Princes, &c.* 2 vols. London: Richard Bentley, 1833.

Aynsley, H.G.M. Murray. *Our Visit to Hindostán, Kashmir, and Ladakh*. London: W.H. Allen & Co, 1879.

Bajwa, Fauja Singh. *Military System of the Sikhs*. Delhi: Motilal Banarsidass, 1964.

Balfour, Edward. *The Cyclopaedia of India and of Eastern and Southern Asia, Commercial, Industrial and Scientific*. 3rd ed. London: B.Quaritch, 1885.

Banerjee, Indubhusan. *Evolution of the Khalsa. Vol. 1, The Foundation of the Sikh Panth*. 2nd ed. Calcutta: Mukherjee, 1963.

Banerjee, Indubhusan. *Evolution of the Khalsa. Vol. 2, The Reformation*. 2nd ed. Calcutta: Mukherjee, 1962.

Banga, Indu, ed. *Five Punjabi Centuries: Polity, Economy, Society and Culture c.1500–1990*. Delhi: Manohar, 1997.

Bayly, C.A. *Empire & Information*. Cambridge: Cambridge University Press, 1996.

Bence-Jones, Mark. *Clive of India*. London: Constable, 1974.

Bhargava, Krishna Dayal, ed. *Browne Correspondence*. Delhi: National Archives of India, 1960.

Bidwell, Shelford. *Swords for Hire: European Mercenaries in Eighteenth-Century India*. London: John Murray, 1971.

Bruce, George. *Six Battles for India: The Anglo-Sikh Wars, 1845–6, 1848–9.* London: Arthur Baker Ltd, 1969.

Buckland, C.E. *Dictionary of Indian Biography.* London: S. Sonnenschein, 1906.

Chaudhury, Sushil. *From Prosperity to Decline: Eighteenth Century Bengal.* New Delhi: Manohar, 1995.

Coley, James (Chaplin to the Honourable East India Company). *Journal of the Sutlej and the Sutlej Campaign of 1845–6 and also Lord Hardinge's Tour in the Following Winter.* London: Smith, Elder and Co, 1856.

Cunningham, J.D. *A History of the Sikhs from the Origin of the Nation to the Battles of the Sutlej.* London: John Murray, 1849. Reprint, New Delhi: S. Chand & Co., 1985.

Cust, Robert Needham. *Linguistic and Oriental Essays, Written from the Years 1846 to 1878.* London: Trubner & Co., 1880.

Dalhousie, James Andrew Broun Ramsay, Marquis of. *Private Letters of the Marquess of Dalhousie.* Ed. J.G.A. Baird. Edinburgh and London: William Blackwood and Sons, 1910.

Daly, Sir Henry Dermot, G.C.B. *Memoirs of General Sir Henry Dermot Daly.* London: John Murray, 1905.

Deane, A. *A Tour through the Upper Provinces of Hindostan; Comprising a Period Between the Years 1804 and 1814.* London: C. & J. Rivington, 1823.

District and State Gazatteers of the Undivided Punjab. Vol. 3, Chamba State, 1910. Republished, Delhi: Low Price Publications, 1993.

Dogra, Ramesh Chander and Gobind Singh Mansukhani. *Encyclopaedia of Sikh Religion and Culture.* New Delhi: Vikas, 1995.

Dua, J.C. *Eighteenth Century Punjab.* New Delhi: Radha, 1992.

Eden, Emily. *Up the Country: Letters Written from the Upper Provinces of India.* London: Richard Bentley, 1866.

Eden, Fanny. *Tigers, Durbars and Kings: Fanny Eden's Indian Journals, 1837–1838.* Transcribed and edited by Janet Dunbar. London: John Murray, 1988.

Elliot, Sir Henry M. *The History of India, as Told by its own Historians.* London: Hertford, 1867–1877.

Francklin, William. *Military Memoirs of Mr. George Thomas.* Calcutta: 1803. Reprint, London: John Stockdale, 1805.

Fraser, J.B. *Military Memoir of Lieut.-Col. James Skinner.* C.B. London: Smith, Elder, 1851. Reprint, Ambala: Civil and Military Press, 1955.

Friedmann, Yohanan. *Shaykh Ahmad Sirhindī: An Outline of His Thought and a Study of His Image in the Eyes of Posterity.* Montreal: McGill-Queen's University Press, 1971.

Gandhi, Surjit Singh. *Sikhs in the Eighteenth Century.* Amritsar: Singh Bros., 1999.

Garrett, H.L.O-, ed. *The Punjab a Hundred Years Ago as Described by V. Jaquemont (1831) and A. Soltykoff (1842).* Lahore: Punjab Government Record Office Publications, 1935.

Gascoigne, Bamber. *The Great Moghuls.* London: Cape, 1971. Reprint, London: Cape, 1991.

Gole, Susan. *Maps of Mughal India Drawn by Colonel Jean-Baptiste-Joseph Gentil, Agent for the French Government to the Court of Shuja-ud-Daula at Faizabad, in 1770.* London: Kegan Paul International, 1988.

Gole, Susan. *Early Maps of India.* Edinburgh: Skilton, 1978.

Gordon, General Sir John. *The Sikhs.* Edinburgh: William Blackwood, 1904. Reprint, ed. S.P. Gulati and Dr Baldev Singh Baddan. Delhi: National Book Shop, 1996.

Grewal, J.S. *From Guru Nanak to Maharaja Ranjit Singh: Essays in Sikh History.* Amritsar: Guru Nanak Dev University, 1974.

Grewal, J.S. and Indu Banga, eds. *History and Ideology: The Khalsa over 300 Years.* New Delhi: Tulika, 1999.

Grewal, J.S. and Irfan Habib, eds. and trans. *Sikh History from Persian Sources.* New Delhi: Tulika, 2001.

Grey, Charles. *European Adventurers of Northern India, 1785 to 1849.* Ed. H.L.O. Garrett. Lahore: Printed by the superintendent, Government printing, Punjab, 1929.

Grierson, G.A., comp. and ed. *Linguistic Survey of India: Part I: Specimens of Western Hindi and Panjabi.* Calcutta: Superintendent Government Printing India, 1916.

Griffen, Lepel, H. *The Rajas of the Punjab, Being the history of the Principle States in the Punjab and their Political Relations with the British.* Lahore: The Punjab Printing Co. Goverment, 1870. Reprint, New Delhi: Manu Publications, 1977.

Gupta, Hari Ram. *History of the Sikhs.* 5 vols. New Delhi: Munshiram Manoharlal, 1978–1991.

Gupta, Hari Ram. *Later Mughal History of the Panjab (1707–1793).* Lahore: Sang-e-Meel Publications, 1976. Reprint of *Studies in Later Mughal History of the Panjab, 1707–1793.* Lahore: Minerva Bookshop, 1944.

Gupta, Hari Ram. *Short History of the Sikhs.* Ludhiana: Sahitya Sangam, 1970.

Hans, Surjit. *Reconstruction of Sikh History from Sikh Literature.* Jalandhar: ABS Publication, 1988.

Hardgrave, Robert L. *Boats of Bengal: Eighteenth Century Portraits by Balthazar Solvyns.* New Delhi: Manohar, 2001.

Hennessy, Maurice Noel. *The Rajah from Tipperary.* London: Sidgwick and Jackson, 1971.

Hopkirk, Peter. *The Great Game: On Secret Service in High Asia.* London: Murray, 1990.

Ibbetson, Sir Denzil. *Punjab Castes: Being a Reprint of the Chapter on "The Races, Castes and Tribes of the People" in the Report on the Census of the Panjab Published in 1883 by the late Sir Denzil Ibbetson,* K.C.S.I. Lahore: Sang-e-Meel Publications, 1994.

Imperial Record Department. *Calendar of Persian Correspondence. Volume 2 (1767–9).* Calcutta: Superintendent Government Printing, 1914.

Irvine, William. *Later Mughals.* Calcutta: M.C. Sarkar & Sons; London: Luzac & Co., 1922

James, Lawrence. *Raj: The Making and Unmaking of British India.* London: Little, Brown, 1997.

Keay, John. *India: A History.* London: Harper Collins, 2000.

Khurana, G. *British Historiography on the Sikh Power in the Punjab.* London: Mansell, 1985.

Kipling, Rudyard. *Kim.* New York: Doubleday, Page & Co., 1901.

Krishen, Indra. *An Historical Interpretation of the Correspondence of Sir George Russel Clerk, Political Agent, Ambala and Ludhiana, 1831–43, etc.* Delhi: printed by Kulab Chand Kapur & Sons, 1952.

Latif, Syad Muhammad. *History of the Panjab from the Remotest Antiquity to the Present Time.* Calcutta: Central Press, 1891. Reprint, New Delhi: Kalyani Publishers, 1997.

Loehlin, Clinton Herbert. *The Granth of Guru Gobind Singh and the Khalsa Brotherhood.* Lucknow: Lucknow Publishing House, 1971.

Long, James. *Selections from Unpublished Records of Government for the Years 1748 to 1767 Inclusive, Relating Mainly to the Social Condition of Bengal, with a Map of Calcutta in 1784.* ed. Mahadevaprasad Saha. 2nd ed. Calcutta: Firma K.L. Mukhopadhyay, 1973.

Losty, Jeremiah P. *The Art of the Book in India.* London: The British Library, 1982.

Macauliffe, Max Arthur. *The Sikh Religion: Its Gurus, Sacred Writings and Authors.* 6 vols. in 3. Oxford: Clarendon, 1909. Reprint, Delhi: S. Chand, 1985.

Mackenzie, Lt.-Gen. Collin. *Storms and Sunshine of a Soldier's Life.* 2 vols. Edingburgh: David Douglas, 1884.

Madra, Amandeep Singh and Parmjit Singh. *Warrior Saints: Three Centuries of the Sikh Military Tradition.* London: I.B. Tauris, 1999.

Malcolm, Lt.-Col. John, *Sketch of the Sikhs.* London: John Murray, 1812.

Malik, Arjan Dass. *An Indian Guerrilla War: The Sikh Peoples War 1699–1768.* New Delhi: Wiley Eastern Ltd., 1975. Later published as *The Sword of the Khalsa.* New Delhi: Manohar Publishers and Distributors, 1999.

Mason, Philip. *The Men who Ruled India.* Abridged ed. London: J. Cape, 1985.

Masson, Charles. *Narrative of Various Journeys in Balochistan, Afghanistan, and the Panjab, Including a Residence in those Countries from 1826 to 1838.* 3 vols. London: Richard Bentley New Burlington Street, Publisher in Ordinary to her Majesty, 1842.

McLeod, W.H. *Historical Dictionary of Sikhism.* Lanham, Md. and London: Scarecrow, 1995. Reprint New Delhi: Oxford University Press, 2002.

Mundy, Peter. *The Travels of Peter Mundy, in Europe and Asia, 1608–1667.* 5 vols. Ed. Sir Richard Carnac Temple. London: Hakluyt Society, 1907–1936.

Murray, J.C. *Our Visit to Hindostan, Kashmir, and Ladakh.* London: Aynsley, 1879.

Narang, K.S. and H.R. Gupta, eds. *History of the Punjab (1500–1858).* Delhi: Uttar Chand Kapur, 1969.

Oberoi, Harjot. The Construction of Religious Boundaries: Culture, Identity and Diversity in the Sikh Tradition. Chicago: The University of Chicago Press, 1994.

O'Malley, Lewis Sydney Steward. *Bengal District Gazetteers.* Calcutta: Bengal Secretariat Book Depôt, 1910.

Oman, John Campbell. *Cults, Customs, and Superstitions of India, Being a Revised and Enlarged Edition of "Indian Life, Religious and Social," Comprising Studies and Sketches of Interesting Peculiarities in the Beliefs, Festivals and Domestic Life of the Indian People; Also of Witchcraft and Demonical Possessions as Known Amongst them.* London: T. Fisher Unwin, 1908.

Oman, John Campbell. *The Mystics, Ascetics and Saints of India: a Study Of Sadhuism, with an Account of the Yogis, Sanyasis, Bairagis, and other Strange Hindu Sectarians.* London: T. Fisher Unwin, 1903.

Orme Robert. *A History of the Military Transactions of the British Nation in Indostan.* London: printed for J. Nourse, 1778.

Osborne, Lord William Godolphin. *The Court and Camp of Runjeet Sing.* London: H. Colburn, 1840.

Phillips, James Duncan. *Salem and the Indies. The Story of the Great Commercial Era of the City.* Boston: Houghton Mifflin Co., 1947.

Polier, Antoine-Louis-Henri. *Shah Alam II and his Court.* Ed. Pratul C. Gupta. Calcutta: S.C. Sarkar and sons, 1947.

Rangaiyar, S. *Diary of Late Maharaja of Nabha: A Biography Based on the Maharaja's Diary.* Lucknow: Indian Daily Telegraph, 1924.

Rennell, Major James. *Memoir of a Map of Hindoostan; or the Mogul's Empire.* London: Printed by M. Brown for the author, 1783.

Rose, H.A. *A Glossary of the Tribes and Castes of the Punjab and North-West Frontier Province.* Vol. 2. Lahore: Civil and Military Gazette, 1911. Reprint, New Delhi: Asian Educational Services, 1990.

Sachdeva, Veena. *Policy and Economy of the Punjab During the Late Eighteenth Century.* Delhi: Manohar, 1993.

Sarkar, Sir Jadunath. *Fall of the Mughal Empire.* 4 vols. Santosh Kumar Sarkar, 1938. Reprint, Hyderabad: Orient Longman Limited, 1999.

Sarkar, Sir Jadunath. *History of Aurangzib: Mainly Based on Persian Sources.* 4 vols. Calcutta: M.C. Sarkar & Sons, 1912–1919.

Schonberg, Baron Erich Von. *Travels in India and Kashmir.* 2 vols. London: Hurst and Blackett, Publishers, 1853.

Seetal, Sohan Singh. *The Sikh Misals and the Punjab.* Ludhiana: Lahore Book Shop, 1981.

Seetal, Sohan Singh. *Rise of the Sikh Power in the Punjab.* Jalandhar: Dhanpat Rai, 1970.

Shackle, Christopher, Gurharpal Singh, and Arvindpal Singh Mandair, eds. *Sikh Religion, Culture and Ethnicity.* Richmond: Curzon, 2000.

Shāh, Muhammad Kasim Ibn Hindu [Astarabadī Ferishtāh]. *The History of Hindostan, from the Earliest Account of Time to the Death of Akbar; Translated from the Persian of Mahummud Casim Ferishtah . . . Together with a Dissertation Concerning the Religion and Philosophy of the Brahmims.* 3 vols. Trans. and commentary Alexander Dow. London: T. Becket and P. A. de Hondt, 1770–1772.

Singh, Bhagat. *History of the Sikh Misals.* Patiala: Punjabi University, 1993.

Singh, Bhagat. *Sikh Polity in the Eighteenth and Nineteenth Centuries.* New Delhi: Manohar Publications, 1978.

Singh, Chetan. *Region and Empire: Panjab in the Seventeenth Century.* Delhi: Oxford University Press, 1991.

Singh, Darshan, ed. *Western Image of the Sikh Religion: A Source Book.* New Delhi: National Book Organisers, 1999.

Singh, Fauja. *Historians and Historiography of the Sikhs.* New Delhi: Oriental, 1978.

Singh, Ganda. *Life of Banda Singh Bahadur.* Amritsar: Khalsa College, 1935. Reprint, Patiala: Punjabi University, 1990.

Singh, Ganda, ed. *Early European Accounts of the Sikhs.* New Delhi: Today & Tomorrow's Printers & Publishers, 1974.

Singh, Ganda, comp. *A Bibliography of the Punjab.* Patiala: Punjabi University, 1966

Singh, Ganda, comp. *A Select Bibliography of the Sikh and Sikhism.* Amritsar: S.G.P.C., 1965.

Singh, Ganda. *Ahmad Shah Durrani: Father of Modern Afghanistan.* Bombay: A.P.H., 1959.

Singh, Gopal. *History of the Sikh People (1469–1978).* New Delhi: World Book Centre, 1979. Revised and updated edition. New Delhi: World Book Centre, 1988.

Singh, Harbans, ed. *The Encyclopaedia of Sikhism.* 4 vols. Patiala: Punjabi University, 1992–1998.

Singh, Harbans and N. Gerald Barrier, eds. *Punjab Past and Present: Essays in Honour of Dr Ganda Singh.* Patiala: Punjabi University, 1976.

Singh, Jodh and Dharam Singh, trans. *Sri Dasam Granth Sahib Text and Translation.* Patiala: Heritage Publications, 1999.

Singh, Kharak and Gurtej Singh, eds. *Episodes from the Lives of the Gurus: Parchian Sewadas.* Chandigarh: Institute of Sikh Studies Chandigarh, 1995.

Singh, Khazan. *History and Philosophy of the Sikh Religion.* Lahore: Printed at the "Newal Kishore" Press, 1914.

Singh, Khushwant. *A History of the Sikhs.* 2 vols. Princeton, NJ: Princeton University Press, 1963, 1966. Revised edition, Delhi: Oxford University Press, 1991.

Singh, Rajwant, comp. *The Sikhs: Their Literature on Culture, History, Philosophy, Religion and Traditions.* Delhi: Indian Bibliographies Bureau, 1990.

Singh, Sirdar Attar, trans. *Sakhee Book or the Description of Gooroo Gobind Singh's Religion and Doctrines, Translated from Gooroomukhi into Hindi, and Afterwards into English.* Benares: Medical Hall Press, 1873.

Singh, Teja and Ganda Singh. *A Short History of the Sikhs (1469–1765).* Vol. 1. Bombay: Orient Longmans, 1950. Reprint, Patiala: Punjabi University, 1989.

Sinha, Narendra Krishna. *The Economic History of Bengal: From Plassey to the Permanent Settlement.* 3rd ed. Calcutta: Firma K.L. Mukhopadhyay, 1981–1984.

Smith, Vincent A. *The Oxford History of India: From the Earliest Times to the End of 1911.* Oxford: Clarendon Press, 1919.

Smyth, Major G.M. Carmichel. *History of the Reigning Family of Lahore.* Calcutta: W. Thaker and Co.-St. Andrew's Library, 1847. Reprint, Delhi: Parampara Publications, 1979.

Solvyns, Balt (Balthazar). *Les Hindoûs.* 4 vols. Paris: Chez L'Auteur, 1808–1812.

Solvyns, Balt (Balthazar). *The Costume of Hindostan, Elucidated by Sixty Coloured Engravings with Descriptions in English and French, Taken in the Years 1798 and 1799. By Balt. Solvyns, of Calcutta.* London: E. Orme, 1804.

Solvyns, Balt (Balthazar). *A Catalogue of 250 Coloured Etchings; Descriptive of the Manners, Customs, Character, Dress, and Religious Ceremonies of the Hindoos.* Calcutta: Mirror Press, 1799.

Solvyns, Balt (Balthazar). *A Collection of Two Hundred and Fifty Colored Etchings: Descriptive of the Manners, Customs, Character, Dress, and Religious Ceremonies of the Hindoos.* Calcutta, 1796, 1799.

Suri, Lala Sohan Lal. *An Outstanding Original Source of Panjab History: Umdat-ut-tawarikh, daftar III, Parts I–IV; Chronicle of the Reign of Maharaja Ranjit Singh, 1831–1839 A.D.* Translated from Persian into English with corresponding notes by V.S. Suri. Delhi: S. Chand, 1961.

Sutton, S.C. *A Guide to the India Office Library.* London: H.M.S.O., 1967.

Taylor, Colonel Philip Meadows. *The People of India. A Series of Photographic Illustrations, with Descriptive Letterpress, of the Races and Tribes of Hindustan, Originally Prepared under the Authority of the Government of India, and Reproduced by Order of the Secretary of State for India.* 6 vols. Ed. J.F. Watson and J.W. Kaye. London: W.H. Allen and Co., 1868–1872.

Wasti, Syed Razi, ed. *Biographical Dictionary of South Asia.* Lahore: Publishers United, 1980.

Wheeler, J. Tallboys. *Early Records of British India.* London: Trubner & Co., 1878.

Williams, Monier. *Religious Thought and Life in India. An Account of the Religions of the Indian Peoples, Based on a Lifes Study of their Literature and on Personal Investigations in their own Country.* London: John Murray, 1883.

Wilson, C.R. *The Early Annals of the English in Bengal.* 2 vols. London: W. Thacker & Co., 1895.

Wolff, Joseph. *Travels and Adventures of the Rev. Joseph Wolff, D.D., LL.D., Vicar of Ile Brewers, near Taunton; and Late Missionary to the Jews and Muhammadans in Persia, Bokhara, Cashmeer, ETC.* London: Saunders, Otely, and Co., 1861.

Yule, Henry and Burnell, A.C. *Hobson-Jobson: A Glossary of Colloquial Anglo-Indian Words and Phrases, and of Kindred Terms, Etymological, Historical, Geographical and Discursive.* Ed. William Crooke. London: Murray, 1903. Reprint with a historical perspective by Nirad C. Chaudhuri. Sittingbourne: Linguasia, 1994.

BOOKS IN PUNJABI

Bhangū, Ratan Singh. *Prachīn Panth Prakāsh.* Amritsar: Vazir Hind Press, 1914. Reprint, ed. by Bhāī Vīr Singh. New Delhi: Bhāī Vīr Singh Sāhit Sadan, 1993, 5th ed.

Chibbar, Kesar Singh. *Bansāvalīnāmā Dasan Padshāhīān dā.* Ed. Piārā Singh Padam. Amritsar: Singh Brothers Amritsar, 1996.

Gurdās, Bhāī. *Vāran Bhāī Gurdās jī,* ed. Giānī Hazārā Singh (New Delhi: Bhāī Vīr Singh Sāhit Sadan, 1999), 667.

Nābhā, Kahan Singh. *Gur-Shabad Ratnākar Mahān-Kosh.* 4 vols., Patiala: Patiala State Government, 1931. Reprint, 1 vol., 1960, 2nd ed.

Narotam, Pandit Tārā Singh. *Gurū Tīrath Samgrahi.* Kankhāl: Srī Nirmal Panchāyātī Akhārā, 1883. Reprint, 1975.

Padam, Piārā Singh. *Rahitnāme.* Patiala: Kalama Mandira, 1974.

Singh, Davinder. *Srī Gurū Nānak Abhinanda.* Amritsar, 1978.

Singh, Gandā. *Mahārājā Kaurā Mall Bahādur.* Amritsar: Khalsa College, 1942.

Singh, Giānī Giān. *Navīn Panth Prakāsh.* Amritsar: Murtazain Press, 1880. Reprint, Punjab: Bhāshā Vibhāg, 1987.

Singh, Giānī Giān. *Twārīkh Gurū Khālsā.* 3 vols. Sialkot: 1891–1894. Reprint, 1 vol., Bhāsha Vibāgh, Punjab, 1970.

Singh, Kavī Santokh. *Srī Gur Partāp Surāj Granth.* Ed. by Bhāī Vīr Singh. 14 vols. Punjab: Bhāshā Vibhāg, 1989.

Singh, Pandit Narayan, trans. *Sri Dasam Granth Sahib Ji.* 10 vols. Amritsar: Bhāī Jawāhir Singh, Kirpāl Singh & Co., 1993, 3rd ed.

INDEX

Variant spellings which are not obvious have been given brackets after page references, e.g. 'Djats' for 'Jats.' Sikh and other Indian names are listed alphabetically by first name whereas European names are listed by surname.